# The Story of God Bible Commentary Series Endorsements

"Getting a story is about more than merely enjoying it. It means hearing it, understanding it, and above all, being impacted by it. This commentary series hopes that its readers not only hear and understand the story, but are impacted by it to live in as Christian a way as possible. The editors and contributors set that table very well and open up the biblical story in ways that move us to act with sensitivity and understanding. That makes hearing the story as these authors tell it well worth the time. Well done."

**Darrell L. Bock**
Dallas Theological Seminary

"The Story of God Bible Commentary series invites readers to probe how the message of the text relates to our situations today. Engagingly readable, it not only explores the biblical text but offers a range of applications and interesting illustrations."

**Craig S. Keener**
Asbury Theological Seminary

"I love the Story of God Bible Commentary series. It makes the text sing, and helps us hear the story afresh."

**John Ortberg**
Senior pastor of Menlo Park Presbyterian Church

"In this promising new series of commentaries, believing biblical scholars bring not only their expertise but their own commitment to Jesus and insights into today's culture to the Scriptures. The result is a commentary series that is anchored in the text but lives and breathes in the world of today's church with its variegated pattern of socioeconomic, ethnic, and national diversity. Pastors, Bible study leaders, and Christians of all types who are looking for a substantive and practical guide through the Scriptures will find these volumes helpful."

**Frank Thielman**
Beeson Divinity School

"The Story of God Bible Commentary series is unique in its approach to exploring the Bible. Its easy-to-use format and practical guidance brings God's grand story to modern-day life so anyone can understand how it applies today."

**Andy Stanley**
North Point Ministries

"I'm a storyteller. Through writing and speaking I talk and teach about understanding the Story of God throughout Scripture and about letting God reveal more of His story as I live it out. Thus I am thrilled to have a commentary series based on the Story of God—a commentary that helps me to Listen to the Story, that Explains the Story, and then encourages me to probe how to Live the Story. A perfect tool for helping every follower of Jesus to walk in the story that God is writing for them."

**Judy Douglass**
Director of Women's Resources, Cru

"The Bible is the story of God and his dealings with humanity from creation to new creation. The Bible is made up more of stories than of any other literary genre. Even the psalms, proverbs, prophecies, letters, and the Apocalypse make complete sense only when set in the context of the grand narrative of the entire Bible. This commentary series breaks new ground by taking all these observations seriously. It asks commentators to listen to the text, to explain the text, and to live the text. Some of the material in these sections overlaps with introduction, detailed textual analysis and application, respectively, but only some. The most riveting and valuable part of the commentaries are the stories that can appear in any of these sections, from any part of the globe and any part of church history, illustrating the text in any of these areas. Ideal for preaching and teaching."

**Craig L. Blomberg**
Denver Seminary

"Pastors and lay people will welcome this new series, which seeks to make the message of the Scriptures clear and to guide readers in appropriating biblical texts for life today."

**Daniel I. Block**
Wheaton College and Graduate School

"An extremely valuable, and long overdue series that includes comment on the cultural context of the text, careful exegesis, and guidance on reading the whole Bible as a unity that testifies to Christ as our Savior and Lord."

**Graeme Goldsworthy**
author of *According to Plan*

# GENESIS

# The Story of God Bible Commentary

## GENESIS

Tremper Longman III

Tremper Longman III & Scot McKnight
*General Editors*

ZONDERVAN

*Genesis*


This title is also available as a Zondervan ebook. Visit www.zondervan.com/ebooks.

Requests for information should be addressed to:
Zondervan, *3900 Sparks Dr. SE, Grand Rapids, Michigan 49546*

ISBN 978-0-310-49607-6 (hardcover)



*Cover design: Ron Huizinga*
*Cover image: iStockphoto®*
*Interior composition: Greg Johnson/Textbook Perfect*

*Printed in the United States of America*

---

15 16 17 18 19 20 /DHV/ 24 23 22 21 20 19 18 17 16 15 14 13 12 11 10 9 8 7 6 5 4 3 2 1

To my wife Alice and our children (*zera*)

Tremper IV and our granddaughters Gabrielle and Mia

Timothy and his wife Kari

Andrew and his wife Tiffany

## Old Testament series

1 ■ Genesis—*Tremper Longman III*
2 ■ Exodus—*Christopher J. H. Wright*
3 ■ Leviticus—*Jerry E. Shepherd*
4 ■ Numbers—*Jay A. Sklar*
5 ■ Deuteronomy—*Myrto Theocharous*
6 ■ Joshua—*Lissa M. Wray Beal*
7 ■ Judges—*Athena E. Gorospe*
8 ■ Ruth/Esther—*Marion Taylor*
9 ■ 1–2 Samuel—*Paul S. Evans*
10 ■ 1–2 Kings—*David T. Lamb*
11 ■ 1–2 Chronicles—*Carol M. Kaminski*
12 ■ Ezra/Nehemiah—*Douglas J. Green*
13 ■ Job—*Martin A. Shields*
14 ■ Psalms—*Elizabeth R. Hayes*
15 ■ Proverbs—*Ryan P. O'Dowd*
16 ■ Ecclesiastes/Song of Songs—*George Athas*
17 ■ Isaiah—*Mark J. Boda*
18 ■ Jeremiah/Lamentations—*Andrew G. Shead*
19 ■ Ezekiel—*D. Nathan Phinney*
20 ■ Daniel—*Wendy L. Widder*
21 ■ Minor Prophets I—*Beth M. Stovell*
22 ■ Minor Prophets II—*Beth M. Stovell*

## New Testament series

1 ■ Matthew—*Rodney Reeves*
2 ■ Mark—*Timothy G. Gombis*
3 ■ Luke—*Kindalee Pfremmer DeLong*
4 ■ John—*Nicholas Perrin*
5 ■ Acts—*Dean Pinter*
6 ■ Romans—*Michael F. Bird*
7 ■ 1 Corinthians —*Justin K. Hardin*
8 ■ 2 Corinthians—*Love L. Sechrest*
9 ■ Galatians—*Nijay K. Gupta*
10 ■ Ephesians—*Mark D. Roberts*
11 ■ Philippians—*Lynn H. Cohick*
12 ■ Colossians/Philemon—*Todd Wilson*
13 ■ 1–2 Thessalonians—*John Byron*
14 ■ 1–2 Timothy, Titus—*Marius Nel*
15 ■ Hebrews—*Radu Gheorghita*
16 ■ James—*Mariam J. Kamell*
17 ■ 1 Peter—*Dennis Edwards*
18 ■ 2 Peter, Jude—*C. Rosalee Velloso Ewell*
19 ■ 1–3 John—*Constantine R. Campbell*
20 ■ Revelation—*Jonathan A. Moo*
21 ■ Sermon on the Mount —*Scot McKnight*

# Contents

# Acknowledgements

In 2009, I had the honor of delivering the annual lecture for the Institute of Biblical Research. I titled the paper "'Of the Making of Many Commentaries ...': The Past, Present, and Future of a Genre," and as I looked to the future, I expressed hope that one day we would have an Old Testament commentary series that not only examined the ancient message of the Old Testament but also looked at the text from a New Testament perspective to describe its continuing relevance for Christian life and, most importantly, how this ancient text anticipated the coming of Jesus. After all, Jesus himself told his disciples that the all the Scriptures looked forward to his coming (Luke 24:25–27, 44–45). Within twenty-four hours Katya Covrett from Zondervan sat down with me to discuss what such a commentary would look like and soon thereafter we launched this series and combined it with the New Testament series edited by Scot McKnight and now titled the Story of God Bible Commentary.

Thus, my first thanks goes out to Katya and Zondervan for allowing this series to take shape. We first recruited associate editors and our top choices agreed to join us: George Athas, Mark Boda, and Myrto Theocharous. George and Myrto read my initial sample and gave me feedback, and I thank them for that.

Special thanks goes to Mark, who was my assigned editor and gave me invaluable feedback. Thanks so much, Mark! Of course, I did not always accept his suggestions (after all, many years ago this now-distinguished Old Testament scholar was my student!), so any problems are my own.

After the editorial team was set in place, we then recruited contributors. I shamelessly confess that I first of all assigned myself the book of Genesis. I wanted to work with this book that is beautifully crafted, historically interesting, and theologically rich. Besides that, now that I am in my sixties (early!) I did not want to wait too long before commenting on this book.

I have enjoyed a long publishing relationship with Zondervan that goes back about thirty years. Over this time I have developed not only professional connections, but friendships with many who work there. In terms of the present book (and series, of which I am the General Edtior), having already mentioned Katya Covrett, I want to express my appreciation for the work of Verlyn Verbrugge who helped us develop this series and with whom I have worked closely on many previous projects. Verlyn passed away this summer (2015), and he is deeply missed. Already before his illness and death, Nancy Erickson had been given the responsibility of working with the Old Testament authors, including of course me, and I want to thank her for her great work in terms of bringing this book to the point of publication.

In a book that is so concerned with descendants (seed, *zera*), I wanted to dedicate this book to Alice, my wife, and my children and grandchildren. This book is ultimately dedicated to the glory of God, to whom I am deeply indebted for giving me such a wonderful, supportive, and fun family.

Tremper Longman III
*Robert H. Gundry Professor of Biblical Studies*
*Westmont College*

# The Story of God Bible Commentary Series

Why another commentary series?

In the first place, no single commentary can exhaust the meaning of a biblical book. The Bible is unfathomably rich and no single commentator can explore every aspect of its message.

In addition, good commentary not only explores what the text meant in the past, but also its continuing significance. In other words, the Word of God may not change but culture does. Think of what we have seen in the last twenty years: we now communicate predominantly through the internet and email; we read our news on iPads and computers. We carry smartphones in our pockets through which we can call our friends, check the weather forecast, make dinner reservations, and get an answer to virtually any question we might have.

Today we have more readable and accurate Bible versions in English than any generation in the past. Bible distribution in the present generation has been very successful; more people own more Bibles than previous generations. However, studies have shown that, while people have better access to the Bible than ever before, people aren't reading the Bibles they own, and they struggle to understand what they do read.

The Story of God Bible Commentary hopes to help people, particularly clergy but also laypeople, read the Bible with understanding not only of its ancient meaning, but also of its continuing significance for us today in the twenty-first century. After all, readers of the Bible change too. These cultural shifts, our own personal developments, the progress in intellectual questions, as well as growth in biblical studies and theology and discoveries of new texts and new paradigms for understanding the contexts of the Bible — each of these elements work on an interpreter so that the person who reads the Bible today asks different questions from different angles.

Culture shifts, but the Word of God remains. That is why we as editors of The Story of God Bible Commentary, a commentary based on the New International Version 2011 (NIV 2011), are excited to participate in this new series of commentaries on the Bible. This series is designed to speak to this generation with the same Word of God. We are asking the authors to explain what the Bible says to the sorts of readers who pick up commentaries so they can understand not only what Scripture says but what it means for today. The Bible does not change but relating it to our culture changes constantly and in differing ways in different contexts.

As editors of the Old Testament series, we recognize that Christians have a hard time knowing exactly how to relate to the Scriptures that were written before the coming of Christ. The world of the Old Testament is a strange one to those of us who live in the West in the twenty-first century. We read about strange customs, warfare in the name of God, sacrifices, laws of ritual purity, and more and wonder whether it is worth our while or even spiritually healthy to spend time reading this portion of Scripture that is chronologically, culturally, and—seemingly—theologically distant from us.

But it is precisely here that The Story of God Commentary Series Old Testament makes its most important contribution. The New Testament does not replace the Old Testament; the New Testament fulfills the Old Testament. We hear God's voice today in the Old Testament. In its pages, he reveals himself to us and also his will for how we should live in a way that is pleasing to him.

Jesus himself often reminds us that the Old Testament maintains its importance to the life of his disciples. Luke 24 describes Jesus' actions and teaching in the period between his resurrection and ascension. Strikingly, the focus of his teaching is on how his followers should read the Old Testament (here called "Moses and all the Prophets," "Scripture," and "the Law of Moses, the Prophets and Psalms"). To the two disciples on the road to Emmaus, he says:

> "How foolish you are, and how slow to believe all that the prophets have spoken! Did not the Messiah have to suffer these things and then enter his glory?" And beginning with Moses and all the Prophets, he explained to them what was said in all the Scriptures concerning himself. (Luke 24:25–27)

Then to a larger group of disciples he announces:

> "This is what I told you while I was still with you: Everything must be fulfilled that is written about me in the Law of Moses, the Prophets and the Psalms." Then he opened their minds so they could understand the Scriptures. (Luke 24:44–45)

The Story of God Commentary Series takes Jesus' words on this matter seriously. Indeed, it is the first series that has as one of its deliberate goals the identification of the trajectories (historical, typological, and theological) that land in Christ in the New Testament. Every commentary in the series will, in the first place, exposit the text in the context of its original reception. We will interpret it as we believe the original author intended his contemporary audience to read it. But, then we will also read the text in the light of the death and resurrection of Jesus. No other commentary series does this important work consistently in every volume.

To achieve our purpose of expositing the Old Testament in its original setting and also from a New Testament perspective, each passage is examined from three angles.

**Listen to the Story.** We begin by listening to the text in order to hear the voice of God. We first read the passage under study. We then go on to consider the background to the passage by looking at any earlier Scripture passage that informs our understanding of the text. At this point too we will cite and discuss possible ancient Near Eastern literary connections. After all, the Bible was not written in a cultural vacuum, and an understanding of its broader ancient Near Eastern context will often enrich our reading.

**Explain the Story.** The authors are asked to "explain" each passage in light of the Bible's grand story. It is here that we will exposit the text in its original Old Testament context. This is not an academic series, so the footnotes will be limited to the kinds of books and articles to which typical Bible readers and preachers will have access. Authors are given the freedom to explain the text as they read it though you will not be surprised to find occasional listings of other options for reading the text. The emphasis will be on providing an accessible explanation of the passage, particularly on those aspects of the text that are difficult for a modern reader to understand, with an emphasis on theological interpretation.

**Live the Story.** Reading the Bible is not just about discovering what it meant back then; the intent of The Story of God Bible Commentary is to probe how this text might be lived out today as that story continues to march on in the life of the church.

Here in the spirit of Christ's words in Luke 24 we will suggest ways in which the Old Testament text anticipates the gospel. After all, as Augustine famously put it, "the New Testament is in the Old Testament concealed, the Old Testament is in the New Testament revealed." We believe that this section will be particularly important for our readers who are clergy who want to present Christ even when they are preaching from the Old Testament.

The Old Testament also provides teaching concerning how we should live today. However, the authors of this series are sensitive to the tremendous impact that Christ's coming has on how Christians appropriate the Old Testament into their lives today.

It is the hope and prayer of the editors and all the contributors that our work will encourage clergy to preach from the Old Testament and for laypeople to study this wonderful, yet often strange portion of God's Word to us today.

Tremper Longman III, general editor Old Testament
George Athas, Mark Boda, and Myrto Theocharous, editors

# Abbreviations

| | |
|---|---|
| AB | Anchor Bible |
| *ANET* | *Ancient Near Eastern Texts Relating to the Old Testament.* Edited by James B. Pritchard. 3rd ed. Princeton: Princeton University Press, 1969 |
| *BA* | *Biblical Archaeologist* |
| *BAR* | *Biblical Archaeology Review* |
| *BASOR* | *Bulletin of the American Schools of Oriental Research* |
| BCOTWP | Baker Commentary on the Old Testament Wisdom and Psalms |
| BZAW | Beihefte zur Zeitschrift für die alttestamentliche Wissenschaft |
| *COS* | *The Context of Scripture*. Edited by William W. Hallo. 3 vols. Ledien: Brill, 1997–2002 |
| *CTJ* | *Calvin Theological Journal* |
| ESV | English Standard Version |
| *HAR* | *Hebrew Annual Review* |
| HCB | Holman Christian Bible |
| IBC | Interpretation: A Bible Commentary for Teaching and Preaching |
| *IEJ* | *Israel Exploration Journal* |
| *JAOS* | *Journal of the American Oriental Society* |
| *JBL* | *Journal of Biblical Literature* |
| *JCS* | *Journal of Cuneiform Studies* |
| *JSOT* | *Journal for the Study of the Old Testament* |
| JSOT Sup | Journal for the Study of the Old Testament Supplement Series |
| NAB | New American Bible |
| NAC | New American Commentary |
| NIBC | New International Biblical Commentary |
| NICOT | New International Commentary on the Old Testament |
| *NIDOTTE* | *New International Dictionary of Old Testament Theology and Exegesis*. Edited by Willem A. VanGemeren. 5 vols. Grand Rapids: Zondervan, 1997 |

| | |
|---|---|
| NIV | New International Version |
| NIVAC | New International Version Application Commentary |
| (N)KJV | (New) Kings James Version |
| NLT | New Living Translation |
| NRSV | New Revised Standard Version |
| SBLDS | Society of Biblical Literature Dissertation Series |
| SPCK | Society for Promoting Christian Knowledge |
| TOTC | Tyndale Old Testament Commentaries |
| UBCS | Understanding the Bible Commentary Series |
| *VT* | *Vetus Testamentum* |
| WBC | Word Biblical Commentary |
| *WTJ* | *Westminster Theological Journal* |
| *ZAW* | *Zeitschrift für die alttestamentliche Wissenschaft* |
| ZIBBC | Zondervan Illustrated Bible Backgrounds Commentary |

# Introduction to Genesis

If asked to name the first book of the Bible, many people think that the correct answer is Genesis, and in a sense they are correct. But in another sense Genesis is not the first book; that distinction goes to the Torah, also known as the Pentateuch.

Pentateuch is a term formed from the Greek whose etymological meaning is "five scrolls." This name reminds us that Genesis, Exodus, Leviticus, Numbers, and Deuteronomy are really one literary composition, but this one literary composition is divided into five parts because an ancient scroll could not contain more than one-fifth of this majestic and powerful work.

The main story is found in Exodus through Deuteronomy. These books are not only a literary unity, but they also tell an uninterrupted story. The story begins with the birth of Moses (Exod 1–2) and ends with an account of his death (Deut 34). The story focusses on the exodus, the salvation event *par excellence* in the Old Testament, and brings the Israelites, freed from Egyptian bondage and brought into the service of Yahweh, to the plains of Moab, poised to enter the promised land.

Genesis is a prequel to the main story of the Pentateuch, giving the background to the events that lead up to Israel's dramatic deliverance. Genesis begins with an account of the creation of the cosmos and of humanity. Though created innocent, humanity chose to rebel against God and thus, as Paul says (Rom 5:12–21), introduced sin and death into the world.

When creator God blessed Adam and Eve, they lived in a harmonious relationship with God and thus in a harmonious relationship with each other and their world. The name Eden, meaning "abundance" or "luxury," conveys a harmony between humanity and the world as well. That harmony was fractured by their rebellion against God, and thus they forfeited a blessed existence. No longer was their relationship with God or with each other or even with themselves harmonious.

Starting with Genesis 3:15, the punishment on the serpent, God declares his intention to defeat evil and Genesis continues by narrating God's passionate pursuit of his sinful creatures. Genesis 4–11 speaks of God's interaction with sinful humanity from the time of the initial rebellion up until the time of Abraham. We have here three stories (Cain and Abel; the flood; the tower of

Babel) connected by genealogies that show the passage of time and contribute to the theological teaching of this section of the book.

As we will explore more fully in the commentary proper, these stories follow the same general pattern as the account of the rebellion. Each speaks of sin and God's judgment, which is first announced by God and then executed by him. Even in the context of judgment of sin, God also extends a token of his grace (a mark on Cain, the preservation of Noah and his family, languages) as he did to Adam and Eve (clothing). In these initial stories, humans show themselves to be addicted to sin and God shows that he will not give sin a free pass, but will judge sin. But, equally significantly, through the token of grace, God shows that he will not give up on us.

Indeed, that passionate pursuit eventually leads God to choose Abraham and his descendants. He promises to make his descendants a "great nation," bless them, and use him and his descendants to bring a blessing to "all peoples on earth" (Gen 12:1–3, citing v. 3).

The story of Abraham in the main follows how the patriarch responds to threats and obstacles to the fulfillment of the promises, most pointedly connected to Sarah's barrenness. Indeed, as we will indicate in the commentary proper, the focus in Genesis 12 and following is on the promised seed and how the covenant promises pass down through the generations.[1] As the commentary will show, Abraham responds mostly with fear and manipulation as he grasps for the fulfillment of the promises, but on occasion (Gen 15:6) and certainly at the end (Gen 22), Abraham displays confidence and trust in God.

After the death of Abraham, the narrator's attention turns next to Isaac, who is the son chosen to carry forward the covenantal promises to the next generation. Isaac is only rarely the main character in a story, though, and most readers find the Jacob story more engaging. Jacob and Esau are Isaac's two sons and, in this case, the younger is the one chosen to continue the line of covenant promise. Esau, and Ishmael before him, are not chosen, but, as we will see, that does not mean God does not care about them and their descendants. Far from it. God blesses them in many ways as well.

Jacob's story ultimately leads to the final section of Genesis, commonly referred to as the Joseph narrative. Indeed, the focus is on Joseph, but all the sons are in view here. They, after all, are the sons of Jacob, who gives his new name Israel to the nation that descends from him, and his twelve sons are the patronyms of the twelve tribes of Israel. Their actions here, particularly Joseph's and Judah's, are relevant to the later history of Israel.

---

1. As explicated well by D. J. A. Clines, *The Theme of the Pentateuch*, 2nd ed. (London: T & T Clark, 1997).

The book of Genesis is, as the name implies, a book of beginnings: the beginning of the cosmos, the beginning of humanity, the beginning of Israel. In narrative terms a beginning leads to a middle and to an end. The book, in other words, is ultimately not to be read isolated from the rest of the Pentateuch, the Old Testament, or finally the Christian canon as a whole.

The ending of Genesis makes it clear that the story of God's work with his people does not end with its close. In Genesis 50:22–26, in anticipation of his death, Joseph anticipates the return of Israel as he makes his brothers swear to take his bones to the promised land and bury them there.

## Composition, Transmission, and Canonicity

### Authorship and Date

The question of the authorship and the date of writing of the book of Genesis has been one of the most contested questions in biblical scholarship for over two centuries. As a matter of fact, in many quarters one's answer to this question is a matter of orthodoxy and thus evokes great passion.

The issue of the authorship of Genesis is inextricably bound to the question of who wrote the Torah (or Pentateuch), which as we observed above is a literary, if not an authorial, whole. On one side, for some, orthodoxy is signaled by the simple statement that Moses wrote the whole of the Pentateuch (with maybe some minor exceptions known as postmosaica [passages that had to be written after the death of Moses, see Gen 11:28 and 14:14 for examples] and amosaica [passages that would be awkward for Moses to write; Num 12:4]). On the other extreme are those who say that Moses wrote none of the Pentateuch, but rather the Pentateuch was composed much later than the time the Bible purported that he lived (if, in the minds of some, he lived at all).

While the extremes can be represented in such a straightforward and simple way (the author is Moses or not), there are a number of variations among scholars that might fall into these two general categories. For the purposes of this commentary, it is not necessary for us to get into the details of these views. No matter who wrote the book of Genesis or how it was written, we are going to concentrate on the final form of the book. The commentary will use the NIV (2011) as a base, which is a translation of the Codex Leningradensis as presented in the Biblia Hebraica Stuttgartensia in consultation with important variant texts (when the NIV departs from Leningradensis, it is noted in a footnote). Such a text, we believe, is not an exact replica of the original text of the final form (the so-called autograph), but we are confident that it is extremely close.

Thus, here we will simply describe our understanding of the composition of Genesis (the Pentateuch) and refer the interested reader to our fuller discussion of the matter elsewhere where we also interact with rival views.[2] In the following discussion, whatever we say about the Pentateuch pertains to the book of Genesis, though we will also on occasion refer specifically to the book of Genesis.

Right from the start it is important to note that the Pentateuch is anonymous. Nowhere in the Pentateuch is an author named, not Moses or any other person. However, that said, a number of passages in the Pentateuch mention that Moses wrote things down. Consider the following:

> Then the LORD said to Moses, "Write this on a scroll as something to be remembered and make sure that Joshua hears it ..." (Exod 17:14)
>
> When Moses went and told the people all the LORD's words and laws, they responded with one voice, "Everything the LORD has said we will do." Moses then wrote down everything the LORD had said. (Exod 24:3–4, in reference to the law God gave Moses)
>
> At the LORD's command Moses recorded [wrote down] the stages in their journey. (Num 33:2)
>
> After Moses finished writing in a book the words of this law from beginning to end ... (Deut 31:24)

And these references are just a sample of a number of other passages that could be cited (see also Exod 24:12; 34:28; Deut 27:3, 8; 31:19). Notice that none of these passages concern the writing of the book of Genesis (see below).

Certainly the passages that speak of Moses writing things down do not claim that Moses wrote the entirety of the Pentateuch, but they do imply that Moses wrote material that was incorporated into the Pentateuch. With this in mind, we turn now to references to the "book of the law of Moses" or "the book of Moses" (with variants) found in biblical books that follow the Pentateuch. The first example comes from Joshua 1, and then they reverberate through the rest of the Old Testament. The following are just a few examples:

> "Be strong and very courageous. Be careful to obey all the law my servant Moses gave you; do not turn from it to the right or to the left, that you may be successful wherever you go. Keep this Book of the Law always on your lips ..." (Josh 1:7–8a)
>
> Yet he did not put their children to death, but acted in accordance with what is written in the Law, in the Book of Moses, where the LORD commanded ... (2 Chr 25:4)

2. See T. Longman III and R. B. Dillard, *Introduction to the Old Testament*, 2nd ed. (Grand Rapids: Zondervan, 2006), 40–51 and idem, *How to Read Genesis* (Downers Grove, IL: InterVarsity Press, 2005), 43–58.

> On that day the Book of Moses was read aloud in the hearing of the people ... (Neh 13:1)

These references to the Book or Law of Moses are not necessarily, and until the postexilic period are unlikely, indicating the Pentateuch in its final form as we know it, but still they attest to some body of writing that was connected to the figure of Moses.

When we come to the New Testament, however, such references are more likely to refer to the final form of the Pentateuch, though still they do not mean that Moses wrote every word. But they do imply a belief that Moses had an integral connection with the composition of the Pentateuch.

In the New Testament, when quoting the Pentateuch, people often spoke of Moses being the author. For example, the disciples, referring to Deuteronomy 24:1–4, questioned Jesus, "'Why then,' they asked, 'did Moses command that a man give his wife a certificate of divorce and send her away?'" (Matt 19:7). Jewish leaders asked Jesus a question based on Deuteronomy 25:5–10 by saying, "'Teacher,' they said, 'Moses told us that if a man dies without having children, his brother must marry the widow and raise up offspring for him'" (Matt 22:24). Jesus himself, quoting the fifth commandment (Exod 20:12; Deut 5:16) and a case law (Exod 21:17; Lev 20:9), said, "For Moses said, 'Honor your father and mother,' and 'Anyone who curses their father or mother is to be put to death" (Mark 7:10). For other New Testament references see Mark 12:26; John 1:17, 5:46, 7:23.

In light of the references to Moses' writing in the Pentateuch and the post-pentateuchal citations to the Pentateuch that associate Moses with its composition, it seems reasonable to affirm that the origins of the Pentateuch are connected to this great biblical figure.

But to say that the composition, even the origins, of the Pentateuch is to be associated with Moses certainly does not mean he wrote every word. Traditional approaches to this question acknowledge that Moses did not write the entirety of the Pentateuch when they point to a so-called postmosaica.

Postmosaica are passages that had to be written after the death of Moses, and of course, the most obvious postmosaica is the account of his death in Deuteronomy 34. There are postmosaica in the book of Genesis as well. While Ur is an ancient city predating Moses, the reference to Ur of the Chaldeans (see Gen 11:31) is a postmosaica since the Chaldeans were an Aramaic-speaking tribe that lived in the first millennium BC, long after the death of Moses. In Genesis 14:14 the narrator reports that Abram chased the four ancient Near Eastern kings who kidnapped Lot "as far as Dan." This reference to the city of Dan is a postmosaica because this city, earlier called Laish, was not named Dan until the time of the Judges (see Judg 18), and of course the name derived from the tribe of Dan named after Jacob's son Dan, Abraham's great grandson.

While some people believe that Moses wrote everything in the Pentateuch except a handful of postmosaica, the postmosaica may only be the tip of the iceberg. These postmosaica establish a principle that later inspired editors/redactors can contribute to the writing of the Pentateuch.

For our next comment, we turn specifically to the book of Genesis. Of course, the narrative speaks of events that take place long before the birth of Moses. It is interesting that Moses is never mentioned in the book even as writing things down. Instead, we encounter a formula that appears eleven times in the book (2:4; 5:1; 6:9; 10:1; 11:10, 27; 25:12, 19; 36:1, 9; 37:2). This formula is introduced by *elleh toledot* PN, "This is the account of PN," where PN is the personal name of the person whose descendants will be the subject of the following section. These indicate the use of oral and/or written sources (see 5:1) for the writing of the book of Genesis.

Taking seriously the indications within the Pentateuch itself, along with the post-pentateuchal references to the Book/Law of Moses, one might conclude that the Pentateuch finds its origins in Moses, who used sources particularly in the writing of Genesis. The postmosaica indicate that there were editorial additions. These additions may only be the most obvious examples of textual material added after the time of Moses and we cannot determine precisely what was authored by Moses or added by later inspired editors. In the final analysis, it is not necessary to do so because what is canonical is not restricted to what Moses wrote, but to the final composition of the Pentateuch, which may not have reached final form until the postexilic period.

## Canonicity

The book of Genesis (as the first part of the five-part Torah) has always been accepted as canon (in Jewish terminology it "makes the hands unclean," since coming into contact with something holy can render a person ritually unclean.)[3] Christians share the same canon as first-century Pharisees. The Sadducees, however, only accepted the Torah as authoritative, but this, of

3. The Old Testament speaks of people either as clean or unclean. These categories are not easy for modern people to understand since they don't correlate simply to ethical categories like righteousness and sin or even simple hygiene. People were normally "clean," but could come become unclean under certain conditions. One might become unclean by coming into contact with something that represents death (like a corpse), but paradoxically one can also become unclean by coming into contact with something that represents life (semen, the blood of a woman's reproductive system). In the case of the later Jewish idea that the scrolls that contain Scripture can make one unclean, it is the latter cause that is in mind. On a practical level, the person who handled Scripture then signified their move from the realm of the common to the realm of holy by washing their hands before and after handling the scroll. For more on the concept of ritual purity, see R. K. Duke, "Priests, Priesthood,"

course, meant that they affirmed the book of Genesis.[4] In brief, the canonicity of Genesis is without controversy.

In Jewish circles, the first book of the Bible is known by its opening phrase *bereshit* ("in the beginning"). In the English Bible tradition, based on the Septuagint, the book's name is Genesis, from a Greek word that means "origins." These names are appropriate because this book is a book of origins, beginning with the origins of the cosmos and humanity and moving on to the story of the origins of the people of Israel in the call of Abraham and the promise that his descendants will be a "great nation" (Gen 12:2).

## Literary Analysis

### Genre

The Bible contains books of different literary types. What kind of book is Genesis?

The book talks about past events and to that extent can be called a work of history. However, its central concern is not politics or economics or military history, but rather it focuses on God's relationship with his human creatures and eventually with Abraham and his descendants. In that sense, Genesis is a theological history.

The argument that all of Genesis is a theological history is rooted in the consistent use of the *waw*-consecutive verbal form, which is the Hebrew form used to narrate past action[5] as well as the appearance of the *toledot* formula throughout the whole book. These two features appear to indicate that Genesis 1 – 11 and 12 – 50 share a similar genre. That said, there is not only similarity in the intent to speak of the past but also a difference between Genesis 1 – 11 and 12 – 50 in how the author presents the past.

Genesis 1 – 11 speaks of the distant past. Attempts to try to date the time of creation by means of the numbers contained in the genealogies fail because the genealogies are not exhaustive and the numbers are likely not to be taken literally; they have different purposes (see discussion at Gen 5). Based on our present knowledge derived from science, the origins of the cosmos are to be located in the Big Bang that happened approximately fourteen billion years ago. The creation of *homo sapiens sapiens* occurred about two hundred thousand years ago. Certainly the biblical author had no knowledge of this expanse of time, but a modern reader knows that the story of creation of the cosmos

---

in *Dictionary of the Old Testament: Pentateuch*, ed. by T. D. Alexander and D. W. Baker (Downers Grove, IL: InterVarsity Press, 2003), 650 – 51.

4. R. Beckwith, *The Old Testament Canon in the New Testament Church* (London: SPCK, 1985).

5. G. C. Aalders, *Genesis* (Grand Rapids: Zondervan, 1981), 45.

and human beings is a depiction of events that happened in the deep past. It is futile for many reasons to try to date the other events of Genesis 1–11, but we do know that the end of this part of Genesis brings us up to the time of Abraham, for whom we have no precise date, but we know he lived sometime around the first quarter of the second millennium BC.

Thus, Genesis 1–11 covers a vast amount of time, and the focus of the narrative is on the whole world. With such wide narrative sweep and scope, no wonder we are left many, many unanswerable questions.

There are many signals that Genesis 1–11, though theological history and thus making claims about the past, speaks of events in a nonliteral and imprecise fashion. These signals include an intense use of obviously figurative language (e.g., the days of creation; God breathing into dust), interplay with ancient Near Eastern mythological texts (Enuma Elish, Atrahasis, Baal Myth, Gilgamesh, Adapa, etc.), and cases of nonchronological sequence (between Gen 1 and 2 and 10 and 11:1–9). We refer the reader to the commentary on Genesis 1–11 where we highlight these narrative features.

When we come to the beginning of the *toledot* of Terah (11:27; the beginning of the patriarchal narratives), we do not have a dramatic shift in genre. The narrator continues to speak of the past with a theological focus. But narrative time slows down and the focus narrows, concentrating on the life of Abraham, then Isaac, then Jacob, and finally the twelve sons of Jacob (with primary attention to Joseph and then also on Judah). There is less figurative language and less interplay with ancient Near Eastern mythology (though ancient Near Eastern texts often inform us of relevant social customs). The author thus signals an interest to communicate actual events in a more precise manner as the narrative turns to events which form the foundation for Israel.

Our discussion has focused on the book of Genesis as a whole. Within the narrative whole, which we have identified as a theological history, the author has incorporated other types of literature into the main narrative genre. Genesis 4:17–5:32 is the first of a number of genealogies for instance. Genesis 14 is a narrative, but of a particular type, the battle report, and Genesis 49 is an example of a poetic testament. These and other types of literature will be discussed, as appropriate, at the relevant place in the commentary.

## Style

Genesis is a work of theological history. While Hans Frei memorably called this type of biblical literature "history-like story,"[6] we believe "story-like history" is more appropriate. While Genesis reports events in the past, it does so

6. H. W. Frei, *The Eclipse of Biblical Narrative: A Study in Eighteenth and Nineteenth Century Hermeneutics* (New Haven, CT: Yale University Press, 1974).

in the form of vivid and gripping stories with compelling characters and plot twists that capture the imagination of the reader.

As scholarly attention turned back to an interest in studying the Old Testament as literature around 1980,[7] Genesis and Samuel were quickly recognized as exceptional examples of narrative artistry. In this section of the introduction, we will simply highlight some of the characteristics of Hebrew storytelling. Modern readers may not be naturally familiar with the conventions of Hebrew narrative. As Alter pointed out:

> Every culture, even every era in a particular culture, develops distinctive and sometimes intricate codes for telling its stories, involving everything from narrative point of view, procedures of description and characterization, the management of dialogue, to the order of time and the organization of plot.[8]

While space does not allow nor is there necessity for a discussion of each of these topics, we will highlight a few of the conventions of the Hebrew storyteller that are particularly relevant for understanding the book of Genesis.

As is typical throughout the Hebrew Bible, a third-person, unnamed, omniscient narrator presents the story. The narrator knows what people are thinking and also what they are doing when alone. Indeed, the narrator depicts the creation even before the emergence of human beings. While there is no explicit connection made, when one reads Genesis as sacred literature, the impression on the reader is that one is getting a divine perspective on the events and the characters.

The narrator is the one who describes action and also presents speech. Indeed, it is fair to say that the story is moved along predominantly through the latter. Genesis 3 is a typical example presenting a story of the first human rebellion against God by a dialogue between the serpent and Eve, followed by God speaking to Adam (whose silence has significance in the earlier episode [see commentary]). Then God speaks to the woman, followed by pronouncements delivered to the serpent, the woman, and the man, in succession and individually. Indeed, it is typical of biblical prose to present two people and no more speaking to each other.

For the purposes of proper interpretation, it is important for the modern reader to understand the reticent style of the narrator of Genesis. Physical

---

7. R. Alter's *The Art of Biblical Narrative* (New York: Basic, 1981) is commonly recognized as a pivotal book in a new interest in the literary artistry of Hebrew narrative.

8. R. Alter, "A Response to Critics," *JSOT* 27 (1983): 113. My own views may be found in T. Longman III, "Biblical Narrative," in *A Complete Literary Guide to the Bible*, eds. L. Ryken and T. Longman III (Grand Rapids: Zondervan, 1993), 69–79.

description is never gratuitous. Esau's ruddy complexion and his hairy chest play a role in the story as of course does the beauty of Rachel and the "weak eyes" of Leah. The narrator is not interested in helping us visualize a scene by such descriptions; they always forward the plot.

The narrator is also reticent in providing evaluations or giving motivations. Why does God prefer Abel's sacrifice to Cain's (Gen 4)? Was Jacob correct in his angry denunciation of Levi and Simeon's slaughter of the Shechemite males (Gen 34)? These are just two of the questions that modern readers often stumble over, expecting explicit narrative statements rather than heeding the subtle clues provided by the narrator's careful presentation.

While Genesis as a whole may be rightfully described as a work of theological history written in narrative prose, it certainly contains other types of writing as well. We will discuss genealogy at Genesis 4:17–5:32, but we should also take note of the occurrence of poetry at various places within the story. Most poems in Genesis are brief like Adam's celebration of the creation of Eve (Gen 2:23), but Jacob's final words of blessing and curse on his twelve sons (Gen 49) constitutes a poem of significant length.

Full descriptions of biblical poetry may be found elsewhere,[9] but here we highlight three characteristics. First, while prose is written in sentences that form paragraphs that form discourses, poetry is made of short, typically two- or three-word clauses (often called cola). Two or three cola make a parallel line (a bi- or tricolon), which forms stanzas. The poet packs a lot of meaning in just a few words, meaning that the reader must slow down and reflect carefully on the message of the poem.

As mentioned, these cola form parallel lines. While these parallel lines often appear to say almost the same thing twice, Kugel has persuaded modern interpreters that a better paradigm is to read the parallel line knowing that the second colon furthers and progresses (or even sharpens) the thought of the first colon.[10]

Finally, poetry utilizes a lot of figurative language. The prose of Genesis is highly literary, so it too, particularly Genesis 1–11, utilizes figurative language, but that use is heightened and intensified in a poem.

## Structure

There is more than one way to describe the structure of the book of Genesis. When we discussed the composition of the book, we took note of the *toledot* formula that occurs eleven times and is an indicator of oral and/or written

9. See the relevant articles in T. Longman III and P. Enns, eds., *Dictionary of the Old Testament: Wisdom, Poetry, and Writings* (Downers Grove, IL: InterVarsity Press, 2008).

10. J. Kugel, *The Idea of Biblical Poetry* (New Haven, CT: Yale University Press, 1981).

sources for the writing of the book. The book can be structured according to the *toledot* formula. The only question that would arise has to do with the first occurrence of the formula that appears at the juncture of the two creation accounts at the beginning of 2:4. Is this the conclusion to the first or the introduction to the second? We cannot be sure, but since all the other formula begin a section, we will treat this verse as the introduction to the second creation account and thus the first account is a type of introduction to the whole. We end up with the following structure:

| | |
|---|---|
| Introduction: | 1:1–2:3 |
| The *toledot* of the heavens and the earth: | 2:3–4:26 |
| The *toledot* of Adam: | 5:1–6:8 |
| The *toledot* of Noah: | 6:9–9:29 |
| The *toledot* of the sons of Noah: Shem, Ham, and Japheth | 10:1–11:9 |
| The *toledot* of Shem: | 11:10–26 |
| The *toledot* of Terah: | 11:27–25:11 |
| The *toledot* of Ishmael: | 25:12–18 |
| The *toledot* of Isaac: | 25:19–35:29 |
| The *toledot* of Esau: | 36:1–8 |
| The second *toledot* of Esau: | 36:9–37:1 |
| The *toledot* of Jacob: | 37:2–50:26 |

For the purposes of the present commentary, however, we will follow a more general structure of the book. Even the reader of the English Bible without special training can, if reading closely, detect three major sections of the book of Genesis:

1. The Primeval History (1:1–11:26)
2. The Patriarchal Narratives (11:27–37:1)
3. The Joseph Story (37:2–50:26)

For ease of reference, the three sections will hereafter typically be described as Genesis 1–11 (primeval history), 12–36 (patriarchal narratives), and 37–50 (the Joseph narrative). The three sections have a different literary feel and theological focus to them, though in the final analysis they tell a single story.

The primeval history spans the time from creation up to the time of Abraham, which, as we described above, represents an incredibly long period, at least as measured in real time. The narrative focus is on the entire world. After presenting two synoptic accounts of creation (Gen 1–2), there follow four stories of divine judgment and continuing grace in response to human sin: Adam and Eve's initial rebellion (Gen 3), Cain and Abel (Gen 4:1–16), the flood and its aftermath (Gen 6:1–9:28), and the tower of Babel (Gen 11:1–9). Genealogies connect these stories with each other and give a sense of the passage of time: genealogies of Cain and Seth (Gen 4:17–5:32), the genealogies of Japheth, Ham, and Shem (Gen 10), and a second genealogy of Shem that leads to Abraham (Gen 11:10–26). This last named genealogy leads to the introduction of the patriarchal narratives.

The patriarchal narratives speak of the founding fathers (and mothers) of the future nation of Israel. As attention turns to the first patriarch, Abraham, narrative time dramatically slows down as does narrative focus. Rather than the story of the world from creation to Abraham being told in eleven chapters, the story of Abraham runs from 11:27 to 25:11, followed by the stories of Isaac and Jacob that run from 25:12 to 37:1. Of course, Isaac plays a significant role in the Abraham story, as Jacob plays a major role in the story of Isaac.

The book ends with the Joseph story, called such because Joseph plays such a dominant role in this last section of the book of Genesis. The Joseph story has a different literary feel than the previous sections of the book, reading like a short story or novella. Joseph is not considered a patriarch (later tradition speaks of God as the God of Abraham, Isaac, and Jacob). In the previous generations, the covenant promises were passed down from Abraham to Isaac (not Ishmael) and then from Isaac to Jacob (not Esau). Though Joseph is the focus of the final section of Genesis, there is no sense in which he uniquely inherits the covenant promises. Jacob, whose name is changed to Israel has twelve sons, all of whom are the founding fathers of tribes in later Israel. The Joseph narrative provides a bridge to the account of the exodus, explaining why the Israelites find themselves in Egypt some centuries later in bondage and requiring divine deliverance.

## Historical Background

### Historical Setting of the Contents of the Book

To summarize the information found above, the contents of the book of Genesis cover the period of time from the creation until the death of Joseph. The period of time from creation until the time of Abraham is covered in a mere eleven chapters. We are not given enough information in the Bible to date creation. We are on slightly better grounds when it comes to the next section, the patriarchal narratives, though it is fruitless to attempt to be precise. At best we can say that Abraham, Isaac, and Jacob lived sometime around the first quarter of the second millennium BC. We can only come to the same uncertain conclusion with regard to the time of Joseph.

### Ancient Near Eastern Background

Since we are uncertain about the precise dates for the historical setting of the contents of the book of Genesis, it is also impossible to be precise about how the events it records fit into broader Near Eastern history. We (and others) can (and occasionally will) speculate about such matters, yet we remain uncertain about such matters as the identity of Nimrod (Gen 10:8–12) or the four Near Eastern kings who invade Canaan at the time of Abraham (Gen 14) or the identity of the unnamed Pharaoh at the time of Joseph.

As we will see in the commentary proper, ancient Near Eastern materials do provide background to the stories of Genesis in other ways. In the first place, our commentary on Genesis 1–11 will show extensive interplay with ancient Near Eastern creation (particularly the Babylonian Enuma Elish, Atrahasis, Adapa, as well as the Ugaritic Baal myth), flood story (especially Tablet 11 of the Gilgamesh Epic), and stories of an original singular human language (Enmerkar and the Lord of Aratta). We will also see how important it is to read the genealogies of Genesis on the background of ancient Near Eastern genealogies and not modern ones.

As we turn our attention to Genesis 12–50, ancient Near Eastern material continues to prove illuminating, but not in quite the same way. In these chapters, ancient Near Eastern material illumines social customs (adopting a household servant and passing through animal parts [Gen 15], taking on a secondary wife [Gen 16], and much, much more). Of course, we will describe and explain all of these ancient Near Eastern connections in the commentary proper.

## Theological Message

### Reading in the Context of the Old Testament

The book of Genesis is theologically rich. As the first book of the canon, it provides a foundation for the knowledge of God and his human creatures' relationship with him. The theological teaching is varied and profound, each part of the book containing its unique focus and making its important theological contribution. The following commentary will bring out many of these themes when they emerge from the text under study.

At this point, however, we will take a look at the larger theological picture of Genesis as the foundational book of the Pentateuch and indeed of the whole Bible. When we think of the message of the Bible as a whole, in particular as a history of God's dealings with his human creatures, we can see that it has four basic parts: creation, fall, redemption, and consummation. The book of Genesis informs the reader about the creation and fall and initiates the story of God's redemption.

Genesis 1–2 speaks of God's creation of the cosmos with a focus on humanity. God created Adam and Eve who are without sin, or, to put it more positively, are moral beings who are innocent. They are in a harmonious relationship with God and thus with each other. They live in a land of abundance and delight (Eden), lacking nothing that they need. In a word, God "blessed" them (Gen 1:22, 28; cf. 5:2), blessing being an important word in the book of Genesis. Those who are blessed by God have a vibrant and healthy relationship with him, with each other, and with the world in which they live.

As we turn to the second act of the biblical story, the fall (Gen 3), we read about Adam and Eve's sin which forfeited the divine blessing. Since sin disrupted humanity's relationship with God, their relationship with each other is fractured, signaled by their inability to be naked and unashamed as well as the punishment leveled at Eve (3:16). Their relationship to the creation also changed for the worse, as noted particularly in the punishment announced to Adam that the land would no longer easily yield its produce to human labor (3:17–19).

Genesis tells us that, rather than human sin being the end of the story, God immediately begins the work of redemption as he passionately pursues his human creatures for the purpose of reconciliation. Indeed, the seed of the third act of redemption begins as early as Genesis 3 with the announcement of judgment on the serpent, that ancient symbol of evil that led to the disruption of relationship. Genesis 3:15 announces hostility between the serpent and the woman and their respective offspring, culminating in a victory over the serpent ("he will crush your head," 3:15). God also shows his intention of staying involved with his human creatures in spite of their sin when he gives them garments to cover their nakedness (3:21). Yes, they will eventually die, but before they do, they have children. Humanity does not come to an end with the initial rebellion.

As the story continues after the fall, humanity does split into two parts, those who follow God and those who reject God: Cain and Abel (Gen 4:1–16), the Cainites and the Sethites (Gen 4:17–5:32). By the time of the flood, there was only one righteous person (Noah), while the rest of the world was wicked (6:5). As with Adam and Eve, God judged the wicked, though he continues to stay involved with his human creatures. At the time of Noah, he shows his continuing grace by telling Noah to build an ark and survive the flood that would eradicate the rest of the wicked world.

As Noah and his family step out of the ark after the flood, Noah offers a sacrifice. We should notice the language here, "Then God blessed Noah and his sons, saying to them, 'Be fruitful and increase in number and fill the earth'" (9:1). Here we see that significant word "bless" again, along with language that echoes back to Genesis 1. In the commentary to follow, we will see that Noah is a kind of new Adam, but as with Adam and Eve before him, humanity will again soon sin and suffer the effects of their rebellion in a broken relationship with God, with each other, and with their world. Even so, as the final story (the tower of Babel) of the first part of Genesis (the primeval history, chapters 1 – 11) tells us, God stays involved with his human creatures. He keeps them from experiencing the full consequences of their actions even while he shows them grace in not removing their ability to communicate, even while he makes it more difficult.

But God is not done seeking reconciliation, and as we move to the second major part of the book of Genesis (the patriarchal narratives, chapters 12 – 36), we see that key word "blessing" right at the beginning. In what is certainly one of the most pivotal passages in all Scripture, God speaks to Abraham:

> Go from your country, your people and your father's household to the land I will show you.
> I will make you into a great nation,
> and I will bless you;
> I will make your name great,
> and you will be a blessing.
> I will bless those who bless you,
> and whoever curses you I will curse;
> and all peoples on earth
> will be blessed through you. (Gen 12:1 – 3)

God continues to seek reconciliation with humanity, and now he will do so through Abraham and his descendants. The patriarchal narratives tell the story of how these promises pass down to Isaac from Abraham and to Jacob from Isaac. From time to time, God reiterates his blessing on the patriarchs and his intention to bless the world through them (14:19; 17:6, 20; 18:18; 22:17; 24:1, 31, 35; 25:11; 26:3, 24, 29; 27:29; 28:14; 32:6; 35:9). As we will note at relevant places in the commentary, God does indeed both bless Abraham and his descendants as well as peoples from other nations, including those who are descendants of Ishmael and Esau, the nonelect sons of the patriarchs.

The third and final part of Genesis focuses on the sons of Jacob, particularly Joseph and secondarily Judah (Gen 37 – 50). That God blesses Abraham and his descendants during Joseph's generation is made clear in the story of Joseph in Potiphar's house. God was with Joseph during this time and everything he did succeeded as a result. Also in keeping with the promise of blessing to Abraham, we see here that blessing flows through Joseph to the nations as Potiphar's household prospers under his management: "From the time he put him [Joseph] in charge of his household and of all that he owned, the Lord blessed the household of the Egyptian because of Joseph. The blessing of the Lord was on everything Potiphar had, both in the house and in the field" (39:5). God used Joseph to make plans for the coming famine so that the family of God would survive, as well as the country of Egypt itself.

The book of Genesis looks to the future as well. First, Jacob blesses Joseph's sons, Ephraim and Manasseh, both future tribes of Israel (48:9, 16). Then, in Genesis 49 he blesses a number of his own sons in a way that will have ramifications for the future of Israel.

Thus, the book of Genesis lays the foundation for all of the history of redemption. It starts by describing the creation of the cosmos and humanity. Humans live a life of blessing, which is soon disrupted by their own rebellion. But right from the start of their rebellion God begins his pursuit of restoration of blessing with his people.

This story of God's work of redemption continues through the rest of the Old Testament. When the book of Exodus begins, some centuries have passed through the close of the book of Genesis. Abraham's descendants are no longer a large family, but now are a numerous people. Yet they are enslaved by the Egyptians. The story of the remainder of the Pentateuch is how God acts on the basis of his covenant promises and frees his people from Egyptian bondage so that they can serve him rather than the false god Pharaoh. They then travel to Mount Sinai where God will constitute them as a nation, giving them the law (Exod 19–24) and commanding them to build a tabernacle, a place where he will make his presence known among his people (Exod 25–40). The remainder of the Pentateuch (Lev 1–Deut 34) reports Israel's rebellion against God and thus their forty-year sojourn in the wilderness.

While the Pentateuch ends with a sense of closure with the death of Moses, the reader knows that more is to come. After all, in the book of Deuteronomy, Moses gave his final sermon to the Israelites, warning the second generation not to disobey like their forefathers; the exodus generation did, and thus die without coming into the promised land.

The book of Joshua then continues the story begun in the Pentateuch as it tells the story of the conquest (Josh 1–12) and the settlement of the land (Josh 13–24). Though the land is not completely taken until the time of David, the fact that the many descendants of Abraham now possess land in Canaan shows the beginning of the fulfillment of the promise God made to Abraham that his descendants will become a "great nation" (Gen 12:2).

With the conquest and settlement behind them, Joshua leads the Israelites in a reaffirmation of their relationship with God in which they determine to continue worshiping him and obeying him (Josh 24). In spite of their commitment, the book of Judges tells us the dark story of the next generations, a time of great moral depravity, political fragmentation, and spiritual confusion. Even the leaders, the so-called judges, are problematic, particularly toward the end of the time period with leaders like Jephthah and Samson.

The books of Samuel and Kings (as well as Chronicles) continue the story, beginning with the transition from the last judge (Samuel) to the first king Saul (1 Sam 1–12). Kingship had been anticipated in God's words to Abraham in Genesis 17:7, but the Joseph narrative in which Judah emerges as an important leader of the brothers would lead us to expect that kingship would originate in the tribe of Judah, not in Saul's Benjamin. Jacob's blessing on Judah affirms that impression (Gen 49:8–12).

Perhaps not surprisingly, Saul disappoints and the story of redemption turns to an account of the kingship of David from Judah. David is not perfect by any stretch of the imagination. He too is a sinner, most notably in the matter of his adultery with Bathsheba and his murder of her husband. Still, the difference between Saul and David is that David sincerely repents and thus models a proper attitude toward God.

The short period of the united monarchy comes to a close with the reign of Solomon, David's son. He begins with great promise, manifesting a loving heart toward God. God thus gave him the gift of wisdom (1 Kgs 3), which characterized the first part of his rule. Sadly, his love of foreign women turned this incredibly wise king who loved Yahweh into a fool who worshiped foreign gods. His apostasy led to the division of the kingdom into two parts with only the southern kingdom of Judah ruled by a descendant of David.

The period of the so-called divided monarchy is told by both the books of Kings as well as Chronicles (which places this period in the context of the entire history of redemption up to that point). The former was written during the exile and intends to answer the question, "Why did God punish us?" The latter came to its final form during the postexilic period and thus addresses different questions: "How do we relate to the past?" and "Now what do we do?"

This is not the place for a full description of the agendas of these two great historical works, nor an individual recounting of the different emphases of each. While Chronicles presents a much more positive account of the period, both agree, though Kings emphasizes, that the kings of Israel and Judah both led God's people in a direction which brought God's judgment on them.

That judgment resulted in the defeat of the northern kingdom by the Assyrians in 722 BC. The Assyrians deported some of the Israelites to other regions of its kingdom, while importing foreign people into Israel. The result was intermarriage and the emergence of the Samaritans.

Judgment on the southern kingdom of Judah, ruled by the descendants of David, came at a later time (586 BC). The Babylonians defeated Jerusalem, destroyed the temple, and exiled the political, military, and religious elites to Babylon. However, they did not force intermarriage or import foreign people into Judah. Thus, after this period of judgment and exile, some of the Jewish exiles returned to Jerusalem after the Persians defeated the Babylonians and Cyrus, the conquering Persian king, permitted those Jews who wanted to return to go back to Jerusalem and rebuild the temple (Ezra 1:1–4).

Accordingly, the Old Testament does not end on a note of judgment, but with restoration. That said, the story of the restoration is rather tepid. Yes, a number of Jewish exiles returned to Jerusalem and eventually the temple was rebuilt. But God's people remained under the political shadow of the Persians and then eventually the Greeks and, moving closer to the New Testament time period, the Romans.

As the Old Testament closes, prophetic voices of the postexilic period (Daniel, Zechariah, etc.) look forward to something more grand than what the people of God had experienced up to that point. That story continues into the New Testament period.

### Reading from the Perspective of the New Testament

In the previous section, we noted that the Bible can be summarized as a plot with four parts: creation, fall, redemption, and consummation. The story of creation and fall are the subject of the first three chapters of Genesis. God starts seeking humanity's redemption right from the start (see Gen 3:15), and his pursuit of reconciliation with humanity continues from Genesis 4 on, indeed throughout the remainder of the Old Testament. We noted that "blessing" played an important role in the book of Genesis. God created humanity in a blessed condition only for them to forfeit that status when they rebelled against God. The goal of redemption is the restoration of blessing to humanity.

The pivotal turning point in the history of redemption in the book of Genesis comes in Genesis 12:1–3, where God chooses Abraham and promises that he will bless him and his descendants and all the nations of the world through him. While we see glimpses of this blessing on both the chosen family as well as peoples from other nations throughout Genesis and beyond in the Old Testament, the Old Testament does not bring us to a point of realization, or consummation, of the promise.

But how does the New Testament relate to the Old Testament? Or to put it another way, how should a Christian read the Old Testament now that Christ has come?

Interestingly, Jesus himself spoke to this issue in the period of time between his resurrection and ascension. According to Luke 24, Jesus told two different groups of followers how he expected them to read the Old Testament as anticipatory of his coming.

The first occasion describes his meeting two disciples as they are walking to Emmaus on the day he rose from the dead. God kept them from recognizing Jesus, so when he inquired why they were so upset, they are amazed he does not know about the events of the past few days where the one in whom they had invested so much hope had been executed.

Jesus responds sharply to them, " 'How foolish you are, and how slow to believe all that the prophets have spoken! Did not the Messiah have to suffer these things and then enter his glory?' And beginning with Moses and all the Prophets, he explained to them what was said in all the Scriptures concerning himself" (Luke 24:25–27).

The second episode involves a larger group of disciples. He tells them, " 'This is what I told you while I was still with you: Everything must be fulfilled that is written about me in the Law of Moses, the Prophets and the Psalms.' Then he opened their minds so they could understand the Scriptures" (Luke 24:44–45).

Using terminology familiar to a first-century-AD audience ("Moses and all the Prophets," "the Law of Moses, the Prophets and the Psalms," and "Scriptures"), Jesus tells his disciples that the whole Old Testament anticipates his coming. Such statements have a major impact on how Christians should read the Old Testament, and, for our purposes, the book of Genesis.

First, we must read Genesis and ask how it was understood by the original audience. This "first reading" of the text leads us to what Brevard Childs called the "discrete voice" or "discrete witness" of the Old Testament.[11] Christians, however, live in the time when the shadows of the Old Testament give way to the reality which they anticipate—Jesus. As Augustine famously stated, "The New Testament is in the Old concealed; the Old Testament is in the New Testament revealed." Thus, Christians go on to read the Old Testament a second time in the light of the resurrected Christ.

In principle, we are encouraging a reading of the Bible that is not different than reading any other book, or watching a movie, for that matter. Jon Levenson, a prominent Jewish academic, recognizes the importance for the Christian of reading the Old Testament in the light of the New Testament. He likens it to reading a Shakespeare play when he says: "Christian exegesis requires that the Hebrew Bible be read ultimately in a literary context that

11. B. S. Childs, *Biblical Theology of the Old and New Testaments: Theological Reflection on the Christian Bible* (Minneapolis: Fortress, 1993), 76.

includes the New Testament. To read it only on its own would be like reading the first three acts of Hamlet as if the last two had never been written."[12]

Thus, throughout this commentary, after explaining the passage in its Old Testament setting in the Explain the Story section, we will often, but not always, provide a reading of the passage from a New Testament perspective in the Live the Story section. These sections will show how the book of Genesis finds its ultimate goal in Christ.

While these Christotelic readings of the individual stories will be presented in the commentary proper,[13] here in the introduction we will continue our broader view begun in the previous section. There we saw how the story of creation (Gen 1–2), fall (Gen 3), and then redemption (Gen 3:15, then chapters 4–50)—the first three parts of the four-part structure of Scripture—are found in the book of Genesis. The story of redemption, God's acts to reconcile himself with humanity, continues through the history of the Old Testament. The Old Testament period ends on a note of expectation of future redemptive events, and so the New Testament understands that that expectation is met in the coming of Christ.

John the Baptist stands at the beginning of Jesus' ministry. He picks up where the last Old Testament prophets left off when he announces, "I baptize you with water for repentance. But after me comes one who is more powerful than I, whose sandals I am not worthy to carry. He will baptize you with the Holy Spirit and fire. His winnowing fork is in his hand, and he will clear his threshing floor, gathering his wheat into the barn and burning up the chaff with unquenchable fire" (Matt 3:11–12).

John recognizes Jesus as the expected one and baptizes him. When Jesus begins his work, John is thrown in jail, where he gets disturbing reports. He hears that Jesus is healing people, exorcising demons, and preaching the good news. When John hears this report, he sends two of his disciples to Jesus with a question: "Are you the one who is to come, or should we expect someone else?" (Matt 11:3).

Behind this question, we should hear another: "Why aren't you burning the chaff with unquenchable fire?" Jesus responds to the question by taking these disciples with him as he heals more people and preaches the good news to the poor.

---

12. J. Levenson, *The Hebrew Bible, the Old Testament and Historical Criticism: Jews and Christians in Biblical Studies* (Louisville: Westminster John Knox, 1993), 9.

13. Christotelic is a relatively recently coined term to refer to reading of Old Testament texts in the light of the resurrection of Christ. See P. Enns, *Inspiration and Incarnation* (Grand Rapids: Baker, 2005).

In this way, Jesus announces to John and to the readers of the Gospels that his work of redemption will not meet certain people's expectations, not immediately at least. While Old Testament prophets like Daniel, Zechariah, and Malachi, and then John the Baptist lead one to expect a warrior messiah who will destroy the enemies of God and his people, Jesus' work of redemption takes him to the cross. It is by dying rather than killing that Jesus defeats the ultimate enemy, Satan.

But were John the Baptist and the Old Testament prophets who preceded him wrong? They were not, though they did not understand the full import of their words. As Peter put it, the prophets, while their message is completely reliable, often spoke better than they knew because "prophecy never had its origin in the human will, but prophets, though human, spoke from God as they were carried along by the Holy Spirit" (2 Pet 1:21).

John spoke not knowing that the Messiah's coming had two parts. When Jesus came the first time, he went to the cross and through his death and resurrection achieved redemption for those who put their faith in him. But he is coming again as he himself announced (Mark 13) and as described in the apocalyptic portions of the New Testament, particularly the book of Revelation. Revelation 19:11–16 describes his second coming as that of a warrior ready to render judgment against human and spiritual enemies of God:

> I saw heaven standing open and there before me was a white horse, whose rider is called Faithful and True. With justice he judges and wages war. His eyes are like blazing fire, and on his head are many crowns. He has a name written on him that no one knows but he himself. He is dressed in a robe dipped in blood, and his name is the Word of God. The armies of heaven were following him, riding on white horses and dressed in fine linen, white and clean. Coming out of his mouth is a sharp sword with which to strike down the nations. "He will rule them with an iron scepter." He treads the winepress of the fury of the wrath of God Almighty. On his robe and on his thigh he has this name written: KING OF KINGS AND LORD OF LORDS. (Rev 19:11–16)

At Christ's second coming, God's enemies are defeated and his people are saved. This great final judgment then ushers in the fourth and final act of God's scriptural drama we have been describing: consummation. The final two chapters of the Bible describe the New Jerusalem. This consummation takes us back to the opening chapters of Genesis. It involves a return to origins, only better, as represented by the fact that two trees of life are planted on the opposite banks of the river that flows through the New Jerusalem (Rev 22:2).

Thus, we see how important it is to read any Old Testament text ultimately in the light of the death and resurrection of Christ. In the commentary that follows a number of the essays will offer readings on the passage being studied that suggest ways in which that passage anticipates Jesus.

## Reading from the Perspective of the Twenty-First Century

While Genesis is interesting as a work of ancient literature, the Jewish and the Christian communities believe that it has continuing relevance for life today. This commentary is written based on the premise that the book of Genesis informs our understanding of God, ourselves, and our world.

Indeed, this commentary series, while hopefully relevant to laypeople, is written with clergy in mind as they prepare to preach and teach God's written Word to their congregations. The series, and this particular volume, is written by Christian biblical scholars primarily for a Christian audience. Of course, this is clear from the previous section where we discussed reading the text from a New Testament perspective as anticipating the coming suffering and glorification of Christ.

In this section we introduce the idea, practiced throughout the commentary, of reading the book of Genesis as informing how to live a life pleasing to Christ. After all, we believe that the book of Genesis is a foundational part of the Christian canon. Canon means "standard," and in the case of the biblical canon, we mean those books that provide the standard of faith and practice for the church. For this reason, in the sections entitled Live the Story, we not only explore how these ancient stories inform our understanding of God and our relationship with him, and not only how they anticipate Christ (see previous section), but we also ask whether and how these stories teach us how to live in a way that is pleasing to God.

Not all Christians agree that the Old Testament, particularly its stories, is relevant for the Christian life today. Indeed, it is not uncommon to hear theologians or preaching professors make fun of those who teach the stories and then apply them by saying "Go thou and do likewise!" or, depending on the story, "Go thou and don't do likewise!" Certainly, there are plenty of examples of bad practical preaching from the Old Testament and below we will acknowledge that proper application of the Old Testament is not always a simple matter due to the matter of continuity and discontinuity between the Testaments.

The whole Bible, including the Old Testament, is a "mirror of the soul." As the great sixteenth century Reformer John Calvin stated (in reference to the Psalms but applicable to the whole Bible):

> What various and resplendent riches are contained in this treasury, it were difficult to find words to describe.... I have been wont to call this book not inappropriately, an anatomy of all parts of the soul; for there is not an emotion of which anyone can be conscious that is not here represented as in a mirror.[14]

When we look into a physical mirror, we find out how we are doing on the outside. We may look at ourselves in the morning and see that we are a mess and then take action to put ourselves in order before going public. Calvin's point when it comes to the Bible as a mirror of the soul is that when we read it as it is meant to be read, then we find out how we are doing on the inside. Are we moving toward God or away from him? Are we living a life pleasing or unpleasing to him?

Let's also remember that in the parable of the sower (Mark 4:1–20) Jesus talked about a farmer scattering the seed all over his field. Some of the seed landed on rock and did not produce; some landed on shallow ground and sprouted up quickly but then withered and died. But some landed on rich soil and that seed produced an abundant crop.

The seed, Jesus said, is the Word of God. What we call the Old Testament is the Word of God and it, like the seed, can, like the seed, move from what looks to be lifeless to fruitfulness. The Word can transform a dead life into an abundant one.

This transformation, while wonderful, is not magical; it must be planted, as Jesus said in the parable, in rich soil. While Jesus does not specify what the soil stands for, it seems likely that it points to an open and receptive heart.

In the Live the Story sections of the following commentary, we will treat the book of Genesis as a seed that can transform our life, and so we will read it as a mirror of the soul.

But this does raise the question of precisely how the Old Testament, and in our case Genesis, functions as seed and mirror for a Christian reader. After all, even a casual reader of the New Testament knows that the task of reading the Old Testament from a Christian perspective is not an easy one. At least, it is not as simple as studying the characters and simply emulating or avoiding their behavior.

In the first place, we will see that it is not unusual for the modern reader to wonder how to evaluate the actions of the characters in Genesis. We earlier talked about the "reticent narrator" (see Style above) who rarely is explicit in

---

14. Quoted from H. Lockyer, "In Wonder of the Psalms," *Christianity Today* 28 (March 2, 1984): 76.

his evaluation of the character's behavior (see example from Gen 34) or about their motivations (see example from the Cain and Abel story in Gen 4).

This calls the interpreter to read closely and attend to the subtle signals given by the narrator. However, even after we do that work, we need to consider the relationship between the testaments before we apply the text to our lives. After all, the coming of Jesus is the redemptive historical event anticipated in the Old Testament. The Old Testament remains canon for the church, but we also recognize that there is discontinuity as well as continuity between the Testaments.

In Matthew 5:17, Jesus did say: "I have not come to abolish [the Law or the Prophets]" (a reference to the entire Old Testament). He also said that not a single stroke of the Law will disappear until "everything is accomplished" (v. 18). As we read the New Testament, we see that Jesus did accomplish (that is fulfill) some aspects of the Law in a way that means Christians do not observe them anymore. To cite just one obvious example, Jesus fulfilled the law of sacrifice because on the cross he offered himself as the once and for all sacrifice (Heb 10), rendering animal sacrifice obsolete. Because Jesus fulfilled aspects of the Old Testament, the New Testament can speak of the Old Testament shadows that are fulfilled by their reality in Christ (e.g. Col 2:16–19).

That said, Paul also pointed out that in the Old Testament we find stories that "occurred as examples [for] us" (1 Cor 10:6, 11). The following commentary will attend sensitively to the issues of continuity and discontinuity as we look to these ancient texts as informative of our present Christian life.

# Resources for Those Teaching or Preaching the Book of Genesis

There are many good resources for the study of the book of Genesis. These include very academic treatments as well as popular writings directed at the laity. Many of these are found in the footnotes including other helpful commentaries to which I would give pride of place to Waltke, Wenham, Hamilton, Brueggemann, McKeown, and Matthews.

In addition I recommend the following books for further study beyond this commentary:

Clines, D. J. A. *The Theme of the Pentateuch*. 2nd edition. London: T & T Clark, 1997.

Duguid, I. M. *Living in the Gap between Promise and Reality: The Gospel according to Abraham*. Phillipsburg, NJ: Presbyterian and Reformed, 1999.

_______. *Living in the Grip of Relentless Grace: The Gospel in the Lives of Isaac and Jacob*. Phillipsburg, NJ: Presbyterian and Reformed, 2002.

Greidanus, S. *Preaching Christ from Genesis: Foundations for Expository Sermons*. Grand Rapids: Eerdmans, 2007.

Hughes, R. K. *Genesis: Beginning and Blessing*. Wheaton, IL: Crossway, 2004.

Kaminsky, J. *Yet I Loved Jacob: Reclaiming the Biblical Concept of Election*. Nashville: Abingdon, 2007.

Longman III, T. *How to Read Genesis*. Downers Grove, IL: InterVarsity Press, 2005.

CHAPTER 1

# Genesis 1:1 – 2:4a

## LISTEN to the Story

[1:1]In the beginning God created the heavens and the earth. [2]Now the
earth was formless and empty, darkness was over the surface of the deep,
and the Spirit of God was hovering over the waters.

[3]And God said, "Let there be light," and there was light. [4]God saw
that the light was good, and he separated the light from the darkness.
[5]God called the light "day," and the darkness he called "night." And there
was evening, and there was morning—the first day.

[6]And God said, "Let there be a vault between the waters to separate
water from water." [7]So God made the vault and separated the water under
the vault from the water above it. And it was so. [8]God called the vault
"sky." And there was evening, and there was morning—the second day.

[9]And God said, "Let the water under the sky be gathered to one place,
and let dry ground appear." And it was so. [10]God called the dry ground
"land," and the gathered waters he called "seas." And God saw that it was
good.

[11]Then God said, "Let the land produce vegetation: seed-bearing
plants and trees on the land that bear fruit with seed in it, according
to their various kinds." And it was so. [12]The land produced vegetation:
plants bearing seed according to their kinds and trees bearing fruit with
seed in it according to their kinds. And God saw that it was good. [13]And
there was evening, and there was morning—the third day.

[14]And God said, "Let there be lights in the vault of the sky to separate
the day from the night, and let them serve as signs to mark sacred times,
and days and years, [15]and let them be lights in the vault of the sky to give
light on the earth." And it was so. [16]God made two great lights—the
greater light to govern the day and the lesser light to govern the night. He
also made the stars. [17]God set them in the vault of the sky to give light on
the earth, [18]to govern the day and the night, and to separate light from
darkness. And God saw that it was good. [19]And there was evening, and
there was morning—the fourth day.

[20]And God said, "Let the water teem with living creatures, and let
birds fly above the earth across the vault of the sky." [21]So God created
the great creatures of the sea and every living thing with which the water
teems and that moves about in it, according to their kinds, and every
winged bird according to its kind. And God saw that it was good. [22]God
blessed them and said, "Be fruitful and increase in number and fill the
water in the seas, and let the birds increase on the earth." [23]And there was
evening, and there was morning—the fifth day.

[24]And God said, "Let the land produce living creatures according to
their kinds: the livestock, the creatures that move along the ground, and
the wild animals, each according to its kind." And it was so. [25]God made
the wild animals according to their kinds, the livestock according to their
kinds, and all the creatures that move along the ground according to their
kinds. And God saw that it was good.

[26]Then God said, "Let us make mankind in our image, in our
likeness, so that they may rule over the fish in the sea and the birds in the
sky, over the livestock and all the wild animals, and over all the creatures
that move along the ground."

[27]So God created mankind in his own image,
in the image of God he created them;
male and female he created them.

[28]God blessed them and said to them, "Be fruitful and increase in
number; fill the earth and subdue it. Rule over the fish in the sea and the
birds in the sky and over every living creature that moves on the ground."

[29]Then God said, "I give you every seed-bearing plant on the face of
the whole earth and every tree that has fruit with seed in it. They will be
yours for food. [30]And to all the beasts of the earth and all the birds in the
sky and all the creatures that move along the ground—everything that has
the breath of life in it—I give every green plant for food." And it was so.

[31]God saw all that he had made, and it was very good. And there was
evening, and there was morning—the sixth day.

[2:1]Thus the heavens and the earth were completed in all their vast array.

[2]By the seventh day God had finished the work he had been doing;
so on the seventh day he rested from all his work. [3]Then God blessed the
seventh day and made it holy, because on it he rested from all the work of
creating that he had done.

*Listening to the Text in the Story:* Ancient Near Eastern Texts: Enuma Elish; Baal Myth; Atum Creation Stories; Memphite Theology (Shabako Stone)

Genesis 1:1 – 2:4a begins the story of God's relationship with humanity, and thus there are no background texts in the Bible itself.[1] Even so, Israel's account of the origins of the cosmos and humanity was not written in a vacuum. The original audience knew rival tales of how the world came into being. Thus, they read Genesis 1 (and 2) with those texts ringing in their minds. Modern audiences make the mistake of reading Genesis 1 and 2 in the light of modern accounts of origins (most notably evolution) and not in the light of these ancient Near Eastern texts. Knowledge of these ancient accounts of creation deepens our understanding of the biblical text.

The texts listed above do not by any means exhaust the number of ancient Near Eastern accounts of creation, but they are the most important in that we can discern similarities and differences between them and the biblical text. In this section, we will simply describe the relevant contents of these compositions, and in the next section we demonstrate how they provide the background for Genesis 1:1 – 2:4a.

Enuma Elish gets its name from its opening words ("When on high"). It is the best known of the Babylonian creation accounts, and it is the ancient text that scholars believe most informs the shape of Genesis 1 and 2. At the opening of the story, there are two deities who are simply there and presumably always were: Tiamat, the female, who represents the fresh waters, and Apsu, who represents the salt waters. Their waters mingle, suggesting sexual intercourse, and produce a new generation of gods. These divine children, who were well-known to the original audience of Enuma Elish as the gods they worshiped, disturbed the sleep of their parents. Apsu, the father, determined to kill the children in spite of Tiamat's objections. However, one of the younger gods, Ea, the god of wisdom, learned of this plot and killed his father by a preemptive strike. He placed his throne on the corpse of his father, the flood waters (see Ps 29:10, where the psalmist applies this motif to Yahweh.)[2] Ea had subdued the dangerous primeval waters represented by his father, but his act enraged his mother, who now sought vengeance. She determined to war against her children with the help of a demonic horde headed by Qingu. When confronted by this threat, Ea knew he was no match for his mother, so he issued a challenge to the divine assembly for a champion to step forward. That champion was none other than his son Marduk. Marduk agreed to fight Tiamat on condition that, if he succeeded, the divine assembly would agree

1. Though there are those who argue that the first creation story originated in the exilic or postexilic period (thus after 586 BC), this volume brackets issues of history of composition in favor of reading the text in its final form.

2. T. Longman III, *Psalms*, TOTC (Downers Grove, IL: InterVarsity Press, 2014), 157.

to make him king of the pantheon. Thus, the Enuma Elish explains how Marduk became the most important god in the Babylonian pantheon.

The battle between Marduk and Tiamat was ferocious, but Marduk eventually conquered and killed Tiamat. After his victory, Marduk created the cosmos as we know it:

> He calmed down. Then the Lord was inspecting her carcass.
> That he might divide(?) the monstrous lump and fashion artful things.
> He split her in two, like a fish for drying.
> Half of her he set up and made as a cover, heaven.
> He stretched out the hide and assigned watchmen,
> And ordered them not to let her waters escape. (Enuma Elish, Tablet IV, lines 135–141)[3]

She was, after all, the primordial waters. His conflict with her led to the creation of the heavens (or skies) from which the rains flow and also the earthly waters. To create land, he pushed back her waters and created boundaries. In a passage that follows, he takes the gods and places them in the heavens as stars. The text also goes on to describe the creation of human beings, but since that is more relevant to the second creation text, we reserve a description of this part of the myth until our discussion of Genesis 2:4b–25.

The date for this composition is hard to pin down with great certainty. It is obviously the narrative justification for the preeminence of the god Marduk in Babylonian religion. Marduk was the chief god of the city of Babylon, so it is likely that this myth was written at a time when Babylon, the city, assumed primacy among other cities in the region. The two most likely occasions were either at the time of Hammurabi (reigned ca. 1792–1750 BC) or Nebuchadnezzar I (reigned ca. 1125–1103 BC).

The Baal Myth is a product of Canaanite culture and thus closer to home for future Israel. Baal was a god that many apostate Israelites worshipped. According to many scholars,[4] this Canaanite story helped shape the Babylonian Enuma Elish. The exact date of this text is debated, and it was likely an oral tale before it was set down in written form sometime between 1800 and 1200 BC. The relevant part of the Baal myth concerns a conflict between Baal, the creator god, and Yam, whose name means "sea." Yam attempted to assume the kingship of the gods and take Baal a prisoner. Baal resisted and successfully entreated the craftsman god, Kothar-waHasis, to make him two clubs with which he attacked Yam. He defeated Yam. At this crucial point,

---

3. *COS* 1:398.

4. See, for instance, T. Jacobsen, "The Battle between Marduk and Tiamat," *JAOS* 88 (1968): 104–8.

however, there is a break in the clay tablet that presents this story. Scholars, though, have little doubt that the missing part contains an account of Baal's construction of the world and perhaps also of human beings.

Egyptian creation ideas are found primarily in magical texts, particularly in coffin texts and inscriptions of the walls of pyramids, though there are exceptions, most notably the Shabaka Stone, which preserves the Memphite Theology to be described below. While there are many similarities between the different descriptions of creation to be found in Egyptian texts, there is also a variety of metaphors that are employed.[5] Acts of creation are also attributed to various deities. Different cult centers in Egypt (Memphis, Hermopolis, Heliopolis) had their own versions of creation, though we can also observe some attempts at synthesis.

For our purpose, we will describe the metaphors of creation as well as quote representative texts for illustration. The basic cosmology of the Egyptians seems somewhat constant. The primeval waters are called Nun, and it is out of these waters that creation emerged. One prominent idea was that the creator god, Atum according to Heliopolitan theology, emerged from the waters through an act of self-creation and from him evolved the other gods and goddesses who represent the various parts and forces of nature.[6] The form of his emergence from Nun was the primeval mound, perhaps mythically reflecting the fertile soil that was the source of life left after the annual Nile flood waters receded.

Coffin Texts Spell 714 expresses the originality of the waters: "I am the Waters, unique, without second."[7] One version of the myth of creation has Atum, depicted as the sun god, arising from the primeval waters. Spell 714 continues with Atum speaking:

> That is where I evolved, on the great occasion of my floating that happened to me. I am the one who once evolved—Circlet, who is in his egg. I am the one who began therein, (in) the Waters. See, the Flood is subtracted from me: see, I am the remainder. I made my body evolve through my own effectiveness. I am the one who made me. I built myself as I wished, according to my heart.

Pyramid Texts Spell 527 informs us that Atum then produced Shu, the god of the air, and Tefnut, the goddess of moisture, by masturbating:

---

5. For a helpful synthesis of Egyptian cosmogonic ideas, see J. Currid, *Ancient Egypt and the Old Testament* (Grand Rapids: Baker, 1997), 53–73.

6. The Ogdoad consist of eight deities, of whom Nun and his consort Naunet are two of the most important, who represent the primeval chaos that pre-existed the birth of the sun.

7. Unless specified, all of the translations concerning Egyptian ideas of creation are taken from J. P. Allen in *COS* 1:5–31.

> Atum evolved growing ithyphallic, in Heliopolis. He put his penis in his grasp that he might make orgasm with it, and the two siblings were born—Shu and Tefnut.

Another version, represented by Pyramid Texts Spell 600, substitutes sneezing for masturbating:

> Atum Scarab! When you became high, as the high ground, when you rose, as the *benben* in the Phoenix Enclosure in Helioplis, you sneezed Shu, you spat Tefnut, and you put your arms about them, as the arms of *ka*, that you *ka* might be in them.

Shu's children are Geb, the earth, and Nut, the upper limit of the heavens. Shu creates space for the sun god and for creation by pushing Geb away from Nut in what Coffin Texts Spell 76 calls the "Uplifting of Shu":

> I am weary of the Uplifting of Shu,
> since I lifted my daughter Nut atop me
> that I might give her to my father Atum in his utmost extent.
> I have put Geb under my feet:
> This god is tying together the land for my father Atum,
> and drawing together the Great Flood for him.
> I have put myself between them
> without the Ennead[8] seeing me.

From Geb and Nut emanated the final four deities of the Ennead: Osiris, Isis, Seth, and Nephthys, further broken down into two pairs. Osiris and Isis represented life; Seth and Nephthys, death and infertility. We will further develop the story of their complex social relationships in the section on the Osiris myth below.

At Memphis, a rival creation myth surrounding the god Ptah was current. The best-known expression of this myth is from the so-called "Memphite Theology,"[9] also known as the Shabaka Stone. The latter name comes from the fact that the text is preserved on a stone that was inscribed at the time of the Nubian pharaoh Shabaqo (716–702 BC), though scholars are agreed that the composition comes from a much earlier time. The stone was used as the bottom millstone, so one side is completely effaced.

In any case, Ptah, amalgamated with Ta-tenen, the god representing the primeval hillock that emerges from Nun, actually engenders Atum and thus

8. The Ennead at Heliopolis was composed of nine gods and goddesses, Atum and those who evolved from him.

9. See *COS* 1:21–3.

displaces that Heliopolitan creation god as the source of the Ennead. Indeed, as opposed to the physical action of masturbation or sneezing, Ptah effects the creation of the world by the words of his mouth:

> So were all the gods born, Atum and his Ennead as well, for it is through what the heart plans and the tongue commands that every divine speech has evolved.

These are the various myths of creation of the Egyptians. In every case, however, creation is seen as the evolution of gods and goddesses from the primeval chaos that is represented as primordially present. In the next section, we will show how these ancient texts provide the background for the story of creation in Genesis 1:1–2:4a.

## EXPLAIN the Story

Genesis 1:1–2:4a is the first of two stories of creation. The second account (2:4b–2:25) focuses on the creation of human beings, while this one describes the creation of the cosmos. Human beings find their place in this story (hereafter Gen 1), but they don't occupy the focus of attention as they will in the next (hereafter Gen 2).

### In the Beginning: From Nothing to Watery Mass (1:1–2)

Genesis 1 begins the story of the Bible and is the foundation of the rest of the Bible. Thus, there is no biblical background to Genesis 1,[10] but as we have demonstrated above, neither was this (or the next) creation account read in a vacuum. Other pagan creation accounts existed at the time, and Genesis 1 provides a powerful alternative to those stories, beginning with its momentous opening words, "In the beginning God created the heavens and the earth." The first radical claim here is that all things were created by God. In contrast, the rival creation accounts describe creation as the result of the activity of multiple gods, even though one god takes precedence (Marduk, Baal, Atum, or Ptah). Furthermore, as the narrative continues, the God of Genesis 1:1 turns out to be none other than Yahweh, the name of the God of later Israel, revealed to Moses and used retroactively in Genesis 2:4b where the creator is described as Yahweh (the Lord) God. It is Yahweh, not Baal, Marduk, or Atum, who created the heavens and earth.

The second significant difference with rival creation accounts in this opening line of Genesis 1 is that there is no preexisting material from which God

10. See footnote 1.

creates creation.[11] The message is clear: everything that exists, animate and inanimate, comes from God and depends on God.

Interestingly, according to the description of creation in Genesis 1, God does not bring everything into existence in a single moment (as he surely could have), but over a period of time and in stages.[12] The first stage of creation moves from nothing to a formless mass of water. In this, most ancient Near Eastern accounts of creation agree; a watery mass precedes the ordered creation. Genesis 1:2 further describes the spirit of God as hovering over the waters. While the Old Testament reader would not have read this in a Trinitarian sense, the fuller revelation of the New Testament allows us to understand that creation was a work of the Father, Son, and Holy Spirit (see below Creation and Christ, the Very Image of God in the Live the Story section of 1:1 – 2:4a).

The Bible continues to differ from Mesopotamian and Canaanite accounts in the next stage. Whereas Marduk and Baal bring order into chaos by conflict against the waters, God shapes the waters into a functioning creation by the power of his word.[13] The Spirit, after all, hovers over,[14] but does not battle, the waters.

## The Six Days of Creation and the Seventh, Sabbath Day (1:3 – 2:4a)

After bringing the watery mass into existence, God then shapes the cosmos into a functioning order over a six-day period. Though the analogy is not explicit, God here acts like a sculptor or a potter who takes the "formless and empty" watery mass (1:2) and shapes it into the functional and ordered creation.

Much controversy attends the nature of the "days" of the creation week. Close reading, though, helps clarify the intention of the author. In the first place, the author wants us to imagine creation taking place in six days with God resting on the seventh. Indeed, all six days end similarly with the expression "there was evening, and there was morning — the X day" (1:5, 8, 13, 19,

---

11. Accepting the NIV's (also NLT, ESV, (N)KJV, HCB) translation of Genesis 1:1 – 2 and rejecting the NRSV's rendition: "In the beginning when God created the heavens and the earth, the earth was a formless void. . . ." Admittedly, the NRSV's translation does not preclude "creation from nothing," since it could be said that the text simply does not address the origin of matter. That said, the NRSV's translation is not necessary according to the rules of Hebrew grammar and the NIV's rendition is theologically supported by later understanding of Yahweh's creation of the cosmos as from nothing (2 Macc 7:28; Heb 11:3; Rev 4:11; cf. Rom 4:17).

12. J. Walton (*Genesis 1 as Ancient Cosmology* [Winona Lake, IN: Eisenbrauns, 2011], 126 – 27) is correct to say that "beginning" (*reshit*) does not refer to a moment of time but rather to "a preliminary period of time," a period of time that will be detailed in the following days of creation.

13. It is interesting that the Memphite creation account also describes the god's word as instrumental in creation.

14. Like a bird, see Deuteronomy 32:11.

23, and 31). On the other hand, the author provides clear signals that we are not to take this description literally, as if God actually created creation in six twenty-four-hour days. Simply put, while the first three days have "evening and morning," there are no stars, moon, or sun until the fourth day. There can be no literal evening and morning without these celestial bodies. Granted, God could manipulate some kind of light source to alternate light and darkness in a twenty-four-hour period, but these would still not be literal days. Thus, describing creation as a week is a literary device to make a theological point (see below on the Sabbath).

We should also recognize that there is an interesting pattern to the days of creation. The first three days describe the creation of realms, and then the second three days describe the creation of the inhabitants of those realms. The creatures (sun, moon, and stars) of day four fill the realm of day one (light; darkness). The creatures of day five (birds and fish) fill the realm of day two (sky and sea). The creatures of day six (animals and humans) fill the realm of day three (land).

| **Day 1** | **Day 2** | **Day 3** | **Day 4** | **Day 5** | **Day 6** |
|---|---|---|---|---|---|
| Light and Darkness | Sky and Sea | Land | Sun, Moon, and Stars | Birds and Fish | Animals and Humans |

The author of Genesis 1 is interested in telling us that God created creation, but not how he did so. Of course, the first creation account does more than inform readers that God is creator. The narrative tells us much about God, ourselves, and our world (see Live the Story).

Of special note in terms of the continuing narrative of the Bible (see Gen 3), the first creation narrative makes special effort to point out that what God creates is created "good." Indeed, once God's creative work is finished the earth is described as "very good" (1:31). Evil does not originate with God and his creation (another point of divergence from the rival creation accounts, as we will see in the next chapter).[15]

As mentioned above, human beings are not the focus of this creation account as they will be in the next, but they are certainly the apex of the account. In the first place, they are the last of God's creative acts. In other words, after everything else is set in place, then humans are created.

15. Disagreeing with R. B. L. Moberly, *The Theology of the Book of Genesis*, Old Testament Theology (Cambridge: Cambridge University Press, 2009), 43 n. 4 where he states that " 'good' concerns aesthetics more than ethics." I would argue that both senses are meant.

Interestingly, God announces his intention to create humanity by saying "let us make mankind in our image ..." (v. 26). The plural ("us") reference has occasioned much speculation over the years. While the New Testament makes it clear (see below in Live the Story after 1:1–2:4a, Creation and Christ, the Very Image of God) that creation is a work of the Father, Son, and Holy Spirit, the Old Testament author and audience would not be aware of the Trinitarian nature of the Godhead. The plural has been understood by some as a "plural of majesty," but we have precious little if any evidence that the plural was used in such a way during the Old Testament time period. It is most likely that the original audience would have thought the reference was to God and his divine assembly, composed of angels (see, for instance, the prose preface to the book of Job).[16] We will see this plural reference again in the tower of Babel story (Gen 11).

Second, the creation account highlights the importance of human beings by the use of the verb *bara* ("create"), as opposed to the more general term for "making" (*asa*) that clusters around their creation (see v. 27). While it is true that *bara* has been over interpreted in terms of its theological import,[17] it nonetheless suggests something special about the creation of humans since the verb only occurs with God as its subject.

Third, humans are created in "the image" and "likeness" of God (1:26–27). What does it mean to be created in the image of God? Since the biblical text never specifically defines "image," its meaning has been debated through the centuries. However, it seems reasonable to understand the "image of God" on analogy with the ancient practice of ancient Near Eastern kings setting up images of themselves throughout their realm. Perhaps the most striking confirmation of this idea can be found in the ninth-century BC Aramaic-Akkadian inscription on a statue from Tell Fakhariyeh in the Upper Habur of Syria, which refers to the statute as a "likeness" and "image" of King Hadad-yis'i.[18] In the words of Brueggemann, "It is now generally agreed that the image of God reflected in human persons is after the manner of a king who establishes himself to assert his sovereign rule where the king himself cannot be present."[19] Like a statue reflects the presence and power and authority of a

---

16. See the excellent discussion by M. S. Heiser, *The Unseen Realm: Recovering the Supernatural Worldview of the Bible* (Bellingham, WA: Lexham, forthcoming), 23–120.

17. See R. Van Leeuwen, "*bara*'," *NIDOTTE* 1:728–35. For instance, it is not true, though often believed, that the verb in and of itself implies creation from no previously existing material contra its use in Psalms 51:10; 102:18; 104:29–30.

18. W. R. Garr, "'Image' and 'Likeness' in the Inscription from Tell Fakhariyeh," *IEJ* 50 (2000): 228, as well as his full study, *In His Own Image and Likeness: Humanity, Divinity, and Monotheism* (Leiden: Brill, 2003).

19. W. Brueggemann, *Genesis*, IBC (Louisville: Westminster John Knox, 1982), 32.

king, so human beings reflect the glory of God. Such a view presents human beings as possessing great dignity, captured by the psalmist:

> When I consider your heavens,
> the work of your fingers,
> the moon and the stars,
> which you have set in place,
> what is mankind that you are mindful of them,
> human beings that you care for them?
> You have made them a little lower than the angels
> and crowned them with glory and honor. (Ps 8:3–5)

Indeed, the Hebrew suggests a more exalted portrait than the NIV's translation allows: "You made them a little lower than God" (see NRSV).

It is particularly important to note that God created both males *and* females in his image (v. 27). He did not create men in his image and women in the image of men. Both men and women reflect God's glory. Thus begins an emphasis that will continue in the second creation account on the equality between men and women.

The preeminence of human beings may also be seen in the charge that God gives to the male and the female in verse 28: "Be fruitful and increase in number; fill the earth and subdue it. Rule over the fish in the sea and the birds in the sky and over every living creature that moves on the ground." As the human population expands in the future, men and women assume the positions of kings and queens among all the creatures of the earth. Here we see the connection between "image of God" and the responsibility to rule. They are to subdue and to rule.[20] As McDowell puts it, "the verb *rdh* is used elsewhere in the Hebrew Bible to describe the dominion of the king (1 Kgs 5:4; Isa 14:6; Ezek 34:4; Pss 8:6; 72:8; 110:2), and both *rdh* and *kbsh* reflect similar terminology used in the court parlance of Egypt and Babylon to describe the king's royal duties."[21] Of course, prior to the fall, this command has no hint of exploitation. As benevolent rulers, who are the earthly counterpart of the heavenly king, they are to care for and protect the rest of the creation. Indeed,

---

20. M. Lanier, "Survey of the Old Testament" (unpublished manuscript, p. 94) gets it right when he says "Image was not physical likeness, but rather a responsibility and identity of role and function."

21. C. McDowell, *The 'Image of God' in Eden: The Creation of Mankind in Genesis 2:5–3:24 in Light of the* mis pi pit pi *and* wpt-r *Rituals of Mesopotamia and Ancient Egypt* (Eisenbrauns, forthcoming), 3. See also the stimulating study of J. Richard Middleton, *The Liberating Image: The Imago Dei in Genesis 1* (Grand Rapids: Brazos, 2005), who states that "the *imago Dei* designates the royal office or calling of human beings as God's representatives and agents in the world, granted authorized power to share in God's rule or administration of the earth's resources and creatures" (27).

as the following verses indicate (vv. 29–30), they are not even to eat the fish and the birds, but rather God gives them "every green plant for food."

The work of creation thus came to an end on the sixth day. The final day of the week was a day of divine rest. God thus consecrated the seventh day, the Sabbath, a status that becomes significant for the later ritual observance of Israel (Exod 20:8–11; 31:12–18; Deut 5:12–15).

Before ending our analysis of Genesis 1 in its Old Testament context, we must observe that upon completing his creation God "blessed" the man and the woman. As the next chapter will underline, at this point, the man and the woman are living in harmony with God and with each other. They have everything they need to survive and thrive. In Brueggemann's words, blessing "refers to the generative power of life, fertility, and well-being that God has ordained within the normal flow and mystery of life."[22] They aren't just given mere existence, but a rich and vital life in the very presence of God. As we will see in the following chapters, divine blessing is a major theme of the book of Genesis.

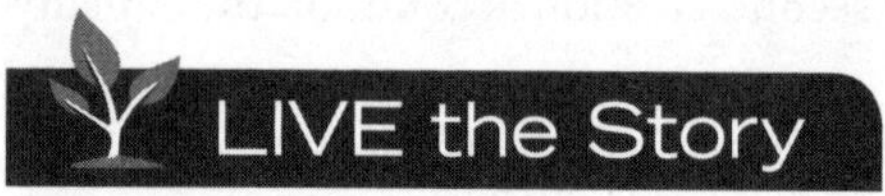


The proclamation of Genesis 1 is that God, and no other, created the cosmos. This remarkable revelation is muted by those who insist that the main purpose of the book is to provide an alternative depiction of the process of creation as that offered by modern science. However, Genesis 1 (and we will see Genesis 2 as well) is not about how God created creation. It is not to be mined for hints about how long creation took or the specific way in which God brought the world and humanity into being. That said, the creation accounts provide profound perspective on the nature of God, ourselves, and the world. Genesis 1 (and 2) imparts to its readers a worldview which affects the way they believe, think, and act. We will here concentrate on the contribution of the cosmic creation of Genesis 1, and in the next on the human-centered account in chapter 2.

### Creator and Creatures

The most fundamental affirmation of Genesis 1 is that God created all things, including humans. God is Creator and we are creatures. The Creator-creature distinction seems obvious but is often forgotten to our great detriment. The second commandment prohibits the making of an idol "in the form of anything in heaven above or on earth beneath or in the waters below" (Exod

22. Brueggemann, *Genesis*, 37.

20:4). In the New Testament, Paul points out that to forget the Creator-creature distinction is the heart of idolatry. Speaking of the "wickedness of people" (Rom 1:18) against whom the wrath of God was being revealed, he says, "For although they knew God, they neither glorified him as God nor gave thanks to him, but their thinking became futile and their foolish hearts were darkened. Although they claimed to be wise, they became fools and exchanged the glory of the immortal God for images made to look like a mortal human being and birds and animals and reptiles" (Rom 1:21–23). Thus, the creation account makes God the Creator the focus of our worship and reminds us of our status as creatures.

### Supremely Other, Yet Involved

Against the backdrop of ancient creation accounts, Genesis 1 is remarkable in presenting the work of creation as that of a single God who does not engage in sexual activity or violence, but rather through the power of his word speaks forth matter and shapes it into functional order.[23] The narrative shows God to be sovereign, self-sufficient, and supreme, a description not appropriate to the other gods of the time. Further, this God is both transcendent and immanent. That is, he is not a part of creation. He makes the cosmos and pronounces it good. Thus, biblical religion is not pantheistic. But neither does God make creation and then let it run on its own. He remains involved. Thus, biblical religion is not deistic. Theism is the proper term for the biblical conception of God. He is both other and present.

### Creation and Gender

Further, Genesis 1 (and 2) informs the reader that gender and sexuality are part of the creation, not a part of the Creator. God may not be described correctly as a male or a female. We have seen that men and women are created in the image of God, showing that both genders reflect the divine glory. For this reason, too, later Scripture will use both male (king, warrior, shepherd) as well as female metaphors (Woman Wisdom [Prov 1; 8–9]; mother [Ps 131]) in reference to God. In keeping with biblical practice, it is wise to refer to God as "he," though not heretical to call God "she," as it would be to refer to God as "it." After all, God is a personal God. Some writers have taken to never using a personal pronoun for God, and thus they avoid the issue. For others, including myself, such a practice is awkward and draws attention to itself. The

---

23. J. Walton, *The Lost World of Genesis 1* (Downers Grove, IL: InterVarsity Press, 2009), is particularly helpful in emphasizing the point that ancient creation texts, including Genesis 1, focuses on function. As he puts it, "people in the ancient world believed that something existed not by virtue of its material properties, but by virtue of its having a function in an ordered system" (26).

important point is to affirm that men and women are equal before God and in relationship to God according to the biblical witness.

### A Good Creation

The repeated emphasis on the fact that God created the cosmos "good" plays a very important role in the formation of a biblical worldview. After all, today we experience the world as "not good," in a moral sense to be sure, but even in a functional sense. The reason for our present experience will be given in Genesis 3, but Genesis 1 and 2 are important reminders that God did not make the cosmos bad. He is not responsible for our present predicament.

### Creation and Sabbath

Finally, the first creation account not only shapes a worldview, but it also points to a practice that was extremely important for later Israel and still informs our thought and action today. The creation week culminates in Sabbath. On the seventh day, God "rested" or perhaps better, "ceased" (from the verb *shabbat*), from his creation work.[24] Granted the human creatures are not commanded to observe this Sabbath, still God "consecrated" (from the verb *qadash*) the seventh day. In other words, he set it apart and made it holy, different from the other six ordinary days. While it is true that God's human creatures are neither invited nor commanded to observe the Sabbath at this time, the fourth commandment, which does mandate Sabbath observance, gives the creation week as the reason:

> Remember the Sabbath day by keeping it holy. Six days you shall labor and do all your work, but the seventh day is a sabbath to the LORD your God. On it you shall not do any work, neither you, nor your son or daughter, nor your male or female servant, nor your animals, nor any foreigner residing in your towns. For in six days the LORD made the heavens and the earth, the sea, and all that is in them, but he rested on the seventh day. Therefore the LORD blessed the Sabbath day and made it holy. (Exod 20:8–11)

Indeed, the Sabbath was the sign of the Mosaic covenant (Exod 31:13), a continual and regular reminder of the commitment Israel had made to be in relationship with God. It was holy (set apart) time when God made his presence especially palpable to his people, Israel. The Sabbath was so important that disobedience resulted in horrible punishment (Exod 31:15; Num 15:32–36).

24. Moberly (*The Theology of the Book of Genesis*, 47) points out that Exodus 31:17 "strikingly depicts even God as 'refreshed' through rest on the seventh day."

Today, Christians disagree over how the coming of Christ affects observance of the Sabbath. Consecrated at creation, mandated at the time of Moses, New Testament appropriation of the Sabbath is a difficult interpretive question. That said, the strongest arguments are on the side of those who say that a radical transformation of the Sabbath has taken place in the light of the coming of Christ. Indeed, all Christians (with the exception of those in the Adventist tradition) recognize some measure of change in that it is the first day of the week, rather than the seventh, which is now set aside in some fashion by most Christians in spite of the fact that there is no divine mandate to do so.[25] After all, Jesus himself signaled a change in attitude and behavior during his earthly ministry. For one example, in Mark 2:23 – 28 the religious authorities charge Jesus with breaking the Sabbath when he and his disciples pick grain.[26] The Pharisees could have cited Exodus 34:21, which prohibits harvesting on the Sabbath, to support their claim.[27] Second, Paul also signals a radical shift in Sabbath observance in Colossians 2:16 – 17: "Therefore do not let anyone judge you by what you eat or drink, or with regard to a religious festival, a New Moon celebration or a Sabbath day. These are a shadow of the things that were to come; the reality, however, is Christ." Christ fulfills the Sabbath. No longer is there a single "holy" day, but all days are holy, given to God. No longer is Sabbath observance a matter of law.[28]

That said, God made us in such a way that we cannot go 24/7 without a break. Furthermore, as Christians, we need a time so we can get together corporately to worship God (Heb 10:25). With these practical needs in mind, it is a matter of wisdom, not law, that Christians agree to name a day for worship and rest. Tradition, dating back into the New Testament period, has chosen Sunday, the first day of the week, for this purpose. Theological rationale has been given in that Sunday was the day of the week on which Jesus was raised from the dead. Also, now that Christ has come, some have reasoned, we can now rest first and work six days, as opposed to working six and resting on the seventh. This last point also reminds us that in an important theological sense, we have not entered the final Sabbath, that day when Christ will return and we will be with him in heaven (Heb 4:1 – 2, 9, 11). Christians anticipate a final Sabbath, a day of ultimate redemption and rest in God.[29]

---

25. Though there are New Testament hints that the first day was the day Christians met (Acts 20:7; 1 Cor 16:2).

26. See also Mark 3:1 – 6; Luke 13:10 – 17; John 5:17.

27. While some readers of this account believe that Jesus' actions are not actually harvesting and therefore not a matter of law, it is important to recall an earlier story, in Exodus 16:25 – 29, concerning the gathering of the manna.

28. See also Romans 14:1, 5 – 6, 10.

29. For more on the biblical theology of Sabbath, see T. Longman III, *Immanuel in Our Place: Seeing Christ in Israel's Worship* (Phillipsburg, NJ: P & R, 2001), 161 – 214.

## Creation and Christ, the Very Image of God

Christians read the story of creation through the prism of the fuller revelation of the New Testament, which also celebrates God as the creator of all that exists (Eph 3:9; Rev 4:11; 10:6). The New Testament, though, bears witness to the triune nature of God as Father, Son, and Holy Spirit and informs Christians that Jesus was involved in the creation of the cosmos:

> In the beginning was the Word, and the Word was with God, and the Word was God. He was with God in the beginning. Through him all things were made; without him nothing was made that has been made. (John 1:1–3)
>
> The Son is the image of the invisible God, the firstborn over all creation. For in him all things were created: things in heaven and on earth, visible and invisible, whether thrones or powers or rulers or authorities; all things have been created through him and for him. (Col 1:15–16)
>
> These are the words of the Amen, the faithful and true witness, the ruler of God's creation. (Rev 3:14)

These passages use the language of Proverbs 8:22–31 that describes Woman Wisdom's observation of and involvement in creation to make the point that Jesus our Savior is also our Creator.[30] Thus, we can appropriately reconsider the language of Genesis 1:26 when God says, "Let us make mankind in our image, in our likeness ..." While it is not likely that the original readers of Genesis understood this in the light of the Trinity, but rather of God and his angelic servants, the divine council, the New Testament allows us a deeper understanding of the language as including intratrinitarian communication. We, and the whole cosmos, are the loving results of the creative work of the Father, Son, and Holy Spirit.

Speaking of the image of God, the New Testament discloses that Jesus himself is the "image of God," who reflects the divine glory (2 Cor 4:4). As image of God, he makes the "invisible God" visible (Col 1:15). As we will see in Genesis 3, humanity has not eradicated, but certainly has marred the divine image. Jesus thus not only reveals God in his person but also reflects perfect humanity. He is fully divine and fully human. Human beings are called to become a new creature in Christ and thus "to be like God in true righteousness and holiness" (Eph 4:24).

---

30. B. Witherington III, *Jesus the Sage: The Pilgrimage of Wisdom* (Minneapolis: Fortress, 1994); T. Longman III, *Proverbs*, BCOTWP (Grand Rapids: Baker, 2006), 208–13.

## Loving Others Created in the Image of God

Sometimes we can be so overwhelmed by the evil in the world and in our own hearts (see Gen 3) that we easily forget that we are created in the image of God. How can we, who are soiled by sin, reflect the glory of God and represent him in his creation?

We should never minimize our sin against God and each other. We are not the glorious creatures that God created and placed in the garden. However, sin does not eradicate the image, and we should never forget this as we consider who we are and who others with whom we interact are.

John Calvin brilliantly describes the impact of recognizing that others are created in the image of God:

> Love of neighbor is not dependent upon the manner of men but looks to God. The Lord commands all human beings without exception "to do good." Yet the great part of them are most unworthy if they be judged by their own merit. But here Scripture helps in the best way when it teaches that we are not to consider that men merit of themselves but to look upon the image of God in all men, to which we owe all honor and love.... Therefore, whatever person you meet who needs your aid, you have no reason to refuse to help him. Say, "He is a stranger"; but the Lord has given him a mark that ought to be familiar to you, by virtue of the fact that God forbids you to despise your own flesh [Isa. 58:7]. Say, "He is contemptible and worthless"; but the Lord shows him to be one to whom God has designed to give the beauty of his image. Say that you owe nothing for any service of him; but God, as it were, has put him in his own place in order that you may recognize toward him the many and great benefits with which God has bound you to himself.... Assuredly there is but one way in which to achieve what is not merely difficult but utterly against human nature: to love those who hate us, to repay their evil deeds with benefits.... It is that we remember not to consider men's evil intention but to look upon the image of God in them, which cancels and effaces their transgressions, and with its beauty and dignity allures us to love and embrace them.

This passage was brought to my attention by Paul C. H. Lim in a lecture where he talked about loving the unlovable involved in the reprehensible sex trafficking trade.[31] He called on us in the light of Calvin's understanding of

---

31. John Calvin, *Institutes of the Christian Religion*, ed. John T. McNeill, trans. Ford Lewis Battles, 2 vols. (Philadelphia: Westminster John Knox Press, 1960), III. Vii. 6. I wish to thank Paul C. H. Lim of Vanderbilt University for drawing my attention to this quote and for his stimulating exposition of it in a paper entitled "Corinth, Calvin, and Calcutta: Trinity, Trafficking, and the Transformation of Theologia," delivered at North Park Theological Seminary on September 26, 2014.

the biblical teaching on the image of God to remember that even sex traffickers, who trade on the vulnerable, are nonetheless created in the image of God and are not beyond redemption.

But we should remember that others are created in the image even when the circumstances are not extreme. Those we love, dislike, annoy us, bring us joy—all are created in the image of God and should be treated with our deepest respect and concern. Those of all races, both genders, different sexual orientations, professions and occupations, rich and poor—all reflect God's glory and represent his presence in the world.

CHAPTER 2

# Genesis 2:4b–25

## LISTEN to the Story

[4]This is the account of the heavens and the earth when they were
created, when the LORD God made the earth and the heavens.

[5]Now no shrub had yet appeared on the earth and no plant had yet
sprung up, for the LORD God had not sent rain on the earth and there
was no one to work the ground, [6]but streams came up from the earth and
watered the whole surface of the ground. [7]Then the LORD God formed a
man from the dust of the ground and breathed into his nostrils the breath
of life, and the man became a living being.

[8]Now the LORD God had planted a garden in the east, in Eden; and
there he put the man he had formed. [9]The LORD God made all kinds of
trees grow out of the ground—trees that were pleasing to the eye and
good for food. In the middle of the garden were the tree of life and the
tree of the knowledge of good and evil.

[10]A river watering the garden flowed from Eden; from there it was
separated into four headwaters. [11]The name of the first is the Pishon; it
winds through the entire land of Havilah, where there is gold. [12](The gold
of that land is good; aromatic resin and onyx are also there.) [13]The name
of the second river is the Gihon; it winds through the entire land of Cush.
[14]The name of the third river is the Tigris; it runs along the east side of
Ashur. And the fourth river is the Euphrates.

[15]The LORD God took the man and put him in the Garden of Eden
to work it and take care of it. [16]And the LORD God commanded the man,
"You are free to eat from any tree in the garden; [17]but you must not eat
from the tree of the knowledge of good and evil, for when you eat from it
you will certainly die."

[18]The LORD God said, "It is not good for the man to be alone. I will
make a helper suitable for him."

[19]Now the LORD God had formed out of the ground all the wild
animals and all the birds in the sky. He brought them to the man to see

what he would name them; and whatever the man called each living creature, that was its name. [20]So the man gave names to all the livestock, the birds in the sky and all the wild animals.

But for Adam no suitable helper was found. [21]So the LORD God caused the man to fall into a deep sleep; and while he was sleeping, he took one of the man's ribs and then closed up the place with flesh. [22]Then the LORD God made a woman from the rib he had taken out of the man, and he brought her to the man.

[23]The man said,

"This is now bone of my bones
and flesh of my flesh;
she shall be called 'woman,'
for she was taken out of man."

[24]That is why a man leaves his father and mother and is united to his wife, and they become one flesh.

*Listening to the Text in the Story:* Biblical Text: Genesis 1:1–2:4a; Ancient Near Eastern Texts: Enuma Elish; Atrahasis

Many biblical scholars believe that Genesis 2:4b–25 is an earlier creation story than 1:1–2:4a, finding the origin of the latter in the P source (typically dated to the exilic [586–539 BC] or the postexilic [after 539 BC] period) and the former to the J source (tenth century BC in the traditional view of the Documentary Hypothesis).[1] Not only do I disagree with this analysis, I do not believe that it matters. In other words, the final form of the text has Genesis 1:1–2:4a preceding Genesis 2:4b–25, and thus the former is the background to the latter, regardless of their origin.

Accordingly, they should be read together, but what is their relationship? Walton believes they are sequential accounts.[2] The first account briefly mentions the creation of humanity (Gen 1:26–30) in the larger story of the creation of the cosmos. The creation of Adam and Eve comes from a later time period. Accordingly, Adam and Eve are not the first human beings. On the contrary, I agree with the traditional viewpoint that Genesis 2:4b–25 is a

1. For a lively defense and description of the Documentary Hypothesis, see Richard E. Friedman, *The Bible with Sources Revealed* (San Francisco: HarperOne, 2005), and for an accessible critique see Longman, *How to Read Genesis*, 43–58.

2. See his treatment of the two accounts in J. Walton in *Four Views on Historical Adam*, ed. by M. Barrett and S. Gundry (Grand Rapids: Zondervan, 2013), 108–11.

second creation account; that is, it is a synoptic, not a sequential, account. It intends to develop the story only briefly mentioned and described as day six in chapter 1.

While Genesis 1 provides a background for the story of the creation of humanity which is the focus of Genesis 2, the latter also interplays with ancient Near Eastern, particularly Babylonian, texts that describe the creation of humanity.

The first text we will examine is Enuma Elish (Tablet 6:11–36), a text described in the previous chapter since it also provides a background for the narration of the creation of the cosmos. We have reserved a discussion of what it says about the creation of humanity until this point.

After pushing back the waters to create the land, Marduk then executes the demon god who was the consort of Tiamat, Qingu. The narrator reports "they [the gods] bound and held him before Ea, they imposed the punishment on him and shed his blood. From his blood he made mankind."[3]

Before commenting on this description of the creation of humanity, we turn now to another Babylonian myth, Atrahasis. We will have reason to come back to this myth again in relationship to the flood story. Atrahasis is the name given to the person who survives the flood, but as a preface to that story, the myth describes the creation of humanity. Atrahasis gives a bit more detail than Enuma Elish when it pictures the creation of humanity as from the clay and the blood of a god, also for the purpose of substituting for the work load of the lesser gods, namely the digging of irrigation ditches (ll. 224–35). After the blood and clay had been mixed, all the gods spit on it. As we will soon see, it is in particular Atrahasis that provides a background for the story of the creation of Adam in Genesis 2:4b–25.

## EXPLAIN the Story

The second creation account is a synoptic, not sequential, telling of the story of creation, but rather than providing a focus on cosmic creation, we now have a close-up account of the creation of humanity. Notably, the sequence of the creation acts is different in the second account. While in Genesis 1 the creation of land was accompanied by the appearance of vegetation (Day 4) before the creation of humanity (Day 6), in Genesis 2 God created Adam before vegetation. The NIV's attempt to harmonize by translating the verbs in the pluperfect ("had yet appeared ... had yet sprung up," etc.) is not the most

3. Translation by B. R. Foster, *COS* 1: 401.

natural translation and is an attempt to harmonize the two accounts.[4] This effort is unnecessary because it is not the intention of these creation accounts to give us a literal description of how God created creation.

### From the Dust of the Ground (2:4b–7)

The account opens with a description of the creation of the man, Adam. He is created from the dust of the ground and the breath of God. This description is obviously figurative since God is a spirit and does not have lungs with which he could literally breathe into dust. The dust too is figurative as we can tell since the psalmist will describe all human beings as created from the dust (Job 4:19; Ps 103:14; implied by the fact that we all return to dust upon death; Ps 104:29; Eccl 12:7).

What is this figurative language teaching us about human beings? Many things. But let's start with a reminder of the Babylonian account in Atrahasis where humans were also created from something from the earth (clay) along with a divine component (the blood of a demon god and the spit of all the gods). The latter description teaches that humans are evil from their origin and also held in contempt by the gods. Indeed, the reason why they were created was to dig the irrigation ditches, a job that previously had been done by the lesser gods. In contrast, the creation of Adam, while affirming the fact that humans are creatures like all other animals (dust) also have a special relationship with God and a dignified status in God's creation (the breath of God).[5]

### The Garden of Eden, Adam's First Home (2:8–16)

The subject now turns to the garden which God creates as the habitat of the newly formed man. It is described as in the east (presumably east of the later Israel). Its description is such that makes it impossible to identify with a known location. Four rivers are said to flow out of Eden, only two of which can be identified with certainty, the Tigris and the Euphrates. But these two rivers flow out of Armenia (which is not east of Israel) and flow toward the Persian Gulf, and their headwaters are not that close together. The third river, the Gihon, is known from later Scripture as a stream in the vicinity of Jerusalem, and the fourth, the Pishon is otherwise unknown. The same difficulties

---

4. The ESV is even more blatant in its attempt to harmonize the sequence of the order of creation acts between the two creation accounts. It not only does this by using the pluperfect tense in the English translation of the verbs, but also by rendering *'erets* as "land" rather than "earth" in 2:5–7. A defense of the attempt may be found in C. J. Collins, *Genesis 1–4: A Linguistic, Literary and Theological Commentary* (Phillipsburg, NJ: P & R, 2006).

5. This does not deny that the animals also had the "breath of life" (see 7:15, 22). However, for the animals we do not get the intimate picture of God actually breathing this "breath of life" into their nostrils.

are found with trying to identify the other geographical references (Havilah, Cush, and Ashur) with a single known locality.[6]

Perhaps Eden is not a real place, but rather contributes to a figurative description of the origin of humanity. If so, we still need to ask what the imagery points to. The best answer is that Eden, whose very name means abundance or luxury, indicates that God provides all of humanity's needs and more when they were first created.

Even so, the man has a divinely given task (v. 15). He must work in the garden and take care of it. Two important observations follow the assignment of these tasks. The first is that work precedes the fall. Even if Adam and Eve did not sin, humans would still have to work. The implications of this observation will be developed below both in the Live the Story section of this chapter as well as the next.

The second observation concerns his assignment to "take care" of the garden. The verb "take care" (*shamar*) elsewhere is often translated "guard." From later events, it seems that this nuance of the verb is at least included. God charged Adam to protect the garden, but from what or whom? Genesis 3 will answer that question as the serpent will invade the garden to bring havoc and disrupt the relationship between God and his human creatures with awful consequences for all of creation.

Adam's assigned role as a guard of Eden, the place where God and humanity lived in perfect harmony, anticipates the rise of the priesthood, which is later assigned to "watch over" (*shamar*) God's word and "protect" (*natsar*) the covenant. This connection supports the broader relationship between Eden and the temple, both are places where God makes his presence known in a palpable way to human beings. As Niehaus points out, "the verbs used here are also used later with respect to the Levitical service in the Mosaic tabernacle. The Levites are to 'do the service' (i.e., 'work') of the tabernacle (e.g., Num 4:26, 28, 31, 33), and they are to 'care for' (i.e., 'keep) it (e.g., Num 1:53, 3:25)."[7]

As he places Adam in the garden and assigns him the task of protecting the garden, he also issues the command not to eat from the "tree of the knowledge of good and evil" (mentioned first in verse 9 along with the "tree of life" which will be discussed in the commentary at chapter 3). This prohibition is the first law in Scripture and it comes with a penalty for breaking it: death. We will

6. Z. Zevit (*What Really Happened in the Garden of Eden*? [New Haven, CT: Yale University Press, 2013]) makes the argument that Eden is described in such a way that it is to be located "as lying somewhere in the western part of Urartu but east of the Halys" (111), just indicating how difficult it is to use the biblical description to come to a definitive conclusion concerning the location of Eden.

7. J. Neihaus, *Biblical Theology: The Common Grace Covenants* (Wooster, OH: Weaver, 2014), 77.

reserve a fuller discussion of the role of the tree for Genesis 3, but for now we should notice that Adam is told he may eat from all the other trees of the garden, which would include the tree of life to be mentioned in chapter 3.

### A Helper Suitable for Him (2:18–25)

Adam had a harmonious relationship with God who has placed him in Eden ("luxury" or "abundance"). But God knows that this is not enough; something is still missing. God realizes that Adam needs relationship with someone who is his peer. Thus, God sets out to create "a helper suitable for him" (v. 18).

Some readers believe that a "helper" implies subordination, but nothing could be further from the truth. The Hebrew word "helper" (*ezer*) is not equivalent to the English word "valet." How do we know this? The psalms frequently refer to God as Israel's helper (Pss 33:20; 89:18–19; see also Deut 33:39), and, of course, God is not Israel's valet. In military contexts, the word *ezer* is well-translated "ally." Indeed, since we will see that there are threats to the garden (the serpent), ally may work well for this context as well. This ally is "suitable to" or "corresponding to" him. The emphasis is on equality throughout the description of the creation of the woman in Genesis 2.

But before we get to the creation of Adam's partner, God tries out some creatures that he either earlier created (as the NIV would have us believe, "had formed") or perhaps he creates now (translating "Now the LORD God formed out of ground …"). In either case, none of the "wild animals" or "birds in the sky" sufficed as a partner to the man. In the process he named them. Naming is a unique ability of humanity among all of God's creatures, indicating language and the ability to categorize. As Alter puts it, "Man is superior to all other living creatures because only he can invent language, only he has the level of consciousness that makes him capable of linguistic ordering."[8]

It is doubtful that God actually thought that the horse or the dog would be appropriate life partners for the man, but this episode creates the narrative tension that leads to the ultimate solution to Adam's loneliness problem, the creation of the woman. God creates a woman from Adam's rib. The Hebrew word (*tsela*) could also be translated "side."[9] In either case, the point of this figurative description of the woman's creation is clear. The woman is not created from Adam's head as if she is superior or from Adam's feet as if she is inferior, but from his side showing mutuality and equality.

When Adam met the woman, he burst out in one of the first poems of the Bible, one that further emphasizes the equality of male and female:

---

8. Alter, *The Art of Biblical Narrative*, 44.

9. For the interesting, but ultimately unconvincing argument that the word refers to the baculum (or penis bone), see Zevit, *What Really Happened?* 146–50.

> This is now bone of my bones
> and flesh of my flesh;
> she shall be called "woman,"
> for she was taken out of man. (v. 23)

The word play on woman and man in English reflects the wordplay in Hebrew where the *ishshah* was taken out of the *ish*.

The poem gives way to the narrative description of the new relationship between the man and the woman. This newly founded relationship has three parts, begininning with leaving parents, then a union of husband and wife, and finally becoming one flesh. Even though the word marriage is not used here, the traditional understanding of this passage as the divine establishment of marriage is correct since one does not need the explicit mention of the word to have the concept. And certainly later Scripture understands this intimate relationship as marriage. The implications of this definition will be explored below (see Live the Story).

The second creation account ends with the statement that the man, who is clearly called Adam only beginning at 4:25, and his not-named wife (see 3:30) were naked in the garden, but without shame. This description highlights humanity's innocence as they were created by God. They had nothing to hide, so they could stand before each other without clothes. This openness is more than physical and sexual, but also indicates their lack of emotional, psychological, and spiritual shame. Genesis 2 thus ends with an emphasis on the harmony between humanity and God and thus among humans and with the creation itself.

## LIVE the Story

Like Genesis 1, the second creation story has been wrongly co-opted into the origins debate. Were human beings specially created or did they evolve from earlier life forms? The highly figurative nature of the descriptions of both Adam and Eve are indications that this question is the wrong one to ask. Genesis 2:4b–25 is not about how God created humans.[10] While the second creation account is not interested in the question of how humans were created, the story is told in a way that informs its readers about the nature of humanity and so much more.

10. For the debate about the relationship between Genesis and science on the issue of cosmic and human origins, see J. D. Charles, *Reading Genesis 1–2: An Evangelical Conversation* (Peabody, MA: Hendrickson, 2013).

### Creatures, Yet with a Special Relationship to God

The creation of Adam illuminates the status of humanity in God's creation and in terms of our relationship with God; in this way, it informs our self-perception of humans and keeps us from avoiding two misconceptions. On the one hand, Adam's creation from the dust of the ground reminds us, that like the animals, which are also created from the ground (2:19), we are creatures, part of creation. We are not divine or even semidivine beings, but rather animals.

On the other hand, we are not just animals, but rather animals that have a special relationship with God. Of course, the first creation account taught this perspective on humanity by noting that humans were made in God's image. In the second creation account, this dimension of our nature is communicated by the fact that humanity is pictured as enlivened by the breath of God. The nobility of this depiction, we should remember, comes out particularly when we contrast it with the contemptuous view of humanity in Babylonian accounts that assign the divine component to the blood or the spit of the gods.

Adam's creation from dust and the breath of God does not attempt to tell us how God created humanity, but rather is giving us insight into who we are and our status in the cosmos. We are not gods, but neither are we mere animals.

Genesis 2 helps us as humans develop a healthy sense of self- as well as other-esteem. The psalmist (see Ps 22:6) and Job (Job 25:9) were told by others that they were worms or maggots. Indeed, in the latter passage Bildad generalizes that all humans are nothing but maggots.

But such a viewpoint is misdirected according to Genesis 1–2. Indeed, the poet who wrote Psalm 8 got it right when he proclaimed:

> You [God] have made them [humans] a little lower than God,
> and crowned them with glory and honor. (v. 5, NRSV)

In the words of the composer of Psalm 139, humans are "fearfully and wonderfully made" (v. 14, NRSV). However, we must not lose perspective. We are lower than God, made from the dust. The perspective given to us from Genesis 2 reminds us that we are creatures.

Not only is this a matter of self-perception; it also gives us a perspective on our fellow human beings. In our encounters with others, whether someone as close as our spouse or a stranger, we must bear in mind that the other person, though a creature, has a special relationship with God by virtue of creation. No matter who the other person is, they are created by God and thus deserve to be treated with the greatest dignity.

## The Importance of Relationship

Genesis 2 also highlights the importance, indeed the necessity of relationship. Of course, the most fundamental relationship at the beginning of the chapter is the one between Adam and God, and in Genesis 2 that relationship is harmonious.

The Bible never addresses the question why God created the cosmos or even more specifically why God created human beings. The Bible, though, beginning with its opening chapters, informs us that God is interested in relationship with his human creatures. Indeed, the consistent biblical picture of God indicates that he pursues relationship with humanity.

Does God need humans? In an important sense, God does not need anyone or anything. He is not dependent on anything else for his existence. He has always existed, even before the creation of humanity. On the other hand, it would betray the biblical witness to deny that God desires relationship with humans and pursues it right from the start. He cares for and loves his human creatures.

At the start that relationship is a healthy one. But even with the strong relationship between God and humans, God himself notes a lack. Adam needs a relationship with a peer ("a helper suitable for him").

We need to bear this in mind when we struggle with our own loneliness or the loneliness of others. Granted that loneliness is now accentuated by the introduction of sin (see Gen 3), but even in Eden God recognized Adam's need for relationship. It just will not do to tell a lonely person that they have God and that is all they need.

In other words, community is important. Even if humanity did not rebel against God, we need to be in relationship with others.

## Gender Equality

A debate rages within the evangelical Protestant church over the relationship between men and women. While there are many nuances to the discussion, it is common to refer to two viewpoints. On the one hand, there are complementarians who believe that men and women have different roles. Men have positions of leadership and ultimate authority in family and church life, while women serve a support role, though they may influence men in their decision making. On the other hand, there are egalitarians, who believe that men and women share responsibilities in these areas.[11]

Though these viewpoints are significantly different, both views would affirm that men and women are both equal before God. Certainly, Genesis 2

---

11. For different perspectives on this issue, see J. Dickson, *Hearing Her Voice: A Case for Women Giving Sermons* (Grand Rapids: Zondervan, 2014) and K. Keller, *Jesus, Justice, and Gender Roles: A Case for Gender Roles in Ministry* (Grand Rapids: Zondervan, 2014).

makes it clear that, as created, both men and women are equal. This view is taught by the picture of Eve's creation from Adam's rib (or side), not from his head or from his feet and is affirmed and clearly taught by Paul when he states, "There is neither Jew nor Gentile, neither slave nor free, nor is there male and female, for you are all one in Christ Jesus" (Gal 3:28).

## The Nature of Marriage and the Gift of Sex

One relationship in particular comes to the fore in Genesis 2—marriage.[12] Marriage is instituted to be the most intimate of all human relationships. Genesis 2 describes marriage as that between one man and one woman; in other words, it is the only human relationship that is mutually exclusive. Granted, after the fall, God allows for polygamy (probably because of the disparity between men and women in a tribal society), but that, like divorce, is not God's ideal, but because of the "hardness" of the human heart (see Jesus' words at Matt 19:8).

As mentioned above, marriage as defined by 2:24 has three essential components, which we will now briefly elaborate.

(1) "that is why a man leaves his father and mother"

For a man to move toward his new wife, he must leave his parents. According to Psalm 45:10, the woman too is to leave her parents ("Listen, daughter, and pay careful attention: Forget your people and your father's house").

It would be wrong to think of this leaving as a physical act. In ancient Israel, newly married couples did not leave town when they got married, but typically moved into the family compound. This leaving is of a more fundamental sort that can best be described as forming a new primary loyalty.

Before marriage, especially in ancient Israel where men and women would have been married at a much younger age than today, children would depend on their parents to help them make life and daily decisions. After marriage, one's spouse is the most important person in life.

(2) "and is united to his wife"

Marriage means a movement away from parents and toward one's spouse. How does this take place?

Genesis does not explicitly say, but experience indicates that two people draw closer together by common experience and through communication. The emotional and spiritual union of a man and a woman does not take place overnight, but is a process that begins before marriage as two people get to know each other by spending time together. The book of Proverbs talks about

---

12. For more see D. Allender and T. Longman III, *Intimate Allies* (Carol Stream, IL: Tyndale House, 1995), and T. and K. Keller, *The Meaning of Marriage: Facing the Complexity of Commitment with the Wisdom of God* (New York: Riverhead, 2013).

the importance of speech in any human relationship, but it is especially critical in a marriage relationship.[13]

Proverbs describes wise speech and foolish speech, and of course a healthy marriage is built on wise speech which tells the truth and speaks from the heart. Through communication a couple shares their past experiences and who they are. Thus, a couple can build a strong relationship over a long period of time.

(3) "and they become one flesh"

John Bettler, the former head of the Christian Counseling and Education Foundation, talked about the three components of marriage in Genesis 2:24 as leaving, weaving, and cleaving. We now come to the cleaving part.

Sexual intimacy is an essential part of a marriage relationship. It is on the basis of Genesis 2:24 that we say that marital sex is the gift of God. In the sexual act, the two become one. This is true not only in a physical sense where the man inserts his penis in his wife's vagina, but they also become one emotionally, psychologically, and spiritually as a husband and wife lose themselves in the other in an orgasm.

Significantly, marriage is not here defined as including childbearing as an essential component. Marriage is leaving, weaving, and cleaving, but not necessarily heaving in childbirth. Of course, the Bible delights in children; they are a gift from God (Ps. 127:3–5), but they are not a part of the divine definition of marriage. An implication of this insight is that sex is God's gift to married couples regardless of whether or not it issues in childbirth. God loves his human creatures to enjoy marital sex; it is his good gift to them.[14]

As instituted in Genesis 2, marriage is between one man and one woman. This raises the question of the occurrence of polygamy later in the Old Testament. Indeed, it is even permitted in the New Testament period. Indeed, polygamy is not condemned by the Mosaic law, though it is regulated (Exod 21:7–11). Abraham, Jacob, David, and many other important figures in the Old Testament have more than one wife.

Even so, on the basis of Genesis 2 we must understand that, though polygamy is permitted, it is not God's ideal for marriage. Like divorce, God appears to be allowing polygamy because of the hardness of the human heart (see Jesus' comments at Matt 19:8–9). Perhaps God permits this at the time because in most tribal cultures there were many more women than men and the fate of a single adult woman in these societies is fraught with danger. That polygamy is not God's ideal is also shown by the stories about polygamous

13. T. Longman III, *How to Read Proverbs* (Downers Grove, IL: InterVarsity Press, 2012).

14. For more, see D. Allender and T. Longman III, *God Loves Sex: An Honest Conversation about Sexual Desire and Holiness* (Grand Rapids: Baker, 2014).

marriages. Having many wives leads to family troubles, not bliss, as we can see from the later stories, including Abraham's marriage to Sarah and Hagar as well as Jacob's marriage to both Rachel and Leah.

### The Goodness of Work

Upon creation Adam was given the responsibility to tend and guard the garden. In short, he was given a work assignment. That means that humans would work even if they did not rebel against God. We will develop this theme more in the next chapter, but here we will just observe that work, which we often experience as onerous and frustrating, is a part of our created nature not a result of sin.

### The Theological Foundation for Creation Care

We have observed that both creation accounts place humanity at their apex. The narrative makes it clear that God cares for his human creatures in a special way. However, humanity's favored status does not mean that the rest of creation does not matter. Indeed, both creation stories provide a theological rationale for concern for the environment and our fellow creatures.

The status of ruler and subduer over creation is not that of an exploiter but of a protector (1:26–28). That God will care for the animals primarily, though not exclusively (see Job 38:39–39:30), through human agency may be seen in God's charge that Adam name the animals (2:19–20). That humans are to care for and protect the environment may be seen in the divine command to "work" and "take care of" (or better "guard/protect") the garden (2:15).

Thus, there are deep biblical and theological roots for the contemporary concern for the environment and we will explore further dimensions of this in later reflections as well (see Was Noah an Environmentalist and Animal Activist? in Live the Story after 6:1–9:17). The critical need of human concern for the environment has only increased in the past few centuries as an unprecedented number of human beings populate the earth and use its rich resources.

Industrialization has added new dimensions to human interaction and interference with the earth's resources that contribute to the complexity of the issues involved in working and taking care of the rest of creation, both animal and natural. In the past decade or two, various Christian leaders have shown themselves sensitive to biblical teaching about creation care.[15] This work is particularly important for the earth and the cause of the gospel.

---

15. See the work of Calvin B. DeWitt, for instance his *Earth-Wise: A Biblical Response to Environmental Issues* (Grand Rapids: CRC Publications, 1994) and the recent work of Katharine Hayhoe and Andrew Farley on climate change (*A Climate for Change: Global Warming Facts for Faith-Based Decisions* [FaithWords, 2009]).

The Bible, and in particular the book of Genesis, leaves us in no doubt about our role as redeemed people who are created in the image of God in terms of caring for the divinely given gift of the earth's animal and natural resources. Precisely how we are to do this takes wisdom since these questions are complex on the level of economics and politics and science. Well-intentioned people will differ in terms of what is the best course of action. For example, while some Christians feel that the science is clear that human activity results in climate change that is potentially disastrous for humanity and creation at large, others feel that the danger is overblown and the proposed remedies are such that it will result in economic hardship not just for the rich but also for the poor who would lose jobs. While neither side should be demonized, the science does seem overwhelming in support of the danger of climate change, but as policies are implemented, and they should be, they should be done mindful of the economic effects and done in a way that would minimize as much as possible the possible impact particularly on the poor.[16]

### Christ: "A Profound Mystery"

As we saw, marriage is the one human relationship that is mutually exclusive and thus it becomes an appropriate metaphor for our relationship with God. Just as we can have only one spouse, so we can have only one God, so the Bible often speaks as if we, the people of God, are the wife of God.

Because of human sin, this metaphor is typically used in a negative sense (see, for example, Hos 1 and 3; Ezek 16 and 23). God's people, through their idolatry, commit spiritual adultery. We will develop this theme in the next chapter. But even in the Old Testament, there are glimpses of the early healthy marriage between God and Israel:

> This is what the Lord says:
> "I remember the devotion of your youth,
> how as a bride you loved me
> and followed me through the wilderness,
> through a land not sown.
> Israel was holy to the Lord,

16. E. Calvin Beisner has been a leader among those Christians who push back on certain forms of Christian environmentalism (see his book *Where Garden Meets Wilderness: Evangelical Entry into the Environmental Debate* [Grand Rapids: Eerdmans, 1994]). Though non-scientists like Beisner should certainly have a voice in the debate, it is telling that there are precious few climate scientists who support the view that the climate is not changing in dangerous ways. Still, he is absolutely correct to expose some of the more extreme forms of environmentalism that would promote the interests of the natural or animal world over the concerns of humans, who are indeed the apex of creation. In this regard, he is fond of quoting Psalm 115:16, "The highest heavens belong to the Lord, but the earth he has given to mankind."

the firstfruits of his harvest;
all who devoured her were held guilty,
and disaster overtook them." (Jer 2:2–3)

Therefore I am now going to allure her;
I will lead her into the wilderness
and speak tenderly to her.
There I will give her back her vineyards,
and will make the Valley of Achor a door of hope.
There she will respond as in the days of her youth,
as in the day she came up out of Egypt. (Hos 2:14–15)

In the New Testament the marriage metaphor is applied to the Christian's relationship with Jesus. In Ephesians 5:21–33 Paul delivers instructions to married couples. In the context of mutual submission of all Christians toward each other (v. 21), he specifically exhorts wives to submit to their husbands (v. 22), and then he tells husbands to love their wives (v. 25). He does so in an analogy with the relationship between Christ and the church. Indeed, he cites Genesis 2:24, which he acknowledges describes the marriage between a man and a woman, but then goes on to say, "this is a profound mystery—but I am talking about Christ and the church" (v. 32).

What Paul here recognizes is that our relationship with Christ is like a wife's relationship with her husband. It calls for our exclusive loyalty, our passion, and our devotion. It is a deeply intimate relationship. Marriage deepens our understanding of our relationship with Christ and our relationship with Christ informs our understanding of marriage.

The book of Revelation utilizes the marriage metaphor to describe our relationship with Christ at the consummation, the time when Christ comes again and initiates the new heavens and the new earth:

Then I heard what sounded like a great multitude, like the roar of rushing waters and like loud peals of thunder, shouting:

"Hallelujah!
For our Lord God Almighty reigns.
Let us rejoice and be glad
and give him glory!
For the wedding of the Lamb has come,
and his bride has made herself ready.
Fine linen, bright and clean,
was given her to wear."
(Fine linen stand for the righteous acts of God's holy people.)

> Then the angel said to me, "Write this: blessed are those who are invited to the wedding supper of the Lamb!" And he added, "These are the true words of God." (Rev 19:6–9)

Our heavenly relationship with Christ is described as a marriage. Through this metaphor we learn that the intimate relationship experienced briefly in the garden will be restored. The desired communion between God and his human creatures will be reestablished, never to be broken again. We will be married to God himself.

CHAPTER 3

# Genesis 3

## LISTEN to the Story

3:1Now the serpent was more crafty than any of the wild animals the
LORD God had made. He said to the woman, "Did God really say, 'You
must not eat from any tree in the garden'?"
2The woman said to the serpent, "We may eat fruit from the trees in
the garden, 3but God did say, 'You must not eat fruit from the tree that is
in the middle of the garden, and you must not touch it, or you will die.' "
4"You will not certainly die," the serpent said to the woman. 5"For
God knows that when you eat from it your eyes will be opened, and you
will be like God, knowing good and evil."
6When the woman saw that the fruit of the tree was good for food and
pleasing to the eye, and also desirable for gaining wisdom, she took some
and ate it. She also gave some to her husband, who was with her, and
he ate it. 7Then the eyes of both of them were opened, and they realized
they were naked; so they sewed fig leaves together and made coverings for
themselves.
8Then the man and his wife heard the sound of the LORD God as he
was walking in the garden in the cool of the day, and they hid from the
LORD God among the trees of the garden. 9But the LORD God called to
the man, "Where are you?"
10He answered, "I heard you in the garden, and I was afraid because I
was naked; so I hid."
11And he said, "Who told you that you were naked? Have you eaten
from the tree that I commanded you not to eat from?"
12The man said, "The woman you put here with me—she gave me
some fruit from the tree, and I ate it."
13Then the LORD God said to the woman, "What is this you have
done?"
The woman said, "The serpent deceived me, and I ate."
14So the LORD God said to the serpent, "Because you have done this,
"Cursed are you above all livestock
and all wild animals!

You will crawl on your belly
and you will eat dust
all the days of your life.
15 And I will put enmity
between you and the woman,
and between your offspring and hers;
he will crush your head,
and you will strike his heel."
16 To the woman he said,
"I will make your pains in childbearing very severe;
with painful labor you will give birth to children.
Your desire will be for your husband,
and he will rule over you."
17 To Adam he said, "Because you listened to your wife and ate fruit
from the tree about which I commanded you, 'You must not eat from it,'
"Cursed is the ground because of you;
through painful toil you will eat food from it
all the days of your life.
18 It will produce thorns and thistles for you,
and you will eat the plants of the field.
19 By the sweat of your brow
you will eat your food
until you return to the ground,
since from it you were taken;
for dust you are
and to dust you will return."
20 Adam named his wife Eve, because she would become the mother of
all the living.
21 The LORD God made garments of skin for Adam and his wife and
clothed them. 22 And the LORD God said, "The man has now become
like one of us, knowing good and evil. He must not be allowed to reach
out his hand and take also from the tree of life and eat, and live forever."
23 So the LORD God banished him from the Garden of Eden to work the
ground from which he had been taken. 24 After he drove the man out, he
placed on the east side of the Garden of Eden cherubim and a flaming
sword flashing back and forth to guard the way to the tree of life.

*Listening to the Text in the Story:* Biblical Text: Genesis 1–2; Ancient Near Eastern Texts: Gilgamesh Epic; Adapa

The first two chapters of Genesis describe the creation of the cosmos (1:1–2:4a) and of humanity (2:4b–25). These two creation accounts provide the immediate background to the story of human rebellion in Genesis 3. In particular, Genesis 3 is a continuation of the second creation account.

At the end of Genesis 2, there is harmony in the garden between God and Adam and Eve, between Adam and Eve, and between Adam and Eve and their living environment (Eden). All is well and everyone is happy. Genesis 3 narrates what happened so that human experience as we know it is anything but blissful.

Besides Genesis 1–2, some scholars see the Akkadian myth of Adapa behind Genesis 3.[1] The latter describes an episode in which a human being forfeits eternal life, but there are enough differences to question whether the myth has any relationship to the biblical text. Adapa has been brought to heaven to appear before the god Anu because he broke the wing of the south wind to save his life. When offered the "food" and the "waters of life" to eat and drink, he refuses based on the advice of his god Ea. We are not told why Ea gives this advice, though it might be because he wanted to keep a devotee rather than having his devotee become a peer. For whatever reason, by not eating he forfeits eternal life. Of course Adam (whose name some people point out is close to Adapa at least in sound) and Eve lose eternal life by eating from the tree of the knowledge of good and evil, an act that makes them forfeit eating from the tree of life.

As we think about the plot of Genesis 3, an episode of the Gilgamesh Epic draws our attention. After the death of his friend Enkidu, Gilgamesh searches for a way to have everlasting life. This search takes him to Utnapishtim, the only human who has achieved such life. As we will see when we recount the story in relationship to the flood account in Genesis 6–9, Utnapishtim's reward came as a result of his role in the flood, so Gilgamesh cannot achieve life in the same way.

The flood hero holds out some hope for Gilgamesh, though, when he tells him about a plant "whose thorns will prick your hand like a rose. If your hands reach that plant you will become a young man again."[2] In response, Gilgamesh dives into the deep waters and retrieves the plant. Before he is able to eat this plant that will give him life, a serpent comes along and eats it. The serpent thus achieves life, or at least perpetual youth as it periodically sheds its skin, while denying Gilgamesh the possibility.

---

1. See *ANET*, 101–3; *COS* 1:129; K. Sparks, *Ancient Texts for the Study of the Hebrew Bible* (Peabody, MA: Hendrickson, 2005), 317–19.

2. Translation from M. G. Kovacs, *The Epic of Gilgamesh* (Stanford: Stanford University Press, 1989), 106.

Here in the Gilgamesh Epic the serpent foils Gilgamesh's chance at life. However, rather than seeing any kind of direct connection between this scene from the Epic and the serpent's role in Genesis 3, it is helpful to note that a serpent played a negative role here and in other Near Eastern texts. John Walton points out that in the Adapa text one of the divine doorkeepers to heaven is Ningishzida who is depicted as a serpent and is the "guardian of demons who live in the underworld."[3] He also talks about how in Egypt serpents were associated with magical, dark wisdom and in the figure of Apophis, a chaos monster. Indeed, Tiamat, the goddess of chaos that resists the forces of creation (see description of Enuma Elish in commentary at Gen 1) is thought to be serpentine in appearance. She certainly gives birth to serpentine demonic figures. In what may be pictorial representations of Tiamat (if not then of demonic power), she is depicted as a walking serpent. Such identification has obvious ramifications for Genesis 3:1 (see below).

## EXPLAIN the Story

### Human Rebellion (3:1–8)

Nothing in the previous chapters prepares us for the appearance of the serpent in 3:1. At the end of Genesis 2, harmony reigned, but here we have a creature who clearly stands at cross purposes with God. The serpent is not good, but evil as it tries to undermine the relationship between God and his human creatures.

Who is the serpent? Christians are too quick to answer "the devil" (but see below). Certainly Adam and Eve would not have thought of the serpent as the devil, nor would anyone among the first audience of the story. That said, we have just discussed how serpents represented forces of evil in ancient Near Eastern literature, and perhaps that is as much as we can say. The serpent was recognizable as an evil force in the story.

We should remember that Adam was charged to guard/protect the garden (2:15). Right from the start, when the serpent first appeared, Adam should have been right there commanding this creature to get out of the garden. But Adam remains silent and does nothing. Indeed, it is Eve who responds to the serpent's question, "Did God really say, 'You must not eat from any tree in the garden'?"

The question is ridiculous on the surface of it. If they did not eat from any of the trees, they would die of starvation. Indeed, as Provan points out,

3. J. Walton, "Genesis," in ZIBBC, vol. 1, ed. J. Walton (Grand Rapids: Zondervan, 2009), 33.

the serpent's question turns God's statement on its head. God said "you are free to eat from any tree in the garden" with the exception of the tree of the knowledge of good and evil. "The vocabulary of God in Genesis 3 indicates freedom and blessing. The vocabulary of the serpent in Genesis 3 indicates prohibition and restriction."[4] But rather than just laughing at the serpent, Eve takes it seriously and engages the serpent in conversation. She does this to defend God from ridicule, and thus she can be considered the first apologist. However, God needs no "defense," so her words will get her into trouble. Indeed, Adam was charged with guarding the garden (2:15), and presumably after Eve was created she would share in this responsibility. Thus, they simply should have ordered the serpent to leave the garden without entering into conversation with it. By so doing, they "turned order on its head, elevating themselves over God while submitting to another creature (the serpent). Instead of exercising their rightful judicial authority over the serpent, they let the serpent be their lawgiver."[5]

Eve points out to the serpent that there is only one prohibited tree, the tree in the middle of the garden, by which she means the tree of the knowledge of good and evil, about which, she says, God instructed them that they are neither to eat nor to touch its fruit.[6] One can look in vain for the command not to touch the tree. Thus, Eve is not only the first apologist, she is also the first legalist. She adds her own restrictions to a divinely given law.

The serpent then mocks God's prohibition and denies that any bad consequence will result from eating of the tree's fruit. Indeed, just the opposite. If they eat the fruit, then "your eyes will be opened, and you will be like God, knowing good and evil" (3:4).

The narrative and the dialogue thus far has highlighted that wisdom is at issue here. We have already heard that the serpent is "shrewd," a word (*arum*) that is connected to wisdom in the book of Proverbs (and translated more positively as "prudent/prudence," 1:4; 8:5, 12; 12:16, etc.). And here the serpent tells Eve that she and her husband will achieve a type of knowledge if they eat. Eve herself comes to believe that she will gain wisdom (v. 6) if she eats. What is really at issue here in the eating of the fruit?

First, we must realize that Adam and Eve already had a kind of knowledge of good and evil. They knew that it was wrong to eat from the tree and that

---

4. I. Provan, *Seriously Dangerous Religion: What the Old Testament Really Says and Why* (Waco, TX: Baylor University Press, 2014), 111.

5. R. Beck and D. VanDrunen, "The Biblical Foundations of Law," in *Law and the Bible: Justice, Mercy and Legal Institutions*, eds. R. F. Cochran Jr. and D. VanDrunen (Downers Grove, IL: InterVarsity Press, 2013), 30.

6. The idea that the fruit of this tree is the apple is because the Latin term for apple (*malum*) is a homonymn for the Latin word for evil. We really have no idea what kind of fruit this tree produced.

it was good to refrain. We must remember that knowledge is more than intellectual awareness in the Bible, but it has to do with experience. When Adam knew (NIV translates "made love to") Eve his wife, she became pregnant (4:1), a good example that knowing is experiencing.

The point is that by eating of the fruit Adam and Eve actually partake in evil. They also assert their own moral independence from God. In essence, through their act, they say to God, "we will not allow you to define what is right and what is wrong, but we will make our own ethical judgments."

The fruit appealed to the woman's senses ("good for food and pleasing to the eye"), so she followed her senses rather than God's instruction and ate the fruit. She then gave some to her husband, who "was with her," and he ate.[7] It is only at this point in the story that we hear that Adam was present, but apparently he witnessed the entire interchange without speaking or acting. To those who want to blame Eve, we say at least Eve presented an argument, Adam just caved in without comment. The bottom line is that both are equally culpable for the first sin against God.

The consequences are immediate, and first registered in their relationship with each other. Up to this point, they have been able to be completely transparent with each other ("naked, and they felt no shame"), but now they must cover themselves. They can no longer stand the gaze of the other because they knew shame. Shame is a form of self-alienation, so there is both a fracture in community relationships as well as a psychological disruption.

### Divine Confrontation (3:9–13)

As the narrative continues, we learn that the rupture in their relationship with each other and their self-alienation is a result of the break in their relationship with God. Accordingly, when they hear the sound of God walking in the garden, they hide themselves from him.

Note the anthropomorphic description of God in this chapter. In other words, he is described in human terms. He walks in the cool of the day. He does not know where Adam or Eve had hidden themselves or what they had done. God has condescended to human understanding by describing himself in these terms. The author uses gripping storytelling in order to communicate important theological truths. These theological truths are not that God is limited in understanding or has legs; this figurative language is used to teach us that humans have placed a huge barrier between themselves and God by their rebellion against him.

---

7. Some translations in antiquity (Vulgate) and more recently (RSV; NJPS) leave out "with her." See J. F. Parker, "Blaming Eve Alone: Translation, Omission, and Implications of *'mh* in Genesis 3:6b," *JBL* 132 (2013): 729–47.

Once Adam reveals his whereabouts to God, he tries to cover up his role in the sin by shifting the blame to his wife and ultimately to God himself. It is God's fault because he "put her here with me" (3:12). God then challenges the woman who also shifts the blame. She blames the serpent for deceiving her.

### God Announces Punishment (3:14–19)

But God himself is not deceived. All three actors are culpable; therefore, God will punish each one in turn in a way that radically affects the future of the world.

The serpent is cursed first in terms of its mode of locomotion. When the serpent first appeared in the garden, apparently it walked on legs and spoke, an appropriate symbol of the force of chaos and evil (see description of Tiamat in Listening to the Text in the Story above). The serpent is now condemned to crawl on its belly and "eat dust," a most undignified way to move.

If the first part of the curse of the serpent may be seen in the current locomotion of the serpent as an animal, the second speaks to the function of the serpent as a symbol of evil. God will cause hostility (enmity) to persist between the offspring (lit. "seed") of the serpent and the seed of the woman. In the conclusion to this enmity, we see the ultimate victory of the latter over the former. In this, we see that the bad news for the serpent is ultimately good news for the woman and her offspring. The victory, though, comes with a cost. In the wording of the NIV, the serpent will strike the heel of the seed of the woman, but he will crush the serpent's head. The damage to the seed of the woman is significant, but pales in comparison to what appears to be the demise of the serpent. If the crushing is done by the foot of the seed of the woman, we are likely to understand that the injury to the heel comes in the act of crushing the serpent's head.

As mentioned, the above exposition uses the language of the NIV, though the footnote on "crush" indicates that there is some question about the exact rendering of the verb. Even though the NIV translates "crush" in the first colon and "will strike" in the second, the verb is the same in both (*shup*). The NIV takes the first occurrence as *shup* I cognate to an Akkadian and Syriac verb, while the second occurrence would be a homophone (*shup* II). However, it seems more likely that they are both instances of *shup* I, even though the idea of "crush" does not work as well for the action of the serpent toward the heel of the woman's seed. Wenham suggests a slightly different nuance when he translates the verb in both places as "batter."[8]

Whatever the exact translation of the verbs, the main thrust of God's curse on the serpent is clear. First, there will be hostility between the seed

8. G. J. Wenham, *Genesis 1–15*, WBC (Nashville: Nelson, 1987), 45.

of the serpent and the seed of the woman. The seed of the woman is clearly the human race. The seed of the serpent on a literal level refers to serpents, and indeed serpents present a threat to human beings, but this meaning is much too banal for this context and certainly is not the way that the New Testament understands this verse (see below). Thus, again, the serpent has a symbolic sense here, standing for the forces of evil. Though it would be wrong to understand the Old Testament author and original audience as having as specific an understanding of the serpent as the New Testament authors (see below), it seems fair to say that the serpent would have been understood as representing the spiritual forces of evil.

Further, as Genesis continues, we will see that humanity itself will be divided between those who follow God and those who chose to reject God (and this as early as the story of Cain and Abel in Gen 4), and in this sense they may be counted as the "seed of the serpent" as well. Even so, God's curse informs the reader at this early point that the forces of evil will eventually be defeated by the "seed of the woman."

Next, we come to the punishment that God applies to the woman. Like the serpent's punishment, it comes in two parts, though both concern relationships and those most dear to her. First, childbearing will come with great pain. I believe that the NIV translation misses an important nuance when it renders verse 16b, "I will make your pains in childbearing very severe." A more literal rendition is found in the NRSV, "I will greatly increase your pangs in childbearing." In other words, even if Adam and Eve did not sin, there would have been pain in childbearing, but sin intensified that pain.

The second affected relationship is with the woman's husband and this punishment comes fundamentally at a psychological level: "Your desire will be for your husband, and he will rule over you." Though this translation is fine, it can easily be misunderstood if the woman's desire for the man is taken as a romantic desire. The word "desire" (*teshuqah*) only occurs two other times in the Hebrew Bible and once in the sense of romantic desire (Song 7:11), but the more telling sense of the word comes in Genesis 4:7 where personified sin desires Cain. Clearly, sin does not desire Cain romantically; it desires to consume or control him. This meaning fits the negative context of our present verse much better and even more significantly fits in with common human experience. When sin affects the marriage relationship, it is not a matter of a woman desiring romance, but rather a woman desiring to control her husband, and, as the next part of the verse indicates, his attempt to control ("rule over") her.[9]

---

9. S. Foh, "What is the Woman's Desire?" *WTJ* 37 (1974/75): 376–83.

Finally, God turns his attention to Adam. In Genesis 2, we saw that God assigned work to Adam. He needed to tend and guard the garden. It wouldn't weed itself and the fruit from the other trees of the garden would not pick itself. God's punishment, however, adds a new degree of frustration to work just as God's punishment added a new degree of pain to childbirth. The consequences of the fall on work are painfully observed by the Teacher in the book of Ecclesiastes:

> What do people get for all the toil and anxious striving with which they labor under the sun? All their days their work is grief and pain; even at night their minds do not rest. This too is meaningless. (2:22–23, see also 2:18–21; 4:4–6)[10]

As the Teacher looks "under the sun," he sees the world affected by the curses that God issues at the time humans rebelled against him, and he notes that work has become toil, filled with frustration. Even if one is successful in life, death comes and "I must leave them to the one who comes after me. And who knows whether that person will be wise or foolish? Yet they will have control over all the first of my toil into which I have poured my effort and skill under the sun. This too is meaningless" (2:18–19). This arduous labor will last the entirety of the man's life until he dies. Death is described as the reversal of the creation of Adam, a return to the dust (see Gen 2:7).

Though announced as part of the punishment of Adam, Eve does not escape death either. As a matter of fact, with one exception (childbirth), we should not understand the punishment of the man and the woman as unique to them. Men as well as women struggle in relationships, and women taste the futility of work as well as men.

And, as we mentioned, both return to the dust. We remember that God had earlier announced that this would be the result of disobedience: "but you must not eat from the tree of the knowledge of good and evil, for when (lit., "on the day") you eat from it you will certainly die" (2:17).

Some interpreters worry that God's warning indicates that death would be an immediate consequence of eating the fruit as if the fruit would be a fast-acting poison that would kill them on the spot. In response, we would point out that, though they did not immediately die in a physical sense, there was a spiritual death upon eating. That is, there was a rupture between God and his human creatures. But even in the physical sense, death at that very moment, to use Paul's later words, "entered" (Rom 5:12) the world.

---

10. For translation and commentary, see T. Longman III, *Ecclesiastes*, NICOT (Grand Rapids: Eerdmans, 1998), 101–6, 136–40.

**Execution of the Judgment (3:20–24)**

The entrance of death into the world is represented by God expelling Adam and Eve from the garden in which stood the tree of life. In his speech to the divine council (see comments on Gen 1:26), God expresses the need to separate the human pair from the tree.

Some people, wrongly in my opinion, understand God as speaking urgently about the need to act quickly lest Adam and Eve make a raid on the tree of life, eat its fruit, and then achieve eternal life without God's permission. This reading is unlikely, since it assumes that the tree had a kind of magical fruit that conferred eternal life.

Let's remember that there was only one tree from which Adam and Eve could not eat, the tree of the knowledge of good and evil (3:3); they ate from all the other trees, which presumably meant they were eating from the tree of life. By expelling Adam and Eve from the garden, God separated them from the tree and thus the effects of aging would set in.

Before being expelled the text informs the reader of two actions. The first is that Adam named his wife Eve, the meaning of this name seems to mean "living," which is connected to the explanation given by the text itself, "she would become the mother of all the living." That death entered the human experience did not mean the end of humanity. Adam and Eve would die, but they would have children. The children would die, but they would have children, and so on and so on. Boda points out that it is here, and not in the traditional understanding of the death of the animals for clothes, that we see the hope of redemption. It is, after all, human seed that will bring about the defeat of sin (see 3:15).[11]

That said, there is a problem with the traditional understanding of the meaning of Eve's name. As Zevit points out, it is not true that she is the mother of all "living" since that would include not just human beings, but "every living creature."[12] Thus, he is almost certainly correct to point to a different understanding of the Hebrew *hayya* by citing an Arabic cognate meaning "kin, related members of a clan, descendants of a father or ancestor"[13] and suggest the translation "And he called her Hawwa, that is, Kin-maker, because she was the mother of all kinfolk."

It is commonly thought that Adam's naming of Eve means that Adam has authority over Eve, leading to the more general assertion that men have

11. Personal communication and M. Boda, *A Severe Mercy: Sin and Its Remedy in the Old Testament* (Winona Lake, IN: Eisenbrauns, 2009), 19.

12. Zevit, *What Really Happened?* 229.

13. Ibid.

authority over women. Provan wisely points out that if this were true then Hagar would have authority over God since she names him at Genesis 16:13.[14]

The second action is of tremendous significance. "The LORD God made garments of skin for Adam and his wife and clothed them" (v. 21). Right after they sinned and lost their innocence, Adam and Eve quickly covered their nakedness using "fig leaves" (v. 7). But this move was a temporary measure, and now God provides them with clothes made of animal skins.

While some try to read the language of animal sacrifice and the shedding of blood in this verse, that seems misplaced. The significance of this act is that God is showing humanity that, though they have sinned and will suffer the consequences of their sin, he will remain involved with them. In other words, God extends his sinful people a token of grace.

The final verse of the chapter narrates the execution of the judgment against the man and the woman as they are expelled from the garden, presumably toward the east since that is where God stations cherubim. With the mention of the cherubim, we see the emergence of the picture of God as a warrior. Now that the world has moved toward chaos, God exerts his energy as a warrior in order to bring back the original creation order. The cherubim are part of his celestial army; indeed, they are the special forces of his army. Adam and Eve were unable to guard (*shamar*, 2:15) the garden, but now the cherubim guard (*shamar*) the garden against unwanted interlopers including God's sinful human creatures.

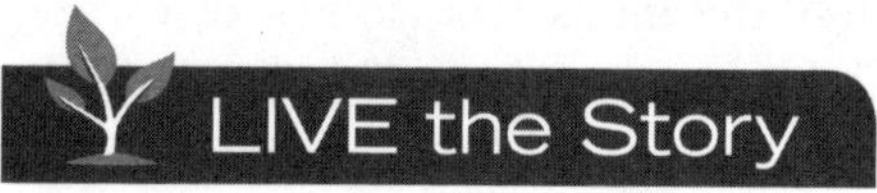


### The Story of the Fall

What purpose does the story of Adam and Eve's rebellion and punishment serve in the Bible? Most Christian readers would be surprised that the question is even asked since it seems obvious in the light of Paul's statement, "just as sin entered the world through one man, and death through sin, and in this way death came to all people ..." (Rom 5:12). In short, for many Christians Adam's sin is the explanation for the presence of sin, guilt, and the experience of death. All human beings are sinners from birth because Adam and Eve broke the commandment not to eat from the fruit of the tree of the knowledge of good and evil. This idea is often referred to as the doctrine of original sin.

But before moving into the Christian perspective on this story, it is important to point out that in the Old Testament human sin, whether collective

14. Provan, *Seriously Dangerous Religion*, 91.

or individual, is never blamed on Adam and Eve. They are hardly ever mentioned in the Old Testament after Genesis 3, and when they are (see only Gen 4:1, 25; 5:3–5; 1 Chr 1:1), it has nothing to do with their sin or anyone else's. Neither Israel nor any individual mentioned in later biblical texts looks at their sin or any other person's sin, guilt, or death as a result of the story of Genesis 3.[15] Perhaps this observation helps explain why Jewish thinkers rarely speak of original sin.[16]

And actually neither does the New Testament. Earlier I only quoted a part of Romans 5:12, the fuller quotation is "Therefore, just as sin entered the world through one man, and death through sin, and in this way death came to all people, *because all sinned*—." We sin, have guilt, and die, not because Adam and Eve sinned, but because we sin.

So is the Christian idea of original sin wrong? And what is the point of Genesis 3 for later readers?

Let's answer the second question first. Genesis 3 (and 1–2 for that matter) is an origins text. What I am about to say does not depend on the highly debated question of whether or to what level of precision (see below) these chapters narrate an actual historical event. In either case, these stories are told not just to satisfy an antiquarian interest, but to tell us why things are the way they are today. Genesis 3 answers many questions, but the primary question it answers is what is sin and why we sin as well as the question why we die.

The answer is that we sin and die, not because of Adam's sin, but because of our own sin. The Bible never teaches that we sin and die because of Adam. The story of Adam, though, does expose the nature of sin. What is sin at its heart? Sin is rebellion against God, a refusal to accept him as Lord. Sin places oneself in the position of God, and, like Adam and Eve, humans substitute their own ideas of right and wrong in the place of God's definition. Sin rejects God ("the fool says in his heart, 'There is no God.' They are corrupt, their deeds are vile" [Pss 14:1; 53:1]). But not only does the story inform us about the fundamental nature of sin it tells us why we sin. In other words, the account of Adam and Eve is a way of telling us what we would all do (and indeed we all do) if we were in their place.

God created humanity morally innocent (not perfect, as some people mistakenly think) and able to make free moral choices. God did not and does not compel humans to bend to his will. The story of the creation of Adam and Eve

15. Some people believe that Hosea 6:7 refers to Adam's sin, but the text clearly refers to the place Adam since it is parallel with the Hebrew *sham* ("there") that denotes a physical place. But even if the prophet refers to Adam the person, it is simply making an analogy with Adam, not blaming Adam for another person's sin, guilt, or death.

16. Zevit, *What Really Happened?* 3–17.

(Gen 2) and the story of their rebellion (Gen 3) make it clear to us that we are sinful not because of the way God made us (that is a Mesopotamian idea, see above in Listening to the Text in the Story), but rather because we choose like Adam and Eve to rebel against God.

But if we are not guilty because of the sin of Adam and Eve, then is it possible for us to act differently and thus be morally innocent? First, there is no doubt, no doubt at all, that the Bible teaches that there is and there will be no morally innocent person. All have sinned and fallen short of the glory of God (Rom 3:23; see 3:9–20). Second, remember that the story of Adam and Eve is not just a story about Adam and Eve (even if it is a specific historical account of a particular couple), but rather tells us what we all would have done in their situation.

But I think we can go even further. Adam and Eve's sin, to use Paul's language, "introduced sin" into the world. Their sin so corrupted the divine-human, human-human, and human-creation relationships that we are born into a warped and distorted world. It is not possible for us not to sin (*non posse non peccare*). We are held guilty for our own sin, not for Adam and Eve's. This view is similar to Walton, who points out, "Humanity was supposed to continue God's process of moving the cosmos from nonorder to order. With the failure of humanity all creation was stuck in ripple effect of sin and the disorder it brought."[17]

In other words, the Bible does not support the idea that we inherit Adam's sin in some kind of genetic way like a disease, thus necessitating a biological connection to Adam. After all, Jesus was human, though he did not inherit a sin nature from Mary his mother. This point is made by John Walton, who adds "that Adam's sin should not be viewed as passed on biologically, since the correlating solution, the death of Christ is not founded on biological parentage but on a representative role."[18]

In short, the idea that we inherit a sin nature, guilt, and death from Adam (and Eve) does not derive from the Old Testament or from Paul, but from the thinking of Augustine. Now Augustine was one of the greatest theological thinkers of all time, but he was not infallible. Augustine got off to a bad start by mistranslating the Greek of Romans 5:12 which properly rendered says "just as sin entered the world through one man, and death through sin, and in this way death came to all people, *because* (*eph hō*) all sinned." Augustine translated "because" as "in whom" (*in quo*), thus changing Paul's point that we all are guilty because of our own sin to the idea that we are all guilty because of Adam's sin.

---

17. J. Walton, "Human Origins and the Bible," *Zygon* 47 (2012): 11.
18. Ibid.

Though much more could be said,[19] we must not lose sight that Genesis 3 tells us that human sin is a result of human rebellion, not a function of our creation by God. He created humans morally innocent. Our guilt and our death are the result of our sin, and Paul reminds us that human rebellion came at the very beginning of human existence.[20]

But Paul in Romans 5 reminds his readers of their sinfulness in order to tell them the good news that just like sin and death was introduced by the one man Adam, so God's gift "came by the grace of the one man, Jesus Christ" (Rom 5:15). For this reason, Jesus is envisioned as the second Adam.

## Is It Wrong to Struggle against the Punishments of the Fall?

We have seen how God announces punishments on the serpent, the woman, and the man that ring true to human experience. Yes, there is hostility in the world. Relationships are certainly troubled, and work is often frustrating. However, we must bear in mind that these punishments are descriptive and not prescriptive.[21]

The difference is significant in two ways. First, we should not live believing that relationships and work are doomed to abject failure. For example, while giving birth to and raising children is often accompanied by both physical and emotional pain, they are also a source of great joy (Ps 127:3–5). Second, knowing that the punishments are descriptive and not prescriptive means that we can work hard against them without sinning against God.

While it is true that the punishment announced against the woman includes the man "ruling" over her, we do not have to submit to the idea that men will dominate women, but we can actively work against any oppression of women particularly through education and laws protecting women's rights. We can further develop technologies and efficiencies with the goal of lessening the burden of work as well as lessening pain in childbirth.

## Helping Us Understand Our Experiences: Loneliness, Frustration, and Hostility

As we have already commented, Genesis 3 is an origins text; it does not simply intend to report an ancient event, but to help us understand who we are as

---

19. And I refer especially to C. M. Hays and S. L. Herring. "Adam and the Fall," in *Strange Bedfellows? Evangelical Faith and Historical Criticism*, eds. C. M. Hays and C. B. Ansberry (Grand Rapids: Baker Books, 2013), whom I am deeply dependent upon in this section.

20. Here I am in agreement with James K. A. Smith (in an unpublished paper, Calvin College Seminar Series: Human Origins, Grand Rapids, Michigan, 2010) who rightly argues that Genesis 3 teaches the "episodic nature" of the fall. See also A. M. McCoy, "Becoming Who We Are Supposed to Be: An Evaluation of Schneider's Use of Christian Theology in Conversation with Recent Genetic Science," *CTJ* 49 (2014): 63–84.

21. See the excellent discussion in Provan, *Seriously Dangerous Religion*, chapter 6.

human beings. In particular, the punishments directed toward the serpent, the woman, and the man may help us understand why we are often lonely, frustrated, and in conflict.

*Why are we lonely and why do we experience pain in relationships?*
In Genesis 2, God knew that "it is not good for the man to be alone" (v. 18). Humans are made for relationship with each other. God's most immediate response to this need was to make a woman who would "become one flesh" (2:24) with the man. Though marriage, according to the Bible, is the most intimate of all human relationships, our loneliness is mitigated by other relationships as well, both kinship relationships as well as voluntary ones like friendship. In a word, "man is not an island" (John Donne), but yearns for, even needs community. At the end of Genesis 2 humanity dwelt in harmony because they had an untroubled relationship with God.

According to our present chapter, human rebellion against God changes the harmonious nature of relationship. Humans asserted themselves against God through their act of pride. Rather than seeking the good of the other, people put themselves first and, according to Genesis 3:16, attempt to control other people for their own benefit.

Sin destroys community, fracturing relationships, both with God and with other people. The biblical narrative is filled with many stories that bear this observation out, but the biblical witness also attests to the possibility of redemption of relationships, first with God and then with each other.

Of the countless texts that illustrate God's pursuit of redemption of relationship and community, we turn to Ephesians 2 for illustrative purposes. Verses 11–13 addresses Gentiles who were separated from Christ as well as from the covenant community (v. 12, "excluded from citizenship in Israel and foreigners to the covenants of promise, without hope and without God in the world") and happily announces that "in Christ Jesus you who once were far away have been brought near by the blood of Christ" (v. 13).

Jesus' death on the cross is not just for our individual redemption, but is for the restoration of human relationships. Christ's death not only creates a relationship with God, but also allows us to have meaningful relationships with other people. Sin creates barriers between people, but Christ "destroyed the barrier, the dividing wall of hostility" (v. 14), for his purpose was "to create in himself one new humanity out of two, thus making peace" (v. 15).

Our sinful, self-serving nature will always try to put ourselves first, thus destroying relationship. If we have a relationship with Christ, we have the foundation for healthy relationships with other people.

*Why is work so frustrating?*

Sin is the cause of loneliness and pain in relationships; sin is also the reason we experience frustration in our work. Genesis 2 informs us that humans would work whether or not they sinned, but Genesis 3 explains why work is difficult, frustrating, and sometimes dehumanizing.

We work to survive—literally. Most readers of this commentary will be participants in a currency-based economy. If we don't work, we don't have any money. If we don't have any money, we don't have shelter or food.[22] But most people want more out of their work than just money; they want a sense of purpose, a sense of accomplishment.

When Adam and Eve worked in the garden, tending and keeping it, they not only provided for their own sustenance, they also were engaged in a noble, God-given task. They reflected their Creator in their work.

But sin troubled work and no one, even those with jobs they generally enjoy, escapes a sense of futility in their work. No one captures it better than the Teacher in the book of Ecclesiastes as he looks at life "under the sun." If we live life apart from God, we will experience the consequences of the covenant curses:

> So I hated life, because the work that is done under the sun was grievous to me. All of it is meaningless, a chasing after the wind. I hated all the things I had toiled for under the sun, because I must leave them to the one who comes after me. And who knows whether that person will be wise or foolish? Yet they will have control over all the fruit of my toil into which I have poured my effort and skill under the sun. This too is meaningless. So my heart began to despair over all my toilsome labor under the sun. For a person may labor with wisdom, knowledge and skill, and then they must leave all they own to another who has not toiled for it. This too is meaningless and a great misfortune. What do people get for all the toil and anxious striving with which they labor under the sun? All their days their work is grief and pain; even at night their minds do not rest. This too is meaningless. (Eccl 2:17–23; see also 4:4; 9:11)

These are depressing words, but most people recognize that they ring true with their experience to a greater or lesser extent. Is there any hope for redemption in our work?

No one escapes the frustration of work to be sure, but we were created to work, thus reflecting in our human way our Creator God. The message of the book of Ecclesiastes is a reminder that the ultimate meaning of life cannot be

22. Of course, many modern currency-based economies also have social systems that will provide people who have no work with money in order to survive.

found in anything, including work, other than in God.[23] But if we put God first and work for this glory, we can certainly find at least glimpses of glory and enjoyment in our labor.

Again, work provides a venue for us to reflect our Creator. We are created in God's image, meaning that we have creative impulses that can be applied to our work as gardeners, janitors, parents, counselors, politicians, ministers, students, accountants, pilots, etc.

***Why is there hostility in the world?***

Genesis 1–3 is the foundation of the Bible. These chapters contain origin stories which help us understand why things are the way they are. Genesis 1–2 informs us that hostility exists not because God made the world that way, but because of human sin. In God's announcement of the punishment of the serpent he speaks of "enmity" that will exist between the serpent and its "offspring" with the woman and her "offspring" (3:15).

But who are the offspring of the serpent and of the woman? Waltke correctly surmises that we are not talking about baby snakes or demons, but those people whom "he [the serpent] has led into rebellion against God."[24] If so, then the offspring of the woman would refer to those who choose to follow God.

The hostility between God's people and those who reject God begin right away as is evidenced by the hostility between Cain and Abel and is illustrated by the genealogy of Cain and the genealogy of Seth (see Gen 4–5). At the root of hostility is, of course, sin. Sinners don't care about others, but only about the self. James much later will ask the question, "What causes fights and quarrels among you?" and then turn around and answer his own question by observing, "Don't they come from your desires that battle within you? You desire but do not have, so you kill. You covet but you cannot get what you want, so you quarrel and fight" (Jas 4:1–2).

The judgment speech to the serpent, thankfully, not only announces the coming conflict, but also envisions its triumphant conclusion as it describes the ultimate crushing of the head of the serpent. The serpent represents evil and so the crushing of the serpent's head signifies the ultimate defeat of evil. Who will crush the serpent's head? The woman's "offspring."

Who is the woman's offspring? The original readers of the book of Genesis would not have had a clear idea. What they would have known is that

---

23. D. Allender and T. Longman III, *Breaking the Idols of Your Heart: How to Navigate the Temptations of Life* (Downers Grove, IL: InterVarsity, 2007), 62–87.

24. B. K. Waltke, *Genesis: A Commentary* (Grand Rapids: Zondervan, 2001), 93.

eventually evil would be silenced. It is interesting to note, though, the interesting interplay between the plural "offspring" and the singular "he."

This observation leads us to the New Testament perspective on this verse which we observe in the following passages:

> The God of peace will soon crush Satan under your feet. (Rom 16:20)
>
> The great dragon was hurled down—that ancient serpent called the devil, or Satan, who leads the whole world astray. He was hurled to the earth, and his angels with him. (Rev 12:9)
>
> And I saw an angel coming down out of heaven, having the key to the Abyss and holding in his hand a great chain. He seized the dragon, that ancient serpent, who is the devil, or Satan, and bound him for a thousand years. He threw him into the Abyss, and locked and sealed it over him, to keep him from deceiving the nations anymore until the thousand years were ended. After that, he must be set free for a short time. (Rev 20:1–3)

The first thing that is obvious from these passages is that, from a New Testament perspective, the serpent is Satan, the ultimate expression of evil in the world. All three of these passages foresee the ultimate defeat of Satan, that "ancient serpent." Who will defeat Satan? The God of peace according to Paul in Romans utilizing the church. How does he do it? That is the story of the Gospel. Jesus defeats Satan by dying on the cross and being raised (Col 1:13–15) and his ascension (Eph 4:8). These redemptive actions provide assurance of the final victory, which will come at the end of the ages when Christ returns again.

### The Disruption of God's Good Gift of Sex

Genesis 2 makes it clear that God intended sexual intercourse to be an essential aspect of what it meant to be married (2:24, "they become one flesh"). In our comments on chapter 2, we pointed out that sex within marriage was not for the utilitarian purpose of producing children, but for mutual pleasure and for developing intimacy between a husband and wife. In the garden, this intimacy was untroubled, "Adam and his wife were both naked, and they felt no shame" (2:25).

The narrative of the fall makes it clear that human rebellion disrupts this precious gift. As soon as they sinned, "they realized they were naked; so they sewed fig leaves together and made coverings for themselves" (3:7). The break in the harmony of the relationship between God and humans results in alienation between a man and a woman.

The story of the fall informs the reader why intimacy is not natural and easy. However, we should not over read the narrative to claim that sexual intimacy is impossible. Here we are informed by the Song of Songs, which should be read as an account of the "redemption of sexuality."[25] The Song is composed of love poems that largely celebrate physical intimacy between a man and a woman, to be understood canonically as a husband and wife.[26] Trible points out that often this unnamed man and unnamed woman make love in a garden setting, evoking the remembrance of the time when Adam and Eve were intimate in the garden. Thus, the Song, read in the light of Genesis 2 and 3, indicates that sex can elicit pleasure and joy even in a fallen world.

I would only add one slight caveat to Trible's insightful comments on the theological significance of the Song.[27] This redemption is an "already-not yet" redemption. There are poems within the Song that remind the reader that such intimacy is not easily achieved. A prime example of such a poem is the one found in Song of Songs 5:2–6:3. Here the woman rebuffs the request that she open her door to let the man in, and by the time she changes her mind and opens the door to him, he has left, requiring her to undergo a strenuous search for him. Thus, Genesis 2–3 and the Song of Songs helps us understand both the joys and the tribulations of sexuality in our lives.[28]

### Is All Suffering and Pain the Consequence of the Fall?

Many people have a utopian picture of life before the fall, which of course has implications for how life would have been lived had sin not entered the world. But is it right to think that there would have been no pain or struggle if Adam and Eve had not eaten of the fruit of the tree of the knowledge of good and evil? Was there and would there have been no death in the original creation? Would there have been no devastating storms, no earthquakes, no hurricanes? Is all suffering and pain the result of human evil and if humans had remained good would there have been no human suffering and pain?

A close look at Genesis 1–3 casts doubt on this idea. We will begin by examining closely the language of the punishment of the woman and the man.

In the Explain the Story section, we have already noted that the NIV obscures the sense of the Hebrew in an unfortunate manner, so here we will cite the ESV which, similar to the vast majority of English translations, more carefully captures the Hebrew: "I will surely multiply your pain in childbearing; in pain you shall bring forth children" (Gen. 3:16). Notice that human

25. See P. Trible, *God and the Rhetoric of Sexuality* (Philadelphia: Fortress, 1978).

26. So B. S. Childs, *Introduction to the Old Testament* (Philadelphia: Fortress, 1979), 575; see also D. Grossberg, "Two Kinds of Sexual Relationships in the Hebrew Bible," *Hebrew Studies* 35 (1994): 7–25.

27. G. Schwab, *The Song of Songs' Cautionary Message concerning Human Love* (New York: Peter Lang, 2002).

28. For extensive treatment, see Allender and Longman, *God Loves Sex.*

sin does not bring pain to childbearing for the first time, but increases that "natural" pain.

Turning now to the punishment of the man, we here too note that sin does not introduce struggle and exertion to the farming process, but rather elevates it to a new intense level of frustration. If humans had not rebelled, they still would have worked hard to produce crops. Their food would not have miraculously appeared like the manna in the wilderness (where of course they still had to go out and collect it).

Indeed, we know from the story of Genesis 3 that not only was there suffering and pain that was "intrinsic" to creation, but there was already the presence of moral evil that was "extrinsic" to it.[29] After all, we have the presence of the serpent before human rebellion. Adam had been commissioned to "guard" the garden against such attacks, thus there is hostility before the fall.

With this in mind we go back now to the account of creation, particularly in Genesis 1, and note that the picture is not so much God creating a world without suffering and pain and chaos, but rather it is the story of his restraint rather than removal of non-moral suffering, pain, and chaos (what Waltke calls absurd or irrational).[30] God doesn't make the darkness, nor does he eradicate it, but rather he restrains it (Gen 1:1–5). Interestingly, the creation account does not explicity say that God created the waters (which often symbolizes chaos in Scripture) either,[31] but rather that he controlled them. Of course, this does not mean that God didn't create everything, but the biblical account purposefully does not narrate the origins of darkness or the waters or does it give us an account of the creation or the serpent nor an explanation of its evil nature. Already before the rebellion of humanity, suffering, pain, and even evil are present in God's good creation.

Thus, even today not all suffering and pain can be ascribed to moral evil today. There is suffering that is intrinsic to God's creation. Earthquakes are the result of the shifting of tectonic plates, which if they did not shift would result in even worse results.

And this is what makes the new creation as described in Revelation 21–22 different from the old creation. The description opens when John says that he

---

29. The language of "intrinsic" and "extrinsic" is borrowed from Provan, *Seriously Dangerous Religion*, 107–9, though I may use and apply his categories slightly differently than he does.

30. B. K. Waltke, *Old Testament Theology: An Exegetical, Canonical, and Thematic Approach* (Grand Rapids: Zondervan, 2007), 180.

31. This is even more explicit in Job's creation account when it cites God who asks Job "Who shut up the sea behind doors when it burst forth from the womb, when I made the clouds its garment and wrapped it in thick darkness, when I fixed limits for it and set its doors and bars in place, when I said, 'This far you may come and no farther; here is where your proud waves halt'?" (Job 38:8–11), see commentary in T. Longman III, *Job*, BCOTWP (Grand Rapids: Baker, 2012), 429.

"saw 'a new heaven and a new earth,' for the first heaven and the first earth had passed away, and there was no longer any sea" (Rev 21:1). The absence of the sea figuratively depicts a place without chaos. And there is no mention of darkness either. Indeed, the new heavens and new earth are described as a city (the New Jerusalem), which "does not need the sun or the moon to shine on it, for the glory of God gives it light, and the Lamb is its lamp" (Rev 21:23). Indeed, there "will be no night there" (Rev 21:25; also 22:5).[32] No sea and no darkness, unlike the first creation. God has not just constrained chaos, but has eradicated it.

### Meeting God in a Fallen World

As we have commented, the real tragedy of human sin is the rupture it creates in our relationship with God. In the garden, Adam and Eve dwelt in the very presence of God. There was no need for a special place to be with him.

All this changed when Adam and Eve were expelled from the garden. From then on, humans needed to approach God at special consecrated locations and with much trepidation.

At first these special places were marked by the construction of an altar, and later we will observe that the first explicit mention of an altar is the one Noah builds as he exits the ark in order to offer sacrifices to God (8:20).[33] An altar was a simple structure composed of stone or dirt (see Exod 20:24–26) and, as the etymology of the Hebrew word for altar (*mizbeah*, the verbal root *zabah* means "to slaughter/sacrifice") indicates, it was a place for the offering of a sacrifice, a ritual by which a worshiper acknowledges their sin and what their sin deserved.

As the people of God transitioned from an extended family to a nation, a larger "holy place" was required and God answered this need by commanding Moses to build a tabernacle (Exod 25–40). A tabernacle is a tent and the bronze altar of sacrifice was placed immediately outside the tent. Thus, the shape of the place where God made his presence known to his people conforms to their sociological setting. Accordingly, when David finishes the conquest by subduing the last of the internal enemies of Israel, God tells his son Solomon to build a temple, a permanent house representing the fact that God had given rest to his people from their enemies and thus signaling the need to centralize worship (so Deut 12).

---

32. This description picks up on the prophetic statement of Zechariah that "on that day there will be neither sunlight nor cold, frosty darkness. It will be a unique day—a day known only to the Lord—with no distinction between day and night. When evening comes, there will be light" (Zech 14:6–7).

33. As we will comment in the next chapter, the sacrifices of Abel and Cain presuppose the presence of an altar.

The temple was built in the mid-tenth century BC and lasted until 586 BC. The book of Kings informs us that the leaders of Judah often placed idols in the Holy of Holies and other kings allowed the flourishing of the rival worship sites known as "high places." For this and for the many other sins of his people, God used the Babylonians to capture the city of Jerusalem and to destroy the temple that symbolized his presence with the people of Judah.

However, the destruction of the temple was not the end of the story for the people of Judah. Ezekiel had a vision of a restored temple (chs. 40–48) and, sure enough, once the Persians had defeated the Babylonians, their king Cyrus encouraged Jews to return to Jerusalem and rebuild their temple (2 Chr 36:22–23; Ezra 1:2–4). The second temple was completed in 515 BC under the leadership of Sheshbazzar and Zerubbabel and the prophetic encouragement of Haggai and Zechariah, but it did not have the glory of the first or meet the full expectation of Ezekiel's prophetic vision. Something greater was yet to come.

That something greater was not a building, but a person, Jesus. The Gospel of John announces that "the Word became flesh and made his dwelling [traditionally, "tabernacled"] among us" (John 1:14). Jesus was the very presence of God.

True, Jesus honored the temple as his Father's house, cleansing it of the money changers (John 2:13–17). But he also spoke radically about the temple, presaging its destruction: "Destroy this temple, and I will raise it again in three days" (2:19). In this way, he anticipated his resurrection and the fact that his presence removed the need for a special holy place like the temple, whose destruction by the Romans in AD 70 he anticipated (Mark 13:2).

That there is no longer any special "holy place" different from any other location is also signaled by the ripping of the curtain of the temple into two pieces from "top to bottom" at the death of Jesus (Matt 27:51). Holiness is no longer contained in that small room but permeates the entire world.

After his resurrection, Jesus ascends to heaven, but he sends the Holy Spirit to dwell in his people both individually as well as corporately just as the glory cloud representing God's presence filled the tabernacle (Exod 40:34–38). It is thus no surprise that the New Testament authors refer to the individual Christian (1 Cor 3:16–17; 6:18–20; 2 Cor 6:14–18) as well as the church (Eph 2:19–22) as the temple.

The Christian can meet with God anywhere and at anytime for intimate fellowship with him. Even so, Eden has not been fully restored. For that we await the return of Christ and the New Jerusalem, which is described in the final two chapters of the Bible. Interestingly, we are given a description of the New Jerusalem which includes the notation that there was no temple. Why?

"Because the Lord God Almighty and the Lamb are its temple" (Rev 21:22). In addition, we learn that there is a river that flows through the city and, reminiscent of Eden, "on each side of the river stood the tree of life, bearing twelve crops of fruit, yielding its fruit every month. And the leaves of the tree are for the healing of the nations" (Rev 22:2).

Two trees of life! In other words, the end is more than a restoration of the Eden; it is better than Eden. In Eden, there was the possibility of a fall; it was a probationary period. But not so the end. The message of the Bible is that we can look forward to dwelling in God's glorious presence forever.[34]

## Excursus: Were Adam and Eve Real People?

One of the most controversial questions today among people who believe that the Bible is God's Word concerns the historicity of Adam and Eve. The literature is voluminous and the issues are complex and emotionally charged. The present discussion is fueled by the recent study of the human genome that provides evidence in favor of human evolution, in particular common ancestry most recently with primates, as well as the conclusion that humanity does not go back to a single couple, but rather to an original population numbering some five to ten thousand individuals.[35]

Does the biblical picture of creation (Gen 1–2) and the fall (Gen 3) contradict these scientific findings, and if so, what is a Christian reader to do?

This commentary is not the place to air out all the issues and the different perspectives offered by different people of faith. Besides requiring much more space than this book can spare,[36] the conclusion to that discussion does not bear on anything we have said about Genesis 1–3. In other words, the above interpretation does not depend on the historicity or non-historicity of Adam and Eve.

Still, the interested reader deserves at least a brief statement of my own views on the matter, even if I cannot provide a full argument and interaction with other views within the confines of this book.

To me, the issue is one of genre. Genre is a type of writing (see Introduction, Literary Analysis: Genre). Authors signal to their readers how to take their words through the conventions of a genre. When the Gospels inform

---

34. For more detail on the biblical theology of the presence of God, see Longman, *Immanuel in Our Place*, 1–74.

35. D. R. Venema, "Genesis and the Genome: Genomics Evidence for Human-Ape Common Ancestry and the Ancestral Hominid Population Sizes," *Perspectives on Science and Christian Faith* 62 (2010): 167–78.

36. See *Four Views on Historical Adam*, ed. by M. Barrett and S. Gundry (Grand Rapids: Zondervan, 2013).

us that Jesus uses a parable to teach his disciples, the term parable leads us to expect Jesus to tell a short, fictional story that creates an analogy that teaches about the Kingdom of God.

Most biblical passages do not provide such an explicit genre label. Therefore, modern readers must be attentive to the genre signals found in the text itself. What are the genre signals of Genesis 1–3? There are four that are particularly relevant, and the first three have been noted above. First, these chapters have a high degree of figurative language (the days of Gen 1; Adam's creation from the dust and the breath of God; Eve's creation from Adam's side/rib). Second, there is a close, seemingly intentional, interaction with ancient Near Eastern literature (see comments above about the Enuma Elish, Atrahasis, etc.). Third, we noted a lack of sequence concord between the depiction of creation in Genesis 1 and 2, thus revealing a lack of interest for telling the reader the actual chronology of creation. These features and others should make us hesitant to take these chapters as historically precise, telling us, for instance, exactly how God created creation. As Lowery insightfully concludes: "it becomes clear that the ancient conventions for history writing—that is, its poetics—were vastly different from those of the present age."[37]

That said, do these features prove that Adam and Eve are not historical? No. Not everything in Genesis 1–3 is figurative. There is a historical impulse in this section of Scripture. The most obvious indicator of that is the presence of the formula "this is the account of (*toledot*). . . ." This phrase, first found in Genesis 2:4 is found an additional ten times (5:1; 6:9; 10:1; 11:10, 27; 25:12, 19; 36:1, 9; 37:2), showing something of a generic continuation throughout the whole book of Genesis.

Thus, if Genesis 12 and following intend to tell us what happened in the past, which is my view, then there is an important sense in which Genesis 1–3 (and through 11) is historical as well.

How does all this evidence come together?

The bottom line is that Genesis 1–3 may be described as theological history. That is, it does intend to tell us about the past, and it is written to tell us about God and our relationship with him.[38] Indeed, all of Genesis may be so described, but since the figurative language, interplay with ancient Near Eastern mythology, and issues of sequencing are not as intense as in the first part of Genesis, there is, in my opinion, a higher degree of literary specificity in Genesis 12–50.

---

37. D. D. Lowery, *Toward a Poetics of Genesis 1–11: Reading Genesis 4:17–22 in Its Near Eastern Context* (Winona Lake, IN: Eisenbrauns, 2013), 8.

38. For a more detailed description, see T. Longman III, *Reading the Bible with Heart and Mind* (Colorado Springs, CO: NavPress, 1997), 97–112.

What are the historical claims of Genesis 1–2? They are that God was the Creator of the cosmos and humanity. He is responsible for the existence of everything and everybody that exists. However, the text is misunderstood if it is taken to tell us how God actually created the world and all its creatures.

What are the historical claims of Genesis 3? They are that God created human beings innocent, and that sin and death arose because of human rebellion. These conclusions remain true whether Adam and Eve are a specific couple (either the first human beings ever created or a representative couple within the original human population[39]) or whether Adam and Eve are not an actual couple but rather stand within the narrative as a representation of the original human population.

39. This is the view of N. T. Wright (*Surprised by Scripture* [San Francisco: Harper One, 2014], 37–38), who believes that Adam and Eve are a representative couple, chosen (like later Israel) "from the rest of the early hominids for a special, strange, demanding vocation."

CHAPTER 4

# Genesis 4:1–16

## LISTEN to the Story

4:1Adam made love to his wife Eve, and she became pregnant and gave
birth to Cain. She said, "With the help of the LORD I have brought forth
a man." 2Later she gave birth to his brother Abel.

Now Abel kept flocks, and Cain worked the soil. 3In the course of
time Cain brought some of the fruits of the soil as an offering to the
LORD. 4And Abel also brought an offering—fat portions from some of
the firstborn of his flock. The LORD looked with favor on Abel and his
offering, 5but on Cain and his offering he did not look with favor. So
Cain was very angry, and his face was downcast.

6Then the LORD said to Cain, "Why are you angry? Why is your face
downcast? 7If you do what is right, will you not be accepted? But if you
do not do what is right, sin is crouching at your door; it desires to have
you, but you must rule over it."

8Now Cain said to his brother Abel, "Let's go out to the field." While
they were in the field, Cain attacked his brother Abel and killed him.

9Then the LORD said to Cain, "Where is your brother Abel?"

"I don't know," he replied. "Am I my brother's keeper?"

10The LORD said, "What have you done? Listen! Your brother's blood
cries out to me from the ground. 11Now you are under a curse and driven
from the ground, which opened its mouth to receive your brother's blood
from your hand. 12When you work the ground, it will no longer yield its
crops for you. You will be a restless wanderer on the earth."

13Cain said to the LORD, "My punishment is more than I can bear.
14Today you are driving me from the land, and I will be hidden from your
presence; I will be a restless wanderer on the earth, and whoever finds me
will kill me."

15But the LORD said to him, "Not so; anyone who kills Cain will
suffer vengeance seven times over." Then the LORD put a mark on Cain so
that no one who found him would kill him. 16So Cain went out from the
LORD's presence and lived in the land of Nod, east of Eden.

*Listening to the Text in the Story:* Biblical Text: Genesis 3; Ancient Near Eastern Texts: Dumuzid and Enkimdu

The story of Cain and Abel falls fast on the heels of the account of the first human rebellion against God. That story told of Adam and Eve's sin, which was followed by a judgment speech in which God announced his punishment on the sinners. The end of the chapter narrates the execution of the punishment, but before that happens, God extends to them a token of grace in the form of clothing to cover their nakedness that for the first time caused them shame.

Interestingly, the story of Cain and Abel presents the very same structure. That is, after Cain sins by killing his brother (4:8), God announces his judgment against him (4:11–12), but before the judgment takes place (4:16), God extends grace to Cain as well (4:15). The details of his story will be given in the next section and the theological significance of the pattern may be found in the essay Token of Grace: God Stays Involved in Live the Story connected to 10:1–11:26.

Some scholars see the Sumerian story of Dumuzid and Enkimdu as the background to the Cain and Abel story. Like Cain, Enkimdu is a farmer, and, like Abel, Dumuzid is a shepherd.[1] Utu, the sun god, is trying to convince his sister to marry the shepherd, but she wants to marry the farmer. This disagreement leads to a debate over the respective benefits of both professions. The composition ends, however, with the shepherd and the farmer collaborating with each other. No substantial connection can be shown between the Sumerian and the biblical story, but it has misled some to think that our biblical story is really about a conflict between the two professions.

### The Birth of Cain and Abel (4:1–2a)

Though Adam and Eve forfeited eternal life, they continue to live for a period of time and give birth to the next generation. Her firstborn was Cain (*qayin*), whose name is formed from the verb translated as "brought forth" (or, as the NIV footnote explains, "acquired," *qaniti*). Eve recognizes that, though on a human level this birth was the result of her sexual intercourse with Adam ("Adam made love to [lit. knew] his wife Eve"), it was also the result of divine grace (lit. "with the LORD," but the NIV captures the sense by translating "with the help of the LORD"). Humphreys helpfully comments that the exposition of the name explains that "Yahweh shares in the activity that continues human life and our story."[2] Boda rightly goes even further to see here "the first

1. For the story, see J. Black, et al., *The Literature of Ancient Sumer* (Oxford: Oxford University Press, 2004), 86–88.

2. W. L. Humphreys, *The Character of God in the Book of Genesis: A Narrative Appraisal* (Louisville: Westminster John Knox, 2001), 53.

signs of the redemption promised in the warning to the serpent regarding the defeat of sin . . . the birth of the seed of the woman."[3] Adam and Eve's second son was named "Abel," (*hebel*) related to the Hebrew word "vapor, bubble" which is translated "meaningless" in the book of Ecclesiastes.[4]

## Cain's Sin: Fratricide (4:2b – 8)

When they grew up, the brothers had different occupations. Cain was a farmer and Abel a shepherd. While some believe these occupations are given in order to highlight the story as a struggle between farmers and shepherds[5] (and connect it to the Sumerian story of Dumuzid and Enkimdu, see above), the better explanation is that it informs the readers why each one brings the type of offering that they do.

Cain the farmer naturally brings some of his crops, while Abel brings an animal sacrifice. God is pleased with Abel's sacrifice, but rejects Cain's. Why?

The narrator does not describe God's motivation, but such reticence is typical of biblical narration.[6] Rather than an explicit statement, the narrator tells the story in such a way that the reader can enter into the story and understand the motivation.

The NIV nicely captures the nuance of the Hebrew when it describes Cain's sacrifice as "some of the fruits of the soil." Abel's sacrifice comes from "fat portions from some of the firstborn of his flock." In a word, Cain offered the ordinary and Abel the best, and of course the quality of their offering reflects the condition of their hearts. Abel is enthusiastic in his worship, while Cain is basically disinterested.[7]

Notice too how Cain responds to God's displeasure with his offering. Rather than wanting to do the right thing, he grows angry and sullen. Even so, God encourages him to change his attitude and his actions. He tells him to "do what is right," that is to worship him with a full heart that manifests itself in a proper offering. But he also warns Cain what will happen if he does not change. Sin will dominate him.

We have already commented on the parallel between God's words here and in his judgment speech against the woman in chapter 3 (v. 16). Here there is no question but that the desire that sin has for Cain is a desire to control him, and here God tells him to "rule over" (*mshl*, compare 3:16) sin.

---

3. Personal communication.

4. Longman, *Ecclesiastes*, 61 – 64.

5. E. Speiser, *Genesis*, AB 1 (Garden City, NY: Doubleday, 1964), 31.

6. A characteristic of Hebrew storytelling noted by Alter, *The Art of Biblical Narrative*, 114 – 30.

7. Contra N. MacDonald (*Genesis and Christian Theology* [Grand Rapids: Eerdmans, 2012], 260) who sees the lack of explicit evaluation of the relative merits of the sacrifices as probably indicating that this story is "a story of unexplained divine preference for the sacrifice of Abel."

After this divine warning, the narrator shows Cain's reaction by narrating his actions. Rather than repenting, he sinks deeper into sin by luring his brother out into the field and then killing him. He thus commits the first murder, an act made more heinous by the fact that the victim was his brother (fratricide).

### Divine Judgment Announced (4:9–12)

As in Genesis 3 (v. 9, God asks Adam "Where are you?"), God introduces his judgment speech with a question, "Where is your brother Abel?" Cain lies to God and also dismissively asks "Am I my brother's keeper?" In the same way that Adam did not guard (*shmr*) the garden so Cain does not keep (*shmr*) his brother.

God is not ignorant of Abel's murder. As Humphreys rightly points out, one effect of Yahweh's question is "to urge the one questioned, and the reader, to view what has happened from the perspective of Yahweh's interest or stake in it."[8] The helpless, who have no one else to aid them, can call out to God for help, and Abel, whose life was like a vapor, is the most helpless of all. The earth, which took in Abel's blood, will take his side and make Cain's efforts frustrating and difficult. Cain's punishment is basically an intensification of the punishment levied on Adam (work becomes even more frustrating) as well as that levied on both of them, their expulsion from Eden. They were expelled to the east from Eden and now Cain will be "a restless wanderer on the earth" (v. 12).

### Token of Grace and Execution of Judgment (4:13–16)

The end of the chapter narrates the execution of the judgment as God expels him to the land of Nod, a place name derived from the Hebrew verb "to wander." However, immediately preceding the judgment, God extends to Cain a token of grace.

Cain is fearful that he will be the prey of hostile people once God expels him further from Eden and from his presence. On the one hand, the principle of retribution would lead one to think that Cain would only get what he deserved. He ruthlessly murdered Abel, so he would be killed by others.

But God is merciful to Cain and protects him. He promises severe retribution ("seven times over") on any who would harm Cain and places a mark on him to warn those who encountered Cain not to kill him. The mark of Cain has been the source of long-standing speculation,[9] but the truth is that we do

8. Humphreys, *The Character of God in the Book of Genesis*, 58.

9. Waltke (*Genesis*, 99) for instance, believes it is "a protective tattoo, allowing him to live out his natural life span," though he provides no argument for this assertion.

not know the exact nature of the mark. Whatever the mark was, it protected Cain from the hostility of whoever finds him (v. 15).

The assumption of the story that there are a number of people beside Adam, Eve, and Cain has mystified many readers who want to take the story as a precise and literal historical narration. While some want to explain the presence of what appears to be a significant number of "others" in the text by appealing to the long lives of the characters in the narrative and the possibility of a passing of many generations by the time this story is set, it is more likely that this is another signal that we should not take the text as a precise literal historical account.

### Heartfelt Worship

In the broader ancient Near East, sacrifices were thought to provide food for the gods. In the Gilgamesh Epic, for example, the god Ea knows that Enlil is making a big mistake by attempting to destroy humanity by virtue of the flood because by doing so he is cutting the gods off from their food supply. Indeed, right after the flood waters receded and Utnapishtim, the Babylonian equivalent of Noah, steps out of the ark to offer a sacrifice, the gods "crowded around the sacrificer like flies"[10] because they were so hungry.

The biblical God does not need sacrifices for food. The psalmist in an oracle in which God tells the Israelites, "If I were hungry I would not tell you, for the world is mine, and all that is in it. Do I eat the flesh of bulls or drink the blood of goats?" (Ps 50:12–13).

So God was not disappointed in Cain because he failed to provide the proper legumes to go along with his main course provided by Abel, but rather because the quality of his sacrifice revealed the insincerity of his worship. The author of Hebrews contrasts the two sacrifices, "By faith Abel brought God a better offering than Cain did. By faith he was commended as righteous, when God spoke well of his offerings. And by faith Abel still speaks, even though he is dead" (Heb 11:4; see also 1 John 3:12; Jude 11).

The biblical witness is consistent in its condemnation of the mere outward exercise of religion. Sacrifice alone does not bring forgiveness, but only a repentant heart. Deuteronomy (10:16; 30:6) and Jeremiah (9:25) both blast those who are circumcised in their body, but not in their heart.

God does not dislike religious ritual, far from it. He commanded the sacrificial system and told Abraham that he and his offspring should be

10. *COS* 1:460.

circumcised, but the physical act itself does nothing unless it is an outward sign of an inward reality.

The point is that God wants us to love him "with all your heart and with all your soul and with all your mind" (Matt 22:37). Unlike Cain, we should not just go through the motions of worship.

Now this observation has nothing to do with worship style. God was not troubled that Cain brought vegetables rather than meat. If Cain had brought the firstfruits, the very best of his produce, then God would have accepted that offering. Worship can take many forms today. In some churches, worship is very orderly. Prayer is offered with folded hands and closed eyes. In other churches, prayers are offered with hands stretched toward heaven, songs are shouted, and people dance in the aisles. In either case, worship can be sincere or insincere. A person with folded hands and closed eyes may be deeply engaged in worshiping God, while another person dancing in the aisles, while looking engaged on the outside, might just enjoy dancing and shouting, getting an emotional high from the experience. That said, one can also have closed eyes and folded hands and be thinking about the next week's tasks, while the people dancing in the aisles have their heart full of thanks and praise of God.

## Unrighteous Anger

Cain's sacrifice was not accepted by God, and this rejection made Cain very angry. Cain's anger gives us a portrait of unrighteous anger.

Notice how easy it would have been for Cain to rectify the matter. God challenged Cain's emotional reaction and asked him a rhetorical question, "If you do what is right, will you not be accepted?" In other words, "try again Cain. Get your heart right and offer me a suitable and acceptable sacrifice that shows me that you love me for all I have done for you." Besides showing Cain the right road to having a good relationship with him, he also warned Cain of the danger of continuing to be insincere in his relationship with him. Sin is waiting to take control of him, but Cain needs to take control of his life and keep sin out.

How does Cain react? He lures his brother out into the field where they are alone and he kills him.

But what did Abel do to him? Abel simply offered his heartfelt sacrifice to God; he did not attack Cain or try to show him up. Why did Cain kill Abel?

Cain kills Abel because he can't kill God, so he kills the one that pleased God. Unrighteous anger results from an interference with satisfaction, a hatred of vulnerability, and a love of control.[11] Unrighteous anger seeks to

11. Dan B. Allender and T. Longman III, *Cry of the Soul* (Colorado Springs, CO: NavPress, 1994), 55–62.

gain independence from God and others. Cain resists the controls that he perceives God trying to put on him. Unrighteous anger delivers us from trusting God who does not comply with what we want.

### "Am I My Brother's Keeper?"

Cain shed the blood of his brother because he was envious of him and hated God who showed him preference. When confronted by God and asked where Abel was, Cain responded, "Am I my brother's keeper?" a phrase that people use even today to coldly distance themselves from responsibility for others, even someone as close as a brother.

What a contrast with Jesus. While Cain shed the blood of his brother, Jesus shed his blood for those who "were still sinners" and "God's enemies" (Rom 5:8, 10, see vv. 6–11).

CHAPTER 5

# Genesis 4:17–5:32

## LISTEN to the Story

[4:17]Cain made love to his wife, and she became pregnant and gave birth to Enoch. Cain was then building a city, and he named it after his son Enoch. [18]To Enoch was born Irad, and Irad was the father of Mehujael, and Mehujael was the father of Methushael, and Methushael was the father of Lamech.

[19]Lamech married two women, one named Adah and the other Zillah. [20]Adah gave birth to Jabal; he was the father of those who live in tents and raise livestock. [21]His brother's name was Jubal; he was the father of all who play stringed instruments and pipes. [22]Zillah also had a son, Tubal-Cain, who forged all kinds of tools out of bronze and iron. Tubal-Cain's sister was Naamah.

[23]Lamech said to his wives,

"Adah and Zillah, listen to me;<br>
wives of Lamech, hear my words.<br>
I have killed a man for wounding me,<br>
a young man for injuring me.<br>
[24] If Cain is avenged seven times,<br>
then Lamech seventy-seven times."

[25]Adam made love to his wife again, and she gave birth to a son and named him Seth, saying, "God has granted me another child in place of Abel, since Cain killed him." [26]Seth also had a son, and he named him Enosh.

At that time people began to call on the name of the Lord.

[5:1]This is the written account of Adam's family line.

When God created mankind, he made them in the likeness of God. [2]He created them male and female and blessed them. And he named them "Mankind" when they were created.

[3]When Adam had lived 130 years, he had a son in his own likeness, in his own image; and he named him Seth. [4]After Seth was born, Adam lived 800 years and had other sons and daughters. [5]Altogether, Adam lived a total of 930 years, and then he died.

6 When Seth had lived 105 years, he became the father of Enosh.
7 After he became the father of Enosh, Seth lived 807 years and had other
sons and daughters. 8 Altogether, Seth lived a total of 912 years, and then
he died.

9 When Enosh had lived 90 years, he became the father of Kenan.
10 After he became the father of Kenan, Enosh lived 815 years and had
other sons and daughters. 11 Altogether, Enosh lived a total of 905 years,
and then he died.

12 When Kenan had lived 70 years, he became the father of Mahalalel.
13 After he became the father of Mahalalel, Kenan lived 840 years and had
other sons and daughters. 14 Altogether, Kenan lived a total of 910 years,
and then he died.

15 When Mahalalel had lived 65 years, he became the father of Jared.
16 After he became the father of Jared, Mahalalel lived 830 years and had
other sons and daughters. 17 Altogether, Mahalalel lived a total of 895
years, and then he died.

18 When Jared had lived 162 years, he became the father of Enoch.
19 After he became the father of Enoch, Jared lived 800 years and had
other sons and daughters. 20 Altogether, Jared lived a total of 962 years,
and then he died.

21 When Enoch had lived 65 years, he became the father of
Methuselah. 22 After he became the father of Methuselah, Enoch walked
faithfully with God 300 years and had other sons and daughters.
23 Altogether, Enoch lived a total of 365 years. 24 Enoch walked faithfully
with God; then he was no more, because God took him away.

25 When Methuselah had lived 187 years, he became the father of
Lamech. 26 After he became the father of Lamech, Methuselah lived 782
years and had other sons and daughters. 27 Altogether, Methuselah lived a
total of 969 years, and then he died.

28 When Lamech had lived 182 years, he had a son. 29 He named
him Noah and said, "He will comfort us in the labor and painful toil
of our hands caused by the ground the LORD has cursed." 30 After Noah
was born, Lamech lived 595 years and had other sons and daughters.
31 Altogether, Lamech lived a total of 777 years, and then he died.

32 After Noah was 500 years old, he became the father of Shem, Ham
and Japheth.

*Listening to the Text in the Story:* Biblical Text: Genesis 3:15; Ancient Near Eastern Texts: Ancient Near Eastern Genealogies; The Sumerian King List

Genesis 4:17–5:32 present the first two of a number of genealogies in the book of Genesis (see also Gen 10; 11:10–26; 26:12–18; 36, among others). Not all these genealogies are of the same type or purpose, but no matter what precise type of genealogy we encounter in Genesis, we must remember that these are ancient Near Eastern, not modern Western, genealogies.

The two main types of genealogies that we find in the Bible are linear and segmented. The former, as illustrated in the present passage, goes from father to one son, while the latter will name a number of sons of one father (see Gen 10). Ancient genealogies are fluid; that is they can change in order to reflect contemporary social and political realities. They can also skip generations, rendering them useless for trying to compute how much actual time is covered by the genealogy.[1] According to Wilson, "genealogies are not normally created for historical purposes. They are not intended to be historical records. Rather in the Bible, as well as in the ancient Near Eastern literature and in the anthropological material, genealogies seem to have been created for domestic, political-jural, and religious purposes, and historical information is preserved in the genealogies only incidentally."[2]

Special mention should be made of the Sumerian King List (SKL) since at least in broad strokes it seems to share the scope and function of Genesis 4:17–11:26. In terms of scope, both texts list prediluvians (in the case of the SKL they are kings), followed by an account of the flood (much more developed in the biblical text than in the SKL), and then a list of postdiluvians. The purpose of the SKL is to rehearse the emergence of kingship as a gift from heaven to the city of Eridu (see below for possible connection with the first city in the biblical account) and then follows the succession of kings down to the last king of Isin (ca. 1816–1794 BC; at least in the latest copy of the SKL that we have). Another striking similarity between the biblical text and the SKL has to do with the length of lives/reigns of those listed, which are spectacularly long, particularly for the prediluvians. While the biblical characters live long (Methuselah being the oldest at 969 years), they pale in the light of the length of the reigns of the prediluvian kings (the longest ruling being Alagar of Eridu at 36,000 years). Life spans/reigns are considerably shorter after the flood. Sparks points out that "the lengths of reigns are absurdly long and seem to have been derived using astronomical figures (for the antediluvian

1. As R. Numbers ("The Most Important Biblical Discovery of Our Time: William Henry Green and the Demise of Ussher's Chronology," *Church History* [2000]: 257–76), points out, it was the mid-nineteenth century Princeton Theological Seminary Old Testament scholar and president W. H. Green who pointed out that genealogies are not consecutive by comparing synoptic genealogies.

2. R. R. Wilson, *Genealogy and History in the Biblical World* (New Haven, CT: Yale University Press, 1977), 199.

chronology) and operations from the sexagesimal mathematics (for the postdiluvian chronology)."[3] Our awareness of the similarity between the SKL and Genesis 5 makes us open to the possibility that we should not press the ages of the prediluvians too literally. The theological significance of their age will be presented below.

Our present passage presents two genealogies, one of Cain and one of Shem, yet another son of Adam and Eve. These genealogies have more than a simple antiquarian function. First, they show that humanity is divided into two camps, one that rejects God and one that follows him.

This division in humanity evokes God's punishment on the serpent in Genesis 3:15: "And I will put enmity between you and the woman, and between your offspring and hers." While in a literal sense both genealogies descend from Eve, who is the "woman" in the context, spiritually, the line of Cain are descendants of the serpent and the line of Seth represents the other line with whom they are in enmity.

Second, these genealogies, particularly Cain's, associate certain developments in civilization with his line of descent, thus suggesting a certain darkness to them.

## EXPLAIN the Story

### The Cainite Genealogy (4:17–26)

We first follow Cain's genealogy, introduced by the same formula as announced his own birth into the world, "Cain made love to [lit. "knew"] his wife, and she became pregnant and gave birth to Enoch" (v. 17). Significantly, this birth notice gives no recognition of God's connection to the gift of a child in contrast to Eve at the time of the birth of Cain (4:1) and later at the birth of Seth (4:25).[4] Interestingly, the genealogy names Cain as the first city builder. He built a city and named it after his son Enoch. This association between Cain and city building elicits several observations.

The first is the most important. By associating Cain with the first city, the narrator makes a comment on cities. Cain's punishment was that he would be a wanderer, but here he is taking steps to create for himself and others a permanent habitation. This act may be seen as an act of resistance against God's punishment and thus sinful. In addition, by identifying Cain as the first city builder, the passage makes a comment on the nature of cities. They are potentially dangerous. If individual sinners are a problem, what happens

3. Sparks, *Ancient Texts*, 346.

4. Thanks to Mark Boda for this insight (personal communication).

when sinners congregate together? The answer is obvious. The sin problem is intensified, not solved. For more, see the Live the Story section below.

Second, that Cain builds a city (see above) raises the question of where all the people have come from. On a literal reading of Genesis 1–4, Cain is the second generation of humanity. Now granting cities are not as big as they are today, we still must be talking about a sizeable population. This detail again raises questions about a literal reading of these chapters that take them as precise history. Other ancient sources as well as archaeology would situate the founding of the first cities long after the emergence of humanity, not in the second generation.[5]

Speaking of ancient sources, we, third, observe that in ancient Sumerian literature (see above on the Sumerian King List), the first city is named Eridu. Some scholars make the interesting observation that the name of this city is similar to the name of Cain's grandson, Irad, not his son Enoch. They speculate (since there is not textual evidence for it) that the Hebrew text that we presently have has a minor corruption and that the original text, in their opinion, would have Enoch as the first city builder who named it after his son Irad.[6] There is much to commend this idea, though we cannot be certain.

Verse 18 quickly moves through three generations (after Enoch comes Irad, then Mehujael, followed by Methshael) to come to Lamech. The narrator shows significant interest in Lamech and his immediate descendants.

Lamech is the first polygamous man, or at least he is the first one so described, in Scripture. Though polygamy is later allowed and regulated by the law of Moses (Exod 21:7–11), we should not forget that marriage as instituted by God was monogamous, the two will "become one flesh" (Gen 2:24). That polygamy emerges in the Cainite line is an implicit critique of the practice, and Lamech's despicable character accentuates its dubious character.

Lamech's character comes out in the speech that he gives to his wives, Adah and Zillah (vv. 23–24). In the first place, he is a man of unjust vengeance. An argument could be made for retributive and equal justice as later stated by the *lex talonis*, "life for life, eye for eye, tooth for tooth, hand for hand, foot for foot, burn for burn, wound for wound, bruise for bruise" (Exod 21:24–25). But Lamech boasts that he will execute disproportionate justice, "life for wound, life for bruise." God had earlier announced that Cain would be avenged sevenfold, but Lamech presumptuously announces that he would

5. A classic study on the development of cities has been recently reissued. R. Adams, *The Evolution of Urban Society* (Piscataway, NJ: Aldine Transaction, 2005).

6. Wilson, *Genealogy and History*, 139–41, and P. D. Miller, "Eridu, Dunnu, and Babel: A Study in Comparative Mythology," *HAR* 9 (1985): 239–40.

be avenged seventyfold. From the perspective of the narrator, people are not getting better as time progresses; they are worsening.

We also hear about his children through Adah and Zillah, and they are associated with certain cultural developments that by association with the evil line are thus revealed as dangerous. They include nomadic herding (Jabal), instrumental music (Jubal), and metal working (Tubal-Cain). In addition to these three men, we are told of a daughter whose name is Naamah. For more on the connection of the Cainite line and civilization, see The Double-Edged Nature of Civilization below.

### The Sethite Genealogy (5:1–32)

For the third time (see 4:1, 17), a birth is announced with the formula that, in this case, Adam "made love to (lit. knew) his wife, and she gave birth to a son" (4:25). The name of this son was Seth (*shet*), and he is introduced as a replacement for Abel, thus a follower of God, unlike his murderous brother Cain. The name Seth reveals his role as a replacement, "God has granted (*shat*) me another child in place of Abel" (4:25).

The genealogy provides no narrative for Seth but quickly passes over to his son Enosh. Here the narrator adds that this was the time that people "began to call on the name of the LORD" (4:26). The exact significance of this phrase is difficult to delineate. The most obvious understanding is that people began to pray to God and offer him worship. But does that mean that neither Adam nor Seth worshiped God? That seems unlikely. A further complication is the phrase "name of the LORD," where LORD translates God's personal name, Yahweh. The difficulty is that the most natural reading of the burning bush incident (Exod 3) is that God revealed his name for the first time to Moses.[7] Even if that natural reading is the correct one, however, we can understand the appearance of LORD here as a retrojection of the name from the later period of time in which the book of Genesis was written.

Though 4:23–26 marks the transition from the line of Cain to the line of Seth, Genesis 5:1 begins a whole new section in the book with an introductory *toledot* formula. We here have the *toledot* of Adam which means as the NIV translation implies, a section that focuses on Adam's "family line."

Verses 1b–2 take us back to Genesis 1, the original description of the creation of humanity. We again hear that they are created in the "likeness" of God (see 1:26), male and female (see 1:27), and in a blessed condition (see 1:28). It also tells us that God named them Adam ("mankind") at their conception.

---

7. T. Longman III, *How to Read Exodus* (Downers Grove, IL: InterVarsity Press, 2009) 101–4.

Verses 3–5 are the first of ten paragraphs that all provide the same information along the lines of the following formula (according to the NIV translation): "When PN (personal name) had lived x years, he became the father (or ancestor) of PN. After he became the father of PN, PN lived x years and had other sons and daughters. Altogether PN1 lived x years, and then he died." The following chapter repeats the formula again placing PN2 in the place of PN1 and then introducing PN3 as the son of PN2.

There are some variations that we will point out in the use of this formula as well as some additional narrative information occasionally given which we will describe, but first we should comment on the question of the relationship between the paragraphs. We have here, in the terminology of R. R. Wilson,[8] a linear genealogy that goes from father to son rather than a segmented genealogy that lists multiple children in a single generation,[9] but the question is whether or not this genealogy intends to skip generations. Since the genealogy extends from Adam to Noah, another way of stating this question is whether or not the narrator believes that the time between the creation and humanity spanned a mere period of ten generations.

Further, the life spans of these pre-flood people are incredibly long. The shortest life span (excluding Enoch, for whom see below) was 777 years (Lamech) and the longest was 969 years (Methuselah). These long life spans, as we observed above, are reminiscent of the life spans of the pre-flood kings and wise men listed in the SKL, though the SKL speaks of the length of reigns not life spans and the numbers dwarf those found in Genesis 5.

A third characteristic of the genealogy in Genesis 5 is that it surprisingly shares names with individuals found in the Cainite genealogy of Genesis 4, specifically Enoch and Lamech (Methushael and Methuselah as well as Cain and Kenan are close). Waltke is likely correct when he suggests that the names of these two genealogies are similar "not to represent variations of the same source, but to parallel and contrast the two offspring of Adam."[10]

How are we to understand these features of the genealogy? Should we take them literally or figuratively? And how do they contribute to the theological message of Genesis 3–11?

The second (literal or figurative?) question is difficult to answer. In our treatment of Genesis 1–3, we have stated reasons for our understanding that the first eleven chapters do present history in broad scope with a heavy use of figurative language and interaction with ancient Near Eastern materials

8. Wilson, *Genealogy and History*.

9. For an excellent and recent analysis of ancient Near Eastern, including Israelite genealogy, see Lowery, *A Poetics of Genesis 1–11*, 77–87.

10. Waltke, *Genesis*, 100.

(see above on the Sumerian King List). Thus, a consideration of the broader literary context provides a reason for not insisting on the long life spans being literally true, but it is also true that, if the numbers are symbolic, we have not "cracked the code." It is interesting that Enoch lived 365 years, the number of days the earth takes to circle the sun (or in the ancient conception, the length of a solar year), however it is not clear that such a connection was intended. It is also interesting that there are exactly ten generations between Adam and Noah and then ten more between Noah and Abraham, suggesting literary artifice rather than historical precision. Even so, no one has yet put forward a persuasive explanation of the symbolic significance of the numbers in the genealogy. Though we cannot be dogmatic about the nature of the numbers we can come to a clear understanding of their theological import (see below).

Now that we have considered the meaning and function of the genealogy as a whole, we may now attend to some of the unique features of the otherwise repetitive formula that describes these ten generations from creation to the flood.

In the first paragraph of the genealogy proper (vv. 3–5), speaking of the birth of Adam's son Seth (already introduced in 4:25), the text does not simply say "Adam became the father of Seth," but rather "he (Adam) had a son in his own likeness, in his own image; and he named him Seth." Here the language of "likeness" and "image" calls for comment since Adam (and Eve) were said to be created in the "likeness" and "image" of God (1:26–27). Is this the language of demotion? That is, Adam was created in the image and likeness of God, but Seth was created in the image and likeness of his father. This conclusion is unlikely considering that later Scripture speaks of all humans as created in the image of God (2 Cor 3:18; Jas 3:9). Perhaps this statement affirms this idea in that Adam was created in the image and likeness of God, so Seth being created in the image and likeness of Adam means that he too is created in the image and likeness of God.

That said, we might not want to limit our understanding of Seth's creation in the image and likeness of his father only to the continuation of the creation of humanity in God's image and likeness. We earlier argued that the language of image and likeness applied to Adam meant that Adam represented God and thus reflected who God is. In the same way a son represents his father and reminds people of the father. As is well known, this may even be seen physically, in that children often reflect the physical features and characteristics of their parents.

The next five generations (Seth is the father of Enosh who is the father of Kenan who is the father of Mehalalel who is the father of Jared who is the father of Enoch) stick to the regular formula described above. The paragraph concerning Enoch, however, adds information about him that is as intriguing as it is enigmatic.

The narrator goes out of his way in order to highlight Enoch's devotion to God (twice [vv. 22 and 24] he says, "Enoch walked faithfully with God"[11] and then adds at the end "then he was no more, because God took him away" [v. 24]). God took him in mid-life (in this genealogy being 365 years old would be middle-age), and since there is no death formula for Enoch as for the others ("and he died"), God's taking him away meant that he avoided the common experience of death.

But where did God take him? The text does not say. However, since God's action toward Enoch is in response to his faithfulness, we might safely imagine that God brought him to himself. Indeed, the only other biblical character who had a similar experience was the prophet Elijah, who, rather than experiencing death, was taken by God "up to heaven" (2 Kgs 2:1).[12]

Before he was brought up to heaven, Enoch had had a son named Methuselah, who lived the longest of any other person (969 years) mentioned in the Bible (and thus is enshrined in the statement that marks someone as ancient, that is "as old as Methuselah"). Methuselah himself had a son named Lamech, and Lamech's child is the famous Noah. Indeed, this genealogy is the link between the story of Adam and his immediate children and the flood story that will occupy the following three chapters, thus there is additional information in the Lamech paragraph. Specifically, attention is drawn to the meaning of his name. Noah is related by sound to the Hebrew word for comfort (*naham*) and a fuller explanation is provided, "He will comfort us in the labor and painful toil of our hands caused by the ground the Lord has cursed." The reference, of course, is to the punishment of Adam (3:17–19) that was intensified in God's punishment of Cain (4:12).

The genealogy concludes with a partial genealogical notice of Noah that only speaks of the birth of his three sons: Shem, Ham, and Japheth (thus shifting from a linear to a segmented genealogy), when he was 500 years old. At this point, the narrative shifts to the story of the flood.

---

11. J. L. Kugel, *The Bible as It Was* (Cambridge, MA: Harvard University Press, 1997), 101, points out that this is twice as many times as the expression is used to describe Noah who is said to be righteous (6:9).

12. The comments concerning Enoch are short but suggestive in the Bible, thus he became an object of fascination among early Jewish interpreters (see Kugel, *The Bible as It Was*, 100–107).

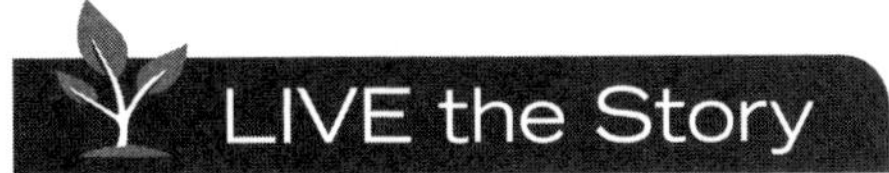


### The Double-Edged Nature of Civilization

To be civilized seems an unquestionably good thing. The opposite of civilized is barbaric, after all. But what is the Cainite genealogy saying by associating the development of civilization to those descended from Cain? In particular, the origins of cities, nomadic herding, music, and metal (bronze and iron) working are connected to the descendants of Cain.

The association between these elements of civilization and Cain's line is a reminder that there is a dark side to civilization. It is not saying that cities, nomadic herding, music, and metal working are an irredeemable evil, but that they can be dangerous to humanity by increasing human strife, oppression, and suffering.

Cities bring large numbers of people together into close proximity. Genesis understands that humans are sinners, at core self-seeking; thus a large mass of humanity can lead to exploitation and violence of all kinds. We can see this in today's cities. At the time of the writing of this commentary, mass murders have taken place at the Naval Yard in Washington, DC, and in a park in Chicago. Globally, a terrorist attack has left scores in an upscale shopping mall in Nairobi and a separate attack has taken place in a church in a major city in Pakistan. In the Bible, we will see that God worries about the evil that a city can precipitate (Gen 11:1–9), and it is not without reasons that cities (Babylon in the Old Testament and Rome in the New Testament) are symbols of the most egregious wickedness. That the Cainite genealogy names Cain (or perhaps Enoch, see above) as the first city builder makes sense.

However, the Bible's teaching about cities should not encourage the faithful to flee cities for the countryside, or even the suburbs. Thanks to God cities can have a redemptive value as well. To counter the negative symbolic value of cities like Babylon and Rome, the Bible presents Jerusalem, the city of God, the place where God chooses to make his presence known most directly during much of the Old Testament time period.

> Great is the Lord, and most worthy of praise,
> in the city of our God, his holy mountain.
> Beautiful in its loftiness,
> the joy of the whole earth,
> like the heights of Zaphon is Mount Zion,
> the city of the Great King.
> God is in her citadels;
> he has shown himself to be her fortress. (Ps 48:1–3)

The book of Revelation depicts heaven itself as a wonderful city, the New Jerusalem (Rev 21–22).

We live in a time between the first and second coming of Christ. Thanks to God's grace, no city is pure evil, but thanks to human sin, no city is an exemplar of holiness and God's presence. In a recent article, Mark Gornik and Maria Liu describe New York City in a way that illustrates this point. While New York is much better in terms of crime than it was a decade or two ago, no one would deny that it still experiences many problems. That said, God has made his presence known in dramatic ways in that city. Gornik and Liu describe a march of members of Latino and black churches through Manhattan, a kind of "rolling prayer meeting," wearing shirts that announced "God Belongs in My City." They are on a mission to spread the presence of God through New York, and they demonstrate that God is not absent even from our largest and most troubled cities.[13]

Not only cities, but music and metalworking have two sides, a dark one and a redemptive side. Music can soothe and lift the human mind and heart toward God. We only have to think of the Psalms as a book of music that praises and petitions God. Music can also fuel violence as a scene from the classic movie *Apocalypse Now* illustrates as the leader of a helicopter attack squadron (played by Robert Duvall) plays the "Ride of the Valkeries" as it strafes innocent civilians from the air during the Vietnam War. It is too simplistic to say that Wagner (or hard rock or rap) is evil and that Bach (and Christian music) is good. But it is important, and the association of music with the Cainite genealogy helps us, to remember that music can lead us toward God and holiness or away from him and toward evil.

Finally (since nomadic herding does not describe the lifestyle of the vast majority of the readers of this commentary), I will comment on the third area associated with the Cainite genealogy— metal working. As we have already observed in regard to cities and music, the connection is not saying that metalworking is an unmitigated evil. Metalworking of a primitive sort is attested among humans starting about 10,000 years ago. Bronze working started about three thousand years later, sporadically, though its heyday was between 3400–1200 BC, a period commonly called the Bronze Age in the ancient Near East. Iron work started even later, during the period we refer to as the Iron Age (post-1200 BC). These dates indicate that it seems fruitless to defend the idea that Cain's immediate descendants actually were engaged in this type of metalworking. By associating this godless line with metalworking, the passage is again reminding its readers that there is real danger associated

13. M. R. Gornick and M. L. Wong, "Christ in the Capital of the World," *Christianity Today* 57 no. 7 (August 2013):13.

with metalworking. As we read through the rest of the Old Testament, we note that metalworking is commonly associated with weapons, weapons that are used to kill and maim.

Should we ban all metal making then? Of course not. Our ability to work with metal has all kinds of beneficial uses, too numerous and well-known even to list. The point is that all technologies can be used for good (nuclear energy to bring light and warmth to houses; the internet to expand knowledge) or for evil (nuclear weapons; internet pornography).

The Cainite genealogy is a reminder that, while much good can come from cities, nomadic herding, music, and metalworking, they also can be used for great evil and harm. The creators, shapers, and participants in civilization need to be mindful that these things are not unqualified goods, but must be redeemed by God in order to be beneficial.

### The Rewards of Righteousness

Today it is only too common to find pastors who preach that godliness will lead to success. Have enough faith and God will heal you and make you wealthy besides. This "prosperity gospel" is deeply problematic, asserting an automatic and mechanical connection between godliness and reward on the one hand and wickedness and punishment on the other.

However, in our appropriate zeal to point out the problems with the prosperity gospel, we should not miss the clear teaching that godliness typically leads to good results. Now these results are not automatic or guaranteed as an immediate consequence of our actions by any stretch of the imagination, but they are guaranteed in the "long run" according to the clear teaching of the New Testament that our relationship with Christ means that he has prepared a room for us in his father's heavenly mansion (John 14:1–4).

But it is not at all untypical that good results arise from our relationship with God and our obedience in the here and now. Such is taught by the very structure of the covenant which connects blessings with obedience to the law and punishments with disobedience (see Deut 27 and 28) or consider the book of Proverbs with the rewards granted to the wise and the bad consequences connected to foolish behavior.[14]

How does the Sethite genealogy teach this connection between godliness and reward? In a number of ways. First of all, those who are godly have long lives. Whether these numbers are literal or symbolic (see above), the long lives of those in the godly line who live before the flood are to be read as a consequence of their "calling on the name of the LORD." After all, God connects the

14. Longman, *Proverbs*, 61–63, 82–86

radical shortening of life spans to human sin (6:3), thus the earlier, longer life spans are a consequence of righteous living. Second, we see this connection in a special way with Enoch. Enoch is highlighted as someone who "walked faithfully with God" (5:22–23) and as a result God "took him away." In other words, he goes into God's presence without experiencing the pain of death.

### The Effects of Sin on Longevity

While there are questions about whether or not we should understand the long ages of the prediluvians as intended to be taken as literal, there is no question about the theological significance of the contrast between the long lives before the flood and the shorter life spans after the flood. With only two exceptions the prediluvians lived into their tenth century.

Adam lived to an age of 930 years
Seth lived to an age of 912 years
Enosh lived to an age of 905 years
Kenan lived to an age of 910 years
Mahalalel lived to an age of 895 years
Jared lived to an age of 962 years
Enoch lived to an age of 365 years before God took him away
Methesaleh lived to an age of 969 years
Lamech lived to an age of 777 years
Noah was 500 years old when the Flood came and died at 950 years

After the Flood, we hear of significantly lower life spans:

Shem died at the age of 600
Arphaxad died at the age of 438
Shelah died at the age of 433
Eber died at the age of 464
Peleg died at the age of 239
Reu died at the age of 239
Serug died at the age of 230
Nahor died at the age of 148
Terah died at the age of 205
Abraham died at the age of 175
Isaac died at the age of 180
Jacob died at the age of 130

As time wears on, life spans grow shorter due to the growing effects of sin. That sin is the cause is affirmed by God's announcement before the flood, "My Spirit will not contend with humans forever, for they are mortal; their days will a hundred and twenty years" (6:3). God makes this statement in the light of the egregious sin of the pre-flood generation.

Of course, as we look at the above list of post-flood persons, they all live more than 120 years, so perhaps we are again dealing with symbolic not literal numbers. This may be most easily seen with the number 120 which may be playing with the symbolic number for a generation which is forty. That 120 is divisible by 40 three times may indicate that God is saying that humans will live long enough to see their grandchildren or great-grandchildren but no more.

Whatever the explanation,[15] again, sin seems the rationale for shorter lives. It is important to see that it is not the sin of the individuals, but of humanity in general. Certainly Abraham does not live a shorter time than his predecessors because he personally was a greater sinner than they were, but again the effects of sin are shortening life.

Today life spans are even shorter than Abraham's even though recent medical advances in certain parts of the world have made it not untypical for a person to live to be 90 or even 100. But even living to a hundred is a brief period of time. According to the prophet Isaiah:

> All people are like grass,
> and all their faithfulness is like the flowers of the field.
> The grass withers and the flowers fall,
> because the breath of the Lord blows on them.
> Surely the people are grass.
> The grass withers and the flowers fall ... (Isa 40:6–8)

One hundred years is nothing for people who were created to live forever but forfeited life through rebellion (Gen 3).

That said, the good news of the gospel is that Jesus, God's Son, has come and died in our place. But death did not keep him in its grasp (Acts 2:22–24; Phil 2:6–8). In this way, he has defeated death (1 Cor 15:12–58).

## The Son of Adam, The Son of God (Luke 3:38)

We encounter the Sethite genealogy again in Luke's genealogy of Jesus. Luke is intent to show that he is not only a descendant of David (so Matthew's genealogy), but that he is a part of all humanity (by virtue of his descent from Adam). As Luke looks back from Jesus, the ten generations (Noah, Lamech,

---

15. Niehaus (*Biblical Theology*, 175) suggests that it is "no argument against this understanding that most humans do not attain that age or that some humans live longer. God is laying down a general standard here, and humans all over the globe live and die under its aegis and will until the Lord returns."

Methuselah, Enoch, Jared, Mahalalel, Kenan, Enosh, Seth, and Adam) are named at the end. From the vantage point of Luke 3, we can see that we are on the way to Jesus, who descends from the godly line of Seth, not the ungodly line of Cain.

Interestingly, Jesus' genealogy does not simply end with Adam. Luke has more than genetic descent in mind here. Theologically, it is important that this census does not end with a statement about Christ's humanity alone. Accordingly, Luke follows "son of Adam" with "son of God." Jesus is fully human, but he is also fully divine. As Nolland insightfully comments, "Luke would have us see that Jesus takes his place in the human family and thus in its (since Adam's disobedience) flawed sonship; however, in his own person, in virtue of his unique origin (Luke 1:35) but also as worked out in his active obedience (4:1–13), he marks a new beginning to sonship and sets it on an entirely new footing. In this human situation Jesus is the one who is really the Son of God."[16]

(See also the related essay, The Nature of Marriage and the Gift of Sex after Genesis 2:2b–25.)

16. J. Nolland, *Luke 1–9:20*, WBC 35a (Dallas: Word Publishing, 1989), 173.

CHAPTER 6

# Genesis 6:1 – 9:17

## LISTEN to the Story

[6:1]When human beings began to increase in number on the earth and daughters were born to them, [2]the sons of God saw that the daughters of humans were beautiful, and they married any of them they chose. [3]Then the LORD said, "My Spirit will not contend with humans forever, for they are mortal; their days will be a hundred and twenty years."

[4]The Nephilim were on the earth in those days—and also afterward—when the sons of God went to the daughters of humans and had children by them. They were the heroes of old, men of renown.

[5]The LORD saw how great the wickedness of the human race had become on the earth, and that every inclination of the thoughts of the human heart was only evil all the time. [6]The LORD regretted that he had made human beings on the earth, and his heart was deeply troubled. [7]So the LORD said, "I will wipe from the face of the earth the human race I have created—and with them the animals, the birds and the creatures that move along the ground—for I regret that I have made them." [8]But Noah found favor in the eyes of the LORD.

[9]This is the account of Noah and his family.

Noah was a righteous man, blameless among the people of his time, and he walked faithfully with God. [10]Noah had three sons: Shem, Ham and Japheth.

[11]Now the earth was corrupt in God's sight and was full of violence. [12]God saw how corrupt the earth had become, for all the people on earth had corrupted their ways. [13]So God said to Noah, "I am going to put an end to all people, for the earth is filled with violence because of them. I am surely going to destroy both them and the earth. [14]So make yourself an ark of cypress wood; make rooms in it and coat it with pitch inside and out. [15]This is how you are to build it: The ark is to be three hundred cubits long, fifty cubits wide and thirty cubits high. [16]Make a roof for it, leaving below the roof an opening one cubit high all around. Put a door in the side of the ark and make lower, middle and upper decks. [17]I am going to bring floodwaters on the earth to destroy all life under the

heavens, every creature that has the breath of life in it. Everything on
earth will perish. [18]But I will establish my covenant with you, and you
will enter the ark—you and your sons and your wife and your sons' wives
with you. [19]You are to bring into the ark two of all living creatures, male
and female, to keep them alive with you. [20]Two of every kind of bird, of
every kind of animal and of every kind of creature that moves along the
ground will come to you to be kept alive. [21]You are to take every kind of
food that is to be eaten and store it away as food for you and for them."

[22]Noah did everything just as God commanded him.

[7:1]The LORD then said to Noah, "Go into the ark, you and your whole
family, because I have found you righteous in this generation. [2]Take with
you seven pairs of every kind of clean animal, a male and its mate, and
one pair of every kind of unclean animal, a male and its mate, [3]and also
seven pairs of every kind of bird, male and female, to keep their various
kinds alive throughout the earth. [4]Seven days from now I will send rain
on the earth for forty days and forty nights, and I will wipe from the face
of the earth every living creature I have made."

[5]And Noah did all that the LORD commanded him.

[6]Noah was six hundred years old when the floodwaters came on the
earth. [7]And Noah and his sons and his wife and his sons' wives entered
the ark to escape the waters of the flood. [8]Pairs of clean and unclean
animals, of birds and of all creatures that move along the ground, [9]male
and female, came to Noah and entered the ark, as God had commanded
Noah. [10]And after the seven days the floodwaters came on the earth.

[11]In the six hundredth year of Noah's life, on the seventeenth day of
the second month—on that day all the springs of the great deep burst
forth, and the floodgates of the heavens were opened. [12]And rain fell on
the earth forty days and forty nights.

[13]On that very day Noah and his sons, Shem, Ham and Japheth,
together with his wife and the wives of his three sons, entered the
ark. [14]They had with them every wild animal according to its kind,
all livestock according to their kinds, every creature that moves along
the ground according to its kind and every bird according to its kind,
everything with wings. [15]Pairs of all creatures that have the breath of life
in them came to Noah and entered the ark. [16]The animals going in were
male and female of every living thing, as God had commanded Noah.
Then the LORD shut him in.

[17]For forty days the flood kept coming on the earth, and as the waters
increased they lifted the ark high above the earth. [18]The waters rose
and increased greatly on the earth, and the ark floated on the surface of

the water. 19They rose greatly on the earth, and all the high mountains
under the entire heavens were covered. 20The waters rose and covered the
mountains to a depth of more than fifteen cubits. 21Every living thing that
moved on land perished — birds, livestock, wild animals, all the creatures
that swarm over the earth, and all mankind. 22Everything on dry land
that had the breath of life in its nostrils died. 23Every living thing on the
face of the earth was wiped out; people and animals and the creatures that
move along the ground and the birds were wiped from the earth. Only
Noah was left, and those with him in the ark.

24The waters flooded the earth for a hundred and fifty days.

8:1But God remembered Noah and all the wild animals and the
livestock that were with him in the ark, and he sent a wind over the earth,
and the waters receded. 2Now the springs of the deep and the floodgates
of the heavens had been closed, and the rain had stopped falling from the
sky. 3The water receded steadily from the earth. At the end of the hundred
and fifty days the water had gone down, 4and on the seventeenth day of
the seventh month the ark came to rest on the mountains of Ararat. 5The
waters continued to recede until the tenth month, and on the first day of
the tenth month the tops of the mountains became visible.

6After forty days Noah opened a window he had made in the ark
7and sent out a raven, and it kept flying back and forth until the water
had dried up from the earth. 8Then he sent out a dove to see if the water
had receded from the surface of the ground. 9But the dove could find
nowhere to perch because there was water over all the surface of the earth;
so it returned to Noah in the ark. He reached out his hand and took the
dove and brought it back to himself in the ark. 10He waited seven more
days and again sent out the dove from the ark. 11When the dove returned
to him in the evening, there in its beak was a freshly plucked olive leaf!
Then Noah knew that the water had receded from the earth. 12He waited
seven more days and sent the dove out again, but this time it did not
return to him.

13By the first day of the first month of Noah's six hundred and first
year, the water had dried up from the earth. Noah then removed the
covering from the ark and saw that the surface of the ground was dry. 14By
the twenty-seventh day of the second month the earth was completely dry.

15Then God said to Noah, 16"Come out of the ark, you and your wife
and your sons and their wives. 17Bring out every kind of living creature
that is with you — the birds, the animals, and all the creatures that move
along the ground — so they can multiply on the earth and be fruitful and
increase in number on it."

18So Noah came out, together with his sons and his wife and his sons' wives. 19All the animals and all the creatures that move along the ground and all the birds—everything that moves on land—came out of the ark, one kind after another.

20Then Noah built an altar to the LORD and, taking some of all the clean animals and clean birds, he sacrificed burnt offerings on it. 21The LORD smelled the pleasing aroma and said in his heart: "Never again will I curse the ground because of humans, even though every inclination of the human heart is evil from childhood. And never again will I destroy all living creatures, as I have done.

22"As long as the earth endures,
seedtime and harvest,
cold and heat,
summer and winter,
day and night
will never cease."

9:1Then God blessed Noah and his sons, saying to them, "Be fruitful and increase in number and fill the earth. 2The fear and dread of you will fall on all the beasts of the earth, and on all the birds in the sky, on every creature that moves along the ground, and on all the fish in the sea; they are given into your hands. 3Everything that lives and moves about will be food for you. Just as I gave you the green plants, I now give you everything.

4"But you must not eat meat that has its lifeblood still in it. 5And for your lifeblood I will surely demand an accounting. I will demand an accounting from every animal. And from each human being, too, I will demand an accounting for the life of another human being.

6"Whoever sheds human blood,
by humans shall their blood be shed;
for in the image of God
has God made mankind.

7As for you, be fruitful and increase in number; multiply on the earth and increase upon it."

8Then God said to Noah and to his sons with him: 9"I now establish my covenant with you and with your descendants after you 10and with every living creature that was with you—the birds, the livestock and all the wild animals, all those that came out of the ark with you—every living creature on earth. 11I establish my covenant with you: Never again will all life be destroyed by the waters of a flood; never again will there be a flood to destroy the earth."

[12]And God said, "This is the sign of the covenant I am making
between me and you and every living creature with you, a covenant for
all generations to come: [13]I have set my rainbow in the clouds, and it
will be the sign of the covenant between me and the earth. [14]Whenever I
bring clouds over the earth and the rainbow appears in the clouds, [15]I will
remember my covenant between me and you and all living creatures of
every kind. Never again will the waters become a flood to destroy all life.
[16]Whenever the rainbow appears in the clouds, I will see it and remember
the everlasting covenant between God and all living creatures of every
kind on the earth."

[17]So God said to Noah, "This is the sign of the covenant I have
established between me and all life on the earth."

*Listening to the Text in the Story:* Biblical Texts: Genesis 3; 4:1–16, 17–24; Ancient Near Eastern Texts: Sumerian King List; The Eridu Genesis; Atrahasis; Gilgamesh Epic

There was a robust flood tradition in Mesopotamian literature. We have already mentioned the notice of the flood in the SKL. After mentioning the eight prediluvian kings, we read that:

> The Flood swept thereover.
> After the Flood had swept thereover,
> when the kingship was lowered from heaven. . . .[1]

A fuller Sumerian account of the flood is provided by the Eridu Genesis (often dated around 1600 BC), which is most significant because it combines a creation story with a flood story similar to Genesis 1–11.[2] Here Enki informs a man named Ziusudra to build an ark in anticipation of a flood. He obeys and after the flood he offers sacrifices.

Atrahasis is the name of the flood hero in Akkadian tradition. The myth known by the name of its main protagonist begins with an account of the creation of humanity (see above in the commentary on Gen 2:4–25). But after a while, humanity's noise disturbs the sleep of the chief gods, particularly the god Enlil who then determines to destroy humanity by means of a flood. Enki thwarts Enlil's efforts by informing his devotee Atrahasis ("extra wise") to build an ark and ride out the flood.

1. Translation from T. Jacobsen, *The Sumerian King List* (Chicago: The University of Chicago Press, 1939), 77.

2. See translation and brief commentary in *COS* 1:513–15; also Sparks, *Ancient Texts*, 310–11.

The most celebrated Mesopotamian account of the flood is the Gilgamesh Epic, known in Old Babylonian as well as neo-Assyrian versions.[3] The flood story is found at the conclusion of the long epic describing the adventures of King Gilgamesh of Uruk. The story is really about the meaning of life, beginning by describing the young king as a pleasure seeker who angers his subjects so that they pray that the gods will aid them against this irresponsible leader. The gods respond by creating Enkidu, a primeval man, who eventually fights Gilgamesh, but is defeated by him. Even so, Gilgamesh befriends Enkidu and sets out on adventures with him.

Gilgamesh attracts the amorous attention of the goddess Ishtar, but he rebuffs her advances and angers her. She convinces her father the god Anu to send the bull of heaven against the upstart, but Gilgamesh kills the bull, tears off its forelock, and throws it in Ishtar's face. Such an affront could not go unanswered, and Anu kills Gilgamesh's comrade Enkidu.

Witnessing the death of his friend up close causes Gilgamesh to set out in search of an answer to death. This search eventually takes him to Utnapishtim, the only human to be given eternal life. Gilgamesh is interested in living forever himself, and he asks Utnapishtim how he achieved immortality, and this question leads him to relate the story of the flood.

The flood story of Gilgamesh is remarkably close to the flood story of the Bible, but there are also significant differences. Utnapishtim responds to Gilgamesh's question by telling him that the god Ea (the Akkadian equivalent of the Sumerian Enki) told him to build an ark to prepare for a flood that the gods under the leadership of Enlil were sending to eradicate humanity since they were disturbing their sleep. Enlil had sworn not to inform any humans of the coming calamity, so he speaks to the reed house of Utnapishtim to build the ark, which is described as a large cube (unlike the boatlike structure of the biblical ark).

After building the ark, he takes animals and his family on board. The storm comes and devastates humanity, but his family and the animals on board the ark survive. As the flood waters recede, it settles on a mountain (Mount Nimush). Utnapishtim then lets three birds out, the first two (a dove and a swallow) returned because there was no dry land, but the third (a raven) did not return, signifying that dry land had emerged from the flood waters. At that point, Utnapishtim disembarked and offered sacrifices. In a rather unflattering portrait of the gods, they are said to have smelled the sweet savor of the sacrifices and then "crowded around the sacrificer like flies."[4] Enlil is

3. J. Tigay, *The Evolution of the Gilgamesh Epic* (Philadelphia: University of Pennsylvania Press, 1982).

4. See the translation of the flood story (Tablet 11 of the Gilgamesh Epic) in *COS* 1:458–60.

irate with Ea for informing a human about the flood, but Ea defends himself by accusing Enlil of overreach. If humans make too much noise then use other means to lessen their number. After all, the gods need the food provided by their sacrifices.

Utnapishtim tells Gilgamesh the flood story in order to tell him that his eternal life is not accessible to others. Though this is not the end of Gilgamesh's attempt to find eternal life, eventually he realizes that he will not live forever. He returns to Uruk knowing that, though he won't live forever, he can achieve an eternal legacy by being a mature, wise ruler of Uruk. We will speak to the most relevant similarities and differences between the Gilgamesh flood story and that of the Bible in the next section.

In terms of the background in Genesis, we have seen that humans have shown themselves to be habitual sinners beginning with Adam and Eve's rebellion (Gen 3) and then continuing with the story of Cain and Abel (4:1–16) as well as the generations that follow Cain (4:17–24).

### Divine Reasons for the Flood (6:1–8)

Technically, Genesis 6:1–8 provides the conclusion to the "account" (*toledot*) of Adam that begins in 5:1. The next "account" (of Noah) begins in 6:9. However, interestingly, the conclusion to the Adam account provides the preface to the story of the flood, so we have decided to treat it separately from chapter 5 and highlight its function as introducing the story of the flood. In essence, we agree with Mathews who says "Genesis 6:1–8 functions as a literary hinge that backtracks to chapter 5 by speaking of marriage and procreation (Gen 6:1–4) and also looks ahead by introducing the consequent flood narrative (Gen 6:5–8)."[5]

According to Utnapishtim in the Gilgamesh Epic, the gods sent the flood because the people were making too much noise. Overpopulation irritated them. The biblical account of the flood provides an entirely different divine rationale.

Genesis 6:1–5 is often treated separately from the flood, but I understand it as a particularly egregious example of the sinfulness of the generations that preceded God's judgment in the flood. All the stories of Genesis 3–11 have a particular structure where a story of sin is followed by a divine judgment speech and ends with the description of the execution of the judgment. We also are told of a token of God's grace that shows God's intent to stay involved

5. K. A. Mathews, *Genesis 1–11:26*, NAC 1 (Nashville: Broadman and Holman, 1996), 296.

with his recalcitrant human creatures. In the light of the expectation of this structure, Genesis 6:1–5 melds into the broader flood story.

Much remains enigmatic to modern readers in the story in these opening verses of Genesis 6. The basic plot is clear. The "sons of God" marry the "daughters of humans," bringing on the anger and judgment of God, who then restricts the human lifespan to a hundred and twenty years (contrast the long life of the pre-flood generations in Gen 5).[6] In addition, the story tells us that the offspring produced by the union of the "sons of God" and the "daughters of humans" are the Nephilim, who are "the heroes of old, men of renown." What are we to make of this story?

As we answer this question, we must distinguish what is clear from what is not. The one thing that is clear, and it contributes to the main message of the story, is that some kind of transgression takes place. Whoever the sons of God and the daughters of humans are, they should not be marrying and having children. It is this transgression that brings on God's wrath.

What we are not certain about is the identity of the main characters of the story. We will only mention the two most plausible theories. One opinion suggests that the "sons of God" are from the godly line (see the genealogy of Seth in Gen 5) and that the "daughters of humans" are the ungodly line (see the genealogy of Cain in Gen 4:17–24). While we might imagine that such unions would be displeasing to God, we are left to wonder why their offspring were so prodigious, especially since the later use of Nephilim (Num 13:33) implies that these Nephilim are unusually tall and fearsome warriors.

In my opinion, the second possibility is more likely. We begin with the observation that "son of God" is often used to refer to angels (Pss 29:1; 82:1; 89:5–10). In this interpretation, angels intermarry with human women, thus producing prodigious offspring, but bringing on God's anger.

Many readers are misled by the idea that angels were incapable of having sex. Indeed, according to Jesus, angels neither marry nor are given in marriage (Luke 20:34–36). However, the heavenly beings in Genesis 6 are not obedient but rebellious angels. They aren't acting according to their divinely given nature. As for their supposed inability, no Israelite/Jewish reader would have thought of the angels as incapable of sexual intercourse. Yes, they are spiritual beings, but they are capable of taking on human appearance (see Gen 18–19; Mark 16:5). The opposite idea is not a biblical one, but one produced by a faulty view on angels developed during the Middle Ages when Christians thinkers were influenced by a neo-Platonic philosophy that radically separated the spiritual from the physical.

---

6. An alternate understanding is that the 120 years refers to the time between this judgment speech and the coming of the judgment in the form of the Flood (see Boda, *A Severe Mercy*, 21).

As I say, no ancient Israelite/Jew would have adopted this perspective. Indeed, we know from the intertestamental book 1 Enoch (see chs. 6–36) that many Jews read Genesis 6:1–5 in precisely this way. Even more compellingly for the Christian reader, the author of the book of Jude also understood the sexual transgression here as that between humans and angels (Jude 6; see also 2 Pet 2:4).

The Nephilim are another enigma in this passage. We know little about them and we should not speculate beyond what we can understand. They are a prodigious offspring: The "heroes of old." While this description sounds good, most translators believe that these are evil people. Perhaps they are the source of myths like the Gilgamesh Epic and other Hercules-like characters. A conquest-period tribe is also named Nephilim, but does that mean they survived the flood? More likely, the presence of an unusually large group of people in the promised land evoked memory of this early story and thus earned them the name Nephilim. Finally, we simply comment that we do not know what to make of their name though we can confidently translate "the fallen ones." Still the question remains, fallen from what? The bottom line, and again what we can confidently say, is that Genesis 6:1–5 narrates a story giving us a particularly horrifying example of the type of sinful activity that leads to the judgment of the flood.

The next paragraph begins (v. 5) with a comprehensive denunciation of humanity. It is not only the human women who consorted with evil angels that have offended God, it is the "human race" whose wickedness is great. Their wickedness is also deep and extensive. It extends into their thought life where "every inclination of the human heart was only evil all the time." Later Jewish thought speaks of the "evil inclination" (*yetser ra*) of humanity, which appears here for the first time.

In one sense, verse 6 fits well following this negative assessment of humanity. God is sad and regrets the decision he made to create humanity in the first place. In another sense, the verse is quite shocking. God is sad? God regrets? God is God after all. Isn't he omniscient? Doesn't he know the future? It sounds like he is surprised how his human creatures have turned out.

These are difficult interpretive waters to navigate. It is appropriate to observe the extensive anthropomorphic language used in these early chapters of Genesis. In other words, we must recognize that God condescends himself to accommodate himself to the reader's understanding. In short, the language is figurative.

That said, it is wrong to simply ignore what the verse says because it is figurative. Figurative language is intentionally chosen to communicate truths. It is inappropriate to say that this language is only a metaphor. The question we must ask is, what does the metaphor point to?

It seems to me a complete overriding of biblical language like we find here to deny that God has an emotional life (as some theologians do as they assert that God is impassable). Our sin saddens God. It does lead him to regret having created us. He created human beings morally innocent and with the ability to make moral choices, and the depressing news is that humans keep choosing to rebel rather than to obey. Thus, he determines to destroy his human creatures and the rest of his animate creation ("the animals, the birds and the creatures that move along the ground," v. 7) by means of a flood.

When we think about it, perhaps the most surprising element of this story is that he refrains from completely destroying us. Verse 8 is the turning point of the story when it informs the reader of God's token of grace in the light of human sin and his declared intention to judge that sin by the flood: "But Noah found favor in the eyes of the Lord."

Thus ends the "account" of Adam. Genesis 6:9 introduces the "account" of Noah and here "a righteous man, blameless among the people of his time, and he walked faithfully with God" (6:9), an assessment also found in 7:1. This raises the question of the relationship between Noah finding God's favor and his righteousness. To put it bluntly, does God show Noah favor because he is righteous?

Kaminski skillfully explores this question and concludes that, though Noah does escape the judgment of his generation, he is not exempt from the negative assessment of humanity presented in 6:5: "The Lord saw how great the wickedness of the human race had become on the earth, and that every inclination of the thoughts of the human heart was only evil all the time." In other words, Noah survived the flood not because he deserved it but because of the unmerited favor of God (see discussion of Gen 6:9 that follows).[7]

## God's Instructions to Noah (6:9–22)

We have treated 6:1–8 as the introduction, but the flood story proper begins with the third occurrence of the *toledot* formula: "This is the account of Noah and his family," prefacing a section that will continue through chapter 9.

6:9b–10 informs the reader that Noah was "righteous" (*tsaddiq*), "blameless" (*tam*), and one who walked faithfully with God. Above, stimulated by Kaminski's fine study of the question,[8] we raised the question of the relationship of this assessment with the earlier statement that "Noah found favor in the eyes of the Lord" (6:8) and concluded that a proper understanding of the

7. C. M. Kaminski, *Was Noah Good?: Finding Favour in the Flood Narrative* (London: T & T Clark, 2014).

8. Ibid.

latter phrase claims that Noah's survival and role was not earned by his righteousness but was a manifestation of God's grace.

But how are we to understand the statement that Noah was righteous? In the first place, Kaminski shows that the term is not to be interpreted in terms of covenant faithfulness,[9] but rather in the light of creation law, understood as acting in conformity with creation norms.[10] Second, and central to her argument, the assessment of Noah as "righteous" in 6:9 is anticipatory of 7:1. In other words, Noah is righteous in the sense of doing "everything just as God commanded him" in regards to the flood (6:22; 7:5). Thus, God's choice of Noah was an act of grace, but Noah responded in obedience and thus becomes a model of faithful response to God (Ezek 14:14, 20).

Along with Noah, the narrator introduces his three sons—Shem, Ham and Japheth—who will survive the flood with their father and play a role in the immediate postlude to God's act of judgment. Verses 11–13 repeat the assessment of humanity as well as God's determination to destroy the earth and its inhabitants found in 6:5–7. The rest of the chapter delineates how God would manifest his grace through Noah allowing the human race to continue after the flood.

God instructs Noah to construct a boat, an ark, on which he and his sons as well as their wives will ride out the flood. In addition, God tells him to bring onto the ark two of every kind of animal as well as food for everyone.

The description of the ark is different from the ark on the Gilgamesh Epic, which is a gigantic cube, which never would have remained stable in the water. The ark is described in the actual shape of a boat. However, its dimensions lead one to wonder whether we are getting a literal description here. Verse 15 describes it as a boat that is 450 feet long (three hundred cubits), 75 feet wide (50 cubits), and 45 feet high (30 cubits). These dimensions describe a boat like no other boat ever built in antiquity.

This is not to deny that this story has a historical kernel. As we have seen throughout the early chapters of Genesis, there is a historical impulse to the narrative, but that the story is told using figurative language and in interaction with ancient Near Eastern accounts. Thus, there is not an interest in historical precision. What is the message of the story then? Humanity grew sinful, deserved punishment, and got it, but, thanks to God, was allowed to continue.

9. So W. J. Dumbrell, *Covenant and Creation: An Old Testament Covenant Theology*, rev. ed. (Milton Keynes, UK: Paternoster, 2013), who argues that there is a previously existing creation covenant.

10. Based on the study by J. K. Bruckner, *Implied Law in the Abraham Narrative* (Sheffield: Sheffield Academic, 2001).

Significantly, God not only informs Noah of his purpose to destroy all living creatures on earth with the exception of Noah himself and his immediate family, but he also announces that he "will establish my covenant with you" (6:18). While we will explain the nature of the covenant in conjunction with the episode that narrates the aftermath of the flood (8:20–9:17), we note here that this passage provides the first explicit mention of this extremely important concept that concerns our relationship with God.

The chapter ends with the simple statement that Noah was perfectly obedient to the divine instructions. The moment of judgment had come.

### The Flood (Genesis 7:1–8:19)

God begins by instructing Noah to board the ark along with his family and representatives of various types of animals and birds. Previously (6:19–21), we heard only that he was to take a single pair of each animal, but the present instructions reveal a distinction between clean and unclean animals. This passage is the first time such a distinction is mentioned in Scripture and its occurrence here is quite surprising. The delineation of clean and unclean otherwise is a Mosaic development (Lev 11). As opposed to unclean animals for which Noah was to have a single pair, he needed to bring seven pairs of clean animals on board and the same for all birds. Again, we learn that Noah was completely obedient to the divine instructions (7:5).

Noah had seven days to comply to God's commands, and after he had successfully accomplished the task, God brought the waters to annihilate the inhabitants of the earth. The waters came from below ("the springs of the great deep") and above ("the floodgates of the heavens").

Verses 13–16 again narrate the entry of Noah, his family, and the animals on the ark, adding the detail that "God shut them in" (v. 16). The following paragraph (vv. 17–23) then describes the flood itself.

There is a debate among conservative scholars about whether or not this story concerns a worldwide deluge or a devastating local flood. The proponents of the latter argue that the word translated "earth" (*erets*) in this paragraph could be translated "land." However, the depth of the water (fifteen cubits=twenty-three feet over the mountains) almost certainly depicts a worldwide flood. Even the alternate translation provided by the NIV footnote is an attempt to make the flood sound local, but in either case the telling phrase is that the waters cover the mountains. Supporting the idea that the passage describes a worldwide flood is the fact that the judgment is said to be worldwide. After the flood waters covered the earth, using language that reflects the creation account in describing the objects of judgment, "Every living thing that moved on land perished—birds, livestock, wild animals, all the creatures that swarm over the earth, and all mankind.... Only Noah was left, and those with him in the ark" (7:21, 23).

Of course, the problem for the position that this is a worldwide flood is that there is not a shred of geological or archaeological evidence for such a flood and, in this case, one might expect there to be.[11] Again, the problem may not be with our translation of the Hebrew text as a worldwide flood or with the lack of evidence for such a flood as it is with an inaccurate understanding of the genre of the text that would wrongly lead one to expect precise and literal historical reportage.

Theologically, the picture of the earth completely covered by water is tantalizingly suggestive. After all, when the world was first created it began as a watery mass (Gen 1:2) which God shaped into a functional and ordered universe over the next six days. The flood is a reversion to pre-creation conditions, what Clines calls un-creation.[12] Indeed, the description of objects of the judgment reflects the language of all the creatures of Genesis 1 and 2, again suggesting the reversal of creation. This observation will be particularly helpful when we consider the immediate post-flood situation in chapter 8 and 9.

The waters of the flood rose for forty days (7:17) and then lasted for another one hundred and fifty (7:24). The narrative moves from an emphasis on the judgment of the flood to the restoration after the flood with the words "But God remembered Noah" (8:1). Finally, the ark came to rest on the mountains of Ararat on the seventh day of the seventh month, but the tops of the mountains only became visible a few months later (the first day of the tenth month). Ararat at the border of Turkey and Iran would have been the tallest peak in the area at over 16,000 feet.

As land started to appear, in a scene very reminiscent of the Gilgamesh Epic, Noah released three birds in succession (raven, dove, dove). The birds are the same as in the Gilgamesh Epic, but in reverse order (dove, dove, raven). The third bird, a dove, first returned with a "freshly plucked olive leaf" (8:11) that told him that the waters had receded significantly and then he sent the dove out a second time and did not return, indicating that it was now possible to emerge from the ark.

He waited a few more months, though, until the ground became completely dry (8:14). God finally instructed the occupants of the ark to exit.

We earlier mentioned that the flood was an act of un-creation in which God reverted the earth to its pre-creation state of *tohu wabohu* ("formless and empty," 1:2). Not surprisingly then, we begin to encounter language that

---

11. D. Young, "Genesis Flood and Geology," in *Dictionary of Christianity and Science*, ed. P. Copan, et al. (Grand Rapids: Zondervan, forthcoming).

12. Clines, *The Theme of the Pentateuch*.

echoes language of the first creation. We move now from un-creation to re-creation. Note for instance the repetition of the creation command (Gen 1:28) to "multiply on the earth and be fruitful and increase in number on it" (8:17).

Noah's first act upon stepping on dry land was to build an altar to God and to offer sacrifices. While this superficially reminds us of Utnapishtim in the Gilgamesh Epic, we should observe the radical difference in the reaction of the Babylonian gods to the response of Noah's God. The Babylonian gods, who had been afraid of the flood waters to begin with, crowd around the sacrifice "like flies." Babylon sacrifices were thought to provide food for the gods, so they had gone hungry during the days of the flood and were now famished. God does not need food, but he does respond to Noah's devotion by vowing never again to destroy humanity by the waters of the flood. The god Ea has to persuade the war god Enlil to the same conclusion, but only by suggesting alternative means by which to reduce human population (famine, plague, war).

**God's Covenant with Noah (Genesis 8:20–9:17)**

In what seems to be part of the covenant agreement (see below) between God and Noah, the former promises to provide continuity in the processes of the creation until the very end ("as long as the earth endures").

Chapter 9 continues the delineation of the content of the covenant with Noah, beginning with the note that God blessed Noah and his sons. Blessing is one of the central themes of the book of Genesis. God created humanity and blessed it (1:22, 28; 5:2). In Eden humanity had a harmonious relationship with God and each other as well as the material blessings of Eden. Such blessing was forfeited by human rebellion, but now with the judgment of the flood, humanity gets a second chance and the people of the earth begin with God's blessing.

The second chance involved a movement back to square one, so again, like at the beginning (1:28), humanity receives the command to "be fruitful and increase in number and fill the earth" (9:1; see a third repetition in v. 7). But there are changes from the original situation that take into account the introduction of hostility in the creation. For instance, at the beginning humans were only to eat vegetables, but now there is a new dimension of conflict among God's creatures ("the fear and dread of you will fall on all the beasts of the earth ..."), and God allows humans to add animals to their diet.

There is, however, one important exception. God prohibits eating meat with its "lifeblood" still in it. This prohibition prevents humans from eating animals that are still alive.

The mention of the "image of God" in verse 6 is yet another intertextual echo to Genesis 1 (see v. 27), but again with a change that takes into account the introduction of hostility in a post-fall world. There will be an "accounting" for the killing of a human being. If another human being takes a life, then that person forfeits their life as is indicated in the *lex talionis* (life for life) provision of verse 6, given in a chiastic poetic form: "whoever sheds (a) the blood (b) of humans (c) by humans (c') will their blood (b') be shed (a')." The rationale for this severe penalty is that humans are made in the image of God. Their life has dignity, and since they reflect the glory of God (see comments on Gen 1:28 and Loving Others Created in the Image of God in the Live the Story section after 1:1–2:4a), an assault on a human is an assault on God himself.

Verses 8–17 contain God's formal proclamation of the covenant with Noah. As mentioned above, this covenant is the first one mentioned in Scripture and thus possessed great importance (though see below concerning the possibility of a covenant with Adam).

The English translation covenant (for *berit*) is a suitable one, denoting a legal agreement between two parties. Since the mid-twentieth century, it has become clear that a particular type of legal agreement stands behind the word covenant, namely a treaty. In particular, God is the sovereign king who enters into a treaty relationship with his vassal people. This agreement is not between equal parties. While the vassals, humanity in this case, have responsibilities, God is the one who sets the terms and makes promises. The emphasis in the Noahic covenant is on God's promise to Noah and indeed "with every living creature that was with" him (9:10) that he would never again destroy the earth by means of a flood. As Provan puts it, "the ongoing stability and fertility of the world until the end of time is assured. God's blessing will sustain this world in the long term, even if evil has now entered into it and is working out its twisted ways within it."[13]

This covenant is accompanied by a sign; indeed, almost all later covenants will have an associated sign. A sign is like a brand, when one sees the sign, in this case the rainbow, one is reminded of the covenant with its promises and obligations.

The sign of a covenant has some kind of integral relationship with the context of the covenant and its content. The most obvious significance of the rainbow for the Noahic covenant is that the rainbow comes out after the rain, but more can be said once it is realized that the Hebrew word for rainbow (*qeshet*) is the word for bow as in the weapon. In essence, the rainbow

13. Provan, *Seriously Dangerous Religion*, 61.

represents the fact that God has ceased from his warfare against sinful humanity. In essence, he has hung up his bow. According to Kline, we can go even further. He suggests that we should derive meaning from the fact that the bow is pointed heavenward, that is toward God. In short, the sign is a self-maledictory oath. In essence, God is saying, "if I break this promise, may I die."

Our first reaction to this idea might be that God cannot die, but that makes the point. Of course God cannot die, but then he cannot lie either. In addition, we should point out that there is at least one clear divine self-maledictory oath in the book of Genesis (see Gen 15). That said, while Kline's idea is interesting and possible, it is not certain.

Before concluding, we should note that, according to the NIV translation, this covenant is an "everlasting covenant." In this covenant God promises that he will never use the waters again to destroy the earth. However, as we will see below, according to Peter, the flood is anticipatory of the final end of the earth, but this time by fire. Though it is literally true that God will not destroy the earth again by a flood, he will bring the earth as we know it to an end by a fire. Is God just talking around the subject and not getting to the point here?

As Niehaus argues, there are reasons to doubt that "everlasting covenant" is the correct translation of *berit olam*.[14] He takes the "root meaning" of *olam* to mean "hidden" with the end result that "long-lasting covenant" is a more accurate translation. Thus, God's words here are not in conflict with the later biblical teaching that God will indeed one day bring the world as we know it to an end (see below).

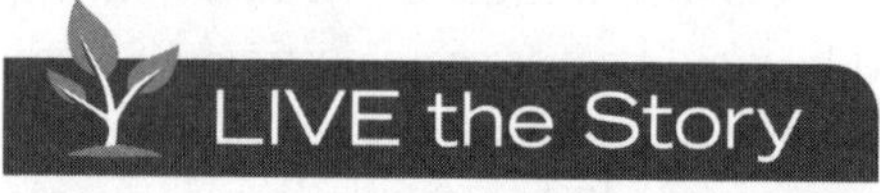


### "The Wages of Sin is Death" (Romans 6:23a)

The flood story is a vivid picture of Paul's statement that the "wages of sin is death." In the generations before Noah, there were two groups of people, those who followed God (Gen 5) and those who did not (Gen 4:17–25). By the time of Noah, humanity had become pervasively and (almost) universally wicked (6:5). Thus God determined to judge all humanity by bringing a flood. The flood represents a reversal of creation, a return to the "formless and empty" (Gen 1:2) condition of the earth before the six days of creation.

The flood also can be seen as an expression of an ancient Near Eastern ordeal. In ancient Babylon a person who is suspected of a crime could be taken to the river and thrown in. If the person is innocent, then they survive the ordeal, but if they are guilty, the river serves as judge and executioner. The

14. See his discussion in Niehaus, *Biblical Theology*, 210–14.

cup ordeal of Numbers 5 shows that the Old Testament is aware of the ordeal ritual. The flood judges and executes the guilty, while allowing the righteous to survive.

According to the New Testament appropriation of the flood tradition, the flood is a preview of the final judgment. As Jesus speaks to his disciples about his eventual return and the final judgment, he draws the analogy when he says:

> Just as it was in the days of Noah, so also will it be in the days of the Son of Man. People were eating, drinking, marrying and being given in marriage up to the day Noah entered the ark. Then the flood came and destroyed them all. (Luke 17:26–27; compare Matt 24:37–41)

While today some teachers and preachers seem almost embarrassed about the Bible's teaching about the last judgment, Jesus wants to warn his disciples, in the words of Paul, that "the wages of sin is death" in order to urge people to abandon their evil attitudes and behavior and thus avoid the judgment.

Peter too draws an analogy between the flood and the final judgment (see 2 Pet 2:4–10). According to Niehaus, "Of course, God will again come to wage war against his foes, only it will not be with water but with fire. That is why Peter can draw such a clear parallel between the Flood and the Lord's eschatological return in judgment (2 Peter 3:5–7)."[15] The similarity is found in the suddenness and thoroughness of God's judgment against evil. The intention of the analogy is to create a sense of urgency for people to drive people to God and his protection (see next section).

### "But the Gift of God Is Eternal Life in Christ Jesus our Lord" (Romans 6:23b)

Paul does not teach that the wages of sin is death in order to gloat over the fate of sinners. He wants those who are "slaves of sin" to become "slaves of God" and "slaves to righteousness leading to holiness" (see the whole argument in 6:19–23).

The flood story not only presents a picture of the judgment of sinners but also the salvation of the righteous. Noah was not chosen at random among the egregious sinners of his generation to survive the flood. There was a reason why it was Noah who "found favor in the eyes of the Lord" (6:8). "Noah was a righteous man, blameless among the people of his time, and he walked faithfully with God" (6:9).

Indeed, while Noah is not mentioned often in later Scripture, when he is, it is his righteousness that is often highlighted. Ezekiel tells the inhabitants of Jerusalem that they will be judged for their sins against God. He says that

---

15. Niehaus, *Biblical Theology*, 209.

"even if these three men — Noah, Daniel and Job — were in it, they could save only themselves by their righteousness" (Ezek 14:14, see also v. 20). The author of Hebrews adds the following: "By faith Noah, when warned about things not yet seen, in holy fear built an ark to save his family. By his faith he condemned the world and became heir of the righteousness that is in keeping with faith" (Heb 11:7). Peter (2 Pet 2:5) calls him a "preacher of righteousness."

What is righteousness? Isn't everyone sinful? No one can really be righteous, can they?

Everyone, including Noah, Job, and Daniel, are sinners, not because of Adam, but because "all sinned" (Rom 5:12, see The Story of the Fall in the Live the Story section after Gen 3). How can Noah be righteous then? Righteousness is not the same as sinlessness. A righteous person is one who seeks to be holy, but when he or she fails, then repents and asks God's forgiveness. In the time of Noah sacrifice was the visible manifestation of the repentant heart, showing awareness that sin deserves death. Sacrifice was the divinely ordained and gracious ritual that allowed for a substitute death in place of the sinner. Thus, when we hear that Noah was righteous, blameless, and that he walked faithfully, we are to understand that he was a repentant sinner who sought to be holy.

And this brings us back to Paul's desire that his readers would become "slaves to righteousness leading to holiness." The pursuit of holiness is often downplayed in our churches and in our lives. Kevin DeYoung suggests various reasons including the fear of being considered "a weird holdover from a bygone era."[16] Others may feel that the pursuit of holiness contradicts the grace of the gospel and verges on salvation by works.

But if we understand righteousness and holiness correctly, we will realize that there is no concession to a salvation by works here. As we have seen, Noah is righteous and blameless because he acknowledged his sin, sought forgiveness, and God graciously restored his relationship with him. He then lived in obedience to his God. Christians are saved by grace alone. We don't offer sacrifices because Jesus, the once-and-for-all sacrifice, died in our place (Heb 7:27). But that is not the end of the story. Now Jesus calls us to obedience and a pursuit of holiness that will please God and attract others to the gospel.

### "This Water Symbolizes Baptism" (1 Peter 3:21)

In his first letter, Peter refers to the flood and makes an analogy between the waters of the flood and the waters of baptism, the ritual that signifies entry

16. K. DeYoung, *The Hole in Our Holiness: Filling the Gap between Gospel Passion and the Pursuit of Holiness* (Wheaton, IL: Crossway, 2014).

into a covenant relationship with God. How are the waters of the flood like the waters of baptism?

The answer to this question may come from understanding the flood as a water ordeal as described above. Someone suspected of a crime was thrown into the waters and the guilty died and the innocent survived. According to Peter, the innocent ("a few people, eight in all") were "saved through the water" (1 Pet 3:20). So too those who turn to Christ and are baptized are saved "by the resurrection of Jesus Christ" (3:21).

By this understanding, we should realize that baptism is a self-maledictory oath like its Old Testament counterpart circumcision (see Circumcision and Baptism in the Live the Story sction of Gen 17), which similarly is a ritual signifying entry into the covenant with God. The cutting off of the foreskin symbolized the possibility if one betrayed their commitment to God that they would be cut off. So baptism is a type of burial from which a Christian is raised, but the implicit assumption is that the insincere person will remain buried in the waters (see Col 2:9–12 for the association with circumcision and burial).

## A Covenant with Humanity

As mentioned above, it is in the flood story that we have the first explicit mention of a covenant between God and his human creatures. The covenant is a major concept throughout the Bible. Indeed, readers of the New Testament understand that Christians have a new covenant established through the work of Jesus (Luke 22:20; Heb 8).

This leads to a number of questions. What is a covenant? How do people today relate to the covenant established with Noah? How does this covenant relate to the other covenants found in the Old Testament? How does the Noahic covenant relate to the new covenant?

A covenant is a formal, legal agreement between two parties. Studies over the past number of decades have shown the close connection between biblical covenants and ancient Near Eastern treaties between a superpower nation and a less powerful nation (so-called vassal treaties). These treaties have a similar structure to certain covenant texts in the Bible (most notably Deuteronomy, which is a renewal of the Mosaic covenant). After an introduction of the two parties entering into a treaty (Deut 1:1–5), there is then a historical preamble outlining the relationship between the great nation as embodied in its king and the lesser nation with an emphasis on how beneficial the relationship has been for the vassal nation and its king (Deut 1:9–3:29). This historical review provides the foundation and rationale for the law that follows (Deut 4–26). In the law, the great king imposes obligations on the vassal and these obligations are reinforced by a series of blessings and curses (Deut 27–28). As a legal document, there is the invocation of witnesses (Deut 30:19).

With the Noahic covenant, we do not have the full spelling out of this treaty-like form. Rather we simply have God initiating, announcing, and establishing a relationship through Noah that he calls a covenant. This covenant is unique in the Bible in that it is a covenant with the entirety of creation. Later covenants, beginning with the covenant with Abraham (see Gen 12:1–3; 15; 17) will have a more specific focus on God's people. The heart of the covenant with creation through Noah is the preservation of creation and a divine commitment to maintain the regular rhythms of created life until the very end ("as long as the earth endures"). No longer will God interrupt that rhythm with a worldwide devastation like the flood.[17] As Beck and VanDrunen point out, "What the Noahic covenant does promise is preservation. God commits himself not to eliminate evil from the world but to mitigate its effects so that the created order might be maintained for a time. The covenant prevents the destruction of the natural order (Gen 8:21; 9:11, 15), sustains the cycles of nature (Gen 8:22), regulates animal-human relations (Gen 9:2–4), and commands human reproduction and the administration of a legal system to maintain the human social order (Gen 9:1, 5–7)."[18]

One might ask whether God in the aftermath of the flood considers the flood a mistake. After all, he realizes that the flood does not resolve the problem of human sin, but "even so" (v. 21) he will not replicate such a judgment. In response, Robertson is correct to say, as we will indicate in the essay Anticipating the Final Judgment, Part 1 (below) that God's purpose was "to provide an appropriate historical demonstration of the ultimate destiny of a world under sin."[19] But now, as we said, God determines to maintain cosmic order until the end, thus creating room for his work of redemption as he seeks to reconcile wayward humanity with himself.

## Situating the Noahic Covenant

Above, we indicated that the covenant with creation through Noah was the first explicit covenant in a series of covenants throughout the Old Testament and into the New. Later in Genesis we will hear of a covenant with Abraham (Gen 12:1–3; see Gen 15 and 17). In Exodus 19–24, God will enter into a

17. Though J. S. Kaminsky (*Yet I Loved Jacob: Reclaiming the Biblical Concept of Election* [Nashville: Abingdon, 2007], 87) points to Zephaniah 1:2–3 as suggesting that even the Noahic covenant of preservation of creation is conditional.

18. R. Beck, R. and D. VanDrunen, "The Biblical Foundations of Law: Creation, Fall and the Patriarchs," in *Law and the Bible: Justice, Mercy and Legal Institutions*, ed. R. F. Cochran Jr. and D. VanDrunen (Downers Grove, IL: InterVarsity Press, 2013), 38–39.

19. O. P. Robertson, *The Christ of the Covenants*, (Phillipsburg, NJ: P & R, 1981), 114.

covenant with Moses which is then renewed by later Israel on the eve of his death (Deuteronomy), on the eve of Joshua's death (Josh 24), in the aftermath of anointing the first king Saul (1 Sam 12), and after the reestablishment of the law under Ezra and rebuilding the wall of Jerusalem under Nehemiah (Neh 9–12). After the covenant with Moses comes a covenant with David that concerns kingship, specifically a dynasty of kings (2 Sam 7). Finally, toward the end of the Old Testament time period God announces through Jeremiah a coming "new covenant" that will be more intense, more internal, more immediate, and more intimate (Jer 31:31–34). It is this new covenant that Jesus makes with his followers (Luke 22:20; Heb 8).

How does the Noahic covenant fit into this developing idea of a covenant? Most especially, how does the Noahic covenant relate to the new covenant, the one that the New Testament announces was established by Jesus and is the one that binds Christians to their God?

First, we must question whether or not the Noahic covenant is really the first covenant in the Bible. Certainly it is the first time the term covenant (*berit*) is used for a relationship between God and his people. However, some scholars have rightly pointed to the relationship between God and Adam and Eve as having the shape of a covenant even though the term itself is not used. After all, in God's relationship with Adam there is a law not to eat of the fruit of the tree of the knowledge of good and evil with attendant blessings and curses for obedience or disobedience.

Another indicator that the earlier relationship with humanity through Adam and Eve has the character of a covenant is hinted at through those intertextual links we noted between Genesis 9 and Genesis 1–2. The relationship with Noah seems to be a reestablishment of the original relationship with Adam and Eve. Thus, we think it is appropriate to understand the relationship between God and Adam and Eve as the original covenant of creation and thus the Noahic covenant is a covenant of re-creation.

After the Noahic covenant, there are the Abrahamic, Mosaic, and Davidic covenants followed by the new covenant. The critical question is, do later covenants abrogate previous ones? If so, then the Abrahamic covenant would have replaced the Noahic covenant which is no longer in effect. Fortunately, Paul answers this question for us. While he is speaking specifically of the relationship between the Mosaic and Abrahamic covenants, the principle still stands in relationship to the Noahic covenant and those that come after it. Paul says, "the law [the Mosaic covenant], introduced 430 years later, does not set aside the covenant previously established by God [the Abrahamic covenant] and thus do away with the promise" (Gal 3:17). On this principle, the Noahic covenant is still in effect.

Paul goes on to say that the Abrahamic covenant is fulfilled in Jesus Christ. Indeed, it appears that all the covenants find their ultimate fulfillment in Christ. As we will see, Jesus is the ultimate seed promised to Abraham (see Jesus the Seed of Abraham in Live the Story after 11:27–12:9). Jesus fulfills the Mosaic covenant by keeping the law as well by suffering the penalty of the law on our behalf. Jesus fulfills the Davidic covenant by virtue of his being the king (messiah) who rules on the throne forever.

But what about the Noahic covenant? Is the Noahic covenant fulfilled in Christ? Here is where it is important to see the Noahic covenant as connected to an earlier covenant with Adam and Eve, the first a creation covenant and the second a re-creation covenant.[20] If we are correct in this assertion, then the fulfillment of these creation covenants may be found both in the language of Jesus as the "last Adam" and in the promise of a new heaven and a new earth.

Jesus is most pointedly presented as such in 1 Corinthians 15:44b–49:

> If there is a natural body, there is also a spiritual body. So it is written: "The first man Adam became a living being"; the last Adam, a life-giving spirit. The spiritual did not come first, but the natural, and after that the spiritual. The first man was of the dust of the earth; the second man is of heaven. As was the earthly man, so are those who are of the earth; and as is the heavenly man, so also are those who are of heaven. And just as we have borne the image of the earthly man, so shall we bear the image of the heavenly man.

Paul's argument is that we are earthly just like Adam who was created from the dust of the ground. But thanks to Jesus, we, who follow him, also bear the image of Jesus, the last Adam, who is a heavenly man. Paul is speaking of these things in the context of the afterlife. He is saying that our relationship with the first Adam, being human, leads to death, but our relationship with Jesus, the last Adam, leads to life.

Second, we have spoken of the movement from Genesis 1–9 as going from creation to un-creation to re-creation. When Noah stepped out of the ark he stepped into a new creation. The previous creation had been corrupted by sin and God made all things new through his awesome judgment.

Peter thinks of the flood as a preview of the final judgment (Anticipating the Final Judgment, Part 1 below). Thus, we should not be surprised that the New Testament picks up on the language of the prophets (Isa 65:17; 66:22) and speaks of the future after the judgment as a new heaven and new earth (2 Pet 3:13; Rev 21:1).

20. For the fullest contemporary argument in favor of an Adamic covenant, see the excellent discussion in Niehaus, *Biblical Theology*, 35–94.

### Was Noah an Environmentalist and Animal Activist?

At the time of the writing of this commentary, a major movie was released on the life of Noah, written and directed by Darren Aronofsky. Aronofsky makes no pretense to presenting Noah according to the depiction given in the biblical account, and certainly a film maker cannot be faulted for taking literary license with an ancient story to address modern issues, but as a biblical scholar, I worry that this popular movie will affect people's perception of the biblical story for decades to come (similar to the way Cecil B. DeMille's portrayal of Moses has affected our culture's understanding of the story of Moses and the exodus).

In brief, Aronofsky's Noah is a radical environmentalist and an animal rights advocate. Noah believes that God judges humanity for its rape of the environment and its poor treatment of animals. Indeed, Noah goes so far as to believe that the purpose of his family is solely to preserve the animals from the flood and after discharging that duty, they should have no children themselves, thus when the last of them die, humanity will cease with the idea that only then does God's creation have a chance at survival. Indeed, Noah goes so far as to tell his pregnant daughter-in-law that if her child is a girl, he will kill it.

The Christian response to the film has been overwhelmingly negative since this film version of Noah is so far removed from the biblical picture.[21] The suggestion that humanity is a cancer that must be removed so that God's creation can thrive reverses the biblical picture of both humanity and nature.

That said, in our reaction to this distorted reading of the Noah story, we should not miss the important teaching of the Noah story (as well as the Adam story before it) as concerns humanity's role and responsibility in creation care.

We begin by going back to the account of the creation of humanity in the first creation account which serves as a background to the Noah story. By way of reminder and further explication, we saw that humans (Adam and Eve) were created in God's image for a purpose.[22] That purpose was to subdue the earth, as well as to "rule over the fish in the sea and the birds in the sky and over every living creature that moves on the ground" (Gen 1:28, see also v. 26). The terms "subdue" and "rule" come from the realm of kingship.

---

21. For a thoughtful Christian and biblical review of the script of the movie, see the remarks of the film writer and novelist Brian Godawa ("Darren Aronofsky's Noah: Environmentalist Wacko," godawa.com/movieblog/darren-aronofskys-noah-enviromentalist-wacko). I am indebted to his thoughtful comments in this essay and find myself in large agreement with his assessment of the biblical material.

22. See Wright, *Surprised by Scripture*, 35: "The image is a vocation, a calling."

Humans are God's vice-regents. He places them in the garden and they are to extend the order and fruitfulness of the garden to the whole earth. They are to rule the animal realm, not in a despotic, irresponsible way, but as wise monarchs who care for the well-being of their subjects.

The second creation account furthers this understanding of humanity as stewards and conservers of the natural creation and the animals. Earlier we explored God's commission that Adam "work" the garden and "take care of" (or guard) it (2:15). In addition, humanity's rule over the animals is further indicated by Adam's naming of them (2:19–20).

Thus, the creation accounts provide the foundation for a robust Christian concern for the well-being of the environment and care for animals. They also are clear, as we saw in the commentary on those chapters, that humanity is the apex or climax of creation.

Between the creation accounts and the story of Noah, however, stands the account of humanity's rebellion against the creator (see commentary on Gen 3). As Paul will later describe it, it was at this time that "the creation was subjected to frustration, not by its own choice, but by the will of the one who subjected it." Thus, the creation is in "bondage to decay" (Rom 8:20–21). God himself tells Adam that the ground is "cursed ... because of you." Adam and Eve are not wise, benevolent rulers, but rather those who foolishly exploit it, and their sin has ramifications not only for themselves, but for all of creation.

We come now to the story of Noah with this background. As Godawa insightfully points out, humanity is judged for the violence perpetrated against humanity, not for ravaging the creation. Aronofsky's version of the Noah story has God punishing humanity primarily for its violation of nature and poor treatment of animals. We might ask, however, if God so cared for animals and vegetation, why would he revert the natural order back to the chaos of the pre-creation state?

That said, Beck and R. and D. VanDrunen are correct when they point out that "much as God had given Adam the task of naming and ruling over animals in the Garden, the task of preserving the animals now falls to Noah."[23] We have above seen that God promises to preserve the rhythms of nature after the flood ("As long as the earth endures, seedtime and harvest, cold and heat, summer and winter, day and night will never cease," Gen 8:22). The Noahic covenant is not just a covenant with humanity but between God "and all life on the earth."

---

23. R. Beck, R. and D. VanDrunen, "The Biblical Foundations of Law: Creation, Fall, and the Patriarchs," in *Law and the Bible: Justice, Mercy and Legal Institutions*, ed. R. F. Cochran Jr. and D. VanDrunen (Downers Grove, IL: InterVarsity Press, 2013), 37.

Noah is the second Adam, and as a human created in the image of God, he and his family and descendants (all of humanity) are called to take care of the creation. They (we) are God's royal representatives in his creation, and we are to discharge our duties toward creation with compassion and wisdom.

### Anticipating the Final Judgment, Part 1

Genesis depicts the flood as God's judgment against pervasive and egregious human sin. As such, the New Testament understands it as a preview of an even more definitive judgment at the end of history when Christ returns again.

The Gospels of Matthew and Luke both connect the future final judgment with the earlier judgment at the time of Noah. Jesus himself presented the analogy:

> But about that day or hour no one knows, not even the angels in heaven, nor the son, but only the Father. As it was in the days of Noah, so it will be at the coming of the Son of Man. For in the days before the flood, people were eating and drinking, marrying and giving in marriage, up to the day Noah entered the ark; and they knew nothing about what would happen until the flood came and took them all away. That is how it will be at the coming of the Son of Man. (Matt 24:36–39)
>
> Just as it was in the days of Noah, so also will it be in the days of the Son of Man. People were eating, drinking, marrying and being given in marriage up to the day Noah entered the ark. Then the flood came and destroyed them all. (Luke 17:26–27)

The flood came suddenly and unexpectedly upon those who were caught up in the judgment of God, and so, says Jesus, will the future, final judgment that will accompany his return. The flood, in essence, is therefore a preview of the final judgment. As such it serves as an encouragement to God's people who are being oppressed by those who reject Christ, but also as a warning to those who will be judged. The judgment can come at any moment without warning.

The faithful then should "keep watch" and "be ready" (Matt 24:42–44) because we do not know when Jesus will return. Those who reject Christ should repent or they will suddenly find themselves the object of God's judgment and like the wicked generation at the time of Noah will find themselves overwhelmed.

We call this essay on the flood Anticipating the Final Judgment, Part 1, because Genesis will provide a second example, the judgment on Sodom and Gomorrah (for this see Anticipating the Final Judgment, Part 2, after Gen 18–19).

CHAPTER 7

# Genesis 9:18–28

## LISTEN to the Story

[18]The sons of Noah who came out of the ark were Shem, Ham and
Japheth. (Ham was the father of Canaan.) [19]These were the three sons
of Noah, and from them came the people who were scattered over the
whole earth.

[20]Noah, a man of the soil, proceeded to plant a vineyard. [21]When
he drank some of its wine, he became drunk and lay uncovered inside
his tent. [22]Ham, the father of Canaan, saw his father naked and told his
two brothers outside. [23]But Shem and Japheth took a garment and laid
it across their shoulders; then they walked in backward and covered their
father's naked body. Their faces were turned the other way so that they
would not see their father naked.

[24]When Noah awoke from his wine and found out what his youngest
son had done to him, [25]he said,

"Cursed be Canaan!
The lowest of slaves
will he be to his brothers."

[26]He also said,

"Praise be to the LORD, the God of Shem!
May Canaan be the slave of Shem.
[27] May God extend Japheth's territory;
may Japheth live in the tents of Shem,
and may Canaan be the slave of Japheth."

[28]After the flood Noah lived 350 years. [29]Noah lived a total of 950
years, and then he died.

*Listening to the Text in the Story:* Biblical Texts: Genesis 1:1–2; 3, 6–9; Ancient Near Eastern Text: The Aqhat Epic

God's judgment of humanity by means of a flood involved a reversal of creation itself. God used unformed matter ("the earth was formless and empty" [*tohu wabohu*]) to create a functional cosmos over six days. Based on ancient Near Eastern analogies, this "formless and empty" matter was a watery blob. The flood took creation back a step making it *tohu wabohu* again. When the waters receded and Noah and his family emerged from the ark, God entered into a covenant with him that reestablished the creation. In essence Noah, through his children, is a second Adam from whom all people descend. The question then is, will things be different now? Or will God's human creatures fall into the pattern of sin familiar from the pre-flood world and as initially manifested by the rebellion of Adam and Eve in Genesis 3? This story answers the latter question with a resounding and sad "Yes."

The Ugaritic Aqhat epic provides a background for the present story. Against the background of its description of the "ideal son," we can see just how badly Ham acts in regards to Noah's nakedness (see below).

## EXPLAIN the Story

God used the flood to execute judgment against humanity, but has not given up on his creatures. He allowed Noah to survive the flood and be the father of future generations beginning with his own sons who also survived the flood, Shem, Ham, and Japheth. In a sense, Noah is a second Adam, and the question arises as to how humanity will react in the aftermath of the flood. Will they now obey God and act with righteousness or not?

Genesis 9:18–28 presents a story about Noah and his sons that does not bode well for the future. Even so, modern readers often miss the point when they identify Noah as the sinner in this account. The real culprit is Canaan and the purpose of this story is largely to explain why Canaanites are a problem.

Verses 18–19 put the focus not on Noah, but on his son, as well as one of his grandsons, namely Canaan. The narrator identifies them as the ancestors of those who were "scattered over the whole earth." This phrase both looks back to God's punishment on Cain (4:12) as well as forward to the story of the tower of Babel (11:1–9, see particularly v. 9 and ch. 10). God punished humanity by so scattering them. In an important sense, there is a redemptive purpose to this punishment since scattering keeps evil people from multiplying their sin through gathering into groups.[1]

---

1. C. M. Kaminski (*From Noah to Israel: Realization of the Primaeval Blessing after the Flood*, JSOTSup 413 [London: T & T Clark, 2004) argues against scholars who see the dispersal of people mentioned here (and later in 10:18; 11:4, 8, 9) as in fulfillment of the mandate to fill the earth in

The plot begins with Noah doing what a "man of the soil" would be expected to do, plant a vineyard. After the crop came in, he made wine, drank it, got drunk, went into his tent and lay down, perhaps passed out, naked.

How are we to evaluate Noah's actions here? Did he sin when he got drunk and passed out naked in his tent? Many modern Christian readers would not hesitate to answer affirmatively. However, interestingly, in the later Mosaic law there is no prohibition against drinking (unless one is a priest on duty [Lev 10:9] or one who has taken a Nazirite vow [Num 6:2–3]). Noah is not the culprit in this story.[2] Drinking alcohol is not a sin; it is enjoying God's good gift to humanity (Judg 9:13; Ps 104:15; John 2:1–12). It is hard to argue that getting drunk is in and of itself a sin. Certainly Noah is not hurting anyone (not that this is the only criterion of sin) as he lies naked in his tent. That said, a clear case can be made that Noah is not acting with wisdom as defined by the later book of Proverbs (Prov 20:1; 21:17; 23:19–21, 29–33; 31:1–9). Getting drunk blurs one's ability to speak and act wisely and, as in the case of Noah in this story, makes one vulnerable to others.

Noah is not the guilty party (notice he is never punished); Ham is. He dishonors his father by seeing his father and not helping him. Indeed, we have evidence from the ancient Near East, in particular Ugarit, of a son's duty in such a circumstance. In the epic of Aqhat, King Dani'ilu describes the "ideal son" whose duties include: "to take his (father's) hand when (he is) drunk, to bear him up [when] (he is) full of wine."[3]

Thus, Ham is the culpable party in this story. In our opinion, certain scholars go too far when they say that Ham's seeing Noah's nakedness is a euphemism for sexual intercourse (incestual rape of either Noah or Noah's wife).[4] It is bad enough that he does not fulfill his filial duty by taking care of his father in a moment of vulnerability. While Ham does not come through, the other two brothers Shem and Japheth do the right thing and tactfully cover their father's naked body.

Thus, Noah is not punished but issues a punishment that has implications for the future. Rather than punishing Ham, he levies a curse toward Ham's son Canaan. The reason for this is not stated in the story. Perhaps Canaan

---

1:28 and then reiterated in 9:1. She argues that this scattering was a matter of judgment. Our view is that there may be a redemptive consequence to God's act of judgment here.

2. Agreeing with W. Brown, "Noah: Sot or Saint?" in *The Way of Wisdom: Essays in Honor of Bruce K. Waltke*, ed. J. I. Packer and S. K. Soderlund (Grand Rapids: Zondervan, 2000), 36–60, against Waltke, *Genesis*, 148.

3. *COS* 1:344. For detailed analysis, see M. Boda, "Ideal Sonship in Ugarit," *Ugarit-Forschungen* 25 (1993): 18–19.

4. See M. Carden, "Genesis," in *The Queer Bible Commentary*, ed. D. Guest, et al. (London: SCM, 2006), 31–2.

was with his father during his egregious neglect, but the text does not make this clear. Perhaps the whole line of Ham was cursed (as all the descendants of Shem and Japheth are blessed), but Canaan is signaled out because of the special role the people who descend from him play in the future biblical narrative. In other words, one of the main purposes of this story is to show the reprehensible origins of the later Canaanite people. No wonder God wants his people to stay away from Canaanites.

On the other hand, Noah blesses his two other children. Shem, who is the ancestor of the Israelites among others (see Gen 10 for the descendants of all three children of Noah), will be the master of Canaan. Japheth and his descendants too will benefit from the subjugation of Canaan. With this episode, the story (*toledot*) of Noah comes to an end.

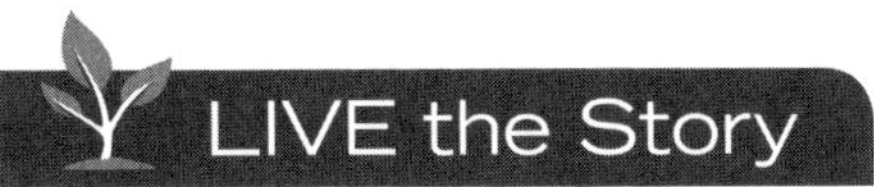


### Honor Your Father and Your Mother (Exod 20:12)

God had just judged the whole earth because of pervasive and deeply ingrained human sin. Only Noah and his family survived because of Noah's righteousness. In the aftermath of the flood, God established a covenant with all creation through Noah, a covenant which might be called a re-creation covenant because, in a sense, the receding flood waters led to what might be called a second creation with Noah as the new first man. This reading of the material is encouraged by all the intertextual echoes between the immediate post-flood narrative and Genesis 1–2 (see Situating the Noahic Covenant in the Live the Story section following 6:1–9:17).

With this understanding, Genesis 9:18–28 stands in the place of the story of Adam and Eve's rebellion, though perhaps not exactly. Above we have argued that Noah is not the sinner in this story. That said, he is a fool in that he lost all capacity in his drunken stupor, leaving himself open to mistreatment at the hands of his son Ham.

We find the sinner proper in Ham and his sin is to dishonor his father. We above cited an Ugaritic text to show that Ham's shameful behavior was condemned even in the broader culture, but of course even more relevant are God's values on the matter. While the Ten Commandments come much later in history, they articulate God's standards and for this reason the fifth commandment is relevant as we evaluate the story of Noah's drunkenness for our lives today. In his actions, Ham violated God's command to "honor your father and your mother, so that you may live long in the land the Lord your God is giving you" (Exod 20:12).

This commandment does not call on children to obey their parents at all times. After all, parents may ask their children to do sinful, godless things and when they do, they should be resisted. But in all things children must honor their parents. Ham is a good example of a person who does not honor his parent and the punishment should encourage readers to seek to honor their parents.

**Misusing Alcohol**

We have argued that the focus of this story is on the sin of Ham, who does not honor his parent (the fifth commandment), not on the Noah's abuse of alcohol. Indeed, nowhere in Scripture is the use of alcohol prohibited.

As a matter of fact, a quick and very selective survey of biblical passages where we find the mention of wine supports the idea that wine is not inherently evil, but actually a blessing. A little later in the book of Genesis, we will see that the priest-king Melchizedek will share bread and wine with Abram (Gen 14:18). Jacob (pretending to be Esau) will prepare a meal including wine for his father Isaac who will then bless his son that God will provide him "an abundance of grain and new wine" (Gen 27:28). In Jacob's deathbed blessing of Judah whose eyes he describes as "darker than wine" (Gen 49:12), he describes him as tethering his "donkey to a vine" and washing "his garments in wine, his robes in the blood of grapes" (49:11). The law encourages offerings of wine to God as a drink offering (Exod 29:40; Lev 23:13; Num 15:5, 7, 10; 18:12; 28:14). According to Proverbs, those who honor God with their wealth will find that their "vats will brim over with new wine" (3:10). Woman Wisdom, who represents Yahweh's wisdom, indeed, Yahweh himself, prepares a feast that includes wine (Prov 9:2) for all the men who seek her. The man in the Song of Songs praises the love of the woman even more than the delight of wine (1:2). The psalmist praises God who has given us "wine that gladdens human hearts" (104:15). In the New Testament Jesus turns water into wine, indeed very good wine (John 2:1 – 12). Paul advises Timothy to drink wine to calm his stomach (1 Tim 5:23).

Thus, it is important to realize that the Bible is positive about the benefits of alcoholic drinks, but it is also crucial to understand that, like many good things, overuse or addiction can be a serious problem. Proverbs clearly speaks to the issue warning about addiction and the problems of drinking too much (20:1; 21:17; 23:19 – 21, 29 – 35; 31:1 – 9). Kings in particular need to be wary of the effects of alcohol since it might dull their decision-making ability (31:4), though it is seen as a benefit for those whose lives are hard (31:6).

There are only two groups for which the consumption of alcohol is prohibited: priests who are on duty at the sanctuary (Lev 10:9) and Nazirites during the period of their vow of consecration (Num 6:1–21). For the rest of us, the moderate consumption of alcohol is a matter of wisdom not of law.

It is in this light that we see Noah's fault (and later Lot's, see Gen 19:30–38). Unlike Boaz who drank enough to be "in good spirits" (Ruth 3:7; a biblical idiom for [slightly] intoxicated) but retain his decision-making capability when Ruth offered herself to him on the threshing floor, Noah (and Lot in the later story) drank so much he did not even realize what was happening to him.

It is quite wrong to condemn people who drink alcohol because they partake of God's good gifts, but it is also wrong to condemn people who decide not to drink alcohol. After all, some people have a propensity to addiction and they should stay far away from temptation. Others may decide for strategic ministry reasons not to drink. I had the enormous privilege of having lunch many years ago with Billy Graham, a well-known Christian evangelist, when the waiter (mistakenly) put a cocktail in front of me. Seeing my discomfort when I told the waiter that the drink was not mine, Dr. Graham calmly said he saw nothing wrong biblically with drinking, but that he would not do so for ministry reasons. For him that was a decision reached through the exercise of wisdom, not the application of law.

CHAPTER 8

# Genesis 10:1 – 11:26

## LISTEN to the Story

This is the account of Shem, Ham and Japheth, Noah's sons, who themselves had sons after the flood.

[2]The sons of Japheth:

Gomer, Magog, Madai, Javan, Tubal, Meshek and Tiras.

[3]The sons of Gomer:

Ashkenaz, Riphath and Togarmah.

[4]The sons of Javan:

Elishah, Tarshish, the Kittites and the Rodanites. [5](From these the maritime peoples spread out into their territories by their clans within their nations, each with its own language.)

[6]The sons of Ham:

Cush, Egypt, Put and Canaan.

[7]The sons of Cush:

Seba, Havilah, Sabtah, Raamah and Sabteka.

The sons of Raamah:

Sheba and Dedan.

[8]Cush was the father of Nimrod, who became a mighty warrior on
the earth. [9]He was a mighty hunter before the LORD; that is why it is said,
"Like Nimrod, a mighty hunter before the LORD." [10]The first centers of
his kingdom were Babylon, Uruk, Akkad and Kalneh, in Shinar. [11]From
that land he went to Assyria, where he built Nineveh, Rehoboth Ir,
Calah [12]and Resen, which is between Nineveh and Calah—which is
the great city.

[13]Egypt was the father of

the Ludites, Anamites, Lehabites, Naphtuhites, [14]Pathrusites,
Kasluhites (from whom the Philistines came) and Caphtorites.

[15]Canaan was the father of

Sidon his firstborn, and of the Hittites, [16]Jebusites, Amorites,
Girgashites, [17]Hivites, Arkites, Sinites, [18]Arvadites, Zemarites and
Hamathites.

Later the Canaanite clans scattered [19]and the borders of Canaan reached from Sidon toward Gerar as far as Gaza, and then toward Sodom, Gomorrah, Admah and Zeboyim, as far as Lasha.

[20]These are the sons of Ham by their clans and languages, in their territories and nations.

[21]Sons were also born to Shem, whose older brother was Japheth; Shem was the ancestor of all the sons of Eber.

[22]The sons of Shem:

Elam, Ashur, Arphaxad, Lud and Aram.

[23]The sons of Aram:

Uz, Hul, Gether and Meshek.

[24]Arphaxad was the father of Shelah,

and Shelah the father of Eber.

[25]Two sons were born to Eber:

One was named Peleg, because in his time the earth was divided; his brother was named Joktan.

[26]Joktan was the father of

Almodad, Sheleph, Hazarmaveth, Jerah, [27]Hadoram, Uzal, Diklah, [28]Obal, Abimael, Sheba, [29]Ophir, Havilah and Jobab. All these were sons of Joktan.

[30]The region where they lived stretched from Mesha toward Sephar, in the eastern hill country.

[31]These are the sons of Shem by their clans and languages, in their territories and nations.

[32]These are the clans of Noah's sons, according to their lines of descent, within their nations. From these the nations spread out over the earth after the flood.

[11:1]Now the whole world had one language and a common speech. [2]As people moved eastward, they found a plain in Shinar and settled there.

[3]They said to each other, "Come, let's make bricks and bake them thoroughly." They used brick instead of stone, and tar for mortar. [4]Then they said, "Come, let us build ourselves a city, with a tower that reaches to the heavens, so that we may make a name for ourselves; otherwise we will be scattered over the face of the whole earth."

[5]But the Lord came down to see the city and the tower the people were building. [6]The Lord said, "If as one people speaking the same language they have begun to do this, then nothing they plan to do will be impossible for them. [7]Come, let us go down and confuse their language so they will not understand each other."

8So the LORD scattered them from there over all the earth, and they
stopped building the city. 9That is why it was called Babel—because
there the LORD confused the language of the whole world. From there the
LORD scattered them over the face of the whole earth.

10This is the account of Shem's family line.

Two years after the flood, when Shem was 100 years old, he became
the father of Arphaxad. 11And after he became the father of Arphaxad,
Shem lived 500 years and had other sons and daughters.

12When Arphaxad had lived 35 years, he became the father of Shelah.
13And after he became the father of Shelah, Arphaxad lived 403 years and
had other sons and daughters.

14When Shelah had lived 30 years, he became the father of Eber.
15And after he became the father of Eber, Shelah lived 403 years and had
other sons and daughters.

16When Eber had lived 34 years, he became the father of Peleg. 17And
after he became the father of Peleg, Eber lived 430 years and had other
sons and daughters.

18When Peleg had lived 30 years, he became the father of Reu. 19And
after he became the father of Reu, Peleg lived 209 years and had other
sons and daughters.

20When Reu had lived 32 years, he became the father of Serug. 21And
after he became the father of Serug, Reu lived 207 years and had other
sons and daughters.

22When Serug had lived 30 years, he became the father of Nahor.
23And after he became the father of Nahor, Serug lived 200 years and had
other sons and daughters.

24When Nahor had lived 29 years, he became the father of Terah.
25And after he became the father of Terah, Nahor lived 119 years and had
other sons and daughters.

26After Terah had lived 70 years, he became the father of Abram,
Nahor and Haran.

*Listen to the Story in the Text:* Biblical Text: Genesis 3–9; Ancient Near Eastern Texts: Genealogies; Enmerkar and the Lord of Aratta

The story of the tower of Babel which speaks of God's division of human speech into different languages and the preceding chapter that describes the languages of the world is the last of the four stories (the fall, Cain and Abel, the flood) that treats human sin and divine judgment and grace. As we will see below, it also anticipates the call of Abraham as God's strategy for addressing the evil of the world.

Genesis 10 is in the form of a genealogy though it functions as a kind of linguistic map and guide to the nations of the world. For more on ancient genealogies see the Listening to the Text in the Story section before Genesis 4:17–5:32.

The Sumerian myth of Enmerkar and the Lord of Aratta is the account of two monarchs, both loved by the goddess Inanna, but engaged in a struggle for dominance. The text as we have it now begins with a passage often called "Nudimmud's (another name for the god of wisdom, Enki) spell." This text mentions a time when there was "but a single tongue." Some interpreters[1] believe this looks back to a primeval time similar to an earlier period before the introduction of languages and thus is often compared to the tower of Babel story. However, it is not clear that the text refers to the past, it might refer to a future blessed time; thus we should not make too much of this connection.[2]

## EXPLAIN the Story

The previous section focused on Noah's sons and one grandson and concluded the *toledot* of Noah (started in 6:9). Genesis 10:1 begins the *toledot* ("account") of the three sons (Shem, Ham, and Japheth) and like all *toledot*, this one focuses in on the descendants of the person or people named in the formula. Thus, we are not surprised that Genesis 10 delineates the descendants of the three sons of Noah.

But what precisely is the purpose of Genesis 10? The form of the chapter is that of a segmented, as opposed to a linear, genealogy,[3] that is, each generation gives more than one descendant. But the content suggests that rather than an interest in descent this chapter intends to comment on ancient perceptions of national and linguistic relationships. As Walton points out, "kinship language is sometimes used in the Bible to reflect political associations (1 Kgs 9:13)."[4]

---

1. See Jacobsen (*COS* 1:547).

2. See the full description of the debate over this text and its relationship to Genesis 11:1–9 in Walton, "Genesis," 64.

3. The terminology and explanation of segmented and linear genealogies may be found in Wilson, *Genealogy and History*.

4. Walton, "Genesis," 56.

This purpose may be seen in the refrain repeated with slight variation at the end of the three sections of the chapter: "by their clans and languages, in their territories and nations," vv. 5, 20, 31. Each section focuses on the "sons" of one of the children of Noah. In Genesis, the sons are always listed in the following order: Shem, Ham, and Japheth; however, it is likely that Japheth is the oldest (10:21, but see NIV note) and Ham is the youngest (Gen 9:24). If Japheth, Shem, and Ham reflects the sons' actual age order, the order Japheth, Ham, and then Shem in this chapter may be the result of wanting to treat the most important (since Israel descends from Shem) last.

Of course, it is theoretically possible, though unlikely, that this ancient linguistic, national map also intends to be a genealogy. That is, that these are actual descendants of these three sons of Noah, who are the founding fathers of nations (and ultimately languages). If so, it is odd that not only people are found in this "genealogy" but also nations (i.e., "the Kittites and the Rodanites," v. 4). In any case, what is important to bear in mind is that these are, as mentioned above, perceptions, not realities, of linguistic and national relationships (as Walton points out, Canaanite is Semitic, not Hamitic [10:6]).[5] It is true that when modern linguistics began some two centuries ago, it adopted its fundamental terminology from this chapter, which persists until today. We still speak of S(h)emitic, Hamitic, and Japhethic languages today. That said, modern linguistics would not make the same connections between languages that are presented in this chapter.

Since medieval times and unfortunately up to the present day, the division of the humanity into these three groups has been abused by being applied to racial politics, with Hamites being described as black races from Africa, Japhetites as white and European, and S(h)emites as Semitic people in Asia. Further, European and other slave traders justified their horrific practices by saying that Ham was cursed (though the account in 9:18–28 does not indicate this) and pointing to Genesis 9:27, which announces that God would extend Japheth's territory. Such views have been thoroughly discredited and rightly condemned.

In terms of the story line, Genesis 10 is clearly not in chronological order with Genesis 11:1–9. Here, as mentioned, we have a primitive linguistic map, but according to the tower of Babel story to follow, there was only one language up to that point in time. As we will see, 10:25 seems to allude to the division of languages, but still the message of Genesis 10 fits chronologically in the narrative after Genesis 11:1–9.

We should further point out that there are seventy descendants in this chapter, each reflecting a later national/linguistic entity. This number fits with

5. Ibid., 55.

later Israelite ideas that there were seventy nations in the world. The number seventy stands for completion or totality.

This "genealogy" is really a primitive linguistic, political map that reflects realties of a later time, certainly no earlier than the time of Moses. Walton is correct to say that "this group of seventy does not reflect the perspective of Noah's generation; rather, it is Israel's perspective at the time of the author, Moses." We should also "note that there is no discussion of anyone outside the known world of the ancient Near East in the middle of the second millennium. The text only seeks to account for groups the Israelites were aware of and does not hint at a world beyond the ancient Near East. In other words, the author has not attempted to provide a comprehensive list of all people(s) descended from the sons of Noah. Instead, he has addressed how all the known peoples and nations of his day are related to the sons of Noah."[6] These connections are drawn from perceptions, and should not be confused with a scientific analysis of language.

### The Japhethites (10:2–5; see also 1 Chr 1:5–7)

Japheth has seven sons. Outside of the repetition of the list in 1 Chronicles, other Bible passages mention some of them. Ezekiel 38 mentions the land of Magog along with Gomer (v. 6), Meshek, and Tubal (vv. 2, 3; 39:1). Meshek and Tubal are also mentioned along with Javan in Ezekiel 27:13 and together (in Sheol) in Ezekiel 32:26. Meshek is also mentioned in Psalm 120:5 along with Kedar an Arabian tribe, but it is not that they are located in the same place, but rather that they both are far, far from Israel.

In terms of location, there is only one relative certainty and that is that Javan stands for the Greeks, or more specifically Ionian Greeks (see also Isa 66:19; Ezek 27:13, 19). The best guess and the general consensus is that the other names represent peoples who live north of Israel and other ancient Semitic peoples in Anatolia and northern Asia. Proposed identifications are made between Gomer and the Cimmerians (known in the second millennium BC in southern Russia and threatening Assyria in the seventh century BC), Magog and what is today part of Turkey, Tubal and Cilicia. Madai and Tiras only appear in Genesis 10 and 1 Chronicles 1, but identifications are proposed based on name association with Medes and the Turscha Sea Peoples respectively.

Verses 3 and 4 give the descendants of Gomer and Javan. Gomer's descendants are Ashkenaz, Riphath, and Togarmah. Ashekenaz is mentioned again only in Jeremiah 51:27, along with Ararat (Urartu) and Minni (Manneans)

6. Walton, "Genesis," 55–56.

located near Lakes Van and Urmia in northeastern Asia Minor. Riphath is only mentioned in Genesis 10 and 1 Chronicles 1 (there Diphath, due to confusion between the similar looking *resh* and *dalet* in Hebrew). Togarmah should be identified with Beth Togarmah mentioned in Ezekiel 27:14, right after Javan, Tubal, and Meshek as well as in Ezekiel 38:6 where it is described as "from the far north" and in alliance with Gomer.

Javan's (Greece) sons are Elishah, Tarshish, the Kittites, and the Rodanites, the first two being individuals and the latter two people groups. Elishah, located generally in the Aegean, is also mentioned in Ezekiel 27:7 as producers of blue and purple awnings and having coasts. Tarshish occurs often in the Bible and is typically identified with Tartessos in southern Spain. The Kittites (see Num 24:24; Jer 2:10) are often connected to Cyprus. The Rodanites are not otherwise mentioned in the Bible, but by sound association are often connected to the island of Rhodes in the Aegean (though a variant has Dodanim).

### The Hamites (Gen 10:6–20; 1 Chr 1:8–16)

The second section of the "genealogy" of Genesis 10 is devoted to the descendants of the disgraced son of Noah, Ham (Gen 9:18–27). 1 Chronicles 1:8–16 replicates the genealogy with the exception of the prose expansions found in 10:9–12 and 18b–20. Ham's descendants are associated with Egyptians, Canaanites, Philistines, Babylonians, and Assyrians. By modern standards there is neither linguistic nor political connection between all these entities, but they are a list of Israel's most vicious enemies through the Old Testament time period.

The list begins by naming the four sons of Ham (Cush, Egypt, Put, and Canaan) and then following the sons' descendants (with the exception of Put) one by one, beginning with Cush. Cush is well-known throughout the Old Testament, occurring about fifty times in reference to a region south of Egypt. In many of these instances, English translations will render Cush as Ethiopia or Nubia. The fact that Cush's brother is Egypt naturally makes one think that such a southern association is intended here.

However, Cush's son Nimrod is clearly associated not with Egypt but with Mesopotamia, since "the first centers of his kingdom were Babylon, Uruk, Akkad and Kalneh, in Shinar" (well-known cities southern Mesopotamia) and then according to verses 11–12, he went on to establish cities in northern Mesopotamia (Nineveh, Rehoboth Ir, and Resen). Indeed, Assyria is called the "land of Nimrod" in Micah 5:6. To further complicate matters, Cush's other sons (Seba, Havilah, Sabtah, Raamah, Sabteka) as well as the sons of Raamah (Sheba and Dedan) are all either Arabian tribes or in the Re(e)d Sea area or south of Egypt.

The identity of Nimrod is also problematic. His name is often thought to be connected to the Hebrew verb for rebellion (*mrd*). He is called a "mighty warrior on the earth" and a "mighty hunter before the LORD" and, as mentioned, connected to southern Mesopotamia and establishing northern Mesopotamia. Theories abound (leading contenders are Sargon the Great, Shulgi, or Hammurabi, though there are problems with each[7]), and we cannot arrive with certainty at identifications of people who may have served as an inspiration of this figure. We can say that Mesopotamian kings were often pictured not only as great warriors but also hunters, typically of lions. According to Niehaus, "we find in Nimrod the very type of the ancient near eastern emperor: a man who is mighty in battle, skilled in the hunt, a builder of cities, and a ruler of nations. The impression (or hoped for impression) is that he is all that a man should be — virtually a god — and of course many ancient rulers claimed divine or semidivine status."[8]

In early Jewish and Christian interpretation, Nimrod was also thought to be the builder of the tower of Babel. There is of course no direct biblical indication of this connection, but it is thought to be implied by the fact that, according to one possible rendering of 10:10, the "beginning of his kingdom" is Babylon. It also explains why he had to leave Babylon to found the other cities.[9]

The second son of Ham is Egypt (Mizraim), of course pointing to the powerful nations that towered over other civilizations beginning at the end of the fourth millennium and waxing and waning throughout the Old Testament period. Egypt's children are people groups not individuals. The Ludites here (as opposed to v. 22) are connected to African nations (also Jer 46:9; Ezek 30:5). Verse 13 associates the Kasluhites with the Philistines and other texts make the same connection for the Caphtorites (Deut 2:23; Jer 47:4; Amos 9:7). It is thought that the Philistines were from the Aegean, making the Egyptian connection here questionable, but some speculate that the origins of the Philistines began in Egypt before they emigrated to the Aegean and then later, as part of the Sea People's movement, came to the eastern coast of the Mediterranean.

Ham's third son is Canaan, the cursed one (9:18 – 27). Canaan, of course, is Israel's later foe, occupants of the promised land as well as regions north of that. Canaanites did not have any genetic connection to Egypt, but often, as on the eve of the conquest, had a political relationship with that great nation,

---

7. For an accessible and thorough discussion of options, see Walton, "Genesis," 57 – 59.

8. Niehaus, *Biblical Theology*, 233.

9. See Kugel (*The Bible as It Was*, 123 – 27), who cites Jewish sources (Philo, Pseudo-Philo, Targum Neophyti, Josephus) and Christian (Jerome and Augustine).

reminding us that this "genealogy" is more a political and linguistic map than one that shows genetic relationships.

Many of the people groups said to be sons of Canaan are the various ethnic entities said to occupy the promised land at the time of the conquest (Hittites, Jebusites, Amorites, Girgashites, Hivites). Sidon, the firstborn son, is connected to the great Canaanite city of that name north of Israel with Arvad north of that. The Hamathites are probably the inhabitants of the Hittite city Hamath in Syria between Damascus and Aleppo. We can assume that the Sinites and Zemarites are in the same region north of the later Israel

Finally, as mentioned, Ham's son Put is the only one who does not have a further genealogy. Elsewhere in Scripture, though, Put is an African nation associated with Egypt and typically identified as Libya.

Verses 18b–19 describe Canaanite expansion until they filled the region from Sidon in the north and then down toward the later Philistine city of Gerar as far as Gaza in the south (bordering Egypt). The infamous "cities of the plain," which would later be destroyed at the time of Abraham (Sodom, Gomorrah, Adman, Zeboyim) and typically located somewhere in the vicinity of the Dead Sea, are the eastern boundary of the Canaanites; the western boundary is assumed to be the Mediterranean coast.

### The Sethites and Summary Statement (Gen 10:21–32; 1 Chr 1:17–20)

We have earlier pointed out that Shem is most likely the middle son of Noah, but he is treated climactically last here since he is the ancestor of Abraham, the chosen one (see Gen 12:1–3). 1 Chronicles 1:17–20 repeats Genesis 10:22–29 verbatim. Genesis 11:10–26, a linear genealogy, contains those elements of the present Shem genealogy, a segmented genealogy, that lead to Abraham.

The present account of the genealogy of Shem begins with an introductory note that, according to the best understanding of the grammar, he was the younger brother of Japheth (though see the NIV variant in the footnote). According to Genesis 9:24, Ham was Noah's youngest son, thus indicating that Shem was the middle son. By mentioning that Shem was the ancestor of Eber (whom we will learn is the ancestor of Abraham [Gen 11:10–26]), the introduction informs the reader that relative importance is the reason for Shem coming third in the genealogy.

Verse 22 presents the five sons of Shem, all but Arphaxad representing a later well-known nation, but not without some confusion in the case of Ashur and Lud. Elam is the patronym of the Elamite nation that was located in what is today southwest Iran and was a frequent rival to Mesopotamian powers in the third through first millennia BC. Elam is mentioned in the

Bible beginning in Genesis 14 where one of the four Near Eastern kings is Kedorlaomer king of Elam (see also Ezra 4:9; Isa 11:11; 21:2; 22:6, etc.).

Ashur certainly is to be understood as the patronym of the great Assyrian empire that dominated the ancient Near East off and on between the middle of the second millennium BC down to the end of the seventh century BC. Some confusion results from the earlier mention of Nimrod as the one who built the great cities of Assyria (v. 11), but there is no doubt that Assyria was a S(h)emitic kingdom, not a Hamitic one.

For the moment, we skip Arphaxad, whose genealogy is furthered in segmented form in verses 24–28 to go to Lud. We already noted that a group known as the Ludites is connected with the Hamitic line (see v. 13). This group may be an African tribe, while the present figure could be the Lydians of Asia Minor, though this connection seems strange because that group is not S(h)emitic.

We again skip Arphaxad to speak of the fifth son Aram, whose name is later given to the Aramaic tribes of Syria and with whom Israel had conflict beginning at the time of David. Aram is the only son besides Arphaxad whose genealogy is extended beyond his time and here only one generation with the mention of his four sons. The first is Uz. While reminiscent with the name of Job's hometown (Job 1:1), the latter is in Edom, not an Aramaic region.[10] Genesis 22:21 mentions another Uz also connected to Aram. Two other sons of Aram are Hul and Gether, about whom nothing additional is known. The NIV names the fourth son Meshek (similar to a Japhethite descendant listed above), but the Hebrew has Mash (see NIV footnote).

The third listed son, Arphaxad, is the only one which is not a patronymic of a later nation, though his line leads eventually to Israel. Verses 24–28 carry forward his genealogy beginning with Shelah. Interestingly, the Septuagint places Cainan between Arphaxad and Shelah and the genealogy of Jesus in Luke 3 follows that order.

Shelah's son Eber has already been mentioned in connection with the introductory verse 21. The importance of Eber is the likelihood that the name Hebrew derives from his name.

Eber's two sons are named Peleg and Joktan. According to verse 25, the name Peleg, which means "division," comes from the fact that "in his time the earth was divided." This division likely refers to the story of the tower of Babel (Gen 11:1–9), where humans' ability to speak was fragmented into different languages. Though the passage dwells on the significance of Peleg's name, the genealogy continues with Joktan, who has thirteen sons (vv. 27–29).

---

10. Longman, *Job*, 78–79.

Only three of the son's names are found elsewhere in Scripture. Sheba is the kingdom whose queen came to experience Solomon's wisdom (1 Kgs 10:1–13; 2 Chr 9:1–12) and is mentioned elsewhere. This kingdom was located in southern Arabia, though it is hard to be certain whether the identification is with this Sheba or the one mentioned in the Hamitic genealogy (v. 7). Ophir is also often mentioned as a gold-producing area elsewhere in Scripture (1 Kgs 9:26–28; 2 Chr 8:18, and elsewhere). While scholars sometimes place Ophir in southern Arabia, this identification is speculative. Havilah is one of the four named areas of the garden of Eden (Gen 2:11–12). It too is often speculatively said to be located in southern Arabia. Jobab is not mentioned elsewhere in Scripture, but in some ancient tradition is erroneously identified with Job.[11]

These thirteen sons and the peoples who descend from them are said to dwell between Mesha and Sephar in the eastern hill country (v. 30), but these locations are otherwise unknown. Verse 31 provides a simple concluding statement for the Shem genealogy and then verse 32 is a summary statement for the entire chapter.

### The Tower of Babel (Gen 11:1–9)

We first note that this passage on language is an example of profound literary artistry and intricate design.[12] There are a number of striking word plays in the story. Certain word groups are bound together by their similar sound: "let's make bricks" (*nilbenah lebenim*); "bake them thoroughly" (*nisrepa serepa*); "tar" and "mortar" (*hemar/homer*). There is also alliteration between "brick" (*lebenah*) and "for stone" (*leaben*). These nearly similar sounds give the story a rhythmic quality that draws the reader's attention not only to the content of the words but to the words themselves.

Other repeated words also sound alike: "name" (*shem*), "there/that place" (*sham*), and "heaven" (*shamayim*). "The place" (*sham*) is what the rebels use as a base for storming "heaven" (*shamayim*) in order to get a "name" (*shem*) for themselves. God, however, reverses the situation because it is "from there" (v. 8) that he disperses the rebels and foils their plans. The ironic reversal of the rebels' evil intentions is highlighted in more than one way by the artistic choice of words. There are a number of words and phrases that appear in the story with the consonant cluster *lbn*, all referring to the human rebellion against God. When God comes in judgment, he confuses (*nbl*) their language. The reversal of the consonants shows the reversal that God's judgment

11. Ibid., 39–40.

12. The following description relies on the analysis of J. P. Fokkelmann, *Narrative Art in Genesis*, Studia Semitica Neerlandica 17 (Assen and Amsterdam: Van Gorcum, 1975).

effected in the plans of the rebels. This reversal is also reflected in Fokkelman's analysis of the chiastic structure of the story:

A 11:1
B 11:2
C 11:3a
D 11:3b
E 11:4a
F 11:4b
X 11:5a "But the LORD came down"
F' 11:5b
E' 11:5c
D' 11:6
C' 11:7
B' 11:8
A' 11:9

Unity of language (A) and place (B) and intense communication (C) induce the people to plans and inventions (D), especially to building (E) a city and a tower (F). God's intervention is the turning point (X). He watches the buildings (F') people make (E') and launches a counter plan (D') because of which communication becomes impossible (C') and the unity of place (B') and language (A') are broken. Literary artistry here is at the service of the message of the passage, which we will now explore further.

The story begins at a time when there was only a single language shared by all humanity. God had earlier punished Cain by making him a wanderer (Gen 4:10–14), though his son is said to have built the first city (Gen 4:17). The people envisioned in 11:1–2 were not yet settled, but were wandering eastward. The eastward direction may pick up on the expulsion from Eden to the east (where the cherubim were stationed) and then Cain's further expulsion to the east of Eden (though we are not certain where Eden was thought to be located); however, it may be using Israel as a fixed point so the text is saying that they are moving east from where Israel is later located.[13]

The most important point, though, is that this scattered people start working together in order to settle down. While this attempt may sound like a good idea to us today, it was not something that pleased God. First of all, they were working against his decreed punishment, but, in addition, we should realize that there was an element of grace to God's punishment. They

13. A further complication is that the Hebrew may be translated "from the east" or "in the east" (see NIV note).

were sinners, and bringing sinners together does not solve, but rather magnifies, the sin problem. So here their corporate efforts are to be understood as an act of rebellion against God, so God takes steps to prevent it.

The place where they chose to settle is a plain in Shinar, Shinar being another name for Babylon. Thus, the reference is to the alluvial plain between the Tigris and the Euphrates in what would come to be known as southern Mesopotamia.

They decide to build a city with a tower where they have settled, using building materials typical for this region, mudbrick and tar, rather than stone and mortar. The tower is described as one that "reaches to the heavens." What kind of structure would this be? The best answer is likely a ziggurat, a stepped pyramid, once again well-known for this region. "These stepped structures were built in Babylonian cities to replicate the concept of a sacred mountain where human and divinity could commune."[14] The most famous Babylonian ziggurat was located in the city of Babylon and had the name *E-temen-an-ki*, which translated from the Sumerian means "the house of the foundation of heaven and earth." In short, this tower was where earth touched heaven; in this sense, it is correct to see this building as a type of assault on heaven. It certainly was an act of hubris. The purpose of the city and the tower was to prevent scattering, but also to "make a name" for the builders. "Name" can be translated reputation.

As mentioned above, the turning point for this story comes in verse 5, when the Lord takes note of the city and the tower. He then turns to the divine council (see discussion at 1:26), where he enlists their aid in confusing the people's language, thus making their communication difficult.

Once their language is confused, they are unable to carry out their intentions and they begin to scatter again. Interestingly, the narrator connects the name of Babylon (Babel) with this event. He claims that the name derives from the confusion of their language based on the similarity in sound between the name Babel and the verb "to confuse" (*balal*). Of course, the narrator/author was fully aware that this explanation was pejorative and not the actual description of how the name came about. Babel is not Hebrew, but Akkadian and derives from the phrase *bab-ilu* which means "gate of the gods."

The tower of Babel account shares the same basic structure as all the major narratives since the story of Adam and Eve's rebellion. It is the story of human sin. In this case, the sin involves the attempt to make a name for themselves by building a city and a tower that reaches to heaven. They act out of pride and put themselves in the place of God who is the one who builds reputations as

14. J. McKeown, *Genesis*, The Two Horizons Old Testament Commentary (Grand Rapids: Eerdmans, 2008), 71.

he promises he will do for Abraham (see Gen 12:2, "I will make your name great").[15] They also try to circumvent his earlier punishments, which we saw included an element of grace, by resisting his call that they should wander.

As in the previous stories, God does not let human sin pass without punishment. He begins with a judgment speech, found in verses 6–7, where he announces his intention to confuse their language, and that is why the passage ends with a description of God's execution of the judgment (vv. 8–9). These elements, we have seen, recur in the previous narratives that recount Adam and Eve's rebellion (Gen 3), Cain and Abel (Gen 4), and the flood (Gen 6:1–9:17).

At first glance, however, a fourth element seems to be missing, namely a token of grace. Where is the token of grace in the tower of Babel story? It is chapter 10, which we have seen is found before Genesis 11, but it is clearly not in chronological order. Genesis 10 must follow Genesis 11:1–9 temporally because Genesis 10 describes the world broken up into language groups.

And here we find the token of grace—languages. After all, God could have simply put an end to all language, effectively abolishing the possibility of human communication. But he does not do this. Communication becomes much, much harder, but it is possible even across linguistic barriers. By preserving the possibility of communication through languages God not only allows for humans to speak to humans, but also for divine-human communication.

Still, though we can rightly speak of languages as the token of grace to the tower of Babel story, we must also recognize that this is the only one of the four stories in Genesis 3–11 where the token of grace is not found in the story itself. Indeed, we should inquire as to why the indication of languages comes before (Gen 10) rather than after the tower of Babel story.

The best explanation is that the tower of Babel story is the last of the primeval narratives. At the end of this first major section of Genesis there is no solution to the sin problem. In God's timing, he introduces something new, and that something new involves a man named Abraham and his wife Sarah.

## From Shem to Abraham (11:10–26)

The primeval history ends with yet another genealogy. The primary purpose of this genealogy is to serve as a bridge between the first two major parts

15. Contra the recent reading of T. Hiebert ("The Tower of Babel and the Origin of the World's Culture," *JBL* 126 [2007]: 29–58), which argues that God is not punishing sin, but rather working to achieve his goal of cultural diversity against the human desire for "identity and cultural solidarity" (58). He achieves this reading by taking the story (which he regards as part of the J source) and reading it independently of its final form.

of the book of Genesis, the primeval history and the patriarchal narratives. While the primeval history has focused on the whole world, the patriarchal narratives will narrow that focus to a single man, namely Abraham, and his descendants. Thus, it is fitting that the final genealogy will lead from Shem, Noah's son, to Abraham.

If this genealogy is taken literally and as an exhaustive account of the line, Shem, Noah's son, lived forty years beyond the death of Abraham. Indeed, Abraham would have been two years old when Noah died. This is not likely, though such a stilted reading of the text is supported by some.[16] Ancient genealogies did not function like modern ones and are often constructed for literary and theological purposes rather than historical ones.[17] The genealogy also has ten names, also suggestive of literary shaping.

The first part of this genealogy covers the same ground as the genealogy of Seth in 10:21–29 and its parallel in 1 Chronicles 1:17–23, but this genealogy is a linear one that goes from father to a single son (constructed similarly to the genealogy in Gen 5) rather than giving multiple descendants in a single generation (a segmented genealogy).Thus, the genealogy moves from Shem to Arhpaxad to Shelah to Eber to Peleg. It is with Peleg's genealogy that we observe divergence for the earlier genealogy (see also 1 Chr 1:24–27). In Genesis 10 Eber's two sons are mentioned, Peleg and Joktan. The genealogy extends to the next generation by enumerating the offspring of Joktan, ignoring Peleg except to explain the meaning of his name. Here the narrator is interested in Peleg because his line leads to Abraham through Reu, Serug, Nahor, and Terah. Interestingly, the final generation of this genealogy is presented in segmented form. Terah's sons are Abram, Nahor, and Haran. Thus, the genealogy prepares us for the account (*toledot*) of Terah, which focuses on Abra(ha)m.

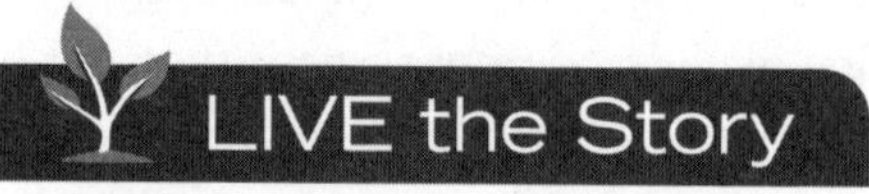


### The Problem of Communication

The tower of Babel story recounts the ancient time when there was a single language. Of course, we live in a world that has thousands of languages, so many we don't know the exact number and it depends on how you count them.

We are so used to the multiple languages of the world that we don't often reflect on the difficulties that arise from the fact that all human beings do not

16. J. Davis, "Unresolved Major Questions: Evangelicals and Genesis 1–2," in *Reading Genesis 1–2: An Evangelical Conversation*, ed. J. D. Charles (Peabody, MA: Hendrickson, 2013), 220.

17. See the Listening to the Text in the Story section before 4:17–5:32.

share the ability to communicate with each other. Not that a single language would eradicate all communication problems, after all consider how often we can misunderstand someone speaking to us in our native language (and this too may be a result of the sin recorded in the tower of Babel story), but the presence of many languages intensifies the problem.

While we could explore this issue from many angles (for instance the problems that result in business, politics, or everyday communication), let's consider just one example, namely the Bible itself. The existence of many languages makes our understanding of the Bible more complex, thus providing an important illustration of how sin has affected our lives.

The Bible is written in ancient Hebrew and Greek with a few chapters of the Old Testament in Aramaic. However, the vast majority of the world's population are not native speakers of these languages (and even those who do speak them speak modern forms). They must be translated into the thousands of languages of the world for them to be understood.

While the Bible, or at least the New Testament, has been translated into the world's major languages, there are still many that do not yet have a translation of any part of the Bible.[18] But even in a language like English, in which there are many versions of the whole Bible, the need for a translation poses problems for communication. In brief, as the saying goes, something is always "lost in translation." No two languages perfectly line up with each other, and this observation is true with English and the three biblical languages.

Now it is important to affirm the point that translators of the Bible would assure readers that no major teaching of the Bible is affected by these translation issues, but they would also admit that nuances of words, especially rare ones, are sometimes not known and often not able to be replicated as we move from the biblical languages to English or any other living language. My point here is not to fully explore all the implications of the existence of multiple languages for Bible translation, but rather simply to provide an example, and an important one, to readers of this commentary, as to how sin has affected our ability to communicate with each other.

### Pentecost: The Reversal of the Tower of Babel

Acts 2 recounts an amazing movement of the Holy Spirit as he fills the followers of Christ who then go out and declare "the wonders of God" (v. 11) to the people who have come from many different nations and thus language groups to celebrate the Jewish festival of Pentecost in the city of Jerusalem. Normally in a post-Babel world, the Aramaic- (and perhaps Greek-) speaking disciples

18. Thus rendering the work of Wycliffe Bible translators of continuing importance.

would not be understood by those Jews who have come to the city from Parthia, Media, Elam, and other parts of the world (see list in Acts 2:9–11), but on this marvelous day God has enabled them to speak directly to them about the gospel. What we see here is a veritable reversal of the confusion of language at the tower of Babel.

This day is best understood as a glimpse of the consummation, the day when God's redemption comes to full realization after the second coming of Christ (see Rev 21–22). This glimpse of heavenly realities should lead us to praise God and to yearn for the coming of that day. For the time being, God's people or at least some of the body of Christ continue to learn foreign languages for the purpose of effective but not perfect communication and translation.

### Tokens of Grace: God Stays Involved

We have now come to the end of the first major section of the book of Genesis, the so-called Primeval History (Gen 1–11 [more precisely 1:1–11:26]). The creation accounts (Gen 1–2) describe a world of harmony. Adam and Eve enjoy a vibrant relationship with God and also with each other and the world in which God placed them.

Human rebellion disrupts the harmony between God and humanity and thus introduces alienation among humans and also between humans and their world (Gen 3). Right from the start we learn that God judges sin. Right after Adam and Eve sinned by eating of the forbidden fruit (3:6), God announces his judgment (3:14–19) and the end of the chapter narrates how he carries out his judgment (3:22–24).

But sin and judgment do not exhaust the story of God's relationship with rebellious humanity. Before he executes his judgment, he extends a token of his grace to Adam and Eve by giving them clothing to wear to cover the nakedness about which they now experience shame because of their sin (3:21). In this way, God shows that he will stay involved with his flawed human creatures in spite of their rebellion.

Three major narratives follow the account of the fall in the primeval narrative and each one bears the same fourfold pattern. That is, they all tell the story of human sin followed by God's judgment which he announces before its execution. Though the final story (the tower of Babel) has an interesting variation on this, they also all describe God extending a token of his grace. While we have described this pattern in the Explain the Story portion of our exposition of the relevant texts, the following chart indicates the relevant texts:

| | Sin | Speech | Grace | Punishment |
|---|---|---|---|---|
| Fall | 3:6 | 3:14–19 | 3:21 | 3:22–24 |
| Cain | 4:8 | 4:11–12 | 4:15 | 4:16 |
| Flood | 6:2, 5, 11–12 | 6:7, 13–21 | 6:8, 18–21 | 7:6–24 |
| Babel | 11:4 | 11:6–7 | 10:1–32 | 11:8 |

As Christians, what do we learn about God and our relationship with him from the repetitive pattern that we see in Genesis 3–11? Actually, we learn the very same lesson that the original readers were to take from it.

We learn that we are sinners. John says as much, "If we claim to be without sin, we deceive ourselves and the truth is not in us.... If we claim we have not sinned, we make him out to be a liar and his word is not in us" (1 John 1:8, 10).

And nothing has changed in God's determination to judge sinful humanity. Christ's coming does not give sinners free passes.

However, the central message of the gospel is that God has extended the ultimate token of grace in his son Jesus Christ. John shares this wonderful news along with all the other New Testament writers. "The blood of Jesus, his Son, purifies us from all sin" (1 John 1:7), so "if we confess our sins, he is faithful and just and will forgive us our sins and purify us from all unrighteousness" (1 John 1:9).

CHAPTER 9

# Genesis 11:27 – 12:9

##  LISTEN to the Story

27This is the account of Terah's family line.

Terah became the father of Abram, Nahor and Haran. And Haran became the father of Lot. 28While his father Terah was still alive, Haran died in Ur of the Chaldeans, in the land of his birth. 29Abram and Nahor both married. The name of Abram's wife was Sarai, and the name of Nahor's wife was Milkah; she was the daughter of Haran, the father of both Milkah and Iskah. 30Now Sarai was childless because she was not able to conceive.

31Terah took his son Abram, his grandson Lot son of Haran, and his daughter-in-law Sarai, the wife of his son Abram, and together they set out from Ur of the Chaldeans to go to Canaan. But when they came to Harran, they settled there.

32Terah lived 205 years, and he died in Harran.

12:1The LORD had said to Abram, "Go from your country, your people and your father's household to the land I will show you.

2"I will make you into a great nation,
and I will bless you;
I will make your name great,
and you will be a blessing.
3I will bless those who bless you,
and whoever curses you I will curse;
and all peoples on earth
will be blessed through you."

4So Abram went, as the Lord had told him; and Lot went with him. Abram was seventy-five years old when he set out from Harran. 5He took his wife Sarai, his nephew Lot, all the possessions they had accumulated and the people they had acquired in Harran, and they set out for the land of Canaan, and they arrived there.

6Abram traveled through the land as far as the site of the great tree of Moreh at Shechem. At that time the Canaanites were in the land. 7The

Lord appeared to Abram and said, "To your offspring I will give this land." So he built an altar there to the Lord, who had appeared to him.

8 From there he went on toward the hills east of Bethel and pitched his tent, with Bethel on the west and Ai on the east. There he built an altar to the Lord and called on the name of the Lord.

9 Then Abram set out and continued toward the Negev.

*Listening to the Text in the Story:* Biblical Text: Genesis 1:4 – 11

Walter Brueggemann helpfully described 12:1 – 3 as a second creation account.[1] Whereas in the first creation account God created the cosmos and all that it contains by the power of his spoken word, here he calls a new people into being by the power of his word.

There is quite a shift in narrative focus that takes place at Genesis 11:27 (the beginning of the account [*toledot*] of Terah). Previously (1:1 – 11:26) the focus has been on the whole world; now there is a close-up on one man, Abraham. Previously narrative time moved with great rapidity, but starting with the Abraham narrative time slows down. After the introduction of human sin, God worked to reconcile all people to himself, but, as we saw, the stories of Genesis 1 – 11 (the fall, Cain and Abel, the flood, and the tower of Babel) devolved into a pattern of sin, judgment, and token of grace. God now seeks to address the sin problem and reconcile humanity to himself through the person of Abraham and the promise he will give him.

## EXPLAIN the Story

### Introducing the Family of Terah (11:27 – 32)

11:27 begins the next major section of the book of Genesis with its announcement of the "account" (*toledot*) of Terah. It is the sixth iteration of the *toledot* formula in the book (see 2:4; 5:1; 6:9; 10:1; 11:10) and, along with the *toledot* of Jacob (37:1), one of the longest since the *toledot* of Terah does not end until 25:11. Of course, as explained already, the *toledot* of someone is really the story of their immediate offspring, so the significance of the *toledot* of Terah is that the story is about his son Abraham, and the importance of Abraham to the drama of the Bible is hard to overemphasize. As Levenson puts it, up to this point God has been involved in "damage control," but now "he is making

1. Brueggemann, *Genesis*, 105.

a new beginning. Abram, and the as-yet-unnamed people promised to derive from him, represent a fundamentally different relationship between God and human beings from that which characterized primordial humanity."[2]

The story of Abraham begins in earnest at 12:1, which surely lies behind the decision of those who made chapter divisions to start a new chapter at that place; however, the *toledot* really begins at 11:27 and then continues with a genealogy of Terah that includes narrative elements that bring us up to the momentous moment when God addresses Abram in 12:1–3.

The genealogy is segmented and names the three sons of Terah. The first is Abram, the original shorter name of the patriarch (see 17:5), followed by his brothers, Nahor and Haran. We assume that they are listed according to birth order. Haran died in Ur of the Chaldeans, also identified as the place of his birth, though we will see that Ur was not the ancestral homeland of this family.

It is interesting that Ur is identified as Chaldean, obviously to distinguish it from other cities named Ur. This Ur, located in southern Mesopotamia, is one of the oldest cities ever built. Archaeological remains at Ur (identified as Tell el-Muqayyar) go back to almost 5000 BC. We cannot precisely date the time when Terah and his family were there except to the Middle Bronze period (2000–1550 BC), but even so it is long after Ur was founded. Its identity as Chaldean Ur is an anachronism to the time of Abraham and even to the time of Moses, the putative author, since the Chaldeans were an Aramaic-speaking tribe that did not live in southern Mesopotamia until the ninth century BC. Thus it is often taken as an addition that helped later readers know which Ur was meant by the narrator.

Haran's genealogy continues to the next generation by naming Lot as his son and thus Abram's nephew. He is named here because Lot will accompany his uncle to the promised land and thus is a significant character in the narrative.

Next, we turn to Abram and Nahor, who was married to his brother's daughter Milkah (whose sister Iskah is otherwise unknown, though some rabbis want to identify her as Sarai, since she is later identified as Abram's half-sister; Gen 20:12). Milkah was Rebekah's grandmother (Gen 24:24). Mosaic law will later prohibit marriages between such close relations (Lev 18:6, 9; 20:17), but at this time they were not prohibited, but even encouraged. At first read, the barrenness of Sarai is stated simply as a matter of fact, but once God gives Abram the promise that he will have many descendants, her inability to have children will be a major motivating factor of the plot.

2. J. D. Levenson, *Inheriting Abraham: The Legacy of the Patriarch in Judaism, Christianity and Islam*, (Princeton and Oxford: Princeton University Press, 2012), 20.

Verse 31 describes Terah as the instigator of the first move from Ur to Harran, a city about sixty miles north from the place where the Euphrates and Balikh rivers meet, in what is today southeastern Turkey on the border with Syria. Harran was well known as a center for the worship of the moon god, perhaps explaining Terah's name which means "moon." Terah took Abram, Sarai, and Lot with him to what is likely their ancestral homeland. While the intention was to move from Harran to Canaan (and thus perhaps assuming the call of Abram in 12:1 – 3 preceded the move, see below), they did not move there until after the death of Terah. Perhaps the delay was a consequence of Terah's status as a pagan (Josh 24:2).[3] He was 205 years old when he died.

## Divine Command and Promise (12:1 – 3)

After this genealogical narrative, the Abraham story begins in earnest in 12:1 – 3. One cannot overestimate the importance of these three verses not only for the Abraham story and the Pentateuch but for the entire Bible, both Old and New Testaments.

God begins by telling Abram to leave his homeland and head to the land he will show him, which turns out to be Canaan. It is unclear where Abram is when God addresses him. The final verse of the previous chapter located the family in Harran, which appears to be the family's ancestral homeland. The NIV departs from most translations by translating the verb as a pluperfect, thus harking back before the time they are in Harran. Based on later references to this text (Gen 15:7; Neh 9:7; Acts 7:2 – 4), it appears that the NIV is correct that God speaks to Abram in Ur.

The way God words his imperative to Abram emphasizes a move from comfort to discomfort. Ur is described as "your country, your people, and your father's household." Thus, God asks Abram to take a step of faith from the known to the unknown, but he bolsters his charge with promises that are contingent on obedience (vv. 2 – 3).

As we read the promises, we are first struck with the repetition of the word blessed (from the Hebrew root *brk*). God will bless Abram and then he in turn will be a blessing to others, ultimately to "all peoples on earth."

The following interpretation follows the translation of the blessing promise as found in the NIV. Before proceeding, however, we should acknowledge that this translation has not gone unchallenged. The debate is over the exact

3. There is a debate about Terah's religious status in connection with 31:53, where Laban says "May the God of Abraham and the God of Nahor, the God of their father, judge between us," which may indicate that Abraham, Nahor, and their father Terah all had the same God, Yahweh. However, as Hamilton notes (*Genesis 11:27–50:26*, NAC [Nashville: Broadman & Holman], 535), the verb "judge" is plural, indicating that the God of Abraham may be different than the god of Nahor and his father.

force of the verb "to bless" in verse 3. The verb is in the *niphal* form, which can have one of three possible renderings. The NIV in the main text takes the verb as a passive, and therefore the sense is that the nations will be blessed through Abram and his descendants. Another possible rendering of the *niphal* is reflexive, that is the nations will "bless themselves." This is the sense that leads to the NIV footnote rendition "will use your name in blessings." In other words, this translation suggests a future not where Abraham's descendants will be instrumental in the blessing on the nations, but that the nations will bless each other by saying something like "may you be like Abraham." The third possible sense is to take the *niphal* as a middle, which would lead to the meaning of "gain blessing." We agree with Anderson, citing Gruneberg, "that the reflexive sense misses the fact that this is a promise from God to Abraham and not to the nations, while the middle sense is without any linguistic corroboration. A passive sense captures the fact that Yhwh directs this word of promise to Abraham, who will be the instrument bringing blessing to all."[4]

But what does it mean to be blessed? Let's begin with the observation that God created Adam and Eve in a blessed condition (1:28). They had a harmonious relationship with God and, as a consequence, with each other. They also had all their physical needs met as they lived in the garden of Eden. Life in the garden defines what blessing looks like and it has spiritual, emotional, psychological, as well as material aspects to it. We can further turn to descriptions of God's blessings on those who obey his covenant found in Deuteronomy 27–28, among other places. The assumption of the blessing is that they have a vibrant relationship with God which leads to material and emotional wholeness.

While Adam and Eve were created in a blessed condition, their sin forfeited that blessing and turned it into curse. They no longer had a harmonious relationship with God or with each other. Not only relationships but also their work was fraught with difficulties.

A major theme of the book of Genesis surrounds blessing, its loss, and God's redemptive work to restore relationship and blessing with humanity. He chooses Abram here in order to be the vehicle through which he will bring blessing to the world.

As part of the future blessing, God promises an obedient Abram that he would make his name great and also would make him a great nation. We earlier observed the sin of the generation that built the tower of Babel when

---

4. See J. E. Anderson, *Jacob and the Divine Trickster: A Theology of Deception and Yhwh's Fidelity to the Ancestral Promise in the Jacob Cycle*, Siphrut 5 (Winona Lake, IN: Eisenbrauns, 2011), 42, citing K. N. Gruneberg, *Abraham, Blessing and the Nations: A Philological and Exegetical Study of Genesis 12:3 in Its Narrative Context*, BZAW 332 (Berlin: de Gruyter, 2003), 84.

they sought to make their name great. Their act was one of pride. But there is nothing inherently evil about having a great name, or better, reputation, but it is God that confers it.

The promise that God will make Abram into a "great nation" may be unpacked as having two major aspects. To be a great nation, Abram must have descendants as well as land. At this point, he has neither and we have already learned that his wife, Sarai, is barren.

As we move next into the various episodes of the Abram story, they will largely focus on the absence of land and especially descendants. To be a great nation, to have many descendants, Abram and Sarai have to begin with one and that birth does not come immediately.

Indeed, the theme of the Abra(ha)m story has rightly been identified as centered on his response to threats and obstacles to the fulfillment of the promises.[5] He makes the bold move to the land, but when he gets there God does not immediately fulfill his promises. Does Abraham respond to these threats and obstacles with faith or with fear?

We should note that nowhere is the word covenant used in this passage. However, when we come to Genesis 15 and 17, God will come to reassure Abraham that he will certainly fulfill his long-delayed promises and in these texts God's relationship with Abraham is called a covenant. While some believe that the Abrahamic covenant comes into existence beginning in Genesis 15, it is best to think of these texts as stories of covenant renewal and that the covenant is made in Genesis 12:1–3 where we have a command ("Go from your country ...") sanctioned by blessings. The Davidic covenant in 2 Samuel 7 is similar in that the relationship between David and God is not called a covenant at that point, but later reflections on the passage use the term (Pss 89 and 132, for instance).

### From Harran to Shechem to Near Bethel and on to the Negev (12:4–9)

Abram heard the promises (Gen 12:2–3) and the command (12:1) and went to the land that God showed him, which turned out to be the land of Canaan. If the command was given in Ur, then there was some delay in his getting to Canaan since they had a stop of unspecified duration (see discussion at 11:27–32). Even so, the narrative accentuates his obedience since "Abram went, as the Lord had told him" follows hard on the heels of God's speech.

Abram did not go alone, of course, but brought Sarai, his wife and Lot, his nephew. Since the presence of Lot leads to future trouble for Abram, some

5. Clines, *The Theme of the Pentateuch.*

speculate that he should not have brought him; however, such an idea may be reading too much into the story. While these are the principal characters who make the journey down to the promised land, they also brought their possessions plus all the people they acquired in Harran. Abram already appears to be a person of means, and his wealth will only increase as time goes on. We are not to picture Abram as a lonely nomad, but rather as a powerful sheik who later will be able to marshal an army of 318 men (14:14) and is called a "mighty prince" in his negotiations with the Hittite Ephron (23:6).

Thus Abram and his retinue arrive in Canaan at the north central site of Shechem with specific mention of a prominent tree at a place called Moreh. Here God reaffirmed his commitment to give Abram and his descendants this land. In response, Abram built an altar and called on God's name.

Altars were places of sacrifice; indeed, the Hebrew word altar (*mizbeah*) is related to the verb "to sacrifice." After the rebellion of humanity in the garden, humans could no longer live easily in God's presence. Thus, special holy places marked by altars had to be constructed for God's people to come into his presence. The mention of an oak tree is particularly interesting since holy places often are connected with trees or symbolic trees like the lampstand which is described as an almond tree in Exodus 25:31–40. The best explanation of this connection between holy place and tree is that it evokes the memory of the garden of Eden where humans dwelt in perfect harmony with God.

After Shechem, Abram went to a location between the towns of Bethel and Ai, a location still in the central hill country but further south, and built an altar there. Finally he traveled much further south to the region known as the Negev where he also built an altar.

In rather short compass, the narrative tells us that Abram reached the promised land and settled successively in three places (north, central, and southern Canaan), each time building an altar. He does not own the land, but he leaves behind markers of God's presence throughout the land.

## The Journey of Faith

As mentioned above, Genesis 12:1–3 reverberates through the rest of the Bible. In large part, the Abraham narrative follows the patriarch's reactions to threats and obstacles to the fulfillment of the promises. We will see in the following episodes of his life that he occasionally responds with faith, but more often he doubts and responds with fear and self-protection. At the end of his life, God will test him to the utmost and he will show himself to be utterly faithful (see Gen 22).

For this reason, the New Testament presents Abraham as a model of the life of faith. After defining faith as "confidence in what we hope for and assurance about what we do not see" (Heb 11:1), the author of Hebrews presents a portrait gallery of examples of faith from the past. The author devotes two parts to Abraham. We will cite portions of the Hebrews passage throughout our study of Abraham in order to remind us of this central theme and its relevance for our lives today:

> By faith Abraham, when called to go to a place he would later receive as his inheritance, obeyed and went, even though he did not know where he was going. By faith he made his home in the promised land like a stranger in a foreign country; he lived in tents ... For he was looking forward to the city with foundations, whose architect and builder is God. (11:8–10)

The author of Hebrews understood the connection with the Christian life of faith. We too have received promises from God. He will be with us during our lives, and he will come again and bring his people into the heavenly city described in Revelation 21–22. But we too, like Abraham, are constantly challenged by threats and obstacles to the fulfillment of that promise. Is God really with me? The disappointments and pain of life seem to provide counter-evidence. Is there really a heaven or is it a figment of my imagination? Doubts plague us. How do we respond? Fear or faith?

Abraham is a model for us, and we will soon see he is far, far from perfect. He will be an encouragement for us to hold on as he did, because we too are far, far from perfect.

## The Myth of Certainty[6]

While we reflect on Abraham's faith journey and our own, it is important to realize that the opposite of faith is not doubt, but unbelief. If we are certain about something, we do not need faith. Paralyzing doubt can hurt faith, but the reflective Christian will often struggle with doubt. As Taylor points out, certainty can only be achieved by a kind of blind acceptance of authority that suppresses questions and doubts. On the other hand, though, doubts that lead to an avoidance of commitment to the object of faith (in our case Jesus) is unhealthy. The church needs to create a culture where healthy, faith-growing doubt can exist and be expressed.

---

6. The title is from D. Taylor's book *The Myth of Certainty: The Reflective Christian and the Risk of Commitment* (Downers Grove, IL: InterVarsity Press, 1986), which has significantly influenced this section.

## Israel, the Seed of Abraham

God promised Abraham that he would make him a "great nation" (12:2). We observed above that the fulfillment of this promise would mean that Abraham would have many descendants and also would come to possess the land. Indeed, the most immediate threat to the fulfillment of the promise will be Sarah's persistent barrenness. To have many descendants a couple has to start with one!

Of course, as we know and will see as the plot continues that one son, Isaac, will eventually be born. But the promise of a great nation entails a large population, not just even a large family, and this aspect of the promise is spelled out in more detail later in the patriarchal narratives. Later God will tell Abraham: " 'Look up to the sky and count the stars — if indeed you can count them.' Then he said to him, 'So shall your offspring be' " (15:5; see also 22:17; 26:4).

This promise is fulfilled in the nation of Israel born in the exodus event as is signaled by the comment at the beginning of the book of Exodus that "the Israelites were exceedingly fruitful; they multiplied greatly, increased in numbers and became so numerous that the land was filled with them" (1:7). The story of Joshua narrates how the numerous people of Israel enter and begin to take possession of the land. It is this great nation, Israel, that is to be blessed by God and to bring a blessing to all the nations of the world. Thus, we can see how the promises to Abraham given in 12:1 – 3 reverberate beyond the book of Genesis and through the rest of the Old Testament as it tells the story of Israel, the seed of Abraham, but not even that is the end of the story. As we turn our attention next to the New Testament, we see that Israel is not only the seed of Abraham, but more importantly Jesus is *the* seed of Abraham.

## Jesus, the Seed of Abraham

Unfortunately, the Old Testament is not a story of triumph but one that is rocky from beginning to end. Like Abraham himself, Israel did not always respond with faith and trust in God. Indeed, Joshua through Kings, while having many bright spots, tells a story of persistent sin. Rather than being a light to the nations Israel received the judgment of God who used the nations (particularly Assyria and Babylon) to remove their status as an independent nation. The exile was not the end of the story to be sure (Ezra-Nehemiah; Esther), but the story of the Old Testament shows that persistent problems remain (see Neh 13).

How does the New Testament look back at the promises to Abraham and in particular the promise of offspring or seed? Paul provides a surprising answer:

> Brothers and sisters, let me take an example from everyday life. Just as no one can set aside or add to a human covenant that has been duly established, so it is in this case. The promises were spoken to Abraham and to his seed. Scripture does not say "and to seeds," meaning many people, but "and to your seed," meaning one person, who is Christ (Gal 3:15–16)

At first sight, Paul's statement is outrageous. As we have just seen, the promise of seed was spelled out in later passages (Gen 15:5, etc.) in a way that clearly points to the nation of Israel, and Paul, who was well trained in Scripture would know that. Paul, though, here exploits the collective singular "seed" to make the bold statement that Jesus is the ultimate fulfillment of the Abrahamic promise. He is the "seed" of Abraham through whom the promise of universal blessing will flow. Notice how Paul ends this part of his argument when he tells the Galatian Christians, and through them us, that we ourselves are Abraham's seed through our relationship with Jesus:

> So in Christ Jesus you are all children of God through faith, for all of you who were baptized into Christ have clothed yourselves with Christ. There is neither Jew nor Gentile, neither slave nor free, nor is there male and female, for you are all one in Christ Jesus. If you belong to Christ, then you are Abraham's seed, and heirs according to the promise. (Gal 3:26–29)

Christians then are also the fulfillment of the Abrahamic promises. The church is a spiritual entity, but metaphorically that "great nation" who receives and dispenses God's blessing to the world. As Peter announced to the church: "you are a chosen people, a royal priesthood, a holy nation, God's special possession, that you may declare the praises of him who called you out of darkness into his wonderful light. Once you were not a people, but now you are the people of God; once you had not received mercy, but now you have received mercy" (1 Peter 2:9–10).

### Leaving Country and Family

God's radical call to Abraham required him to leave "your country, your people and your father's household." God was calling him to a life journey of faith that focused on his primary relationship with him. He left Ur of the Chaldeans and his ancestral homeland of Haran. He also left his broader family back in Paddan Aram (or Northwest Mesopotamia). Both Isaac's and Jacob's wives will come from their extended family back there, but nonetheless Abraham struck out on a different path than they did. He did bring his wife with him as well as his nephew Lot. It is unclear why he brought the latter and debated whether he should have. While the narrator never states that Lot should have been left behind, Lot's presence brings more than its share of trouble to Abraham and may be a way of showing that Abraham would have been more consistently obedient by leaving him behind. Apart from that, Abraham's obedience led him to a radical separation from his extended family, something quite unusual for the ancient Near East.

God would never ask us to do such a thing today. Or would he? Reading 12:1 makes us think of what Jesus said to a large crowd gathered to hear him: "If anyone comes to me and does not hate father and mother, wife and children, brothers and sisters — yes, even their own life — such a person cannot be my disciple. And whoever does not carry their cross and follow me cannot be my disciple" (Luke 14:26–27).

Hate their family? Jesus himself had great affection for his mother. It appears that those commentators who say that Jesus here is using hyperbole are correct. His point is that his disciples must put him first not their parents, and certainly not their country. God may not call us, like he did Abraham, to leave family and to leave country, but we need to be ready to do so if he calls us to do so.

The great third-century AD interpreter Origin understood this, as Layton points out: "The command, Origen holds, to depart from country, kin, and land is 'said not to Abraham alone but to whoever would be his child. For each of us has before the decree of God a certain country and relative who is not good and a house of our father before the Word of God comes to us, from all of which we must depart, according to the word of God.'"[7]

Of course, this is not an excuse to neglect our duties and responsibilities to those who are our family and also our country, but it is a matter of priority. Indeed, if we do so, the reward is great. The twelve disciples had left family and their homeland to follow Jesus. Peter, speaking for the disciples, then asked Jesus, "We have left everything to follow you! What then will there be for us?" And Jesus replied, "at the renewal of all things, when the Son of Many sits on his glorious throne, you who have followed me will also sit on twelve thrones, judging the twelve tribes of Israel. And everyone who has left houses or brothers or sisters or father or mother or wife or children or fields for my sake will receive a hundred times as much and will inherit eternal life. But many who are first will be last, and many who are last will be first" (Matt 19:27–30).

---

7. R. A. Layton, "Interpretation in the Early Church," in *Reading Genesis: Ten Methods*, ed. R. Hendel (Cambridge: Cambridge University Press, 2010), 151.

## Living in the Presence of God

12:4–9 emphasizes Abram's obedience to the divine command to come to Canaan and also describes Abram's intention to live in God's presence. The latter is signaled by the repeated emphasis on Abram building an altar and calling on God's name.

Abram's journey of faith starts out on a good footing. He obeys and maintains close fellowship with God. As we think of our own journey of faith, we can learn from this phase of Abram's life to maintain a relationship with God characterized by continual prayer (1 Thess 5:17).

As we think about our relationship with God, we are struck by the tremendous impact that Christ's work and the Holy Spirit's presence makes in our lives with God. As I said above, after the rebellion, sin created a barrier that did not let humans come naturally into the presence of God. This intimate fellowship could only happen at a designated holy place accompanied by a sacrifice. As we move on in the story of God, we see that when Israel becomes a nation and not just an extended family, the simple altar is accompanied by a tabernacle and then when the people are once and for all settled in the land the tabernacle is replaced by the temple.[8]

Christians, on the other hand, do not need to go to a holy place to have intimate communion with God. Jesus came and "dwelt [the Greek word could be translated "tabernacled"] among us" (John 1:14). At his death, the veil of the temple separating the holy from the common rips apart (Matt 27:51) signaling the eruption of holiness throughout the world. The Holy Spirit now dwells in us so we individually (1 Cor 6:19) and corporately are the temple of God (2 Cor 6:16).

What an encouragement to constant and intimate fellowship with God. Like Abram, we too should "call on the name of God."

---

8. A detailed account of the theological reasons for the shift from the tabernacle to the temple may be found in Longman, *Immanuel in Our Place*, 3–74. Also, see the essay Meeting God in a Fallen World in the Live the Story section after Genesis 3.

CHAPTER 10

# Genesis 12:10–20

## LISTEN to the Story

[12:10]Now there was a famine in the land, and Abram went down to
Egypt to live there for a while because the famine was severe. [11]As he was
about to enter Egypt, he said to his wife Sarai, "I know what a beautiful
woman you are. [12]When the Egyptians see you, they will say, 'This is
his wife.' Then they will kill me but will let you live. [13]Say you are my
sister, so that I will be treated well for your sake and my life will be spared
because of you."

[14]When Abram came to Egypt, the Egyptians saw that Sarai was a very
beautiful woman. [15]And when Pharaoh's officials saw her, they praised
her to Pharaoh, and she was taken into his palace. [16]He treated Abram
well for her sake, and Abram acquired sheep and cattle, male and female
donkeys, male and female servants, and camels.

[17]But the LORD inflicted serious diseases on Pharaoh and his
household because of Abram's wife Sarai. [18]So Pharaoh summoned
Abram. "What have you done to me?" he said. "Why didn't you tell me
she was your wife? [19]Why did you say, 'She is my sister,' so that I took
her to be my wife? Now then, here is your wife. Take her and go!" [20]Then
Pharaoh gave orders about Abram to his men, and they sent him on his
way, with his wife and everything he had.

*Listening to the Text in the Story:* Biblical Texts: Genesis 12:1–3; Genesis 37–Exodus 15; Ancient Near Eastern Text: Papyrus Anastasi VI

We have already remarked (see The Journey of Faith in Live the Story after 11:27–12:9) that the divine promises to Abram found in 12:1–3 propel the plot of the Abraham narrative. How does Abram respond to threats and problems to the fulfillment of the promises? Here the threat is famine, a common problem of the day. We see that Abram addresses the problem of famine by seeking refuge and provision in Egypt. Ancient sources such as the Egyptian

Papyrus Anastasi VI and tomb paintings from as early as the nineteenth century BC show us that it was not untypical for Semitic people to seek such help in Egypt.[1] The result is a story, as we will see, that has the basic outline of the later Exodus from Egypt (Gen 37–Exod 15).

## EXPLAIN the Story

"Now there was a famine in the land" (v. 10); thus, Abram faces the first obstacle to the fulfillment of the promise given to him in Genesis 12:2 that he would become a "great nation." He had left his comfortable home to come to this land, which God had promised would be his and his descendants. But now that land could not even sustain his and Sarai's life, so they decided to move down to Egypt to weather the crisis. As Abram moves from the promised land to Egypt, what is the state of his faith? Does he respond with faith or with fear?

The answer comes quickly in the story as Abram turns to his wife Sarai and instructs her to lie about her relationship with him by saying that she is his sister, not his wife. While true that Sarai was his half-sister (20:12), he asks her to suppress the most important part of his relationship with her, their marriage, for one and only one purpose, namely to save his own life. And not only that, but he plans to use her beauty in order to be "treated well" (v. 13). She is beautiful and he expects that she will be desired by the powerful men of Egypt. As her "brother," he will be in a position to negotiate her marriage proposal since that was the role of brothers in the ancient Near East (see Levi and Simeon in Gen 34).

And, indeed, events unfolded as Abram expected that they might. When they arrive, the Egyptians were struck by her beauty. They informed the Pharaoh about her and he took him into his palace. He thinks Abram is her brother, so Pharaoh enriches Abram, including giving him male and female servants. Among the latter was likely Hagar, the woman who would later become his concubine and give birth to Ishmael (see Gen 16–17).

By making Sarai act this way, he treats his wife like property; indeed, he uses her like he is her pimp, hoping to benefit from her sexual favors. Even further, he puts the promise of descendants at risk. If she has a child with Pharaoh, then that would compromise her status as the matriarch.

In this way, Abram demonstrates that he is acting out of fear, lacking confidence in God's ability to take care of him and protect him. He interprets the famine as God's inability or unwillingness to take care of him.

1. Walton, "Genesis," 74.

But God does protect him and the promise even in the midst of his doubt. God sends "serious diseases" (v. 17) on Pharaoh and his household. Interestingly, the passage does not make it clear whether or not Sarai had had sexual intercourse with Pharaoh. Later, when Abram again lies about the status of Sarai to a foreign king, the narrator makes it very clear, not that they did not have sex, but that she did not conceive. After all, the second story occurs on the eve of the birth of Isaac and there can be no doubt as to who the father is, thus God made it impossible for the women of the royal court of Philistia to conceive.

Once Pharaoh found out that Abram had deceived him and that the serious diseases were due to his adding Sarai to his harem, he called Abram into his presence demanding to know why. Why would Abram do such a thing? The passage does not report Abram's response to the question, so Pharaoh simply orders him to take Sarai and leave. He allows him to take all the possessions he gained while in Egypt, perhaps fearing Abram's God who had sent the devastating diseases on his royal court.

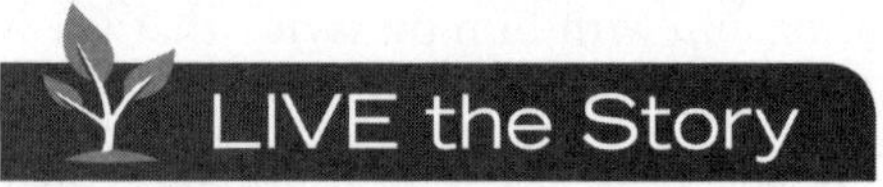


### Trusting God In Spite of Appearances

God made promises to Abram, but there is a time lag between the promise and its fulfillment. God calls on Abram to trust him, even when experiences of life suggest that these promises will never be fulfilled. God, in a word, is asking Abram to live a life of faith. Hebrews 11:1 describes faith as "confidence in what we hope for and assurance about what we do not see." Abram clearly lacks this confidence in God as he heads down to Egypt in the midst of the famine.

God has made promises to those who follow him today as well. He promises that we will be his children and he will watch over us. He promises that eventually we will live in his presence forever.

Like Abram, Christians have life experiences that raise questions about God's ability or willingness to take care of us. We wonder whether he will eventually bring us into his presence forever as he promises:

> Do not let your hearts be troubled. You believe in God; believe also in me. My Father's house has many rooms; if that were not so, would I have told you that I am going there to prepare a place for you? And if I go and prepare a place for you, I will come back and take you to be with me that you also may be where I am. You know the way to the place where I am going. (John 14:1–4).

While it is true that God never promises a problem-free life, when troubles do come into our life, we still often take it as a threat or obstacle to the fulfillment of the promises. And how do we react? Do we react with fear as Abram does in this story or with faith? Fear has us act in self-protective ways or to manipulate events for our own advantage. God, of course, calls us to trust in him, to have confidence in him.

## God Delivers His People

Biblical history is never written for a purely antiquarian purpose; that is, the authors are not interested in the past for the sake of the past. Enns and Byas got it right when they said about the story of Abram's descent into Egypt, "The Israelites who shaped this story were writing for their present time. God has a long track record of delivering his people—even Abraham, the first Israelite—from a foreign land."[2]

As we noted in the Introduction (Composition), it is a matter of debate exactly when the book was written and whether or not it was done at one discrete moment or was the result of a process over time, but whether it was written at the time of Moses (as traditionally thought) or at the time of the Babylonian exile or the return from exile (or both), this story would have resonated with contemporary events of the time. The message that God delivers his people, even his sinful people from trouble, is a message that has relevance for the time of Moses, the time of the Babylonian exile, indeed for all time including today.

First, we should observe how similar Abram's experience here is to that of his later descendants as described in Genesis 37–Exodus 15, the time of Joseph and Moses. At the time of Joseph, Abram's descendants descended to Egypt to weather a severe famine. They ended up staying in Egypt and eventually becoming enslaved to a later, suspicious Pharaoh. God sent plagues against Egypt until he let the Israelites go, and as they left, the Egyptians enriched them with silver, gold, and clothing (Exod 12:35).

But, second, we should also notice how someone living during or just after the Babylonian captivity could also be encouraged by the story of Abram in Egypt. After all, the biblical prophets saw an analogy between the rescue of Israel from Egypt and the future rescue of later Israel from their exile. Scholars today commonly call this strand of teaching in prophets like Isaiah, Jeremiah, Ezekiel, and Hosea the second exodus theme. Let's take as an example Hosea, the eighth-century prophet, who begins his prophetic work by talking about God's judgment on his sinful people (Hos 1:1–2:13). In 2:14 and following,

2. P. Enns and J. Byas, *Genesis for Normal People: A Guide to the Most Controversial, Misunderstood, and Abused Book of the Bible* (Englewood, CO: Patheos, 2012), 69.

however, we read an oracle of salvation or restoration that describes a return of God's sinful people from the wilderness. This return is likened to the earlier sojourn from Egypt through the wilderness back into the promised land:

> Therefore I am now going to allure her;
> I will lead her into the wilderness
> and speak tenderly to her.
> There I will give her back her vineyards,
> and will make the Valley of Achor a door of hope.
> There she will respond as in the days of her youth,
> as in the day she came up out of Egypt. (Hos 2:14–15)

This second exodus expectation has an initial fulfillment at the time of return from exile under the leaders Sheshbazzar and Zerubbabel. When Cyrus issues the decree that allows for their return to the land, he also encourages people to give them precious metals and other valuables (Ezra 1:2–4). When we read of this, we are reminded not only of the time when the Egyptians gave the Israelites gold and silver when they left Egypt (Exod 12:33–36), but also of the Egyptian wealth which Abram and Sarai brought back with them after their sojourn in Egypt.

The return of God's people from Babylonian captivity is indeed a fulfillment of the second exodus expectation of the prophets, but not its full expression. Indeed, the books of Ezra and Nehemiah make it clear that the return was not all that it was expected to be. We should particularly take note of the final chapter, Nehemiah 13, which shows that there were still significant problems among the people of God, not to speak of the few Jews who decided to return.

The message of the New Testament is that the ultimate fulfillment of the second exodus expectation, plus the most powerful expression of the fact that God rescues his people, takes place in the work of Jesus Christ who saves his people from sin, guilt, and death. That Jesus' life and ministry follows the pattern of the exodus story is signaled by the opening of the Gospel of Mark, quoting Isaiah and Malachi's oracles that looked forward to a second exodus: "I will send my messenger ahead of you, who will prepare your way—a voice of one calling in the wilderness, 'Prepare the way for the Lord, make straight paths for him'" (Mark 1:2–3).

Those who have a good knowledge of the exodus tradition will see the multiple connections, often highlighted by the Gospel writers, particularly Matthew. Due to Herod's persecution, Joseph and Mary take Jesus to Egypt when he is a youth. When Herod died, Jesus returned and the Gospel writer cites Hosea 11:1, "Out of Egypt I called my son."

John the Baptist baptizes Jesus at the beginning of his earthly ministry (Matt 3:13–17) and then spends forty days and forty nights in the wilderness. The baptism is his Re(e)d Sea crossing (see 1 Cor 10:1–6 where the sea crossing is called a baptism), and in the wilderness Jesus experienced the same three temptations that Israel confronted in the forty years in the wilderness (hunger, testing God, worshiping a false God). While Israel succumbed to the temptations in the wilderness, Jesus showed himself to be faithful by resisting the temptations and citing Deuteronomy, Moses' final sermon in the wilderness, against the devil's seductions (Matt 4:1–11).

Many other connections between Jesus' life and ministry have been highlighted by scholars, but that the exodus stories (particularly Gen 37–Exod 15, but including Gen 12:1–10) point ultimately to Jesus and culminate with his death on the eve of the Jewish Passover, the ritual celebration of the exodus from Egypt. Jesus is indeed the fulfillment of the exodus; he is the Passover Lamb (2 Cor 5:7–8).

CHAPTER 11

# Genesis 13

## LISTEN to the Story

13:1So Abram went up from Egypt to the Negev, with his wife and everything he had, and Lot went with him. 2Abram had become very wealthy in livestock and in silver and gold.

3From the Negev he went from place to place until he came to Bethel, to the place between Bethel and Ai where his tent had been earlier 4and where he had first built an altar. There Abram called on the name of the LORD.

5Now Lot, who was moving about with Abram, also had flocks and herds and tents. 6But the land could not support them while they stayed together, for their possessions were so great that they were not able to stay together. 7And quarreling arose between Abram's herders and Lot's. The Canaanites and Perizzites were also living in the land at that time.

8So Abram said to Lot, "Let's not have any quarreling between you and me, or between your herders and mine, for we are close relatives. 9Is not the whole land before you? Let's part company. If you go to the left, I'll go to the right; if you go to the right, I'll go to the left."

10Lot looked around and saw that the whole plain of the Jordan toward Zoar was well watered, like the garden of the LORD, like the land of Egypt. (This was before the LORD destroyed Sodom and Gomorrah.) 11So Lot chose for himself the whole plain of the Jordan and set out toward the east. The two men parted company: 12Abram lived in the land of Canaan, while Lot lived among the cities of the plain and pitched his tents near Sodom. 13Now the people of Sodom were wicked and were sinning greatly against the LORD.

14The LORD said to Abram after Lot had parted from him, "Look around from where you are, to the north and south, to the east and west. 15All the land that you see I will give to you and your offspring forever. 16I will make your offspring like the dust of the earth, so that if anyone could count the dust, then your offspring could be counted. 17Go, walk through the length and breadth of the land, for I am giving it to you."

[18]So Abram went to live near the great trees of Mamre at Hebron, where he pitched his tents. There he built an altar to the LORD.

*Listening to the Text in the Story:* Biblical Text: Genesis 12:1–3

In Genesis 12:1–3 God promised that Abram would become a great nation, which would entail both descendants as well as land. Up to this point, Abram possesses none of the land, though the promise would give him a sense that the land was his and not Lot's. This understanding provides an important background to the story of Genesis 13 in which Abraham and Lot have become so rich that they have to settle in separate parts of the land.

## EXPLAIN the Story

After returning from Egypt, Abram, accompanied by Sarai and Lot, returned to Negev in the most southern part of the promised land, the place from which he had descended into Egypt. Verse 2 reminds us that Abram has grown in wealth as measured by number of livestock as well as precious metals (silver and gold). After all, his wealth had grown tremendously because of the time he spent in Egypt (see Gen 12:10–20).

From the Negev, Abram then retraced his steps (by stages) to the area between Bethel and Ai, where he had previously encamped and built an altar. The NIV translation is open to misunderstanding when it says "where he had first built an altar" (v. 4). This rendering makes it sound as if this earlier occasion was the first time that Abram built an altar in the promised land, which is problematic since according to 12:6–7 he had earlier built one in Shechem. Thus, the NRSV rendering is better when it says "where he had made an altar at the first," in other words at his first encampment there. Thus, the point is that Abram did not have to build another altar since one was already present from his earlier time there.

There is no indication that Lot had gone to Egypt with Abram and Sarai, though the text may have just been silent about his presence. In any case, whether he had weathered the famine in Canaan or gone with Abram, Lot too had possessions, so many that, taking into account the presence of the native inhabitants of the land (the Canaanites and Perizzites), there were too few land and water resources to sustain the large numbers of flocks and herds. The abundance of flocks and herds, not to speak of people, led to fights between Abram's herders and Lot's. They had to split.

This situation provided yet another test of Abram's faith, though of a different sort than that described in 12:10–20. In the earlier story, a negative situation (famine) made Abram question God's goodness and ability to take care of him. On his return, he worships God in the land again (v. 4), presumably having seen his protective hand even when Abram himself expressed no confidence in him.

The present situation requires that he separate from Lot due to his abundant wealth, a more positive test of faith than the previous one. Even so, it provides an occasion to test Abram's faith. He, after all, was Lot's uncle; he could simply tell Lot to fend for himself or relegate to Lot an inferior part of the land promised to Abram. Abram could further cite the divine promises that God would make him, not Lot, into a "great nation" (12:2). What does Abram do?

He takes a very reasonable approach to Lot as he seeks a solution to the problem. He wants to avoid conflict on the basis of the fact that they are "close relatives" (v. 8). He then allows Lot to choose whatever part of the land he wants for himself. Abram will then take something from what is left over.

The significance of Abram's approach to this issue is that he is not grasping for the fulfillment of the promise. He is not showing any sign of self-protection or manipulation. We are to see in Abram's speech and actions a response of faith. He does not feel like he has to do the work to gain the promises, but can trust God to fulfill them. We will see that this moment is rare compared to the times that Abram feels like he has to manipulate the situation for his benefit rather than waiting for God to act.

Lot then chooses the land that looked the best, at least on the surface of things. He chose the "whole plain of Jordan toward Zoar" (v. 10) that is near the "cities of the plain" including the one city here named Sodom (v. 12). After all, this area was the most lush available, even being compared to Egypt and to Eden ("the garden of the LORD," v. 10). Egypt was well watered by the annual flooding of the Nile and extensive irrigation. And of course Eden is described as having four rivers flowing out of it (Gen 2:10–14).

Of course, a reader at the time when the book of Genesis was written would have a different picture of this area in their mind. For that reason, the author anticipates the events of Genesis 18–19 by adding as a kind of parenthetical expression, "This is before the LORD destroyed Sodom and Gomorrah" (10). The readers of this story would know this region as a salt plain incapable of growing vegetation, not as a well-watered area that would sustain life. The judgment that will come on the area Lot chose is also anticipated by verse 13,

"Now the people of Sodom were wicked and were sinning greatly against the LORD." We will pick up this story when we come to Genesis 18–19.

God is pleased with Abram and his decision. After Lot leaves, God renews his promise of land to him. He has him look in every direction and then reaffirms that he and his descendants will come to possess the land. He also reaffirms the second component of the promise to be a great nation by saying that his offspring will be as numerous as the "dust of the earth" (v. 16). Though at present Abram does not officially possess any land, God urges him to journey throughout the land and, as he does, to realize that the land is coming into his possession.

At the end of the chapter the narrator reports that Abram goes to a new location, Hebron (today identified with Tel al-Khalil, eighteen miles south and slightly east of Jerusalem in the Judean highlands). Mamre is a location near Hebron (approximately two miles north) identified with Haram Ramet el-Khalil. In particular, the text mentions the great trees of Mamre, perhaps because the narrator goes on to inform the reader that Abram once again built an altar in this new location. We have already commented on the specific significance of the juxtaposition of trees and altars in the commentary at 12:4–9. Later in the Abra(ha)m story we will learn that the patriarch will actually purchase and thus own the first part of the promised land in this vicinity (Gen 23:17–20).

**Seeing Versus Believing**

How do we relate to God when things are going well? At this point in his life, Abram is very successful. He is extremely wealthy and powerful as a pastoral nomadic chief. Lot, his nephew, is also thriving. They both have abundant flocks and herds, but due to their plenty, the land that they share can no longer sustain both their interests, so they must split up.

Above, we discussed how Abram's approach to the problem revealed his heart toward God. He does not manipulate and grasp for the fulfillment of the divine promise, but actually lets Lot choose what land to take.

Above, we also analyzed the nature of Abram's actions and concluded that they derived from his trust in God. What about Lot? Much is revealed when the narrator reports that "Lot looked around and saw that the whole plain of the Jordan toward Zoar was well watered, like the garden of the LORD, like the land of Egypt" (13:10). The reference to the garden of the LORD evokes the memory of Eden and the story of Adam and Eve. As we do, we can see a parallel with the progression of their sin, which began when the woman "saw that the fruit of the tree was good for food and pleasing to the eye" (3:6). The similarity between Eve and Lot, on the one hand, and Abram, on the other, becomes obvious. Lot decides based on what they see and Abram decides by faith, on what he does not see.

That God approves of Abram's approach here is made clear by the reiteration and explication of the promise of land and descendants implied by the assurance that Abram's descendants will be a "great nation" (12:2, see 13:14–17). The consequences of Lot's choice will not be made known until chapters 18–19, which narrate the destruction of Sodom and Gomorrah and their surrounding area.

Abram becomes a model of godliness in the midst of prosperity and as a "mirror of the soul" (see Introduction: Reading from the Perspective of the Twenty-First Century) causes us to reflect on how to we react when things are going smoothly in our lives. Only we can answer that question for ourselves, but here are some typical responses.

The Lot response is to forget about God and go with what we see without thinking about whether it is spiritually healthy for us. While the area around Sodom and Gomorrah is lush on the surface, these cities are evil. Either Lot knew this about the cities or else he didn't and he should have before he moved in that direction. It is more than doubtful that these cities became as perverse as they are described in Genesis 18 and 19 when Lot's family are the only one's counted righteous enough to survive the judgment on them.

Lot exemplifies how many of us react when things are going well. God is important to us when we need help, but when things are going great, we tend toward self-reliance. The psalmist confesses that this happened in his life in Psalm 30:

> When I felt secure, I said,
> "I will never be shaken."
> LORD, when you favored me,
> you made my royal mountain stand firm;
> but when you hid your face,
> I was dismayed. (vv. 6–7)

God had made the psalmist prosperous, but then the psalmist presumptuously became self-reliant. In his case, God then abandoned him, so that he felt what it was like to live without God's presence. This was an act of grace on God's part, because as the rest of the psalm celebrates, God's abandonment evoked an urgent desire for the psalmist to restore his relationship with God.

If we are in a vibrant relationship with God, we can say along with Paul, "I have learned to be content whatever the circumstances. I know what it is to be in need, and I know what it is to have plenty. I have learned the secret of being content in any and every situation, whether well fed or hungry, whether living in plenty or in want. I can do all this through him who gives me strength." (Phil 4:11–13)

## Seeking Peace

Abram seeks peace in the midst of conflict with his nephew Lot. He is willing to give up what he might have seen as his rights to all the land in order to reconcile with him. Abram is a peacemaker and they are those who are blessed "for they will be called children of God" (Matt 5:9).

Peace results from harmony between humans and God. Such harmony leads to peace between human beings. Such peace was the natural condition of Eden, but due to sin, which puts the self at the center, conflict is the norm. Jesus came to work reconciliation between God and humans and among humanity. According to Paul, Jesus "is our peace, who has made the two groups one and has destroyed the barrier, the dividing wall of hostility.... His purpose was to create in himself one new humanity out of the two, thus making peace" (Eph 2:14–15). For that reason, the author of Hebrews exhorts his Christian audience to "make every effort to live in peace with everyone" (12:14).

## Jesus and the Land

God implicitly promised land to Abraham's descendants when he told him that they would become a "great nation" (12:2), but it is in 13:14–17 that the promise of land becomes explicit and more specific. Burge rightly understands the significance of land for Abraham's descendants when he says that "land is not simply about possessing real estate; land is about security and identity, it is about cultural cohesion and purpose. Land in its most profound sense is about place, possessing a locale which is ours, which can be defended, which can give us safety from the world."[1]

As we continue through Genesis, we will see that the primary focus of the narrative is on the promise of descendants, also originally implicit in the promise that Abraham's descendants will be a "great nation." Even so, the land promise will be repeated to Abraham (15:18–21; 17:7–9) and then passed on to Isaac (26:2–4) and to Jacob (28:13–15). Just as with the birth of the first descendant of Abraham and Sarah, Isaac, so the land is not easily acquired. At the end of Abraham's life, the most he will own will be a small burial ground near the city of Hebron (see Gen 23) and that will be the extent

1. G. Burge, *Jesus and the Land: The New Testament Challenge to "Holy Land" Theology* (Grand Rapids: Baker, 2010), 33.

of it for generations. Indeed, at the end of the book of Genesis, the chosen family is not even living in the land, but rather is living in Egypt.

It is not until the time of Joshua, many centuries later, that the promised land comes into the possession of the people of God, and even at that time, it is only the beginning. The account of the distribution of the land to the tribes in Joshua 13–24, as well as the events following the death of Joshua as recorded in Judges 1, makes it clear that only a portion of the promised land is actually controlled by Israel. It is not until the time of David, who subdues the last of the internal enemies of Israel, that Israel truly possesses the land. While it is God who owns the land (Lev 25:23), he had gifted it to his people.

Sadly, beginning with the end of the reign of Solomon, the history of Israel particularly as recounted by the book of Kings is the story of disobedience and even apostasy. As Burge points out, the promise of the land is deeply embedded in covenant theology and "life in the land is contingent on upholding the righteousness expected by God."[2] To support Burge's point, we need only look at the curses that follow covenant disobedience in Deuteronomy 27–28, a number of which concern dispossession of the land. And, not surprisingly considering Israel and Judah's behavior, they lost the land first to the Assyrians and then to the Babylonians.

Thus, at the time of the New Testament, the Romans, who had replaced the Seleucid Greek Empire who had replaced the Persians who had replaced the Babylonians, were controlling the land. There were those who expected God to send a Davidic king, a messiah, to win back the land for the Jewish people. Indeed, there were those who followed Jesus who expected that of him. We can see this in the disappointment of the two disciples after the death of Jesus, when on the way to Emmaus they said that they "had hoped that he was the one who was going to redeem Israel" (Luke 24:21). We can also detect this misunderstanding when, at the time of his ascension, the disciples ask him, "Lord, are you at this time going to restore the kingdom to Israel?" (Acts 1:6).

While Jesus doesn't directly respond to their question with a "Yes" or "No," his answer changes the nature of their expectation, when he says "you will receive power when the Holy Spirit comes on you; and you will be my witnesses in Jerusalem, and in all Judaea and Samaria, and to the ends of the earth" (Acts 1:8). In other words, Jesus here changes focus. He is not interested in possession of real estate, but rather he is interested in reaching the whole earth with the gospel. As Burge summarizes Paul's important teaching,

2. Ibid., 11.

he says that "Paul universalizes faith in Christ in order to include all people; Paul universalizes the promises to Abraham in order to include all lands."[3]

In the Old Testament, only certain locales are holy, that is, permeated with the special presence of God. Certainly the sanctuary is such a place and by extension Jerusalem and also the land of Israel. With the coming of Christ all space is holy. We can meet with God anywhere. In the light of the New Testament, we see that the sanctuary, Jerusalem, and the land of Israel were anticipations of something far, far greater—living in the presence of God eternally. The Christian is not interested in the restoration of real estate to God's people, but rather to the new heavens and the new earth. As the author of Hebrews puts it, "here we do not have an enduring city, but we are looking for the city that is to come" (13:14). Even more to the point of the Abraham promise of land, we think of the same author's reflections on that subject. He points out that the patriarchs "did not receive the things promised; they only saw them and welcomed them from a distance, admitting that they were foreigners and strangers on the earth. People who say such things show that they are looking for a country of their own. If they had been thinking of the country they had left, they would have had opportunity to return. Instead, they were longing for a better country—a heavenly one" (Heb 11:13–16).

Here is where contemporary Christian Zionism (the view that the land promises of the Old Testament are fulfilled in the modern state of Israel) goes wrong. They do not follow the biblical theology of the land as it moves from the Old Testament to the New Testament. They cite the promise of the restoration of the land after the exile found in the prophets (Jer 16:15; Isa 9:1–9; Hos 2:14–23; 11:8–11) and don't see that they found initial fulfillment in the returns recorded in the books of Ezra and Nehemiah, but ultimately in Jesus, whom the New Testament presents as the ultimate fulfillment of the exodus, not by leading a specific people back to a specific land but rather by rescuing people from the ultimate enemy of sin and death and bringing them into an eternal relationship with him.

---

3. Ibid., 92.

CHAPTER 12

# Genesis 14

## LISTEN to the Story

14:1At the time when Amraphel was king of Shinar, Arioch king of Ellasar, Kedorlaomer king of Elam and Tidal king of Goyim, 2these kings went to war against Bera king of Sodom, Birsha king of Gomorrah, Shinab king of Admah, Shemeber king of Zeboyim, and the king of Bela (that is, Zoar). 3All these latter kings joined forces in the Valley of Siddim (that is, the Dead Sea Valley). 4For twelve years they had been subject to Kedorlaomer, but in the thirteenth year they rebelled.

5In the fourteenth year, Kedorlaomer and the kings allied with him went out and defeated the Rephaites in Ashteroth Karnaim, the Zuzites in Ham, the Emites in Shaveh Kiriathaim 6and the Horites in the hill country of Seir, as far as El Paran near the desert. 7Then they turned back and went to En Mishpat (that is, Kadesh), and they conquered the whole territory of the Amalekites, as well as the Amorites who were living in Hazezon Tamar.

8Then the king of Sodom, the king of Gomorrah, the king of Admah, the king of Zeboyim and the king of Bela (that is, Zoar) marched out and drew up their battle lines in the Valley of Siddim 9against Kedorlaomer king of Elam, Tidal king of Goyim, Amraphel king of Shinar and Arioch king of Ellasar—four kings against five. 10Now the Valley of Siddim was full of tar pits, and when the kings of Sodom and Gomorrah fled, some of the men fell into them and the rest fled to the hills. 11The four kings seized all the goods of Sodom and Gomorrah and all their food; then they went away. 12They also carried off Abram's nephew Lot and his possessions, since he was living in Sodom.

13A man who had escaped came and reported this to Abram the Hebrew. Now Abram was living near the great trees of Mamre the Amorite, a brother of Eshkol and Aner, all of whom were allied with Abram. 14When Abram heard that his relative had been taken captive, he called out the 318 trained men born in his household and went in pursuit as far as Dan. 15During the night Abram divided his men to attack them and he routed them, pursuing them as far as Hobah, north of Damascus.

16He recovered all the goods and brought back his relative Lot and his
possessions, together with the women and the other people.
17After Abram returned from defeating Kedorlaomer and the kings
allied with him, the king of Sodom came out to meet him in the Valley of
Shaveh (that is, the King's Valley).
18Then Melchizedek king of Salem brought out bread and wine. He
was priest of God Most High, 19and he blessed Abram, saying,

"Blessed be Abram by God Most High,
Creator of heaven and earth.
20And praise be to God Most High,
who delivered your enemies into your hand."

Then Abram gave him a tenth of everything.
21The king of Sodom said to Abram, "Give me the people and keep
the goods for yourself."
22But Abram said to the king of Sodom, "With raised hand I have
sworn an oath to the LORD, God Most High, Creator of heaven and
earth, 23that I will accept nothing belonging to you, not even a thread
or the strap of a sandal, so that you will never be able to say, 'I made
Abram rich.' 24I will accept nothing but what my men have eaten and the
share that belongs to the men who went with me—to Aner, Eshkol and
Mamre. Let them have their share."

*Listening to the Text in the Story:* Biblical Text: Genesis 12:1–3

We have described the major theme of the Abraham story (see The Journey of Faith in the Live the Story section after 11:27–12:9) as connected to his journey of faith: How does Abraham respond to threats and obstacles to the fulfillment of the promises given in Genesis 12:1–3? It has often been pointed out that Genesis 14 seems an intrusion into the flow of the story from Genesis 13 to Genesis 15, both of which fit nicely into the major theme of the Abraham story. In many ways, the story of Abraham battling the four Near Eastern kings seems like an isolated story, not connected to reactions to threats or promises.

That said, on a closer examination, Genesis 14 certainly does relate to the promises of Genesis 12:1–3. In the present chapter, we observe the patriarch coming to the aid of the kings of Sodom, Gomorrah, Admah, Zeboyim, and Bela [Zoar]. He does so by attacking and defeating the kings of Shinar (Babylon), Ellasar, Elam, and Goyim. What plunged Abram into the fray was the kidnapping of Lot. Thus, this story illustrates God's promise to Abram: "I will bless those who bless you, and whoever curses you I will curse; and all peoples on earth will be blessed through you" (12:3). The four kings harmed Abram by kidnapping Lot and so God brought defeat on them through the agency of Abram and in the process he blesses the five Canaanite kings. At the end of the story Abram receives a blessing from an unlikely source, the priest-king of Salem, Melchizedek. Though unusual, there is no question but that Melchizedek is a divinely authorized representative of the true God that Abram himself worships.

As we will explain below, the ancient Near Eastern background to this story is not certain. We reserve a discussion of this topic until after an exposition of the chapter itself.

Genesis 14 gives an account of Abram's involvement in an international conflict between four kings from the east and five kings from within the land of Canaan. These kings and their lands are named (unlike the king of Egypt mentioned in 12:10–20) and this raises the possibility of situating Abram in a concrete and specific time period. As we will see, our hopes are ultimately frustrated, but first we will simply follow the story and then we will explore the possibility of identifying the time of this event.

### The Kings of the East Plunder the Kings of Canaan (14:1–12)

The opening paragraph (vv. 1–4) introduces the main players of the conflict. On the one hand, we have four kings from the east. Amraphel is the king of Shinar, which is another name for Babylon. Kedorlaomer is the king of Elam, which is a known nation in southwestern Iran. While we can identify the nations ruled by these two kings, much less certainty surrounds the other two. Arioch is the king of Ellasar and Tidal the king of Goyim. What is clear is that all four are associated with significant national powers in the ancient Near East. We will discuss various possibilities below.

On the other side are five local kings. Bera and Bersha are kings of Sodom and Gomorrah respectively, cities that are well known from Genesis 13 and 18–19, but we do not know exactly where these cities are located, though most think in the vicinity of the southern part of the Dead Sea. The other three kings (only two of whom are named, Shinab of Admah, Shemeber of Zeboyim and the king of Bela, also known as Zoar [probably the name by which it was known at the time of writing]) are presumably smaller locations that were in the vicinity of Sodom and Gomorrah. These cities are often mentioned together as a whole or in part elsewhere (Gen 10:19; Deut 29:23; Hos 11:8).

The narrator informs the reader that the latter kings had been subject to Kedorlaomer for twelve years, but in the thirteenth year they rebelled, leading to a reprisal raid by the Elamite king and his allies. The Canaanite coalition gathered together in the Dead Sea Valley (also known as the Valley of Siddim).

Though the rebellion took place in the thirteenth year of the Canaanites' vassalage to Kedorlaomer, the raid took place in the fourteenth year, presumably because it took a year for Kedorlaomer to amass his forces and make the long march from Elam to Canaan. The text then lists a number of tribes with their locations that the allied Near Eastern forces subdued on arriving in Canaan (vv. 5–7). They include the Rephaites (also known as Anakites, perhaps a giant tribe; Num 13:33; Deut 2:11; 3:11; Josh 12:4) in Ashteroth Karnaim (a city in Gilead), the Zuzites (perhaps also known as Zamzummites, known for their height; Deut 2:20) in Ham, the Emites (also mentioned for their height in Deut. 2:10–11) in Shaveh Kiriathaim (or "plain of Kiriathaim," a town in the Transjordan), the Horites (a Semitic people also known as Hurrians) in the hill country of Seir (an area south of the Dead Sea, which later was occupied by the Edomites), as far as El Paran (perhaps Elath on the northern tip of the R[e]ed Sea) near the desert. After this they went to En Mishpat ("spring of judgment," an early name for Kadesh, also known as Kadesh Barnea in the northern Sinai) and conquered the Amalekites (a particularly fearsome tribe in the Negev that will have a long history of conflict with the people of God beginning at Exod 17:1–8) and the Amorites (a name sometimes used generally of Canaanites) living in Hazezon Tamar. Not a lot is known about these tribes (or their locations) except that they had fearsome warriors.

After the initial conquests, the five kings introduced in the first paragraph of the chapter now take the field in the Valley of Siddim (the Dead Sea Valley, v. 3) to confront the four kings of the east. The four decisively rout the five local kings, scattering their armies. The narrator mentions tar pits in the area because some men fall into them during their retreat. The grammar of verse 10 is a bit ambiguous, literally the text reads, "when the kings of Sodom and Gomorrah fled, they fell into them," making it sound as if the kings were the ones swallowed up by the pits. Since these kings show up later in the chapter, some scholars believe that this tension indicates the weaving of different sources (see the Introduction). The NIV takes a different approach by translating "some of the men fell into them." Those who did not die on the battlefield or fall into the pits ran for the hills for protection.

The victorious kings then collected the plunder and captives. This included Lot, who as we know from chapter 13 resettled in the vicinity of Sodom. His capture will motivate Abram to enter the fray in order to rescue his nephew.

### Abraham Recovers the Plunder and Captives (14:13–16)

Abram was informed of Lot's capture by one of the people who successfully fled from the battlefield. The text then reminds us that Abram was located "near the great trees of Mamre" (see Gen 13:18), who here is identified as a person and either related to or allied with (see NIV note) two men named Eshkol and Aner (otherwise unknown). Abram was allied with all of them. Note that Mamre is identified as an Amorite, a general term sometimes equivalent with Canaanite, the occupants of Hazezon Tamar, earlier defeated by the coalition of four eastern kings (v. 7).

Abram mobilized his allies and the 318 "trained men born in his household," and they pursued the kings up to the city of Dan. The mention of Dan has long been recognized as a postmosaica (see Authorship and Date in Introduction) since this city (previously known as Laish) is not given this name until the period of Judges (18:29), and it gets its name from Abram's not-yet-born great grandson.

We don't get the details of Abram's strategy, but during the night, he divided his men and attacked them, likely by surprise. He defeated them, and then pursued them as they tried to retreat back to their homeland via Damascus. He succeeded in recapturing the plunder and the captives, including Lot, at an otherwise unknown spot north of Damascus called Hobah.

We should pause here to reflect on the nature of this victory. On the surface, it seems unbelievable that Abram with a limited force should be able to defeat four Near Eastern kings. No doubt the latter had a superior force, but there is no indication that they brought their national armies with them. To them, their intrusion into Canaan was probably little more than a raiding party. That said, we should not underestimate what the priest-king of Salem, Melchizedek, will say upon Abram's return, "praise be to God Most High, who delivered your enemies into your hand" (v. 20). That is, God provided the victory for Abram as he will throughout the history of Israel under the leadership of Moses, Joshua, David, and others.

### Abram and Melchizedek (Gen. 14:17–24)

After his victory, Abram then met the king of Sodom in the Valley of Shaveh, which the narrator tells the reader is also known as the King's Valley. If this is the same King's Valley in which Absalom later will build a monument to himself (2 Sam 18:18), then it is likely located to the south of Jerusalem. The meeting with the priest-king of Salem (an earlier name of Jerusalem) confirms this location.

From almost out of nowhere appears Melchizedek, one of the most mysterious figures of the Old Testament. He is identified as the king of Salem. The later name Jerusalem is likely formed from the Sumerian determinative *uru* prefixed to Salem.

He brought out bread and wine as a good host would. What is remarkable and mystifying about Melchizedek is that Abram recognizes him as someone who worships the same God as he does, quite surprising coming from a Canaanite king who is also acting like a priest of God Most High (*el elyon*). This name could be at home in a Canaanite religious context, though the Ugaritic texts that we have do not use this exact name. The chief god of the Canaanite pantheon was called *el*, but so was Abraham's God, since it is simply a generic word to refer to G/god. The epithet Most High (*elyon*) is never used with the god El in Canaanite texts, but it is used with Baal, but then again it is used with Abraham's God as well. The bottom line is that Abram clearly recognizes Melchizedek as one who shares his faith in the same God, and we should leave it at that, though we cannot tell how the Canaanite priest-king came to this knowledge. Not only does Abram consider Melchizedek a fellow worshiper of the true God, he also shows him deference when he receives a blessing from him (a superior blesses and an inferior receives the blessing), and he responds by giving him a tithe (a tenth) of the plunder.

Melchizedek is a priest before the institution of priesthood among the later descendants of Abraham, and he acts like one conferring blessing upon the people of God (see Num 6:22–27), here Abram. By blessing Abram, he asks God to live in harmony with him and grant him good relationships with other people as well as to meet his material needs (for blessing, see Reading in the Context of the Old Testament in the Introduction). Melchizedek invokes God as "Creator of heaven and earth" and thus more than able to provide for Abram. Melchizedek is acting as God's agent and acting in harmony with God's intention that Abram would be blessed (Gen 12:2–3). Further, the king-priest praises God and attributes Abram's victory over the four kings of the east to him. The last sentence of verse 20 simply says he "gave him a tenth of everything," leading some to think that it is Melchizedek who gives a gift to Abram, but in context and also according to later Scripture, this understanding is wrong. It is Abram who responds by giving Melchizedek a tenth of the plunder, the first time a tithe is given in the Bible. We will explore the significance of this gift in the Live the Story section.

Abram's response and actions in regard to Melchizedek contrast quite sharply with those toward the king of Sodom. The latter appears appreciative and generous when he asks Abram to return the captives but to keep the plunder for himself.

Abram makes it quite clear that he wants absolutely nothing to do with Sodom and its king, having taken an oath to the LORD (for the use of LORD in Genesis, see commentary at 26:23–35), whom he also refers to by the nomenclature used by Melchizedek in verse 19, giving us no doubt that Abram sees Melchizedek as a worshiper of the true God. By refusing to accept the plunder to enrich himself, he makes it clear that he is unwilling to be in a formal relationship with the king of Sodom. He will accept absolutely nothing ("not even a thread or the strap of a sandal," v. 23). He will allow his allies (Aner, Eshkol and Mamre) to benefit from the victory, but he will not be beholden to the king of Sodom.

It is not that Abram is loath to accept gifts from foreign kings (see 12:10–20). The reason must be that Sodom's exceptional evil (13:13) keeps him from any involvement that might show him dependent on that city. In this he also differentiates himself from Lot, who now freed will return to Sodom.

## Excursus: Fitting Genesis 14 into Ancient Near Eastern History

Before turning to the implications of this story for our lives today, we will address how this account might fit into the history of the broader ancient Near East. In the Introduction (Historical Setting of the Content of the Book), we talked about how it was difficult to situate the patriarchs into a precise point in the chronology of the ancient Near East. Here we have a story that names kings of well-known locations (at least in the case of Shinar=Babylon as well as Elam). We have fairly extensive lists of kings from these areas. However, there are complications. We will now explore what we know and what we do not know as we try to connect Genesis 14 to extrabiblical history.

For our purposes, the discussion of the identity of the kings of the chapter has proven the most salient and, in the final analysis, both the most tantalizing and frustrating.[1] Discussing the kings one by one is the best approach.

1. Two of the most interesting discussants of these issues are M. Astour and J. A. Emerton ("Some False Clues in the Study of Genesis xiv," *VT* 21 [1971]: 24–47). Astour ("Political and Cosmic Symbolism in Genesis 14 and Its Babylonian Sources," in *Biblical Motifs: Origins and Transformations*, ed. A. Altmann and J. A. Emerton, [Cambridge, MA: Harvard University Press, 1966], 65–112) argues that Genesis 14 was a product of the Deuteronomic school from the late sixth century BC and reflects political realities of that time period. He believed that the four kings represent Babylon, Assyria (Ellasar), Elam, and Hatti, the four corners of the world. Furthermore, he believes that the Deuteronomic historian found a kindred spirit in, and thus was inspired by, the so-called

Kedorlaomer king of Elam is the first, who is said to be the head of the foreign coalition. No doubt attends the fact that this king has an authentic-sounding Elamite name. Kedor stands for a common first element in Elamite royal names, Kudur. However, the second part, which certainly could stand for something authentic in Elamite, does not sound like anything associated with a known Elamite king.[2] Then, Amraphel king of Shinar is clearly meant to indicate a king from Babylon from other references in the Bible. At first Amraphel was thought to be Hammurapi, but the philological differences were too large to be overcome, so that identification has been universally dropped. The identification of Arioch of Ellasar has had a similar journey. At first, the geographical location was thought to be the city of Larsa, but more recently identifications include lesser-known areas like Alsi in northern Mesopotamia or Ilansura near Carchemish. Arioch at first was thought to be Arriwuk, the fifth son of Zimri-lim of Mari (from the early Old Babylonian period), but this assertion is now considered unlikely. Tidal, the fourth king, has a name that is attested for four Hittite kings (Tudhaliya). He is identified as king of Goyim, which means "nations." This identification is quite strange, but may be like the well-attested ancient name Umman-manda, which is a general term like "people," used in reference to Scythians and Cimmerians.

The names sound authentic, then,[3] even if we cannot with certainty identify the particular kings with names mentioned outside the Bible. In addition, Kitchen may well be correct that the period before the Old Babylonian period, though not directly attesting this group of kings, may be the only period where such a coalition was even possible.[4]

After all, the period before Hammurapi was a time when Mesopotamia was carved up between a number of less powerful leaders. He was the one who subjected many of them because of his imperial tendencies.[5] Beyond this review, however, not much can be said. Genesis 14 does not, after all, provide

---

Spartoli texts. Emerton provides an effective refutation of Astour's thesis, however, showing how much speculation is involved in it. In a second article ("The Riddle of Genesis xiv," *VT* 21 [1971]: 403–39), he presents a very complex five-stage redactional history of the passage.

2. We do have a list of Elamite kings from 2100 to 1100 BC. Albright first identified Kedorlaomer with an unknown king named Kudur-Lagamar, but later argued that it is Kudur-Nahuti, who was an aggressive military presence in the ancient Near East from 1625 to 1610 BC. W. F. Albright, "A Third Revision of the Early Chronology of Western Asia," *BASOR* 88 (1842): 28–36.

3. V. P. Hamilton, *The Book of Genesis Chapters 1–17* (Grand Rapids: Eerdmans, 1990): 402, also points out that the itinerary of the four kings is given with "geographical exactness."

4. K. Kitchen, *Ancient Orient and Old Testament* (Downers Grove, IL: InterVarsity Press, 1966), 45. See his more recent discussion in *On the Reliability of the Old Testament* (Grand Rapids: Eerdmans, 2003), 319–23.

5. Note the recent article by O. Margalith, "The Riddle of Genesis 14 and Melchizedek," *ZAW* 112 (2000): 501–8. He argues that the text is a *para-mythe* that fits in with the events of the thirteenth century BC.

us with a specific connection to extrabiblical history—at least, not to extrabiblical history as we currently know it.

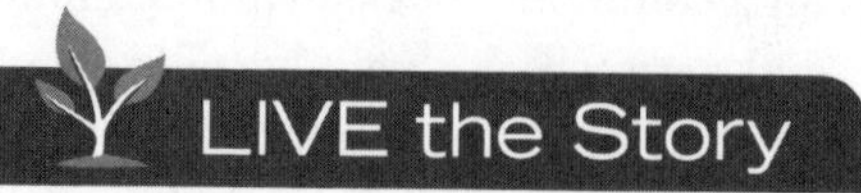


**"Who Delivered Your Enemies into Your Hand" (14:20b)**

Abram led his men and his allies in a successful raid on the four eastern kings who had raided Canaan. He recovered the plunder and returned the people that they had kidnapped, including Lot. We do not get a lot of the detail about the size of the enemy army or the strategy that Abram used. It is Melchizedek who points out the really determinative factor in the victory when he says that it was God "who delivered your enemies into your hand" (v. 20b).

This phrase indicates that God took an active part in Abram's military success and introduces us, for the first time really, to the idea that God is a warrior who fights for his people against their enemies who are often much stronger than they are. After the crossing of the R(e)ed Sea, this picture of God becomes explicit when Moses and the Israelites sing:

> The Lord is my strength and my defense;
> he has become my salvation.
> He is my God, and I will praise him,
> my father's God, and I will exalt him.
> The Lord is a warrior;
> the Lord is his name. (Exod 15:2–3)

Throughout the pages of the Old Testament, God comes to fight for his beleaguered people. He is with Joshua at Jericho (Josh 6), Gideon against the Midianites (Judg 7), David in his battle with Goliath (1 Sam 17:45–47), Jehoshaphat at the battle of Tekoa (2 Chr 20), and the list goes on and on.[6]

But what relevance does the picture of God as a warrior have for the Christian today? Indeed, many people have found the idea that God is a warrior disturbing and embarrassing even when God's violence is directed toward evil people like the four kings of the east.[7] While we cannot engage in a full interaction of this understandable but misguided sentiment, we need to recognize that the picture of God as a warrior is not an Old Testament versus a New Testament idea.

---

6. See T. Longman III and D. Reid, *God is a Warrior* (Grand Rapids: Zondervan, 1995).

7. E. Siebert, *The Violence of Scripture: Overcoming the Old Testament's Legacy* (Minneapolis: Fortress, 2012); P. Enns, *The Bible Tells Me So...: Why Defending the Scripture Has Made Us Unable to Read It* (San Francisco: HarperOne, 2014).

Indeed, the Christian needs to know, and take encouragement from, the fact that Jesus is our warrior. In the Old Testament, God not only fought for his people, but also against them when they were disobedient, ultimately leading to God coming "like an enemy" against Jerusalem to destroy it (Lam 2). However, before the Old Testament comes to a close, God directed his prophets (see Dan 7; Zech 14; Mal 4) to announce the coming of the divine warrior who would save his people from the oppression of the wicked.

When the New Testament opens, we hear the voice of John the Baptist who echoes the sentiments of these Old Testament prophets. He announces one who comes after him, who "will baptize you with the Holy Spirit and fire. His winnowing fork is in his hand, and he will clear the threshing floor, gathering his wheat into the barn and burning up the chaff with unquenchable fire" (Matt 3:11–12).

After his baptism, John gets thrown in jail, while Jesus begins his ministry. John starts to hear reports that disturb him. Rather than bringing judgment against the wicked, Jesus is preaching the good news and healing people. Stunned, John sends his disciples to Jesus with a question, "Are you the one who is to come, or should we expect someone else?" (Matt 11:3). Jesus responds by doing more of the same, healing the sick and preaching the good news. Through his actions, Jesus is telling John that he is the divine warrior, but that he has heightened and intensified the battle so that it is focused on the spiritual powers and authorities and this enemy is not defeated by killing but by dying.

Thus, Jesus' redemptive work on the cross is likened to a military victory (Eph 4:8; Col 2:13–15). His work secured the ultimate victory against the forces of evil, but the battle will not end until he returns again.

Thus, the New Testament pictures Christians as engaged in battle with the "powers and authorities" just as Abram was in conflict with the four kings who were human embodiments of evil. And, according to Paul, it is in the power of God that we fight these enemies (Eph 6:10–20).

The New Testament tells Christians that we are engaged in a battle all throughout our lives with the powers of evil. But we can take heart in the fact that we fight this battle in God's armor and with God's weapons. When we have victory, we, like Abram, need to recognize that we do so because God has delivered the enemy into our hands.

### Keep Me from Evil

Abram will have nothing to do with the king of Sodom, so that the king cannot say "I made Abram rich" (14:23). Though not explicitly stated, Abram's motive for distancing himself is almost certainly because "the people of Sodom were wicked and were sinning greatly against the LORD" (13:13). Abram's actions here contrast with that of his nephew Lot, who, as we have already seen, chose to live in the vicinity of Sodom. His choice has already earned him trouble since he was kidnapped by the invading Near Eastern kings. Abram has bailed him out, but he will return to Sodom where we will find him again in Genesis 18–19. We will explore his actions and choices when we come to those chapters, but for now we will look at Abram.

Abram's choice to separate himself from evil must first be understood within the context of the Old Testament. At this time, God does not want his people to mix with other nations. He does not want them even to associate with those nations for fear that their evil will influence their actions and turn them away from proper worship. Joshua exhorted Israel not to "associate with these nations that remain among you ..." (Josh 23:7). This divine desire will lead to the command to kill all the Canaanites (see Deut 20:16–18). And, of course, anyone who has read the books of Judges or Kings knows that Israel did not obey God in keeping separate from evil, but rather frequently succumbed to the temptation to worship other gods and act in corrupt ways.

God's desire for Abram and his descendants to stay separate from evil was not because he hated the nations. We must remember that the purpose of Abram's election (Gen 12:1–3) was to ultimately lead to the blessing of the nations, but this blessing would not be accomplished if Abram simply blended in.

And in any case, Abram's harsh refusal to accept anything from the king of Sodom is to be contrasted with his affirmation of Melchizedek. Melchizedek is also a Canaanite king, but far from evil, this priest-king of Salem worshipped the same God as Abram.

The godly do not associate with evil people. According to Psalm 1:1:

> Blessed is the one who does not walk in step with the wicked
> or stand in the way that sinners take
> or sit in the company of mockers...
>
> Do not set foot on the path of the wicked
> or walk in the way of evildoers.
> Avoid it, do not travel on it;
> turn from it and go on your way.
> For they cannot rest until they do evil;
> they are robbed of sleep till they make someone stumble.
> They eat the bread of wickedness
> and drink the wine of violence. (Prov 4:14–17)

Abram, in this story at least, is a model of someone who keeps his distance from evil people, a virtue extolled in the Old Testament. The blessing that would extend from Abram and his descendants would come as they kept themselves holy and God blessed them drawing the attention of the surrounding people. They would realize that God's people lived prosperous and meaningful lives because of God's blessing on his obedient people and they would be drawn into a relationship with him.

However, due to the people's sin, it did not work out that way. As we turn to the New Testament, we certainly hear the call to be holy (1 Cor 1:2; 1 Thess 3:13; 4:7; 1 Tim 2:8), but rather than keeping separate from the godless, Jesus sent his church into the midst of the world: "go and make disciples of all nations, baptizing them in the name of the Father and of the Son and of the Holy Spirit, and teaching them to obey everything I have commanded you. And surely I am with you always, to the very end of the age" (Matt 28:19–20).

Paul does tell Christians not to associate with sinners, but specifically those within the church, not outside of it: "I wrote to you in my letter not to associate with sexually immoral people—not at all meaning the people of this world who are immoral, or the greedy and swindlers, or idolaters. In that case you have to leave this world" (1 Cor 5:9–10).

The point is that, while we associate with unbelievers for the purposes of the gospel, we do not associate with them in their evil activities and thoughts. Jesus sends his disciples out into an evil world ("I am sending out like sheep among wolves"), but to be wise in the interaction and to remain distant from its evil ("be as shrewd as snakes and as innocent as doves, " Matt 10:16).

## The Tithe

"Then Abram gave him a tenth of everything" (14:20). Here we have the first mention of a tithe in Scripture. The second occurrence is also found in Genesis (28:22), when Jacob promises a tenth to God if God brings him safely back from Paddan Aram. Even today, some churches will encourage their members to give a tenth of their income to the work of the church. Is this a scriptural principle that should be followed today?

The two occurrences in Genesis are voluntary offerings, not obligatory. Abram's offering indicates his recognition that Melchizedek as king of Sodom was the leader of the Canaanite coalition (studies have shown that it was an ancient Near Eastern custom to give the king a tenth[8]) and also that this king was priest of the same God that Abram himself worshiped. Jacob's vow was also a voluntary offering.

Though these gifts were voluntary, there is no doubt but that later Mosaic law mandated that Israelites give a tenth. Nowhere do these later laws ground

8. Walton, "Genesis," 83.

the practice in the earlier events recorded in Genesis. Indeed, there is some question as to how the various tithing laws in the Torah relate to one another.

In Numbers 18:21–24 (see also Lev 27:30–33) God announces that he grants to the Levites "all the tithes in Israel as their inheritance in return for the work they do while serving at the tent of meeting" (v. 21). In the next paragraph (vv. 25–29), he tells Moses to inform the Levites that they are to take a tithe of the tithe they receive and give that to the priesthood. Here, in other words, we learn how God provided for the provision for the Levites and priests.

The book of Deuteronomy also addresses the issue of the tithe (Deut 12:6, 11, 17; 26:12–15; esp. 14:22–29), but in a way that some believe conflicts with the law as found in Numbers (and Leviticus). According to Deuteronomy 14:12–15, the tithe brought to the sanctuary would be consumed by the offerers. Either a tenth of the grain, new wine, and olive oil and firstborn of the herds and flocks were brought or, if the distance to the sanctuary was too great, these goods could be exchanged for silver and then "use the silver to buy whatever you like: cattle, sheep, wine or other fermented drink, or anything you wish. Then you and your household shall eat there in the presence of the Lord your God and rejoice" (Deut 14:26). In addition, there is the provision that every three years the tithes would not be brought to the sanctuary but stored in the various towns for the Levites, poor, and other disadvantaged people.

The early rabbis posited three different tithes (the first tithe to the Levites and priests [Num 18:21–29], the second that was used for the celebration of the worshipers [Deut 14:22–27], and a third in the third year for the Levites and the poor in the various towns [Deut 14:28–29]). Other, more modern, scholars try to reconcile these laws by positing a historical development in the tithe, but Averbeck disagrees and provides a reasonable perspective on how these laws complement each other.[9] There was one tithe and that was presented during an annual festival at the sanctuary. From that tithe, resources were expended for celebration of the worshipers themselves in keeping with Numbers 18, but this would not expend more than a fraction of the tithe itself. A tithe of the tithe for the Levites would be used for the maintenance of the priests. And the tithe of every third year (the third and sixth year of the sabbatical year cycle) would be placed not at the central sanctuary, but in the local towns and used for the sustenance of the local Levites and the poor and the vulnerable.

Thus, there is no question but that the tithe was a legal requirement imposed on God's people from the time of Moses. Those familiar with the

9. See R. E. Averbeck, "*ma'aser*," *NIDOTTE* 2:1035–55.

history of the Israelite people as described in the Old Testament will not be surprised to realize that Israel did not live up to this ideal.

However, the question for the Christian today is whether the tithe is still a legal requirement. Must Christians set apart a tenth of their income for donation to the church or at least to the furtherance of the gospel?

The Gospels only mention the tithe as the practice of the Jewish people of the time. Indeed, Jesus criticizes the Jewish leaders for keeping the tithe but ignoring the broader principles of justice, mercy, and faithfulness (Matt 23:23; Luke 11:42; see also Luke 18:12). The only other place in the New Testament where the tithe is mentioned is in Hebrews 7:1–10 where the author cites the story of Genesis 14 where Abraham pays a tithe to Melchizedek in order to argue that Jesus is the ultimate high priest.

In other words, the New Testament, after the death and resurrection of Christ, never appeals to the law of the tithe as a requirement for New Testament Christians. Averbeck points out that this observation is more than an argument from silence, since there are ample opportunities in Paul's many appeals for Christians to be generous in their giving for him to cite the requirement of a tithe (Rom 15:25–28; 1 Cor 9:16–18; 16:1–3; 2 Cor 8–9; Eph 4:28, etc.).[10]

Rather than thinking that these biblical-theological observations on the tithe relieve the Christian of giving a tenth of their income to God's work, one needs to wonder whether a tenth is sufficient. If the Old Testament believer gave a tenth, what should the Christian give who is the recipient of God's grace and mercy in Jesus? There is no legal formula here. We should give out of our gratitude and joy in the Lord's work in our life.

### Jesus, a "High Priest Forever, in the Order of Melchizedek" (Heb 6:20)

Melchizedek is an enigmatic figure, a priest-king who is a fellow worshiper of the true God with Abram, making a sudden appearance after the battle with the four eastern kings. The mystery deepens as Abram treats him as a superior as the patriarch receives his blessing and then also gives him a tenth of the plunder. Melchizedek leaves the scene quietly and almost as quickly as he appeared in it.

He is only mentioned one other time in the Old Testament and his second appearance in Psalm 110 does nothing to clarify his first appearance. If Genesis 14:18–20 is one of the more enigmatic narrative passages in the Old Testament, Psalm 110 certain vies for one of the most, if not the most, enigmatic passages in the book of Psalms.

10. Ibid., 1054.

The title of Psalm 110 associates it with David and begins with the announcement of a divine oracle to "my lord." If David is speaking, the identity of his lord is unclear. Recent research comparing Psalm 110 with Assyrian royal prophecies suggests that "Psalm 110 was delivered at the temple by a prophet, possibly a temple functionary, as part of Israel's cultus and pertains to the newly minted king."[11] The prophet would be speaking on behalf of God when he announces to the Davidic king:

> Sit at my right hand
> until I make your enemies
> a footstool for your feet. (v. 1)

The next two verses pronounce victory for the king over his enemies. Then in verse 4, the psalmist presents a second divine oracle:

> The LORD has sworn
> and will not change his mind:
> "You are a priest forever
> in the order of Melchizedek."

The final stanza describes how God will support this king who is a priest in the order of Melchizedek by again announcing his victory.

The announcement in verse 4 is enigmatic in that other texts suggest that kings should not infringe on priestly duties (1 Sam 13:8–15), even though it is true that David, the putative composer of the psalm, occasionally acted like a priest (2 Sam 6), and his sons are called priests (2 Sam 8:18). Perhaps it is because kings were not permitted priestly prerogatives in Israel that the composer cites Melchizedek rather than Aaron as the founder of the king's priestly order.

We are left with questions about both Genesis 14 and Psalm 110 when we turn to the New Testament to see how the Melchizedek tradition is used in the book of Hebrews. The unnamed and unknown author of Hebrews cites the Melchizedek tradition in order to make a very important theological point, namely that Jesus is the ultimate high priest.

Let me begin by saying that it is precisely the mystery of the two Old Testament references to Melchizedek that appeals so much to the author of Hebrews. The author exploits the ambiguities of the Old Testament figure in order to make his important point concerning Christ as priest. He is an exalted priest — so exalted that he transcends the normal categories. He is

---

11. B. Waltke and J. Houston, *The Psalms as Christian Worship: A Historical Commentary* (Grand Rapids: Eerdmans, 2010), 500, who cite J. Hilber, *Cultic Prophecy in the Psalms*, BZAW 352 (Berlin: Walter de Gruyter, 2005).

so much better than Aaron, the priests, and the Levites that he is of a whole different order.

It is not the purpose of the author of Hebrews to tell us more about the Old Testament figure Melchizedek, and he is clearly not saying that Melchizedek was a pre-incarnate appearance of Jesus. The author's allusion to Melchizedek is his way, in keeping with first-century literary practices, of saying that Jesus is the priest *par excellence*.

With this in mind, we will follow the argument of Hebrews in regard to Jesus as the ultimate high priest. Hebrews 4 begins by describing the future rest that God provides for those who follow him. But the tone is one of warning about the possibility of God's judgment. The author's audience is told to "be careful that none of you be found to have fallen short of it" (Heb 4:1). This section concludes by describing how God's Word exposes our souls with surgical precision: "it penetrates even to dividing soul and spirit, joints and marrow" (v. 12). Our God is a God of judgment and justice.

Once this somber note of warning is given, Hebrews turns to the comforting thought that Jesus is there for us. Hebrews 4:14 says: "Therefore, since we have a great high priest who has ascended into heaven, Jesus the Son of God, let us hold firmly to the faith we profess." The road is hard, but Jesus is there to bring us spotless before God.

A priest is someone who brings the people before God. He also brings the people's gifts to God. Aaron and his sons did that, and now Jesus does that as well. Hebrews further informs us that Jesus, just like human priests, experienced temptations. Since we are all tempted, the priests are one with us and can well represent who we are.

However, it is precisely at this point that Hebrews points to the huge difference between Jesus and typical human priests. The priests were tempted and often fell into sin. Jesus was tempted, but never sinned. He is a sinless priest. This has monumental ramifications. Priests not only offered sacrifices for the people; they had to offer sacrifices for themselves as well. The high priest even had to offer sacrifices for himself on the Day of Atonement (Lev 16:6). Jesus, though, does not have to offer sacrifices for his own sins. He has none. He exclusively represents us before God.

It is at this point that the author associates Jesus with the priestly order of Melchizedek for the first time. After quoting Psalm 2 and thus identifying Jesus as God's Son, he cites Psalm 110:4 in Hebrews 5:6 (see above).

Before developing the relationship between Jesus and Melchizedek, the author urges the reader to move from the simple things of the faith (milk) to the more complex concepts of a mature believer (solid food). While not making an explicit connection, the context suggests that the relationship between

Christ and the enigmatic figure of Melchizedek is no simple teaching. Those who have easy answers to the questions of this passage (for instance, insisting that Melchizedek is really Jesus) go against the tone of this admonition.

We return to the subject of Melchizedek at the end of Hebrews 6, and it is developed in chapters 7 and 8. It begins with an interpretive recap of Genesis 14 and the encounter between Abraham and Melchizedek. However, there is an interpretive slant that we will now bring to the fore.

Hebrews 7:3 comments that the priest-king of Salem was "without father or mother, without genealogy, without beginning of days or end of life, resembling the Son of God, he remains a priest forever." If we read this statement with modern lenses on, we will misunderstand it to say that Melchizedek was not born in a human way and is still alive. But if we put ourselves back into the ancient world that produced Hebrews, we will know that the author is speaking about Melchizedek as a literary figure. Nowhere is his birth or death recorded. He pops into the narrative in Genesis and pops right out again. The author of Hebrews exploits this literary fact in order to make the overriding point that Jesus is better than Levi and his priesthood surpasses the Levitical priesthood.

Indeed, the text is saying that Melchizedek was Abraham's superior! Abraham was the father of the faith, but he submitted himself to Melchizedek. Again, according to first-century Jewish thinking, if Abraham bowed to Melchizedek in homage, so Levi his descendant, a product of his loins, so to speak, also showed his obeisance to Melchizedek. This is the force of Hebrews 7:9–10:

> One might even say that Levi, who collects the tenth, paid the tenth through Abraham, because when Melchizedek met Abraham, Levi was still in the body of his ancestor.

The association between Christ and Melchizedek rather than Levi also helps the author of Hebrews explain one other well-known fact. An Aaronic priest was a descendant of Levi, while Jesus was from the royal tribe of Judah. Associated with this is the fact that Melchizedek was not only priest, but also king of Salem. There was a clear and important distinction between priests and kings in Israel. Indeed, Saul got himself into a lot of trouble by offering sacrifices (1 Sam 13).

The teaching of Hebrews is summarized by the statement that begins chapter 8: "Now the main point of what we are saying is this: We do have such a high priest, who sat down at the right hand of the throne of the Majesty in heaven, and who serves in the sanctuary, the true tabernacle set up by the Lord, not by a mere human being." This passage combines the teaching about place of worship with the agent of worship. Indeed, it continues by talking about the mode of worship—Jesus goes to the sacred tent to offer sacrifice.

CHAPTER 13

# Genesis 15

## LISTEN to the Story

[15:1]After this, the word of the LORD came to Abram in a vision:

"Do not be afraid, Abram.
I am your shield,
your very great reward."

[2]But Abram said, "Sovereign LORD, what can you give me since I remain childless and the one who will inherit my estate is Eliezer of Damascus?" [3]And Abram said, "You have given me no children; so a servant in my household will be my heir."

[4]Then the word of the LORD came to him: "This man will not be your heir, but a son who is your own flesh and blood will be your heir." [5]He took him outside and said, "Look up at the sky and count the stars— if indeed you can count them." Then he said to him, "So shall your offspring be."

[6]Abram believed the LORD, and he credited it to him as righteousness.

[7]He also said to him, "I am the LORD, who brought you out of Ur of the Chaldeans to give you this land to take possession of it."

[8]But Abram said, "Sovereign LORD, how can I know that I will gain possession of it?"

[9]So the LORD said to him, "Bring me a heifer, a goat and a ram, each three years old, along with a dove and a young pigeon."

[10]Abram brought all these to him, cut them in two and arranged the halves opposite each other; the birds, however, he did not cut in half. [11]Then birds of prey came down on the carcasses, but Abram drove them away.

[12]As the sun was setting, Abram fell into a deep sleep, and a thick and dreadful darkness came over him. [13]Then the LORD said to him, "Know for certain that for four hundred years your descendants will be strangers in a country not their own and that they will be enslaved and mistreated there. [14]But I will punish the nation they serve as slaves, and afterward they will come out with great possessions. [15]You, however, will go to your ancestors in peace and be buried at a good old age. [16]In the

fourth generation your descendants will come back here, for the sin of the Amorites has not yet reached its full measure."

[17]When the sun had set and darkness had fallen, a smoking firepot
with a blazing torch appeared and passed between the pieces. [18]On
that day the LORD made a covenant with Abram and said, "To your
descendants I give this land, from the Wadi of Egypt to the great river, the
Euphrates — [19]the land of the Kenites, Kenizzites, Kadmonites, [20]Hittites,
Perizzites, Rephaites, [21]Amorites, Canaanites, Girgashites and Jebusites."

*Listening to the Text in the Story:* Biblical Text: Genesis 12:1–3; Ancient Near Eastern Texts: Nuzi and other Old Babylonian Texts (described below)

As will be explained in the Explain the Story section, Genesis 15 is a reaffirmation of the promises given to Abraham in Genesis 12:1–3. God has promised that his descendants will become a "great nation" that will be blessed and will bless the world, but so far he hasn't even had a son.

The dialogue between God and Abram as well as the ritual performed at the end of the chapter sound strange to modern ears, but would have been clear to ancient readers. Modern readers are helped by the recovery of ancient Near Eastern social customs on texts found at the ancient site of Nuzi (Yorgham Tepe) and other Old Babylonian sites. We will explain their relevance while explaining the story.

## EXPLAIN the Story

### God Reassures Abram (15:1–6)

We do not know how long a period elapsed between the events of chapter 14 when God gave Abram victory over the four eastern kings and chapter 15 when God presents himself to the patriarch through a vision ("After this," v. 1). God approaches Abram in order to reassure him, and from the latter's reaction, the reassurance was needed because Abram again doubted God's intention to fulfill his promises, particularly the promise that he would become a "great nation" (12:2), which includes the idea that he would have many descendants. Sarai still had not gotten pregnant and Abram was getting desperate.

God begins by asserting the benefit he brings to Abram. The most likely translation of God's initial speech is found in the NIV text, wherein God reminds Abram of his protective role in his life ("I am your shield") and also the source of all the good things that he experiences ("your very great reward"). We should also note that the noun shield (*magen*) finds a connection to Melchizedek's statement that God "delivered" (*miggen*) your enemies into your hand," 14:20. The alternative translation (NIV notes) is possible, but not likely. The translation of *magen* as "sovereign" involves an emendation to *magan* and is based on a doubtful Ugaritic cognate. The alternative translation of the following colon ("your reward will be very great") changes the focus from God being the reward himself to being the actor who will bring the reward to Abram.

In either case, God speaks these words to move Abram from fear to confidence ("Do not be afraid"). That Abram's fear is not easily allayed is made clear by his reaction to God's short speech, which also identifies the cause of his anxiety. He remains without child and natural heir, even though he continues to grow older and older.

Since he has no child of his own, he then identifies a person named Eliezer of Damascus as his heir (vv. 2–3). Eliezer is described as a "servant of my household." Randall Garr points out that behind the NIV's clear translation of Abram's words here is gibberish that literally would be translated "Benmesheq's my family; that is, Damascus Eliezer." This, though, as Garr points out, is not textual confusion but reflects Abram's frustrated state of mind.[1]

But why would this Eliezer be his heir, rather than, say, Lot, his nephew? In the light of discoveries of a number of cuneiform tablets at the ancient site of Nuzi (=Yorgham Tepe) in the 1930s, modern readers have a better understanding of Abram's comment here. Nuzi was a city in the general area of Harran, Abram's ancestral homeland (Gen 11:27–32). Not only do these tablets come from the general vicinity of Abram's ancestral homeland, but they also come from the same general time period (first half of the second millennium BC). The texts discovered there were written in Akkadian and revealed a number of social customs that are also observed in the patriarchal narratives. At first, these texts were used to try to establish the essential historicity of the patriarchal narratives,[2] but since such an argument depended on these customs being unique to this time period and region, once it became clear that they had broader use, the apologetic argument became much weaker.[3] Even

1. W. Randall Garr, "Abram's Election in Faith," in *The Call of Abraham: Essays on the Election of Israel in Honor of Jon D. Levenson*, ed. Gary A. Anderson and Joel S. Kaminsky (Notre Dame: University of Notre Dame Press, 2013), 23–43.

2. W. F. Albright, "Abram the Hebrew: A New Archaeological Interpretation," *BASOR* 163 (1961): 36–54; C. H. Gordon, "Biblical Customs and the Nuzi Tablets," *BA* 3 (1940): 1–12.

3. For critiques of the use of the Nuzi materials in relationship to the patriarchal narratives, see T. L. Thompson, *The Historicity of the Patriarchal Narratives*, BZAW 133 (Berlin: De Gruyter, 1974); J. Van Seters, *Abraham in History and Tradition* (New Haven, CT: Yale University Press, 1975).

so, the Nuzi texts help to illuminate the significance of certain patriarchal statements and actions, including Abram's claim that Eliezer of Damascus was his heir.[4]

The adoption of a household servant was an attempt to solve one of the gravest consequences of not having a child. As a couple grew older, they would need assistance as their physical and mental abilities deteriorated. In the absence of a child, who would take care of them? After all, there were no retirement centers in the ancient world. A solution was offered by the adoption of a household servant like Eliezer, who would take care of them in their old age and then, in return, would inherit their possessions.

Thus, we can now see that Abram's statement uncovers his attempt to manufacture an heir in the absence of a child. Thus, he does not trust that God will follow through on his promise. Once again Abram is at a low point in his journey of faith (See The Journey of Faith after the commentary on 12:4–9). Indeed, he directly blames God for his predicament and the reason why he has resorted to manipulation of a social custom to manufacture an heir ("you have given me no children," an accusation which certainly implies that Abram does not think the future will be any different, v. 3).

Even so, God does not react with anger, though he immediately denies Abram's charge. He rejects the idea that Eliezer will be Abram's heir and again promises that he and Sarah will have a child. And from that child will come multiple descendants. God asks Abram to look at the stars and understand that he will have as many descendants as the stars. Modern urban dwellers should remember that their experience of a night sky surrounded by the lights of the city or a town is nothing like the celestial scene that Abram would have observed. To him the sky would indeed be filled with a countless number of stars. He would have, or at least should have, remembered that the God who was making this analogy was also the creator of those stars. Certainly, he could give a child to an aging Abram and Sarah.

God's speech appears to have had its desired effect of reassuring Abram. In what to Christians (see below, Abram as a Model of Justification by Faith) is one of the most significant verses in the Old Testament, the narrator tells the reader that Abram believed God and God credited it to him as righteousness.

On this occasion, God also reminded Abram of his identity as well his presence in his life in the past ("I am the Lord, who brought you out of Ur of the Chaldeans," v. 7), while also evoking the second feature of the promise

4. M. J. Selman, "Comparative Customs and the Patriarchal Age," in *Essays on the Patriarchal Narratives*, ed. A. Millard and D. J. Wiseman (Winona Lake, IN: Eisenbrauns, 1983), 91–140; B. L. Eichler, "Nuzi and the Bible: A Retrospective," in *DUMU-E-DUB-BA-A: Studies in Honor of Ake W. Sjoberg*, ed. H. Behrens et al., (Philadelphia: Samuel Noah Kramer Fund, 1989), 107–19.

that he would be a great nation (12:2). To be a great nation, Abram would need multiple descendants and also land. Abram's focused concern in this chapter is on the first part, but God here reminds him of the second and his intention to fulfill both. But now that God has raised the issue of the land promise, Abram requests assurance that God will indeed give him the land, in which he now lives as a sojourner.

### A Ritual of Reassurance (15:7–21)

God does not dismiss Abram's concern or simply reiterate the promise, but rather gives the patriarch instructions in order to perform a ritual. The ritual strikes a modern reader as bizarre and opaque, but ancient Near Eastern analogues help make its significance clear, at least in broad contours.

In brief, the ritual can be illuminated by reference to ancient Near Eastern documents from Alalakh, Mari, and Hatti. All these texts are from the second millennium BC.[5] The Alalakh text is from the seventeenth century BC and has been translated as: "Abban placed himself under oath to Iarimlim and had cut the neck of a sheep (saying): '(Let me so die) if I take back that which I gave thee!"[6]

The similarity with Genesis 15 is found in the connection between a sacrifice and the establishment of a covenant treaty. In particular, we see the superior party (Abban in the Alalakh text), who is assuring the fulfillment of the agreement, taking a self-curse. God, who takes the form of fire and smoke in Genesis, takes such a self-curse on himself.

However, what is missing here is the passing through the divided parts. For that we appeal to another ancient Near Eastern text, this time from the Hittites. A text that describes a ritual after a military defeat says:

> If the troops have been beaten by the enemy they perform a ritual "behind" the river, as follows: they "cut through" a man, a goat, a puppy, and a little pig; they place half on this side and half on that side, and in front of them they make a gate of ... wood and stretch a ... over it, and in front of the gate they light fires on this side and on that, and the troops walk right through, and when they come to the river they sprinkle water over them.[7]

When these and other similar texts are studied together in conjunction with Genesis 15, we can understand the significance of the ritual of slaughtering these animals and God's passing through them. As in the ancient Near

5. I am indebted to the discussion found in Hamilton, *The Book of Genesis 1–17*, 430–34.
6. D. J. Wiseman, "Abban and Alalah," *Journal of Cuneiform Studies* 12 (1958): 129.
7. O. Gurney, *The Hittites* (Baltimore: Penguin, 1954), 151.

Eastern examples, God is performing a self-curse ritual, saying in effect that he will be like those killed and divided animals if he does not keep his promises. He is reassuring Abram, using a custom known in his day.

The broad contours of the ritual are that it constitutes a self-maledictory oath. As a human custom of the age, two people who walk together between the animal halves are saying to themselves and each other "if I betray this agreement, may I die a horrible death like these animals."

But it is only God who goes through the animal parts, and he in the form of a "smoking firepot with a blazing torch" (v. 17). Nowhere else in the Bible does God make his presence known in precisely this form, but this theophany makes use of a very common element, namely fire. God often makes his presence palpable through the medium of fire. We only need to think of the burning bush (Exod 3), the fire and smoke emanating from Mount Sinai (Exod 19:16–19), and the pillars of smoke and fire during the wilderness wandering (Exod 40:34–38).

Thus, God undertakes a ritual that, in essence, says to Abram, "if I do not keep my promise, may I become like these animals." Of course, God cannot die, but that is precisely the point, he cannot lie either. He will certainly keep his promise of providing for descendants and land so that Abram's descendants might become a "great nation" (12:2) and thus be blessed and become a blessing for the nations (12:3).

Interestingly, while Abram is arranging the halves of the animal opposite each other, "birds of prey" attempt to carry away the carcasses, but Abram successfully chases them away. The birds listed as unclean in Leviticus 11:13–19 are birds of prey, presumably because they come into contact with carcasses. It is unlikely that the birds of prey would be mentioned in this ritual unless they carried some symbolic significance, but there is no clear consensus on what that would be. However, some credence can be given to the idea that they represent hostile forces, perhaps foreign nations, who will in the future threaten Israel's covenant relationship with God.

While Abram slaughtered and positioned the animal carcasses while he was awake, God did not make his appearance known until he had fallen into a deep sleep. This sleep brought a "deep and dreadful darkness upon him" (v. 12), setting a solemn mood for God's appearance.

God announces to Abram that the promise of land will not happen immediately or even in the near future. For four hundred years they will be "strangers" in a land that will enslave and mistreat them. Absent any other chronological indications within the Bible, it is uncertain whether this four hundred year period (clearly a round number if not a symbolic one for ten generations[8]) includes the time in Canaan or is only referring to the time period of actual enslavement within Egypt. It certainly focuses on the latter and anticipates the exodus and the gifts that the Egyptians gave the Israelites as they left the land of their enslavement (Exod 12:36).

Verse 16 refers to the population of Canaan as the Amorites and suggests that their eventual removal from the land is the result of their egregious sin. At this point in history, their behavior does not deserve this punishment, but it implies that it is inevitable that they will ultimately come to the point where their destruction is deserved. This verse justifies the view that the command to eradicate the Canaanites from the land is an act of judgment and judicially deserved.[9]

Interestingly, God tells Moses that Abram's descendants will come back to the promised land in the fourth generation after their mistreatment in a foreign country (Egypt). Since this reference comes after God's statement that his descendants will be in that foreign country for four hundred years, the reference to four generations must be referring to four complete durations of time rather than a literal reference to four generations, which would place the exodus in the time of Joseph's children.[10]

For the first time, the extent of the promised land is detailed as extending from the Wadi of Egypt to the Euphrates and as encompassing the land presently held by ten people groups (Kenites, Kenizzites, Kadmonites, Hittites, Perizzites, Rephaites, Amorites, Canaanites, Girgashites, and Jebusites). While Abram will not live to see the fulfillment of the promise of the land, an integral part of becoming a "great nation," he will die in a dignified and honored manner.

God's promises to Abraham are here for the first time given a specifically covenantal context. This covenant is the second one explicitly so named in Genesis (see comments on the Noahic covenant in Gen 6:18; 9:8). A covenant is a legal agreement between two parties and recent studies have likened the covenant specifically to a vassal treaty between two countries.

However, there is nothing new here in the agreement that God has made to Abram. Thus, it is perhaps more accurate to think that this is a renewal of the covenant that God made with Abram in 12:1–3. The lack of the specific

---

8. Similar to the argument that the 480 years between the exodus and the fourth year of Solomon is symbolic of twelve generations of forty generations each (Kitchen, *On the Reliability of the Old Testament*, 307–10).

9. T. Longman III, "The Case for Spiritual Continuity," in *Show Them No Mercy: God and the Canaanite Genocide* (Grand Rapids: Zondervan, 2003), 108; contra Siebert, *The Violence of Scripture*; P. Enns, *The Bible Tells Me So....*

10. K. A. Mathews, *Genesis 11:27–50:26*, NAC 2 (Nashville: Broadman and Holman), 175; Waltke, *Genesis*, 242.

term covenant there is not troubling in the light of the lack of the term in the text that establishes the Davidic covenant.

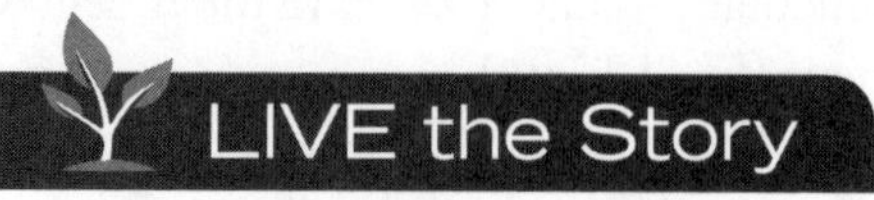


**Dealing with Disappointment**

I became a Christian in 1970, during the height of the so-called Jesus Revolution. During that time, God's Spirit moved across college campuses of the United States, and many people turned their life over to Christ. A number of people who are presently leaders in evangelical churches and ministries became Christians during that time and then eagerly shared the gospel with their dorm mates and their friends on campus. It was not unusual for someone to share with another person that "God loves you and has a wonderful plan for your life!"

Abram heard that God had a wonderful plan for his life as well. That plan included moving to Canaan where God would make his descendants a great nation which would be blessed and provide a blessing to the whole world.

Abram took the plunge, just as many people in our present time make the plunge and turn their life over to God and his "wonderful plan" for their lives. But it wasn't long before Abram realized that "wonderful" included famine, wandering, barrenness, warfare, loss, and more. In this, Abram is no different from my contemporaries who turned their lives over to Christ in the 1970s, nor will those who turn their lives over to God's plan for their life in the present find that their lives are devoid of sickness, suffering, pain, abandonment, and loss.

We have been studying the life of Abram and charting how he responds to threats and obstacles to the fulfillment of the promises. Already by this point in the story we see that he has sometimes responded with faith, but more often responded with fear and disappointment. Certainly that is his initial response in the present episode. He has attempted to manipulate the fulfillment of the promise by adopting his household servant Eliezer, and he responds bitterly to God when God approaches to reassure him of the integrity of the promise of a child.

How do we respond when it looks like God is not following through on his promise of a "wonderful life"? In the first place, we need to question the impression that many of us were given (and gave) at the time we became Christians. Nowhere in the Bible is there a promise that those who turn over their lives to Christ will have a problem-free, happy life. We are told that we will experience joy, but it is a joy in the midst of suffering. As Jesus put it, "so that in me you may have peace. In this world you will have trouble. But take heart! I have overcome the world" (John 16:33).

How do we have joy in the midst of suffering? We have joy because God is with us through the pain. God comes to Abram in order to reassure him of his loving presence and his commitment to fulfill the promise in spite of appearances. For the Christian, we know that God is with us. Jesus made his presence known to us and the Holy Spirit dwells in our hearts. We know that this life will be filled with struggle, but that a time is coming when "he will wipe every tear from their eyes. There will be no more death or mourning or crying or pain, for the old order of things has passed away" (Rev 21:4).

### Abram as a Model of Justification of Faith

In response to God's reassurances in the light of his doubts that God would keep the promise of "seed," Abram believed him. According to the narrator, God then "credited it to him as righteousness." That is, thanks to his faith that God would follow through on his promise, God treated him as acting and believing correctly. Abram's doubt threatened the intimacy of his relationship with God and now his trust solidified that relationship.[11]

Paul considers this moment pivotal in his argument with those who want to make obedience to the law a precursor to a relationship with God. Contra this position, he states that "we maintain that a person is justified by faith apart from the works of the law" (Rom 3:28). He then points back to Genesis 15:6 to argue that Abram "believed God, and it was credited to him as righteousness" (Rom 4:3). He points out that God pronounced Abraham righteous before he was circumcised. Thus, Abram is not only the father of those who are circumcised (Jewish believers), but also those who are not (Gentile believers). Paul firmly believed that our relationship with God comes through our faith and not by our works. He cites Genesis 15:6 also in Galatians 3:6, where he is making the argument that faith and not works bring Jews and Gentiles into relationship with God. In Romans, Paul utilizes chronology when he points out that God credited righteousness to Abraham even before he was circumcised in Genesis 17.[12] Paul is vitally interested in making sure that Christians realize that they do not earn their salvation, but it is a gift from God, and Abraham, the father of the Jewish faith, is his prime example.

Of course, Paul is not the only one to cite Genesis 15:6. James also cites the passage (see Jas 2:23). Contrary to those who see Paul and James in tension, they both agree that justification is by faith alone, but that faith without

---

11. This comment depends on God being the subject, which is supported by the context, though Abram is the most immediate antecedent (see J. Hartley, *NIDOTTE* 2:306).

12. D. Moo, *Romans*, NIVAC (Grand Rapids: Zondervan, 2000), 157.

works is dead (see further discussion in Gen 22 and in the essay that follows the commentary on that chapter Faith With Deeds).

### "Your Descendants Will Come Back Here, for the Sin of the Amorites Has Not Yet Reached Its Full Measure" (15:16)

God speaks to Abraham in a way that anticipates the exodus from Egypt. They will be enslaved and mistreated "by a country not their own" (Egypt). But God will punish the country (the plagues) and bring them out enriched.

In other words, God here anticipates the exodus, the time Jacob's descendants will come back and possess the land of Canaan. The exodus is the salvation event *par excellence* in the Old Testament and ultimately points forward to the greater deliverance provided by Jesus (see the essay God Delivers His People, in the Living the Story section connected to Gen 12:10–20).

The inhabitants of the promised land are here described as Amorites. The reason why God does not immediately give Abraham the land is because their sin "has not yet reached its full measure." This statement is extremely important for a theological understanding of the conquest. God does not disinvest the previous inhabitants of the promised land just to make room for the Israelites. It is a matter of judgment for their sin. God indicates that at the time of Abraham the Amorites do not deserve such a judgment, but in the future they will. And it is at that moment that God will give the land to Israel. And the conquest itself is anticipatory of Jesus Christ, who is the divine warrior who will defeat the spiritual powers and authorities and ultimately usher in the final defeat of evil in the end days (see "Who Delivered Your Enemies into Your Hand" [Gen 14:20b], an essay found at the commentary at Gen 14).

CHAPTER 14

# Genesis 16

## LISTEN to the Story

16:1Now Sarai, Abram's wife, had borne him no children. But she had
an Egyptian slave named Hagar; 2so she said to Abram, "The Lord has
kept me from having children. Go, sleep with my slave; perhaps I can
build a family through her."

Abram agreed to what Sarai said. 3So after Abram had been living
in Canaan ten years, Sarai his wife took her Egyptian slave Hagar and
gave her to her husband to be his wife. 4He slept with Hagar, and she
conceived.

When she knew she was pregnant, she began to despise her mistress.
5Then Sarai said to Abram, "You are responsible for the wrong I am
suffering. I put my slave in your arms, and now that she knows she is
pregnant, she despises me. May the Lord judge between you and me."

6"Your slave is in your hands," Abram said. "Do with her whatever
you think best." Then Sarai mistreated Hagar; so she fled from her.

7The angel of the Lord found Hagar near a spring in the desert; it
was the spring that is beside the road to Shur. 8And he said, "Hagar, slave
of Sarai, where have you come from, and where are you going?"

"I'm running away from my mistress Sarai," she answered.

9Then the angel of the Lord told her, "Go back to your mistress and
submit to her." 10The angel added, "I will increase your descendants so
much that they will be too numerous to count."

11The angel of the Lord also said to her:

"You are now pregnant
and you will give birth to a son.
You shall name him Ishmael,
for the Lord has heard of your misery.
12He will be a wild donkey of a man;
his hand will be against everyone
and everyone's hand against him,
and he will live in hostility
toward all his brothers."

[13]She gave this name to the LORD who spoke to her: "You are the God who sees me," for she said, "I have now seen the One who sees me." [14]That is why the well was called Beer Lahai Roi; it is still there, between Kadesh and Bered.

[15]So Hagar bore Abram a son, and Abram gave the name Ishmael to the son she had borne. [16]Abram was eighty-six years old when Hagar bore him Ishmael.

*Listening to the Text in the Story:* Biblical Text*:* Genesis 12:1–3; Ancient Near East Texts: Various Marriage Contracts

This chapter finds Abram again frustrated at the lack of fulfillment of the divine promise of a son, implicit in God's promise that his descendants will become a great nation (Gen 12:1–3). In this episode, Abram will avail himself of the ancient Near Eastern practice of concubinage in order to have children when one's primary wife is barren. Walton cites two particularly relevant marriage contracts in reference to Abram's and Sarai's action here. One is a tablet from Nuzi (for more information on Nuzi, please see the commentary on 15:1–6) in which a man named Shennima marries Gilimninu and will not take a concubine unless she cannot have children. The other is from the Old Assyrian period, also close to the time of the patriarchs, a certain Laqipum marries Hatala with the provision that he can take on a concubine if she does not give birth to a child within two years.[1]

### Sarai Gives a Concubine to Abram (16:1–4a)

Verse 1 begins with the painful reminder that Abram's wife had not yet given him any children. In the previous chapter (15), God assured Abram that he and Sarai would indeed have a child, but here he is already doubting what he had earlier believed.

Sarai is the one who initiates the plan that Abram readily accepts which is to have a child with her Egyptian concubine Hagar. Hagar would almost certainly have been a part of the gifts that the Egyptian Pharaoh gave to Abram as he was in Egypt (12:16). Sarai, at this point, wants Abram to impregnate Hagar in order to have a baby so they could have a family. Levenson

1. Walton, "Genesis," 87.

insightfully notes that Sarai's act of giving Hagar to Abraham is presented in a way parallel to Eve giving the fruit to Adam and by thus connecting the two indicates the negative nature of Sarai's act:

> So Sarai, Abram's wife, took (*wattiqqah*) her maid, Hagar the Egyptian—after Abram had dwelt in the land of Canaan ten years—and gave (*wattitten)* her to her husband (*ishah)* Abram as a concubine. (Gen 16:3)
>
> When the woman saw that the tree was good for eating and a delight to the eyes, and that the tree was desirable as a source of wisdom, she took (*wattiqqah*) of its fruit and ate. She also gave (*wattitten*) some to her husband (*le'ishah*), and he ate. (Gen 3:6)[2]

In short, Abram and Sarai are utilizing contemporary ancient Near Eastern customs in order to manufacture an heir. Again, they do not wait for God to fulfill the promise but manipulate a contemporary social custom to produce an heir. It was a well-known and accepted practice of couples, particularly but not exclusively those that were unable to produce children on their own, to use a surrogate, or concubine, to produce children.

## The Birth of Ishmael (16:4b–16)

Their strategy was successful in producing a child. Abram slept with Hagar and she became pregnant. Hagar's pregnancy leads her to make a fundamental mistake in her relationship with Sarai. She believes her pregnancy makes her superior to her mistress. Perhaps she feels that Abram would be so happy that she was pregnant that he would favor her over his wife, but if so, she woefully miscalculated. As Proverbs 30:21–23 points out, "Under three things the earth trembles; under four it cannot bear up: a servant who becomes a king, a godless fool who gets plenty to eat; a contemptible woman who gets married, and a servant who displaces her mistress." After Sarai informs him of the situation, Abram simply places Hagar's fate in the hands of his offended wife. Sarai then abuses her ("Sarai mistreated Hagar," v. 6), and Hagar understandably flees the camp.

She escapes the human couple, but not God's angel who confronts her and asks her where she is going. This confrontation takes place at a spring in the desert near the "road of Shur," which is the southernmost route from Canaan to Egypt.[3] She honestly confesses that her only goal is to get away from Sarai, who is oppressing her.

---

2. J. Levenson, *The Death and Resurrection of the Beloved Son: The Transformation of Child Sacrifice in Judaism and Christianity* (New Haven, CT: Yale University Press, 1993), 91.

3. J. K. Hoffmeier and S. O. Moshier, "'A Highway Out of Egypt': The Main Raod from Egypt to Canaan," in *Desert Road Archaeology in Ancient Egypt and Beyond*, ed. F. Forster and H. Reimer, Africa Praehistorica 27 (Cologne: Heinrich-Barth-Institut, 2013), 485–86.

The angel of the Lord then tells her to return and submit to Sarai. This command is not necessarily a requirement to go back to an abusive relationship. Since the abuse was because Hagar lorded it over Sarai, the hope was that the former's submission to the latter would also alleviate the abuse. But even further her return would be rewarded with a blessing that she (like Sarai) would have innumerable descendants. Further, God delivers an oracle concerning her and her future offspring (vv. 11–12).

She will give birth to a son, and he will be called Ishmael. This name is formed from the root "to hear" and is explained as referring to God who has heard of Hagar's misery. He will be like a wild donkey, not easy to control and dangerous. Since dangerous, others (including the descendants of his future brother Isaac) will try to control him. He will be in a constant state of hostility with others.

Hagar now reveals that she believes that the angel is none other than God himself when she names God the God who sees her, and then notes that she has seen God ("the One who sees me," v. 13). This event gives name to the place since Beer Lahai Roi means "the well of the Living One who sees me." God's seeing implies his care here. He is not simply observing her from afar, but taking action in order to save her. This location is between Kadesh and Bered, which is in the Negev.

Thus Hagar returns and gives birth to Ishmael. Abram is eighty-six years old at this time. His age is mentioned to signal to the reader that even now he is well beyond the age for giving birth.

The story of the birth of Ishmael is one that shows that Abram, having ultimately reacted in faith in the previous chapter, is once again flagging in his confidence that God will provide him with an heir. Thus, we are not surprised that God once again returns to the patriarch in order to set him straight.

### Enduring Difficulty

In the story of Hagar and Ishmael, we once again observe Abram grasping at the fulfillment of the promise by exploiting contemporary custom. On this occasion, he follows his wife's advice and impregnates his concubine. However, Hagar miscalculates the situation and "despises" her mistress. She has forgotten her place in the household, not remembering who really, for right or wrong, has the power. Sarai may be barren, but Hagar's fate still depends on the decisions of her mistress. Thus, Sarai begins to "mistreat" Hagar. We are not told the details or the extent of this mistreatment, but we can be sure that it has made life so difficult that the pregnant Hagar runs away.

Who can blame her? Who wouldn't run away from such unpleasantness? Isn't that our first response to trouble—to run away?

What is mystifying, though, is God's reaction. "Go back to your mistress and submit to her" (v. 9). Really? Is that fair? Doesn't God want us to enjoy ourselves? He certainly does not want us to persist in a difficult situation, does he? Well, apparently he does want Hagar to go back and submit to her mistress. His instruction though comes with an incentive. She will give birth to Abram's son, and though he is not the promised son, her descendants will become numerous and powerful. God asks Hagar to endure in a hard situation for his purposes, but also to bless her and her future son.

We have to be careful here. Sometimes we should leave a difficult situation. Indeed, in a later story we will see that God wants Hagar and Ishmael to leave (see Gen 21), but for now God wants her to stay. The point is that a hard situation is not in and of itself an excuse to leave. Sometimes we are called to endure.

Take marriage for instance. I would tell any woman or man who was the object of physical abuse to leave the relationship immediately and seek help from the police and from the church. I am not saying that reconciliation is impossible; nothing is impossible with God, but the work toward reconciliation in such a case can only take place after separation and with help of others.

However, I have observed and counseled in situations where a husband or wife has left a marriage because the relationship has become too much work. One man I know left his wife when she got terminal cancer; another because his wife struggled with anxiety. On too many occasions the marriages of friends and family have broken up because the passion of the relationship had diminished.

Also sad is the destruction of a friendship because the friend just isn't fun anymore. A person is more work "than they are worth." When it comes to work relationships, it is more understandable why someone might leave one job for another because the work or the relationships at work have become difficult. That said, one must wonder at someone who leaves a job and a steady income for no alternative job and no money to pay for bills because they just don't enjoy it.

Every situation must be treated differently, but just because something is difficult isn't in and of itself a reason to leave. Again, sometimes we are called to endure.

### The Angel Who Saves

Hagar flees the mistreatment of Sarai her mistress and soon finds herself alone in the wilderness. However, the angel of the Lord encounters her and orders her back. Though, as we have seen in the previous essay, this duty is difficult, God also encourages her with a blessing on her and on her soon to be born son.

But who is this angel of the Lord exactly? This story is not the only one in which he makes an appearance.

In Genesis 21, Hagar again will be out in the wilderness, but this time forced to go by Abraham and Sarai. There the angel of the Lord will come and provide help to Hagar and her son Ishmael. Indeed, if it were not for the intervention of the angel of the Lord, it is likely that Hagar and Ishmael would have died in the wilderness.

The angel of the Lord makes another appearance in Genesis 22, the binding of Isaac. It is the angel of the Lord who stays Abraham's hand and provides the substitute ram. The angel also speaks to Abraham and reasserts the covenantal promises to him (22:15–18).

The angel of the Lord makes an appearance in the story that recounts the journey of Abraham's servant to northwest Mesopotamia (Paddan Aram) to find a wife for Isaac. Before he departs, Abraham confidently tells him that God "will send his angel before you so that you can get a wife for my son from there" (24:7, see also v. 40).

After his long sojourn in northwest Mesopotamia, Jacob determined to go back to the promised land. But he was determined to get paid, so when Laban agreed finally to pay him wages, Jacob devised a plan to increase his flock by saying that he would take the speckled and spotted sheep, every dark-colored lamb, and every spotted or speckled goat (30:32). Later, when he explained his strategy to Rachel and Leah, he told them that this plan was given to him by the angel of the Lord (31:11). Toward the end of his life, Jacob blessed Joseph's two sons Ephraim and Manasseh, and as he did, he invoked the angel, referring to him as "the Angel who has delivered me from all harm" (48:16).

The angel of the Lord is an angel who helps his people. He helped Hagar in the wilderness on two occasions. He interceded so Abraham did not sacrifice Isaac and then he reaffirmed the promises. He helped Abraham's servant find a wife for Isaac. He aided Jacob in his efforts against Laban who had mistreated him, and at the end of his life he reflects on the angel as the one who delivered him from harm.

Who is the angel? Walton believes the angel is God's messenger, and as such, the messenger speaks as if he is the one who sent him.[4] However, this viewpoint does not seem to take account of the close connection between the angel and God. From Hagar's reaction in the present chapter under consideration, it is clear that she recognized that the angel of the Lord was none other

4. Walton, "Genesis," 87–88.

than God himself ("You are the God who sees me. . . .I have now seen the One who sees me," 16:13).

The relationship between God and the angel of the Lord is not as clear in Genesis 21:17–21. One way of reading it is that when God heard the boy crying, he then had a second party, the angel of God, call rather than calling directly, but it is more likely, especially considering the close relationship in Genesis 16, to think that the angel of the Lord is God himself. The same may be said for Genesis 24 where the angel could be understood as a representation of God himself or a messenger of God.

The angel's appearance in Genesis 22, though, again, is most naturally read if the angel is God himself. This may be seen in particular in verse 15, "The angel of the LORD called to Abraham from heaven a second time and said, 'I swear by myself,' declares the LORD. . . ." The same close connection may also be heard in Jacob's speech to Rachel and Leah: "The angel of God said to me in the dream, 'Jacob.' I answered, 'Here I am.' And he said, 'Look up and see that all the male goats mating with the flock are streaked, speckled or spotted, for I have seen all that Laban has been doing to you. I am the God of Bethel, where you anointed a pillar and where you made a vow to me. Now leave this land at once and go back to your native land' " (31:11–13). The same close connection between God and the angel may be seen in Jacob's blessing of Ephraim and Manasseh, where the "Angel who has delivered me from all harm" is invoked in parallel with "the God who has been my shepherd all my life to this day" (48:15–16).

Thus, the angel is God himself. It is God who helps and saves by taking the form of an angel and appearing to Hagar here and then Abraham and Jacob later.

But some object to this identification because they know that no one can look at God and live. God is too majestic and powerful and glorious. Even the powerful cherubim must look down rather than look at God enthroned in the Holy of Holies above them (Exod 25:17–22). God tells Moses, "But. . .you cannot see my face, for no one may see me and live" (Exod 33:20).

But Hagar here says that she has seen God in the angel of the Lord. What are we to make of this?

Some have recourse to the Trinity. John 6:46 states "No one has seen the Father except the one who is from God; only he has seen the Father." Thus, the angel of the Lord is considered by some a Christophany (a pre-incarnate appearance of Jesus) rather than a theophany (an appearance of God himself).

The problem, though, is that the teaching on the Trinity develops over time in Scripture and it not clearly taught in the Old Testament. In short, no one reading Genesis at the time it was written or during the Old Testament time period would have thought in those terms.[5]

Hagar saw God. One is reminded of Samson's parents at a later time, when the angel of the Lord came to them and announced that they would have a son. Once they realized who it was, Manoah, Samson's father, says "We are doomed to die! . . . We have seen God!" (Judg 13:22), but his wife responded, "If the Lord had meant to kill us, he would not have accepted a burnt offering and grain offering from our hands, nor shown us all these things or now told us this" (13:23).

How are we to make sense of what seems contradictory teaching? Humans cannot see the face of God, but they can see God.

The fact is that God appears to humans all the time, but never directly in the full force of his glory. He appears in a flaming torch in a smoking firepot (Gen 15), in a burning bush (Exod 3), and as an angel in the passages under consideration.[6] God appears in these forms to communicate his presence, but not his full presence, which would certainly overwhelm those who would experience his power and majesty.

In conclusion, it is not correct to think of the angel as a pre-incarnate appearance of Christ, but rather as an appearance by God. Reading from a Christian perspective, however, we know that the God who appears to Hagar here is the Triune God, whom Jesus reveals most clearly, "The Word became flesh and made his dwelling among us. We have seen his glory, the glory of the one and only Son, who came from the Father, full of grace and truth" (John 1:14). Christians experience the presence of God in a way longed for by Hagar, Abraham, and Jacob.

---

5. See A. Malone, *Knowing Jesus in the Old Testament?* (Leicester, England: InterVarsity Press, 2014).

6. We will treat Genesis 18–19 as a special case because there is no explicit reference to the angel of the Lord, but there are three men who appear to Abraham, and two of them are later referred to as angels.

CHAPTER 15

# Genesis 17

## LISTEN to the Story

17:1 When Abram was ninety-nine years old, the LORD appeared to
him and said, "I am God Almighty; walk before me faithfully and be
blameless. 2 Then I will make my covenant between me and you and will
greatly increase your numbers."
3 Abram fell facedown, and God said to him, 4 "As for me, this is my
covenant with you: You will be the father of many nations. 5 No longer
will you be called Abram; your name will be Abraham, for I have made
you a father of many nations. 6 I will make you very fruitful; I will
make nations of you, and kings will come from you. 7 I will establish
my covenant as an everlasting covenant between me and you and your
descendants after you for the generations to come, to be your God and
the God of your descendants after you. 8 The whole land of Canaan,
where you now reside as a foreigner, I will give as an everlasting possession
to you and your descendants after you; and I will be their God."
9 Then God said to Abraham, "As for you, you must keep my
covenant, you and your descendants after you for the generations to
come. 10 This is my covenant with you and your descendants after you, the
covenant you are to keep: Every male among you shall be circumcised.
11 You are to undergo circumcision, and it will be the sign of the covenant
between me and you. 12 For the generations to come every male among
you who is eight days old must be circumcised, including those born in
your household or bought with money from a foreigner—those who are
not your offspring. 13 Whether born in your household or bought with
your money, they must be circumcised. My covenant in your flesh is to
be an everlasting covenant. 14 Any uncircumcised male, who has not been
circumcised in the flesh, will be cut off from his people; he has broken my
covenant."
15 God also said to Abraham, "As for Sarai your wife, you are no longer
to call her Sarai; her name will be Sarah. 16 I will bless her and will surely
give you a son by her. I will bless her so that she will be the mother of
nations; kings of peoples will come from her."

[17]Abraham fell facedown; he laughed and said to himself, "Will a
son be born to a man a hundred years old? Will Sarah bear a child at the
age of ninety?" [18]And Abraham said to God, "If only Ishmael might live
under your blessing!"

[19]Then God said, "Yes, but your wife Sarah will bear you a son,
and you will call him Isaac. I will establish my covenant with him as an
everlasting covenant for his descendants after him. [20]And as for Ishmael,
I have heard you: I will surely bless him; I will make him fruitful and will
greatly increase his numbers. He will be the father of twelve rulers, and I
will make him into a great nation. [21]But my covenant I will establish with
Isaac, whom Sarah will bear to you by this time next year." [22]When he
had finished speaking with Abraham, God went up from him.

[23]On that very day Abraham took his son Ishmael and all those born
in his household or bought with his money, every male in his household,
and circumcised them, as God told him. [24]Abraham was ninety-nine
years old when he was circumcised, [25]and his son Ishmael was thirteen;
[26]Abraham and his son Ishmael were both circumcised on that very day.
[27]And every male in Abraham's household, including those born in his
household or bought from a foreigner, was circumcised with him.

*Listening to the Text in the Story:* Biblical Texts: Genesis 12:1–3; 15

Genesis 17 begins similarly to Genesis 15, and as we read on, we note that this chapter is a second covenant renewal in which God comes to Abram, whose faith once again is flagging, in order to reassure him of his commitment to fulfill his promises as given originally in Genesis 12:1–3.

### God Reassures Abraham a Second Time (17:1–6)

In verse 1 we learn that Abram is now ninety-nine years old. No wonder he doubts God! Ninety-nine and still no promised heir! He (and of course Sarai) are well beyond human ability to reproduce.

God begins his reassurance by reminding him that he is God Almighty (El Shaddai), thus emphasizing his power. The exact meaning of El Shaddai is not clear, but the best explanation is that this title means "God of the mountains," with the mountains representing his great strength.

After reassuring the patriarch, El Shaddai then calls Abram to covenant obedience. Granted that Abram's relationship with God is based on God's grace (Gen 15:6 and see Paul in Rom 4:3 and Gal 3:6), he nonetheless must be obedient (see Jas 2:22, based on Gen 22:15–18). The logic of verse 2 is that, in some sense, the fulfillment of the promises does depend on his obedience. Initially, the promises depended on Abram leaving Ur and heading to the promised land. No wonder Abram is both the model of salvation by faith as well as covenant obedience (Gen 26:6). Abram's life is a journey, and he is to undergo his life journey with obedience.

Abram demonstrates his proper fear of God by falling prostrate before him (v. 3), and God responds to this act of obeisance by reaffirming his covenant and also bringing out further nuances of the wonderful things he will do for him and his descendants. In 12:2, God promised him that his descendants would become "a great nation," but now we learn that he will be "the father of many nations." Because of this, God gives him a new name with great significance. Up to this point in the story, he has been called "exalted father" (Abram), but now he receives the name Abraham ("father of many nations").

Not only will Abraham give birth to many nations, these nations will have kings. At this point it is not clear that Israel will be among the nations that will derive from Abraham that has a king, but later developments will indicate that this is so (see comments on the Judah oracle in Gen 49:8–12 below). This covenant is called everlasting, and indeed it will be, though perhaps not in the way one might have imagined at the time (see Jesus, the Seed of Abraham in the Live the Story section after 11:27–12:9).

As God reassures Abram of his intention to fulfill the promise that he would have an heir that would lead to many descendants, he also speaks to the other dimension of the promise that his descendants would be a "great nation" (12:2) and that is the promise of the land. Right now Abram does not possess any of the land; he resides as a "foreigner" or, perhaps better, a sojourner in the land (the verb in v. 8 is from *gur*, related to the noun *ger*). Though that is Abram's present status, the land of Canaan will one day come to him and his descendants as an "everlasting possession" (see Gen 23:3, 9, 20; 48:4; 49:30; 50:13).

In the next paragraph (vv. 9–14), God makes it very clear that Abram and his descendants have obligations as they respond to God's covenant promises. Keeping the covenant is more than a state of mind or an attitude; it involves obedience. Specifically, God mentions circumcision as the "sign of the covenant between me and you" (v. 11).

We earlier noted that the Noahic covenant had a sign, the rainbow (9:13–16). These signs of the covenant function as a brand, reminding the covenant people of the relationship that they have with God. These signs have a meaningful connection to the specific nature of the covenant, and circumcision is no exception. The focus of God's promise to Abraham is presently on descendants or "seed" (*zera*). Thus, it is appropriate that the sign of this covenant is connected to the male reproductive organ.

Also similar to the rainbow, circumcision suggests a self-maledictory oath, but this time on the human partner of the covenant. Indeed, in terms of the Abrahamic covenant, God had already undergone a ritual of self-curse on himself (see Gen 15), but here it is the human partner who enacts one. Circumcision, in essence, is a covenant initiation ritual, performed on a male child when they reach eight days, probably the earliest time the operation can be safely done. When the foreskin is cut off, the implicit significance of the ritual is that it indicates that if this child breaks the covenant, he will be cut off from God and the community and thrown away. Indeed, not to circumcise a member of a household would in itself constitute covenant rebellion and would result in that person being cut off.

Note that the entire household must be circumcised, not just the biological heirs of the head of the household. This includes foreigners who are purchased as slaves. At this point we should remember that God's promise includes not only those who are directly descended from Abraham, but "all peoples on earth" (12:3).

We should also point out, contrary to some popular understandings, that Abram and his descendants are not the first people to employ a ritual of circumcision (see Jer 9:25–26).[1] We know that other ancient Near Eastern people practiced some form of circumcision. God's institution of the ritual of circumcision is innovative in terms of its theological significance as described in the previous paragraph.

Not only does Abraham receive a new name at this point, but so does Sarai, underlining the fact that the matriarch is of crucial importance to God's program. That said, the significance of her name change is not as clear as was Abraham's. God tells Abraham that his wife will no longer be called "Princess" (Sarai), but now will be called "Princess" (Sarah). While there does not appear to be a change in the meaning of her name, perhaps we are to see significance in the fact that Sarai is an east Semitic pronunciation and that Sarah is a west Semitic pronunciation of "Princess." If so, then God is saying that she no longer is a part of their old world in Mesopotamia, but both she and Abraham are now part and parcel of their new world in the promised land.

---

1. See Walton, "Genesis," 89, citing J. Sasson, "Circumcision in the Ancient Near East," *JBL* 85 (1966): 473–76 and P. J. King, "Circumcision: Who Did It and Who Didn't, and Why," *BAR* 32/4 (2006): 48–55.

**Isaac and Not Ishmael (17:7–27)**

In spite of God's reassurances, Abram still doubts God's intention or ability to fulfill the promise of descendants. He maintains his proper place before God by once again prostrating himself before God, but inwardly he laughs and questions whether he and Sarah at their advanced ages (one hundred years and ninety years respectively) can have a child. They are, after all, well beyond the time in which people can have children.

While Abraham does not directly verbalize his doubts, he implies them when he then says out loud to God, "If only Ishmael might live under your blessing!" (v. 18), perhaps believing that "a bird in the hand is worth two in the bush." God responds by reasserting his commitment to give Abraham and Sarah a son. The NIV begins God's response to Abraham with a "Yes, but," while the NRSV translates the opening particle (*'abal*) "No, but." The Hebrew term *abal* is a word that marks a "reversal of beliefs or expectations,"[2] so an argument can be made for both. NRSV captures the point that Abraham is wrong to think that the covenant blessing of 12:1–3 will fall on Ishmael and his descendants. The NIV translation, though, can be justified by the fact that, though not the recipient of the promises originally given to Abraham, Ishmael too will receive God's blessings, as he makes clear in verse 20 (see also 21:18 and especially 25:12–18, where his twelve sons who are "tribal rulers" are named). His blessing, like Abraham's, includes the promise that he will have many descendants (v. 20). In short, Ishmael will be the father of one of the many nations that will come from Abraham (see below).

That said, it is the son born to Abraham and Sarah who will be the recipient of the "everlasting covenant" that is the focus of the narrative. For the first time, we hear his name. God calls him Isaac, a name that, as we will later hear, is connected to the laughter elicited by the fact that a couple of such advanced age actually gave birth to a son (see comments at 21:1–7). Just before he withdraws his presence from Abraham, God makes it very clear that Isaac will be the promised child and that this child will be born within a year ("my covenant I will establish with Isaac, whom Sarah will bear to you by this time next year," v. 21).

The chapter ends describing Abraham's obedience to the divine command to circumcise his household. Ishmael, though not the son of the promise, is also circumcised. Abraham's obedience in this matter contributes to God's assessment of him at the end of his life as one who "obeyed me and did everything I required of him, keeping my commands, my decrees and my instructions" (26:5).

---

2. *NIDOTTE* 4, 1031.

**Doubt and the Persistence of God**

Unbelief is the opposite of faith; doubt straddles the two. Faith is a firm conviction in something or someone that they will be true to their word. Unbelief is also a firm conviction that they will not. Doubt entertains both possibilities. In the case of Abraham, doubt tends toward unbelief—at least until God reassures him that he will indeed provide him with a son.

Christians too struggle with doubt. We have received promises from God. He tells us through his Word that he is in control, though evil rages in the world. He tells us that he loves us, though our lives are marred by pain and suffering. He tells us that he is coming again to bring us to himself, but time stretches on and on.

Abraham is transparent with God about his doubt, and Christians should also be honest with him. In his book, *The Myth of Certainty*, Dan Taylor shares his struggles with a Christian community that does not tolerate doubt[3] (see the Myth of Certainty in the Live the Story section after Gen 11:27–12:9).

God does not respond to Abraham's doubt with prohibition or censure, but rather with calm and concrete reassurances. Jesus did the same with his disciples. On one occasion, his disciples saw him walking on the water and responded in fear. Jesus reassured them, "Take courage! It is I. Don't be afraid" (Matt 14:27). Peter responded with a confident faith and was able to walk on the water. That is, until his faith wavered and he sank into the water. Jesus grasped his hand and brought him out of the water, saying to him "You of little faith...why did you doubt?" (Matt 14:31). Rather than rejecting his weak disciple, he brought him into the boat where they all worshiped him. As with God's persistence in his relationship with Abraham, so Jesus maintains and builds his relationship with his doubting disciples.

Of course, he does not want us to doubt. It is faith, and not doubt, that leads to a great answer to prayer: "Truly I tell you, if you have faith and do not doubt, not only can you do what was done to the fig tree, but also you can say to this mountain, 'Go throw yourself into the sea,' and it will be done. If you believe, you will receive whatever you ask for in prayer" (Matt 21:21–22; see also Mark 11:22–25).

The persistence of Jesus in the face of his disciples' doubts can also be seen in his appearance after his resurrection. After questioning them ("Why are you troubled, and why do doubts rise in your minds?"), he then reassures them, "Look at my hands and my feet. It is I myself! Touch me and see; a

3. Taylor, *The Myth of Certainty*.

ghost does not have flesh and bones, as you see I have" (Luke 24:37–38; see also John 20:26–27).

To be sure, we are urged to faith and not to doubt ("when you ask, you must believe and not doubt, because the one who doubts is like a wave of the sea, blown and tossed by the wind" (Jas 1:6). Even so Jesus treated his doubting disciples with kind reassurances rather than rejection, so, according to Jude, we too are to "be merciful to those who doubt" (v. 22).

### "... I Will Make Nations of You, and Kings Will Come from You" (17:6)

God not only reassures Abraham that he will have a son who will be the precursor to his descendants becoming a "great nation" (12:2), but he expands upon the promise. In the first place, he will be the father not just to one "great nation" (Israel), but to many nations. We have already heard, for example, that Hagar, Abraham's concubine, will have descendants that "will be too numerous to count" (Gen 16:10), and indeed, the descendants of Ishmael will be known as the Ishmaelites, a nomadic and tribal people (Gen 25:12–18). In addition, after the death of Sarah, Abraham took another wife, Keturah, who gave birth to a number of sons, who were the patriarchs of yet other nations (see Gen 25:1–4).

Readers of the New Testament know that Abraham is the spiritual father of peoples from many nations:

> So in Christ Jesus you are all children of God through faith, for all of you who were baptized into Christ have clothed yourself with Christ. There is neither Jew nor Gentile, neither slave nor free, nor is there male and female, for you are all one in Christ Jesus. If you belong to Christ, then you are Abraham's seed, and heirs according to the promise. (Gal 3:26–29)

Here too for the first time we hear that kings will descend from Abraham. Being the father of many nations, we are not only speaking about future kingship in Israel, but certainly kingship in Israel is included and perhaps foregrounded in this statement. The importance of God's statement about kingship here is that it tips the balance in favor of those who understand that it was always God's intention that Israel have a monarchy at the right time.

The reason to doubt that comes from reading 1 Samuel 8–12, which recounts the rise of the monarchy in Israel. After all, kingship comes about in response to a sinful request of the people to have a leader like the other nations. This request is the result of a lack of confidence in both Samuel and God's ability to protect them against their foes. Samuel is irate with their request, and God takes offense at it, but still he accedes to their demand and the first king, Saul, is eventually anointed in spite of his resistance to the idea. Saul turns out to be such an inept king that one can come away from 1 Samuel 8–12 wondering if kingship was really God's hope for Israel.

The promise to Abraham that kings would descend from him puts kingship in a much more positive light. At the end of the book of Genesis, we hear that kingship will emerge from the tribe of Judah (see commentary on 49:8–12). Other positive anticipations of kingship occur in the fourth oracle of Balaam (Num 24:15–19) and the law of kingship in Deuteronomy (17:14–20).

Though kingship gets off to a rocky start in Israel with Saul, David soon replaces him, and he is a king "after God's own heart." It is not that David is without sin (see 2 Sam 11), but that he, as opposed to Saul, sincerely repents of his sin and seeks God's forgiveness (2 Sam 12; Ps 51). For this reason, God grants him a covenant, assuring him that he will have a son who will sit on the throne "forever" (2 Sam 7:16).

While it is true that David establishes a dynasty whose length is unprecedented in the ancient Near East (lasting from ca. 1004 to 587 BC), it does come to an end when understood simply as a descendant of David on the literal throne of Israel/Judah. However, once the Davidic dynasty ended with the Babylonian exile, hope emerged, based on the promises of the Davidic covenant, that a future Davidic ruler would once again lead God's people. The clear message of the New Testament is that that descendant of David who definitively fulfills the promise of the Davidic covenant is none other than Jesus, the Christ ("the anointed" king). Thus the promise that "kings will come" from Abraham ultimately points to Jesus Christ, the King of Kings and Lord of Lords (Rev 19:16).

### Abra(ha)m in Judaism, Islam, and Christianity

Abraham is an important figure in the three great monotheistic religions: Judaism, Christianity, and Islam. Abraham is given the promise that his descendants will become a "great nation," and that great nation is Israel, the precursor to Judaism. Christians, following Paul, also lay claim to Abraham as their great precursor: "The promises were spoken to Abraham and to his seed. Scripture does not say 'and to seeds,' meaning many people, but 'and to your seed,' meaning one person, who is Christ ... If you belong to Christ, then you are Abraham's seed, and heirs according to the promise" (Gal 3:16, 29). Muslims believe that their religion descends from Abraham via Ishmael. Accordingly, three religions lay claim to Abraham as their father figure.

Some argue that Abraham thus is the foundation for the belief that the three religions are really one religion.[4] We may have different histories and different traditions, but we worship the same God and have the same founding figure.

John Levenson has subjected such views to a thorough and devastating critique.[5] We may all look back to the same person until we look more closely. In other words, the three great religious traditions look back to Abraham but emphasize different aspects of his story.

In a previous essay ("Abram as a Model of Justification of Faith" Gen 15), we noted that the New Testament often cited Genesis 15:6. To Christians, Abraham is the model of justification by faith alone. For Jews, Genesis 26:4–5 is key: "I will make your descendants as numerous as the stars in the sky and will give them all these lands, and through your offspring all nations on earth will be blessed, because Abraham obeyed me and did everything I required of him, keeping my commandments, my decrees and my instructions." On the one hand, words like "commandments," "decrees," and "instructions" are anachronistic for Abraham, anticipating the Mosaic law. But the point is clear. Abraham is the paradigmatic keeper of Torah. The attention of Islam is focused not on Abraham's faith or law keeping, but his utter submission to the will of God as displayed in Genesis 22. Here Abraham is willing to offer his son, his only son, the son he loves so much. There has been different opinion in the Muslim tradition as to whether that son was Ishmael (the father of the Arab people who for the Koran usually plays the role that Isaac plays in the Hebrew Bible), but no doubt that the Akedah was an act of utter submission that is a model for Muslim piety.

Thus, while there is similarity between these three religions in the important part played by Abraham in the founding of their religion, the similarity also highlights the differences between them. Thus, Abraham does not provide the grounds for saying that Judaism, Christianity, and Islam are really one and the same religion. That said, it does provide one of many reasons why the three religions should relate to one another with deep respect and civility. When there are differences, they should be discussed in the context of love.

---

4. W. Moberly (*The Theology of the Book of Genesis* [Cambridge: Cambridge University Press, 2009]) cites K. J. Kuschel (*Abraham: A Symbol of Hope for Jews, Christians and Muslims* [London: SCM, 1995]) as an example.

5. Especially in Levenson, *Inheriting Abraham*. Moberly argues essentially the same position for a Christian viewpoint in *The Theology of the Book of Genesis*, 200–24.

**Circumcision and Baptism**

In Genesis 17 God instructs Abraham concerning circumcision, a ritual that indicates membership in the covenant community normally performed on the eighth day after birth. We have noted above that the symbolism of circumcision is connected to the "cutting off" of the foreskin. Just as the foreskin was cut off, so would the person who later violated the covenant. In essence, circumcision is a covenant initiation ceremony.

However, even in the Old Testament the physical act of circumcision was not sufficient to maintain a good relationship with God. Bodily circumcision was totally useless unless one's heart was also circumcised:

> Circumcise yourselves to the LORD,
> circumcise your hearts,
> you people of Judah and inhabitants of Jerusalem,
> or my wrath will flare up and burn like fire
> because of the evil you have done—
> burn with no one to quench it. (Jer 4:4; see also Deut 10:16; 30:6;
> Lev 26:41; Jer 6:10; 9:26; Ezek 44:7, 9; cf. also Rom 2:25–29)

Thus understood, circumcision occupied a central and critical place in Israel's relationship with God. But as we turn to the New Testament, we observe an intense conflict over the status of circumcision as uncircumcised Gentiles enter into covenant relationship with God. One party argued that Christians needed to be circumcised as a sign that they are now in covenant relationship with God (Acts 15:1; Titus 1:10). Paul, however, resisted this idea:

> Those who want to impress people by means of the flesh are trying to compel you to be circumcised. The only reason they do this is to avoid being persecuted for the cross of Christ. Not even those who are circumcised keep the law, yet they want you to be circumcised that they may boast about your circumcision in the flesh. May I never boast except in the cross of our Lord Jesus Christ, through which the world has been crucified to me, and I to the world. Neither circumcision nor uncircumcision means anything; what counts is the new creation. Peace and mercy to all who follow this rule—to the Israel of God. (Gal 6:12–16; see also Col 3:11)

As it well known, Paul's view won the day (Acts 15:1–21).

Moberly helps us understand how a ritual that was said in Genesis to be "an everlasting covenant" can be rendered irrelevant with the coming of Christ. He says:

Another factor concerns the reception of the Old Testament in the New Testament and the difference that Jesus makes to God's dealings with Israel. An obvious example is the fact that God's covenant of circumcision with Abraham is explicitly "everlasting" (*berit 'olam*; see Gen 17:7, 13), again in the sense that it is an arrangement "in perpetuity" whose termination is not envisioned. Yet in the New Testament, this arrangement is terminated (as, already within the Old Testament, God's promise to the house of Eli is terminated). According to Paul — whom mainstream Christian theology has followed — circumcision is no longer necessary; rather, it becomes at best optional and may be problematic.[6]

Thus, for the Christian circumcision no longer functions as a required covenant initiation ritual. However, biblical Christianity is not without its rituals, and the New Testament establishes baptism as the mark of initiation into the new covenant. Indeed, Paul relates baptism to circumcision in a rich and complex passage in Colossians:

> For in Christ all the fullness of Deity lives in bodily form, and in Christ you have been brought to fullness. He is the head over every power and authority. In him you were also circumcised with a circumcision not performed by human hands. Your whole self ruled by the flesh was put off when you were circumcised by Christ, having been buried with him in baptism, in which you were also raised with him through your faith in the working of God, who raised him from the dead. (Col 2:9 – 12)

The Christian has been circumcised by Christ, but not by a rabbi cutting off the foreskin. The circumcision not performed by human hands is a reference to the death of Christ. Garland persuasively argues that the NIV's rendition of the Greek genitive as subjective ("you were circumcised by Christ") is incorrect and should rather be understood to be an objective genitive, that is in reference to a circumcision experienced by Christ, thus a reference to his death.[7]

According to Paul, Christians are those who have been circumcised not by human hands but through the circumcision (death) of Christ. In him, Christians experience the circumcision of the heart as described in Deuteronomy 30:6 and elsewhere. Furthermore, Paul relates this to the ritual of baptism ("having been buried with him in baptism"). In this passage, therefore, baptism is not so much a symbol of cleansing but rather of death. But of course, one does not stay under the waters, but emerges from them as Jesus emerges

6. Moberly, *The Theology of the Book of Genesis*, 173.

7. David Garland, *Colossians, Phileman*, NIVAC (Grand Rapids: Zondervan, 1998), 148.

from death through the resurrection ("in which you were also raised with him through your faith in the working of God, who raised him from the dead").

Thus, one can see the parallel between circumcision and baptism not only as a covenant initiation ritual but also as a self-maledictory oath of the human partner of the covenant. If one violates the new covenant it is as if they have not emerged from the waters.

See related essays: Jesus, the Seed of Abraham (after 11:27–12:9) and A Promise for All Nations (after 25:12–18).

CHAPTER 16

# Genesis 18–19

## LISTEN to the Story

18:1The LORD appeared to Abraham near the great trees of Mamre while he was sitting at the entrance to his tent in the heat of the day. 2Abraham looked up and saw three men standing nearby. When he saw them, he hurried from the entrance of his tent to meet them and bowed low to the ground.

3He said, "If I have found favor in your eyes, my lord, do not pass your servant by. 4Let a little water be brought, and then you may all wash your feet and rest under this tree. 5Let me get you something to eat, so you can be refreshed and then go on your way — now that you have come to your servant."

"Very well," they answered, "do as you say."

6So Abraham hurried into the tent to Sarah. "Quick," he said, "get three seahs of the finest flour and knead it and bake some bread."

7Then he ran to the herd and selected a choice, tender calf and gave it to a servant, who hurried to prepare it. 8He then brought some curds and milk and the calf that had been prepared, and set these before them. While they ate, he stood near them under a tree.

9"Where is your wife Sarah?" they asked him.

"There, in the tent," he said.

10Then one of them said, "I will surely return to you about this time next year, and Sarah your wife will have a son."

Now Sarah was listening at the entrance to the tent, which was behind him. 11Abraham and Sarah were already very old, and Sarah was past the age of childbearing. 12So Sarah laughed to herself as she thought, "After I am worn out and my lord is old, will I now have this pleasure?"

13Then the LORD said to Abraham, "Why did Sarah laugh and say, 'Will I really have a child, now that I am old?' 14Is anything too hard for the LORD? I will return to you at the appointed time next year, and Sarah will have a son."

15Sarah was afraid, so she lied and said, "I did not laugh."

But he said, "Yes, you did laugh."

16When the men got up to leave, they looked down toward Sodom,
and Abraham walked along with them to see them on their way. 17Then
the Lord said, "Shall I hide from Abraham what I am about to do?
18Abraham will surely become a great and powerful nation, and all nations
on earth will be blessed through him. 19For I have chosen him, so that he
will direct his children and his household after him to keep the way of the
Lord by doing what is right and just, so that the Lord will bring about
for Abraham what he has promised him."

20Then the Lord said, "The outcry against Sodom and Gomorrah
is so great and their sin so grievous 21that I will go down and see if what
they have done is as bad as the outcry that has reached me. If not, I will
know."

22The men turned away and went toward Sodom, but Abraham
remained standing before the Lord. 23Then Abraham approached him
and said: "Will you sweep away the righteous with the wicked? 24What if
there are fifty righteous people in the city? Will you really sweep it away
and not spare the place for the sake of the fifty righteous people in it?
25Far be it from you to do such a thing—to kill the righteous with the
wicked, treating the righteous and the wicked alike. Far be it from you!
Will not the Judge of all the earth do right?"

26The Lord said, "If I find fifty righteous people in the city of Sodom,
I will spare the whole place for their sake."

27Then Abraham spoke up again: "Now that I have been so bold as to
speak to the Lord, though I am nothing but dust and ashes, 28what if the
number of the righteous is five less than fifty? Will you destroy the whole
city for lack of five people?"

"If I find forty-five there," he said, "I will not destroy it."

29Once again he spoke to him, "What if only forty are found there?"

He said, "For the sake of forty, I will not do it."

30Then he said, "May the Lord not be angry, but let me speak. What
if only thirty can be found there?"

He answered, "I will not do it if I find thirty there."

31Abraham said, "Now that I have been so bold as to speak to the
Lord, what if only twenty can be found there?"

He said, "For the sake of twenty, I will not destroy it."

32Then he said, "May the Lord not be angry, but let me speak just
once more. What if only ten can be found there?"

He answered, "For the sake of ten, I will not destroy it."

33When the Lord had finished speaking with Abraham, he left, and
Abraham returned home.

19:1The two angels arrived at Sodom in the evening, and Lot was sitting in the gateway of the city. When he saw them, he got up to meet them and bowed down with his face to the ground. 2"My lords," he said, "please turn aside to your servant's house. You can wash your feet and spend the night and then go on your way early in the morning."

"No," they answered, "we will spend the night in the square."

3But he insisted so strongly that they did go with him and entered his house. He prepared a meal for them, baking bread without yeast, and they ate. 4Before they had gone to bed, all the men from every part of the city of Sodom—both young and old—surrounded the house. 5They called to Lot, "Where are the men who came to you tonight? Bring them out to us so that we can have sex with them."

6Lot went outside to meet them and shut the door behind him 7and said, "No, my friends. Don't do this wicked thing. 8Look, I have two daughters who have never slept with a man. Let me bring them out to you, and you can do what you like with them. But don't do anything to these men, for they have come under the protection of my roof."

9"Get out of our way," they replied. "This fellow came here as a foreigner, and now he wants to play the judge! We'll treat you worse than them." They kept bringing pressure on Lot and moved forward to break down the door.

10But the men inside reached out and pulled Lot back into the house and shut the door. 11Then they struck the men who were at the door of the house, young and old, with blindness so that they could not find the door.

12The two men said to Lot, "Do you have anyone else here—sons-in-law, sons or daughters, or anyone else in the city who belongs to you? Get them out of here, 13because we are going to destroy this place. The outcry to the Lord against its people is so great that he has sent us to destroy it."

14So Lot went out and spoke to his sons-in-law, who were pledged to marry his daughters. He said, "Hurry and get out of this place, because the Lord is about to destroy the city!" But his sons-in-law thought he was joking.

15With the coming of dawn, the angels urged Lot, saying, "Hurry! Take your wife and your two daughters who are here, or you will be swept away when the city is punished."

16When he hesitated, the men grasped his hand and the hands of his wife and of his two daughters and led them safely out of the city, for the LORD was merciful to them. 17As soon as they had brought them out, one of them said, "Flee for your lives! Don't look back, and don't stop anywhere in the plain! Flee to the mountains or you will be swept away!"

[18]But Lot said to them, "No, my lords, please! [19]Your servant has found favor in your eyes, and you have shown great kindness to me in sparing my life. But I can't flee to the mountains; this disaster will overtake me, and I'll die. [20]Look, here is a town near enough to run to, and it is small. Let me flee to it — it is very small, isn't it? Then my life will be spared."

[21]He said to him, "Very well, I will grant this request too; I will not overthrow the town you speak of. [22]But flee there quickly, because I cannot do anything until you reach it." (That is why the town was called Zoar.)

[23]By the time Lot reached Zoar, the sun had risen over the land. [24]Then the LORD rained down burning sulfur on Sodom and Gomorrah — from the LORD out of the heavens. [25]Thus he overthrew those cities and the entire plain, destroying all those living in the cities — and also the vegetation in the land. [26]But Lot's wife looked back, and she became a pillar of salt.

[27]Early the next morning Abraham got up and returned to the place where he had stood before the LORD. [28]He looked down toward Sodom and Gomorrah, toward all the land of the plain, and he saw dense smoke rising from the land, like smoke from a furnace.

[29]So when God destroyed the cities of the plain, he remembered Abraham, and he brought Lot out of the catastrophe that overthrew the cities where Lot had lived.

[30]Lot and his two daughters left Zoar and settled in the mountains, for he was afraid to stay in Zoar. He and his two daughters lived in a cave. [31]One day the older daughter said to the younger, "Our father is old, and there is no man around here to give us children — as is the custom all over the earth. [32]Let's get our father to drink wine and then sleep with him and preserve our family line through our father."

[33]That night they got their father to drink wine, and the older daughter went in and slept with him. He was not aware of it when she lay down or when she got up.

[34]The next day the older daughter said to the younger, "Last night I slept with my father. Let's get him to drink wine again tonight, and you go in and sleep with him so we can preserve our family line through our father." [35]So they got their father to drink wine that night also, and the younger daughter went in and slept with him. Again he was not aware of it when she lay down or when she got up.

[36]So both of Lot's daughters became pregnant by their father. [37]The older daughter had a son, and she named him Moab; he is the father of the Moabites of today. [38]The younger daughter also had a son, and she named him Ben-Ammi; he is the father of the Ammonites of today.

*Listening to the Text in the Story:* Biblical Texts: Genesis 12:1–3; 15; 17 (for 18:1–15); Genesis 11:31–12:5; 13; 14 (for 18:16–19:29); Genesis 9:18–28 (for 19:30–38)

Time continues to pass, but Sarah remains barren. The promise that Abraham's descendants will be a "great nation" (12:2) has yet taken its first step toward fulfillment. God had already twice come to Abraham to reassure him of his intention to fulfill the promise of "seed," and here he comes yet a third time accompanied by two angels to reassure the chosen couple yet one more time. However, as the story continues, we see that the heavenly trio is en route to investigate the wickedness of the cities of Sodom and Gomorrah.

Abram, now Abraham, brought his nephew Lot with him and his wife Sarai, now Sarah, when they responded to God's call to go to the promised land. Our reticent narrator never tells the reader outright whether bringing Lot was a good thing or not, but whether good, bad, or indifferent, he will now show us that Lot was a source of concern for the patriarch, and this was not the first time.

When Abraham and Lot had to find separate areas to live in order to pasture their extensive flocks, Lot chose to go to the city of Sodom (Gen 13). The very next episode of the Abraham story finds the patriarch needing to battle four Near Eastern kings in order to rescue Lot who had been kidnapped by them during their plundering raid of Canaan. Abraham's cold reaction to the king of Sodom shows that, though Lot had chosen to live there, Abraham wanted nothing to do with him (14:21–24). In our present story, the patriarch will intercede for Sodom and his motivation is almost certainly that Lot and his family live there.

Genesis 19:30–38 should also be read with Genesis 9:18–28 in mind. There Noah was sexually violated by a close family member while under the influence of alcohol.

**Abraham Hosts Three Visitors (18:1–8)**

While not given an explicit indication of how much time has passed since the episode in chapter 17, it could not have been too long. After all, God had told Abraham that he and Sarah will have a son "by this time next year" (17:21), which is the same message delivered by the messengers who visit Abraham in the present story (v. 10). But who are these messengers?

At first, their identity is not clear, to the reader at least. Indeed, it is not obvious exactly who Abraham thinks they are at the beginning of the chapter. He certainly treats them with great respect. His hospitality to these visitors will contrast dramatically with the lack of hospitality provided to them by the inhabitants of Sodom, though Lot, like his uncle, will extend to them protection and sustenance (ch. 19).

Abraham sees them approach as he is resting at the entrance of his tent during the hot part of the day. His urgency and deep respect for the visitors may well indicate that he is a aware that they are more than ordinary guests. He does not wait for them to come to him, but hurries out from the tent to greet them, and when he meets them, he bows low to the ground. At a minimum, he recognizes that he is their inferior, but it is much more likely that he understands that one of them is none other than God himself.

There are three visitors, but one obvious leader to whom Abraham addresses himself. The NIV translation of *adonay* ("my lord" and not Lord) indicates uncertainty among the translators whether Abraham recognizes that the one to whom he speaks is God. He presses them not to continue journeying (we will later understand that they are on their way to Sodom), but to spend time refreshing themselves in Abraham's tent.

As a good host, he offers them the opportunity to wash their feet, drink some water, have something to eat, and rest under the tree. After all, it is the "heat of the day" (v. 1). They agree to accept Abraham's magnanimous hospitality.

He then hurries to Sarah to tell her to prepare bread from the finest flour. He specifically tells her to use "three seahs" of flour. Waltke tells us that a seah is "two gallons (eight liters) of grain,"[1] and the NIV footnote points out that this would be about 36 pounds of grain. By mentioning such a large amount, the narrator indicates Abraham's tremendous largesse toward his guests.

Besides the bread from the "finest flour," he also takes a "choice, tender calf" and tells a servant to prepare it. These he served with curds and milk. The emphasis on hurrying throughout this passage emphasizes urgency and

1. Waltke, *Genesis,* 267.

this along with the quality of the food demonstrates both Abraham as an excellent host and his recognition of the importance of his guests. He lets them eat while he attends to their needs standing by the tree.

### The Promise of a Son (18:9–15)

As we have suggested, it is likely that Abraham already knows something about the true identity of his guests, but if he didn't before, he would after their conversation during the meal. They begin by asking about the whereabouts of Sarah. How would they know her name? Further, the question would likely have been considered rude if asked by a normal visitor.

Abraham, however, does not take offense, but rather tells them that she is in the tent. At this point, one of the three, surely the leader—God himself—then reiterates the promise and its near fulfillment, "I will surely return to you about this time next year, and Sarah your wife will have a son" (v. 10).

Sarah was not present for this conversation, but she was within earshot. When she overheard the visitor, she laughed internally ("to herself"), and then to herself she thought about their advanced age. The idea that she might have sexual pleasure (the apparent meaning of the word here translated simply "pleasure") struck her as funny.

Her reaction is said to be internal, not public. Yet the visitor heard, and for the first time the visitor is identified explicitly as the Lord. God can read minds and hearts. He can accomplish anything as he asserts through the rhetorical question, "Is anything too hard for the Lord?" If God can create the cosmos ("Ah, Sovereign Lord, you have made the heavens and the earth by your great power and outstretched arm. Nothing is too hard for you" [Jer 32:17]), he can certainly cause an old couple to have a child.

Surely shaken by the visitor's knowledge of her inner thoughts, she tries to deny her reaction to his announcement, but to no avail. God simply reiterates that she laughed at the prospect of having a child.

### Abraham Intercedes for Sodom (18:16–33)

The visitors finished their rest at Abraham's tent and continued on their journey. We now learn that their destination is the city of Sodom, the place where Lot had chosen to live. We have already been told that Sodom was an evil place, so the reader is filled with a sense of foreboding as the one we now know is God moves toward that place.

God then determines to tell Abraham, who accompanies him at the beginning of his journey, about his mission in Sodom. He does so because Abraham and his descendants will play a pivotal role in his redemptive purposes. This episode also reveals that Abraham is a prophet since God does not keep his plans from his prophetic messengers (Gen 20:7; Jer 23:16–22; Amos 3:7; John 15:13).[2] Abraham needs to know what will happen to an evil city as the patriarch will teach his own descendants how to act in a manner which is "right and just" (v. 19) unlike the city of Sodom and its surroundings.

He informs Abraham that he is going to Sodom to check if the city is as evil as those who cry out to him for help leads him to believe it is. God is just and fair and will not punish a people who do not deserve it. The anthropomorphic description of God as needing to actually go to the city to determine the extent of their wickedness serves the purpose of communicating that he is utterly just in his judgments since the Bible elsewhere teaches that God is omniscient (Pss 139:1–6; 147:5).

As Bruckner has argued, the narrator uses legal language to describe this scene. The "outcry" against Sodom and Gomorrah that has reached God has the status of "legal complaint, requesting deliverance."[3] God has come to adjudicate the charge.

Abraham now intercedes with God on behalf of the innocent. As the NIV note indicates, the translation follows the Masoretic Text in picturing Abraham standing before God, but the original text is almost certainly preserved in the ancient scribal tradition (*tiqqune sopherim*) that indicates that the text has "the LORD stood before Abraham," which likely made the scribes nervous because the inferior always stands before the superior. Could the original be indicating God's willingness to assume an inferior position to listen to Abraham's appeal? Indeed, Bruckner points out the one bringing a legal case stands before the judge.[4]

He looks for assurance from God that he will not bring judgment on the innocent along with the wicked. We are not told, but perhaps his motivation is stirred by his knowledge that Lot and his family are residents of that wicked city. Whatever the motivation, Abraham's intercession with God on behalf of the innocent in the city of Sodom associates the patriarch with later prophets like Moses (Exod 32:31–33:23), Samuel (1 Sam 12:19–25), Jeremiah, and others who intercede on behalf of others with God. Indeed, it is precisely Abraham's role as intercessor that leads God to direct Abimelek, the king of Gerar, to Abraham to intercede on his behalf "for he is a prophet" (Gen 20:7).

Interestingly, Abraham's intercession involves bartering between himself and God. Abraham calls on God to spare (or forgive) the city if he is able to find fifty righteous people in it. Abraham is not just calling for the sparing of the righteous, but because of the presence of righteous people in the city, he was asking that the whole city be spared.

---

2. Ibid., 268.

3. J. Bruckner, *Implied Law in the Abraham Narrative: A Literary and Theological Analysis* (Sheffield: Sheffield Academic Press, 2001), 91–92.

4. Bruckner, *Implied Law*, 95, citing 1 Kings 3:16; Jer. 15:1, 18.

Abraham engages in a type of bartering that is still well known in the ancient Near East (or an American car dealership) today. He starts with fifty. "If there are fifty righteous people in the city God, won't you spare them?" And then he talks God down to ten. God agrees that if there are ten righteous people in the city that he would spare the city. With that God and Abraham part ways, God heading toward Sodom and Abraham going home. This episode depicts Abraham as a person who is willing to advocate for the righteous and God as one who is willing to hear the pleas of his people when they speak on behalf of the righteous.

### The Angels Arrive at Sodom (19:1–3)

At the end of the previous chapter, God had set out toward Sodom and Gomorrah with two attending angels (they are identified explicitly as angels for the first time in 19:1). However, only the two angels actually enter the city of Sodom. Perhaps the sinfulness of the city kept the holy God from actually entering into its precincts.

When they enter, Lot is the first to greet them. He is in the gateway of the city. The gate of an ancient city was not only its public square but also a place where the leaders of the city would meet. His presence in the gate may well imply that he is a leader in the city. The fact that he offers hospitality to the unknown visitors to the city indicate that he has not fully been corrupted by the evil city. He offers them shelter and protection, thus differentiating himself from the inhabitants of the city who will soon seek to exploit them. Through his hospitality, he not only distinguishes himself from the other inhabitants of the city, but likens himself to his uncle Abraham who was quick and generous in his hospitality to the strangers who visited him.

However, though Lot is more similar to Abraham than the inhabitants of Sodom, there is still a noticeable difference of degree between the two. Levenson puts its well:

> Abraham runs; Lot only rises. Abraham offers water and food; Lot does not. And the food that Abraham actually provides—"a calf tender and choice ... curds and milk" as well as the cakes that he bids Sarah to rush to bake—contrasts with Lot's "feast," of which the only item mentioned is "baked unleavened bread" (18:6–8; 19:3).... the largest contrast lies in the initial purpose of the visitations of the two men. The one to Abraham is for the purpose of announcing a birth; the one to Lot, for the purpose of announcing impending death.[5]

5. Levenson, *Inheriting Abraham*, 59.

The angelic visitors at first refuse his invitation, saying that they will spend the night in the square. Lot, however, will not hear of it, probably aware of the danger to which they would be exposed if they stayed in the square. "Lot ... by insisting on hospitality, he exercises his power not only to protect them from harm but also to bind them to an implicit social contract not to harm his household."[6] He successfully persuades them to spend the night in his house, and he provides food for them. The meal includes bread without yeast that makes one think of the future exodus (Exod 12:8 and throughout the account of the first Passover and the actual exit from Egypt), which of course had already taken place by the time the book of Genesis was written, so we must imagine that this connection was intended by the author of the story. Perhaps even more to the point Lot's offer of bread without yeast contrasts with Abraham's abundant bread made out of choice flour.

### Attempted Rape (19:4–11)

As the day ends, the reader now learns why Lot was so insistent on the visitors leaving the public square where they would be totally unprotected. The men of the city, and the emphasis is on the whole city's male population ("men from every part of the city of Sodom—both young and old"), come and essentially lay siege to Lot's house, demanding that he turn over the visitors so they can have sex with them. In an ancient context, such lack of hospitality and protection to visiting strangers is horrendous, not to speak of the attempt to coerce sex (see The Sin of Sodom, in Live the Story below).

Lot, at least, steps forward as the one who has offered them shelter, not yet knowing their true identities (see Angels Unawares, in Live the Story below). He names their intended action a "wicked thing," but then he goes ahead and offers his two virgin daughters in their stead, raising questions about Lot's moral thinking as well. The law of hospitality was an important one in this ancient society ("they have come under the protection [literally 'shade,' a metaphor of protection] of my roof"), and by offering protection and sustenance to strangers who might otherwise be vulnerable, it is a virtuous custom. Lot, though, perverts it by attempting to substitute his daughters for the men. Lot tries to maintain his virtue as a host only to shame himself as a father.

The fact that the men reject Lot's offer does not focus their crime on homosexuality as such. The sin is still coercive sex and an attack on strangers who are due hospitality.

---

6. Hendel (ed.), *Reading Genesis*, 79.

Also, modern audiences need to be aware that the desire of the men of the city to have sex with the visiting men was almost certainly not because the former were gay themselves. Rather, it was a way of exerting power over these visiting foreigners.

These men now threaten Lot, who is a foreigner who lives in their town. He himself is a stranger, though he has lived there for some time, and now he becomes the object of their violence. It is at this point that Lot's visitors take action in a way that indicates they are more than regular travelers. They grab Lot and pull him inside while striking the spiritually blind men of Sodom with physical blindness so they can't find the door to break it in.

### The Escape from Sodom (19:12–26)

The supernatural visitors now announce to Lot their intention to destroy Sodom. Sodom's wickedness is such that it will now experience God's judgment. It is interesting to note that God is not just responding from his own revulsion to the evil of Sodom, but he is acting in response to the "outcry ... against its people," though we are never explicitly told who exactly is crying out to God. Certainly, whoever they are, they experienced the oppression and violence of the people of Sodom. God's judgment comes from his holy nature, but it also provides help to the oppressed.

While Lot, in his misguided way, worked to protect them, now they will protect Lot and his family. They call on him to gather his children and their spouses so they can all escape from the city before it is destroyed and its inhabitants killed. Those pledged to be (or "already," see NIV note, but since these daughters are earlier described as having "never slept with a man," v. 8, the main text is probably correct) married to Lot's daughters laugh off Lot's suggestion that they flee the city. Their reaction indicates their lack of spiritual sensitivity and reveals that they participate in the sin of the city.

Even Lot along with his wife and the two daughters are not quick to leave, so that the angels have to grab them and pull them out of the city. By virtue of his offer of his daughters to the sex-craved men of Sodom, we have observed that Lot is not a paragon of virtue. In the stories to come, we will see the same about his wife and his daughters. Unlike Noah (6:9), Lot and his family are not saved because of his or their righteousness. It is perhaps fair to say that Lot is relatively righteous compared to the inhabitants of Sodom, but even so, it is tempting to see that they are saved rather out of concern for Abraham, who pressed God not to destroy the city even if there are ten righteous people living in it (19:27–29). When it comes down to it, there are less than five who are even only relatively righteous in the city. God does not spare the city, but he does act to save Lot, his wife, and his two daughters.

The angels urge Lot to take his families far far away from the city, because they intend not just to destroy the city but the entire area. They are not to stop and they are not to look back. Lot, though, beseeches the angels to allow them to seek refuge in a small town within the area. Indeed, the name of the city is "Small" (Zoar).

In his request, Lot acknowledges the grace and kindness that the angels have extended to him, even as he requests even more mercy. He does not feel like he can make it to the mountains before the destruction comes, perhaps because of his age. The angels agree to let him seek refuge in Zoar, and this story perhaps explains how this small city managed to avoid the destruction of the general area. Even so, the angels press on Lot the need for urgency.

The men of the city had tried to storm Lot's house to take the men at the beginning of the evening, now the sun had arisen on the next morning (v. 23) when Lot and his family reached Zoar. At this moment God brought his punishment in the form of raining burning sulfur on Sodom and Gomorrah. According to Bruckner, "the morning is the preferred time for an intervention or judgment by God."[7] We are likely to think here of volcanic activity, of which there are signs today in the region around the location of these ancient cities. Indeed, even today this area around the Dead Sea looks like a wasteland.

God's angelic messengers had warned Lot and his family not to look back on the city. We are not told why, though it is often thought that looking back signifies a longing for the city which God will destroy. Verse 26 simply states that Lot's wife looked back and God turned her into a pillar of salt. Waltke (citing Fensham) gets at the significance of the salt here when he points out that "in the biblical world, a site was strewn with salt to condemn it to perpetual barrenness and desolation (e.g., Deut 29:23; Judg 9:45; Ps 107:34; Jer 17:6)."[8]

### He Remembered Abraham (19:27–29)

The scene now shifts from Lot in Zoar to Abraham standing at the place where he interceded with God. As he looked toward the area in which Sodom and Gomorrah stood, he saw smoke rising up. This was like smoke from a furnace, again consistent with the description of a volcano.

At this point, he knew that God did not find ten righteous people in the city, and also at this point, we have no reason to think that even Lot survived.

---

7. Bruckner, *Implied Law*, 107, citing Exod 14:24; Josh 6:15; Isa 13:10.

8. Waltke, *Genesis*, 279; Fensham, "Salt as Curse in the Old Testament and the Ancient Near East," *BA* 25 (1962): 48–50.

But the episode ends by telling us that God saved Lot and his family because he "remembered" Abraham. This is the second time Abraham saved Lot (see 14:1–16).

That God saved Lot because he remembered Abraham might have several meanings. God might have remembered his special relationship with Abraham, which led him to save his close relative. On the other hand, he might have remembered Abraham's passionate speech on behalf of the "righteous" in the city (see 18:22–31), and though there were not the requisite ten righteous which would have led to the preservation of the city, he did save Lot and his family along with him because he was righteous. While the Genesis text does not call Lot "righteous," his act of hospitality clearly differentiates him from the other citizens of that wicked city. Later biblical tradition also calls him righteous (particularly 2 Pet 2:6–8).

### The Perverse Origins of Moab and Ammon (19:30–38)

After God's judgment of the world at the time of the flood, we had an account of Noah and his sons, exposing a dysfunctional family. Now, the account of the judgment of Sodom and Gomorrah is followed by a story focusing on the family of the man who survived the judgment due to his righteousness (see below on the righteousness of Lot).

Lot's wife died in the conflagration, being turned into a pillar of salt (19:26), leaving him with his two daughters. The angels had permitted them to seek refuge in Zoar, and then they spared Zoar from the destruction. However, for reasons that are not explicit, Lot was afraid to stay in Zoar, which likely participated in the evil of Sodom and Gomorrah and only survived because of the presence of Lot. Perhaps now the inhabitants would turn on them. Or perhaps the devastation was a continual reminder of potential danger. For whatever reason, Lot took his two daughters and they sought refuge in a cave. The area around the cities on the plain are filled with caves.

Thus, Lot's family was isolated. The girls were of marriageable age, having been engaged back in Sodom, though their faithless fiancées (or possibly husbands) refused to leave the city and were thus killed in the judgment.

They have no husbands; there are no men around, yet they want children. They thus devise an evil plan to get their father drunk and have him impregnate them. Their father had offered them to be raped by the men of Sodom and now they will take advantage of him sexually. As we have commented, there are some similarities with the earlier story of Noah and his sons. In both accounts, the child(ren) take advantage of the father while the latter is under the influence of wine. Their transgression is clearly sexual in both stories.

The two daughters get their father so drunk that he does not have any idea what is happening when the older sister sleeps with him the first night and the younger sister sleeps with him the second. While this story (and the one concerning Noah) does not condemn the drinking of alcohol, it does raise warnings about overindulgence which leads to the inability to make good decisions. (See Using Alcohol Wisely in the Live the Story section below.) That his sons-in-law ridiculed him and his daughters abuse him in this way shows that Lot, while not evil like the Sodomites, is a weak and ineffective person.

The daughters succeeded in their goal of getting pregnant by their father. They eventually gave birth, each to a son. Their names highlight the fact that they were born from an incestuous relationship. Their names also highlight the broader significance of this story for later Israelite history.

The first child is named Moab, which as the NIV note indicates can be understood to mean "from father," and the second child is named Ben-Ammi, which can be understood as "son of my father's people." The Moabites and the Ammonites who descend from them will be rivals to and enemies of the people of Israel who descend from Abraham through Isaac and Jacob.

Future Moab is directly to the east of Israel on the western shores of the Dead Sea. Today, this region is occupied by the country of Jordan. It is a region typified by deep wadis and extensive plateaus. The future relationship between Israel and the Moabites will be full of hostility and conflict. When Israel is freed from Egyptian bondage and travels toward the promised land, they have to pass through Moabite territory. King Balak of Moab recruits a pagan prophet named Balaam to try to stop or even destroy them (Num 21–23). When this strategy fails, the women of Moab seduce the men to worship foreign gods (Num 25). Only the quick actions of a priest named Phinehas saves the day. For this reason, the law of Moses forbids any Moabite or their descendants for ten generations to enter the sacred assembly (Deut 23:3–6).

During the period of Judges, Eglon of Moab oppressed part of Israel until Ehud the judge delivered them. Conflict continued with the Moabites down through Israelite history. From the Moabite side, we have a document now known as the Moabite stone which documents a conflict between that country and its king Mesha with Omri the king of Israel. With this difficult history in mind, the reader can appreciate the length and intensity of the various prophetic oracles against Moab (Isa 15–16; Jer 48; Ezek 25:8–11).

Just to the north of Moab lay Ammon, to the east of the Jordan River and extending to the desert on its eastern boundary. Israel under Moses came into contact with the Ammonites as they journeyed toward the promised land.

God told Israel not to bother the Ammonites (Deut 2:19), but the Ammonites tried to stop the Israelites from reaching their destination. Deuteronomy 23:3–6 names them along with the Moabites as responsible for hiring Balaam in the abortive attempt to curse the Israelites.

At the time of the settlement, the tribe of Gad was given "the territory of Jazer, all the towns of Gilead, and half the Ammonite country as far as Aroer, near Rabbah" (Josh 13:25). War plagued Ammon and Israel all throughout their common history. Citing only the notorious examples, the judge Jephthah had to counter their attempt to push into territory Israel claimed (Judg 10–11). Saul fought with Nahash the Ammonite king over the city of Jabesh Gilead (1 Sam 11). It was while Joab was leading the armies of Israel against the Ammonites that David impregnated Bathsheba (2 Sam 10). Second Chronicles 20 records a battle between Jehoshaphat and the combined forces of the Ammonites and Moabites.

In history more recent to Jeremiah, Ammon had become a vassal of Babylon helping Babylon when Jehoiakim rebelled in 597 BC (2 Kgs 24:2). But later Ammon worked against the interests of Judah, wanting to take advantage of its weakened position. King Baalis was reportedly behind the successful assassination of Gedaliah, the Babylonian-appointed governor of post-destruction Judah (Jer 40:7–41:15). Eventually, though, Babylon did subjugate Ammon (582 BC), the event that this oracle most likely anticipated. For related oracles against Ammon, see Ezekiel 25:1–7 and Zephaniah 2:8–11. From our historical vantage point, we can understand how later Israel would have read this story as explaining the dark origins of their enemies.

### The Redemptive Presence of the Righteous

God indicates his willingness to preserve a city of wicked people if there are even only ten righteous people living there. As it turns out, there are not ten righteous people living in Sodom, so God does destroy the city, though he does preserve Lot, his wife (who later dies because she looks back on the city), as well as their two daughters. Later we expand more fully on why God rescued Lot and his family from the judgment brought on Sodom, but at this point we should recognize the redemptive effect that the righteous have on a community. After all, as Peter points out, God rescued Lot because he was a righteous man and thus illustrates that "the Lord knows how to rescue the godly from trials and to hold the unrighteous for punishment on the day of judgment" (2 Pet 2:9).

That God is willing to preserve a whole city of extremely wicked people if there are only ten righteous people there illustrates the teaching of the book of Proverbs. Proverbs is often wrongly thought to concern the ethics of the individual and the benefits or punishments that come on the individual, but a close reading shows that the wisdom, righteousness, and godliness of individuals benefits the community.

> Through the blessing of the upright a city is exalted,
> but by the mouth of the wicked it is destroyed. (Prov 11:11)
>
> Righteousness exalts a nation,
> but sin condemns any people. (Prov 14:34)

Proverbs here articulates the two sides of the same truth and this truth is illustrated by the story of Sodom and Gomorrah. That truth is that righteous people lead to the betterment of a society while wicked people destroy it. It is particularly important, again according to Proverbs, that leaders be righteous.

> When the righteous triumph, there is great elation;
> but when the wicked rise to power, people go into hiding.
> (Prov 28:12)
>
> When the wicked rise to power, people go into hiding;
> but when the wicked perish, the righteous thrive. (Prov 28:28)
>
> When the righteous thrive, the people rejoice;
> when the wicked rule, the people groan. (Prov 29:2)

This principle is relevant on many levels today including the family (note Prov 20:7; "the righteous lead blameless lives; blessed are their children after them"), society, and the church.

There are too many sad stories of Christian leaders who have gone bad, destroying their churches and bringing shame on Christianity. These are often the subject of public display and ridicule, but there are many other stories where God's people have been a healing presence to a community. Let's consider the story of New Song Church, where its leaders and members brought a redemptive presence into a difficult neighborhood in the city of Baltimore.

Mark Gornik gives an account of the transformation of a part of that city known as Sandtown, which, while at one point was a thriving community, was hit hard when manufacturing jobs left for other regions and countries to be replaced by destitution and drug dealing. Many houses were left vacant for a long time and, besides the drug trade, the majority of businesses were liquor stores and same-day loan shops.

Mark and his wife Rita, along with Allan and Susan Tibbels, moved into this neighborhood, and while the story of the transformation of Sandtown is much too long and detailed to be told here,[9] it demonstrates how the presence of God's people can lead to real and positive change. As the Gorniks and the Tibbels came to know the community and in particular the Christians who lived there, the church became an agent of reconciliation, intercession, and change. Over the next decade, the church, working through Habitat for Humanity, rebuilt hundreds of homes, helped people find jobs, and encouraged the next generation to go to college. Besides the positive transformation of this community, this example speaks to "the promise and possibility of God's peace for the changing of the American inner city."[10]

## Abraham the Teacher

In a recent article, Fretheim has pointed to Genesis 18:19 as a passage that highlights Abraham's role as a teacher.[11] Here God states to his angelic companions that "I have chosen him [Abraham], so that he will direct his children and his household after him to keep the way of the LORD by doing what is right and just, so that the LORD will bring about for Abraham what he has promised him." Thus, one of Abraham's divinely given tasks is to teach his children and his household. The subject of his teaching is "the way of the Lord" and the result will be that they will do "what is right and just." The consequence of his instruction ("so that") will be that God will bring about what he has promised, which seems best understood as a reference back to Genesis 12:1–3 where God promises Abraham that he will make him a great nation and will bless him and his descendants who in turn will bless the nations (see 12:1–3). That Abraham followed through on his divinely commissioned teaching may be seen in Genesis 26:5 which states that "Abraham obeyed me and did everything I required of him."

Fretheim connects this charge to Abraham with the later admonitions in the Torah that all godly parents have a duty to teach their children about "the way of the Lord." Parents are to teach their children about the exodus and specifically the Passover (Exod 12:26–27; 13:8–10). They are to tell them about God, his great deeds, and his law (Deut 4:9–10; 6:4–9, 2–25; 11:13–21; 31:9–13).

---

9. For such an account, see M. R. Gornik, *To Live in Peace: Biblical Faith and the Changing Inner City* (Grand Rapids: Eerdmans, 2002).

10. Ibid, 1.

11. T. E. Fretheim, "'God Was with the Boy' (Genesis 21:20): Children in the Book of Genesis," in *The Child in the Bible*, ed. M. J. Bunge, T. E. Fretheim, and B. R. Gaventa (Grand Rapids: Eerdmans, 2008), 3–23.

But it is not only the Torah which speaks of instructing the children in the way of the Lord. The psalmist speaks about God's great deeds in the past as well as the importance of teaching the children about the law, "so the next generation would know them, even the children yet to be born, and they in turn would tell their children. Then they would put their trust in God and would not forget his deeds but would keep his commandments" (Ps 78:6–7).

Wisdom literature puts a heavy emphasis on parents teaching their children. This is particularly true of the book of Proverbs, in which a father (but notice also the role of the mother in 1:8) teaches his son about how to live in a productive and godly way in the world. The dynamic of a father teaching his son is also found in the book of Ecclesiastes where an unnamed wise man teaches his son to "fear God and obey the commandments" (12:13–14) by exposing him to the thought of another wise man referred to as the Teacher.[12]

Thus, parents were to teach children about God, his mighty deeds, as well as the law. They were not the only teachers in Israel, of course. The priestly tribe of Levi was divinely commissioned to teach Israel about the law as Moses stated in his blessing on the tribe of Levi: "He teaches your precepts to Jacob and your law to Israel" (Deut 33:10).

Interestingly, toward the end of the Old Testament period, Jeremiah announced the coming of a new covenant that would fulfill and replace the old covenant of Moses. Notable in the description of this new covenant was the fact that "no longer will they teach their neighbor, or say to one another, 'Know the LORD,' because they will all know me, from the least of them to the greatest" (Jer 31:34). In the new covenant the people will have such a close and immediate relationship with God that they will not need a teacher to mediate that relationship. The New Testament announces that Jesus Christ initiates and mediates this new covenant (Luke 22:20; Heb 8:7–13; 10:15–18).

We should not over read the description of the new covenant and think that teachers have no role at all. While people do not need a human mediator to teach them about a relationship with God, teachers are still important to guide Christians. Indeed, many New Testament passages speak of the high calling and deep responsibility of the teacher in the Church. Indeed, it is Christ himself who gave the church " ... teachers, to equip his people for works of service, so that the body of Christ may be built up until we all reach unity in the faith and in the knowledge of the Son of God and become mature, attaining to the whole measure of the fullness of Christ" (Eph 4:11–13). Indeed, the job is so important that James warns that "not many of you should become teachers, my fellow believers, because you know that we

12. See Longman, *Ecclesiastes*.

who teach will be judged more strictly" (Jas 3:1). After all, teachers influence others in terms of the knowledge of God and his ways.

In a sense, every Christian is a teacher. We teach others whenever we talk about God or whenever we tell people how God wants us to live. We teach our friends and associates, we teach our children and our spouses. In this we follow Abraham's example, and we should do so boldly but also carefully.

### The Sin of Sodom

What was the sin of Sodom that led to their judgment? To many the answer is obvious; it is the sin of homosexuality or at least homosexual practice. It is from this biblical story that the term "sodomite" came to be applied to male homosexuals. Indeed, the narrative of the destruction of Sodom and Gomorrah finds currency in modern culture wars due to the controversy over the issue of homosexuality more than any other reason. Is this justified? To answer this question, we will first consider the story itself, then we will explore how it is handled in later biblical passages.

As we look at the story itself, it is hard to be certain that it is homosexuality or the practice of it as such that is the sin that leads to God's judgment on the city. After all, we are not talking about consensual sex in this story, but rather rape, and gang rape at that. Indeed, any sex outside of marriage, homosexual or heterosexual, would be considered wrong. Even if the story concerned heterosexual sex, it would be sinful since the sex was intended to be forced upon unwilling parties.

Further, the story itself also concerns a lack of hospitality, which was considered an egregious crime in the ancient world. After all, the Bible was written in a time where there were not an abundance of hotels and restaurants in which a traveler can find shelter and food. A stranger's sustenance and safety depended on the willingness of people to offer them lodging and food.

Indeed, later Scripture typically cites the destruction of Sodom and Gomorrah as paradigmatic of the type of horrific judgment that would come on God's own people or some other foreign people because of their sin without specifying the nature of the sin that led to their punishment (Isa 1:9, 10; 13:19; Jer 23:14; 49:18; 50:40; Amos 4:11; Zeph 2:9; see Anticipating the Final Judgment, Part 2 below).

On the occasion that the sin is specified, it is typically not homosexuality that is singled out or even mentioned. The prophet Ezekiel announces, "Now this was the sin of your sister Sodom: She and her daughters were arrogant, overfed and unconcerned; they did not help the poor and needy. They were haughty and did detestable things before me" (16:49–50a). In the Gospels, Jesus says that those cities that do not show hospitality to his disciples are worse than Sodom and Gomorrah, suggesting that it is in the lack of hospitality that we are to locate the sin of those cities (Matt 10:9–15; Luke 10:8–12).

There is one passage that names the sin of Sodom and Gomorrah as a sexual perversion. Jude is warning his readers about the sexual transgressions of the false teachers who are leading them astray by comparing them to "Sodom and Gomorrah and the surrounding towns [who] gave themselves up to sexual immorality and perversion. They serve as an example of those who suffer the punishment of eternal fire" (Jude 7). But even here, the sexual immorality could be gang rape rather than specifically homosexuality.

Thus, one must be careful about bringing the sin of Sodom and Gomorrah into the modern discussion of homosexual practice. It is not clear from the story itself or from its later citations that homosexuality per se was what led to the horrific judgment of those cities.

That acknowledged, there are other passages that are appropriately cited to support the idea that the canon witnesses that homosexual practice is a transgression of God's will for his human creatures. As Waltke points out, "homosexuality is a capital offense in the Old Testament (Lev 18:22; 20:13)"[13] and further, the New Testament reaffirms the Old Testament's assertion that homosexual acts constitute sinful behavior (Rom 1:24–27; 1 Cor 6:9). In the light of that consistent scriptural teaching, one cannot help but think that the homosexual intentions of the citizens of Sodom contribute to the dark picture of that notorious city.

Of course, recognizing that the Bible identifies homosexual behavior as sinful is not the end of the discussion, particularly in the twenty-first century in the West, where more permissive attitudes are on the up-rise, even within the church. While churches that consider Scripture as canon (the standard of faith and practice) cannot ignore the biblical teaching on homosexuality, its leaders and members must be very careful not to demonize and shun gays.

How to stand for biblical teaching on homosexuality and also show love toward our gay friends and relatives is not an easy issue. One thing is clear. Churches should not drive gays or others away from the church where they can, along with the rest of us sinners, hear the gospel. Indeed, that seems to be an important consideration as we think about this issue. We need to remember that none of us are without sin and we all need a Savior. We need to remember Jesus' teaching about the need to take the plank out of our eye as we tell our brothers about the speck in theirs (Matt 7:1–5).

Again, how this works out in practice is difficult and may differ from church tradition to church tradition. It is heartening to hear reports of

13. Waltke, *Genesis*, 276.

churches, like the massive Southern Baptist Church, which while not backing off on its recognition of biblical teaching on homosexuality, has adopted a more open attitude toward dialogue with gay activists as well as exhorting families not to shun gay relatives.[14] The Roman Catholic Church under the leadership of Pope Francis, while not changing its basic stance on homosexual activity, has also considered more loving attitudes toward gays who identify as believing Christians.

A large evangelical church in the Midwest in which I have recently preached has adopted the policy of allowing gay Christians to join the church, but not serve as leaders within the church. While they consider homosexuality as pastoral issues on a par with unmarried heterosexual couples who live together, they do not consider it a "pulpit issue." Such an approach appears to be working for this church, though it is unsatisfactory to some on both sides of the issue.

Again, the purpose of this essay is not to provide a pat answer to how churches should respond to the changing attitudes toward homosexuality in our culture today. The Bible's teaching is clear, but so is the mandate to love all others. Church leaders will continue to struggle with this issue for a long time to come. What God calls us to do is to struggle recognizing our own brokenness as we consider the brokenness of others.

## Who Are Those Men?

Genesis 18–19 begins with the appearance of three visitors at first described as "three men" (18:2). Abraham enthusiastically greeted them and extended hospitality to them (see the next essay). But who are these men?

The narrative soon makes it clear that their leader is none other than the Lord himself (18:13). In 19:1, the other two "men" are called "angels." This lends support to the idea that the Lord himself is making his presence known to Abraham as the "angel of the Lord." We have encountered the angel of the Lord as early as Genesis 16 where we discussed a number of passages that explicitly refer to the angel of the Lord as one way in which the Lord made his presence known to the patriarchs (see The Angel Who Saves at Genesis 16). We did not include God's appearance to Abraham on the eve of his destruction of Sodom and Gomorrah there because the Lord's appearance as angel of the Lord is only implied here.

But if we are correct, then, like in those earlier discussed passages, we are to understand the angel as a theophany and not specifically as a pre-incarnate appearance of Jesus, also known as a Christophany. That said, Christians are

14. See "Southern Baptists Soften Tone on Gays," *Wall Street Journal* (vol. 264, number 104, A6) on October 31, 2014.

not incorrect to think of this physical manifestation of God to his people in relationship to the coming of Jesus, who makes God's presence more palpable than anything that the patriarchs could imagine.

**Angels Unawares (Heb 13:2)**

In our study, we have noted more than once the role that hospitality plays in the narrative concerning the cities of Sodom and Gomorrah. Lot distinguishes himself from the people of Sodom by displaying hospitality to strangers, though his hospitality pales in comparison to that of Abraham. Hospitality to strangers seems correlated to godliness, and God responds accordingly, blessing Abraham, saving Lot, and destroying the cities of Sodom and Gomorrah.

Of course, hospitality for travelers was critical in the age before hotels. Perhaps we should think that God does not care so much about hospitality these days.

Before we come to such a conclusion, we need recognize that the New Testament authors urge their readers to display hospitality to others, including strangers. Indeed, the author of Hebrews alludes to our narrative in Genesis when he instructs his readers to "not forget to show hospitality to strangers, for by so doing some people have shown hospitality to angels without knowing it" (Heb 13:2). The admonition to hospitality is shared by other New Testament authors (Rom 12:13; 1 Tim 5:10; 1 Peter 4:9; 3 John 1:8). Indeed, officers in the church must be hospitable (1 Tim 3:2; Titus 1:8).

While some of these passages focus in on Christians showing hospitality to each other, our responsibility does not end there. And our Genesis passage as well as Hebrews specifies the "stranger" as the object of our hospitality.

Telling is Jesus' statement about the sheep and the goats (Matt 25:31–46). He speaks of himself as the Son of Man, who when he returns in his glory and sits on his throne will separate people into two categories, the sheep and the goats. The sheep he invites into glory, while goats go to eternal punishment. What makes one a sheep as opposed to a goat? Jesus says that the sheep are those who gave him something to eat when he was hungry and drink when he was thirsty, clothed him when he was without clothes and visited him in prison. "I was a stranger and you invited me in" (v. 35). The righteous sheep are incredulous, not remembering when they did these kind acts for him. Jesus then tells them "Truly I tell you, whatever you did for one of the least of these brothers and sisters of mine, you did for me" (v. 40).

Does this biblical admonition have anything to say to our contemporary debates about immigration? It is to this question that we turn in our next section.

**Showing Hospitality to Strangers: The Issue of Immigration**

The migration of individuals, families, and communities has taken place throughout human history. At the time of the writing of this commentary, immigration is one of the most controversial issues facing America and other Western nation states. This year (2014) the number of unaccompanied children illegally crossing the border in the southern states of the US is unprecedented, and our society is divided over what to do in response. Since these questions have troubled nations for decades and even centuries, I suspect that the issue will not soon go away in the future.

So, does the Bible, and in particular the book of Genesis, address the issue of immigration? Can we devise modern policy based on a biblical blueprint? Not directly and definitively.

The Old Testament situation is considerably different from our modern situation. The New Testament is speaking to the church and not a nation state. The Bible does not provide an argument in favor of or against open borders or accepting people as citizens. That said, the approval of Abraham and even Lot as those who show hospitality to strangers (and the New Testament affirmation of Abraham's actions as one who showed hospitality to strangers unaware that they were angels) certainly does prohibit a callous and uncaring response on the part of God's people to immigrants who come to our country for work and survival. Christians should not be the angry voices calling for the quick deportation of people, particularly children. We must show love and provide care and compassion to all strangers even at our own expense while debating the wisest way to handle the immigration issue. Vilifying and abusing those who cross our borders is the very opposite of the biblical admonition of care for the stranger. In this, we find agreement with Beck and VanDrunen who helpfully remark:

> Though Genesis 19 and 20 certainly do not provide concrete guidance for immigration policy, it is striking how the relatively righteous city of Gerar is distinguished by its respect for Abraham, the alien among them, and how the condemned city of Sodom demonstrated its wickedness by violent threats against aliens within its walls. How people treat those who are different from them seems to be a fundamental test of their righteousness. In the present day, when issues of immigration and the place of (especially illegal) immigrants are widely debated in many societies, these Genesis narratives confirm the importance of such matters and provide much grist for reflection.[15]

15. R. Beck, and D. VanDrunen, "The Biblical Foundations of Law: Creation, Fall and the Patriarchs," in *Law and the Bible: Justice, Mercy and Legal Institutions*, ed. R. F. Cochran Jr. and D.

In addition, we commend the judicious and sensitive treatment of the biblical material that impinges on the question of immigration provided by M. Daniel Carroll R.[16]

## The Dangers of Living in a Toxic Culture

Lot was different from the rest of the inhabitants of the city of Sodom where he lived. He offered the strangers hospitality, while the rest of the city tried to violate them. That said, a close reading of Genesis 19 shows that Sodom's toxic culture had influenced Lot and his family. He maintained his fundamental relationship with God, but he found himself attracted to and caught up in Sodom's evil culture as well.

We can see Sodom's influence on Lot when he offers his own two daughters in place of the strangers (vv. 6–8). That Lot did not always speak forthrightly likely explains why his sons-in-law think he is joking when he tries to warn them about the coming destruction of Sodom (v. 14). Lot was hesitant to leave the city (v. 16) and refused to follow the angels' instructions to flee to the mountains, talking them into letting him go instead to a small, nearby town (vv. 18–20). Lot's wife's actions speak even more loudly of a toxic influence of the evil culture in which she lived, when she looks back and is turned into a pillar of salt.

Lot's story is a timely reminder that we are all influenced subtly and even more blatantly by the culture in which we live. We all live in a toxic culture. We can debate how much our modern Western culture resembles the culture of Sodom, but we are on very dangerous grounds if we do not recognize that our culture is toxic and dangerous to our faith.

That said, there is not a simple formula for how faithful Christians are to live in the context of a toxic culture. It does not seem right that we should simply treat our faith as a different compartment of our life. Faith affects all of life. But should we withdraw or fight against our culture? Should we infiltrate the culture and change it from within? Should we try to change the laws of the land in order for it to be less toxic? Should we develop a separate distinct Christian culture?

In our opinion, there is not one correct approach to how we live as faithful people in an environment that is toxic and sometimes hostile to our faith. In terms of the biblical narrative, while Lot gives us a negative example, Daniel, particularly in the first two chapters of the book that bears his name, gives us a more promising, positive example of a person of faith living in a culture

---

VanDrunen (Downers Grove, IL: InterVarsity Press, 2013), 46.

16. M. Daniel Carroll R., *Christians at the Border: Immigration, the Church, and the State* (Grand Rapids: Brazos, 2013).

that is extremely toxic and hostile to faith. As we look at how he chooses to live in Babylon, we see that he doesn't always object, even when he has his name changed and is forced to study the hostile curriculum in the school that Nebuchadnezzar had set up in order to train Daniel and his three friends as wise men in a Babylonian system. However, they exercise their faith, though privately, by refusing the food and drink that Nebuchadnezzar had prescribed for them.[17]

The stories of Lot and of Daniel remind us that even today and even in the West we live in a culture that is not friendly to our faith. These stories do not give us a formula for how to live, but they do call us to give thoughtful consideration to how we should preserve and even stimulate our faith.

## Anticipating the Final Judgment, Part 2

Earlier, we discussed how the New Testament describes the flood as an anticipation of the final judgment that accompanies the return of Christ at the end of the age (see Anticipating the Final Judgment, Part 1, after Gen 6:1–9:17). The destruction of Sodom and Gomorrah is also a vivid example of God's sudden and decisive judgment against a sinful community. As such, it becomes a harbinger of future judgments. As Beck and VanDrunen point out, "This extraordinary divine judgment on these very wicked cities serves, through the rest of Scripture, as the preeminent paradigm of divine judgment on the last day.... Human judgment must answer to divine justice, and God will call all people to account."[18]

Moses, for example, invoked the destruction of Sodom and Gomorrah when he warned people not to break God's covenant law. Such violation would lead to judgment that will be "like the destruction of Sodom and Gomorrah, Admah and Zeboyim, which the Lord overthrew in fierce anger" (Deut 29:23; see also Isa 1:9–10; 3:9; Jer 23:14; Amos 4:11). In the Old Testament, the destruction of pagan nations is also compared to the destruction of Sodom and Gomorrah (Isa 13:19; Jer 50:40 [Babylon]; Jer 49:18 [Edom]; Zeph 2:9 [Moab]).

When we turn to the New Testament, we hear that God's future and final judgment will be like the destruction of Sodom and Gomorrah. After citing the judgment that came on the disobedient angels (a reference to Gen 6:1–3), and the flood, Peter focuses in on the story of Sodom and Gomorrah as an object lesson of what will happen when God comes in the future to judge sinners:

---

17. For the reasons why they choose to separate themselves from their culture in this way, see T. Longman III, *Daniel*, NIVAC (Grand Rapids: Zondervan, 1997).

18. Beck and VanDrunen, "The Biblical Foundations of Law," 44.

> ... if he condemned the cities of Sodom and Gomorrah by burning them to ashes, and made them an example of what is going to happen to the ungodly; and if he rescued Lot, a righteous man, who was distressed by the depraved conduct of the lawless (for that righteous man, living among them day after day, was tormented in his righteous soul by the lawless deeds he saw and heard) — if this is so, then the Lord knows how to rescue the godly from trials and to hold the unrighteous for punishment on the day of judgment. This is especially true of those who follow the corrupt desire of the flesh and despise authority. (2 Pet 2:6–8)

The story of Sodom and Gomorrah is a warning to us today to avoid sin for fear that we will suffer the fate of those two cities. Peter is urging us to emulate Lot, a righteous man, who was saved by God from meeting the fate of the rest of the citizens of the cities.[19]

It has become popular these days to downplay or even deny the idea of God as a judge of sin.[20] However, the New Testament's evocation of the memory of Sodom and Gomorrah to parallel the future judgment is a reminder of what lays in store for those who reject God or who, after following God, decide to look longingly back on a life of sin. Indeed, according to Jesus, the fate of Sodom and Gomorrah will be nothing compared to those who reject his message: "If anyone will not welcome you or listen to your words, leave that home or town and shake the dust off your feet. Truly I tell you, it will be more bearable for Sodom and Gomorrah on the day of judgment than for that town" (Matt 10:14–15). On another occasion, according to the Gospel of Luke, we learn that on the day Jesus returns, it will be similar to the days of Lot. "People were eating and drinking, buying and selling, planting and building. But the day Lot left Sodom, fire and sulfur rained down from heaven and destroyed them all. It will be just like this on the day the Son of Man is revealed" (Luke 17:28–30). He goes on and warns his hearers not to be like Lot's wife who looked back and lost her life (17:33).

## "When He Hesitated ..." (Gen 19:16)

Lot's experience is one with which many of us can identify. Let's remember that, as Calvin said, the Bible is a mirror of the soul. As we read it, we discover

---

19. The biblical account of Lot does not specifically describe him as righteous, though God does promise to spare the cities if there were at least ten righteous people there (Gen 18:32). There were not ten, but the rescue of Lot and his family shows that he considered Lot righteous. Peter expands upon the biblical story when he talks about Lot's torment.

20. Perhaps the leading example these days is R. Bell, *Love Wins: A Book about Heaven, Hell, and the Fate of Everyone Who Ever Lived* (San Francisco: HarperOne, 2012); see also Siebert, *The Violence of Scripture.*

how we are doing in terms of our relationship with God. Are we moving toward God or away from him?

When we read historical narrative, it is typical for us to identify with the characters and often find that our own experience is reflected in their actions. The best character in the story of Sodom and Gomorrah is Lot, and he is only relatively better. We certainly can question his integrity as he offers his virgin daughters in place of the "strangers" to whom he offers hospitality. Lot stands out from his fellow citizens, but he has, as we explained above, been influenced by the company he has kept. God promised Abraham that he would not judge Sodom if there were ten righteous in the city. But there are not even ten, and even Lot cannot be described as righteous except in relative terms.

That said, God graciously, and because of Abraham, determined to remove Lot and his family (wife and daughters) from the judgment that was about to fall on the city. Even so, Lot is surprisingly reluctant to be rescued! When God's angels tell him to hurry and get out of the city (v. 15), he hesitates, and the angels have to forcibly drag him out of the city. He also does not trust the angels to take him to safety but begs them to let him go to a small nearby town, Zoar.

The angels react by grabbing Lot by the wrist and dragging him out of town. They even acceded to his request to go to the small nearby town.

Many of us can identify with Lot. God saves us, but we are reluctant to leave the pleasures of our previous life even when we know that to stay means we will be destroyed. The story of Lot points out the folly of a life that wants to dwell in sin. If Lot had stayed, he would have died in the conflagration of judgment that came on the city. And thereby we too are warned against keeping one foot in our previous life when God wants to bring us to safety.

### The Consequences of Living by Sight and Not by Faith

The daughters of Lot are desperate. They have escaped the destruction of their homeland, but now they are in a cave with each other and their father. Perhaps they can see the smoke rising from the area in which they used to live. For all they know it is not just Sodom, but the whole world that has just come to an end. All they know is that there are three of them, and this drives them to an act of desperation.

They act on the basis of what they see, and this leads them to deceive their father by getting him drunk and sleeping with him. They think they have limited options and this drives them to sin, the sin of incest, a daughter sleeping with her father. They would likely argue that their situation made this act necessary, though they clearly understood it was wrong and that their father in his right, sober mind would never agree to it.

Most of us cannot relate to the specifics of this story, but, if we are honest, we sometimes rationalize our actions based on what we perceive to be our circumstances. If it weren't for the fact that I can't pay the bills, I wouldn't cheat on my taxes, deceive my customers, shoplift ... If it weren't for the fact that my spouse ignores me, I wouldn't find myself in an emotional or physical affair. If it weren't for the fact that I desperately need this job, I wouldn't lie about my past employment history. The list can go on and on.

We need to live by faith and not by sight. Our sight is limited and flawed. We need to follow God and his requirements, because no matter what short-term discomfort or suffering we have to undergo, it is the better, that is the right, way.

**Using Alcohol Wisely**

As mentioned, this story is the second one where a biblical character gets into trouble through overindulgence of alcohol. Noah drank too much and Ham "saw his father naked" (9:22). Here on two occasions Lot's daughters got him drunk and he impregnated them. Both events connect the overuse of alcohol with illegitimate sex, not an uncommon connection even today. These biblical stories clearly warn about the dangers of alcohol.

But do they lead to the conclusion that any consumption of alcohol is bad? The biblical answer is no. We find the use of wine in positive as well as negative contexts. Remember that Melchizedek, the king of Salem, brought wine and bread to Abraham (Gen 14:18). God blesses Jacob, thinking he is Esau, by saying "May God give you heaven's dew and earth's richness — an abundance of grain and new wine" (Gen 27:28). In his blessing on Judah, Jacob says "He will tether his donkey to a vine, his colt to the choicest branch; he will wash his garments in wine, his robes in the blood of grapes. His eyes will be darker than wine, his teeth whiter than milk" (Gen 49:11 – 12). More examples could be given, but we will conclude this paragraph by citing Psalm 104:15, which praises God as the one who provides "wine that gladdens human hearts."

The problem is not with wine per se, but a lack of self-control in drinking it. Like with many things, overindulgence is the problem, a serious problem and Noah and Lot are prime examples. And it is a real danger for everyone. God's good gift of alcohol is so enjoyable that it can be addictive.

Proverbs will speak of wine as a sign of God's blessing ("Honor the LORD with your wealth, with the firstfruits of all your crops, then your barns will be filled to overflowing, and your vats will brim over with new wine," 3:9 – 10). It is part of the feast that Woman Wisdom offers to men who seek her (9:2, 5). But Proverbs also addresses the dangers of addiction and overuse:

Who has woe? Who has sorrow?
Who has strife? Who has complaints?
Who has needless bruises? Who has bloodshot eyes?
Those who linger over wine,
who go to sample bowls of mixed wine.
Do not gaze at wine when it is red,
when it sparkles in the cup,
when it goes down smoothly!
In the end it bites like a snake
and poisons like a viper.
Your eyes will see strange sights,
and your mind will imagine confusing things.
You will be like one sleeping on the high seas,
lying on top of the rigging.
"They hit me," you will say, "but I'm not hurt!
They beat me, but I don't feel it.
When will I wake up
so I can find another drink? (23:29–35)

Excessive alcohol lowers inhibitions and dulls decision making and leads to bad acts, a lesson taught King Lemuel by his mother: "It is not for kings, Lemuel—it is not for kings to drink wine, not for rulers to crave beer, lest they drink and forget what has been decreed, and deprive all the oppressed of their rights" (31:4–5). Though she goes on to allow for the poor to drink and forget their sorrows (31:6–7), the advice she gives to kings not to drink to the point of losing decision making capacity is true for all of us.

## The Consequences of Incest

By all measures, the twenty-first century West has one of the most permissive attitudes toward sexual expression. Same-sex marriage, gender-reassignment surgery, living together outside of marriage, and bisexual relationships are no longer censured by society at large. Indeed, those who have qualms or disagreement with this general cultural norm are themselves censured and marginalized.

That said, there is still universal rejection of marriage and/or sexual relationships between close relatives. No one in the public square is presenting an argument in favor of incest. That said, incest continues to be a major problem behind closed doors. In particular, young women are taken advantage of by their fathers, uncles, brothers, or other close relatives. But it is not only female family members who are abused sexually. While according to the best statistics provided by an article by Mia Fontaine in *The Atlantic*, one in three to four girls are abused by the time they are eighteen, so are one in five to seven boys.[21] Many of these violations are perpetrated by close family members. According to statistics reported in Fontaine's article, there were approximately 105,000 reported cases of incest in California in 2010, 92,000 were cases where parents violated their children and another 4,600 by other relative.

Incest is a modern American, indeed global, problem. Studies have also suggested that there is a close correlation between being a victim of incest and later addictions as well as criminal behavior, particularly prostitution.

Due to the high incidence of incest in the world, in spite of public expressions of revulsion, it is worth taking the opportunity provided by the story of Lot and his daughters to remind us of the Bible's decisive rejection of incestuous relationships, especially since incest is not only a problem in society at large, but sadly within the church.[22]

The seventh commandment prohibits adultery, which means any sexual intercourse outside of marriage. The case law further specifies the meaning and significance of the commandments and Leviticus 18 and 20 as well as Deuteronomy 27 help us understand the application of the commandment on adultery by prohibiting sexual relations between close relatives (incest), men (homosexuality), with animals (bestiality), and with a woman who is having her period.

Not all the case law continues to be operative in the New Testament time period to be sure. Some of the case law is only relevant during the Old Testament time period, but in the case of incest there is no reason to think that the coming of Christ has abolished the continuing relevance of the laws on incest. Indeed, Paul admonishes the Corinthian church for not disciplining a man sleeping with his mother (1 Cor 5). Though our present passage speaks of an unusual form of incest (daughters raping their drunk father), it still warns against all incest by presenting the act in such an ugly manner.

---

21. Mia Fontaine, "America Has an Incest Problem," *The Atlantic*, Jan 24, 2013, www.theatlantic.com/national/archive/2013/01/america-has-an-incest-problem/272459/.

22. See the excellent and groundbreaking work done by D. Allender, *The Wounded Heart: Hope for Adult Victims of Child Sexual Abuse* (Colorado Springs, CO: NavPress, 2008).

CHAPTER 17

# Genesis 20

## LISTEN to the Story

20:1 Now Abraham moved on from there into the region of the Negev
and lived between Kadesh and Shur. For a while he stayed in Gerar, 2 and
there Abraham said of his wife Sarah, "She is my sister." Then Abimelek
king of Gerar sent for Sarah and took her.

3 But God came to Abimelek in a dream one night and said to him,
"You are as good as dead because of the woman you have taken; she is a
married woman."

4 Now Abimelek had not gone near her, so he said, "Lord, will you
destroy an innocent nation? 5 Did he not say to me, 'She is my sister,'
and didn't she also say, 'He is my brother'? I have done this with a clear
conscience and clean hands."

6 Then God said to him in the dream, "Yes, I know you did this with
a clear conscience, and so I have kept you from sinning against me. That
is why I did not let you touch her. 7 Now return the man's wife, for he is
a prophet, and he will pray for you and you will live. But if you do not
return her, you may be sure that you and all who belong to you will die."

8 Early the next morning Abimelek summoned all his officials, and
when he told them all that had happened, they were very much afraid.
9 Then Abimelek called Abraham in and said, "What have you done to us?
How have I wronged you that you have brought such great guilt upon me
and my kingdom? You have done things to me that should never be done."
10 And Abimelek asked Abraham, "What was your reason for doing this?"

11 Abraham replied, "I said to myself, 'There is surely no fear of God in
this place, and they will kill me because of my wife.' 12 Besides, she really
is my sister, the daughter of my father though not of my mother; and
she became my wife. 13 And when God had me wander from my father's
household, I said to her, 'This is how you can show your love to me:
Everywhere we go, say of me, "He is my brother." ' "

14 Then Abimelek brought sheep and cattle and male and female slaves
and gave them to Abraham, and he returned Sarah his wife to him. 15 And
Abimelek said, "My land is before you; live wherever you like."

[16]To Sarah he said, "I am giving your brother a thousand shekels of silver. This is to cover the offense against you before all who are with you; you are completely vindicated."

[17]Then Abraham prayed to God, and God healed Abimelek, his wife and his female slaves so they could have children again, [18]for the LORD had kept all the women in Abimelek's household from conceiving because of Abraham's wife Sarah.

*Listening to the Text in the Story:* Biblical Texts: Genesis 12:1–3; Genesis 12:10–20; Ancient Near Eastern Texts: Akkadian text at Ugarit (PRU IV, 139) and Egyptian Marriage Contracts

The background of this story is in the initial promises to Abraham that his descendants would be a "great nation" (12:2), which includes not only descendants but also land. As earlier (12:10–20), famine threatens the viability of the land promise, thus creating a threat to its fulfillment. As in the earlier famine story when Abraham sought refuge in Egypt, this famine too raises a challenge to Abraham's journey of faith. Will he again react with fear and manipulation or will he respond with faith?

Abraham thought there was no "fear of God" in Gerar, and therefore the king would simply kill him and take his wife from him. But ancient Near Eastern societies tended to prohibit adultery. Indeed, we have an Ugaritic text that accuses the wife of King Ammishtamru of committing the "great sin" of adultery. And indeed, that language of "great sin" likely stands behind Abimelek's reference to adultery bringing "great guilt (better, sin [*hata'a*])" on the land. This language is also found in Egyptian marriage contracts.[1]

## EXPLAIN the Story

### Abraham Lies about Sarah Again (20:1–2)

We last left Abraham in Mamre near Hebron where he received and interacted with three visitors, one of whom was none other than God himself (18:1). After the destruction of Sodom and Gomorrah and their environs, Abraham, for reasons that are left unexplained, moves south through the Negev, the

1. G. Hugenberger. *Marriage as Covenant: Biblical Law and Ethics as Developed in Malachi* (Eugene, OR: Wipf and Stock, 1994), 291–92.

region through which he traveled to go to Egypt (Gen 12:9). The reference to the Negev likely intends to remind us of that earlier episode when Abraham lied to the king of Egypt about Sarah. It appears that he then traveled even further south for a period of time and lived between Kadesh and Shur. Kadesh is also known as Kadesh-barnea, the place in the north part of the Sinai where Israel will later sojourn for a period of time as they journey from Egypt to Canaan (Num 20:1; 33:16). "Shur may indicate the defensive wall erected by the Egyptians to create a buffer with the Asiatics (14:7; 16:7) or it may refer to Cenomanian limestone wall-like escarpment of Gebel Halal and Gebel Maghara."[2]

The action begins, though, when Abraham and Sarah arrive in Gerar, a Philistine city (implied by Gen 21:32, 34) that is between Beersheba and Gaza. This is the first mention of the Philistines (outside of the Table of Nations [Gen 10:14]) who will play such an important role in the history of Israel. Indeed, the Philistines will be rivals to Israel for possession of the promised land until David successfully subdues them. Hartley interestingly points out that there is an interesting parallel between this story and Israel's future relationship with Israel, particularly in the account of the Philistine capture of the ark of the covenant, which we will point out below.[3]

In verse 2, we learn that Abraham used the same ruse that he employed during his sojourn in Egypt. He said that Sarah was his sister and not his wife, and the narrator is then quick to inform the reader that Abimelek king of Gerar took her into his harem.

The reporting of Abimelek's taking of Sarah is terse and to the point. As opposed to the narrative in Genesis 12:10–20, there is no request for Sarah's agreement to the plan or explanation for why Abraham would do such a thing. He just does it, and the explanation comes later after Abimelek becomes aware of Abraham's plot (see below).

## God Confronts Abimelek (20:3–7)

The narrative moves quickly from the report that Abimelek has taken Sarah to the account of a dream in which God warns him that his relationship with the matriarch will lead to the death penalty. God tells Abimelek what Abraham has not, namely that Sarah is a married woman. The prohibition of adultery was not exclusive to later Israel, but was pervasive through the ancient Near East. Waltke rightly points out that "adultery was considered a 'great sin' among many Semitic groups, as evidenced at Ugarit and in Egyptian marriage contracts (see Gen 26:10; 39:9 . . .)."[4] Sarna agrees, saying:

2. Hoffmeier and Moshier, "'A Highway Out of Egypt,'" 485–86.
3. Hartley, *Genesis*, NIBC (Peabody, MA: Hendrickson, 2000),196.
4. B. K. Waltke, *Genesis* (Grand Rapids: Zondervan, 2001), 285–86.

> Literally, "great sin" (v. 9, NIV translates "great guilt") [is] a phrase that reflects ancient Near Eastern legal terminology found in Akkadian documents from Ugarit and in Egyptian marriage contracts. The "great sin" is adultery . . . Ancient Mesopotamia seems to have held a similar view of adultery, i.e., as an offense to the deity.[5]

Abimelek's defense is to point out that he was just acting on the knowledge that Abraham and Sarah (v. 5) had given him. He thought she was unmarried, and so he has a "clear conscience and clean hands." He points out that punishment would be unfair in such a situation. He fears not only for his own life, but the welfare of his nation. Indeed, we saw how God brought suffering on Egypt earlier (12:17).

We now learn that this divine intervention happened so quickly that Abimelek had not yet consummated his relationship with Sarah. Interestingly, in the Egyptian episode there was no clear statement that the Pharaoh had not had sexual relations with Sarah. The narrator here goes to great pains to announce that Abimelek had not touched her. Indeed, at the end of the chapter (vv. 17–18), we hear that God had afflicted Abimelek, his wife, and his female slaves and prevented them from becoming pregnant. This information is extremely important at this stage of the Abraham story because in the next chapter Sarah is pregnant and there can be no doubt over who the father is.

God next instructs Abimelek to seek out Abraham and to ask him to intercede for him. How ironic that it is the one who created the problem in the first place who is the one who must intercede to save the king of Philistia, though Jacobs rightly points out that "this is not the only time that the Deity is portrayed as overlooking the faults of the favored and placing the harmed under the control of the one who is responsible for the harm (16:5),"[6] indicating that "God's purpose is more important than the person involved."[7] The reason given is equally remarkable. Abraham is a prophet.

This is not only the first mention that Abraham is a prophet, but the very first time the term is used in the Bible. In one sense, then, Abraham is the first prophet, though Moses will become the paradigmatic prophet (Num 12:6–8; Deut 18:15–22; 34:10–12).

Certainly Abraham is not a prophet in the commonly understood sense as one who delivers oracles of judgment and salvation along the lines of Isaiah, Jeremiah, or Ezekiel. Indeed, calling Abraham a prophet in this context

---

5. N. Sarna, *Genesis*, JPS of America Torah Commentary (Philadelphia: Jewsih Publication Society, 1992), 143, cited by Bruckner, *Implied Law*, 113–14.

6. M. R. Jacobs, *Gender, Power, and Persuasion: The Genesis Narratives and Contemporary Portraits* (Grand Rapids: Baker, 2007), 98.

7. Ibid., 92.

highlights a central function of prophets, namely intercessory prayer. We have already seen Abraham function in this way earlier (18:16–33) when he interceded with God concerning the fate of the city of Sodom. Here he is being asked to intercede on behalf of the king of Abimelek so God will not punish him for taking Sarah into his harem.

Once we recognize that Abraham's designation as a prophet is connected to his intercession, we then see just how central intercessory prayer is to those who are better known as prophets later in Israel's history, including Moses (Exod 33; Deut 9–10), Samuel (1 Sam 12), Jeremiah (Jer 14:1–9, 19–22; 18:18–23), Joel (Joel 2), and others.[8]

## Abimelek Confronts Abraham (20:8–13)

After God confronts him, Abimelek informs his officials, and they respond with fear just as the king himself did. Then he called for Abraham, whom he confronts, asking him why? Why would the patriarch put the Philistine king in such a position?

Abraham's response is revealing and a study in rationalization. He suspected that there was no "fear of God" in Gerar, which strikes the reader as ironic after reading the Philistines' reaction to God's demands. This occasion is the first where this important phrase and concept appears in Scripture, being most fully developed in wisdom literature (among the most important occurrences are found in Job 28:28; Prov 1:7; Eccl 12:13, though these are just representative of many occurrences). One who fears God obeys him, recognizing God's superior power and wisdom. The irony may be seen that if anyone can be said not to fear God in this story it is Abraham himself.

Abraham tries to rationalize his actions by saying that Sarah really is his sister, more precisely his half-sister since she was the daughter of his father and a different mother. Interestingly, such a marriage was prohibited by later Mosaic law (Lev 20:9). Since God blesses his marriage with Sarah, it is unlikely that such a marriage was considered wrong at this time. Indeed, this marriage, out of keeping with later Israelite sensibilities, provides an argument against attempts to late date the writing of the patriarchal narratives.[9]

But in this case a half truth is a full lie. After all, Abraham omitted the most relevant part of his relationship with Sarah, the fact that she was his wife as well as his sister. It is true that not all lying is wrong in the Bible. A classic example is the lie told by the midwives to Pharaoh (Exod 1:15–22).

---

8. M. Widmer, *Standing in the Breach between Divine Mercy and Judgment: An Old Testament Theology and Spirituality of Intercessory Prayer*, Siphrut 13 (Eisenbrauns: forthcoming).

9. For more on this, see I. Provan, V. P. Long, and T. Longman III, *A Biblical History of Israel* (Louisville: Westminster John Knox, 2003), 112–17.

This example illustrates well the conditions under which a lie is appropriate, namely when the safety of God's people is at stake. At such times, one can (and should) lie to the one(s) who want to perpetrate harm.

Abraham (wrongly) anticipated harm, but he put his wife, and even worse from the perspective of the narrative, the promise of descendants at great risk. And to cap it all off, Abraham here says that he did this "everywhere" they went (v. 13).

This comment shows that Abraham not only lied in Egypt (12:10–20) and here in Gerar, but all the time and everywhere they went to a potentially hostile location. The significance of hearing about this occasion, though, is to demonstrate that Abraham has not yet broken through to a position of utter trust in God.

Earlier we described how the Abraham narrative can be read as an account of the patriarch's journey of faith. How does Abraham respond to threats and obstacles to the fulfillment of the promises? We have seen that Abraham's faith is an up-and-down, indeed mostly down, proposition. While occasionally reacting with confidence, typically he reacts with fear, self-protection, and manipulation. To hear that he still tries to protect himself by putting his wife at risk shows that Abraham is still the same old Abram of Genesis 12.

### God Enriches Abraham (20:14–18)

Even so, God cares for his chosen servant. Because of his fear of God, he not only restores Sarah to Abraham but he also enriches him (vv. 14–16) reminding us again of the episode in 12:10–20. He also permits Abraham to live anywhere in his land that the patriarch so chooses. Very importantly, Abimelek vindicates Sarah publicly and gives Abraham a thousand shekels of silver, which, as the NIV note indicates, is twenty-five pounds of metal, a considerable amount. According to Walton, this large payment, is Abimelek's "guarantee that Sarah has been untouched, a fee to Abraham for his intercessory role, and an appeasement of the deity who has virtually cut off all fertility in his family."[10]

The account ends with Abraham praying for Abimelek and his family and court. God responds to the prayer by restoring the Philistine women's ability to have children.

Modern readers struggle with the fact that Abraham appears to act in such a cowardly way, but still ends up benefitting. Brueggemann gets it right when he says:

> Abraham emerges from the narrative with his power and authority not only intact but enhanced. That is, the one who lies ... is still the

10. Walton, "Genesis," 95.

> one preferred. The morally upright one [Abimelech] is still dependent on Israel. The preeminence of Abraham here rests not on Abraham's virtue, but on God's promise ... The story has a strangeness about it, perhaps because the theological narrator wanted to make a point that ill-fitted the traditional material with which he had to work. As it stands, the text makes the claim that Abraham is the chosen of God, not by words, nor even by faith (which is feeble here), but only by God's incredible grace. Thus, we can hardly advance on Calvin's summary, "The infirmity of man and the grace of God ..." The infirmity of both men is evident. But God's grace overrules.[11]

The time has now come to point out the details of Hartley's description of the analogy between this episode and the account of the later Philistine capture of the ark. It begins with a capture, in the present story the capture of Sarah, in 1 Samuel 3, the capture of the ark of the covenant (vv. 1–11). In the former, we saw that God brought a sickness that brought infertility on the Philistine women, in the later story, he brought disease on the Philistines who took the ark to the temple of Dagon. He also caused the Dagon statue to fall at night (1 Sam 5:1–8) just as he confronted Abimelek at night. Finally, Israel was enriched upon the return of the ark (1 Sam 6:3–6).[12]

### Habitual Sin

We have two stories of Abraham lying about the status of his wife, putting her in danger (not to speak of the divine promise of descendants) in order to protect himself. In the present account, we learn that these two stories are just the tip of the iceberg, so to speak. Abraham tells Abimelek that he instructed Sarah, "Everywhere we go, say of me, 'He is my brother'" (Gen 20:13).

Here we have an example of a habitual sin. After the first occurrence when he went to Egypt (Gen 12:10–20), he knew that God was displeased with his behavior, but he continued to struggle with his self-protective lying until at least this point in his life.

Everyone struggles with habitual sins or, to put it another way, bad behavior or attitudes that we cannot shake. We might call it sexual addiction, alcohol dependency, or an anger-management problem, but when it comes right down to it, they are sins that we keep coming back to again and again. We sin

---

11. Brueggemann, *Genesis*, 178, cited by Bruckner, *Implied Law*, 190–91.
12. Hartley, *Genesis*, 196–97.

and repent. We may manage our actions and feelings for a period of time, but we do it again, and again, and again. What can we learn from Abraham's life about habitual sins and our relationship with God?

First, God does not let our sin slide. In the present story, it takes God's actions to prevent the typical serious ramifications that might result from such behavior. In this situation, the consequences of Abraham's sin affected others who got sick and threatened Sarah who could have gotten pregnant. It was through the grace of God that things weren't worse. And that leads to a second point, God does not let Abraham's habitual sin derail his relationship with Abraham or the purpose of his life.

Of course, we have to remember that Abraham does have a special place in God's plan of redemption, and we have to be careful to too quickly apply the stories about his life too easily to our own. Indeed, if anything, the consequences of our habitual sin might be more severe and troublesome than they were, as far as we can tell from the text, for Abraham. God had a vested interest in Abraham's survival.

Further, we have to be careful not to let the fact that God does not cut Abraham off in spite of his persistent sin lead to a complacent attitude toward our sin. The author of Hebrews recognizes that there is a sin that "hinders and . . . so easily entangles," but he also exhorts us to "throw off" these sins (Heb 12:1). But that said, the story of Abraham's life gives us hope that, though God punishes sinners, he also continues to work for our redemption no matter whether we have committed a sin once or many times. The one who calls on his followers to forgive someone who hurts them not just seven times "but seventy-seven times" (Matt 18:22) himself will forgive the repentant habitual sinner. In the next section we will consider resources that are available to us as we confront our habitual sins.

### Imperfect Intercessors

The story of Abraham in Gerar is a sad one on many levels. Abraham is up to his old sinful tricks, lying about the status of his wife, putting her in danger, in order to save his own life (see Habitual Sin). He is acting out of fear, rather than faith. Even so, God tells Abimelek to go to Abraham so that the patriarch can intercede for him. How amazing. Even a person like Abraham who needs to repent for his own actions can intercede with God on behalf of another.

Now it is true, as we mentioned in the Explain the Story section above, that Abraham's intercession is connected with his special status as a prophet. At the heart of the prophetic task is intercession. Intercessory prayer is not restricted to the prophet of the Old Testament, but it is especially connected to that office.

The Scriptures suggest that all Christians are, in an important sense, prophets. Just like the New Testament speaks of a "priesthood of all believers" (1 Pet 2:9) so it suggests a "prophethood of all believers." This may in particular be seen in the citation of Joel 2:28–32 on the occasion of Pentecost: "In the last days, God says, I will pour out my Spirit on all people. Your sons and your daughters will prophesy, your young men will see visions, your old men will dream dreams. Even on my servants, both men and women, I will pour out my Spirit in those days, and they will prophesy" (Acts 2:17–18, citing Joel 2:28–29).

Much can be said about the Christian as a Spirit-filled prophet, but here we will only highlight our call to intercede with God on behalf of others. We should be engaged in unending prayer (1 Thess 5:17) for our family, friends, communities, and selves. While James tells us that "the prayer of the righteous person is powerful and effective" (5:16), we must remember that even sinful Abraham's prayers are effective and that a "righteous person" is not a sinless person, but rather one who has confessed their sins to each other and then pray for each other (again, v. 16).

When it comes to the subject of intercession, the most important point to remember is that it is the Spirit that lives in us who intercedes for us. As Paul states it: "In the same way, the Spirit helps us in our weakness. We do not know what we ought to pray for, but the Spirit himself intercedes for us through wordless groans. And he who searches our hearts knows the mind of the Spirit, because the Spirit intercedes for God's people in accordance with the will of God" (Rom 8:26–28). Knowledge of the Spirit's intercession ought to give us confidence in how we live our lives and also confidence as we intercede on behalf of others.

### Jesus, the Perfect Prophetic Intercessor

While in an important sense, all believers are prophets (just as they are also all priests), Jesus is the ultimate prophet (just as he is the ultimate priest, see the essay Jesus, a "High Priest Forever, in the Order of Melchizedek" [Heb 6:20] in the Live the Story section of Gen 14). The primary text for that assertion is found in Acts when Peter, exploiting the collective singular of Deuteronomy 18:15, 18, 19, states: "The Lord your God will raise up for you a prophet like me from among your own people; you must listen to everything he tells you. Anyone who does not listen to him will be completely cut off from their people" (Acts 3:22–23).

Jesus as the ultimate prophet is also the one who intercedes on behalf of his people. Jesus' prayer in John 17 is often, not incorrectly, called the high priestly prayer, but it could just as well be called his Prophetic Intercessory prayer. As he anticipates his death, resurrection, and ascension to heaven he calls on God to protect his followers. Though explicitly connected with his priestly role, Hebrews 7:25 tells us that his intercession for us continues even after his ascension to heaven: " … he is able to save completely those who come to God through him, because he always lives to intercede for them."

See related essay: Does God Communicate to Us through Our Dreams? (after Gen 41).

CHAPTER 18

# Genesis 21:1 – 21

## LISTEN to the Story

21:1Now the LORD was gracious to Sarah as he had said, and the LORD
did for Sarah what he had promised. 2Sarah became pregnant and bore a
son to Abraham in his old age, at the very time God had promised him.
3Abraham gave the name Isaac to the son Sarah bore him. 4When his son
Isaac was eight days old, Abraham circumcised him, as God commanded
him. 5Abraham was a hundred years old when his son Isaac was born
to him.

6Sarah said, "God has brought me laughter, and everyone who hears
about this will laugh with me." 7And she added, "Who would have said to
Abraham that Sarah would nurse children? Yet I have borne him a son in
his old age."

8The child grew and was weaned, and on the day Isaac was weaned
Abraham held a great feast. 9But Sarah saw that the son whom Hagar
the Egyptian had borne to Abraham was mocking, 10and she said to
Abraham, "Get rid of that slave woman and her son, for that woman's son
will never share in the inheritance with my son Isaac."

11The matter distressed Abraham greatly because it concerned his son.
12But God said to him, "Do not be so distressed about the boy and your
slave woman. Listen to whatever Sarah tells you, because it is through
Isaac that your offspring will be reckoned. 13I will make the son of the
slave into a nation also, because he is your offspring."

14Early the next morning Abraham took some food and a skin of
water and gave them to Hagar. He set them on her shoulders and then
sent her off with the boy. She went on her way and wandered in the
Desert of Beersheba.

15When the water in the skin was gone, she put the boy under one of
the bushes. 16Then she went off and sat down about a bowshot away, for
she thought, "I cannot watch the boy die." And as she sat there, she began
to sob.

17God heard the boy crying, and the angel of God called to Hagar
from heaven and said to her, "What is the matter, Hagar? Do not be

afraid; God has heard the boy crying as he lies there. [18]Lift the boy up and take him by the hand, for I will make him into a great nation."

[19]Then God opened her eyes and she saw a well of water. So she went and filled the skin with water and gave the boy a drink.

[20]God was with the boy as he grew up. He lived in the desert and became an archer. [21]While he was living in the Desert of Paran, his mother got a wife for him from Egypt.

*Listening to the Text in the Story:* Biblical Texts: Genesis 12:1–3; 15; 17; 18:9–15 (for 21:1–7); Genesis 16 (for 21:8–21)

At the very start of the Abraham story, God told Abraham that he would make his descendants a "great nation" (12:2). But for his descendants to be a great nation, Abraham and Sarah had to have a child, and Sarah was barren. The lack of offspring led to Abraham's crisis of faith to which God responded by coming and assuring him that he and Sarah would indeed have a child. Twice God came and reassured Abraham by reaffirming his covenant with him (Gen 15 and 17). Most recently, he came with two angels to announce that the great event would take place in about a year's time (Gen 18:9–15).

Once the promised child came into the world, a new problem arose (21:8–21). Thanks to Abraham and Sarah's impatience, Abraham had a child, Ishmael, with the concubine given to him by his wife (Gen 16) and whom Abraham had tried to pass off as his heir to God (17:18). The bitterness that Sarah felt toward Hagar and led the slave woman to flee from her mistress earlier (Gen 16) now returns but with a vengeance.

## EXPLAIN the Story

### A Son is Born! (21:1–7)

As we have observed from time to time since we began the Abraham story, the central theme of the narrative has to do with Abraham's journey of faith. Abraham received momentous promises from God that he would be a "great nation," and that he and his descendants would be blessed and would be a blessing to the nations (Gen 12:1–3). Abraham, however, encountered numerous obstacles and threats to the fulfillment of the promises and the extent of his faith was demonstrated by how he reacted when it appeared that the promises would not come to fulfillment. Of all the promises the one that he would become a great nation was most severely tested. To be a great nation, Abraham would have to begin by having that first son to pass on the promise to the next generations. But Abraham and Sarah could not have children — until now.

We thus come to the climax of the plot of the Abraham story. Finally Abraham and Sarah have the long-anticipated child, a son named Isaac. What strikes the reader first is the relatively brief and straightforward presentation of the birth of Isaac. Verse 1 emphasizes the point that God was behind the birth. Indeed, it could be presented in a poetic format as if it were a two-part parallelism:

> Now the Lord was gracious to Sarah as he had said,
> and the Lord did for Sarah what he had promised.

The ancient rabbis treated this formulation as if the two parts referred to two different matters, perhaps the birth of the child and then the fact that God allowed Sarah to nurse him. Indeed, verse 7 shows Sarah marveling that she, a ninety-year-old woman, not only gave birth to a child, but was able to nurse him. But this interpretation is driven by the belief that God would not repeat himself, so there must be two different referents.[1] Though this verse is not truly poetic, we nonetheless can learn from the proper reading of a parallel line that the second part continues the thought of the first while bringing in a slightly different perspective. The first part talks about God's grace, that he "took care" (a slightly different rendition of the verb *pqd*) of Sarah, and then the second part highlights that this was done in fulfillment of the earlier promise. But both parts refer to the marvelous fulfillment of the promise of a descendant.

Indeed, though, rather than unexpected, the time this child was born was anticipated. The child was born "at the very time God had promised him" (v. 2). Most immediately, this reference points back to 18:14 where the Lord said to Abraham, "I will return to you at the appointed time next year, and Sarah will have a son," but behind this statement is the idea that God planned for the child to be born in Abraham and Sarah's old age from the very start. But why?

Certainly, the delay in the birth created the conditions that tested Abraham's faith. We have seen that his confidence often wavered, but he never completely abandoned his trust in God. We will soon see that this test of faith is far from over.

But more importantly, the birth at this "appointed time" clearly demonstrates that this child is not simply the result of natural human processes, but

1. Kugel, *The Idea of Biblical Poetry*, 98–99.

is rather a divine gift. That a one-hundred-year-old man and a ninety-year-old woman could have a child is a crystal clear demonstration that Isaac's birth is the result of God's intervention.

Abraham named his son Isaac, a name foretold already in Genesis 17 (vv. 19–22), a name that means "he laughs," referring to the earlier reaction of both Abraham and Sarah (see 18:10–15). Sarah even here laughs (v. 6), but rather than a laugh of skepticism or disbelief, here Sarah laughs happily because of the fulfillment of the promise of a child. Further, in keeping with God's earlier command (17:9–14), Abraham circumcised Isaac on the eighth day after his birth.

### Household Conflict (21:8–13)

The next episode occurs a few unspecified years in the future at the time that Isaac was weaned. It was a gift of God that Sarah could give birth and a further gift that she could nurse the child (21:7). To celebrate the transition from unweaned to weaned child, Abraham threw a feast. According to Jacobs, "because of the high infant mortality rate, children were apparently weaned during their third year, and a feast celebrated their survival."[2]

We have already read about friction between Sarah and Hagar. Indeed, in Genesis 16 Sarah so abused Hagar that she ran away. She only returned because the angel of the Lord directed her to do so, promising her that her soon-to-be-born child will himself give rise to multiple descendants (16:9–12). This tension reaches a new fever pitch when Sarah observes Ishmael "mocking," presumably Isaac. Here we see another instance of the verb *tsahaq* that forms the basis of Isaac's name ("he laughs"), but here appearing in the *piel* form, which can be used for derisive laughing and thus mocking (see also Judg 16:5). In some examples, the verb actually has a sexual meaning (Gen 26:9; 39:17; Exod 32:6), though it is not clear that this meaning is intended in this context. In either case, Sarah was incensed and seized the opportunity to be rid of her rival and her son and any claims that they might have on the inheritance (which is her main motivation for having Ishmael sent away). She pressed Abraham then to "Get rid of that slave woman and her son, for that woman's son will never share in the inheritance with my son Isaac" (v. 10).

Abraham was torn. He recognized Ishmael as his son and cared for him. We do not really know what Abraham might have done if God did not intervene, but God does speak to him and makes it clear that it is also his will that Hagar and Ishmael separate from the family, though this does not necessarily include an approval of her motives. Indeed, while Sarah just wants to get rid of the

2. Jacobs, *Gender, Power, and Persuasion*, 150.

mother and her son and couldn't care less about what happens to them, God assures Abraham that he has plans for them, important and significant plans.

First, God again makes it clear that the covenant promises of Genesis 12:1–3 will pass through Isaac and not Ishmael. But then God comforts Abraham by telling him that the descendants of Ishmael will also form a nation in the future. The angel of the Lord had earlier informed Hagar that Ishmael's descendants will be many (16:10), but now we learn that his many descendants will be a nation, a promise that finds its fulfillment in a later section of Genesis (see commentary at 25:12–18, as well as Gen 37:25–36 and 39:1; not also Judg 8:24; Ps 83:6). Though not mentioned here, 16:12 ("he will live in hostility toward all his brothers") anticipates conflict between the descendants of Ishmael and the descendants of Isaac. Note that God's care for Ishmael and his descendants is motivated by his relationship with Abraham, illustrating that blessing comes not just to the so-called elect line, but also to other nations.

### Hagar and Ishmael Sent Away (21:14–21)

At God's urging, Abraham then "sent her off" (v. 14) along with their son Ishmael. The verb translated "sent off" (*shalah*) is used elsewhere for a legal divorce (Deut 22:19, 29; 24:1, 3; Jer 3:1; Mal 3:16). Abraham thus severed any kind of legal obligations he had toward them, particularly in the area of inheritance.

While the patriarch supplied them with food and water, they soon ran out of the latter, thus they were in danger of dying of thirst in the Desert of Bathsheba, just outside of Gerar where they had been living with Abraham. We cannot speculate about why Hagar and Ishmael find themselves in this predicament. It is too much to assert that Abraham did not care or intentionally did not give them enough water. After all, his reaction to Sarah's insistence that he rid himself of them revealed that he had concern for them. Perhaps Hagar got lost. Unfortunately, we cannot be certain.

Hagar thought they certainly were going to die, so she took her son and placed him under a bush so she could not see him. This detail raises the question of Ishmael's age. We do not know exactly how much older Ishmael, whose birth is described in Genesis 16, was at the time Isaac was born, but he was at least beyond toddler age and certainly not an infant. Perhaps he had passed out from weakness, and his mother just dragged him there. Later he is said to be crying (v. 17), so he may just be in an incredibly weakened condition. In any case, the picture is quite pathetic. The reader cannot help but feel great sympathy for the two, forced out of their home and into the desert heat with insufficient supplies.

God shares the readers' sympathy and soon the angel of the Lord, who appears to be none other than God himself, speaks to Hagar from heaven to comfort and encourage her (v. 17). God has responded to Ishmael's tears and tells her to endure by getting Ishmael and continuing on their journey. He had told Abraham earlier that Ishmael's descendants will become a nation, but we do not know whether the patriarch informed her. In any case, now God makes the promise known to her. His descendants will not just be a nation, but a "great nation" (v. 18).

At this point he also opened her eyes to show her a well of life-giving water. So refreshed, they are able to continue their journey. They do not enter a city though, but stay in the desert; indeed, as we will see, the later Ishmaelites are desert Bedouins (25:12–18).

It is significant that the narrator informs us that God was "with the boy." While the text has made it very clear that it is Isaac and not Ishmael who inherits the covenant promise, this phrase resonates with the idea of covenant. At a minimum, the fact that God was with Ishmael again shows that God does not have contempt but rather love for the nonelect offspring of the patriarchs and those nations that ultimately derive from them.

Besides the most important fact that God was with him, the narrative concludes by informing us of facts about Ishmael which indicate that he had a good life. He became an archer and married a woman from Egypt. In terms of the latter, we should remember that Hagar herself was an Egyptian (16:1), probably given to Abraham by Pharaoh during his sojourn there (12:16). They settled in the Desert of Paran, most likely a region within the Negev, not too far north of the Sinai and Kadesh.

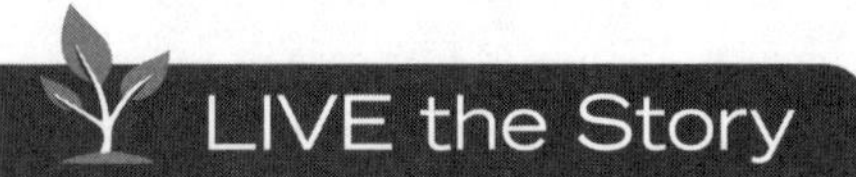


### God Keeps His Promises[3]

God had promised Abraham that he would make his descendants a "great nation" (12:2), but for this promise to come true Abraham and Sarah would have to have a child. We have followed the story of Abraham as the journey of his faith. Does he respond with faith or fear in the face of threats and obstacles to the fulfillment of the promises? But the Abraham narrative not only focuses on the patriarch, it also reveals God. Here we learn that God indeed does keep his promises. He promised that Abraham would have a son and, though

3. I was greatly helped in the writing of this article by the entry on promise written in the *Baker Illustrated Bible Dictionary*, ed. T. Longman III (Grand Rapids: Baker, 2013), 1361–63. The article was written by Dr. JinKyu Kim.

both Abraham and Sarah are long beyond the regular time to have children, Sarah gets pregnant and gives birth to Isaac. This miraculous birth is just the beginning of the fulfillment of the promise of becoming a great nation which will be blessed and which will bring a blessing to the world (12:1–3; see also 13:14–17; 17:4–8; 22:17–18; 26:1–5; 28:13–15), but it is an event which gives confidence that God will indeed follow through on all dimensions of the promise.

As we read through the book of Genesis and into the rest of the Old Testament, we see that God makes many promises. A survey of the highlights (in particular connected to God's covenant) begins with his promise that he will put enmity between the serpent's offspring and the woman's with the result that evil will be crushed. In the aftermath of the flood, he promises Noah that he will never send a flood to destroy the earth again (Gen 8:21–22). At the foot of Mount Sinai, he promises that his people, Israel, will be his "treasured possession" (Exod 19:5). Later he promises David that he will have a descendant on the throne forever (2 Sam 7:11–16).

As we think of these promises and many others that we have not mentioned in Scripture, we should remember that Balaam, the pagan prophet, proclaimed that "God is not human, that he should lie, not a human being, that he should change his mind. Does he speak and then not act? Does he promise and not fulfill?" (Num 23:19).

As we turn to the New Testament, we are struck by Paul's understanding that Jesus is the fulfillment of God's promises. According to Paul, "For no matter how many promises God has made, they are 'Yes' in Christ" (2 Cor 1:20). He is, after all, the son of David, the Messiah, who sits on the throne forever. He is true Israel, God's obedient son, who is God's "treasured possession." He is the seed of Abraham (Gal 3:16). He is the offspring of the woman who will crush the head of the serpent (Rom 16:20; Rev 12:9).

God makes promises that he keeps and thus Christians should trust that God will fulfill the promises that he has made to us. Christ has promised that he will be with his people as they make disciples of the nations "to the very end of the age" (Matt 28:16–20). He has promised that those who believe in him "will not perish but have eternal life" (John 3:16). He has promised that his followers will "have life, and have it to the full" (John 10:10). He has promised that the Holy Spirit will be with us (John 14:16) and that we will live in his peace and joy (John 14:27; 16:20–24). And, last but not least, that Jesus will return again to usher in the new heavens and the new earth and give us eternal life (John 5:28–29; 11:25–26; 1 Cor 15:48–57; 2 Cor 4:14; 1 Thess 4:13–18).

In the light of this teaching, then how should we live? Returning to Paul in 2 Corinthians 1:20, after stating that all God's promises are "Yes" in Jesus, he tells his readers "so through him the 'Amen' is spoken by us to the glory of God." Thus, our response to the question "How should we live?" is with confidence, "so be it." As Kent Hughes puts it, "you and I can, and must, trust every syllable of God's word. This is the way every Christian is meant to live—in deepest trust in all of God's word—just as Jesus lived."[4]

### God's Gift of a Child—to a Virgin!

> Children are a heritage from the Lord,
> offspring a reward from him. (Ps 127:3)

Certainly parents are right to think that the birth of their children is God's good gift to them. But God makes it clear that Isaac is a gift in a special way, signaling that he is the one through whom the covenant promises will carry on to the next generation. Indeed, we learn of a number of births to barren mothers in the Old Testament (Jacob and Esau to Rebekah; Samson to his unnamed mother; Samuel to Hannah) as well as a variant on that theme in the Moses birth story. In all these cases, God is making it clear that he is the one who provides these very special individuals to his covenant people.

It is on this background that we should read the story of Jesus' birth. According to the Gospels (e.g., Matt 1:18–25), Mary was a virgin when she gave birth to Jesus. Read against the background of the narratives of barren women giving birth to important children in redemptive history, Jesus' birth story stands out with its message that this child was truly special, far surpassing the importance of Isaac or any of the other children born to barren women.

### Two Kinds of Laughter

Genesis 21 records two instances of laughter, but as we look closely, they are two different types. The first is laughter of joy at the incredible gift of a child in Abraham and Sarah's old age (21:6–7). Sarah's laughter of joy replaces her early laughter of incredulity when God informed Abraham that they would have a child in about a year's time (18:10–15). But even Sarah's early laughter of incredulity differs radically from Ishmael's mocking laughter (21:9). While Ishmael may have been mocking the young Isaac, ultimately he is mocking God since Isaac is the child of the promise.

According to the book of Proverbs, fools are wicked and godless, but the worse type of fool is a mocker because a mocker not only acts foolishly, but

---

4. R. K. Hughes, *Genesis: Beginning and Blessing* (Wheaton, IL: Crossway, 2004), 293.

ridicules the godly righteous person. They mock those who try to point them in the right way (Prov 9:7, 8, 12; 13:1; 15:22). Thus, the psalmist advises to avoid the company of a mocker (Ps 1:1: "Blessed is the one who does not ... sit in the company of mockers").

When we read the Gospels, we see that Jesus was mocked (Matt 9:24; Mark 5:40; Luke 8:53). Thus, as followers of Christ we should not be surprised when we too are mocked by those who dismiss or hate God. Our reaction should not be to hate or mock back. Rather like Jesus, we should patiently bear the ridicule, hoping through our words and actions to lead people to a relationship with God.

### God's Care for the Abused Wife and Neglected Child

In a provocative essay on children in the book of Genesis, Fretheim draws our attention to God's care for Ishmael, who is unchosen and neglected by his father.[5] We might also add that the story is also about God's care for Hagar, the abused wife of Abraham.

Abraham's treatment of Hagar and Ishmael is driven primarily by his first wife's jealousy and worry about her own son Isaac. The situation gets so bad that Hagar takes Ishmael and flees into the wilderness where they are soon in dire straits. Above, we have seen how God does not abandon them as unimportant or expendable, but rather reaches out to them to rescue them.

Just at the point where Hagar is convinced that she and her crying child will die in the wilderness, God comes to them and not only saves their lives but also informs them that Ishmael's descendants will become a "great nation." Indeed, God did not merely come to save them and then leave them on their own, rather the text makes a point of the fact that "God was with the boy as he grew up" (21:20). For all practical purposes Ishmael was a child without a father, but God cared for him.

Fretheim suggests that "this text about Ishmael in Genesis is a lens through which to read the many references to orphans and other underprivileged children in the Old Testament, for his is the first such biblical individual."[6] As far as we know, there were no orphanages in the ancient Near Eastern world. Perhaps a close relative would take care of an orphan, but it was not uncommon that they would have to fend for themselves. Thus, the life of an orphan was a life of suffering (Lam 5:2; John 14:18), and God cares for those who suffer. The Old Testament texts that teach that God cares for the fatherless are numerous (Deut 10:18; Pss 10:14, 18; 68:5; 146:9; Jer 49:11; Hos 14:3).

5. T. E. Fretheim, "'God Was with the Boy,'" 3–23.

6. Ibid., 14.

God's love provides for the orphan (Exod 22:21–24). The book of James exhorts Christians to care for widows and orphans (Jas 1:27).

It should be needless to say, but this robust biblical teaching about care for orphans should lead the church today to exercise special concern for those children who have no living parents or who are neglected by their parents. They are special objects of God's care and thus should be the special object of concern for Christians. This concern does not necessarily mean that all Christian families should adopt or take on a foster child, but all of us can help. If we don't adopt, how can we come alongside a family who has adopted a child to help them? Can we help them with babysitting, even giving the parents time away to reenergize for the difficult task of raising children? Can we provide meals during difficult times? There are a host of ways in which we as a community can come alongside those who are raising orphaned or neglected children. Fortunately, there are some excellent Christian organizations that can help those who want to adopt and or who want to come alongside those who do.

Angels Foster Care Santa Barbara: *https://www.angelssb.com*; *https://www.facebook.com/AngelsFosterCare*

Arrow Child and Family Ministries: *http://www.arrow.org*

### "The Women Represent Two Covenants" (Gal 4:21–31)

In the book of Galatians, Paul addresses a group known as the Judaizers. They are Christians who believe that obeying the law is critical to salvation. Paul utilizes the story of the relationship between Sarah and Hagar to make the point that the type of legal religion promoted by the Judaizers is a form of slavery but that the gospel represents freedom.

Paul here acknowledges that he is taking the story of Hagar and Sarah figuratively (Gal 4:24). He is not interested in what today we would call a historical-grammatical interpretation of the text with the purpose of getting back to the original meaning intended by the author of the Genesis story. He sees an analogy, however, between the ancient story and his modern situation, and he will now make his point vividly by drawing out the connections for his readers. Whether this is an allegorical reading or a typological one or, as is probably the case, a combination of the two, is beside the point and not particularly important to the meaning.[7]

Paul's point is clear enough. He uses the child of Hagar, the slave woman, to represent those who relate to God through the law. Hagar represents the Sinaitic (or Mosaic) covenant of law and those who use law to enter into a

7. See the helpful discussion in S. McKnight, *Galatians*, NIVAC (Grand Rapids: Zondervan, 1995), 227–41.

relationship with God are like Ishmael (never called by name but implied) who was the product of the wife of a slave. Ishmael was the product of a compelled marriage between Abraham and Hagar. On the other hand, Sarah was a free woman who was married to Abraham and her child Isaac was a child of the promise (he, not Ishmael, was the fulfillment of God's promise that Abraham would have descendants).

The child of the slave woman did not have a secure relationship with his father Abraham. Indeed, he and his mother were ultimately expelled from the household. They were expelled because Ishmael made a mistake by laughing at Isaac and he was not forgiven. So those who try to relate to God by the law do not have a stable relationship with him, because they will be expelled when they violate that law.

Paul's message to us is clear. Be like the child of the free woman Sarah, not the slave woman Hagar. Realize your relationship is that of a son to a father whose love is not based on performance but on grace.

### Israel and the Arabs

As is well known, Jewish people trace their past back to Abraham through Isaac, whereas Arabs trace theirs back to Abraham through Ishmael (a view that goes back at least to the book of Jubilees [20:12]). In the Judeo-Christian Bible, Isaac is the chosen son, the one who will carry on the covenant promises, the one whom Abraham will take to Moriah in order to sacrifice him at the command of God (Gen 22). For Muslims informed by the Koran, it is Ishmael who plays that role.[8] Ishmael and Abraham are also the ones who are said to build the Ka'bah[9] (in *al-Baqara*).

We have already considered the role that Abraham plays as a founding father figure for the three great monotheistic religions (Judaism, Christianity, and Islam, see Abra(ha)m in Judaism, Islam, and Christianity in the Live the Story section after Gen 17). In this essay, we want to offer a few observations about the present political climate that sees such animosity between elements of all three religions. Certainly nothing approaching a full analysis can be offered here due to the availability of space and my own lack of expertise in modern politics. But I can perhaps challenge the use of the biblical picture of Isaac and Ishmael as a tool in the political rhetoric of the present situation.

Accepting the biblical picture of Isaac and Ishmael, it would be wrong minded to see in the account the roots of future conflict specifically between

8. The son to be sacrificed is not actually named in the Koran, but that is the common understanding of readers of the Koran.

9. The Ka'bah is a building in the form of a cube found at the mosque (Al-Masjid al-Haram in Mecca) considered the most holy site in all Islam.

the descendants of Isaac and the descendants of Ishmael. While it is true that the divine oracle delivered in 16:11–12 includes the comment that Ishmael will be "a wild donkey of a man; his hand will be against everyone and everyone's hand against him, and he will live in hostility toward all his brothers" speaks more to the nomadic condition of his future descendants than a multimillennial conflict between Israel and Arab people.[10]

Indeed, Ishmael was not the chosen son according to the biblical account, but, using Kaminski's persuasive three-part categorization, neither was he antielect, but rather he was nonelect. And Isaac's chosen status was not just for his own betterment, but for all the nations, (12:3) including those that descend from Ishmael. Indeed, Ishmael is himself blessed of God and told that his descendants too would be a "great nation" (21:18).

Indeed, God twice shows his special concern for Hagar and Ishmael (Gen 16 and 21). And indeed, though Ishmael may have mocked the young Isaac, they are last seen peaceably together at the burial of Abraham (25:7–11). As for the future Ishmaelites, they are surprisingly rarely mentioned in the following literature, playing the role simply as those who take Joseph to Egypt (Gen 37:25–28).

See related essay: The Angel Who Saves (after Gen 16).

10. Indeed, it is not certain what exactly the real connection is between Arabs and Ishmael.

CHAPTER 19

# Genesis 21:22 – 34

## LISTEN to the Story

[21:22]At that time Abimelek and Phicol the commander of his forces said to Abraham, "God is with you in everything you do. [23]Now swear to me here before God that you will not deal falsely with me or my children or my descendants. Show to me and the country where you now reside as a foreigner the same kindness I have shown to you."

[24]Abraham said, "I swear it."

[25]Then Abraham complained to Abimelek about a well of water that Abimelek's servants had seized. [26]But Abimelek said, "I don't know who has done this. You did not tell me, and I heard about it only today."

[27]So Abraham brought sheep and cattle and gave them to Abimelek, and the two men made a treaty. [28]Abraham set apart seven ewe lambs from the flock, [29]and Abimelek asked Abraham, "What is the meaning of these seven ewe lambs you have set apart by themselves?"

[30]He replied, "Accept these seven lambs from my hand as a witness that I dug this well."

[31]So that place was called Beersheba, because the two men swore an oath there.

[32]After the treaty had been made at Beersheba, Abimelek and Phicol the commander of his forces returned to the land of the Philistines. [33]Abraham planted a tamarisk tree in Beersheba, and there he called on the name of the Lord, the Eternal God. [34]And Abraham stayed in the land of the Philistines for a long time.

*Listen to the Story in the Text:* Biblical Text: Genesis 12:1 – 3; 20; Ancient Near Eastern Texts: Correspondence between the kings of the city of Larsa and Eshnunna

We have already been introduced to Abimelek, the king of the Philistine region named Gerar as the one to whom Abraham lied concerning the status of Sarah (Gen 20). At that time, Abimelek allowed Abraham to "live wherever you like" (20:15). The present story picks up on the relationship between Abraham and this Philistine king.

How this story fits into the narrative flow of the Abraham story is not immediately obvious. The focus so far has been on Abraham's offspring as the beginning of the fulfillment of the promise that his descendants would be a "great nation" (12:2). However, the other aspect of being a great nation is having land, and the present episode does deal with land.

In terms of the ancient Near East, we can certainly imagine that the dealings between Abraham and Abimelek are not unique. Water was scarce in the region and so water rights would have been the subject of negotiations between clans, tribes, and nations. Walton cites an interesting correspondence between King Rim-Sin of Larsa and the king of Eshnunna over water rights during the Old Babylonian period (ca. eighteenth century BC).[1]

**Abraham Swears an Oath (21:22–24)**

Abimelek has since that time observed that God is with Abraham in everything he does (v. 22). From the use of the phrase in Genesis 39, which narrates Joseph's work in Potiphar's house, we can derive the implication of Abimelek's statement as meaning that Abraham is growing wealthier and more powerful (see 39:2–6). Accordingly, Abimelek wants to enter into a treaty with the patriarch and brings along his main military commander Phicol in order to offer such a relationship. Abraham resides as a foreigner within his borders, and he wants to assure himself that Abraham will not take advantage of him. We might see behind his demand that Abraham not "deal falsely" with him the sting of the first moment when they met and Abraham lied to him about Sarah thus bringing God's judgment on him.

The term translated "live as a foreigner" is from a Hebrew verbal root (*gwr*) that can be translated "dwell as a stranger" or "become a refugee." The sense of the verb and its associated noun (*ger*) is that they refer to people who are not native to the land in which they live, but neither are they just passing through. They are somewhat like permanent residents.

1. Walton, "Genesis," 96, citing M. Rowton, "Watercourses and Water Rights in the Official Correspondence from Larsa and Isin," *JCS* 21 (1969): 267–74.

We are not, however, to picture Abraham as some poor Bedouin eking out an existence in the land. If that were so, then Abimelek would not be interested in a treaty relationship. Indeed, in the not too distant future, other native inhabitants of the promised land will refer to him as "a mighty prince among us" (23:6), and, of course, we have already seen that even earlier he was able to amass a significant fighting force in order to take on the four Near Eastern kings (Gen 14). That said, the term does remind us that Abraham does not yet formally possess any of the land. The land promise implied in Genesis 12:1–3 will not be fulfilled during the time of Abraham, though future events will provide him with a token of the future reality (see commentary at Gen 23).

Abimelek wants Abraham to commit himself not only to refrain from dealing falsely with him and his descendants, but also to show him and the country "kindness." The word kindness (*hesed*) is often used in treaty/covenant contexts, referring to the type of love that the partners of this legal relationship are obligated to show to each other. "God's *khesed* is the kind of love that is devoted and loyal."[2] Indeed, the term treaty (*berit*), as this formal relationship between Abraham and Abimelek is later called, and the verb used for the procedure of making the treaty ("made a treaty," but literally "cut a treaty"; see vv. 27, 32) refer to the human institution which is elsewhere used metaphorically to describe the relationship between God and his people, including earlier when God "cut a treaty/covenant" with Abraham (see, for instance, Gen 15:18).

## A Treaty between Abraham and Abimelek (21:25–33)

Abraham agrees to the arrangement (v. 24) and immediately issues a complaint about the seizure of one of the wells that he used (vv. 25–26). Abimelek demonstrates that he will be a good treaty partner, and he disowns any knowledge or participation in the seizure with the implication that the well will be restored to Abraham's use.

As a good faith gesture, Abraham gave Abimelek a gift of seven ewe lambs (vv. 27–29), which might also be seen as a type of payment for the use of the well, though Abraham himself apparently dug the well. And, as we have often seen already in Genesis (for instance 16:13–14), this event gave the place where it occurred its name, Beersheba. The name can mean either the "well of seven" or "well of the oath." The motive clause in verse 31 ("because the two men swore an oath there") points to the viability of the second possibility.

2. Provan, *Seriously Dangerous Religion*, 62.

Nevertheless, it is always possible that there is a double meaning at play here, and if so perhaps it is a reference to the gift of the seven ewe lambs.

The final paragraph of the story tells us of the immediate aftermath of this treaty making. Abimelek and Phicol simply go home, and the narrative stays with Abraham, who plants a tamarisk tree in Beersheba and then calls on the name of the Lord. The collocation of calling on God and planting a tree reminds us of the fact that earlier Abraham built an altar next to prominent trees (12:6). Thus perhaps we are to think that Abraham built an altar here at Beersheba, thus continuing his practice of setting up what in essence are memorials to Yahweh throughout the land of promise (see 12:7; 13:18).

The chapter ends with the notice that Abraham remained in Abimelek's Philistine region of Gerar for a long time. It is thus at this place that Abraham receives God's chilling demand that he should sacrifice Isaac.

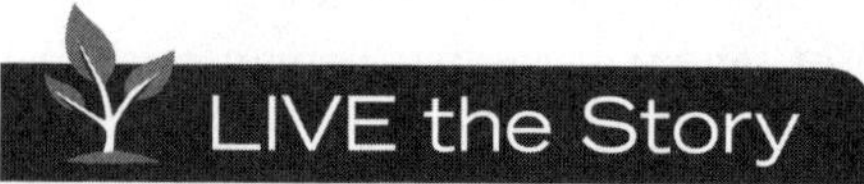


### Growing in Faith[3]

We have followed Abraham's tumultuous faith journey from his initial entry into the promised land until now. The ride is not over yet, the biggest test is yet to come, but we have observed that his faith, like our own, has been tested and tried and sometimes, perhaps often found wanting. We can derive some measure of encouragement from the fact that even Abraham struggled in his faith and, even more, from the fact that God stayed with him and pursued him in some of his darkest moments.

The present story indicates that Abraham has grown in his faith through the years. Perhaps this positive development has been spurred by the recent birth of the long-awaited child Isaac, but we can see signs of his growth in the present story by virtue of his interaction with Abimelek.

In the past, Abraham feared interaction with foreign kings and made self-protective moves out of his lack of confidence in God's ability to protect him. We see this most notably when he moves to Egypt (12:10–20) and when he initially moved into the region of Gerar, where Abimelek, also featured in this story, was king (v. 20). Both times he lied about his relationship with Sarah in order to lay low and avoid interaction. In our present story, however, Abraham speaks boldly and honestly with Abimelek. He enters into a treaty with this king and his military commander and even brings up a violation on the part of some of Abimelek's people who have stolen his well. His planting of the

3. The following essay has been greatly helped by the thoughts of Hughes, *Genesis*, 296–97.

tamarisk tree is a gesture that indicates he will be in the area for a while and that he belongs there.

As we reflect on Abraham's journey of faith and notice the similarities to our own struggles in our life and our relationship with God, we should gain confidence from the accounts of Abraham's growing trust in God and his growing confidence in living in a difficult world.

See related essay: Jesus and the Land (after Gen 13).

CHAPTER 20

# Genesis 22:1–19

## LISTEN to the Story

[22:1]Some time later God tested Abraham. He said to him, "Abraham!"

"Here I am," he replied.

[2]Then God said, "Take your son, your only son, whom you love—Isaac—and go to the region of Moriah. Sacrifice him there as a burnt offering on a mountain I will show you."

[3]Early the next morning Abraham got up and loaded his donkey. He took with him two of his servants and his son Isaac. When he had cut enough wood for the burnt offering, he set out for the place God had told him about. [4]On the third day Abraham looked up and saw the place in the distance. [5]He said to his servants, "Stay here with the donkey while I and the boy go over there. We will worship and then we will come back to you."

[6]Abraham took the wood for the burnt offering and placed it on his son Isaac, and he himself carried the fire and the knife. As the two of them went on together, [7]Isaac spoke up and said to his father Abraham, "Father?"

"Yes, my son?" Abraham replied.

"The fire and wood are here," Isaac said, "but where is the lamb for the burnt offering?"

[8]Abraham answered, "God himself will provide the lamb for the burnt offering, my son." And the two of them went on together.

[9]When they reached the place God had told him about, Abraham built an altar there and arranged the wood on it. He bound his son Isaac and laid him on the altar, on top of the wood. [10]Then he reached out his hand and took the knife to slay his son. [11]But the angel of the Lord called out to him from heaven, "Abraham! Abraham!"

"Here I am," he replied.

[12]"Do not lay a hand on the boy," he said. "Do not do anything to him. Now I know that you fear God, because you have not withheld from me your son, your only son."

[13]Abraham looked up and there in a thicket he saw a ram caught by its horns. He went over and took the ram and sacrificed it as a burnt offering instead of his son. [14]So Abraham called that place The LORD Will Provide. And to this day it is said, "On the mountain of the LORD it will be provided."

[15]The angel of the LORD called to Abraham from heaven a second time [16]and said, "I swear by myself, declares the LORD, that because you have done this and have not withheld your son, your only son, [17]I will surely bless you and make your descendants as numerous as the stars in the sky and as the sand on the seashore. Your descendants will take possession of the cities of their enemies, [18]and through your offspring all nations on earth will be blessed, because you have obeyed me."

[19]Then Abraham returned to his servants, and they set off together for Beersheba. And Abraham stayed in Beersheba.

*Listening to the Text in the Story:* Biblical Text: Genesis 11:27–21:34

The plot of the Abraham narrative came to a clear climax with the birth of Isaac, Sarah and Abraham's long anticipated child (21:1–7). The main theme of the preceding narrative connected to Abraham's journey of faith. How does he react when he encounters threats and obstacles to the fulfillment of the promises, including the promise of "seed" or "descendants"? That theme seemed to come to an end once the promised child was born.

As we turn to Genesis 22, we realize that the birth of Isaac was not the final conclusion to the story of Abraham's faith, rather it is the story of his binding (the Akedah in Jewish tradition). Abraham's faith will be tested one more time and in the most horrifying way imaginable. The test will reveal the quality of Abraham's trust in God. Will he respond with faith or will he again respond with fear?

## EXPLAIN the Story

### Divine Command (22:1–8)

An undetermined amount of time has passed since the events recorded in chapter 21. We will have to speculate about the age of Isaac in connection with his actions (see below). The narrator begins by announcing God's intention to test Abraham yet one more time (v. 1). God calls his name and Abraham quickly responds, "Here I am." After this brief introduction, God delivers his demand: "Take your son, your only son, whom you love—Isaac—and go to the region of Moriah. Sacrifice him there as a burnt offering on a mountain I will show you" (v. 2).

At the beginning of the Abraham narrative, God had commanded Abraham to leave his native country and to go, by faith, to the land that God would show him, offering him rewards if he would obey. Here, there are no rewards listed on the condition of obedience, and the demand is ever so much more difficult.

Notice how God highlights the cost to Abraham by the multiple descriptions of his special relationship with Isaac. As if he would need a reminder, he refers to Isaac as "his son," but then goes on to call him the patriarch's "only son," and finally the child that he "loves so much." He is to take him to the region of Moriah, a place near the future site of Jerusalem (see below for the significance of this name). He is to take him to a specific mountain in Moriah that God will choose and show to Abraham. Once there, he is to sacrifice the boy as a burnt offering.

The burnt offering (*ola*) is later described as one of the most fundamental types of animal sacrifice (Lev 1). It is distinctive in that the animal so offered is slaughtered and then completely burned. God was commanding Abraham to offer his own son as a human sacrifice.

We know that human sacrifice was practiced in the broader ancient Near East (2 Kgs 3:26–27), but it does not seem to be a regular ritual practice anywhere. It was a special sacrifice used in emergency situations to get a god's help. We do not know what Abraham knew or did not know about the practice of human sacrifice or even what practices were current at his exact time period. It is virtually certain, though, that this would have been the first occasion that God placed such a demand on his follower. Abraham would not have known whether this God desired human sacrifice or not.

We can speculate endlessly about what went through Abraham's mind that night. Perhaps he was angry, depressed, confused, or some combination of these emotions. The narrator does not tell us. What he emphasizes is Abraham's ready obedience as he moves straight from the divine command to Abraham's preparations for the journey.

He wastes no time, setting off early in the morning with not only Isaac but also two servants. In terms of supplies we hear only that Abraham brought the wood from his home base in the Philistine territory of Gerar.

The journey from Gerar to Moriah took three days. When he saw the place, he instructed his servants to stay with the donkeys as he and Isaac traveled alone to the location of sacrifice. It is striking that Abraham informed the servants that he and Isaac "will worship and then we will come back to you" (v. 5).

What was going through Abraham's mind when he says this to his servants? In typical fashion, the narrator reports the statement without commenting or evaluating it. Is he misleading the servants out of embarrassment, saving explanations until later? Considering the nature of the master-servant relationship at the time, it seems unlikely that Abraham would owe them such an explanation. A better understanding, though it is not certain, leads us to detect a note of hope in Abraham's voice as he tells them that both he and Isaac will return to them.

The same type of ambiguity attends to the interchange between Isaac and Abraham as they make the final ascent up the mountain. Isaac has a question for his father, "The fire and wood are here, ... but where is the lamb for the burnt offering?"

Isaac has noted the absence of the sacrificial animal. How old was he at this time? It is unclear, though he had to be of a certain age in order to carry the wood. Even so, we are left with uncertainty. He could be as young as six or seven, though many interpreters through the ages have seen him to be an adolescent or young adult. This will lead to further speculations about Isaac's precise role in the Akedah, as we will observe later in the text.

In answer to his son's question, Abraham responds, "God himself will provide the lamb for the burnt offering, my son" (v. 8). What are we to make of this? Could it be that Abraham was deflecting Isaac's question to spare both him and his son the emotional trauma till the bitter end? It is possible, though it is hard to think of Abraham muttering to himself, "and it's you my son."

Again, we cannot be certain, but I believe we are justified in seeing in Abraham's statement a measure of hope, hope that God would indeed provide a substitute for his son. However, it is important to the integrity of the story to recognize that Abraham was determined to obey God no matter what the cost. Hope was one thing, but submission to the will of God by his obedience was his primary goal as can be seen by the next paragraph (vv. 9 – 11).

### A Substitute (22:9 – 14)

When they reached the place on the unnamed mountain in the Moriah region, Abraham built an altar, something he had done many times in the past. The altar would have been dirt or more likely undressed stones. He then placed the wood for the fire on top of it. At that point he bound Isaac on the altar on top of the wood.

Here the matter of Isaac's age comes to the fore again. Just by virtue of the fact that he could carry the wood means that Isaac would have been able to put up resistance to his aged father's attempt to sacrifice him. Of course, if he were a young adult, then the old man would not have stood a chance.

Thus, through the ages, interpreters have suggested that Isaac himself came to participate in this act of obedience by his independent decision.[1] Again, we cannot be certain since the text itself does not make it clear.

Verse 10 makes it clear that Abraham intended, though he far from desired, to go through with the sacrifice. At the point that his actions indicated his intent, the angel of the Lord called out his name from heaven. The angel of the Lord is often identified with God himself.[2] The double repetition ("Abraham! Abraham!") shows urgency, which of course is fitting for the occasion. For the second time, Abraham responds to the heavenly voice with a "Here I am!" (*hinneni*; see also v. 1[3]), making himself available to the angel and his new instructions. He is not to kill Isaac, and then the angel tells Abraham that the earlier command was a test.

Abraham passed the test, demonstrating that he feared God. The phrase "fear God" and the related "fear of the Lord" describe a proper relationship with God. One who fears God knows their proper place in the cosmos. This fear does not make one run away, but does reveal an attitude that is willing to submit and obey. Indeed, it "expresses the idea of covenantal service."[4]

In the case of Abraham, his willingness to sacrifice his son, the one who represented the future to him, shows that he is willing to obey God even at great personal cost. It is this Abraham who amazes Johannes de Silento, Soren Kierkeguard's pseudonymous author, who exclaims:

> There was the one who relied on himself and gained everything, and the one who, secure in his own strength, sacrificed everything, but the one who believed God was greater than everybody. There was the one who was great by his wisdom, and the one who was great by his hope, and the one who was great by his love, but Abraham was greater than everybody—great by that power whose strength is powerlessness, great by that wisdom whose secret is folly, great by that hope whose form is madness, great by that love which is hatred of oneself.[5]

---

1. This view is represented by Josephus in his Antiquities (1:232), so J. Levenson, *The Death and Resurrection of the Beloved Son: The Transformation of Child Sacrifice in Judaism and Christianity* (New Haven, CT: Yale University Press, 1993), 190–92.

2. The angel of the Lord is a theophany, not specifically a Christophany. See Malone, *Knowing Jesus in the Old Testament?*

3. Note Abraham also similarly responds to Isaac's inquiry in verse 7, though the NIV simply translates the Hebrew word (*hinneni*) as "Yes."

4. Levenson, *Inheriting Abraham*, 80.

5. From Soren Kierkegaard, *Fear and Trembling*, ed. C.S. Evans and Sylvia Walsh (Cambridge: Cambridge University Press, 2006), 13–14. My thanks to Dr. Mark Nelson of Westmont College for this reference.

At that moment, Abraham saw a ram caught by its horn in the thicket. He apparently took the "coincidence" as a sign that God was indeed providing a substitute sacrifice. Notice God does not direct him to offer the animal, though the divine intention can be discerned through the coincidence.

This event then gave a new name to the place. The NIV and many other translations render the name *Yahweh-yireh* as "The LORD will provide," though this rendering is not a common translation of the verb *raah*. A more obvious translation of the phrase would be "The LORD will see" (see NAB). Either version makes sense in the context. God had indeed seen Abraham's great act of faith. But, and perhaps the stronger argument is here, the naming may be the way to definitively but indirectly teach that God had indeed provided the substitute sacrifice.

In verse 14 Moriah is called "the mountain of the LORD," in other words a place where God makes his presence known. Perhaps here we are to hear an anticipation of Sinai, the "mountain of God" (Exod 3:1) where God will make his presence known to Israel and reveal his law to them. In addition, due to Moriah's association with Jerusalem, the site of the future temple (see below The Journey to Moriah), we should also recognize a connection with Zion, the place where God makes his presence known in an enduring way among his people.

### The Angel's Second Speech (22:15–19)

Abraham has shown himself faithful. Again, the main theme of the Abraham story is his journey of faith. How does he respond to threats and obstacles to the fulfillment of the promises found at 12:1–3? Much of the time the answer is not positive. He manipulates and acts out of fear. But here at the end, during his most difficult test, he admirably succeeds. He demonstrates the kind of trust that will make him an example of faith in the New Testament (see below).

But here there is a further dimension to God's determined affirmation that he will fulfill the promises given at the beginning of the Abraham story. Genesis 15:6 emphasized the importance of Abraham's faith. Now God remarks that the promises will be fulfilled because Abraham has demonstrated his faith through obedience ("because you have obeyed me," 22:18), a point picked up by James in the New Testament (see below).

The angel's explication of God's promises to Abraham is rooted in their original expression in 12:1–3; see also 15:12–16; 17:3–8. God will bless Abraham and all the nations of the earth will be blessed. But what does it mean to be blessed? Let's begin with the observation that God created Adam and Eve in a blessed condition (1:28). They had a harmonious relationship with God and as a consequence with each other. They also had all their physical needs met as they lived in the garden of Eden. Life in the garden defines what blessing looks like, and as we look at the garden, we discover that blessing has spiritual, emotional, psychological, as well as material aspects to it. We can further turn to descriptions of God's blessings on those who obey his covenant found in Deuteronomy 27–28 among other places. The assumption of the blessing is that they have a vibrant relationship with God which leads to material and emotional wholeness.

The blessing on the nations will flow from Abraham's "offspring" or more literally "seed" (22:18). In 12:1–3, God had promised that Abraham's descendants would become a great nation. To be a great nation, they would have to be numerous. Here the angel uses the striking metaphor of stars in heaven and sand on the seashore. They will be countless. This expression will be cited in the future when Abraham's descendants become a great nation (2 Sam 17:11; 1 Kgs 4:20; see also Heb 11:12). In addition, the second component of a "great nation" is land, and the angel reaffirms that by speaking of future possession of the "cities of their enemies" (22:17). The angel assures Abraham of God's intention by telling him that God has "sworn by himself" (22:16), recognizing that God cannot swear by any higher authority than himself.

After the angel's second speech, the episode comes to an end with the narrator telling us that Abraham set off for Beersheba (22:19), the place where the patriarch had entered into a treaty with Abimelek, the king of Gerar (see chapter 21:22–34).

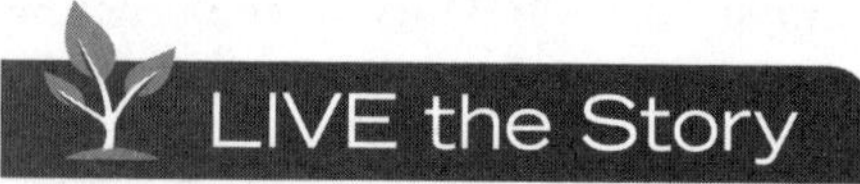


### Does God Test Us?

At the end of his life, God subjects Abraham to the most severe test of his life when he instructs the aged patriarch to take his son, his only son Isaac, to Moriah in order to sacrifice him there. The thought that God tests his people is a horrifying one to say the least. Will God test us like he tested Abraham? Or is this unique to his experience?

Before going further, we can say without a shadow of a doubt that God would not test us in the exact same way that he tested Abraham. We can be sure that if we think that God is telling us that he wants us to kill our child, or anyone for that matter, we are wrong. It is not God who is asking us to do it. After all, he has made it clear in a way that it was likely not clear at the time of Abraham that he does not want human sacrifice (Lev 18:21; 20:2–5; Deut 18:9–12; Micah 6:6–8 as well as the frequent prophetic attacks on the practice), and God would not instruct a person to do something that he has clearly forbidden as we now understand in a way that Abraham could not. Indeed, Deuteronomy 19:10 forbids the killing of the innocent.

That said, while God would never test anyone again in the same way that he tested Abraham, we know from later Scripture that he does on occasion test his people to expose the quality of their faith. Perhaps the best known example in later Old Testament Scripture is the account of the wilderness wanderings. It begins with the manna. God provides manna for Israel in the wilderness, but tells them only to collect enough for one day. The temptation will be to gather more and hoard the food for the future. What if God doesn't send the manna the next day? But God had said that he would supply manna six days a week (allowing them to gather enough for two days on the day before the Sabbath). Can they trust God to collect only enough manna for that day? Thus God tested Israel (Exod 16:4), as he did throughout the wilderness period (Exod 20:20; Deut 8:2, 16). As is well known, Israel miserably failed the test rebelling against God in the wilderness, so that the generation that emerged from Egypt died in the wilderness.

God also tested later generations of Israelites. At the time of the judges, God tested Israel using the nations that Joshua did not drive out of the land. Will Israel continue to follow God in spite of their presence (Judg 2:22; 3:1, 4)? As one reads the book of Judges, the answer to this question becomes sadly clear.

It is interesting to observe that on occasion the psalmist will call on God to test him. For instance, at the end of Psalm 139 the psalmist cries out: "Search me, God, and know my heart; test me and know my anxious thoughts. See if there is any offensive way in me, and lead me in the way everlasting" (vv. 23 – 24). The broader context of the psalms suggests that the psalmist has been accused of some crime, but he calls on God who knows his every thought to search him and exonerate him.[6]

So it seems clear that God does test his people in the Old Testament period to expose the quality of their faith. But what about the New Testament? What about today?

Interestingly, Paul, God's appointed spokesperson, calls on the Corinthian Christians to "Examine yourselves to see whether you are in the faith; test yourselves" (2 Cor 13:5). Paul does not want his hearers to be complacent, but rather to look at their lives to see if indeed their obedient lives are reflecting their professed faith. If a Christian lives like anyone else, their actions expose their hypocrisy. No one is perfect, but the Christian life reflects the truth and

6. T. Longman III, *Psalms*, 451 – 53.

Christians "cannot do anything against the truth, but only for the truth" (2 Cor 13:8). Paul is saying this to a church that has rebelled against Paul's apostolic authority, which is a signal that Christ is not with them. Thus, to "stand the test" will be manifested by "showing support for Paul's ministry by manifesting the life of the new creation that flows from trusting his gospel (5:17)."[7]

That the Christian life is tested is also indicated by Peter's admonition to his readers: "Dear friends, do not be surprised at the fiery ordeal that has come on you to test you, as though something strange were happening to you. But rejoice inasmuch as you participate in the sufferings of Christ, so that you may be overjoyed when his glory is revealed" (1 Pet 4:12–13). Thus, Peter tells us that life's difficulties, their tragedies, are means of testing the mettle of our faith. Do we respond with faith to life's hardships or with fear and withdrawal? The answer to that question exposes the strength of our faith. We suffer, but we can experience joy in the midst of our suffering. Indeed, James reminds us that the trials of life that test us are occasions for joy and the building up of our faith: "Consider it pure joy, my brothers and sisters, whenever you face trials of many kinds, because you know that the testing of your faith produces perseverance" (Jas 1:2–3).

In this life, the Christian can expect to be tested and we should heed the encouragement of Paul, Peter, and James to "stand the test." However, we know that we will do so only imperfectly. The only one who has indeed been tested and come out perfectly is Jesus himself. Three times he is tested/tempted by Satan and each time he withstands the temptation (Matt 4:1–11; see fuller treatment of this theme in the essay God Delivers His People in the Live the Story section after 12:10–20). Jesus is the perfectly obedient child of God, and he is the role model as well as the object of our own faith.

**Can We Test God?**

The story of God's testing of Abraham naturally raises the question considered in the previous essay "Does God Test Us?" Indirectly, it raises the question can we test God? It only seems fair after all that if he can test us than he ought to let us test him. "If you are there God, then. . . ." And we can fill in the blank, "heal me," "help me pay the bills," "reveal yourself to me," "make it rain," "let me get pregnant." The potential list is endless.

About this issue, Scripture is perfectly clear: "Do not put the Lord your God to the test" (Deut 6:16; see also Exod 17:2). The psalmist cites Israel's testing God as a sign of their rebellion against God (Pss 78:18, 41, 56; 106:14). Jesus understood this when Satan tried to get him to test God, and he utterly refused (Matt 4:7, citing Deut 6:16).

---

7. S. J. Hafemann, *2 Corinthians*, NIVAC (Grand Rapids: Zondervan, 2000), 493.

It is in the light of these consistent and clear prohibition of testing God that we are to read the narratives about those who are coming out to test Jesus (Matt 19:3; Mark 8:11; Luke 10:25; John 6:6; see also Acts 15:10; 1 Cor 10:9). In other words, those who come out to test him are pictured in a negative light as not trusting him.

Thus, it is clear in Scripture that we are not to test God, but rather to trust him. But, someone might object, isn't it OK to "put a fleece out before the Lord"? This reference is to Gideon's testing God's command that he lead an army against the Midianites (Judg 6). The angel of the Lord came to Gideon and commissioned him to save Israel from Midian. The angel, who is the Lord himself, assures Gideon that he will be with him in the battle. The Lord assures Gideon of his presence by creating the fire of the sacrifice. Because of this, he is certain that he was in the presence of God (Judg 6:22). On this basis, he demolished the altar of Baal. But he remains uncertain about leading an army against the Midianites and he put out a dry fleece and asks God to make the fleece wet and the ground dry. God did it, but Gideon tests God even further, and he then asks God to reverse it making the fleece dry and the ground wet.

Though God did this for Gideon, it does not give blanket approval to the practice of testing God, which is, as we have seen, prohibited in the rest of Scripture. And when we think about it, Gideon's persistent testing of God is clearly an indication of his fundamental distrust of God even after God made his presence absolutely clear to him. Indeed, a close reader of the story of Gideon sees that he is hardly a model to be emulated. God uses him, but like with so many of the judges, he is a deeply flawed individual, even creating the occasion for an act of idolatry at the end of his life (Judg 8:22–27).[8]

God tests us, but we are not to test God. After all, we are weak, fallible creatures who do waver in our faith. On the other hand, God is totally faithful. To test him is to cast doubt on that unassailable fact.

Before we leave the subject of testing, however, we need to clarify a possible misapprehension. While it is wrong to test God, there is nothing wrong with testing whether something is from God or not. John tells us to "not believe every spirit, but test the spirits to see whether they are from God" (1 John 4:1). There is a lot of false religion and even false Christian voices out there. We need to test, that is think about, ask questions, investigate those who claim to speak about or in the name of God. Thankfully, John also gives us a criterion to distinguish true from false voices: "Every spirit that

8. G. Wenham, *Story as Torah: Reading the Old Testament Ethically*, Old Testament Studies (Edinburgh: T & T Clark, 2000), 119–27.

acknowledges that Jesus Christ has come in the flesh is from God, but every spirit that does not acknowledge Jesus is not from God" (1 John 4:2–3).

### Faith with Deeds

As we have seen, Paul often appeals to Abraham as an illustration of what today we would call justification by faith alone (see Abraham as a Model of Justification by Faith in the Live the Story section after Gen 15). In particular, he appeals to Genesis 15:6 ("Abram believed the LORD, and he credited it to him as righteousness") and notes the significance that God credits him as righteous before he is circumcised.

However, we should avoid the mistake of believing that Paul thought that good deeds have nothing to do with faith. James makes clear that there is no such misunderstanding when he appeals to the Akedah to make his point that faith without works is dead:

> What good is it, my brothers and sisters, if someone claims to have faith but has no deeds? Can such faith save them? Suppose a brother or a sister is without clothes and daily food. If one of you says to them, "Go in peace; keep warm and well fed," but does nothing about their physical needs, what good is it? In the same way, faith by itself, if it is not accompanied by action, is dead.
>
> But someone will say, "You have faith; I have deeds."
>
> Show me your faith without deeds, and I will show you my faith by my deeds. You believe that there is one God. Good! Even the demons believe that—and shudder.
>
> You foolish person, do you want evidence that faith without deeds is useless? Was not our father Abraham considered righteous for what he did when he offered his son Isaac on the altar? You see that his faith and his actions were working together, and his faith was made complete by what he did. And the scripture was fulfilled that says, "Abraham believed God, and it was credited to him as righteousness," and he was called God's friend. You see that person is considered righteous by what they do and not by faith alone. (Jas 2:14–24)

I have quoted this passage at length because it is, unsurprisingly, an extremely sensitive and profound theological reflection on not only the Akedah, but the Abraham story as a whole. Further, for mostly good reasons, Protestant theology tends to downplay James on this point, preferring to emphasize Paul's emphasis on faith without works. As we will see, however, there really is no difference between the two and their viewpoints are easily harmonized.

Paul wants to make it perfectly clear that our salvation is not earned but graciously given to us as a gift from God. James would not disagree. James, though, wants to speak against those who would say that faith does not have to manifest itself through good deeds. Faith will always issue forth in good deeds. James is not making the case that people of faith will do only good deeds. He is not even setting a minimum requirement. But if our new relationship with God does not have any effect on our thoughts, attitudes, relationships, and behavior, then we have to question whether or not we are people of faith.

Again to be clear, this is not an infringement on the clear biblical teaching that we are justified by faith alone. And certainly, we should not use James' teaching as a tool to evaluate the faith of others. Indeed, some people may have been so evil before they became a Christian that even what to outside observers is still bad behavior really is a manifestation of faith.

I knew an old man who had harmed many during his long lifetime. Even in the retirement center, he cursed and even hit the attendants and any others who came too close. He heard the gospel about three weeks before his death and God graciously saved him. He did not become an angel in his final weeks, but people could discern a notable change in his attitude and behavior. He was less angry and less violent. I believe in his last three weeks his faith was not without works.

### Heavenly Rewards

But, speaking pragmatically (and a bit crassly), what benefit are good works or at least what advantage is there to really pursuing good works? Of course, the reason why this question is a bit crass is because we should not be motivated by such self-interest. Our transformed hearts should desire to help others for the glory of God, not because of any benefit to ourselves.

That said, the Scriptures themselves point to rewards in heaven as the consequence of our good works. Let's survey a few, beginning with Paul's statements in his Corinthians correspondence.

> By the grace God has given me, I laid a foundation as a wise builder, and someone else is building on it. But each one should build with care. For no one can lay any foundation other than the one already laid, which is Jesus Christ. If anyone builds on this foundation using gold, silver, costly stones, wood, hay or straw, their work will be shown for what it is, because the Day will bring it to light. It will be revealed with fire, and the fire will test the quality of each person's work. If what has been built survives, the builder will receive a reward. If it is burned up, the builder will suffer loss but yet will be saved—even though only as one escaping through the flames. (1 Cor 3:10–15)

> Therefore we are always confident and know that as long as we are at home in the body we are away from the Lord. For we live by faith, not by sight. We are confident, I say, and would prefer to be away from the body and at home with the Lord. So we make it our goal to please him, whether we are at home in the body or away from it. For we must all appear before the judgment seat of Christ, so that each of us may receive what is due us for the things done while in the body, whether good or bad. (2 Cor 5:6–10)

In the first passage, Paul describes the believer as a building, whose foundation is Christ. The believer then builds on this foundation, a metaphor which points to a person's works. One might use gold, silver, or costly stones—these materials represent good works that will survive the fire of the day of judgment. But others will use wood or hay or straw. When the fire comes, they will be shown for what they are—perishable. The latter group will be saved, but barely, while the good works of others will survive and the builder will receive a reward.

In his second letter to the Corinthians, Paul straight out tells his readers that they will receive their proper reward when they "appear before the judgment seat of Christ." Thus, we need to please God while we can in this life.

The New Testament's teaching, based on the Old Testament, is clear. We are saved by faith, but that faith must manifest itself in works. The quality of the works determines what our reward will be in heaven (see also Col 3:23; Rev 2:23).

## Not Ethnicity, But Faith and Obedience

What makes a person a true child of God? God called Abram and said that he would make his descendants a great nation, blessed by God (12:1–3). Does that mean that all his biological descendants are in and that those who are not genetically related to him are on the outside? What does it mean to be a descendant of Abraham?

The New Testament is clear on this matter. Physical descent from Abraham is not sufficient in and of itself. John the Baptist blasted those who came to him proclaiming privilege due to physical descent from Abraham: "Produce fruit in keeping with repentance. And do not think you can say to yourselves, 'We have Abraham as our father.' I tell you that out of these stones God can raise up children for Abraham" (Matt 3:8–9).

In John 8, Jesus addresses those who press their claim that they have a special relationship with God by saying "Abraham is our father," by responding "If you were Abraham's children, . . . then you would do what Abraham did" (8:39). In other words, the true children of Abraham are not those who are related to him by ethnicity but those who follow him in his faith (Gen 15:6) and his obedience (22:15–19). These physical descendants of Abraham were "looking for a way to kill" Jesus (John 8:40) and thus disqualified themselves as true (spiritual) children of Abraham since they working against the purposes of God.

Are you a child of Abraham? In biblical terms, this question is not a matter of physical but rather of spiritual descent. The prophet Jeremiah said that even Judaeans who were circumcised "only in the flesh" were not part of the covenant community and "even the whole house of Israel is uncircumcised in heart" (Jer 9:25–26). According to Paul, "if you belong to Christ, then you are Abraham's seed, and heirs according to the promise" (Gal 3:29).

### Human Sacrifice: What Does God Want from Us?

It is debated how widespread was the practice of child sacrifice in ancient Near Eastern religion.[9] It is unlikely that it was a regular feature of any one of them, but there is no doubting that it was practiced on occasion. Indeed, the one report of a child sacrifice in the Bible, that of the child of Mesha the king of Moab, indicates that it was done only as a last resort to gain the attention of one's deity:

> When the king of Moab saw that the battle had gone against him, he took with him seven hundred swordsmen to break through to the king of Edom, but they failed. Then he took his firstborn son, who was to succeed him as king, and offered him as a sacrifice on the city wall. The fury against Israel was great, they withdrew and returned to their own land. (2 Kgs 3:26–27)

We don't know all the details of the background that led to Mesha's horrific act, but it is likely that Mesha thought of this as the ultimate sacrifice. If a sacrifice is taking something dear and precious (even an animal is costly) and offering it to the deity, what is more dear and precious than a firstborn son to a Moabite king?

We observed above that it is likely that Abraham did not know God's policy on human sacrifice. If he did, we imagine he might have objected on those grounds. Indeed, one way of reading the Abrahamic narrative is as a revelation of God's rejection of human sacrifice as a means of worshiping him, and instead substituting the sacrifice of an animal, a practice already known (for instance, see Gen 8:20–21).

9. R. W. Green, *The Role of Human Sacrifice in the Ancient Near East* (Missoula, MT: Scholars Press, 1975); M. Selman, "Sacrifice in the Ancient Near East," in *Sacrifice in the Bible*, ed. R. T. Beckwith and M. Selman (Grand Rapids: Baker, 1995), 99–100.

The Mosaic law makes such a prohibition official and public. It is true that God demanded the firstborn son: "You must give me the firstborn of your sons" (Exod 22:29), but as a later passage of the same book reveals, these sons, as opposed to the firstborn animal, are all to be redeemed and not executed ("The first offspring of every womb belongs to me, including all the firstborn males of your livestock, whether from herd or flock. Redeem the firstborn donkey with a lamb, but if you do not redeem it, break its neck. Redeem all your firstborn sons, " [34:19–20]).

Of course, Christian readers share the prophets' revulsion of even the idea of human sacrifice (e.g., Jer 19:5–6). But what then is the ultimate sacrifice? In one of the most moving and memorable passages of the Old Testament, the prophet Micah both asks and answers the question:

> With what shall I come before the Lord
> and bow down before the exalted God?
> Shall I come before him with burnt offerings,
> with calves a year old?
> Will the Lord be pleased with thousands of rams,
> with ten thousand rivers of olive oil?
> Shall I offer my firstborn for my transgression,
> the fruit of my body for the sin of my soul?
> He has shown you, O mortal, what is good.
> And what does the Lord require of you?
> To act justly and love mercy
> and to walk humbly with your God. (6:6–8)

The prophet makes it clear the sacrifice that God wants from us is our heart and our obedience. He does not want human sacrifice to be sure, as God himself declared through Jeremiah, the idea is something that never even "enter[ed] my mind" (7:31). According to the Torah (Lev 1–7), God did want animal sacrifice, but that is not the ultimate sacrifice and unless one is humble, just, and merciful, all the sacrifices in the world will do a person no good.

Jesus makes the same point as he confronted the Pharisees and the teachers of the law (see Matt 23:13–39). These people observed all of the religious practices and more, but they exploited others and were proud of themselves. Jesus thus pronounced a series of five "woe oracles" against them.

Can we fall into the same trap today? Of course. We may be active in church, give generous offerings, take communion, even study the Bible and regularly pray, but unless our hearts are in it, unless we act with justice and mercy toward others, unless we are humble, these religious acts mean nothing.

### Christ and the *Akedah*

Though never quoted in the New Testament, attentive Christian readers of the Akedah cannot help but think of the crucifixion of Christ. Indeed, early church fathers were not slow to note the connection. To cite one example, consider the poem of Melito in the second century:

> As a ram he was bound,
> he says concerning our Lord Jesus Christ,
> and as a lamb he was shorn,
> and as a lamb he was crucified.
> And he bore the wood on his shoulders,
> going up to slaughter like Isaac at the hand of his father.
> But Christ suffered.
> Isaac did not suffer,
> for he as a type of the passion of Christ which was to come.[10]

God commanded Abraham to sacrifice "your son, your only son, whom you love" (22:2). This reminds us of God's words at Jesus' baptism, "You are my Son, whom I love; with you I am well pleased" (Mark 1:11; see also Matt 3:17; Luke 3:22; 2 Pet 1:17, passages that also reflect Isa 42:1 in their background). When he went to Moriah, God provided a ram as a substitute. In the New Testament, it was the Father's will that Jesus go to the cross ("He who did not spare his own Son, but gave him up for us all"; Rom 8:32). The Father loves the Son, so such a determination was sacrificial on the part of the Father as well as the Son. As Paul states, "What, then, shall we say in response to these things? If God is for us, who can be against us? He who did not spare his own Son, but gave him up for us all . . ." (Rom 8:31 – 32). We saw that, because of his age, it was possible, but far from certain, that Isaac participated in the decision to comply with the divine command. The episode at the garden of Gethsemane (Mark 14:32 – 42) makes it clear that it wasn't easy for Jesus to follow his Father's will to die on the cross, but in the end he voluntarily submitted and went to the cross. He did so on our behalf.

### The Journey to Moriah

God commanded Abraham to take Isaac and sacrifice his beloved son Isaac at a specific location — Moriah. What is the significance of this location? The answer comes in the only other place in all of Scripture where this site is mentioned, 2 Chronicles 3:1: "Then Solomon began to build the temple of

10. Melito of Sardis, *On Pascha: With the Fragments of Melito and Other Material Related to Quartodecimans*, trans. Alistair Stewart – Sykes (Crestwood, NY: Saint Vladmir's Seminary, 2001), 76, quoted by Levenson, *Inheriting Abraham*, 102.

the Lord in Jerusalem on Mount Moriah." The place where Abraham built an altar in order to sacrifice his son is none other than the future location of the temple that was the place God chose to make his presence known among his people. After it was built the temple was the only place where God's people could come in order to make sacrifices to God (see the Law of Centralization in Deut 12).

Thus Moriah is Zion located in the holy city of Jerusalem. Perhaps it is another name for Zion (as Horeb is another name for Sinai) or Zion is a peak in the Moriah range. But there is no doubt about the association of Moriah with the future Jerusalem and the mountain that made it famous.

Indeed, as Moberly points out, the name which Abraham gives this place ("The Lord will Provide [or Sees]") also points to Jerusalem.[11] After all, as he points out, the distance from Beersheba is only three days (a number which means a short period of time) which is appropriate for Jerusalem. Second, the reference to "the mountain of the Lord" in verse 14 is right for Jerusalem.

Moberly also suggests an interesting connection between the name Moriah, the name "The Lord will Provide (or Sees)," and Jerusalem. The verbal root of "provide" or "sees" is *ra'ah*, which may be the root at play in the name Moriah, though there may also be a *double entendre* there with the verb *yare'* ("to fear"). The latter would be relevant because this is the place where God learns that Abraham fears him. Then, as the location of the later temple where God makes his presence known, Jerusalem is the place where God is "seen."

In summary, Moriah turns out to be a place of great significance once we know of its association with Jerusalem, specifically Zion, the location of the later temple. It is the place where God makes his presence known. As we learned in the essay Living in the Presence of God in the Living the Story section after 11:27–12:9, the temple itself is anticipatory of Jesus, the Word who became flesh and dwelt among us (John 1:14).

See related essays: The Angel Who Saves (after Gen 16).

11. R. W. L. Moberly, *The Bible, Theology, and Faith: A Study of Abraham and Jesus* (Cambridge: Cambridge University Press, 2000), 110–12.

CHAPTER 21

# Genesis 22:20–23:20

## LISTEN to the Story

[22:20]Some time later Abraham was told, "Milkah is also a mother; she has borne sons to your brother Nahor: [21]Uz the firstborn, Buz his brother, Kemuel (the father of Aram), [22]Kesed, Hazo, Pildash, Jidlaph and Bethuel." [23]Bethuel became the father of Rebekah. Milkah bore these eight sons to Abraham's brother Nahor. [24]His concubine, whose name was Reumah, also had sons: Tebah, Gaham, Tahash and Maakah.

[23:1]Sarah lived to be a hundred and twenty-seven years old. [2]She died at Kiriath Arba (that is, Hebron) in the land of Canaan, and Abraham went to mourn for Sarah and to weep over her.

[3]Then Abraham rose from beside his dead wife and spoke to the Hittites. He said, [4]"I am a foreigner and stranger among you. Sell me some property for a burial site here so I can bury my dead."

[5]The Hittites replied to Abraham, [6]"Sir, listen to us. You are a mighty prince among us. Bury your dead in the choicest of our tombs. None of us will refuse you his tomb for burying your dead."

[7]Then Abraham rose and bowed down before the people of the land, the Hittites. [8]He said to them, "If you are willing to let me bury my dead, then listen to me and intercede with Ephron son of Zohar on my behalf [9]so he will sell me the cave of Machpelah, which belongs to him and is at the end of his field. Ask him to sell it to me for the full price as a burial site among you."

[10]Ephron the Hittite was sitting among his people and he replied to Abraham in the hearing of all the Hittites who had come to the gate of his city. [11]"No, my lord," he said. "Listen to me; I give you the field, and I give you the cave that is in it. I give it to you in the presence of my people. Bury your dead."

[12]Again Abraham bowed down before the people of the land [13]and he said to Ephron in their hearing, "Listen to me, if you will. I will pay the price of the field. Accept it from me so I can bury my dead there."

[14]Ephron answered Abraham, [15]"Listen to me, my lord; the land is worth four hundred shekels of silver, but what is that between you and me? Bury your dead."

[16]Abraham agreed to Ephron's terms and weighed out for him the price he had named in the hearing of the Hittites: four hundred shekels of silver, according to the weight current among the merchants.

[17]So Ephron's field in Machpelah near Mamre—both the field and the cave in it, and all the trees within the borders of the field—was deeded [18]to Abraham as his property in the presence of all the Hittites who had come to the gate of the city. [19]Afterward Abraham buried his wife Sarah in the cave in the field of Machpelah near Mamre (which is at Hebron) in the land of Canaan. [20]So the field and the cave in it were deeded to Abraham by the Hittites as a burial site.

*Listening to the Text in the Story:* Biblical Texts: Genesis 11:27–32 (for 20:20–24); Genesis 12:1–3; 15:17–21 (for 23:1–20)

The present episode of the Abraham story begins by reminding the reader of Abraham's eastern relatives, and thus picks up on developments in that side of the family since the genealogy of 11:27–32. As we will see, the purpose for the reminder is to introduce the story of the marriage between Isaac and Rebekah.

However, before proceeding to the story of the marriage of Isaac and Rebekah, Sarah dies and is buried. As we will explain in the Explain the Story section, the background for this story is the promise of land that is implicit in the God's covenant with Abraham where he tells the patriarch that his descendants will be a great nation (12:1–3 and expanded upon in 15:17–21).

### Abraham's Eastern Relatives (22:20–24)

Abraham learns that his brother Nahor has had children with both his wife Milkah, who was the daughter of his now dead brother Haran (11:29), and also by his concubine Reumah, a woman mentioned here for the first time. Nahor had stayed in Harran when Abraham descended into the promised land. The genealogy is mentioned here to remind the reader that there is an eastern branch of the family, because soon the narrative will describe Abraham sending a servant to his ancestral homeland to find a woman for Isaac to marry rather than marrying one of the Canaanites. That woman is Rebekah, the granddaughter of Nahor and Milkah through their son Bethuel (see ch. 24).

Besides the introduction of the later important character, Rebekah, the most interesting feature of this short family history is their connection with

Arameans. Kemuel is called "the father of Aram," while later texts refer to Bethuel as "the Aramean" (25:20; 28:5; 31:20, 24). Later Israel will have frequent interaction with the Aramean tribes that descend from this family. As Hartley points out, it is significant that Nahor has twelve sons that are the putative fathers of the Arameans, paralleling the later twelve tribes of Israel (49:28) and the twelve tribes that descend from Ishmael (25:12–16).[1]

## Abraham Buys Ephron's Land (23:1–20)

The main significance of the story of Sarah's burial is that Abraham comes into possession of a portion of the promised land. With his purchase of the field and the cave of Ephron the Hittite, Abraham now receives a down payment on the land implied by the promise that his descendants will become a "great nation" (12:2).

Sarah lived a long life, but not as long as Abraham. She lived to be one hundred and twenty-seven years old. She died in Kiriath Arba, which was likely the name of the place at the time of the story, though the narrator informs the reader that this city is known during his time as Hebron. This city is in the Judean highlands, about eighteen miles south-southwest of Jerusalem.

Abraham mourned her death, but after weeping over her deceased body, he began the process of purchasing a burial place. The narrative informs us that Hittites lived in this region. These Hittites do not seem to be related to the famous Hittite nation located in Anatolia from about 1800–1200 BC. It may be a different group or the text may be using Hittite ("sons of Heth") to refer in a general sense to the "other."

These Hittites are part of Canaan and presumably then part of Canaanite culture (Gen 15:18–21; Exod 3:8). They will become foes of Israel and God will drive them out of the land (Exod 23:28). Indeed, God told later Israel to completely annihilate them (Deut 7:1–2; 20:17).

However, this conflict is in the future. For now, Abraham engages in a real estate transaction to purchase the grave. He speaks first to a group of Hittites whom we presume are the decision makers in the community. He acknowledges his identity as an "outsider" ("foreigner and stranger," v. 4), and then asks for permission to buy land as a grave site. The bartering that ensues will be familiar to those who have bought something in a modern Middle Eastern bazaar.

The Hittites first respond to Abraham as a group by honoring him as a "mighty prince among us" (v. 5). Thus, they inform Abraham that they do not think of him as just any "foreigner and stranger," but as one who has real power among them. In the light of the fact that "mighty prince" can be

1. Hartley, *Genesis*, 215.

rendered "prince of God," they may also recognize his favored divine status. The final result is that Abraham can have the choice of any piece of land. No one will refuse him.

It appears that Abraham already had a burial place in mind, and so he asks the group to intercede for him with a man named Ephron son of Zohar. He is not looking for a deal; he is more than willing to pay the full price for the "cave" at the "end of the field" owned by Ephron (v. 9). We might compare his refusal to take the land for free with his rejection of gifts from the king of Sodom in Genesis 14. The patriarch does not want to be beholden to the Canaanites.

As it turned out Ephron was already in attendance, and in traditional fashion he offers to simply give the land to Abraham, and then he expands the "offer" to include the field (though it is possible, but not likely, to translate the verb "sell" instead of "give," see NIV note). Abraham, also in the traditional fashion (courteous and indirect), refuses to simply take the land. He insists on paying (of course Ephron expects this; he is not really going to give Abraham the land) the substantial price of four hundred shekels, an amount cited by Ephron as if the money was of little matter to him. But it is significant that Abraham paid the full amount, so there can be no future question about ownership.

Thus, the real estate transaction is complete and Abraham for the first time is in possession of a token of the promised land (vv. 17–18). This transaction was public (v. 18), so there can be no future question about ownership. The land constituted a field, a cave (where presumably Sarah's body would be placed), and some trees. The location here is described as the field of Machpelah near Mamre which is near Hebron. Today this place is known as the Tomb of the Patriarchs, since not only Sarah, but eventually also Abraham, Isaac, Rebekah, Jacob, and Leah were all buried there (49:31).

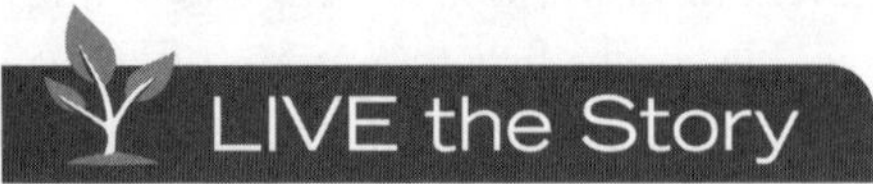


### Sarah: "Who Obeyed Abraham and Called Him Her Lord" (1 Pet 3:5–6)

Peter offers Sarah as a model submissive wife. He begins by exhorting wives to submit to their husbands in such a way that if the husbands were not Christians, they would be won over to the faith. He further tells them to put their emphasis on inner and not outward beauty. He concludes his instructions for wives by saying "for this is the way the holy women of the past who put their hope in God used to adorn themselves. They submitted themselves to their own husbands, like Sarah, who obeyed Abraham and called him her lord. You are her daughters if you do what is right and do not give way to fear" (1 Pet 3:5–6).

We have now come to the end of Sarah's life after having been introduced to her by the name Sarai as Abraham's childless wife in 11:29–31. She went with Abraham from Ur to Harran and eventually to the promised land according to God's instructions in 12:1–3. She was not only Abraham's wife, but also his half-sister, and she colluded with Abraham on two known occasions (12:10–20; 20, see especially v. 13) and apparently other unreported instances when the patriarch passed her off as his sister in order to save his own skin. She traveled with Abraham throughout the promised land, though they did not actually possess any of the land until now when Abraham bought land that would serve as her burial place.

Sarah is the one who told Abraham to sleep with Hagar so she, Sarah, could "build a family through her" (16:2). Apparently, she too came to doubt that God would fulfill his promise through her. She did come to regret her decision when her handmaid Hagar began to feel superior to her, bitterly complaining to Abraham and asserting that it was all Abraham's fault. In response, Abraham allowed Sarah to do whatever she wanted to Hagar and the abused Hagar fled only to be told by God to return and submit to Sarah (16:9). Sarah was still childless at the age of eighty-nine when the Lord and two other visitors appeared to them near the great trees of Mamre (18:1). After preparing a feast to show exemplary hospitality to her guests, she retired to her tent where she overheard the Lord reaffirm his intention to give Abraham a son with Sarah. Sarah vainly tried to hide that she had laughed in disbelief at this, to her, outrageous claim. But sure enough Sarah became pregnant and gave birth to Isaac when she was ninety years old (21:1–6). Sarah laughed again, but this laughter was one of joy.

Still, the animosity between Sarah and Hagar continued to fester, and she demanded that Abraham expel her and her child (21:8–21). Abraham was against the idea until God gave him permission. Sarah, interestingly, plays no part in the story of the "binding of Isaac" (22:1–19), and it is mere speculation to think about how she might have responded to the event and her husband's actions. Indeed, after the episode that led to Hagar's expulsion we do not hear about her again until her death and burial at the age of one hundred and twenty-seven (ch. 23).

It is this Sarah that Peter points to as a role model of wifely submission. In particular, he says to Christian wives that they are "her daughters" if they do what is right and do not fear.

Now our survey of Sarah's life indicates that she did not always do what is right and at times she acted as if she, along with Abraham, was afraid. Thus, women are to look at those moments in Sarah's life when she did what was right and she was not afraid as indicative of their submission. In the same way, the New Testament uses Abraham as a role model for a life of faith (Rom 4:18–25; Heb 11:9–12, 17–19), though even a surface reading of the story of Abraham in the book of Genesis indicates that he too lacked confidence in God on many occasions.

Submission is not simply doing what one's spouse wants no matter what. It is not a matter of blind obedience. When Sarah went along with Abraham's deceptions, she was not "doing what was right" and she was not unafraid. She was not submitting to her husband but enabling him to dangerous behavior. Submission means putting the other person's best interests ahead of your own and sometimes that means the opposite of obedience.

Of course, today we live in a culture that puts "me" before anyone else. And that is true of men as well as women. A true biblical perspective on submission in marriage recognizes that not only should wives submit to husbands but husbands should submit to their wives. For cultural reasons, Peter as well as Paul put an emphasis on wives submitting to their husbands, but Paul makes it very clear that submission is mutual when he says to men and women, husbands and wives: "Submit to one another out of reverence for Christ" (Eph 5:21). Husbands are to put their wife's best interest ahead of their own and wives are to put their husband's best interest ahead of their own. That is pivotal to a successful marriage.[2]

### An Earnest of the Promise: Tomb of the Patriarchs

As mentioned above in the exposition, when Abraham purchases a plot of land for the burial of Sarah, he now officially owns a piece of the land of promise. When God promised that his descendants would become a "great nation" (12:2), that promise included not only the promise of many descendants but also the promise of land. Indeed, the promise of land is spelled out explicitly by God when he reconfirmed his promise to Abraham by passing through the divided parts of animals and proclaimed: "To your descendants I give this land, from the Wadi of Egypt to the great river, the Euphrates — the land of the Kenites, Kenizzites, Kadmonites, Hittites, Perizzites, Rephaites, Amorites, Canaanites, Girgashites and Jebusites" (Gen 15:18–21; see also 13:14–17; 17:7–9; 26:2–4; 28:13–15),

2. See D. Allender and T. Longman III, *Intimate Allies* (Wheaton, IL: Tyndale House, 1995), 157–96.

Indeed, this small piece of real estate was the extent of the holdings of Abraham and his descendants for many years. It is not until Joshua and the Israelites cross the Jordan River centuries later that the extent of their holdings are expanded, but even the conquest left much of the promised land still in possession of the Canaanites. It is not until the time David subdued the last of the internal enemies of Israel that the promise of the land came to full realization (for more on the theology of the land, see the reflection on "Jesus and the Land" after the exposition of Gen 13).

This little plot of land may be seen as a down payment on the divine promise of land, an earnest, so-to-speak, of the blessing that would come to the descendants of Abraham. The Christian can relate to this. After all, as we have pointed out more than once, we too are on a faith journey, having received divine promises of an eternal relationship with God, a restoration, yet even better, of an Edenic life in God's presence (Rev 21 – 22). Paul tells us that, though the fulfillment of this promise is still future, that we have received a down payment, or earnest, of that promise in the Spirit. In 2 Corinthians, Paul is assuring his readers that God will come through on his promises: "For no matter how many promises God has made, they are 'Yes' in Christ" (1:20). He goes on to inform us that Christ "anointed us, set his seal of ownership on us, and put his Spirit in our hearts as a deposit, guaranteeing what is to come" (1:21b – 22). The implication of having received this deposit is that we should live confidently in a troubled present and with certain hope as we face the future.

See related essay: Jesus and the Land (after Gen 13).

CHAPTER 22

# Genesis 24

## LISTEN to the Story

24:1Abraham was now very old, and the LORD had blessed him in every way. 2He said to the senior servant in his household, the one in charge of all that he had, "Put your hand under my thigh. 3I want you to swear by the LORD, the God of heaven and the God of earth, that you will not get a wife for my son from the daughters of the Canaanites, among whom I am living, 4but will go to my country and my own relatives and get a wife for my son Isaac."

5The servant asked him, "What if the woman is unwilling to come back with me to this land? Shall I then take your son back to the country you came from?"

6"Make sure that you do not take my son back there," Abraham said. 7"The LORD, the God of heaven, who brought me out of my father's household and my native land and who spoke to me and promised me on oath, saying, 'To your offspring I will give this land'—he will send his angel before you so that you can get a wife for my son from there. 8If the woman is unwilling to come back with you, then you will be released from this oath of mine. Only do not take my son back there." 9So the servant put his hand under the thigh of his master Abraham and swore an oath to him concerning this matter.

10Then the servant left, taking with him ten of his master's camels loaded with all kinds of good things from his master. He set out for Aram Naharaim and made his way to the town of Nahor. 11He had the camels kneel down near the well outside the town; it was toward evening, the time the women go out to draw water.

12Then he prayed, "LORD, God of my master Abraham, make me successful today, and show kindness to my master Abraham. 13See, I am standing beside this spring, and the daughters of the townspeople are coming out to draw water. 14May it be that when I say to a young woman, 'Please let down your jar that I may have a drink,' and she says, 'Drink, and I'll water your camels too'—let her be the one you have chosen for

your servant Isaac. By this I will know that you have shown kindness to
my master."
[15]Before he had finished praying, Rebekah came out with her jar on
her shoulder. She was the daughter of Bethuel son of Milkah, who was
the wife of Abraham's brother Nahor. [16]The woman was very beautiful,
a virgin; no man had ever slept with her. She went down to the spring,
filled her jar and came up again.
[17]The servant hurried to meet her and said, "Please give me a little
water from your jar."
[18]"Drink, my lord," she said, and quickly lowered the jar to her hands
and gave him a drink.
[19]After she had given him a drink, she said, "I'll draw water for
your camels too, until they have had enough to drink." [20]So she quickly
emptied her jar into the trough, ran back to the well to draw more water,
and drew enough for all his camels. [21]Without saying a word, the man
watched her closely to learn whether or not the LORD had made his
journey successful.
[22]When the camels had finished drinking, the man took out a gold
nose ring weighing a beka and two gold bracelets weighing ten shekels.
[23]Then he asked, "Whose daughter are you? Please tell me, is there room
in your father's house for us to spend the night?"
[24]She answered him, "I am the daughter of Bethuel, the son that
Milkah bore to Nahor." [25]And she added, "We have plenty of straw and
fodder, as well as room for you to spend the night."
[26]Then the man bowed down and worshiped the LORD, [27]saying,
"Praise be to the LORD, the God of my master Abraham, who has not
abandoned his kindness and faithfulness to my master. As for me, the
LORD has led me on the journey to the house of my master's relatives."
[28]The young woman ran and told her mother's household about these
things. [29]Now Rebekah had a brother named Laban, and he hurried out
to the man at the spring. [30]As soon as he had seen the nose ring, and
the bracelets on his sister's arms, and had heard Rebekah tell what the
man said to her, he went out to the man and found him standing by the
camels near the spring. [31]"Come, you who are blessed by the LORD," he
said. "Why are you standing out here? I have prepared the house and a
place for the camels."
[32]So the man went to the house, and the camels were unloaded. Straw
and fodder were brought for the camels, and water for him and his men
to wash their feet. [33]Then food was set before him, but he said, "I will not
eat until I have told you what I have to say."

"Then tell us," Laban said.

[34]So he said, "I am Abraham's servant. [35]The Lord has blessed my master abundantly, and he has become wealthy. He has given him sheep and cattle, silver and gold, male and female servants, and camels and donkeys. [36]My master's wife Sarah has borne him a son in her old age, and he has given him everything he owns. [37]And my master made me swear an oath, and said, 'You must not get a wife for my son from the daughters of the Canaanites, in whose land I live, [38]but go to my father's family and to my own clan, and get a wife for my son.'

[39]"Then I asked my master, 'What if the woman will not come back with me?'

[40]"He replied, 'The Lord, before whom I have walked faithfully, will send his angel with you and make your journey a success, so that you can get a wife for my son from my own clan and from my father's family. [41]You will be released from my oath if, when you go to my clan, they refuse to give her to you—then you will be released from my oath.'

[42]"When I came to the spring today, I said, 'Lord, God of my master Abraham, if you will, please grant success to the journey on which I have come. [43]See, I am standing beside this spring. If a young woman comes out to draw water and I say to her, "Please let me drink a little water from your jar," [44]and if she says to me, "Drink, and I'll draw water for your camels too," let her be the one the Lord has chosen for my master's son.'

[45]"Before I finished praying in my heart, Rebekah came out, with her jar on her shoulder. She went down to the spring and drew water, and I said to her, 'Please give me a drink.'

[46]"She quickly lowered her jar from her shoulder and said, 'Drink, and I'll water your camels too.' So I drank, and she watered the camels also.

[47]"I asked her, 'Whose daughter are you?'

"She said, 'The daughter of Bethuel son of Nahor, whom Milkah bore to him.'

"Then I put the ring in her nose and the bracelets on her arms, [48]and I bowed down and worshiped the Lord. I praised the Lord, the God of my master Abraham, who had led me on the right road to get the granddaughter of my master's brother for his son. [49]Now if you will show kindness and faithfulness to my master, tell me; and if not, tell me, so I may know which way to turn."

[50]Laban and Bethuel answered, "This is from the Lord; we can say nothing to you one way or the other. [51]Here is Rebekah; take her and go, and let her become the wife of your master's son, as the Lord has directed."

[52]When Abraham's servant heard what they said, he bowed down to
the ground before the LORD. [53]Then the servant brought out gold and
silver jewelry and articles of clothing and gave them to Rebekah; he also
gave costly gifts to her brother and to her mother. [54]Then he and the men
who were with him ate and drank and spent the night there.

When they got up the next morning, he said, "Send me on my way to my master."

[55]But her brother and her mother replied, "Let the young woman remain with us ten days or so; then you may go."

[56]But he said to them, "Do not detain me, now that the LORD has granted success to my journey. Send me on my way so I may go to my master."

[57]Then they said, "Let's call the young woman and ask her about it."
[58]So they called Rebekah and asked her, "Will you go with this man?"

"I will go," she said.

[59]So they sent their sister Rebekah on her way, along with her nurse
and Abraham's servant and his men. [60]And they blessed Rebekah and said
to her,

"Our sister, may you increase
to thousands upon thousands;
may your offspring possess
the cities of their enemies."

[61]Then Rebekah and her attendants got ready and mounted the camels and went back with the man. So the servant took Rebekah and left.

[62]Now Isaac had come from Beer Lahai Roi, for he was living in the
Negev. [63]He went out to the field one evening to meditate, and as he
looked up, he saw camels approaching. [64]Rebekah also looked up and saw
Isaac. She got down from her camel [65]and asked the servant, "Who is that
man in the field coming to meet us?"

"He is my master," the servant answered. So she took her veil and covered herself.

[66]Then the servant told Isaac all he had done. [67]Isaac brought her into
the tent of his mother Sarah, and he married Rebekah. So she became his
wife, and he loved her; and Isaac was comforted after his mother's death.

*Listening to the Text in the Story:* Biblical Text: Genesis 12:1–3

Isaac was God's fulfillment of the promise that Abraham and Sarah would have many descendants. At least it was a start. Of course, for the promises to continue into the future Abraham and Sarah would need grandchildren. That story begins with the account of Isaac's marriage to Rebekah.

### Abraham Commissions His Servant (24:1–9)

Genesis 24 takes place at an unspecified future time in the aging Abraham's life. We can perhaps speculate that it is in the not-too-distant future from the momentous events of Genesis 22–23 since we can assume that Isaac got married at a typical age for the time which would have been not too long after puberty. Fortunately, Abraham's age at the time does not really bear on the meaning of the story. The narrator adds the notice that God has blessed Abraham in every way, which of course brings us back once again to Genesis 12:1–3 and in particular the promise that God would bless Abraham and his descendants.

Of course, it has not been an easy road, but Abraham had his heir and a portion of land. Now his son would be married.

It was important to Abraham, and to the fulfillment of the promises, that his son not marry one of the Canaanites. Thus, the patriarch commissioned his "senior servant" to go to his ancestral homeland (in the region around Harran from which he descended to the promised land after the death of his father Terah) and to find a wife from among his own relatives.

Abraham's determination on this matter is indicated by making his servant so swear by placing his hand under his "thigh" when he took the oath. The "thigh" here is a euphemism for his genitals, which of course is the repository of his "seed," and thus a sacred part of the body. The oath is taken by the name of "the God of heaven and the God of earth" (v. 3), a name emphasizing the universality of Abraham's God. He is not simply the God of the promised land. Hughes points out that the significance of the gesture is connected to circumcision, which is the "sign of the covenant," which was borne by all the men of Abraham's family, including the servants (Gen 17:12). "The oath therefore invoked the power and presence of the Lord God Almighty who gave the covenant. The highly personal formalizing of this oath by his servant suggests that for Abraham the fulfillment of the vow was as important as life itself."[1]

The servant responds to Abraham's request by asking what will happen if the chosen woman refuses to come back, but wants to stay in her homeland.

1. Hughes, *Genesis*, 315.

Abraham insists that under no circumstances is Isaac to go there. He then reiterates the divine promise of land that God had made under oath to Abraham and had informed him that this promise would pass to his heir Isaac. He believes that God will prepare the way for the servant by sending his angel ahead of him, but in case the woman is unwilling, the servant can simply return to Abraham, released from his oath. Abraham thus expresses some measure of confidence that God, through his angel, will provide a spouse for Isaac, but the slight hint of uncertainty increases the narrative tension of the story. Will the servant successfully find Isaac a wife in Abraham's ancestral homeland? Under these conditions, the servant places his hand under Abraham's "thigh" and swears that he will find a wife for Isaac, not among the Canaanites but among their relatives who live in Aram Naharaim.

### The Servant Travels to Aram Naharaim (24:10 – 11)

Aram Naharaim is in the transitional zone between Mesopotamia and Syria (or as the NIV note puts it "northwest Mesopotamia"). Nahor is the name of Abraham's brother (Gen 11:27), who apparently gives his name to the town where the family resides. The servant went well provided with ten camels carrying goods from Abraham's household. These goods would not only provide for the caravan headed by the servant, but would also demonstrate to the family back home that Abraham had prospered in his new land.

The servant heads to the well upon arrival. This episode is not the only one in the Bible where a marriage relationship is initiated. Isaac and Rebekah's son Jacob will meet his future wife at a well (Gen 29:1 – 14), and Moses met his wife Zipporah at a well (Exod 2:15 – 25).

### Rebekah, an Answer to Prayer (24:12 – 27)

The servant prayerfully devises a test in order to identify an appropriate mate for Isaac. Moberly, comparing this test to the one Joseph applies to his brothers (will they sacrifice Benjamin to save themselves? Gen 44), points out that the servant is not requesting some kind of prophetic sign from God, but rather setting up a test of character. "The girl who comes to the well to draw water must not only offer him a drink (i.e., be hospitable) but also offer to water his camels (i.e., be self-sacrificially generous with her time and energy)."[2] As Levenson puts it, the unnamed emissary and God intend "to ensure that the girl that is found is also ethically suitable to marry into the family of the generous and hospitable patriarch."[3]

---

2. Moberly, *The Theology of the Book of Genesis*, 241.
3. Levenson, *Inheriting Abraham*, 88.

God's answer is immediate since the text indicates that Rebekah approached the well to retrieve water even before the prayer ended (v. 15). The narrator then presents Rebekah's background information, beginning with her family connections. She is the "daughter of Bethuel son of Milkah, who was the wife of Abraham's brother Nahor" (v. 15b, see the family genealogy at 22:20–24, which anticipated this meeting). Thus, Rebekah is Abraham's grandniece and a cousin to Isaac, a perfect match for what Abraham was looking for. Besides her genealogy, the narrator adds that she was beautiful and a virgin. Indeed, the latter is stated twice since it is an important matter especially for someone who is going to give birth to a child who will inherit the promises.

Rebekah not only passes the test that the servant set for choosing a wife for Isaac, she surpassed all expectations. Upon request, she not only gives him a drink but does so "quickly" (v. 18). He does not even have to ask about the camels, she volunteers to give them water. She "quickly" emptied her jar into the trough, and then "ran" (v. 20) back to the well to get even more water so they could drink until they were fully sated.

During this whole process, the servant wordlessly watches "to see if the LORD had made his journey successful" (v. 21). Apparently he wanted to make "the test as searching as possible. Rebekah must not only show willingness, but she must also stay with it to the end; if she gives up halfway 'I've had it with these camels, I'm going home!'), she is not the one."[4] His hesitation may also be related to the fact that he is not yet sure exactly who she is and to whom she is related.

But she is the one; she completes the task with alacrity. So the servant bestows gifts of a nose ring weighing a beka (one fifth of an ounce) and two gold bracelets weighing ten shekels (four ounces), which may be seen as the down payment on the marriage price.[5] Afterward he asks after her family, and whether they will extend hospitality to him and his fellow travelers. She tells him what the narrator has already told the reader that she is the daughter of Bethuel and the granddaughter of Nahor and Milkah. She also assures him that they have plenty of space and provisions to extend hospitality to them.

Now the servant is fully certain that God has answered his prayers, so he praises God for bringing him to this place so he can fulfill the task that Abraham gave him. God has shown his "kindness" and "faithfulness" (v. 27) to Abraham. These two words are closely connected to the covenant and communicate that God is following through on his promises to the patriarch.

4. Ibid.

5. Walton, "Genesis," 102.

**Negotiations with Laban (24:28–61)**

Rebekah again demonstrates her energy and excitement in the service of hospitality and runs to tell her "mother's household." The first family member to respond is Laban, who will become a major figure in the following chapters. Our first impressions, guided by the narrator's description, anticipate a cunning, greedy, opportunistic young man. His excitement is generated by the gifts that the servant has given to his sister. Even so, his involvement is not inappropriate since it was the custom of the day for brothers to be involved in marriage negotiations (see Gen 34:11–17; Song 8:8–12). And he does greet the servant warmly, urging him to receive the hospitality of his household.

Once the unnamed servant and his entourage reach the household of Bethuel, they are treated according to the highest standards of ancient hospitality. The camels were unloaded and fed, and water was brought so that the men could wash their feet, dusty from their travel.

They also brought them food to eat, but the servant will not think of eating until he has discharged the duty he swore to Abraham that he would accomplish. That duty, of course, was to secure a bride for Isaac from this household. Though it seems clear that Rebekah is the right woman, it is not yet clear that she or her family will consent to the union.

At this point, he informs Bethuel and Laban (v. 50), Rebekah's father and brother of Abraham's hope to find a wife for Isaac among their family. Laban is involved in the negotiations, as is typical for a brother in this ancient setting, and thus he is the one who encourages the servant to speak. He tells them of Abraham's wealth and the fact that he and Sarah had given birth to a son in their old age. Abraham, he says, does not want a wife for his son from among the daughters of the Canaanites, but rather from his own family. He also informs Bethuel and Laban that Abraham would release him from his oath if "they [the clan of the woman] refuse to give her to you" (v. 41).

The servant continues by telling the story of his meeting with Rebekah at the well. He had prayed to God and set up a test, which Rebekah passed admirably. He then turns to Bethuel and Laban for a decision, "if you will show kindness and faithfulness [see above for these terms] to my master, tell me; and if not, tell me, so I may know which way to turn" (v. 49).

The fact that Laban is mentioned before Bethuel in verse 50 may indicate that he is the moving force in the decision about which there is no doubt. They wholeheartedly agree and believe that "this is from the Lord." Who are they to stand in the way? Besides that, they will marry off their sister/daughter to a very rich and successful man.

Abraham's servant knows that it is God whom he should thank and does so. Afterward, he bestowed gifts on Rebekah (perhaps to be seen as the remainder of the marriage price, see v. 22), her brother Laban, and her mother. Now that this essential business had been dealt with, they all ate together and then they spent the night.

Now that the deal had been struck, the servant is anxious to return to Abraham, but Laban and his mother wanted to delay the departure. We are not certain why they were concerned to delay their return for a significant period of time ("ten days or so," v. 55). Certainly there is no reason to think that they were not in favor of the union, a motive that can be read into the concubine's father's attempt to delay the departure of his daughter with the abusive Levite in Judges 19. Perhaps they would sincerely miss her or worried that she would not be ready to leave her home.

If the latter were the case, Rebekah herself puts their worries to rest by saying, "I will go," in verse 58. Thus, Rebekah's family sent her off with a blessing that her offspring would be numerous and that they would overpower their enemies. Perhaps we should read this blessing with the knowledge that later Israel would grapple with the Aramean descendants of Bethuel and Laban during the period of kingship (1 Sam 14:47 ["the kings of Zobah]; 2 Sam 8:3–8; 10–12; 1 Kgs 15:16–22; 22:1–38, etc.).

### Isaac Meets Rebekah (24:62–67)

Upon their return to the region in the Negev where Abraham and Isaac were living, Isaac and Rebekah meet for the first time. He is out in the field when she arrives, and according to the NIV translation he is "meditating" (v. 63). However, as the NIV note makes clear, we are not certain this is the correct understanding of the difficult verb and so there are some who think he is not meditating or praying, but rather he is grieving his departed mother. Unfortunately, we cannot be certain.[6]

When she is informed as to the identity of Isaac, she covered herself up, demonstrating her modesty. Isaac took her then into the tent of his now deceased mother Sarah, a location indicating that they there consummated their relationship. While an arranged marriage, the text makes it clear that Isaac loved her and found comfort in their relationship after the loss of his mother.

### Marrying the Right Person

Abraham is very concerned that his son, Isaac, marry the "right" woman. For him, the "right" woman is not a Canaanite. Canaanites, after all, did

6. For the details of the difference of opinion, see Mathews, *Genesis 11:27–50:26*, 347.

not worship his God, but others like Baal and Asherah.[7] It was Abraham's descendants who were to receive the promised land, not the Canaanites, who would be judged once their sin "reached its full measure" (Gen 15:16). Thus, Abraham sent his servant back to northwest Mesopotamia to find a proper wife for Isaac, and we have just read the successful story of the encounter with Rebekah.

The story of Isaac and Rebekah is not the last account of patriarchs' children finding wives. Indeed, in the next generation we will observe a dramatic contrast between Isaac's two sons, Esau and Jacob. Indeed, it is Esau's marriage to Hittite women who disgust Rebekah (Gen 27:46) that motivates her to instruct Isaac to send Jacob back to northwest Mesopotamia to find a wife for himself. Later, Esau will try to rectify his mistake by marrying close relatives descended from Ishmael (28:6–9). Indeed, as we read through the remaining stories of the book of Genesis we will encounter a number of texts that deal in one way or another with the marriages of those in the chosen line descended from Abraham.

It would be a mistake to think of this as a matter of ethnic purity rather than one of proper worship of the true God and character. We have seen that the servant of Abraham was not just interested in any woman in the family, but one who had the proper character as revealed by the test that he devised in order to discover the right woman.

As time goes on, there will be examples of non-Israelite women who marry men who are important to the story of redemption. We think here of Rahab and Ruth as prime instances. It is hard to determine if Bathsheba is herself a Hittite, but her first husband, Uriah, certainly was. These foreigners who marry into the redemptive line are mentioned in the Bible because of their importance to the history of redemption, leading to the presumption that there were many, many more that aren't mentioned. When Ezra and Nehemiah later challenge Jewish men who have divorced their Jewish wives and remarried foreign women, they do so not because they are foreign, but because they do not share the worship of Yahweh. Thus, they worry that they commit the same sin as Solomon who married many foreign women and whose love for them led him to worship those same false gods (1 Kgs 11:1–13).

Can we learn anything about marriage from Genesis 24 and the other accounts of marriage in Genesis? We must be very careful here as always that we don't simply assume continuity between the ancient Old Testament world and our own. After all, for instance, the culture of marriage has changed from a patriarchal, semi-nomadic clan setting to a modern urban environment.

---

7. With exceptions, like Melchizedek (see Gen 14:18–20).

We should not assume that, to put it somewhat technically, mate-selection and marriage customs will remain the same. Indeed, it is not strictly the same even in the patriarchal custom of Genesis. While Abraham sends his servant to find a wife for Isaac, Isaac will send his son Jacob to the same location to find a wife for himself. And certainly there is not a single biblical pattern for finding a spouse and marriage through the entirety of the Bible. While at times it appears that parents chose their children's spouses, the Song of Songs testifies to a time when it was romantic desire that brought a couple together.

Enough has been said here to undermine the attempt to find a biblical blueprint for choosing a spouse. There is nothing inherently unbiblical, and much to appreciate, about internet dating services like E-Harmony. One doesn't have to go to a well of water to be biblical in their finding a mate.

But if we can't learn about how to pick a spouse, can we learn something about the type of spouse we should pick? I believe we can if we look at the underlying purpose of Abraham's strategy here. He wants his son to marry someone who shares his most fundamental values, thus he sends his servant out of Canaan to his homeland to find a godly woman who is a woman of character.

What is important after all? If we may cite a later text that we believe is not foreign to Abraham's thinking here: "Charm is deceptive, and beauty is fleeting; but a woman who fears the Lord is to be praised" (Prov 31:30). The Song of Songs tells us that beauty has its place, but the sages put it in the right, secondary, place. The one crucial characteristic in a spouse is the proper attitude toward God (see Ps 112:1 for a similar point about a man).

With this background, we should listen to the apostle Paul in 2 Corinthians 6:14–18:

> Do not be yoked together with unbelievers. For what do righteousness and wickedness have in common? Or what fellowship can light have with darkness? What harmony is there between Christ and Belial? Or what does a believer have in common with an unbeliever? What agreement is there between the temple of God and idols? For we are the temple of the living God. As God has said:
>
> "I will live among them
> and walk among them,
> and I will be their God,
> and they will be my people."
> Therefore,
> "Come out from them
> and be separate,
> says the Lord.

> Touch no unclean thing,
> and I will receive you."
> And,
> "I will be a Father to you,
> and you will be my sons and daughters,
> says the Lord Almighty."

Granted, this passage is not specifically about marriage, but considering there is no more intimate human relationship than marriage, it would be unimaginable that Paul would not have been including marriage in his warning. After all, even common sense makes it clear that if a couple does not share the most important, basic, life-shaping relationship (that with God) in common, that true intimacy becomes very difficult. If one's relationship with God is central to their life, then sharing that with the person who is the most important in their life would be crucial. If the decisions in life are to be made with God at the center, then that becomes difficult if the person with whom one is making decisions does not acknowledge God. At best the unbelieving spouse will be tolerant or respectful or perhaps just choose to treat it as a separate part of their believing spouse's life.

Thus, read in the context of the whole Bible, Genesis 24 can be an encouragement to people who are not yet married to choose the "right," that is, godly, spouse. To those who are already married to an unbeliever, Paul gives hope when he says the unbelieving spouse is "sanctified" through the believing spouse and that the believing spouse should stay with their spouse unless the latter leaves the relationship (1 Cor 7:12–16). While, according to Blomberg, verse 16 makes clear that this does not mean the unbeliever is saved, it does point to the "spin-off blessings for the non-Christian spouse and children that come from having even one member of the family follow the Lord."[8]

**Our Divine Spouse**

Genesis 24 is a sweet, relatively untroubled, story of the meeting and wedding of Isaac and Rebekah. Abraham does not try to hasten matters but trusts God as he sends his household servant to northwest Mesopotamia to find a bride for Isaac. That God brings Rebekah to Isaac as wife is shown clearly when Rebekah conforms to the character test that the servant poses prayerfully to God. Indeed, as Hughes points out, "it is reasonable to conclude that Rebekah had left her house before the servant had begun to pray. Therefore we are meant to see that the providence was all of God."[9] Not even Laban,

---

8. C. Blomberg, *1 Corinthians*, NIVAC (Grand Rapids: Zondervan, 1994), 135.
9. Hughes, *Genesis*, 318.

whom we will soon see is typically self-serving, gets in the way. The servant faithfully takes Rebekah back to Isaac where they are married. The story ends well: "So she became his wife, and he loved her; and Isaac was comforted after his mother's death" (24:67).

This idyllic story will contrast with the other tumultuous wedding in the book of Genesis, namely, Jacob's to Leah, thinking his bride was Rachel (29:14–30). As such, it is a picture of a marriage as it was meant to be ("That is why a man leaves his father and mother and is united to his wife, and they become one flesh," 2:24). Granted, the story of Isaac and Rebekah's relationship does not end here, and there will be plenty of times when their marriage will reflect the consequences of the fall ("Your desire [to control] will be for your husband, and he will rule over you," 3:16b), but the end of Genesis 24 allows us to reflect a moment on marriage as it was supposed to be: a reflection of our intimate relationship with God and from a Christian perspective of our relationship with Christ.

We have already seen that marriage is a pervasive image used to describe our intimate, passionate, and exclusive relationship with Christ back in Genesis 2 (see Christ: "A Profound Mystery") and will not rehearse that material here but refer back to it. Instead, we turn to John 4 and the account of Jesus meeting the woman at the well.

As we mentioned above in Explain the Story, this story is the first of three occasions in the Old Testament when a man (the servant—a surrogate for Isaac, Jacob, Moses) meets a woman (Rebekah, Rachel, Zipporah) that serves as a precursor to marriage. This background would not have been lost on the disciples (as well as the readers of the Gospels) when they see Jesus talking to a woman at a well. Indeed, the memory of Jacob would have been stirred since the well is one associated with the life of that patriarch in a town called Sychar in Samaria.

No wonder the disciples were "surprised to find him talking with a woman" (John 4:27). The setting at the well suggests that this meeting might lead to a more intimate relationship than modern readers might imagine. And he was inviting her to an intimate relationship, not a marriage or sexual relationship, but something much more significant, a relationship with God himself. Indeed (and here we are reflecting on our earlier study after Gen 2), Jesus invites all of us to a spiritual marriage with him, one that will culminate in the "marriage supper of the Lamb" (Rev 19:1–10).

See related essay: The Angel Who Saves (after Gen 16).

CHAPTER 23

# Genesis 25:1–11

## LISTEN to the Story

[25:1]Abraham had taken another wife, whose name was Keturah. [2]She bore him Zimran, Jokshan, Medan, Midian, Ishbak and Shuah. [3]Jokshan was the father of Sheba and Dedan; the descendants of Dedan were the Ashurites, the Letushites and the Leummites. [4]The sons of Midian were Ephah, Epher, Hanok, Abida and Eldaah. All these were descendants of Keturah.

[5]Abraham left everything he owned to Isaac. [6]But while he was still living, he gave gifts to the sons of his concubines and sent them away from his son Isaac to the land of the east.

[7]Abraham lived a hundred and seventy-five years. [8]Then Abraham breathed his last and died at a good old age, an old man and full of years; and he was gathered to his people. [9]His sons Isaac and Ishmael buried him in the cave of Machpelah near Mamre, in the field of Ephron son of Zohar the Hittite, [10]the field Abraham had bought from the Hittites. There Abraham was buried with his wife Sarah. [11]After Abraham's death, God blessed his son Isaac, who then lived near Beer Lahai Roi.

*Listening to the Text in the Story:* Biblical Texts: Genesis 12:1–3; 17:3–8; 23

God had initially promised Abraham that his disciples would become a "great nation" (12:2) and so the emphasis in the Abraham narrative has been on the birth of Isaac. However, when God came to reassure Abraham of his intentions to fulfill this promise the second time, he told him "I will make you very fruitful; I will make nations of you, and kings will come from you" (17:6). The descendants of Ishmael the son of his concubine Hagar comes into view at this point, but so, as we will see, do the sons of his other concubine Keturah.

The final paragraph of our passage refers back to Genesis 23, where we read the account of Abraham's purchase of the burial cave from Ephron. As we noted there, besides providing a burial place for Sarah, this story also informs the reader that at this time Abraham came into possession of a small piece of the promised land in fulfillment of the promise of land implicit in God's statement that Abraham's descendants would become a "great nation" (12:2). Just as the birth of Isaac is the first of many Abrahamic descendants, so the purchase of the cave is the earnest on the fulfillment of the land.

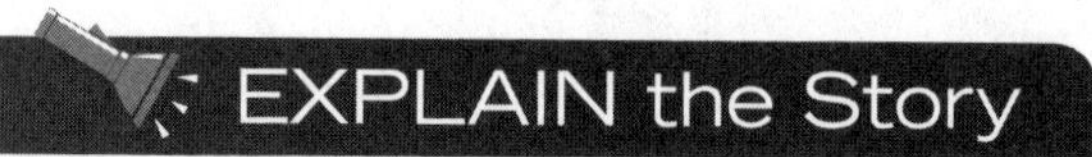


### Abraham and Keturah (25:1–4)

We now come to the end of the *toledot* of Terah (11:27–25:11) before proceeding to the short *toledot* of Ishmael (25:12–18) and the longer *toledot* of Isaac (25:19–35:29). Preceding an account of his death, we learn that Abraham had another wife in his old age, a woman named Keturah. The significance of the notification of this wife is connected to the fact that their offspring were the patronyms of many other nations. In Genesis 17, God had promised Abraham that Sarah would be "the mother of nations; kings of peoples will come from her" (17:16). The nations that derive from Abraham and Keturah (see also 1 Chr 1:32–33 for a shorter list, note that Keturah here is called "the concubine of Abraham") are not connected to that promise, but perhaps we are to understand God as surpassing even the marvelous promise given at that earlier point in his life.

We can only speculate about Zimran, but Jokshan fathered two sons, who were the ancestors of the Sabeans and the Dedanites (though the connection between this Semitic Dedan and the descendant of Ham in Gen 10:7 is unclear, see Jer 25:23–24; 49:8; Ezek 25:13; 27:20). The descendants of Dedan are said to be the Ashurites, maybe the Assyrians but more likely a smaller tribe, the Letushites, and the Leummites, about which nothing further is known.

Midian, the fourth listed son of Abraham and Keturah is the patronym of the Midianites, a nomadic people who wandered in the Sinai Peninsula and the western wilderness of the Arabian peninsula. His children are considered to be clan heads of the Midianites (see Isa 60:6, which mentions Ephah with Midian [and Sheba]).

### Abraham's Inheritance (25:5–6)

Abraham demonstrated his care and love for these children by giving them gifts while he was still alive. But, as with Ishmael, he sent them away while he was still alive. In particular he sent them to the east (of the promised land) where the nations that will descend from them took root.

Though Abraham had many children, Isaac was the child that would inherit the promise. Thus, the narrative goes to pains to indicate that Isaac was the one who inherited Abraham's wealth upon his death (vv. 5 – 6).

### Abraham's Death and Burial (25:7 – 11)

Verses 7 – 11 give us a short account of the death of Abraham, which brings the *toledot* of Terah to a close. He lived until he was one hundred and seventy-five years, an advanced age that shows the blessing of God. Indeed, Abraham's age surpasses the limit set by God at the time of the flood (Gen 6:3). He not only lived a long life, but a full one. Of course, his long, full life was at times not at all easy, but this death notice gives us the impression that at the end of it all, it was a satisfying life.

He was buried with Sarah at the site that he purchased from Ephron the Hittite (Gen 23), which is in the cave of Machpelah near Mamre, a place where Abraham lived for a period of time early in his sojourn in the promised land (Gen 13:18; 14:13; 18:1). It is particularly interesting and touching to see that Ishmael joined Isaac at the burial site to see their father off. The last we had seen of Ishmael was when Abraham had sent him away along with his mother Hagar (Gen 21:8 – 21). At that time, we learned that they survived the wilderness trek and had settled in the Desert of Paran. He had married. We should be careful not to read too much into the mention of Ishmael, but his presence does seem to indicate some kind of relationship between the two brothers; otherwise, how could he have known of his father's death? The mention of Ishmael also prepares us for the first episode after the narration of the patriarch's death, namely the *toledot* of Ishmael.

### Ending Well

Abraham lived a long and tumultuous life. The narrative of the previous chapters began when he was already seventy-five years old (12:24). He died when he was one hundred and seventy-five years old, though most of the stories about Abraham focus on the time period between coming to the promised land and the birth of Isaac (when he was one hundred). The story of the binding of Isaac (Akedah; Gen 22) and the choice of Isaac's bride (Gen 24) take place after this, so much happened that the biblical author chooses not to mention.

That said, the depiction of Abraham's life is such that we can say that he ended his life well. We have seen how during much of his life he struggled in his relationship with God and often responded with fear and manipulation when confronted with obstacles to the fulfillment of the promises. But after the birth of Isaac, he demonstrates a steady confidence in his God. Indeed, in spite of his earlier faults, God will later tell Isaac that his father "obeyed me and did everything I required of him, keeping my commands, my decrees and my instructions" (26:5). When the New Testament looks back on Abraham, it does not see the problems of his character or life, but rather it sees a man of faith (Heb. 11:8–12, 17–19). This depiction is not a distortion, but an assessment made through the lens of how he ended his life.

The account of the end of Abraham's life is an inspiration to all, but perhaps particularly to those of us who are over sixty. Short of unexpected medical breakthroughs, none of us will live as long as Abraham, but it is possible that these days we might make it to seventy, eighty, ninety, maybe even a hundred years. We do not know when we will die, and the question all of us want to ask ourselves is, how will we end this life? Will we live lives of fear, doubt, withdrawal, and caution? Or will we, no matter what our age or even our physical ability, live our lives with confident faith, seeking to impact our world for Christ? Truth be told, all of us, no matter what our age, should live our lives anticipating our reception by God and striving for the greeting, "Well done, good and faithful servant! You have been faithful with a few things; I will put you in charge of many things. Come and share your master's happiness!" (Matt 25:21).

CHAPTER 24

# Genesis 25:12–18

## LISTEN to the Story

25:12This is the account of the family line of Abraham's son Ishmael,
whom Sarah's slave, Hagar the Egyptian, bore to Abraham.
13These are the names of the sons of Ishmael, listed in the order of
their birth: Nebaioth the firstborn of Ishmael, Kedar, Adbeel, Mibsam,
14Mishma, Dumah, Massa, 15Hadad, Tema, Jetur, Naphish and Kedemah.
16These were the sons of Ishmael, and these are the names of the twelve
tribal rulers according to their settlements and camps. 17Ishmael lived a
hundred and thirty-seven years. He breathed his last and died, and he was
gathered to his people. 18His descendants settled in the area from Havilah
to Shur, near the eastern border of Egypt, as you go toward Ashur. And
they lived in hostility toward all the tribes related to them.

*Listening to the Text in the Story:* Biblical Texts: Genesis 12:1–3; 16; 17:6; 21:8–21

We now come to the *toledot* of Ishmael, the first son of Abraham with his concubine Hagar (Gen 16). The preceding passage included a paragraph (25:1–4) in which Abraham's nonelect offspring through Keturah are named. Ishmael and his offspring occupy the same relationship to the covenant, but Ishmael is a more prominent character being featured as a potential rival to Isaac's place as heir. Still, like with Keturah's offspring, Ishmael and his descendants were also a fulfillment of God's promise to Abraham: "I will make many nations of you, and kings will come from you."

## EXPLAIN the Story

Genesis 25:12 introduces the short *toledot* ("account") of Ishmael by explaining that he is the son of Abraham through Hagar the Egyptian. As the previous narrative has made abundantly clear, he is not the one through whom the covenant promise would continue from Abraham to the following generations. Even so, the narrative does not simply drop interest in Ishmael. Indeed, the narrator treats the nonelect son Ishmael before turning attention to the elect son Isaac, a pattern that we will also see with Esau and Jacob. At her moment of desperation in the desert after having been turned out by Abraham and Sarah, God had assured Hagar that he would "make him into a great nation" (21:18). Indeed, as Kaminsky has pointed out "the non-chosen sibling (in this case Ishmael) is not necessarily excluded from all divine favor. Ishmael, while not the chosen child and thus excluded from the covenant, does receive some of the elements of the original Abrahamic promise in Gen 12: being blessed, being fruitful, and becoming a great nation."[1]

The *toledot* then lists his twelve sons, who are said to be "the twelve tribal rulers according to their settlements and camps" (v. 16). Thus, God's promise is coming into fulfillment. They are a nomadic people, who, according to verse 18, "settled in the area from Havilah to Shur, near the eastern border of Egypt as you go toward Ashur" (v. 18). We have already seen (16:7) that Shur is connected to the Sinai Peninsula, while most think that Havilah here indicates the Arabian peninsula. Of course, Ashur is in northern Mesopotamia. The geographical region is rather large and not precisely defined, which is in keeping with the nomadic nature of the Ishmaelites. In Genesis 37:25–28, we will see that they engage in trade. The final notification is that they were hostile with unspecified tribes that were related to them. This hostility was anticipated by the divine oracle given to Hagar when Ishmael was very young,

> He will be a wild donkey of a man;
> his hand will be against everyone
> and everyone's hand against him,
> and he will live in hostility
> toward all his brothers. (Gen 16:12)

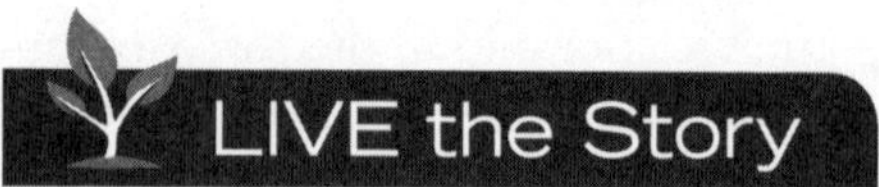


### A Promise for All Nations

This short *toledot* of Ishmael (as well as the longer, but still relatively short *toledot* of Esau [Gen 36]) sends an important and powerful message concerning the status of the non-chosen in the book of Genesis. Ishmael may not be the one through whom the promise descends, but nonetheless he is a beneficiary of the covenant promises as are, at least potentially, all the nations of

1. J. S. Kaminsky, *Yet I Loved Jacob: Reclaiming the Biblical Concept of Election* (Nashville: Abingdon, 2007), 41.

the world (12:3, "all peoples on earth will be blessed through you"). Again, we must constantly keep in mind that not only will Abraham and his descendants receive God's blessing, but through them so will the nations. God is far from hostile or even indifferent to the non-chosen; he deeply cares for all the nations of the world.

However, it is possible, to use Joel Kaminsky's categories, that the nonelect become the antielect if they set themselves against God and his chosen people. After all, God not only announces to Abraham that he will "bless those who bless you," but also he will "curse those who curse you" (12:3).

When Christians read Genesis 12:3 (see also 17:4–6; 22:18; 26:4; 28:14), they think of the inclusion of the Gentiles ("nations") into the new covenant after the coming of Jesus, and rightly so. The New Testament authors understand that Gentile participation in the covenant is a fulfillment of Old Testament prophetic expectations (see, for instance, Isa 2:2–5; 49:22–23; 51:4–5; 60:3–16; 66:12–13; Mic 4:1–5; 7:12–15; Zech 14:16–21) that are ultimately derived from Genesis 12:3 (see Rom 3:21–4:25; 8:1–17; 9:30–10:17; 11:13–32; Gal 2:11–4:7; Eph 2:11–22; 3:4–6).

Gentile Christians today should realize that we are not afterthoughts in God's plan of redemption. Gentiles who aligned themselves with Yahweh, observed the law, and identified with Israel could participate in the covenant during the Old Testament period (Rahab; Ruth; Shamgar; Uriah; Naaman). But once Jesus came, rather than Gentiles coming to Israel, the disciples are sent out to "make disciples of all nations" (Matt 28:19).

CHAPTER 25

# Genesis 25:19 – 34

## LISTEN to the Story

25:19This is the account of the family line of Abraham's son Isaac.
Abraham became the father of Isaac, 20and Isaac was forty years old
when he married Rebekah daughter of Bethuel the Aramean from Paddan
Aram and sister of Laban the Aramean.

21Isaac prayed to the LORD on behalf of his wife, because she was
childless. The LORD answered his prayer, and his wife Rebekah became
pregnant. 22The babies jostled each other within her, and she said, "Why
is this happening to me?" So she went to inquire of the LORD.

23The LORD said to her,

"Two nations are in your womb,
and two peoples from within you will be separated;
one people will be stronger than the other,
and the older will serve the younger."

24When the time came for her to give birth, there were twin boys in
her womb. 25The first to come out was red, and his whole body was like
a hairy garment; so they named him Esau. 26After this, his brother came
out, with his hand grasping Esau's heel; so he was named Jacob. Isaac was
sixty years old when Rebekah gave birth to them.

27The boys grew up, and Esau became a skillful hunter, a man of the
open country, while Jacob was content to stay at home among the tents.
28Isaac, who had a taste for wild game, loved Esau, but Rebekah loved
Jacob.

29Once when Jacob was cooking some stew, Esau came in from the
open country, famished. 30He said to Jacob, "Quick, let me have some of
that red stew! I'm famished!" (That is why he was also called Edom.)

31Jacob replied, "First sell me your birthright."

32"Look, I am about to die," Esau said. "What good is the birthright
to me?"

33But Jacob said, "Swear to me first." So he swore an oath to him,
selling his birthright to Jacob.

[34]Then Jacob gave Esau some bread and some lentil stew. He ate and drank, and then got up and left.

So Esau despised his birthright.

*Listening to the Text in the Story:* Biblical Text: Genesis 12:1–3

Genesis 12:1–3 continues to exert its influence on the narrative as we come to the story of the transition from the second to the third generation after the promises were given to Abraham. Who will be the chosen son who will be the non-chosen son of Isaac and Rebekah?

## EXPLAIN the Story

### The Birth of Jacob and Esau (25:19–26)

Genesis 25:19 announces the *toledot* ("account") of Isaac, the son through whom the covenantal promises given to Abraham in Genesis 12:1–3 will flow to future generations. Thus, his *toledot* is considerably longer than that of Ishmael. Even so, Isaac is a rather undeveloped character in Genesis with very few distinctive stories that focus on him. The narrative rather focuses on his children, particularly Jacob, but also Esau. This is not unusual for *toledot*; they tend to focus on the children, but it does highlight the absence of a *toledot* of Abraham that would have focused on Isaac, thus giving the sense that Isaac is something of a transitional figure whose story is of secondary interest in comparison with his father and his son.

The *toledot* of Isaac thus begins by telling the story of the birth of his two children, Esau and Jacob. The manner of the birth of the twins anticipates later relationships and developments of the plot.

The birth story starts by reminding us of the previous narrative. Abraham was Isaac's father and he married Rebekah, the daughter of Bethuel and the sister of Laban (Gen 24). We learn that Rebekah, like her mother-in-law, was childless. Her condition moves Isaac to prayer, and she became pregnant (see below on the Power of Relentless Prayer). As we noted in regard to Sarah's inability to have a child, God opening the womb of the matriarch there and here indicates that the offspring are important for God's purposes with humanity. In other words, the offspring are God's gift, brought into the world by his action in opening up their wombs.

Our first anticipation of the future comes when Rebekah turns to God because the children appeared to be fighting even within the womb. In response to her question why this was happening to her, God delivered an important oracle:

> Two nations are in your womb,
> and two peoples from within you will be separated;
> one people will be stronger than the other,
> and the older will serve the younger. (25:23)

Thus, Rebekah is apprised from the start that her children will both be the fathers of future nations, but of unequal strength. And, contrary to custom of the day, it will be the older who will serve the younger.[1] Thus, it has great significance which of the two would emerge first from the womb.

Sure enough, there were twins in her womb, and the fight seemed to continue from the womb through the birth canal and into the world. Baby Jacob was grabbing baby Esau's heel as he followed him out of the womb as if he was trying to pull him back in and take precedence. Rebekah who had heard the divine oracle, though, would know that God would give precedence not to the elder but to the younger one.

The parents gave them names that described them at birth. Esau was so hairy that it was almost as if he was wearing a hair coat, so they named him Esau, which means "hairy." Jacob, as we commented was grabbing Esau's heel, thus they named him Jacob or "he grasps the heel." The latter, as the NIV note points out, has a further idiomatic meaning of "he deceives." While it is doubtful that that meaning was intended by the parents, as the story goes on, we will see that it aptly fits Jacob's character. Isaac was sixty years old at the time of the birth. While not as old as Abraham at the time of his birth, he is still up there in age for a first time father. It will not be long before Rebekah and Jacob take advantage of his old age.

### Esau Sells His Birthright (25:27–34)

The story does not dwell on the boys' youth, but turns immediately in verse 27 and following to a significant moment in their adolescence or young

---

1. Some scholars (Anderson, *Jacob and the Divine Trickster*, 50–51) want to suggest a different translation than "the older will serve the younger." While it is true that the expression could be rendered "the greater will serve the lesser," thus adding an element of ambiguity to the oracle, it is clear from Rebekah's actions and later developments that the NIV translation is the best. If Anderson is correct, then one wonders why the birth account puts such emphasis on birth order. See also Kaminsky, *Yet I Loved Jacob*, 44.

adulthood. Esau is an outdoorsman, while Jacob is a stay-at-home young man.[2] Indeed, Esau's hairy body and his love of the field have invited comparison with Enkidu, the primeval man in the Gilgamesh epic.[3] Esau is a hunter and is preferred by his father, while Jacob prefers the company of his mother and likes to cook.

One day when Esau returned from hunting, he entered the tent to find his brother cooking some red stew. He asked his brother for some stew since he was famished. Alter suggests that the word Esau uses for eating (the *hiphil* of *l't*) is used only for animals (though he does not indicate that this is in rabbinic Hebrew, since this is the only clear use of the verb in the Bible), and suggests rendering "let me cram my maw."[4] But before Jacob will give him anything, he sets a condition that Esau sell him his birthright.

Esau was the firstborn son and thus by custom of the day would inherit the lions' share of his father's property. Jacob is asking him to trade this birthright for a pot of lentil stew, and Esau swears to do so.

The trade is quite disproportionate since it is extremely unlikely that Esau would actually have died of starvation ("Look, I am about to die" is a dramatic exaggeration). The story thus characterizes Esau as someone who cares about the present more than the future. It also marks him as a person who is interested in sensual things, not spiritual things. We will see that this characterization continues in future episodes of the *toledot* of Isaac.

This story also gives Esau a second name, Edom, which means "red," after the color of the lentil soup that he consumed in exchange for his birthright. Later readers would immediately know that this announces Esau's connection to the later Edomites, a people who lived to the east of Israel across the Jordan River, south of Moab to the southeast of the Dead Sea. There would be conflict between Edom and Israel at a number of points in later history (Num 20:14–21; 2 Sam 8:14; 1 Kgs 22:47; 2 Kgs 8:20). At the time of the Babylonian destruction of Jerusalem, Edom had taken advantage of the situation in some way. While not precisely described, this point can be established by reference to texts like Psalm 137:7; Lamentations 4:22; Ezekiel 35:15; Obadiah 10–14.

2. The description of Jacob as "content" (*tam*) to stay at home (v. 27) is a word that often has moral significance ("blameless"). Noah and Abraham are described as *tam* in its moral sense (Gen 6:9 and 17:1 respectively). Of course, the difficulty of describing Jacob as *tam* in the moral sense is that he is clearly a deceiver. This leads some to suggest that his deception should not be negatively evaluated. While deception is not always evil (Michael Williams, *Deception in Genesis* [New York: Peter Lang, 2001]), it is hard to make that case with Jacob, as we will see.

3. Speiser, *Genesis*, 196, and, more recently, Anderson, *Jacob and the Divine Trickster*, 65.

4. Alter, *The Art of Biblical Narrative*, 59.

The story also serves to introduce us to Jacob's character. He is a manipulator and, while thinking of the future, does so in order to gain advantage for himself.

So Esau sold his birthright to his brother for "some bread and some lentil stew" (v. 34). The exact significance of this sale is not clear. It does not appear to have any kind of legal force, since later Rebekah and Jacob must deceive Isaac for Jacob to get the blessing that Isaac intended for his older son. This story probably sets up that later story through its characterizations of Jacob and especially Esau. The thought that the storyteller wants us to leave the episode with is the idea expressed in the final verse of the chapter, that "Esau despised his birthright." Alter gets it right when he says that this scene indicates that "Esau ... is not spiritually fit to be the vehicle of divine election, the bearer of the birthright of Abraham's seed. He is too much the slave of the moment and of the body's tyranny to become the progenitor of the people promised by divine covenant to have a vast historical destiny to fulfill."[5] In contrast, Jacob shows himself interested in the future, though the calculating way he seeks to secure the future does not commend himself as a person to the reader. Still, when Jacob tricks Isaac into blessing him, the reader has lost sympathy for Esau, a shortsighted person who seems more interested in his stomach than in the birthright.

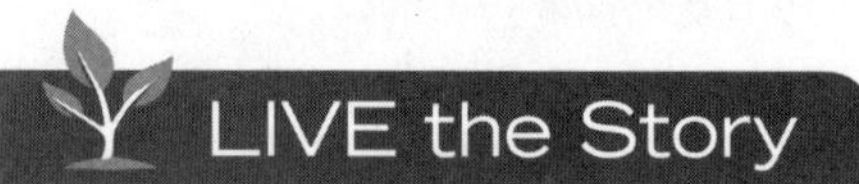


**"God Chose the Foolish Things of the World" (1 Cor 1:27)**

Walter Brueggemann sees in Jacob an illustration of Paul's comments in his first letter to the Corinthians: "But God chose the foolish things of the world to shame the wise; God chose the weak things of the world to shame the strong. God chose the lowly things of this world and the despised things—and the things that are not—to nullify the things that are" (1 Cor 1:27–28). He then goes on to point out that the story of Jacob "presents Jacob in his crude mixture of motives. This grandson of the promise is a rascal compared to his faithful grandfather Abraham or his successful father Isaac."[6]

Indeed, the story of Jacob reminds us that God uses the foolish, weak, and despised, not the worldly wise, powerful, and respected in order to accomplish his purpose. The consequence? According to Paul, God does this "so that no one may boast before him. It is because of him that you are in Christ Jesus, who has become for us wisdom from God—that is, our righteousness,

5. Ibid., 60.

6. Brueggemann, *Genesis*, 204.

holiness and redemption. Therefore, as it is written: 'Let the one who boasts boast in the Lord'" (1 Cor 1:29–31).

Christians were and are considered fools and weak in the eyes of unbelievers both at the time of Jesus as well as today. But Paul wants us to take encouragement from the fact that, in the eyes of the world, so was Jesus. According to Paul, "Jews demand signs and Greeks look for wisdom, but we preach Christ crucified: A stumbling block to Jews and foolishness to Gentiles" (1 Cor 1:22–23). So also, and preeminently, God chose Jesus, who was considered foolish and weak and was despised to save the world. Thus, "to those whom God has called, both Jews and Greeks, Christ the power of God and the wisdom of God" (1 Cor 1:24).

**Not by Works But by Him Who Calls (Rom 9:12)**

According to Moo's excellent exposition of Romans 9, Paul is speaking in the context of a message that has been largely resisted by Jewish people, but welcomed by many Gentiles.[7] This situation raises a question since the Old Testament promises seem directed toward Israel. He responds to this issue by declaring that "it is not as though God's word had failed" and then turning to the Old Testament to make the point that "not all who are descended from Israel are Israel" (Rom 9:6). In other words, not everyone who is a physical descendant of Abraham (Isaac but not Ishmael) receives the promise, but only those children whom God chooses. In short, "God never promised salvation to all of Israel."[8] Thus, the fact that only a fraction of the Jewish people has affirmed the gospel is not out of keeping with the promises of the Old Testament. In Romans 9:10–13, Paul turns to the story of Jacob and Esau in order to make his point.

The story of Isaac and Ishmael makes the point that relationship with God is not the result of human effort or status but rather the consequence of divine mercy. Both are descendants of Abraham, but one is chosen and the other is not. This same point is made even more pointedly in verses 10–13 with Jacob and Esau. After all, Isaac and Ishmael, though both children of Abraham, were born at different times and also to different mothers. Not so with Jacob and Esau. They had the same father and mother and were "conceived at the same time by our father Isaac" (v. 10). Granted, one was born slightly before the other, but God reversed the expected order by choosing the younger rather than the older. Indeed, Paul tells his audience, God chose Jacob rather than Esau even before either "had done anything good or bad" (v. 11).

7. D. J. Moo, *Romans*, NIVAC (Grand Rapids: Zondervan, 2000), 290–324.

8. Ibid., 298.

Paul is using the story of Jacob and Esau to demonstrate that God's Old Testament promises have not failed in spite of the fact that only a minority of Jews have responded to the gospel. As he does so, he also affirms that anyone who has responded to the gospel has done so not because of their own goodness or status or efforts, but because of God's mercy.

The section ends with a rather jarring quotation of Malachi 1:2–3. "Jacob I loved, but Esau I hated" (Rom 9:13). It is possible that this is Semitic hyperbolic rhetoric, but, as Moo points out, it is more likely that this language is to be interpreted as covenant language meaning that God chose Jacob, but rejected Esau as the recipient of the promises.[9]

The significance of this use of the Jacob-Esau story in Romans has the same ramifications for us as it did for the original audience. In the first place, it assures us that God was faithful to his Old Testament promises. But it also reminds us that our own relationship with God through Christ is not the result of our own efforts, but rather the result of God's merciful choice. Thus, we should not feel that we are any better than anyone else, but rather we should thank God for bringing us into a relationship with him. Our proper response is worship and obedience.

We should also remember that the choice of Isaac and Jacob does not mean that God abandoned Ishmael and Esau. Indeed, in both cases the book of Genesis makes it clear that God cares for the nonelect. The Old Testament stories are not talking about election to salvation, but rather election to a particular role in redemptive history. That said, Paul's use of these Old Testament stories has a different purpose, and to make his argument, in this case Esau is not so much nonelect as antielect.[10] This is signaled by his ending quotation from Malachi, which is directed in its original context not to the individual Esau but to the nation that descended from him, the Edomites, who had violently opposed Israel. The difference between the Genesis depiction of Esau and the prophet's treatment of him in the light of the Edomites is well expressed by Zakovitch, who reflects on Malachi 1:2–5 (and Amos 1:11–12): "In this new prophetic light, Esau is no longer the blameless, duped brother but rather has become the villain who deserves vengeance and who must be punished, measure for measure."[11]

## Despising One's Spiritual Birthright

"So Esau despised his birthright" (25:34). Thus ends our present story.

---

9. Ibid., 301.

10. To use the language of Kaminsky, *Yet I Loved Jacob*.

11. Y. Zakovitch, "Inner-Biblical Interpretation," in *Reading Genesis: Ten Methods*, ed. R. Hendel (Cambridge: Cambridge University Press, 2010), 116.

How could he do it? How could he give away such a precious gift for such an insignificant price as a bowl of soup? Mignon Jacobs puts it well when she says, "By seeing food as more desirable than his birthright, Esau is persuaded to resolve a temporary problem with a solution that has permanent consequences. He is a caricature of one who gives away his home for a bottle of whiskey or a drug fix."[12]

We need to learn a lesson from Esau's actions. Disciples of Jesus have a tremendous spiritual gift, but how often do we take it for granted and trade it in for something trivial? I became a Christian while I was in college and was excited about my new-found faith. I remember heading off to seminary, burning with desire to go to a school that followed Jesus and believed deeply and intelligently about the Scriptures. Of course, in seminary I encountered many like-minded people, but was also struck by the diffidence of a number of students who attended class and talked about Jesus in a kind of ho-hum way. Interestingly, most of these students were people who were children of believers. In other words, they grew up in the church and always thought of themselves as Christians. Even though they decided to go on to seminary, there were many things that excited them more than their faith. It made me almost glad that I had become a Christian as a young adult.

Of course, that was about forty years ago. As I look back on the past four decades, I am embarrassed to say that there have been many times where I have taken Christ and my faith for granted. I now understand a bit better the attitudes of some of my fellow seminarians.

In other words, I think most of us have Esau moments, where we would be willing to sell our spiritual birthright in Christ for a bowl of soup. After all, following Christ does not lead to immediate gratification like a good bowl of soup or a steak does when you are hungry. The Christian life is deeply meaningful and brings significance to our lives, but if we understand the "abundant life" it offers as a perfectly happy, suffering-free life, then we will be quickly let down and be susceptible to the less than spiritual joys of what offer themselves to us in the present.

We do well to listen to the warning of the author of Hebrews, who evokes the wilderness wanderings when he tells his readers to press on in the faith and, in spite of the many obstacles of this life, look forward to the reward of entering the promised land, which for the Christian means heaven. Our spiritual birthright is life forever in the presence of our God in a new heaven and a new earth. Don't sell it for a bowl of soup or any sensual pleasure that may lead to immediate gratification but forfeits our glorious future.

---

12. Jacobs, *Gender, Power, and Persuasion*, 232.

### The Power of Relentless Prayer

"Isaac prayed to the Lord on behalf of his wife, because she was childless. The Lord answered his prayer, and his wife because pregnant" (25:21). Isaac prayed and God answered his prayer. A surface reading of this verse makes it sound like God answered Isaac's prayer quickly; almost as if he prayed one night and the next morning God answered.

But we should read more closely. In verse 20 we learn that "Isaac was forty years old when he married Rebekah" and in verse 27 we read that "Isaac was sixty years old when Rebekah gave birth to them." Isaac prayed for two decades before he got an answer to his prayers.

In our technological age, we demand immediate gratification. If God does not answer our prayers right away, then there must be something wrong with our prayers, or maybe there is something wrong with God. We often think of God as someone who meets our needs and desires, and if he doesn't or doesn't do so immediately, then what good is he?

God is not our celestial valet. Sometimes he does not give us what we want or even need. In terms of the latter, there are godly people whom God in his wisdom did not answer their prayers to "give us this day our daily bread" and have starved to death. We don't understand why he answers some prayers and doesn't answer others. We only know that he invites us to approach him with our praises and our petitions. If we don't ask, we will not receive. And sometimes we, like Isaac, have to ask persistently. Isaac's prayers may have been fueled by his own father and mother's experience and the knowledge that he was the one through whom God would pass the promises to the next generation.

Isaac's twenty-year prayer odyssey reminds us of Jesus' parable of the persistent widow (Luke 18:1–8). While the object of prayer is a matter of justice, the parable has been and can be used to motivate all of us to persist in our petitions to God. The parable features a widow who is trying to seek justice from a judge who does not care about God or other people. But she keeps showing up and asking for justice which he finally gives her just to keep her from pestering. Jesus draws the conclusion, "Will not God bring about justice for his chosen ones, who cry out to him day and night? Will he keep putting them off?" (Luke 18:7). The lesson from the parable and from Isaac's example is to persist in our prayers to God, holding out continual hope that he will indeed respond in the right way and at the right time.

CHAPTER 26

# Genesis 26

## LISTEN to the Story

26:1Now there was a famine in the land—besides the previous famine
in Abraham's time—and Isaac went to Abimelek king of the Philistines in
Gerar. 2The LORD appeared to Isaac and said, "Do not go down to Egypt;
live in the land where I tell you to live. 3Stay in this land for a while, and
I will be with you and will bless you. For to you and your descendants I
will give all these lands and will confirm the oath I swore to your father
Abraham. 4I will make your descendants as numerous as the stars in the
sky and will give them all these lands, and through your offspring all
nations on earth will be blessed, 5because Abraham obeyed me and did
everything I required of him, keeping my commands, my decrees and my
instructions." 6So Isaac stayed in Gerar.

7When the men of that place asked him about his wife, he said, "She
is my sister," because he was afraid to say, "She is my wife." He thought,
"The men of this place might kill me on account of Rebekah, because she
is beautiful."

8When Isaac had been there a long time, Abimelek king of the
Philistines looked down from a window and saw Isaac caressing his wife
Rebekah. 9So Abimelek summoned Isaac and said, "She is really your
wife! Why did you say, 'She is my sister'?"

Isaac answered him, "Because I thought I might lose my life on
account of her."

10Then Abimelek said, "What is this you have done to us? One of the
men might well have slept with your wife, and you would have brought
guilt upon us."

11So Abimelek gave orders to all the people: "Anyone who harms this
man or his wife shall surely be put to death."

12Isaac planted crops in that land and the same year reaped a
hundredfold, because the LORD blessed him. 13The man became rich, and
his wealth continued to grow until he became very wealthy. 14He had so
many flocks and herds and servants that the Philistines envied him. 15So
all the wells that his father's servants had dug in the time of his father
Abraham, the Philistines stopped up, filling them with earth.

16Then Abimelek said to Isaac, "Move away from us; you have become too powerful for us."

17So Isaac moved away from there and encamped in the Valley of Gerar, where he settled. 18Isaac reopened the wells that had been dug in the time of his father Abraham, which the Philistines had stopped up after Abraham died, and he gave them the same names his father had given them.

19Isaac's servants dug in the valley and discovered a well of fresh water there. 20But the herders of Gerar quarreled with those of Isaac and said, "The water is ours!" So he named the well Esek, because they disputed with him. 21Then they dug another well, but they quarreled over that one also; so he named it Sitnah. 22He moved on from there and dug another well, and no one quarreled over it. He named it Rehoboth, saying, "Now the LORD has given us room and we will flourish in the land."

23From there he went up to Beersheba. 24That night the LORD appeared to him and said, "I am the God of your father Abraham. Do not be afraid, for I am with you; I will bless you and will increase the number of your descendants for the sake of my servant Abraham."

25Isaac built an altar there and called on the name of the LORD. There he pitched his tent, and there his servants dug a well.

26Meanwhile, Abimelek had come to him from Gerar, with Ahuzzath his personal adviser and Phicol the commander of his forces. 27Isaac asked them, "Why have you come to me, since you were hostile to me and sent me away?"

28They answered, "We saw clearly that the LORD was with you; so we said, 'There ought to be a sworn agreement between us'—between us and you. Let us make a treaty with you 29that you will do us no harm, just as we did not harm you but always treated you well and sent you away peacefully. And now you are blessed by the LORD."

30Isaac then made a feast for them, and they ate and drank. 31Early the next morning the men swore an oath to each other. Then Isaac sent them on their way, and they went away peacefully.

32That day Isaac's servants came and told him about the well they had dug. They said, "We've found water!" 33He called it Shibah, and to this day the name of the town has been Beersheba.

34When Esau was forty years old, he married Judith daughter of Beeri the Hittite, and also Basemath daughter of Elon the Hittite. 35They were a source of grief to Isaac and Rebekah.

*Listening to the Text in the Story:* Biblical Texts: Genesis 12:1–3; 12:10–20; 20

Chapter 26 is one of the few places where we have stories that focus on Isaac. Most of the *toledot* of Isaac focuses on Jacob, but here we learn about Isaac himself.

The first episode of this chapter describes Isaac's response to a famine in the land. Indeed, the opening verse of the chapter evokes memory of the famine in Abraham's time (see 12:10–20 as well as ch. 20). The Abraham story fits into the theme of Abraham's life of faith as it charted his reaction to threats and promises to the fulfillment of the promises. There we observed that he reacted with fear and manipulation as he tried to protect himself by lying about the status of Sarah, saying that she was his sister and suppressing her status as his wife. By doing so, he put the matriarch (and her womb, which would bear the promised child) at risk. Isaac here will act much like Abraham, and, though we do not have as developed a theme of the journey of faith as we did with Abraham, we see here that the son acts just like the father, and that is not good news.

Abraham had twice entered foreign territory during a famine and had lied about Sarah to save himself. The present story is closer to the second one (ch. 20) since in both the patriarch entered the Philistine region of Gerar, a city in the southern part of the promised land between Beersheba and Gaza, which is under the leadership of a king named Abimelek. However, we do not have to think that the Abimelek Isaac encountered was the same individual with whom his father dealt. Abimelek, "my father is king," may be, and indeed sounds like, a throne name.

## EXPLAIN the Story

### Isaac Goes to Gerar (26:1–6)

God did not want Isaac to go farther south and enter Egypt in response to the famine, so he instructed him to stay in Gerar, which is still within the borders of the promised land. God also uses this occasion to reaffirm the covenant promises to Isaac (vv. 3–4). Indeed, all the major elements of the promises as they were first given to Abraham are repeated here. God will make Abraham and Isaac's descendants a great nation, here unpacked as having numerous offspring as well as land. God will bless Abraham and Isaac's offspring and they will be a blessing on "all nations on earth" (v. 4).

Verse 5 is particularly interesting. Here God says that he is moved to fulfill these promises because of Abraham's obedience (see discussion at Gen 22). What is doubly interesting is that Abraham's obedience is described using post-Mosaic language. "Abraham obeyed me and did everything I required of him, keeping my commands, my decrees and my instructions" (v. 5). In a word, Abraham is a model law keeper and thus deserves the blessings conferred on those who keep the law. Jon Levenson identifies this verse as the heart of a Jewish appropriation of Abraham. To many Jewish readers, according to Levenson, his most important virtue is not his faith attitude (as it is for Christian readers), but rather his obedience. We have suggested that both are very important.[1]

### Isaac Lies about Rebekah (26:7–11)

Verse 7 shows Isaac lying about Rebekah, just like his father earlier lied about Sarah. And he does so for the same reason—to protect himself from those who would kill him to get his beautiful wife.

Apparently, this situation continued a "long time" (v. 8) until Abimelek saw Isaac being physically intimate with Rebekah. Thus, Isaac's lie was exposed. Just like in the Abraham and Abimelek story in chapter 20, so here the Philistine king shows himself to be morally outraged at the patriarch's lies. Abimelek shudders to think what would have become of them had they acted on the information that Isaac had given them. Isaac justifies himself, just as his father had, by telling the king that he feared for his life if he hadn't lied. Abimelek makes it clear that that would not have happened, and thus Isaac did not need to compromise himself by lying, by forbidding anyone from harming Isaac or Rebekah.

### Isaac Prospers (26:12–22)

In the previous section, we saw that Isaac acted just as Abraham did on two occasions (actually more, see 20:13) when his father moved into foreign territory. Indeed, the second account was very close to the Isaac story because Isaac moved into the same territory as his father had earlier, the Philistine city of Gerar, whose king's name was Abimelek.

The story that follows the story of Isaac's lying about Rebekah interestingly sounds familiar, though not exactly, to the story that follows Abraham's lying about Sarah. The earlier story, found in Genesis 13, recounts how Abraham and his nephew Lot had to part ways because of their growing wealth. Here, particularly in verses 12–17, Isaac must move further from Abimelek because of Isaac's growing wealth.

Isaac's wealth is a sign that God was with him and "blessed him" (v. 12). But the blessing of God that led to such prosperity had a price. The Philistines

1. Especially in J. D. Levenson, *Inheriting Abraham*. Moberly argues essentially the same position for a Christian viewpoint in *The Theology of the Book of Genesis*, 200–224.

envied him and tried to thwart his efforts by stopping up the wells that had been dug by Abraham in the previous generation (see 21:22–34). This situation leads King Abimelek to tell Isaac to move away from them.

Thus, Isaac moved away, but not too far, to the Valley of Gerar. Here there were more wells that the Philistines had earlier stopped up. He unplugged them and settled there. He had also restored the names that Abraham had given them.

When they arrived at their new location, Isaac's servants dug a new well, but they still had a conflict with the herders of Gerar. They named that well, Esek, or "dispute." The second well was also disputed, and they named it Sitnah, or "opposition." The third well was not disputed; they could use it as their own, so they named it Rehoboth, or "room." In this, Isaac and his men saw the hand of God.

From the Valley of Gerar, Isaac traveled to Beersheba. We are thus reminded of Abraham's fight over water rights with the earlier Abimelek and the Philistines of Gerar (Gen 21:22–34). When he came to Beersheba, God once again reaffirmed the covenant promises, identifying himself as the "God of Abraham" and promising to bless him and increase his offspring because of his relationship with Abraham.

In response, Isaac did what his father had done on such occasions, he built an altar. Of course, an altar is a place of sacrifice and worship and it also marks the place as part of Yahweh's land. Isaac settled in Beersheba and dug a well.

### The Treaty between Isaac and Abimelek (26:23–35)

At this point, Abimelek comes to him again with two high officials. We have seen the name Phicol before at the time of Abraham (21:22, 32), but since six or seven decades have passed since that event, it is best to think that this is a descendant and the position was handed down from father to son. Besides Phicol, Ahuzzath, described as Abimelek's personal advisor, accompanied the king. We know nothing further about this man, but the presence of these three important officials shows that they have important business with Isaac and recognize him as a powerful man.

Isaac, however, greets them warily since they had sent him away (26:16), a move that Isaac believed was an act of hostility. He wonders why Abimelek has now come to him. Abimelek answers that it is because they know that the Lord was with him. Typically, this is indicated to outsiders like Abimelek by the prosperity of the one whom God is with (see Gen 39:2).

It is interesting that Abimelek gives the credit to Yahweh (the Lord). For a number of reasons, it is surprising to hear him use the name Yahweh. First, this name might have only been revealed for the first time to Moses at the burning bush (see Exod 3). If so, then the composer of this story in Genesis would have retroverted the name back to this early time. We can't be certain, though, since it is also possible to read the revelation of the divine name at the burning bush not as a first time use of the name, but as a deeper explanation of that name.

But whatever the answer to this question, it is surprising to hear a Philistine invoke the name. However, though a Philistine, the earlier Abimelek showed that he was a God-fearer, so, though likely not a monotheist, Abimelek certainly demonstrates great respect for Isaac's God.

And so he wants to enter into a formal treaty relationship with him. Isaac agrees, so they share a meal and swear oaths to each other. Of course, relationship with Philistines will not continue to be so positive in the future. Perhaps this story serves the purpose of putting blame on the Philistines for this later trouble.

The episode, and the focus on Isaac, concludes with an announcement of the discovery of water and the digging of a well, so important to life in this part of the world. This is likely the well already mentioned in verse 25, but its announcement here may be a way of indicating divine pleasure over the treaty concluded with Abimelek.

This well, like the previous ones, is given a name—Shibah. Shibah can mean "seven" or it can mean "oath." The well also gives its name to the town Beersheba, "the well of seven" or "the well of the oath."

Scholars have long commented on the fact that Beersheba had already received its name at the time of Abraham (21:31). While some believe that the similarities are explained by the weaving together of originally separate documents, it is also possible that the discovery of this new well, after Abraham's had gone dry, gives impetus for naming the town the same as at the time of Abraham.

### The Sins of the Father...

As noted in the exposition of the story of Isaac and Abimelek, Isaac here repeats the sin of his father Abraham. The Abraham narrative includes two accounts of his lying about the status of his wife in order to protect himself (Gen 12:10–20; 20). Indeed, he admits that this deceit was common practice whenever he entered foreign land (20:13; see Habitual Sin after Gen 20). Isaac here, like his father before him, acted out of fear and lack of confidence in God's ability to protect him. Their deceit may have kept them from harm, but it certainly risked their wives and also the vitality and integrity of the promise of a descendant. We see that God intervened in each situation to assure the fulfillment of the promise. The special nature of the promise for the furtherance of God's redemptive purpose keeps us from presuming that God's intervention to keep the patriarchs' sins from their worse consequences is a principle that applies to all God's people.

However, Isaac's repetition of Abraham's recurrent sin does lead us to reflect on the tendency of children to follow in the footsteps of their parents. One might think that the exact opposite would be the case, and sometimes it is. But more often than not one might expect children to grow up susceptible to the sinful behaviors of their parents. Children who are abused are more likely to grow up to be abusers themselves.[2] Children of alcoholics are more likely to misuse alcohol. These are well-known and discussed trends, but it is likely that children of parents of all kinds of unhealthy behavior are more susceptible to those patterns, even when they themselves have suffered the consequences of their parents' actions.

It is likely that this sorry tendency is behind the Bible's often criticized statement that the sins of parents will be visited on the children. The most notable example is the second commandment where God announces that he will punish those who worship idols and their children "to the third and fourth generation of those who hate me" (Exod 20:5). That the principle works in a positive direction as well may be seen by the next verse where God says he will show "love to a thousand generations of those who love me and keep my commandments" (Exod 20:6).

These verses are a warning, not a mechanical principle. They serve to warn children not to follow in the sin of their parents to which they are particularly susceptible. Unfortunately, this warning can be misunderstood as a statement of fatalism and misunderstood to say that children will be punished for the sin of their parents in spite of their own behavior. Jeremiah and Ezekiel react to those of their own generation who have made such a conclusion. Their generation faced God's judgment for the accumulated sins of generations of God's people. There was likely a tendency to blame their parents, but not themselves.[3] To these individuals, the prophets proclaim: "In those days people will no longer say, 'The parents have eaten sour grapes, and the children's teeth are set on edge.' Instead, everyone will die for their

---

2. Child Welfare Information Gateway, "Long-Term Consequences of Child Abuse and Neglect," 5. https://www.childwelfare.gov/pubs/factsheets/long_term_consequences.pdf#page=5&view=Behavioral%20Consequences.

3. See T. Longman III, *Jeremiah/Lamentations*, UBCS (Grand Rapids: Baker, 2008), 210.

own sin; whoever eats sour grapes — their own teeth will be set on edge" (Jer 31:29–30; see also Ezek 18:2–3).

What do we learn from these texts? We learn that we are often more susceptible to the sins of our parents. Wisdom suggests that we recognize that and take steps to avoid thinking and behaviors that put us at risk. If our parents abused alcohol, we need to be extremely careful ourselves about drinking. However, we should also be careful of the kind of fatalistic attitude that leads to a self-fulfilling prophecy. We are responsible for our own actions, not the actions of our parents.

For Christians, we realize that we do not have to depend on our own strength to resist sin, but we can turn to God, whose Spirit dwells in us. And, when we do sin, we can turn to Jesus who died on our behalf and was raised in power.

### Learning to Live in the Presence of God

Kent Hughes helpfully points out how in this story God makes it clear to Isaac that he was present to him in the past ("the Lord has been with you," v. 28), is with him in the present ("I am with you," v. 24), and will be present to him in the future ("I will be with you and bless you," v. 3). He goes on to say that "Isaac's growth in awareness of the dynamic all-presence of God in his life lifted him from cowardice to confidence. Isaac recovered from the disgrace of passing off Rebekah as his sister as he stood tall amidst the hostile Philistines and prospered."[4]

Isaac's world was a hostile one. He was a sojourner in a land where at least initially he had no power or control over his circumstances. But, you know, his world is no different from anyone else's. In this story, no one had more power than Abimelek, but thanks to Isaac's lie and God's desire to protect him, Abimelek's kingdom was struck by disease over which he had no control.

Whether we are a helpless sojourner or a powerful political figure or business leader, we live in a dangerous world, and it is perfectly natural to live in fear. We don't want to be hurt, physically, emotionally, or in any way. Some people try to protect themselves by amassing money and power, but we have already seen that that does not work. What can give us peace to live in a dangerous present as we face an uncertain future? Only the knowledge that God has been with us, is with us, and will be with us.

Jesus understood that as he promised his disciples that he would be with them till the end of the ages (Matt 28:20). The Gospel of John records his

4. Hughes, *Genesis*, 347.

prayer for those who follow him. Here he promises that he will leave us as orphans, but will come to us (John 14:18).

How do we develop the awareness of the fact that Jesus is with us and thus move from, as Hughes puts it in regard to Isaac, "from cowardice to confidence"? Nowhere do we get a manual containing "how-to's," but the Bible advocates developing a healthy relationship with God through speaking to God (prayer) and listening to God (through Scripture reading). Other spiritual disciplines also can encourage our awareness of God's presence. For those seeking to explore such disciplines as silence and solitude, service, sacrificial living as well as prayer and meditation on Scripture are well directed to the writings of Dallas Willard.[5]

5. D. Willard, *The Spirit of the Disciples: Understanding How God Changes Lives* (San Francisco: HarperOne, 1999).

CHAPTER 27

# Genesis 27:1 – 28:9

## LISTEN to the Story

27:1When Isaac was old and his eyes were so weak that he could no longer see, he called for Esau his older son and said to him, "My son."

"Here I am," he answered.

2Isaac said, "I am now an old man and don't know the day of my death. 3Now then, get your equipment—your quiver and bow—and go out to the open country to hunt some wild game for me. 4Prepare me the kind of tasty food I like and bring it to me to eat, so that I may give you my blessing before I die."

5Now Rebekah was listening as Isaac spoke to his son Esau. When Esau left for the open country to hunt game and bring it back, 6Rebekah said to her son Jacob, "Look, I overheard your father say to your brother Esau, 7'Bring me some game and prepare me some tasty food to eat, so that I may give you my blessing in the presence of the LORD before I die.' 8Now, my son, listen carefully and do what I tell you: 9Go out to the flock and bring me two choice young goats, so I can prepare some tasty food for your father, just the way he likes it. 10Then take it to your father to eat, so that he may give you his blessing before he dies."

11Jacob said to Rebekah his mother, "But my brother Esau is a hairy man while I have smooth skin. 12What if my father touches me? I would appear to be tricking him and would bring down a curse on myself rather than a blessing."

13His mother said to him, "My son, let the curse fall on me. Just do what I say; go and get them for me."

14So he went and got them and brought them to his mother, and she prepared some tasty food, just the way his father liked it. 15Then Rebekah took the best clothes of Esau her older son, which she had in the house, and put them on her younger son Jacob. 16She also covered his hands and the smooth part of his neck with the goatskins. 17Then she handed to her son Jacob the tasty food and the bread she had made.

[18]He went to his father and said, "My father."
"Yes, my son," he answered. "Who is it?"
[19]Jacob said to his father, "I am Esau your firstborn. I have done as
you told me. Please sit up and eat some of my game, so that you may
give me your blessing."
[20]Isaac asked his son, "How did you find it so quickly, my son?"
"The LORD your God gave me success," he replied.
[21]Then Isaac said to Jacob, "Come near so I can touch you, my son,
to know whether you really are my son Esau or not."
[22]Jacob went close to his father Isaac, who touched him and said,
"The voice is the voice of Jacob, but the hands are the hands of Esau."
[23]He did not recognize him, for his hands were hairy like those of his
brother Esau; so he proceeded to bless him. [24]"Are you really my son
Esau?" he asked.
"I am," he replied.
[25]Then he said, "My son, bring me some of your game to eat, so that
I may give you my blessing."
Jacob brought it to him and he ate; and he brought some wine and
he drank. [26]Then his father Isaac said to him, "Come here, my son, and
kiss me."
[27]So he went to him and kissed him. When Isaac caught the smell of
his clothes, he blessed him and said,
"Ah, the smell of my son
is like the smell of a field
that the LORD has blessed.
[28]May God give you heaven's dew
and earth's richness—
an abundance of grain and new wine.
[29]May nations serve you
and peoples bow down to you.
Be lord over your brothers,
and may the sons of your mother bow down to you.
May those who curse you be cursed
and those who bless you be blessed."
[30]After Isaac finished blessing him, and Jacob had scarcely left his
father's presence, his brother Esau came in from hunting. [31]He too
prepared some tasty food and brought it to his father. Then he said to

him, "My father, please sit up and eat some of my game, so that you may
give me your blessing."

32His father Isaac asked him, "Who are you?"

"I am your son," he answered, "your firstborn, Esau."

33Isaac trembled violently and said, "Who was it, then, that hunted
game and brought it to me? I ate it just before you came and I blessed
him—and indeed he will be blessed!"

34When Esau heard his father's words, he burst out with a loud and
bitter cry and said to his father, "Bless me—me too, my father!"

35But he said, "Your brother came deceitfully and took your blessing."

36Esau said, "Isn't he rightly named Jacob? This is the second time he
has taken advantage of me: He took my birthright, and now he's taken
my blessing!" Then he asked, "Haven't you reserved any blessing for me?"

37Isaac answered Esau, "I have made him lord over you and have made
all his relatives his servants, and I have sustained him with grain and new
wine. So what can I possibly do for you, my son?"

38Esau said to his father, "Do you have only one blessing, my father?
Bless me too, my father!" Then Esau wept aloud.

39His father Isaac answered him,

"Your dwelling will be
away from the earth's richness,
away from the dew of heaven above.
40You will live by the sword
and you will serve your brother.
But when you grow restless,
you will throw his yoke
from off your neck."

41Esau held a grudge against Jacob because of the blessing his father
had given him. He said to himself, "The days of mourning for my father
are near; then I will kill my brother Jacob."

42When Rebekah was told what her older son Esau had said, she
sent for her younger son Jacob and said to him, "Your brother Esau is
planning to avenge himself by killing you.
43Now then, my son, do what
I say: Flee at once to my brother Laban in Harran.
44Stay with him for a
while until your brother's fury subsides.
45When your brother is no longer
angry with you and forgets what you did to him, I'll send word for you to
come back from there. Why should I lose both of you in one day?"

46Then Rebekah said to Isaac, "I'm disgusted with living because of
these Hittite women. If Jacob takes a wife from among the women of this
land, from Hittite women like these, my life will not be worth living."

28:1So Isaac called for Jacob and blessed him. Then he
commanded him: "Do not marry a Canaanite woman. 2Go at once
to Paddan Aram, to the house of your mother's father Bethuel. Take
a wife for yourself there, from among the daughters of Laban, your
mother's brother. 3May God Almighty bless you and make you
fruitful and increase your numbers until you become a community
of peoples. 4May he give you and your descendants the blessing
given to Abraham, so that you may take possession of the land where
you now reside as a foreigner, the land God gave to Abraham."
5Then Isaac sent Jacob on his way, and he went to Paddan Aram, to
Laban son of Bethuel the Aramean, the brother of Rebekah, who
was the mother of Jacob and Esau.
6Now Esau learned that Isaac had blessed Jacob and had sent him
to Paddan Aram to take a wife from there, and that when he blessed
him he commanded him, "Do not marry a Canaanite woman,"
7and that Jacob had obeyed his father and mother and had gone to
Paddan Aram. 8Esau then realized how displeasing the Canaanite
women were to his father Isaac; 9so he went to Ishmael and married
Mahalath, the sister of Nebaioth and daughter of Ishmael son of
Abraham, in addition to the wives he already had.

*Listening to the Text in the Story:* Biblical Texts: Genesis 12:1–3; 25:19–34

The roots of this story are found back in the promises God gave to Abraham in 12:1–3. The question continues to be who will be the divinely chosen son who will mediate the covenant promises to the next generation. At the birth of Isaac's twin sons, God had announced that the "older will serve the younger" (25:23), and when they grew up, the older, Esau, had sold his birthright to the younger, Jacob, for a bowl of lentil soup. Now it was time for their father, Isaac, to confer his blessing on the one who would receive the status of chosen son.

## EXPLAIN the Story

### Jacob Deceives Isaac (26:34–27:40)

Before chapter 26 ends, the narrator shifts quickly to Esau, Isaac's older son, reporting that he married two Hittite women, one named Judith the daughter of Beeri and the other named Basemath the daughter of Elon.

He later marries Mahalath, the sister of Nebaioth and daughter of Ishmael. There is some at least superficial tension with the names of his wives given in 36:2–3 where the daughter of Elon the Hittite is called Adah and only an Ishmaelite (not a Hittite as in 26:34) Basemath is mentioned. Scholars speculate as for the reasons for this, some arguing that it shows different documentary traditions being woven together without regard for the resulting tensions and others proposing harmonization or suggesting a textual transmission problem.

What is clear from the text and what is important for the story is that Rebekah and Isaac are none too pleased about the marriage to the Hittite girls. That Esau married women of whom his parents did not approve again indicates his self-centered, impulsive, and sensuous nature, which was also displayed in the story about the purchase of the birthright (25:19–24).

This background of Esau's marriages leads to the story of the stolen blessing. Earlier we saw that Esau sold his birthright to Jacob for a bowl of lentil stew (25:19–34). We suggested that this sale had no legal standing. That said, Esau had sworn to it, and it is obvious from the present account that he had no intention at all of honoring his oath, thus again darkening his reputation. Thus, Rebekah will take the matter into her own hands. After all, she loves Jacob more than Esau, and Esau's wives are irritating to her.

The story begins with the now aged and blind Isaac calling for his favorite son, Esau, to ask him for a special meal provided by his hunting skill. He realizes that he is near death, and it is time for him to confer his patriarchal blessing on his older son.

Rebekah had overheard the conversation and now acts quickly to undermine her husband's attempt to give the blessing to Esau. Before judging Rebekah too severely for acting out of her favoritism for Jacob, we need to remember that she heard the divine oracle at the time of her children's birth to the effect that Jacob would be the recipient of the blessing:

> Two nations are in your womb,
> and two peoples from within you will be separated;
> one people will be stronger than the other,
> and the older will serve the younger. (25:23)

On the other hand, it might have been better had she let God work the matter out in his mysterious way rather than taking matters in her own hands. In the Abraham narrative, we frequently observed the troubles that arise when the patriarch (and matriarch in the case of Sarah) tried to fulfill the promise in his own wisdom and power rather than waiting for God. In Genesis, and indeed, throughout Scripture, waiting on God to fulfill his promises is a virtue and grasping and manipulating is a vice that often leads to trouble (see The Danger of Manipulation below in the following Live the Story section).

Rebekah creates a ruse that will confuse the aged and blind Isaac into thinking that Jacob is Esau, which is quite a trick because Esau is so hairy. She also uses two young goats rather than fresh game in order to prepare the dish that her husband wants Esau to provide.

Jacob worries that the blessing will turn into a curse if he is discovered, but his mother encourages him and even says that she will take the curse on her own head if need be. Rebekah then prepares Jacob for the ruse and sends him in to bring his father the meal.

One can certainly appreciate why Jacob would be worried. After all, couldn't Isaac have discerned the difference between wild game that he loves so much and the meat of domesticated goats? And, really, could Rebekah fool Isaac by giving him goat hair gloves and clothing him with a goat skin chest piece? (Esau must have been extremely hairy!)

The narrator does not say, and we should not be dogmatic. Perhaps Isaac was senile and blind. Or perhaps he too found Esau's wives annoying. Or perhaps he was simply duped.

Whatever the reason, Rebekah's plan succeeded, though Isaac was clearly suspicious. Jacob identifies himself as Esau and tells Isaac that he brought him the game and requests the blessing. Isaac, though, wonders how Esau hunted and cooked so quickly. Jacob then claims that "the LORD your God" allowed it to happen.

Still, Isaac remains suspicious, asking to touch his son to make sure. He touches him and the hair pieces did their job. Isaac is easily duped since he trusts his touch rather than his ears since he admits that the voice was that of Jacob, not Esau.

For a second time, Isaac asks Jacob whether he is Esau, and for a second time, Jacob lies to him in order to receive the blessing. Isaac does not immediately bless him, but first enjoys the food and drink that Jacob brought to him.

We have seen that Isaac was convinced that Jacob was Esau by touch and now taste as he ate the food. At the last, he asks for a kiss, and when Jacob comes forward and kisses him, Isaac smells him, and to him, the smell is that of Esau. Thus, Isaac follows his senses, at least those of smell, taste, and touch, though he does ignore his hearing. This leads him to his blessing on Jacob, whom he thinks is Esau.

He leads with the smell of his son, which is the smell of the outdoors, which is one of the reasons he preferred Esau, the outdoorsman, over Jacob, the one who preferred to stay with his mother and cook. He asks that God bless Esau, who is really Jacob, with fertile fields that will produce food and drink that will sustain and enrich him. He then also blesses him with superiority over his brothers, which may indicate that there were other siblings besides Esau and Jacob.[1] The most direct contact with the promises to Abraham comes at the end when he says "May those who curse you be cursed and those who bless you be blessed" (v. 29, compare 12:3).

Soon after the blessing, Jacob left and then Esau came in with the meal of game and ready to receive the blessing. At this moment Isaac realizes that he has been deceived. He has blessed Jacob and there was nothing he could do about it. Esau desperately wants his father to bless him too, but Isaac tells him that he has expended the blessing of superiority over his brothers to Jacob.

Esau is overwhelmed with sorrow and implores his father to bless him too. Isaac then tells him that Jacob had stolen his blessing and done it with deceit (*mirmah*). Esau picks up the theme of deception and calls attention to the significance of his name Jacob, which as the NIV note points out means "he grasps the heel" (an allusion to his birth, 26:21–26), but has an idiomatic meaning of "he takes advantage of" or "he deceives." Esau remarks that this is the second time he was deceived, the first time being the time he gave Jacob his birthright (25:27–34). However, while there is no doubt that Jacob used deception in this present story, it is not clear that this is the case in the matter of the birthright. Jacob was not so much deceiving Esau as appealing to his sensuous and impulsive nature to give up something important in the future for something to eat in the present.

Isaac's response is chilling to Esau. He has made Jacob, the younger, the superior over Esau and also has blessed him with abundant crops. He has nothing left for Esau, though Esau presses him for a blessing. Kaminsky is surely correct when he states that "Isaac's refusal to retract his blessing in Gen 27:33 [is] less an indication that blessings once spoken are irrevocable than as evidence that Isaac came to recognize that Jacob's and Rebekah's actions were somehow merged with God's intentions, a fact that he glimpsed in the light of the way events transpired."[2]

In answer, Isaac pronounces what sounds like a blessing formally, but is really not one. Esau, as opposed to Jacob who has been blessed with "an abundance of grain and new wine" (v. 28), will dwell in an impoverished land that is not conducive to agriculture. Thus, Esau will "live by the sword" not the plow. Many nations will serve Jacob, but Esau will serve his brother, though he will rebel against his brother's rule.

---

1. Or, according to Kaminsky (*Yet I Loved Jacob*, 53) it is a standardized blessing, or perhaps reckons with the fact that "Esau is the ancestor of other rival peoples, such as the Amalekites (Gen 36:16)."

2. Ibid., 51.

This blessing makes sense in the light of the later relationships between Jacob's descendants, Israel, and Esau's descendants (Edom). There would be conflict between Edom and Israel at a number of points in later history (Num 20:14–21; 2 Sam 8:14; 1 Kgs 22:47; 2 Kgs 8:20). At the time of the Babylonian destruction of Jerusalem, Edom had taken advantage of the situation in some way. While not precisely described, this point can be established by reference to texts like Psalm 137:7; Lamentations 4:22; Ezekiel 35:15; Obadiah 10–14.

### Jacob Must Flee (27:41–28:9)

For obvious reasons, Esau wants to kill his brother who has robbed him of birthright and blessing. Out of respect for his father, he decides to wait until Isaac dies, which he believes is near.

Rebekah catches wind of Esau's murderous intentions and tells Jacob that he has to leave. She tells Isaac that she cannot stand the thought that Jacob would marry Hittite women like Esau had (see 26:34–35), and so she encourages Isaac to let Jacob go back to their ancestral homeland in Harran in order to find a wife.

Isaac agrees, but before he sends Jacob to Harran, he calls him to him and again blesses him. Though Isaac was clearly upset when he discovered that he was deceived into giving Jacob the blessing, it appears that he has come to terms with it.

He instructs Jacob not to take a wife from among the women of the land (as Esau had). But rather he advises him to marry a woman from his ancestral homeland (as he had), specifically from among the "daughters of Laban, your mother's brother" (28:2). Finally, Isaac blesses Jacob with a blessing that more explicitly connects with the blessing that God had given his father Abraham (12:1–3). He asks that God bless him so that he has multiple descendants that will eventually become "a community of peoples" (28:3). He also asks God to give him and his descendants the land promised to Abraham, namely the land of Canaan. In other words, though Isaac is sending him out of the land, he presumes that he will eventually return. Thus, the next phase of Jacob's tumultuous life begins. But before he reaches Paddan Aram (northwest Mesopotamia), he has an important encounter with God.

Before we read of this important encounter, the narrator shifts attention back to Esau for a moment. Isaac and Rebekah's advice to Jacob leads Esau to realize that it was a mistake for him to marry Hittite (Canaanite) women. Thus, he decides to marry again and this time from within the extended family. Of course, he cannot go to Paddan Aram where his mother's blood relatives lived to find his new wife since that is the direction that Jacob took, but he can go to Ishmael's family. Ishmael, of course, is the half-brother of his father and the son of Abraham. He marries Mahalath, "the sister of Nebaioth and daughter of Ishmael son of Abraham" (28:9). We never hear of his parents' reaction. But it is interesting that this move is an attempt to assuage his parents. He does not react as Cain did when his sacrifice was rejected; that is, just stewing in anger. The next time we see Esau, we will see that he is no longer the angry brother who wants to murder his brother. Though somewhat speculative, perhaps it is right to see here a shift in his thinking in the right direction.

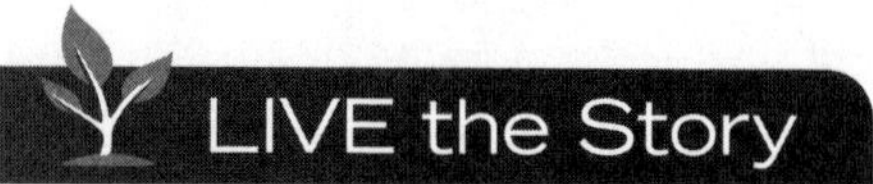


### The Danger of Manipulation

In our exposition of this story, we discussed the ethics of Rebekah's and Jacob's actions in deceiving Isaac. As is typical with our reticent narrator, he does not evaluate or judge whether or not their actions were commendable. On the one hand, careful reading of Genesis and other biblical narratives show that deception is not always wrong (see Is Deception Ever Permissible? after Gen 31:22–55). And there is no doubt that their deception of Isaac leads to the choice of Jacob over Esau that was God's intention according to the divine oracle at their birth (25:23). That said, we have seen as early as the Abraham story (especially Gen 15 and 17) that grasping for the fulfillment of the divine promises by manipulating the situation is always wrong. A close reading of our present story would also lead us to believe that Rebekah and Jacob's ruse was unethical and problematic.

But the end result was God's plan all along. Don't the ends justify the means? Of course not.

In the first place, to manipulate in this way shows an utter lack of confidence in God. As he made clear with the birth of Isaac, God will fulfill his promises and he will achieve his ends no matter how unlikely it looks from a human perspective. In the second place, though Jacob rightly receives the blessing, the deceptive way in which he was chosen and blessed by his father led to undesirable consequences.

Those negative consequences will play themselves out in the remainder of the book of Genesis. Indeed, they will play out through the history of the Old Testament and, arguably, into the New Testament.

The most immediate consequence is Esau's threat to the life of Jacob, causing Rebekah to convince Isaac to send Jacob away, and we will see that his sojourn in Paddan Aram (northwest Mesopotamia) will be a difficult period in his life. More long term, even though Jacob and Esau appear to reconcile later (Gen 34; 35:29), the latter's descendants, the Edomites, will become long term adversaries of Jacob's descendants, the Israelites. As we noted in the Explain the Story section, the rivalry begins at the time the Edomites refuse the wilderness generation to cross through their land to get to the promised land (Num 20:14–21) down to the exilic and postexilic periods (Ps 137:7; Lam 4:22; Ezek 35:15; Obad 10–14).

It may not be too much of a stretch to see this rivalry continuing into the time period of the New Testament. After all, Herod the Great and his family were Idumeans, the descendants of the Edomites. They came into power when their ancestor Antipater was appointed procurator of Judea by Caesar in AD 47. Herod the Great was the procurator at the time of the birth of Jesus, of course a descendant of Jacob. Alerted by the Magi who came looking for the "one who has been born king of the Jews" (Matt 2:2), Herod was determined, yet failed, to kill Jesus (Matt 2). Later, Herod the Great's son, Herod Antipas, had Jesus' precursor John the Baptist killed (Matt 14:1–12; Mark 6:14–29). Antipas also tried to kill Jesus but failed (Luke 13:31–32). Later descendants of Herod the Great, the Idumean (Edomite), also persecuted the early church (Acts 1:1–24).

Rebekah and Jacob used unethical means to achieve a good end. God still used them to achieve his redemptive purposes, but he would have accomplished those purposes without their "help." Their lack of integrity did not hamper God, but it brought unnecessary suffering into their lives and the lives of their descendants.

The lesson for us is to avoid using unethical means to achieve God's purposes. We will later (see Leading with a Limp after Genesis 32:22–32) consider the case of a seminary whose leadership used strong-arm techniques to change the ethos of the institution. I have no doubt that these people believe, in my opinion wrongly, that their tactics are saving the seminary. They feel that their "good" ends must be achieved in part by ridding the school of certain tenured and long-serving faculty members. Even if one disagrees with their goals, one could be sympathetic if they made their case publicly and through the normal means provided by the faculty handbook and the ethics of ecclesiastical academic institutions.

However, they did not choose that route. Rather than using the seminary's normal procedure for firing one young professor and hiring another one more to their liking according to the normal channels of hiring and firing, they simply issued an executive order without consultation of the relevant department. They also forced a senior faculty member to "retire" by presenting him with a choice: sign a severance agreement or suffer a long review process that might have a financially devastating result. These are just two examples out of many that could be cited.

I am a college and seminary professor, so it is not surprising that my example comes from that world. The business world, the legal world, the medical world, the labor union world, the political world—you name it—have their examples of those who use inappropriate means to achieve their ends. All of us have heard, seen, or even experienced such treatment in our lives. Unfortunately, some of us have perpetrated injustices against others in the service of what we think are important and right goals.

What we need to remember if we are tempted to use shortcuts to get our desired ends is that often, if not always, as in the case of Rebekah and Jacob, such behavior backfires or has unintended negative consequences. The seminary in my example is now experiencing heavy criticism from former students and retired former professors as well as the general public. Students are deciding not to enroll there; some who are there are considering leaving. Churches and denominational leaders are hesitant to employ their graduates. The reputation of the school has received a major blow.

And if we see such injustices perpetrated against us or against others, then it is right and just to protest such behaviors. It is necessary to hold our institutions and their leaders accountable. Even so, while a proper reaction to such injustices is righteous anger and to protest and work to right an injustice, we must also temper that with the knowledge that ultimately the matter is in God's hands.

After all, the most egregious example of injustice known to humanity is that which Jesus suffered. The high priest Caiaphas felt that Jesus was a threat to the stability of Judea when he stated his motivation to pursue the death of Jesus: "You do not realize that it is better for you that one man die for the people than that the whole nation perish" (John 11:50). Then, using trumped-up charges, they convicted Jesus of a capital crime.

Caiaphas thought what he was doing was a good thing, saving his people from turmoil that would force the Roman army to reestablish peace. But what an injustice! Nonetheless, God used this evil act for his good purposes: "This man was handed over to you by God's deliberate plan and foreknowledge; and you, with the help of wicked men, put him to death by nailing him to the cross. But God raised him from the dead, freeing him from the agony of death, because it was impossible for death to keep its hold on him" (Acts 2:23–24). The knowledge that it is ultimately God who holds people responsible should not lead to a passive approach to injustice, but it will keep our righteous anger from turning into a vindictive bitterness.

### The Danger of a Good Meal

Isaac prefers Esau. Why? Well one of the reasons is that Esau is a hunter and can provide him with the type of game he loves to eat. Indeed, we have seen that Isaac wants Esau to bring him that tasty meal before he confers the blessing on him.

It is not absolutely certain, but it seems highly likely that Isaac was aware of the divine oracle delivered at the time of the birth of the boys that the older will serve the younger. Could his spiritual discernment be dulled by his desire for the sensual pleasures of life? We have already seen Esau trade in his birthright for a cup of soup (25:19–24). Twice in the Jacob narrative food leads to trouble.

I don't think the storyteller is telling readers that there is anything inherently evil with a good, tasty meal. But he is warning that the craving for sensual pleasure—whether it is culinary, sexual, or the like—can distort our spiritual life. We must put God first and our legitimate sensual pleasures second. Only God can satisfy our deepest longings and desires.

Of course, the book of Ecclesiastes makes this point well. The Teacher tries to find meaning in all the wrong places—pleasure, wisdom, relationships, power, money, and more. His conclusion? Life is meaningless. After all, he is trying to find meaning "under the sun," in other words, in a fallen world.

At the end of the book, a second unnamed wise man steps in (12:8–14) to speak to his son about the Teacher's search for meaning. After affirming the truth of what the Teacher has been saying (there is no meaning "under the sun"), he points his son in a better direction: "Fear God and keep his commandments, for this is the duty of all mankind. For God will bring every deed into judgment, including every hidden thing, whether it is good or evil" (12:13b–14). In other words, put God first and everything else can find its proper place.[3]

See related essays: Marrying the Right Person (after Gen 24) and Is Deception Ever Permissible (after Gen 31:22–55).

3. For an extensive treatment, see Allender and Longman, *Breaking the Idols of Your Heart.*

CHAPTER 28

# Genesis 28:10–22

##  LISTEN to the Story

[28:10]Jacob left Beersheba and set out for Harran. [11]When he reached a certain place, he stopped for the night because the sun had set. Taking one of the stones there, he put it under his head and lay down to sleep. [12]He had a dream in which he saw a stairway resting on the earth, with its top reaching to heaven, and the angels of God were ascending and descending on it. [13]There above it stood the Lord, and he said: "I am the Lord, the God of your father Abraham and the God of Isaac. I will give you and your descendants the land on which you are lying. [14]Your descendants will be like the dust of the earth, and you will spread out to the west and to the east, to the north and to the south. All peoples on earth will be blessed through you and your offspring. [15]I am with you and will watch over you wherever you go, and I will bring you back to this land. I will not leave you until I have done what I have promised you."

[16]When Jacob awoke from his sleep, he thought, "Surely the Lord is in this place, and I was not aware of it." [17]He was afraid and said, "How awesome is this place! This is none other than the house of God; this is the gate of heaven."

[18]Early the next morning Jacob took the stone he had placed under his head and set it up as a pillar and poured oil on top of it. [19]He called that place Bethel, though the city used to be called Luz.

[20]Then Jacob made a vow, saying, "If God will be with me and will watch over me on this journey I am taking and will give me food to eat and clothes to wear [21]so that I return safely to my father's household, then the Lord will be my God [22]and this stone that I have set up as a pillar will be God's house, and of all that you give me I will give you a tenth."

*Listening to the Text in the Story:* Biblical Texts: Genesis 12:1–3; 15; 17; 27:27–29

The main theme of the patriarchal narratives concerns the divine promises delivered to Abraham in Genesis 12:1–3 and reaffirmed to him in Genesis 15 and 17. Though nowhere are these promises explicitly stated by God to Isaac, there is no question but he is the chosen one of his generation that mediates the blessing on to his son Jacob (27:27–29). In the present episode, God himself will confirm that Jacob is the proper recipient of the promises.

**A Stairway to Heaven (28:10–15)**

The narrator shares one story that takes place in his journey from Beersheba in the southernmost part of the promised land to Harran in northwest Mesopotamia. At the beginning of the story, we do not know how much time has elapsed or the location of the event ("a certain place," v. 11). Indeed, the episode will give the place its name.

After taking a stone and using it as a pillar, Jacob fell asleep and then had a dream that he knew was a message from God. At the center of the dream, there was a stairway connecting heaven and earth. Perhaps these were like the steps on a ziggurat (a stepped pyramid typical of Mesopotamia); others conceive it as a ladder. The Hebrew word (*sullam*) only occurs here, but presumably from the verb *sll* "to heap" or "to pile up." Though we might debate the precise meaning of this term, there is no doubt that the dream depicts a place where there is a connection between heaven and earth. Spiritual beings, angels, can move back and forth between heaven and earth in this place.

God then speaks. It is unclear whether God is speaking down from heaven ("above it," namely the stairway) or next to Jacob (translating the prepositional phrase, "beside him"); either is possible. The important point is that God now addresses Jacob and uses the occasion to do what Isaac has done, assure Jacob that he is the recipient of the covenant promises given to Abraham (12:1–3).

God begins by identifying himself as the Lord (Yahweh), the name revealed, and if so then here projected back in time, or explained to Moses at the burning bush (Exod 3).[1] Yahweh also identifies himself as the God of Jacob's ancestors ("the God of your father Abraham and the God of Isaac," v. 3). God then tells Jacob that he will give him and his descendants the land where he is now lying, and that his descendants will be so numerous that they will populate the land in all directions from his present location. Finally, the Lord reiterates the promise that Jacob and his offspring will be a blessing to

1. T. Longman III, *How to Read Exodus* (Downers Grove, IL: InterVarsity Press, 2009), 101–4.

"all peoples on the earth" (v. 14). God then assures Jacob that he will be "with you" (v. 15) and take care of him. He is leaving the promised land now, but God will see that he returns. Thus, not only did his father pass on the covenantal promise to Jacob (27:27–29; 28:3–4), but now God has affirmed that it is Jacob, not Esau, who will carry on the promises into the next generation. As Anderson points out, "How striking and revelatory it is, then, that YHWH does give Jacob the ancestral promise in 28:13–15, on the very heels of a family-shattering deception."[2]

### An Oath at the House of God (28:16–22)

All of this happened in a dream vision, but Jacob had no doubt that the vision communicated reality. Yahweh made his presence known to him in this place and thus he recognizes it as the "house of God" and "the gate of heaven" (v. 17). Thus, he gives the place the name Bethel, which means "house of God," replacing its old name Luz. He consecrated the location by taking the stone he used as a pillar and pouring oil on it. Such a ritual will be prohibited in later Israel since the erection of standing stones could be conceived as a kind of idol, thus breaking the second commandment. However, we have no indication that Jacob's actions here are anything but the right thing to do at the time. Rather than representing a false deity, here the stone pillar is a memorial stone, marking an important meeting between God and his servant. That the stone is not intended to be a false image is supported by Jacob freely offering God a tenth (tithe) of what God will give him.

We now know where Jacob is in the promised land since Bethel becomes a prominent town in later biblical narrative. Today, we identify Bethel with Beiten which is a bit over ten miles north of Jerusalem. The town is first mentioned in Genesis 12:8 when Abram camped soon after entering the promised land for the first time. Presumably, the narrator gives the site its post-Jacob name in the text rather than the name (Luz) which would have been current during the time of Abraham. When Abram first settled there he built an altar to the Lord there. Abram would live there again briefly after returning from Egypt (Gen 13:3). In later history, Bethel is best known as the location of one of Jeroboam's two calf shrines, which he set up to keep his people from going to Jerusalem to worship (1 Kgs 12:26–33). Perhaps it was the reputation of this town as a place that God made his presence known to the patriarchs that motivated Jeroboam to choose this site. Whatever the reason, Bethel, "the house of God," was transformed into a place of false worship. The book of Kings makes it clear that it was the perpetuation

2. Anderson, *Jacob and the Divine Trickster*, 81.

of this false place of worship that was one of the key factors that led to the judgment that ultimately came on the northern kingdom (Jer 48:13; Hos 10:15; Amos 5:5–6).

In response to God's promises, Jacob himself makes a promise. He sets certain conditions, namely that God will remain with him and take care of him, including providing food and clothes, and finally will bring him back to the promised land after his sojourn to Paddan Aram. If God does all these things, then Yahweh will be his God and the stone pillar will be God's house, and Jacob will give Yahweh a tenth of all he has (a tithe: see Gen 14:20 and the essay on The Tithe in the Live the Story section of that chapter).

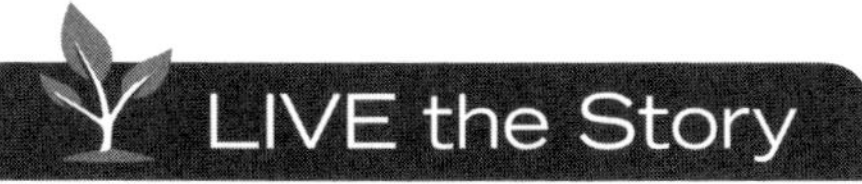


**Jesus: The Axis Mundi**

At Bethel, Jacob witnessed the connection between heaven and earth, the *axis mundi*, the navel of the world, a ladder where angels came down the earth and went back up to heaven. God made his presence known to Jacob at this place, whose name translates into English as the "house of God." Indeed, in the eighth century BC, the prophet Hosea will refer to this incident: "He [God] found him at Bethel and talked with him there" (Hos 12:4).

As we turn to the Gospel of John, we learn about an encounter between Jesus and a man named Nathanael. His friend Philip had just become a disciple and told Nathanael that he was the expected one. Nathanael is incredulous since Jesus is from Nazareth, and he does not believe that anything good can come out of Nazareth. His disbelief dissipated when Jesus greets him as one whom he knows. In response, Jesus evokes the memory of Jacob at Bethel when he tells Nathanael " 'You believe because I told you I saw you under the fig tree. You will see greater things than that.' He then added, 'Very truly I tell you, you will see heaven open, and the angels of God ascending and descending on the Son of Man' " (John 1:50–51). This interchange is enriched by remembering that Nathanael was a man "in whom there is no deceit" (1:47), whereas Jacob, who had the initial revelation was a man whose very name means deceit.[3]

Jesus here claims to be the one who connects heaven and earth. In the words of Burge, "if the location of Jacob's sleep was the focus of God's descent into the world—if this also came to be known as 'God's house,' then it is clear

3. Thanks to Mark Lanier in his *Old Testament Survey* (unpublished manuscript), 189, for pointing this out.

that Jesus subsumes these to himself. He is the 'gateway to heaven' as well as 'the house of God.' "[4]

## Bethel: The House of God Becomes a House of Idols

Bethel is the "house of God," its significance connected to God's appearance to Jacob (note also Abraham's altar, Gen 12:8) and his reaffirmation of the covenant promises. In the Old Testament God's presence renders space holy, and Bethel was a particularly holy location.

However, the later history of Bethel is a sad one, particularly as we turn to the beginning of the divided monarchy. After Jeroboam led the northern tribes away from the Davidic dynasty in Jerusalem, he worried that if his citizens went to the temple, they might become disloyal to him. Thus, he chose Bethel (along with Dan in the north) as a site where he would build an altar that featured the worship of golden calves (2 Kgs 12).

The choice of Bethel was almost certainly because of its connection to God's appearance to Jacob in the past, but by building the altar at this sacred site, he made it a place of false worship. Indeed, God almost immediately sent a prophet to condemn the altar and to anticipate its eventual destruction (2 Kgs 13). The later prophets joined in the chorus of distain for this previously glorious location (Jer 48:13; Hos 10:15; Amos 4:4; 5:5–6).

In the New Testament era, we do not have distinctively holy places; all places are holy in the sense that we can be in God's presence anywhere.[5] In the same way, there is no place that is inherently profane either. That said, the lesson of Bethel, a place of great holiness that becomes a profane place, can serve as a warning to churches, organizations, and individuals that, though they may glorify God at one point in their history/lives, they can turn into a place of sin and degradation.

In America, for instance, we have many fine universities and colleges. They are places where one can get a great education. Not everyone knows that the vast majority of our universities were founded by churches, and the reason why this comes as a surprise to many is that these same great universities downplay their religious roots. As a matter of fact, at most universities and colleges today, Christianity, indeed religion in general, is treated neutrally at best and harshly at worse.

The story of Bethel serves as a warning against presumption and a call to be vigilant, though not heavy handed, in our care and concern for our religious institutions. We cannot simply rely on institutional history or live on the spiritual capital of the past. Institutions are made up of people, and the

4. Burge, *Jesus and the Land*, 49.

5. Longman, *Immanuel in Our Place*, 1–74.

people who work at churches and para-ecclesiastical organizations, as well as Christian universities and colleges, should attend to their own spiritual health and encourage others to grow in their relationship with God.

See related essay: Does God Communicate to Us through Our Dreams? (after Gen 41).

CHAPTER 29

# Genesis 29:1 – 30:24

## LISTEN to the Story

29:1Then Jacob continued on his journey and came to the land of the
eastern peoples. 2There he saw a well in the open country, with three
flocks of sheep lying near it because the flocks were watered from that
well. The stone over the mouth of the well was large. 3When all the flocks
were gathered there, the shepherds would roll the stone away from the
well's mouth and water the sheep. Then they would return the stone to its
place over the mouth of the well.

4Jacob asked the shepherds, "My brothers, where are you from?"

"We're from Harran," they replied.

5He said to them, "Do you know Laban, Nahor's grandson?"

"Yes, we know him," they answered.

6Then Jacob asked them, "Is he well?"

"Yes, he is," they said, "and here comes his daughter Rachel with the
sheep."

7"Look," he said, "the sun is still high; it is not time for the flocks to
be gathered. Water the sheep and take them back to pasture."

8"We can't," they replied, "until all the flocks are gathered and the
stone has been rolled away from the mouth of the well. Then we will
water the sheep."

9While he was still talking with them, Rachel came with her father's
sheep, for she was a shepherd. 10When Jacob saw Rachel daughter of his
uncle Laban, and Laban's sheep, he went over and rolled the stone away
from the mouth of the well and watered his uncle's sheep. 11Then Jacob
kissed Rachel and began to weep aloud. 12He had told Rachel that he
was a relative of her father and a son of Rebekah. So she ran and told her
father.

13As soon as Laban heard the news about Jacob, his sister's son, he
hurried to meet him. He embraced him and kissed him and brought him
to his home, and there Jacob told him all these things. 14Then Laban said
to him, "You are my own flesh and blood."

After Jacob had stayed with him for a whole month, [15]Laban said to him, "Just because you are a relative of mine, should you work for me for nothing? Tell me what your wages should be."

[16]Now Laban had two daughters; the name of the older was Leah, and the name of the younger was Rachel. [17]Leah had weak eyes, but Rachel had a lovely figure and was beautiful. [18]Jacob was in love with Rachel and said, "I'll work for you seven years in return for your younger daughter Rachel."

[19]Laban said, "It's better that I give her to you than to some other man. Stay here with me." [20]So Jacob served seven years to get Rachel, but they seemed like only a few days to him because of his love for her.

[21]Then Jacob said to Laban, "Give me my wife. My time is completed, and I want to make love to her."

[22]So Laban brought together all the people of the place and gave a feast. [23]But when evening came, he took his daughter Leah and brought her to Jacob, and Jacob made love to her. [24]And Laban gave his servant Zilpah to his daughter as her attendant.

[25]When morning came, there was Leah! So Jacob said to Laban, "What is this you have done to me? I served you for Rachel, didn't I? Why have you deceived me?"

[26]Laban replied, "It is not our custom here to give the younger daughter in marriage before the older one. [27]Finish this daughter's bridal week; then we will give you the younger one also, in return for another seven years of work."

[28]And Jacob did so. He finished the week with Leah, and then Laban gave him his daughter Rachel to be his wife. [29]Laban gave his servant Bilhah to his daughter Rachel as her attendant. [30]Jacob made love to Rachel also, and his love for Rachel was greater than his love for Leah. And he worked for Laban another seven years.

[31]When the Lord saw that Leah was not loved, he enabled her to conceive, but Rachel remained childless. [32]Leah became pregnant and gave birth to a son. She named him Reuben, for she said, "It is because the Lord has seen my misery. Surely my husband will love me now."

[33]She conceived again, and when she gave birth to a son she said, "Because the Lord heard that I am not loved, he gave me this one too." So she named him Simeon.

[34]Again she conceived, and when she gave birth to a son she said, "Now at last my husband will become attached to me, because I have borne him three sons." So he was named Levi.

35She conceived again, and when she gave birth to a son she said, "This time I will praise the Lord." So she named him Judah. Then she stopped having children.

30:1When Rachel saw that she was not bearing Jacob any children, she became jealous of her sister. So she said to Jacob, "Give me children, or I'll die!"

2Jacob became angry with her and said, "Am I in the place of God, who has kept you from having children?"

3Then she said, "Here is Bilhah, my servant. Sleep with her so that she can bear children for me and I too can build a family through her."

4So she gave him her servant Bilhah as a wife. Jacob slept with her, 5and she became pregnant and bore him a son. 6Then Rachel said, "God has vindicated me; he has listened to my plea and given me a son." Because of this she named him Dan.

7Rachel's servant Bilhah conceived again and bore Jacob a second son. 8Then Rachel said, "I have had a great struggle with my sister, and I have won." So she named him Naphtali.

9When Leah saw that she had stopped having children, she took her servant Zilpah and gave her to Jacob as a wife. 10Leah's servant Zilpah bore Jacob a son. 11Then Leah said, "What good fortune!" So she named him Gad.

12Leah's servant Zilpah bore Jacob a second son. 13Then Leah said, "How happy I am! The women will call me happy." So she named him Asher.

14During wheat harvest, Reuben went out into the fields and found some mandrake plants, which he brought to his mother Leah. Rachel said to Leah, "Please give me some of your son's mandrakes."

15But she said to her, "Wasn't it enough that you took away my husband? Will you take my son's mandrakes too?"

"Very well," Rachel said, "he can sleep with you tonight in return for your son's mandrakes."

16So when Jacob came in from the fields that evening, Leah went out to meet him. "You must sleep with me," she said. "I have hired you with my son's mandrakes." So he slept with her that night.

17God listened to Leah, and she became pregnant and bore Jacob a fifth son. 18Then Leah said, "God has rewarded me for giving my servant to my husband." So she named him Issachar.

19Leah conceived again and bore Jacob a sixth son. 20Then Leah said, "God has presented me with a precious gift. This time my husband will treat me with honor, because I have borne him six sons." So she named him Zebulun.

[21]Some time later she gave birth to a daughter and named her Dinah.
[22]Then God remembered Rachel; he listened to her and enabled her to conceive. [23]She became pregnant and gave birth to a son and said, "God has taken away my disgrace." [24]She named him Joseph, and said, "May the LORD add to me another son."

*Listening to the Text in the Story:* Biblical Texts: Genesis 12:1 – 3; 21:1 – 7; 24; 25:19 – 26

Stories of marriage (24) and childbearing (21:1 – 7; 25:19 – 26) are important to the patriarchal narratives. After all, these narratives are following how the divine promises in Genesis 12:1 – 3 pass down from generation to generation. To have a new generation there must be a marriage followed by childbearing. As we will develop in the Explain the Story section, there are echoes, particularly concerning the setting at the well, that bind the story of the meeting of Isaac and Rebekah (Gen 24) with that of Jacob and Rachel, though there are significant differences as well.

## EXPLAIN the Story

### Jacob Meets Rachel (29:1 – 14a)

After his encounter with God at Bethel, Jacob continued his journey and the next episode takes place near his ultimate destination of Harran. A number of commentators draw attention to the verbal clause that begins the chapter.[1] The phrase that the NIV translates as "Jacob continued on his journey" is more literally rendered "Jacob picked up his feet." This is an unusual idiom, but it may be too much to say that it indicates a new "bounce in his step," to use the modern idiom, as a result of his recent encounter with God.

As he nears Harran, he sees a well in the open field. It is not clear that this is the same well where Abraham's servant met Rebekah (Gen 24), but the mention of a well, especially in a story about a man seeking a wife, raises the readers' anticipation of an important meeting between a man and a woman, an expectation that is not disappointed.

However, the romantic encounter is delayed, building up narrative tension. Jacob sees three flocks of sheep waiting at this well. The narrator then explains

1. See I. M. Duguid, *Living in the Grip of Relentless Grace: The Gospel in the Lives of Isaac and Jacob* (Phillipsburg, NJ: P & R, 2002), 65.

that this well is covered by a large stone, and that the three shepherds who are present wait until all the other shepherds come to remove this stone. Once the sheep are watered then they would roll the stone back in place (vv. 2–3).

Jacob arrives and enters into a conversation with the shepherds who have congregated around the well. He asks after Laban, whom he identifies as Nahor's (Abraham's brother) grandson. After assuring him that Laban is well, they then point out Laban's daughter Rachel who is shepherding her father's sheep.

While the narrator has already informed the reader that the stone covering the well was not rolled away until all the shepherds got there, Jacob now inquires what the wait is for, and they explain to him that they have to wait until all the shepherds get there. Even so, when Rachel arrived, Jacob rolled the stone away. Perhaps we are to understand that his emotions permit him an extraordinary physical feat of moving a large and heavy stone, or perhaps he is not bound by the alliance of the shepherds to wait until all were there to move the stone, but in any case it is an act that reveals that he is in love at first sight with Rachel, a love that will not diminish over time.

Alter suggests that the specific mention of the stone develops our understanding of the character of Jacob as "the man who seizes his fate, tackles his adversaries, with his own two hands."[2] He further believes that the stone anticipates the obstacles he will encounter, thanks to Laban (see 29:15–30), to consummate his relationship with Rachel.

After moving the stone, he then watered the sheep of his uncle. Jacob knows that Rachel is the one, so he kisses her with great emotion and identifies himself to her. With the Isaac-Rebekah marriage in the background, the implication is clear. Jacob is here to meet his wife, and he has identified Rachel as the one. Thus, she goes off to inform Laban, who enthusiastically welcomes Jacob into his household. Laban was also enthusiastic when he met Abraham's servant who represented Isaac in his eventual marriage to Rebekah. There we saw that he was enamored more by Abraham's wealth and gifts than anything else. While Jacob is a refugee and not carrying gifts, he may have thought that marriage with this grandson of Abraham would naturally lead to wealth. He will be frustrated in the matter of gifts, but, we should not be surprised, he will find a way to exploit the situation to his own advantage—at least at first.

### Jacob Marries Leah and Rachel (29:14b–30)

Apparently Laban put Jacob right to work, and about a month into his labors, Laban asked him how he might repay him. In his question, "because you are a relative of mine, should you work for me for nothing?" sounds like the kind

---

2. Alter, *The Art of Biblical Narrative*, 73.

of thing for which Laban might hope, but for whatever reason, he puts the issue to Jacob, who, as we earlier observed, arrived with nothing.

After the meeting at the well, we are not surprised that he identifies Rachel as his desired wages for his work, but we are also here introduced to her older sister Leah, who will play a major role in the chapters to come. For the first time, we hear that Rachel is beautiful, though again we are not surprised since Jacob seemed immediately attracted to her when he met her at the well. Leah is also described as having "weak" (*rakkot*) eyes. The difficulty of understanding this description is signaled by the NIV footnote which suggests an alternate meaning of "delicate," which would be a much more positive trait. The Hebrew word can produce either of these meanings, so context is going to determine the proper interpretation. What is clear is that Leah is being contrasted with Rachel, so if she is beautiful, then Leah is not. But how can eyes be weak?

While some have suggested that Leah's appearance makes men's eyes weak, it is more likely that it is a characteristic of Leah's eyes. We do know that a woman's eyes are a source of fascination in the Song of Songs (4:1, "your eyes behind your veil are doves"). There, thus, must have been something peculiar about her eyes. Perhaps they were dull or listless, perhaps she was cross-eyed. Something marred her beauty, and thus she was not attractive to Jacob.

We have yet to learn anything about her character, though later God will take pity on her because Jacob does not love her. She will indeed be driven by jealousy of her sister to engage in what we will call a "baby war," which is generated by the manner in which she is treated by Jacob and her sister. In other words, we see no great character flaws in her that would justify Jacob and Rachel's ill-treatment of her. We earlier saw that Esau was a sensuous person, drawn to the here and now, perhaps in this area of life, Jacob too has a weakness. In any case, his favoritism for Rachel will lead to all kinds of strife later in life.

But we are getting ahead of ourselves. Because of his love for her, Jacob agrees to work for seven years in order to marry Rachel, Laban's younger daughter. Why seven years? It is hard to say, except that it is a symbolic number that indicates a significant and full length of time. In the Mosaic law (Exod 21:1–6), we learn that a Hebrew slave must be freed in the seventh year. Perhaps a post-Moses readership would make a connection here since, according to Deuteronomy (15:12–18), the released slave would be given a payment at the completion of his service. It is likely that Jacob's seven-year labor was in lieu of the payment of a bride-price.

Laban agrees, though his affirmation is hardly enthusiastic (v. 19, "it's better that I give her to you than to some other man"). To Jacob, the time seemed to fly by since he was working in the presence of and for the hand of his beloved, the beautiful Rachel.

The time flies by for the reader as well, since verse 20 narrates the seven-year period, and thus in verse 21 we come to the end of Jacob's seven years, and, accordingly, he makes his request, "Give me my wife. My time is completed, and I want to make love to her." Jacob makes his point simply and forcefully, perhaps indicating that he must prod Laban to follow through on his promise. After all, he had a productive worker based on Jacob's belief that his labor will result in his marriage to Rachel. In any case, Laban agreed to a wedding, but with a surprise attached to it.

The wedding seemed to go without controversy, which indicates that Rachel was the bride during the ceremony. But for a marriage to be valid, it has to be consummated (see Gen 2:24), and the next morning when Jacob woke up, he found that he had slept with Leah and not with Rachel!

How could this happen? How could Jacob not know that the woman he had intercourse with on his wedding night was not his beloved Rachel, but rather the "weak-eyed" Leah?

First, of course, we are reminded of the deception that Jacob himself perpetrated on his blind father Isaac that raised the same questions. There we noted that Isaac was blind and perhaps also a tad senile. Jacob was not blind, but it was night, so the episode took place in the darkness. Jacob was not senile, but then, though the text does not make a point of it, he was almost certainly drinking heavily at the wedding feast, apparently so heavily that he could not tell Leah from Rachel.

The trickster has been deceived by another trickster. Laban has outdone Jacob in this instance. But perhaps we should also see God's hidden work here. After all, his marriage to Leah will produce six of his sons plus a daughter Dinah. We also hear at this time that Laban gave Leah a servant, Zilpah, who will also produce two sons for Jacob. After all, these children, along with the two sons born to Rachel and the two born to her handmaiden Bilhah, are the founding ancestors of the tribes of Israel.

The deceiver, Jacob, then confronted Laban and asks him, "Why have you deceived me?" The deal, after all, was for Rachel, and he ended up with Leah. Laban, who may have worried that he could not marry off his "weak-eyed" daughter, tells him that it is the custom of the area to marry off the oldest first. Of course, Jacob had been there for seven years, if it was the custom he probably would have been aware of it. Furthermore, Laban could have told him this before the wedding, but he chose to conceal the custom from him, if indeed it was a custom. He was stuck.

For Laban's part, he not only married off his oldest daughter, but he also now coerced Jacob to work for him for another seven years in order to earn the second daughter, the one he really wanted. Fortunately for Jacob, but perhaps not for Leah, he does not have to wait until the end of another seven years, but marries her at the end of the first week of marriage to Leah. Even so, he is now obligated to work for another seven years for Laban. As he did with Leah, Laban gave a servant, Bilhah, to Rachel. She too will play an important role in the narrative to follow. Once again (v. 30, see also vv. 16 – 18), the narrative makes it clear that Jacob loved Rachel more than Leah.

## Leah Provides Sons for Jacob (29:31 – 35)

In the ancient Near East in general, children are important. In Abraham's family, with the promise that God will make his descendants a "great nation" (12:2), they are crucial. Jacob is married to Leah and Rachel. He loves Rachel; he does not care so much for Leah, who was forced on him. Interestingly, God has compassion for Leah, who was likely lonely in the marriage, so he opened her womb and kept Rachel's closed. God's care for Leah makes us sympathetic for her even more than we might be otherwise. We get the sense that she does not deserve the neglect and abuse that she receives from Jacob and Rachel.

God's opening her womb and not Rachel's begins what we might call the baby wars, since having children will be a bone of contention between the two sisters We grow even more troubled by Rachel since she is not content with her husband's love. Of course, these children are not just any children, they are the founding ancestors of the future tribes of Israel. Thus, the narrative will focus on their birth and also will find great significance in their names.

The firstborn is Reuben, whose name sounds like the Hebrew for either "he has seen my misery" or possibly "see, a son," either being appropriate for the situation. The explanation that Leah gives for the name supports the first meaning, though perhaps both are intended to be heard in the name. She hopes that her giving Jacob his first son will lead him to change his attitude toward her and love her as a husband should love his wife. That her hopes for a change of attitude from Jacob are vain is clear from her explanation of the name that she gives her second son, Simeon. She says that the Lord has given her this son because he understands that she is still not loved by Jacob. The name Simeon is connected to the verb "to hear," and likely means something like "one who hears."

Her hopes for a change in Jacob's attitude toward her persists with the birth of her third son, Levi, a name that is connected by sound or meaning with the Hebrew verb that means "to attach." She hopes that this third child means that her husband will grow in his attachment for her.

It is with her fourth child with Jacob that she seems to give up hope, not naming him in a way that expresses her desire for a closer relationship with Jacob. This child is Judah, whose name is related to the verb "to praise." She explains it by saying "this time I will praise the Lord" (v. 35). At this point she stops having children.

Rachel is beside herself with jealousy at her sister's ability to have children. She demands that Jacob give her children. Jacob will have none of it, since there is little that he can do about it. He is, after all, able to have children with Leah, thus he believes the fault does not lie with him. Rather he (rightly) asserts that it is God who has kept her from having children.

### Bilhah, Rachel's Servant, Provides Sons for Jacob (30:1–8)

Rachel thus makes Jacob sleep with her servant, Bilhah, on the grounds that children with her servant would be counted in her tally of children, not Leah's. Her request, or perhaps the word "demand" captures her tone better, is that he sleep with Bilhah so that, translating the Hebrew idiom literally, "she can give birth on my knees." The idiom expresses the idea that even though her servant will do the physical labor, the child will count as Rachel's. This understanding is confirmed by her final point that Rachel "can build a family through her." This language is the same as Sarah's words to Abraham concerning her desire that he sleep with Hagar to "build a family through her" (Gen 16:2).

Jacob concedes to Rachel's demands, and we learn that Bilhah has a number of children with Jacob. The first is Dan, a name formed from the Hebrew verb "to vindicate," which fits with Rachel's explanation of the name. She sees in Dan's birth a divine vindication in that God has answered her appeal for a son. Such an interpretation could be doubted, since it is not her womb that has yet opened, and all we know about God's interest is that he allowed Leah to have children out of compassion for her unloved status.

We also seem to get Rachel's perspective on the situation in the naming of Bilhah's second son, Naphtali. The name means something like "my struggle," and she says that the struggle has been with Leah, and that she, Rachel, has won the battle. The name seems a bit presumptuous in that, in terms of children, Leah's side still dominates with four versus two sons.

### Zilpah, Leah's Servant, Provides Sons to Jacob (30:9–13)

Indeed, Leah rises to the challenge by now getting her servant into the act. Zilpah has two children, thus recovering the numerical advantage that Leah enjoyed before Bilhah had her two children.

Leah names the first son born to Zilpah, Gad. As the NIV footnote indicates, Gad can mean either "good fortune" or a "troop." The former seems, on the surface of it at least, the best for the context. The meaning "good fortune" also fits nicely with the meaning of Zilpah's second son whom Leah names Asher, which means "happy." The names of these two boys show that

Leah is made happy by her ability to "build" a bigger family for Jacob than her favored sister.

### More Sons for Leah (30:14–21)

But, as it turns out, Leah herself is not finished. The simple listing of births and names is interrupted by an episode that explains how Leah's reproduction kicks into gear once again. It begins with Leah's oldest son Reuben out in the fields during the wheat harvest and discovering some mandrakes. Hearing of this discovery, Rachel requests some of the mandrakes, which her jealous sister at first refuses to give her.

Modern readers may miss the point here unless they understand that in the ancient context of the story mandrakes were considered either an aphrodisiac or something that allowed the user to conceive and have a child. Note the following passage from the Song of Songs:

> Come, my love.
> Let's go out to the field,
> let's spend the night in the villages.
> Let's go early to the vineyards;
> let's see if the vine has budded,
> the bud has opened,
> the pomegranates have bloomed.
> There I will give my love to you!
> The mandrakes give forth their scent,
> and on our entrance is every precious gift.
> The new as well as the old,
> I have treasured up for you, my love. (Song 7:11–13)[3]

The Hebrew word translated in Genesis and the Song as mandrake is *dudaim* which is very close in spelling and pronunciation to a common word for love or lover in the Hebrew of the Song (*dwd*), and this may explain its presence in the poem and the superstition that the plant was an aphrodisiac and something that helped women to conceive. Indeed, as Marvin Pope points out, the mandrake "is actually more of a soporific and narcotic than a stimulant."[4] However, a physiological reaction may not be in view here—at least it may not be what generated the belief that the mandrake was an erotic stimulant. The roots of the mandrake have the appearance of genitalia; the analogy today may be with the ginseng plant, an Asian aphrodisiac that is

---

3. Translation from Longman, *Song of Songs*, NICOT (Grand Rapids: Eerdmans, 2001), 199–200.

4. M. H. Pope, *Song of Songs*, AB 7c (Garden City, NY: Doubleday, 1977), 649.

becoming increasingly popular in the West. Indeed, we should note that not everyone agrees that that *duda'im* is the mandrake, some even preferring ginseng. The translation mandrake goes back to the Septuagint which translated the Hebrew word *mandragoras* (the Vulgate followed suit), which is the official name of the genus of the mandrake. Whatever the precise identification of the plant, the role it plays in the narrative is clear enough. Rachel thinks it will help her have a baby, thus she is willing to barter an evening with Jacob for Leah in return for the plants.

Unfortunately for Rachel, her plan backfired. Though she will eventually give birth to two sons, the narrative does not connect this turn of events to her use of the mandrakes (see, v. 21, "some time later"). On the other hand, Leah's time with Jacob appears to trigger three more births.

Verse 17 pictures Jacob as no more than a pawn in these baby wars. Indeed, he is a "bought man," though instead of him getting paid, he gets sold by one wife to another. Leah names the first son from this new round of births, Issachar, because "God has rewarded me for giving my servant to my husband" (v. 18). Issachar sounds like the Hebrew word for "reward." The second son in the new round, and the sixth overall born to Leah, is Zebulun. From the explanation, it appears that the name is connected to the meaning "honor." She thinks having six of his sons means that Jacob will start to show her honor. Finally, we hear about the birth of a daughter named Dinah. We do not know that this is the only daughter they had. Dinah is singled out for mention because she will play an important role in the story found in chapter 34.

### Rachel Finally Has a Son (30:22–24)

After the birth of ten sons, Rachel's time has finally arrived. God has kept her from having children, but now he opens her womb. Her child is named Joseph, whose story will dominate the last major section of the book of Genesis (chs. 37–50). The name comes from the Hebrew verb for "to add" or "to increase." Thus, she names her child as an appeal that God grant her yet more. God will indeed finally add a second son, but at the cost of Rachel's life (Gen 35:16–20).

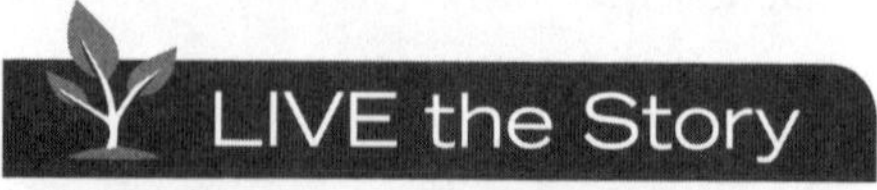


### A Woman in a Man's World

"For she was a shepherd" (v. 9). Rachel may have been beautiful, at least in Jacob's estimation, but there was more to her than beauty. It was not easy being a shepherd in the ancient Near East. A shepherd was responsible for the sheep, not only to guide them to water but also to protect them from predators and perhaps also human thieves. Rachel is the only female shepherd mentioned in the Bible, and so it isn't much of a stretch to think that it was a male-dominated profession. Indeed, the three shepherds who showed up before her were male. She would have to know how to handle herself in a male-dominated world—especially if she were pretty.

In some parts of the evangelical church today, there is a tendency to talk about roles that are appropriate for men and those which are appropriate for women. "Men should be in the work force and women in the kitchen."

Of course, the casual mention of Rachel as a shepherd does not in and of itself undermine that viewpoint, but it does make us wonder whether a case for distinct roles for men and women has a biblical basis at all, particularly when a passage that describes the "wife of noble character" describes her as an active business woman (Prov 31:10–33). We have already seen that, while Esau liked the outdoors and was "wild at heart," Jacob loved the indoors and cooking with his mother. Neither is criticized for their preferences, and indeed, the male in the kitchen is the one whom God choses to receive and pass on the promises. The bottom line is that a careful reading of the Bible does not support stereotyped roles for men and women.

### What Goes Around Comes Around

Jacob, whose very name indicates that he is a deceiver, is himself deceived by his uncle Laban. The trickster is tricked. Jacob had disguised himself as Esau to his father to receive the blessing and now Laban has disguised Leah as Rachel in order to force him to marry her. When Jacob challenges Laban with the question "Why have you deceived me?" (29:25b), the attentive reader remembers Isaac telling Esau, "Your brother came deceitfully and took your blessing" (27:35).

The book of Proverbs makes a point of warning its readers that evil actions can circle back and hurt the perpetrator rather than the intended victim. "The violence of the wicked will drag them away, for they refuse to do what is right" (Prov 21:7). In the first lecture of the father to his son (1:8–19), the father tells the son not to join with those who want to harm the innocent. He tells him that "these men lie in wait for their own blood; they ambush only themselves! Such are the paths of all who go after ill-gotten gain; it takes away the life of those who get it" (1:18–19). Just as Jacob used deception to get an advantage over others; Laban uses it to take advantage of him. As Paul will put it, "a man reaps what he sows" (Gal 6:7).

The story of Mordecai and Haman in the book of Esther is a classic case of someone reaping what they sow and having done to them what they intend for another. Haman wanted to kill Mordecai, so he erected a large sharpened pole on which to impale him (Esth 5:14). However, events conspired (thanks to God's hidden providence) so the king orders that his men impale Haman on the pole and honor Mordecai (Esth 6–7). As the story continues, Haman's attempt to eradicate the Jews also provides the occasion that the Jews eradicate Haman's people (Esth 8:15–9:19) on a day that is still annually celebrated—Purim (Esth 9:20–32).

About three decades ago at a well-known American Bible college and seminary, a senior faculty member was fired for departing from the theological standards of his institution. What is significant about this event is that this same senior faculty member's efforts had led over the years to the firing of more than twenty-five of his junior colleagues. He was well-known for using his influence among powerful donors and constituents to root out people he did not like on trumped-up charges and minor departures from the school's statement of faith. What goes around comes around.

But not always. The principle of reaping what one sows is not an iron-clad rule of life. Even so, it should serve as a warning. As the Golden Rule states, we should treat others as we would want to be treated ourselves.

We should also be mindful of the fact that if we all reaped what we sowed, we would all be in significant trouble. In the eyes of God, we all deserve to die because we are all sinners.

But why don't we? As Christians, we believe that Christ reaped on the cross what we sow. Jesus took our sins on himself and died so that we might live. Our response should be gratitude and obedience. We should be Christ-like in our treatment of others.

## Leah: The Futility of Grasping for Jacob's Love

Leah rejoiced that she had children because she thought that if she provided Jacob with sons, she would finally win his love (29:22). However, though she has his first four sons and ultimately six of his twelve (plus a daughter), Jacob never apparently changed his attitude toward her. Jacobs, who rightly believes that "many aspects of modern life are analogous to the characters and situations in the biblical narratives,"[5] offers the following reflection:

> Leah epitomizes women who in both the private and the public domain of their lives tailor their behavior toward the goal of being loved by the men around them. This may mean having sex with a man to secure a relationship with him, becoming pregnant to get a man to marry her; or having a child to keep a husband in marriage. In the public domain,

5. Jacobs, *Gender, Power, and Persuasion*, 241.

> some women may seek inappropriate attention from their male colleagues or allow inappropriate behavior in order to be accepted.[6]

Jacobs feels that women should take heed of Leah's example and realize that such attempts at manipulation don't work because one can't "control peoples' emotions" this way.[7]

Her advice is sound and also applies to men who try to manipulate others in order to win love. That said, we need to remember that it is God who opens up Leah's womb because he "saw that Leah was not loved" (29:31). However, it is not at all clear that God thought children would change Jacob's attitude toward Leah. More likely, God may have felt that having children would soften the harshness of the loneliness Leah likely experienced in the family.

### God Loves the Unloved

"When the Lord saw that Leah was not loved, he enabled her to conceive, but Rachel remained childless" (29:31). Jacob was forced to marry Leah; he did not love her. Rachel was no friend of her sister, as the ensuing baby wars will make very clear. Laban only acted for his own benefit. As far as we know, there was no one there for Leah. Except God. God doesn't care what we look like; he loves us as his creation. Good looking or not, we are created in his image. God expressed his care toward Leah concretely by allowing her to have children, while the favored wife, who had Jacob's affection, was unable to have children.

Of course, this divine love for unlovely people issues forth in Jesus' sacrifice on the cross. "For God so loved the world that he gave his one and only Son, that whoever believes in him shall not perish but have eternal life" (John 3:16). He loved us though we did not love him, and he died on the cross for our sins.

There, accordingly, should be no Leahs among us. Though she enjoyed the concrete expression of God's love for her in her ability to have children, she should also have felt the love of her family and friends in spite of the circumstances, beyond her control, that brought her to the place where she found herself.

Jesus' love for us should lead us to love each other. "My command is this: Love each other as I have loved you. Greater love has no one than this: to lay down one's life for one's friends" (John 15:12–13).

### Monogamy: God's Plan for Marriage

Many readers of the Old Testament are shocked by the prevalence of polygamous marriage among some of the Bible's best known characters. Indeed, the

---

6. Ibid., 237.
7. Ibid.

later Mosaic law does not prohibit such marriages, but simply regulates it so that a less favored wife is not completely neglected (Exod 21:7–11). The surprise arises because, as we have already seen (see The Nature of Marriage and the Gift of Sex in the Live the Story section after Gen 2:4b–25), God clearly establishes marriage as a monogamous institution; the two become "one flesh" (Gen 2:24).

How are we to understand polygamous marriages in the Bible? Before addressing this question, we should also realize that polygamy was not prohibited among Christians in the New Testament era either. Below we will see that there are indications within the New Testament that polygamy is not God's ideal, but we don't get an explicit prohibition of the practice of having more than one wife.

To understand how this all fits together, we need to realize that the Mosaic law does not necessarily express God's ideal or his ultimate aspirations for how God's people should live. In the Old Testament, God condescends to his people's weakness and then pushes them toward that ideal. That is clearly the case with the topic of divorce. In the Old Testament period, it was relatively easy for a man to divorce his wife (Deut 24:1–4). For this reason, the disciples are taken back when Jesus teaches that divorce could only be permitted under certain conditions (Matt 19:3–6). Jesus explains the difference between the period of the Old Testament and their present when he says, "Moses permitted you to divorce your wives because your hearts were hard. But it was not this way from the beginning" (Matt 19:8).

On analogy with divorce, the Old Testament's allowance for polygamy was because "their hearts were hard." Now that Jesus Christ has come, God moves us toward what we might call his creation ideal of monogamy. But the push comes slowly at first. As Paul teaches, an elder must be "the husband of one wife," which is the literal translation of 1 Timothy 3:2. In other words, he must not be in a polygamous marriage.

Now, granted that the Old Testament period allows for polygamy, the stories of characters who are in polygamous relationships are showpieces for the dangers in such relationships. We have just seen it in the incredible family dysfunction of Jacob and his two wives and the two concubines. We have earlier observed it in Abraham's relationship with Sarah and Hagar. And Abraham and Jacob are in relationship with God. We commented briefly on the first mentioned polygamous marriage, that of Lamech, whose goal was to surpass Cain in evil (Gen 4:19–24).

The point is that polygamy is not God's ideal even when it was tolerated by God. Polygamy is not an issue in the West, since most western societies prohibit marriage with more than one wife. But it has been and still is occasionally an issue on the global South. What happens when a man who has multiple wives becomes a Christian? I remember speaking to Jacob Akpira of the Tiv tribe of Nigeria, one of my many brilliant advanced students, when I taught at Westminster Theological Seminary. Jacob, now sadly deceased as a result of an accident, told me how his father was the husband of eight wives when he became a Christian. In a previous generation, he would have been told to leave seven of them so he could have a monogamous relationship. Of course, such a requirement led, unnecessarily considering the biblical allowance of polygamy, to great harm to the women who were abandoned. Jacob's father was wisely told that he could be a Christian with eight wives, but, because of passages like 1 Timothy 3:2, he could not be an officer in the church. He was also taught biblically to raise his children to only have one wife, which of course Jacob, his son, who was now a leader in the church, had done.

In the West, we may not have a general problem with polygamy (except in parts of Utah), but God's principle of monogamy is frequently violated by adultery or even flitting from one spouse to another when divorce occurs for other than biblical reasons. Marriage is a divinely established institution which calls on a husband and a wife to commit to each other in an exclusive relationship.

See related essays: Marrying the Right Person (after Gen 24) and Our Divine Spouse (after Gen 24).

CHAPTER 30

# Genesis 30:25–31:55

## LISTEN to the Story

30:25After Rachel gave birth to Joseph, Jacob said to Laban, "Send me on my way so I can go back to my own homeland. 26Give me my wives and children, for whom I have served you, and I will be on my way. You know how much work I've done for you."

27But Laban said to him, "If I have found favor in your eyes, please stay. I have learned by divination that the LORD has blessed me because of you." 28He added, "Name your wages, and I will pay them."

29Jacob said to him, "You know how I have worked for you and how your livestock has fared under my care. 30The little you had before I came has increased greatly, and the LORD has blessed you wherever I have been. But now, when may I do something for my own household?"

31"What shall I give you?" he asked.

"Don't give me anything," Jacob replied. "But if you will do this one thing for me, I will go on tending your flocks and watching over them: 32Let me go through all your flocks today and remove from them every speckled or spotted sheep, every dark-colored lamb and every spotted or speckled goat. They will be my wages. 33And my honesty will testify for me in the future, whenever you check on the wages you have paid me. Any goat in my possession that is not speckled or spotted, or any lamb that is not dark-colored, will be considered stolen."

34"Agreed," said Laban. "Let it be as you have said." 35That same day he removed all the male goats that were streaked or spotted, and all the speckled or spotted female goats (all that had white on them) and all the dark-colored lambs, and he placed them in the care of his sons. 36Then he put a three-day journey between himself and Jacob, while Jacob continued to tend the rest of Laban's flocks.

37Jacob, however, took fresh-cut branches from poplar, almond and plane trees and made white stripes on them by peeling the bark and exposing the white inner wood of the branches. 38Then he placed the peeled branches in all the watering troughs, so that they would be directly in front of the flocks when they came to drink. When the flocks were in

heat and came to drink, 39they mated in front of the branches. And they
bore young that were streaked or speckled or spotted. 40Jacob set apart
the young of the flock by themselves, but made the rest face the streaked
and dark-colored animals that belonged to Laban. Thus he made separate
flocks for himself and did not put them with Laban's animals. 41Whenever
the stronger females were in heat, Jacob would place the branches in the
troughs in front of the animals so they would mate near the branches,
42but if the animals were weak, he would not place them there. So the
weak animals went to Laban and the strong ones to Jacob. 43In this way
the man grew exceedingly prosperous and came to own large flocks, and
female and male servants, and camels and donkeys.

31:1Jacob heard that Laban's sons were saying, "Jacob has taken
everything our father owned and has gained all this wealth from what
belonged to our father." 2And Jacob noticed that Laban's attitude toward
him was not what it had been.

3Then the LORD said to Jacob, "Go back to the land of your fathers
and to your relatives, and I will be with you."

4So Jacob sent word to Rachel and Leah to come out to the fields
where his flocks were. 5He said to them, "I see that your father's attitude
toward me is not what it was before, but the God of my father has
been with me. 6You know that I've worked for your father with all my
strength, 7yet your father has cheated me by changing my wages ten
times. However, God has not allowed him to harm me. 8If he said,
'The speckled ones will be your wages,' then all the flocks gave birth to
speckled young; and if he said, 'The streaked ones will be your wages,'
then all the flocks bore streaked young. 9So God has taken away your
father's livestock and has given them to me.

10"In breeding season I once had a dream in which I looked up and
saw that the male goats mating with the flock were streaked, speckled or
spotted. 11The angel of God said to me in the dream, 'Jacob.' I answered,
'Here I am.' 12And he said, 'Look up and see that all the male goats
mating with the flock are streaked, speckled or spotted, for I have seen all
that Laban has been doing to you. 13I am the God of Bethel, where you
anointed a pillar and where you made a vow to me. Now leave this land at
once and go back to your native land.'"

14Then Rachel and Leah replied, "Do we still have any share in the
inheritance of our father's estate? 15Does he not regard us as foreigners?
Not only has he sold us, but he has used up what was paid for us. 16Surely
all the wealth that God took away from our father belongs to us and our
children. So do whatever God has told you."

[17]Then Jacob put his children and his wives on camels, [18]and he drove all his livestock ahead of him, along with all the goods he had accumulated in Paddan Aram, to go to his father Isaac in the land of Canaan.

[19]When Laban had gone to shear his sheep, Rachel stole her father's household gods. [20]Moreover, Jacob deceived Laban the Aramean by not telling him he was running away. [21]So he fled with all he had, crossed the Euphrates River, and headed for the hill country of Gilead.

[22]On the third day Laban was told that Jacob had fled. [23]Taking his relatives with him, he pursued Jacob for seven days and caught up with him in the hill country of Gilead. [24]Then God came to Laban the Aramean in a dream at night and said to him, "Be careful not to say anything to Jacob, either good or bad."

[25]Jacob had pitched his tent in the hill country of Gilead when Laban overtook him, and Laban and his relatives camped there too. [26]Then Laban said to Jacob, "What have you done? You've deceived me, and you've carried off my daughters like captives in war. [27]Why did you run off secretly and deceive me? Why didn't you tell me, so I could send you away with joy and singing to the music of timbrels and harps? [28]You didn't even let me kiss my grandchildren and my daughters goodbye. You have done a foolish thing. [29]I have the power to harm you; but last night the God of your father said to me, 'Be careful not to say anything to Jacob, either good or bad.' [30]Now you have gone off because you longed to return to your father's household. But why did you steal my gods?"

[31]Jacob answered Laban, "I was afraid, because I thought you would take your daughters away from me by force. [32]But if you find anyone who has your gods, that person shall not live. In the presence of our relatives, see for yourself whether there is anything of yours here with me; and if so, take it." Now Jacob did not know that Rachel had stolen the gods.

[33]So Laban went into Jacob's tent and into Leah's tent and into the tent of the two female servants, but he found nothing. After he came out of Leah's tent, he entered Rachel's tent. [34]Now Rachel had taken the household gods and put them inside her camel's saddle and was sitting on them. Laban searched through everything in the tent but found nothing.

[35]Rachel said to her father, "Don't be angry, my lord, that I cannot stand up in your presence; I'm having my period." So he searched but could not find the household gods.

[36]Jacob was angry and took Laban to task. "What is my crime?" he asked Laban. "How have I wronged you that you hunt me down? [37]Now that you have searched through all my goods, what have you found that belongs to your household? Put it here in front of your relatives and mine, and let them judge between the two of us.

38“I have been with you for twenty years now. Your sheep and goats have
not miscarried, nor have I eaten rams from your flocks. 39I did not bring
you animals torn by wild beasts; I bore the loss myself. And you demanded
payment from me for whatever was stolen by day or night. 40This was my
situation: The heat consumed me in the daytime and the cold at night, and
sleep fled from my eyes. 41It was like this for the twenty years I was in your
household. I worked for you fourteen years for your two daughters and six
years for your flocks, and you changed my wages ten times. 42If the God of
my father, the God of Abraham and the Fear of Isaac, had not been with
me, you would surely have sent me away empty-handed. But God has seen
my hardship and the toil of my hands, and last night he rebuked you.”

43Laban answered Jacob, “The women are my daughters, the children
are my children, and the flocks are my flocks. All you see is mine. Yet
what can I do today about these daughters of mine, or about the children
they have borne? 44Come now, let’s make a covenant, you and I, and let it
serve as a witness between us.”

45So Jacob took a stone and set it up as a pillar. 46He said to his
relatives, “Gather some stones.” So they took stones and piled them in a
heap, and they ate there by the heap. 47Laban called it Jegar Sahadutha,
and Jacob called it Galeed.

48Laban said, “This heap is a witness between you and me today.”
That is why it was called Galeed. 49It was also called Mizpah, because he
said, “May the Lord keep watch between you and me when we are away
from each other. 50If you mistreat my daughters or if you take any wives
besides my daughters, even though no one is with us, remember that God
is a witness between you and me.”

51Laban also said to Jacob, “Here is this heap, and here is this pillar I
have set up between you and me. 52This heap is a witness, and this pillar
is a witness, that I will not go past this heap to your side to harm you
and that you will not go past this heap and pillar to my side to harm
me. 53May the God of Abraham and the God of Nahor, the God of their
father, judge between us.”

So Jacob took an oath in the name of the Fear of his father Isaac. 54He
offered a sacrifice there in the hill country and invited his relatives to a
meal. After they had eaten, they spent the night there.

55Early the next morning Laban kissed his grandchildren and his
daughters and blessed them. Then he left and returned home.

*Listening to the Text in the Story:* Biblical Texts: Genesis 12:1 – 3; 28:10 – 30:24

Jacob was the recipient of the divine promises that God spoke to Abraham (12:1–3), which assured him that his descendants would become a great nation and that they would be blessed and would be a blessing to the nations. Jacob had to leave the promised land because of the threat that Esau posed and because he needed to find a spouse among his relatives in northwest Mesopotamia. On his way to the city of Harran, God encountered him at Bethel where he reiterated the promises to him and added that he "would bring you [Jacob] back to this land" (28:15).

Now it was time for him to return. However, due to his complicated relationship with Laban, it would not be an easy departure. Even so, Jacob devised a plan that would enrich him and his family

### Jacob Deceives Laban and Grows Wealthy (30:25–43)

The birth of Joseph was a key moment in Jacob's life. His beloved Rachel had finally given birth. Jacob's thoughts start to think of returning home. Earlier (27:42–45) his mother Rebekah had told him that she would let him know when it would be safe to return to the land. As far as we know (and we might expect the text to say so if she had), she had not sent him any such assurance. Thus, it appears that Jacob feels ready to return even in the light of such uncertainty. As far as he knows, Esau still wants to kill him.

Of course, as will become increasingly clear, life in Paddan Aram (northwest Mesopotamia) with Laban was not easy or comfortable to say the least. He had already basically extorted an additional seven years of labor from Jacob after the seven years that he volunteered to win the hand of Rachel.

But when Jacob approached Laban for permission to go home along with his wives and his children, Laban urges him to stay. Of course, Laban wants him to stay for his own welfare. God has informed Laban that his success is due to the fact that Jacob was with him. Notice here, the presence of a descendant of Abraham has led to the blessing of another outside the line ("all the peoples of the earth will be blessed through you," Gen 12:3). We will see a similar situation in Joseph's life first to the benefit of the household of Potiphar (ch. 39) and then for all of Egypt. It is interesting that God communicated this to Laban through the latter's divination, a practice condemned in later Scripture (Deut 18:9–13). We have no reason to doubt, though, that God did use this unusual method of communicating with Laban (see later the reference to Joseph's divining cup, Gen 44:5).

In any case, Laban does not want to lose Jacob, so he offers to pay him. Interestingly, in verses 29–30, Jacob responds in a way that indicates that Laban did not need divination to realize that it is because of the presence of Jacob that he has prospered. The livestock that he has taken care of have prospered. God has blessed everything Jacob has undertaken on behalf of Laban. Thus, Jacob does want Laban to do something that would prosper Jacob's household, rather than simply prospering Laban's.

At this point, the two master deceivers set to work against each other. Jacob suggests that he remove "every speckled or spotted sheep, every dark-colored lamb and every spotted or speckled goat" (v. 32), and, based on the fact that the mating of such animals will not lead to white lambs and goats, Laban and his people can easily tell which are Jacob's. He claims that this method will remove the possibility of the charge of theft. Under such conditions, Jacob will continue to watch over all the flocks of Laban.

Laban agrees and Jacob then removes the lambs and goats that are not pure white, puts them in charge of his sons, and moves Laban's flock a three day journey away from his new flock.

Jacob remains with Laban's flocks where he devises a plan to increase his flock at the expense of Laban's. Verses 37–39 describe his strategy. He took branches from poplar, almond, and plane trees and then peeled the bark on them so they exposed white stripes. Thus, from this description it appears that the branches are striped like many of the animals. He placed these branches near the watering place so the animals would see them when they came to drink. Those in heat mated in front of the branches. He worked it in particular when the stronger females came. The end result was that those white animals that mated in front of the branches were speckled, spotted, or dark in some way and so would become part of Jacob's flock. Thus, Jacob's flock grew at the expense of Laban's.

But why would two white lambs or goats have speckles, stripes, or dark color just because they mated in front of Jacob's branches? Is there a scientific answer for this?

The answer is no. There is no good scientific reason why Jacob's procedure should have worked. Nothing in modern science would lead us to think that there is anything to Jacob's procedure. Indeed, there is no ancient Near Eastern background that we are aware of behind this practice. That leads us to one conclusion: God caused this to happen so Jacob could get his fair share (see Gen 31:9). Indeed, the chapter ends (see v. 43) with the statement that Jacob grew extremely prosperous.

**Jacob Departs for the Promised Land (31:1–21)**

Jacob prospered due to his strategy with the lambs and goats. However, now he had a new problem. Since his success came at the expense of Laban, Laban's sons were now upset at their loss of wealth, as was Laban himself.

At this point, God told Jacob to return to the promised land. God promises to be "with [him]," a sure indication that Jacob enjoyed a special covenant relationship with Yahweh.

Jacob first of all convinces Rachel and Leah of the need to return to his ancestral homeland. They are easy to persuade. Jacob points out that Laban is now against him, though Jacob's God is for him. He also indicates that Laban had cheated him of wages that were due him by continually changing the conditions of his pay. He can't be trusted. In the previous section, we saw that all the animals that were streaked, speckled, or simply not white were Jacob's, but Laban kept changing the conditions. He would say only the speckled, but not the streaked were Jacob's. God then would make all the offspring speckled. Then Laban would say only the streaked, and God would make all the offspring streaked. Indeed, the angel of the Lord made it clear to Jacob that the reason why his strategy for producing a large flock succeeded was due to God's intervention. It was not the shaved branches, but God himself who assured that the flock would produce Jacob's brand of sheep rather than Laban's. The angel of the Lord then identifies himself as none other than the "God of Bethel," thus informing Jacob that he is the same God that appeared to him at Bethel on his journey up to Paddan Aram (see 28:10–22). At Bethel, God had promised him that he would "bring you back to this land" (28:15). He also reminds Jacob at this time that he had "anointed a pillar" and "made a vow" to him at Bethel (31:13). The vow that Jacob took was that if God would take care of him in his sojourn to Paddan Aram and then would bring him back safely, then this God would be "my God and this stone that I have set up as a pillar will be God's house, and of all that you give me I will give you a tenth" (28:21–22). As we follow Jacob, we will see whether he carried through on his part of the arrangement.

As mentioned, Rachel and Leah, who have not agreed on much up to this point, agree that it is more than right to leave their father Laban. He has, after all, cut them off from family and inheritance ("Do we still have any share in the inheritance of our father's estate? Does he not regard us as foreigners?" vv. 14–15). Indeed, he has sold them to Jacob for fourteen years of his labor, and, they claim, he has already consumed the benefit that that arrangement had accrued for him. Perhaps their statement explains why Laban is trying to exploit Jacob and his labor even further.

They recognize that God is simply working justice with Laban by causing Jacob's flocks to grow while Laban's grow smaller. In essence, they are getting the wealth due to them, even if the means are "irregular." Perhaps here we are to see yet another anticipation of the exodus in Genesis. After all, the Israelites were forced to labor for the Egyptians, receiving no payment for their work. However, when finally they departed from Egypt, God "made the Egyptians favorably disposed toward the people, and they gave them what they asked for; so they plundered the Egyptians" (Exod 12:36). Granted Laban did not willingly or even knowingly give Jacob anything, but the similarity is found in that God created the conditions whereby Jacob and eventually the Israelites got the payment due to them.

Thus, Jacob mobilized his family and the flocks that belonged to him in order to leave Paddan Aram and head back to his father's household in Canaan (vv. 17–18). They left deceptively in that they did not inform Laban of their departure. They left while he was gone shearing the sheep. Unknown to Jacob, Rachel also stole Laban's household gods, which, as we will see, will give Laban additional motivation to set out in pursuit of his son-in-law.

**Laban Overtakes Jacob (31:22–55)**

Jacob managed a three day head start, but traveling with family, flocks, and other possessions, they were eventually overtaken by an embarrassed and angry Laban. Again, we have another anticipation of the exodus story where after Israel departs from Egypt, an angry and embarrassed Pharaoh pursues and overtakes the Israelites. However, it was the purpose of God to destroy the Egyptians. With Laban, it is a different story and God issues a stern warning, instructing Laban not even to say anything "good or bad" to Jacob. In other words, God makes it clear that he does not want Laban to harm Jacob. After this warning, Laban caught up with Jacob in the "hill country of Gilead" (v. 23).[1]

After overtaking Jacob, the two men enter into discussions. He tells Jacob that God had warned him not to say anything "good or bad" to him (v. 29). Apparently, he does not believe that this divine command precludes questions to get an explanation from Jacob.

Thus, he asks "why?" Why did he leave without telling him? Laban, the deceiver, takes exception at being deceived by Jacob's actions here (v. 26). He implicitly accuses him of kidnapping his daughters, which of course, we know is not true. Why did he not let him give his grandchildren a proper good-bye? Why not let him send them off properly? He understands the motive of

1. Waltke (*Genesis*, 428) addresses the problem of Jacob and his group covering what might be up to a 350-mile trip in seven days by suggesting that the seven days start not at Harran, but at a point closer to Gilead within northwest Mesopotamia.

returning to his father's homeland, or so he suggests. But he saves the most stinging accusation for last. Why did he steal his gods?

The mention of Laban's gods is the first explicit indication that he does not worship the same God as Jacob (and Isaac and Abraham), or at least he does not worship the true God exclusively. He certainly acknowledges the patriarch's God, since he heeds God's warning not to harm Jacob. Indeed, he informs Jacob of that fact by telling him that if it weren't for God's intervention, he would certainly have exerted his superior power against his son-in-law.

Jacob explains himself by telling Laban that he expected him to try to take his daughters away from him if he discovered his plans. Indeed, from what we know about Laban at this point, he surely would have tried something to thwart Jacob's intention to return to the promised land. However, he takes umbrage at Laban's accusation that someone stole his household gods. He wants to distance himself from the theft, and he does not know or, apparently, even suspect that Rachel stole them. Thus, he announces publicly that if a thief is discovered then that "person shall not live" (v. 32). In this way Rachel's theft and Jacob's announcement puts Rachel at great risk. Even if Laban did not insist on her death since she is his daughter, he certainly could demand that she return with him to Paddan Aram.

But what is the significance of these idols, and why did Rachel steal the household gods in the first place? Our reticent narrator does not tell us and perhaps the motivation would have been obvious to the ancient reader. After the discovery of cuneiform tablets at Nuzi, a place relatively near Abraham's ancestral homeland of Harran and also a time not too distant from that of the patriarchs, scholars realized that many of the strange actions of the patriarchs were explained by contemporary social customs (see below).[2] Or perhaps Rachel simply wanted to hurt the father who had hurt her so badly by stealing something that was meaningful to him.

The very existence of the household gods, of course, indicates that Laban was not an exclusive worshiper of the true God. But what does it indicate about Rachel? It is possible, but not certain, that she too worshipped other gods along with the true God at this time. Indeed, it will only be later that Jacob's family will give up the worship of multiple gods to worship only the true one (35:1–5).

Household gods were used for rituals connected to ancestor worship and provided a link with one's departed relatives. The Nuzi tablets (for more information on Nuzi, please see the commentary on 15:1–6) indicate that there might have been some connection with inheritance since the main heir would

2. See Provan, Long, and Longman, *A Biblical History of Israel*, 113–16.

receive these household deities. This certainly explains Laban's anger and anxiety. Perhaps Rachel only wanted to anger her father.

Jacob is confident that no one stole the household gods, but the reader knows better. Thus, narrative tension escalates as Laban begins his search. He first searches Jacob's tent and then Leah's. After Leah's tent, he then investigates the tents of the two maidservants, Bilhah and Zilpah. He finds nothing, so he heads to Rachel's tent.

Verse 33 shows that he searched Rachel's tent last, thus building the readers' suspense since they know that it is Rachel who stole them. Interestingly, the first part of the verse gives the following order: Jacob, Leah, and then the two maidservants, but the second part of the verse indicates that it was after he left Leah's tent that he went into Rachel's. If the first part gives the actual order, it might show more distrust for the older daughter than the younger whose tent is not even searched until after the two maidservants. But searching Leah's tent before Rachel's may simply be the result of the fact that the former is older than the latter.

The narrator informs the reader that Rachel had hidden the household gods in her camel's saddle, on which she is sitting when her father enters the tent. Laban then finds nothing in his search. Rachel cleverly deceives her father by telling him that she cannot get up from her seat because she is having her period. Of course Laban is an Aramean living in the patriarchal period, but later Mosaic law is likely still relevant in helping us understand the effect of her statement. After all, Mosaic categories are relevant for other stories in Genesis including the clean and unclean animals brought on the ark by Noah (7:6–10) and the narrator's judgment of Abraham as one who "did everything I required of him, keeping my command, my decrees and my instructions" (26:6). Judging this by later Levitical law, the comment is brilliant because if Laban touched Rachel or anything on which she sat he would become ritually unclean: "When a woman has her regular flow of blood, the impurity of her monthly period will last seven days, and anyone who touches her will be unclean till evening. Anything that she lies on during her period will be unclean, and anything she sits on will be unclean ... Anyone who touches anything she sits on will be unclear ..." (Lev 15:19–20, 22). Of course, Laban avoids touching her or her camel's saddle, but the reader understands a further implication as they picture the household idols themselves embedded under the ritually unclean Rachel. They are not only false gods, but they are ritually defiled (for more on the household idols, see commentary on 35:1–2).

Laban comes up empty handed even though his charges were true; his household idols were indeed stolen. Of course, the reader should have no sympathy for this opportunistic, exploitative deceiver when he himself is deceived. Thus when Jacob unleashes his anger on him we feel nothing but satisfaction.

He asks Laban to bring the evidence forward to back up his accusations. He cannot because he has not been able to find the stolen objects. Of course, there is more than an element of truth in Jacob's saying "how have I wronged you?" It was not Jacob, after all, who stole the gods, indeed, he didn't even know about it.

From present "injustice," Jacob turns to those of the past. He had worked for Laban for twenty years, and Laban was a hard taskmaster. He worked under difficult conditions and for as meager a pay as Laban could dole out. Jacob himself, he claims, was fair, while Laban cheated him. Indeed, he asserts, Laban would have let him leave with nothing unless God had worked things out. The latter claim is a reference to God allowing the speckled, colored, and spotted animals to multiply so that he had a large flock to take with him back to the promised land.

It is significant that in his speech to Laban, in spite of all the pain and suffering of his life so far, he sees that the good has come from "the God of Abraham and the Fear of Isaac" (v. 42). The reference to the "Fear of Isaac" is particularly arresting. Of course, to fear God is very positive in the wisdom literature (see especially Prov 1:7; Job 28:28; Eccl 12:13). One can point to Genesis 22, the Akedah, to see a moment when indeed Isaac might learn fear of God, though it is hard to say whether Isaac developed a positive or negative fear of God and that story only comments on Abraham's fear (22:12). Considering the context of the present reference to Isaac's fear of God, it should be taken in a positive sense.

Laban is unwilling to concede the principle. He insists that everything that Jacob has—his wives, his children, and his flocks—really belong to him and not to Jacob. But he does concede on a practical level. There is nothing he can do about it. Everyone—most especially Jacob's God—is against him and he knows it. Thus, he asks Jacob to enter into a covenant with him.

A covenant in this context is a treaty, a legal agreement between two parties, typically representing nations or people groups, to regulate their relationship into the future. It will serve as a witness between them. A covenant/treaty contains law that binds both parties and the law is supported by rewards for obedience and punishments for disobedience.

Jacob signals his agreement by setting up a stone and then telling his relatives to pile up stones. Such a move reminds us of the role that stones play in the Jacob narrative (28:11, 18, 22; 31:45–46; 35:14). Though stones play a special role in the Jacob story, other covenant/treaty agreements are also commemorated by the erection of some kind of stone monument (e.g., Josh 24:25–27). They function as witnesses to the legal agreement. If one party breaks the agreement, the other party can point to the stone and say, "remember the agreement we made here!" Indeed, the names both sides give to this particular stone monument highlights its function as witness. Laban's party gives it the Aramaic name Jegar Sahadutha and Jacob's side the Hebrew name Galeed, both of which mean "witness heap."

Laban then speaks and defines the significance of the pillar which Jacob erected and the stone heap made by the people. He begins by asserting what we already know from the narrator, that the heap is a witness to the treaty made between the two parties, again explaining the Hebrew name, Galeed, or "witness." The narrator then goes on to explain that the heap had yet a third name, namely Mizpah, which is Hebrew for "watchtower." Laban then appeals to the Lord to keep watch over this new relationship ("between you and me," v. 49), thus requesting God himself to be a witness to this relationship. Though he has not shown a lot of familial affection up to this point, Laban expresses his concern for his daughters' welfare now that Jacob is moving them beyond his reach. He tells Jacob not to take any more wives or to mistreat them.

In verses 51–53a Laban continues by calling on the heap, and now in addition the pillar, to function as a witness against the possibility of violence between the two groups. In effect, the heap and the pillar function as a boundary marker between Laban's people and Jacob's people. Laban insists that neither should cross the border in order to harm the other.

This provision has ramifications for later history since Laban's people become the Arameans and Jacob's people become the Israelites. Later history attests to numerous incursions of Arameans against the Israelites. Second Kings 24:2, for instance, mentions that Nebuchadnezzar sent Aramean raiders against Jerusalem sometime before the siege of that city in 597 BC and these may have come from the Damascus region. Later audiences would certainly understand that it was the Arameans, the descendants of Laban, who violated the trust that Laban himself had requested from Jacob.

It was typical in an ancient Near Eastern treaty to appeal to the gods of both sides of the agreement to serve as guarantors of the relationship. Thus, it is interesting that Laban concludes his speech by invoking "the God of Abraham and the God of Nahor." Of course, Abraham was Jacob's grandfather and his God was the Lord. There is some question about who the God of Nahor is. Nahor is Abraham's brother, but did he worship the same God? We are not sure. Abraham and Nahor's father, Terah, was a pagan (Josh 24:2). Nahor himself did not go to the promised land. His grandson Laban had household idols. So we are not certain about the identity of Nahor's God, but in any case, the covenant/treaty was now presented to Jacob for ratification.

Accordingly, we learn in verses 53b–54 that Jacob does exactly that. First he swears an oath to abide by the oath, again invoking God by the name of "the Fear of Isaac" (see discussion above). Then he offered a sacrifice to God followed by a covenant-sealing meal shared between his family and Laban's.

With their disagreements resolved or at least now regulated, Laban can take a dignified departure from Jacob. He kissed his children and grandchildren and blessed them. We are not told the content of his blessing, unlike the blessings of Jacob on his children in chapter 49, because, again unlike Jacob's, it carries no effects into the future.

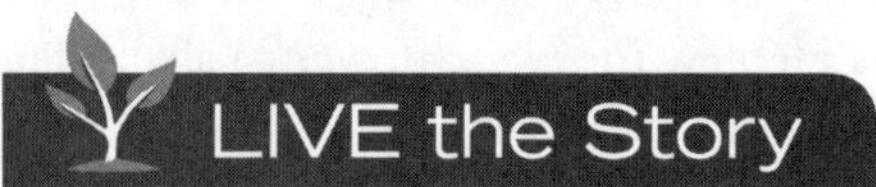


### "The Lord Has Blessed Me Because of You" (30:27)

Perhaps for the first time, and under the pressure that he might lose Jacob's presence, Laban acknowledges to his son-in-law that he has brought blessing to his household because God was with him. Jacob wants to leave because Laban has exploited him even though the blessing has come through him, but we should still note that here God's chosen is a source of blessing to his family and his community in a way that leads Laban to desire Jacob's presence. We will see this same theme play out when we read about Joseph. Since God was "with Joseph," those around him prospered and wanted to be associated with him (see Gen 39 in particular).

Laban's words to Jacob struck me because I wonder how many non-Christians would say that today about the church and the individual Christians who people the church. My impression, based on local and national media reports, is that the broader culture sees Christianity as a bane and a curse. While we are quick to blame the "world" for their hardheartedness and resistance to the gospel, a fair-minded self-reflection leads us to see some measure of fault with Christians as we approach our culture.

After all, the society sees Christian ecclesiastical and political leaders who are judgmental, petty, trying to push their "Christian" agenda on the rest of society. When they don't get their way, these same Christian leaders whine about how our original (supposed) Christian nation is heading to hell. In addition, as the world looks on, they see Christians fighting with each other over the most petty of theological, ecclesiastical, or even just personal matters. During the summer when I am writing, the president of the college where I am teaching has gotten attacked over simply having an audience with the

Pope. My readers certainly know many other examples of what I am referring to here.

What does Jesus say? In his high priestly prayer, he asks God that "all of them [Christians] may be one ... just as you are in me and I am in you. May they also be in us so that the world may believe that you have sent me. I have given them the glory that you gave me, that they may be one as we are one — I in them and you in me — so that they may be brought to complete unity. Then the world will know that you sent me and have loved them even as you have loved me" (John 17:21–23). Jesus' urgent prayer is that Christians demonstrate love toward each other before, to quote the title of a Francis Schaeffer book on this subject, a "watching world."[3]

## God, the Righter of Wrongs

In an earlier essay (What Goes Around Comes Around, after 29:1–30:24), we noted that often God works situations out so that an evil person "reaps what he sows" (Gal 6:7). In the earlier passage, we observed how Laban out deceived Jacob the deceiver. But in that story, there was no sense that what Jacob wanted — namely Rachel as a wife — was sinful or wrong. Laban was not righting a wrong, but rather just exploiting Jacob so that he would marry both of his daughters, not just the attractive one.

In our present story, we see that Laban will get what is coming to him. Jacob deceives Laban when Laban is trying to cheat him out of his wages (see Is Deception Ever Permissible? below). We have seen how Jacob comes up with a plan to produce the kind of sheep that would be his, not Laban's, that just should not work, but in this case does. Why? As Jacob later tells his wives, "God has taken away your father's livestock and has given them to me" (31:9). God was the one who made sure that Laban could not cheat Jacob out of his deserved wages.

God never promises that he will turn every wrong into a right in this life. He calls us to be faithful even if we are exploited. No one was more exploited in life and death than Jesus. God did not render quick and immediate judgment on those who harmed Jesus. And Jesus did not seek their punishment. Even though he was tortured and executed for no crime, he asks his heavenly Father to forgive those who humiliated and crucified him (Luke 23:34). Of course, and the Christian knows this, his life is not the end of the story. Jesus died at the hands of wicked men, but "God raised him from the dead, freeing him from the agony of death" (Acts 2:24).

---

3. F. Schaeffer, *The Church before the Watching World: A Practical Ecclesiology* (Downers Grove, IL: InterVarsity Press, 1971).

What should we learn from this? We can affirm that God indeed protects the exploited (Ps 140:12; Prov 14:31; 23:11; Isa 3:14). He may not do so immediately, but he will right all wrongs. Thus, we should be warned not to take advantage of others, particularly those in a vulnerable position. On the other hand, if we are victims ourselves, we should turn to God and ask his intervention, even if it may not happen immediately. Like Jacob, we might take action against our exploiter within the bounds of biblical ethics and contemporary law, and God may honor our efforts. But we must also follow Paul's admonition:

> Do not repay anyone evil for evil. Be careful to do what is right in the eyes of everyone. If it is possible, as far as it depends on you, live at peace with everyone. Do not take revenge, my dear friends, but leave room for God's wrath, for it is written: "It is mine to avenge; I will repay," says the Lord. On the contrary: "If your enemy is hungry, feed him; if he is thirsty, give him something to drink. In doing this, you will heap burning coals on his head." Do not be overcome with evil, but overcome evil with good. (Rom 12:17–21)

### Time to Leave

It is time for Jacob to gather his family and his possessions together and depart from Paddan Aram. God has told him to leave, and Jacob is ready to follow God's instructions in this matter. But Jacob also knows it is time to leave to get away from Laban, who has been exploiting him and abusing him. To stay would mean a continuation of the abuse.

Some Christians labor under the impression that we must always forgive those who harm us. After all, when Peter asked Jesus, 'Lord, how many times shall I forgive my brother or sister who sins against me? Up to seven times?,' Jesus responded, 'I tell you, not seven times, but seventy-seven times.' (Matt 18:21–22). As is well-known, seven and its multiples are often used symbolically, and here Jesus seems to be saying that our willingness to forgive needs to be unlimited. Indeed, the parable of the unmerciful servant that follows (18:23–35) teaches that if we do not forgive those who harm us, then God will not forgive us.

The ability to forgive those who hurt us is extremely important not just to the other person but also to ourselves. If we hold on to our resentments, then the anger and anxiety that follows from abuse allow the person who harmed us to continue to do so.[4]

---

4. D. Allender and T. Longman III, *Bold Love* (Colorado Springs, CO: NavPress, 1992).

That said, elsewhere Jesus indicates that our forgiveness, like God's forgiveness of us, is not free of conditions. In Luke 17:3–4, we read "If your brother or sister sins against you, rebuke them; and if they repent, forgive them. Even if they sin against you seven times in a day and seven times come back to you saying 'I repent,' you must forgive them." Notice the "if" clause—if they repent. Repentance involves more than an acknowledgement of harm but also a change of behavior. If there is no acknowledgement and there is no change of behavior, then it could be, in some situations, quite dangerous to forgive someone. And if someone asks for forgiveness and keeps committing the same sin against another, then one has to doubt whether there is sincere repentance. This leads me to think when Jesus says to forgive someone who repents seven times a day, we are not talking about the repetition of the same sin because in such a case the person would make it perfectly clear that they hadn't really repented.

What does this biblical teaching boil down to? First, we must be quick to accept the sincere repentance of someone who harmed us. Again, Jesus teaches clearly that we will not be forgiven if we are not ourselves forgiving people. But even in cases where we extend our forgiveness to an abuser, it still may be wise to remove ourselves from that person if they have shown themselves to be dangerous. Jacob knows it is time to leave his abuser Laban and remove his family from the possibility of harm. In the next episode, we will see an angry Laban overtake Jacob, and though we do not get a record of repentance on Laban's side, he and Jacob will be able to reach an amicable settlement between them, entering a treaty that will keep them separate and avoid conflict.

### The True Source of Jacob's New Found Wealth

In a section of his helpful book on Isaac and Jacob, Iain Duguid provides an excellent perspective on how the story of Jacob and his growing flocks provides an object lesson to warn us from misreading providence.[5] We have seen how Jacob devised an elaborate scheme in order to increase his flocks at the expense of Laban's (see 30:37–43). He worked hard and likely thought himself quite clever and industrious. In the exposition of this passage, we pointed out, however, that there was no real merit to his plan. The only reason he succeeded, and he comes to recognize this himself (31:9–13), is because God made it happen.

Duguid is correct to say that Jacob would have been wrong to continue to believe that it was his scheme that led to his wealth. I would add that if he

5. Duguid, *Living in the Grip of Relentless Grace*, 97–98.

had, he would have been in the position of the psalmist, whom God blessed with prosperity, but came to put all his trust in himself not God ("when I felt secure, I said, 'I will never be shaken,'" Ps 30:6). God reminded the psalmist that it was because of God that he had what he had by temporarily abandoning him.

I would also go further and say that it is not just when we, like Jacob in this instance, achieve success in spite of our misguided plans and efforts that we should see the hand of God. Even when we, as we should, plan wisely and engage in diligent effort, we should see God giving us whatever success comes our way.

### Anticipation of the Exodus from Egypt and Even Further...

Kent Hughes helpfully points out that Jacob's return from Paddan Aram (or northwest Mesopotamia) looks back on Abraham's initial entry into the promised land (Gen 12:1–9) as well as forward to the exodus from Egypt: "Here Jacob's large family flees from Laban; there a multitude of his descendants will flee Pharaoh. Here his family plunders Laban; there they will plunder Pharaoh and his people. Here Laban is forced to let Jacob's family go; there Pharaoh will be forced to let Jacob's descendants go."[6] Thus, too, this story not only reminds the reader of Abraham's initial descent into the promised land but also his return from Egypt after the famine (12:10–20). And here we refer the reader to the essay after the exposition of that passage that shows the connection between the exodus event and its anticipations in the book of Genesis with the ultimate Exodus accomplished by Jesus (see God Delivers His People in the Live the Story section after 12:10–20).

### Is Deception Ever Permissible?

The attentive reader of Genesis will notice there has been a lot of lying in the book up to this point.[7] The serpent deceives Adam and Eve (Gen 3:1–19), Abraham twice deceives a foreign ruler concerning the status of his wife (12:10–20; 20:1–18), an example followed by his son Isaac (26:6–11). Jacob's very name is connected to the act of deception, and he has deceived (29:15–30, and some think also at 27:1–40) and been deceived (31:4–9, 38–42). There is more to come as well, not only in the Jacob story (34:1–31) but also in the story of his sons Joseph (37:29–35; 39:1–20; 42:7–28; 44:1–34) and Judah (38:1–26).

---

6. Hughes, *Genesis*, 389.

7. Williams (*Deception in Genesis*, 12–38) provides a helpful catalogue of scenes of deception in Genesis.

Is deception always wrong? Many people think that a simple citation of the ninth commandment ("you shall not give false testimony against your neighbor," Exod 20:16) makes it clear that the answer to this question is yes. Indeed, most of the episodes listed above either receive an explicit negative evaluation or an implicit one.

However, as Williams rightly points out in his book *Deception in Genesis* (see footnote #7), not all of them are negatively assessed. In our present story, Jacob deceives Laban by secretly leaving Paddan Aram with his family and his possessions. While there is not a direct evaluation (there rarely is), the fact that God has told Jacob to return to the promised land and God's warning to Laban to "be careful not to say anything to Jacob, either good or bad" (31:24) is a strong indication that God approved of Jacob's deception of Laban in this situation.[8]

As we go on, we will see other stories in which deception serves a good purpose and is positively evaluated, including Levi and Simeon deceiving the Shechemites (34), Joseph lying to his brothers about his identity (42:7–28), and Joseph accusing Benjamin of stealing his divining cup (44:1–34). For details, the reader should consult the commentary at those places.

What differentiates good deception from sinful deception in the book of Genesis? I agree with Williams when he concludes: "Within the book of Genesis, deception is positively evaluated only when the perpetrators deceive one who has previously wronged them in order to restore their own situations to what they would have been had they not been disrupted."[9] In our present story, Laban certainly had previously and often wronged Jacob, beginning with his marriage to Leah when Jacob thought he was marrying Rachel.

However, Williams goes further and adds: "Moreover, in their efforts to restore their situations to what they should be, the deceivers must not negatively affect the 'normal' situation of their targets for their behavior to be positively evaluated."[10] This describes well our present story as well as Joseph's deception of his brothers. Neither Laban nor Joseph's brothers are harmed. But this is not true of the objects of Levi and Simeon's deception, namely the Shechemites. Granted that Williams does not believe the latter is a story of positive deception, he would so evaluate (expanding beyond Genesis) Moses' attempted deception of Pharaoh when he tells him that he is only interested in taking the Israelites out for a short three day trek for a religious observance or, for that matter, God's directive to deceive Pharaoh by circling back and encamping by the Re(e)d Sea (Exod 14:1–4). As we look at these examples,

8. Ibid., 22.
9. Ibid., 221.
10. Ibid.

we may want to add the following principle. Deception is permissible if the person asking for the truth wants to use it to harm us or others.

What does this tell us about truth telling today? First of all, we must underline the ninth command. We must tell the truth. The narrative texts do, however, provide a caveat that actually treats lying in certain situations a virtue and not a vice. During the Second World War, some Christians (and others) bravely resisted the Holocaust by hiding Jews in their homes. What were these Christians to do when the Gestapo knocked on their door and asked if they knew where any Jews were? Here the person asking for the truth wants it for great harm to others? I think the biblical answer to this question is to say that they should lie (think of the Egyptian midwives; Exod 1:15–22). Such people forfeit the right to the truth because of their evil intentions.

We would be remiss not to point out that such circumstances are very rare. While it is too simplistic and also dangerous to simply say that we must speak the truth at all times no matter what the circumstances, we need to be aware of the temptation to lie not to avoid certain undeserved harm to ourselves or others, but for our own convenience.

See related essay: Does God Communicate to Us through Our Dreams? (after Gen 41).

CHAPTER 31

# Genesis 32:1 – 21

## LISTEN to the Story

32:1Jacob also went on his way, and the angels of God met him. 2When
Jacob saw them, he said, "This is the camp of God!" So he named that
place Mahanaim.
3Jacob sent messengers ahead of him to his brother Esau in the land
of Seir, the country of Edom. 4He instructed them: "This is what you are
to say to my lord Esau: 'Your servant Jacob says, I have been staying with
Laban and have remained there till now. 5I have cattle and donkeys, sheep
and goats, male and female servants. Now I am sending this message to
my lord, that I may find favor in your eyes.' "
6When the messengers returned to Jacob, they said, "We went to your
brother Esau, and now he is coming to meet you, and four hundred men
are with him."
7In great fear and distress Jacob divided the people who were with
him into two groups, and the flocks and herds and camels as well. 8He
thought, "If Esau comes and attacks one group, the group that is left may
escape."
9Then Jacob prayed, "O God of my father Abraham, God of my
father Isaac, Lord, you who said to me, 'Go back to your country and
your relatives, and I will make you prosper,' 10I am unworthy of all the
kindness and faithfulness you have shown your servant. I had only my
staff when I crossed this Jordan, but now I have become two camps.
11Save me, I pray, from the hand of my brother Esau, for I am afraid
he will come and attack me, and also the mothers with their children.
12But you have said, 'I will surely make you prosper and will make your
descendants like the sand of the sea, which cannot be counted.' "
13He spent the night there, and from what he had with him he
selected a gift for his brother Esau: 14two hundred female goats and
twenty male goats, two hundred ewes and twenty rams, 15thirty female
camels with their young, forty cows and ten bulls, and twenty female
donkeys and ten male donkeys. 16He put them in the care of his servants,

each herd by itself, and said to his servants, "Go ahead of me, and keep some space between the herds."

[17]He instructed the one in the lead: "When my brother Esau meets you and asks, 'Who do you belong to, and where are you going, and who owns all these animals in front of you?' [18]then you are to say, 'They belong to your servant Jacob. They are a gift sent to my lord Esau, and he is coming behind us.'"

[19]He also instructed the second, the third and all the others who followed the herds: "You are to say the same thing to Esau when you meet him. [20]And be sure to say, 'Your servant Jacob is coming behind us.'" For he thought, "I will pacify him with these gifts I am sending on ahead; later, when I see him, perhaps he will receive me." [21]So Jacob's gifts went on ahead of him, but he himself spent the night in the camp.

*Listening to the Text in the Story:* Biblical Texts: Genesis 25:19–34; 26:34–46

Right from the start Jacob and Esau were rivals for dominance. They fought in the womb (25:22). Esau was firstborn, but Jacob was grasping the heel of Esau (indeed, one meaning of his name is "to grasp the heel") in what could be construed as an attempt to pull him back into the womb. Though Esau was the first born, God had spoken to Rebekah during her pregnancy and informed her that "the older will serve the younger" (25:23). When they grew up, Jacob convinced Esau to sell him his birthright (25:27–34), and Rebekah and Jacob together deceived Isaac so that he conferred the blessing meant for the firstborn on Jacob rather than Esau (26:34–46).

Not surprisingly, Esau hated Jacob and vowed to kill him. When Rebekah found out Esau's intentions, she convinced Isaac to send him away to Paddan Aram to find a wife and to avoid Esau. At that time, she told Jacob that she would let him know when Esau's anger dissipated and advised him to wait until that time to return home (27:45).

But Jacob has returned home before receiving word from his mother. Therefore, he does not know what Esau's attitude is toward him. Jacob's ignorance of Esau's present attitudes and intentions are what drives the suspense of the following narrative.

**Jacob Informs Esau of His Return (32:1–6)**

After Laban departs (see previous section), Jacob now continues his journey. His first encounter is with "the angels of God" (v. 1). The angels' presence makes him name this location Mahanaim, which means "two camps," presumably the "camp of God" and his own camp. His encounter with the angels after his departure from Laban and the establishment of the boundary between the two distant parts of the family, indicates that he has re-entered the promised land. It also likely presages his coming encounter with God himself in the second part of the chapter.

In later Israelite history Mahanaim plays a significant role. It was a Levitical city on the border of Manasseh and Gad (Josh 13:23, 30; 21:38). During the United Kingdom, it was Ish-bosheth's, Saul's son, capital (2 Sam 2:8, 12, 29). David fled there during Absalom's rebellion (2 Sam 17:24, 27; 19:32).

At this point, Jacob's attention now turns to his brother Esau. When we last left Esau (27:41), he was plotting to murder his brother for stealing his birthright and his inheritance. Rebekah had urged Jacob to flee to Paddan Aram and start a family there in order to avoid falling into his brother's hands. Indeed, Rebekah had warned him to wait until he heard from her that it was safe to return (27:45). We have no indication at all that Rebekah had so communicated with him. Jacob decided to return anyway because conditions had deteriorated in Paddan Aram and, even more importantly, God had told him to return (31:3).

Rather than arriving unannounced, Jacob thinks it wise to contact his brother to inform him of his return. We should note that it was not absolutely necessary for Jacob to alert Esau of his return. Jacob did not have to cross Esau's tribal territory to go where he wanted to go, so it is significant that Jacob takes the risk of alerting his brother that he has returned.

Thus, he sends messengers to Esau who now lived in the region of Seir, the country of Edom. We have already seen that Edom is Esau's second name. Edom is a country located to southeast of the Dead Sea just below the nation state of Moab. It should be stated that it may be an anachronism to refer to Edom as a "country" at this point. Esau had just emigrated there recently. His people would be an extended family and their attendants and perhaps associates. Edom would emerge as a nation state later in history, but right now Edom (also identified as the hill country of Seir) was inhabited by migrating tribal groups.

His message oozes with respect for his brother. He shows humility toward him by calling him "my lord" and refers to himself to Esau as "your servant" (v. 4). He reports to his brother that he has returned to the land after a lengthy sojourn with Laban. He also informs him that he is returning a wealthy person in terms of herds, flocks, and servants. The purpose of his message is "to find favor in your eyes" (v. 5).

Jacob's message is interesting to read in terms of the oracle God delivered to Rebekah at the time of the twins' birth: "the older will serve the younger." Here the younger Jacob calls his older brother Esau "lord" and himself the "servant" of Esau, and we will see this throughout the story of their reunion.

However, this should not get us to rethink the nature of the oracle. Jacob is willing to grovel in order to survive what he thinks is the hostile approach of his brother. But there is no doubt that the ultimate fulfillment of the oracle lodged in Jacob's chosen status. That said, the type of lordship that the chosen must practice is one that mediates the promised blessing to others, including Esau and his descendants (see 12:1–3).

When the servants return, they come with disturbing information. Esau did not give a verbal response to Jacob, but rather was on his way with four hundred men, a veritable army!

### Jacob Prepares for Esau (32:7–21)

Jacob's reaction indicates that he believes that Esau is coming to fight. Why else bring four hundred men with him? Thus, Jacob prepares for the worst case scenario by dividing his people and his animals into two "groups" (v. 7). The word translated "groups" here is the same word as "camps" in the name Mahanaim. Thus, if Jacob's naming of the site was due to the fact that there was a human camp and an angelic one at this place, now his own people are divided into two camps.

His plan is simple and desperate. If Esau is coming to destroy him, then the second group may have an opportunity to escape while Esau is attacking the first group.

After devising his plan, Jacob then turns to God in prayer for help. He knows that he can plan all he wants, but unless God is with him, he is doomed. He thus illustrates the wisdom encapsulated in Proverbs 16:1–3, 9:

> To humans belong the plans of the heart,
> but from Yahweh comes a responding tongue.
> All paths of people are pure in their eyes,
> but Yahweh measures the motives.
> Commit your acts to Yahweh,
> and your plans will be established.

> Human hearts plan their path,
> but Yahweh establishes their step.[1]

Jacob begins his prayer by appealing to God who was the God of his fathers, Abraham and Isaac. He thus implicitly calls to God's attention the covenant promises that began with Abraham and were then passed down to Isaac and now have come to Jacob. He reminds God that he was the one who told Jacob to return at this time. Indeed, Jacob did not determine to leave Paddan Aram until God had told him, "Go back to the land of your fathers and to your relatives, and I will be with you" (31:3). Interestingly, in Jacob's quotation of God's command for him to return, he changes the last sentence to "and I will make you prosper" (32:9). As we will see in chapter 39, God's presence often leads to the prosperity and success of the recipient and those around him. Indeed, Jacob himself was the beneficiary of prosperity because of God's presence while he was in Paddan Aram (30:27 – 28). Thus, Jacob's change of wording brings out his understanding of the effect of God's promised presence in his life. If not prosperity, God had certainly assured Jacob of survival at least.

Even though Jacob begins his case with God by reminding him of prior promises, Jacob is careful not to express disappointment with God. Indeed, he confesses that he has been unworthy of God's care and concern. God's blessing is clearly manifest in the fact that, though he came to Paddan Aram with nothing but his walking staff, he is now coming back to the land a rich man, so rich that he has become "two camps." We see that once again we come back to the theme of two camps in this chapter.

God has also shown his fidelity to Jacob by expressing "kindness" (or "loyalty;" *hesed*) and "faithfulness" (*emet*) to him. These words indicate Jacob's awareness that up to this moment God has followed through on his covenantal commitments to Jacob, and, of course, he is implicitly asking God to continue to do so, particularly in the matter of his brother Esau.

His final appeal makes explicit his most pressing need. He asks God to save him from his brother. He appeals to God's pity by mentioning the women ("the mothers") as well as children ("their children"). If God is not moved by concern for Jacob, surely he will move to protect the defenseless women and children.

He concludes his prayer with one final reference to earlier divine promises. In verse 12, he cites God as saying "I will surely make you prosper and will make your descendants like the sand of the sea, which cannot be counted" (32:12). It is not impossible that God had said this directly to Jacob, though,

---

1. For translation and commentary, see Longman, *Proverbs*, 327 – 29, 331.

if so, it is not recorded in the earlier chapters. More likely, Jacob refers to God's words to Abraham after the Akedah, which comes closest in wording: "I will surely bless you and make your descendants as numerous as the stars in the sky and as the sand on the seashore" (Gen 22:17). If this is the reference to which Jacob refers, it is again interesting that the one major change is from "I will surely bless you" to "I will surely make you prosper." Again, the change is not unwarranted in that Jacob would appropriately think that blessing would include survival if not prosperity.

After his appeal to God, Jacob continues to implement his strategy of "divide to survive." He prepared an elaborate gift for Esau from his flocks and herds (vv. 13–16). He divided them up and put them in charge of his servants, whom he told to put distance between themselves, presumably again in an attempt to gain time for those who follow behind. He instructs these servants to offer them to Esau as a gift from Jacob with the hope that by the time Esau reaches Jacob who will be "coming behind us" (v. 20), his anger will be pacified. With his preparations thus completed, Jacob then spent the night before the encounter with Esau in camp where we will see that he has an unexpected encounter of another kind.

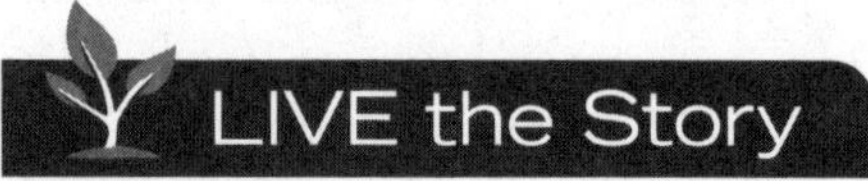


### Greeted by Angels

As Jacob left the promised land, God gave him a vision at Bethel of angels descending and ascending a ladder (Gen 28:12), now that he has returned God sends his angels to greet him as he enters the promised land. What a wonderful picture of God's concern for the patriarch!

What are we as Christians to make of this? Are there angels involved in our lives? Do they watch over us? Do they guide us? Do they protect us? Today there is a tremendous fascination with angels, but is there any substance to the claims that they are involved in our lives?

According to Hebrews 1:14, the answer is yes: "Are not all angels ministering spirits sent to serve those who will inherit salvation?" A little later the author of the book tells us that we are presently in a joyful assembly with "thousands of angels" (Heb 12:22). We are also reminded what Jesus said concerning children, "See that you do not despise one of these little ones. For I tell you that their angels in heaven always see the face of my Father in heaven" (Matt 18:10).

In our highly secularized society, we are often blind to the spiritual world. The thought of angels interacting with our lives sounds fanciful and maybe a little ditsy. But, according to the Bible, they are alive and well and involved in our everyday lives. We should thank God for them.

And, of course, that is the most important thing to remember. They are "ministering spirits sent," and it is God who sent them. We should not make more of angels than we should. Even at the time of the New Testament, there was always the temptation to pay too much attention to angels to the detriment of our devotion to Jesus. Paul rebukes those who worship angels (Col 2:18), and the author of Hebrews feels he has to debunk the idea that angels are superior to Jesus (Heb 1:4–14; 2:5). The New Testament also makes it clear that humanity, not angels, are the apex of God's creation and that the angels were created in order to serve and worship God (Pss 103:20; 148:2) and carry out God's will concerning humans (1 Cor 6:3; Heb 2:16).

Yes, angels are involved in our lives even in the twenty-first century secularized West. We should realize this and, with them, worship God who sent them to minister to us.

### The Risk of Reconciliation

In the exposition above, we commented on the risk involved in Jacob alerting Esau to his return to the promised land. He could have tried to slip quietly back, hoping that if Esau did learn of his return, it would be after he could have dug in his defenses. Jacob instead chooses to approach his brother with the hope that he "would find favor in his eyes." In other words, he was to seek a rapprochement with his brother and live in peace with him.

This move, of course, is risky. The last he knew Esau wanted to kill him.

Kidner is helpful when he sees in Jacob an illustration of Jesus' future instructions to his disciples about how to deal with conflict, particularly conflict initiated by our own sin.[2]

> Therefore, if you are offering your gift at the altar and there remember that your brother or sister has something against you, leave your gift in front of the altar. First go and be reconciled to them; then come and offer your gift. Settle matters quickly with your adversary who is taking you to court. Do it while you are still together on the way, or your adversary may hand you over to the judge, and the judge may hand you over to the officer, and you may be thrown into prison. (Matt 5:23–25)

Today we too are called to take the risk involved in seeking reconciliation with those whom we have harmed. It's dangerous work, because as we are vulnerable with others, they may use it as an occasion to harm us in revenge. But, as Jesus says, it is absolutely important to work for this kind of reconciliation,

2. D. Kidner, *Genesis*, TOTC (Downers Grove, IL: InterVarsity Press, 2008).

particularly as we come into the presence of God. Jacob takes the risk and we will see what happens as the story unfolds (see Gen 33:1–20 and the following essay Reconciliation among Brothers).

## Approaching Conflict Wisely

Jacob anticipates serious conflict. His presumably angry brother is bearing down on him with what looks to be an army of four hundred men. Jacob has few fighting men at best and probably no weapons to speak of, certainly not enough to counteract Esau and his men.

He begins by trying to mollify his brother by sending him greetings and a gift. As we turn to the book of Proverbs, we learn that bribes are bad when they try to change the course of justice (Prov 15:27; 17:8; 21:14; 25:14; 28:21), but that gifts can be helpful when they smooth the way for the giver. According to the sages, "A gift opens the way and ushers the giver into the presence of the great" (Prov 18:16) and "many curry favor with a ruler, and everyone is the friend of one who gives gifts" (Prov 19:6). Both of these proverbs suggest that gifts, when appropriately and wisely given, can lead to good results. Surely Jacob is hoping for that here.

But he certainly isn't sure. He may hope for the best, but he prepares for the worst. For this reason, he divides his family into two parts, so if the first is attacked, there is a chance that the second could get away.

But the most important and the wisest part of his preparations is his prayer to God to help him. We can, and should, take all the precautions and make all the preparations we can in the face of conflict, but if we make it through, it will be because of God's good grace. We continue our reflections on this theme in the next essay.

## To Depend on God or to Take Action?

The ad for a popular internet dating site for Christians says to people looking for a spouse, "Sometimes we wait for God to make the next move when God is saying it is your time to act." The message is not subtle — use our service to find someone; don't just sit back and wait for someone to suddenly appear on your doorstep. But is it true? Should we plan and act or should we pray and wait?

Again, we turn to the book of Proverbs to begin to consider this question. The sages promote the importance of good planning and the execution of those plans. According to Proverbs 21:5, "the plans of the diligent lead to profit as surely as haste leads to poverty." Jacob has a goal — to mollify Esau — and he plans and acts on the plan in order to achieve his intention. Wise planning and action can lead to great confidence in the future such as that displayed by the "wife of noble character" (Prov 31:20), who can "laugh at the days to come" (31:25b) because she is ready for whatever comes her way.

But Proverbs also teaches a very important lesson about planning. The outcome of our plans depend entirely on the Lord:

> To humans belong the plans of the heart,
> but from the LORD comes the proper answer of the tongue.
> All a person's ways seem pure to them,
> but motives are weighed by the LORD.
> Commit to the LORD whatever you do,
> and he will establish your plans. (Prov 16:1 – 3)

And Jacob does exactly that. He commits his plans to the Lord by praying to him in order to establish his plans.

We now see the answer to the question that we posed at the beginning of the essay, do we depend on God or do we take action? We do both. As Proverbs points out we fall far short if we just take action, but we also fall far short if we only pray about something and wait for God to act.

Last Sunday, our pastor (Reed Jolley) told a story, not original to him, that illustrates this point. When a tremendous flood started pouring water into a man's house, he turned to God in prayer, asking God to rescue him from the flood. Soon the flood waters were so high, he had to seek refuge on his roof. A policeman in a boat came by and urged him into the boat, but he refused, saying that God was going to rescue him. After a while a helicopter appeared overhead sending down a lift to bring him up to safety. He refused to go, yelling to the pilot that God was going to save him. Eventually the flood waters overwhelmed him, he died and soon was in the presence of the Lord. He complained, "I prayed to you to rescue me and you didn't!" God responded calmly, "Well, I sent a boat and a helicopter; what more did you want?"

Jacob acts wisely in this episode. He neither prays and waits passively nor does he act without appealing to God for help. We too should avoid the presumption of prayer without action or the arrogance of action without prayer.

# Genesis 32:22 – 32

## LISTEN to the Story

[32:22]That night Jacob got up and took his two wives, his two female servants and his eleven sons and crossed the ford of the Jabbok. [23]After he had sent them across the stream, he sent over all his possessions. [24]So Jacob was left alone, and a man wrestled with him till daybreak. [25]When the man saw that he could not overpower him, he touched the socket of Jacob's hip so that his hip was wrenched as he wrestled with the man. [26]Then the man said, "Let me go, for it is daybreak."

But Jacob replied, "I will not let you go unless you bless me."

[27]The man asked him, "What is your name?"

"Jacob," he answered.

[28]Then the man said, "Your name will no longer be Jacob, but Israel, because you have struggled with God and with humans and have overcome."

[29]Jacob said, "Please tell me your name."

But he replied, "Why do you ask my name?" Then he blessed him there.

[30]So Jacob called the place Peniel, saying, "It is because I saw God face to face, and yet my life was spared."

[31]The sun rose above him as he passed Peniel, and he was limping because of his hip. [32]Therefore to this day the Israelites do not eat the tendon attached to the socket of the hip, because the socket of Jacob's hip was touched near the tendon.

*Listening to the Text in the Story:* Biblical Text: Genesis 32:1 – 21

After entering the promised land returning from his sojourn in northwest Mesopotamia (Paddan Aram), Jacob sent messengers to inform his estranged brother of his return. In response, Esau mobilized a group of four hundred men, a veritable army, who were now heading their way.

Jacob did not know what to expect, but he had reason to think that his angry brother was ready to seize the opportunity to seek revenge for Jacob's theft of his birthright and his blessing. Thus, Jacob began urgent preparations for the confrontation. While waiting for this potentially dangerous meeting, Jacob is unexpectedly attacked by another apparent and mysterious foe.

## EXPLAIN the Story

### Jacob Wrestles a "Man" (32:22–25)

We now come to one of the most memorable, dramatic, and enigmatic stories in the Bible. Part of the reason for the enigma is that the action is narrated without much explanation as to motivation, evaluation, and character identification. While Hebrew prose is famous for its reticent style, this episode is spectacularly sparse in its narrative guidance.

Thus, Jacob's wrestling match is the type of story that lends itself to all kinds of interpretive embellishments, but we will try to tread carefully here. There are certain points that are crystal clear to us, and others about which we can only speculate, and still others that we want to throw up our hands in frustration. We will try to be careful to indicate our level of certainty or lack thereof as we exposit the story of Jacob's nocturnal wrestling match.

Jacob spends the night alone after sending his wives, children, and possessions across the ford of the Wadi Jabbok. Jabbok is a river that flows into the Jordan River from the east about twenty miles north of the Dead Sea. There appears to be a word play on the river's name (*yabboq*), the verb "wrestled" (*yeabeq*), and Jacob's name (*yaaqob*).

Upon telling us that Jacob was alone, the narrative immediately informs the reader that a man wrestled Jacob until daybreak. There is no introduction that explains the identity of the "man" or the reason for the fight. We are not informed of any specific action or speech until just before the sun comes up. For reasons that are not clear, the "man" must go before daybreak. He sees that he cannot overpower Jacob, so he chooses to cripple him by simply touching the socket of his hip and thus wrenching it. Such power raises the question why he could not defeat Jacob. Perhaps we are to think at this point that the wrestler limits his power for some unspecified reason.

### Exchanging Names (32:26–32)

The limits of the man's power, whether self-imposed or not, come to the fore again when he appeals to Jacob to let him go before the sun rises. Jacob agrees but only on the condition that the "man" bless him. Jacob's desire for a blessing would indicate that he believes that this person is his superior, because it is the superior who blesses the inferior.

In response to Jacob's request, the man asks for Jacob's name. In response, the man changes the name from Jacob ("to grasp the heel" with a secondary meaning "to deceive") to Israel, a name perhaps best understood to mean (in accordance with the NIV study note) "he struggles with God," though the explanation of the name given by the man is "because you have struggled with God and with humans and have overcome" (v. 28). Jacob's struggle with humans may be seen in his relationship with Laban and proleptically in his relationship with Esau. As the present narrative continues, his struggle with God seems to be most pointedly a reference to his just-concluded nocturnal wrestling match.

With the name change, we should note a change of character. The deceiver is changed in the process of striving with God. It is not a stark change from someone who deceives to someone who is now perfect in character. No, Jacob will continue to have his flaws. He will mislead Esau in the next scene, and he will show harmful favoritism in the Joseph story. That said, Jacob has learned a new level of reliance on God. He had a tendency to rely on himself and his own resources, but now he has come to rely more on God.[1]

Of course, we are not to miss the implications of this name change for later history. This man is the person who will give his name to the nation that will descend from his family. Israel has fathered children who are the patronyms of the future tribes of Israel. The name Israel not only describes Jacob's relationship with God but also his future descendants. They too will struggle with God as they try to be self-reliant. They will only succeed when they give up confidence in themselves and rather put their trust in God.

Jacob then asks the "man" his name, but the "man" refuses to give it. Instead, he blesses him and then apparently departed before the sun arose. Thus, the "man" never clearly identified himself to Jacob, but Jacob's naming of the location of the fight indicates that he knew that this mysterious figure was none other than God himself. He names the place Peniel, "the face of God." To encounter the face of God is to be in his presence. He saw God face to face and survived, again reminding us of the man's explanation of Jacob's new name "because you struggled with God ... and have overcome" (v. 28). The account ends with a focus on Jacob's hip. He may have struggled with God and overcome, but he walks away with a limp. The narrator explains this as the origin of the custom that Israelites not eat the tendon attached to the

1. See the helpful comments by S. Greidanus, *Preaching Christ from Genesis: Foundations for Expository Sermons* (Grand Rapids: Eerdmans, 2007), 315–34.

socket of the hip. Apparently, God's touching that area in Jacob's body has rendered that joint holy.

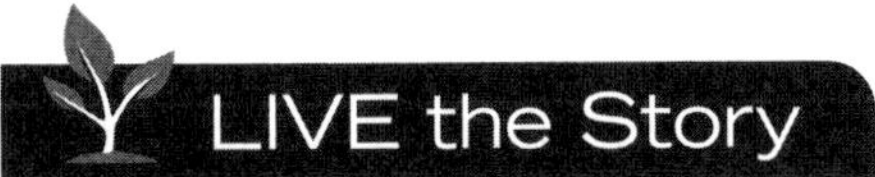

## LIVE the Story

### Self-Reliant or God-Reliant?

Sidney Greidanus successfully identified a major theme of the story of God's wrestling with Jacob: "Before self-sufficient Jacob can enter the Promised Land, God needs to change Jacob into Israel, a person who strives with God for his blessing."[2] In other words, only people who depend on God, not on themselves, can enter the promised land. It is important to emphasize, as we did in the Explain the Story section, that this statement does not mean that Jacob is perfect. Indeed, we will see that he continues to be a deeply flawed person, but he certainly takes a substantial step forward in this important moment of his life.

Greidanus goes on to rightly point out that when we read the story of Jacob/Israel, we should also think that he anticipates the nation of Israel. The prophet Hosea (see 12:5) alludes to the story in reference to the later history of Israel.

Indeed, the book of Genesis was written when the nation of Israel existed. Even assuming a Mosaic authorship of the book, Israel, the nation, had already learned the lesson that Jacob learned on this occasion. We see this, Greidanus points out, in the aftermath of the spies report in Numbers 13–14. When Israel hears about the presence of fearsome warriors in the land, they panic rather than trust God to bring them safely into the promised land. In other words, Israel was unwilling to be God-reliant and as a result, God would not permit them to enter the land.

What about the Christian? The promised land for the Christian is the kingdom of God and ultimately life with God in the new heavens and the new earth. The same principle holds for Christians as it did for the Israelites. Only the God-reliant and not the self-reliant will enter the promised land.

The author of the book of Hebrews even uses the picture of the wilderness wanderings to encourage his readers to adopt a God-reliant, faithful attitude. He reminds Christians that they are wandering in the wilderness; they are not yet in the promised land (heaven). He encourages them to maintain their faith in God in spite of opposition and persecution; otherwise, they will end up perishing in the wilderness just like the exodus generation that died during the forty years (Heb 3:7–4:13).

2. Ibid., 322.

### Jesus Wrestles God

It wasn't easy for Jesus to go to the cross. His way was the way of suffering and, being fully human as well as fully divine, pain and death were something to be avoided, not embraced. Thus, in the garden of Gethsemane (Matt 26:36–46), Jesus strives with God. "Going a little further, he fell with his face to the ground and prayed, 'My Father, if it is possible, may this cup be taken from me' " (v. 39). Notice that he does not flee from God or simply abandon his Father-given responsibility, but he does ask God to relieve him of it. However, when the Father does not relent, Jesus accepts his will for his life ("Yet not as I will, but as you will," v. 39). Jesus is the model of the God-reliant, not the self-reliant person.

### Wrestling with Jesus

After his wrestling match with God, Jacob stands amazed, "It is because I saw God face to face, and yet my life was spared" (v. 30). This assertion leaves no doubt that Jacob understood the one he wrestled was none other than God himself. While it is true that no human can stand in the full presence of the holy God and survive, God does allow some of his servants to get a glimpse of his presence (see Moses in Exod 33:18–32). That said, it is an act of God's grace that Jacob could come into the presence of God and survive, though not unscathed.

We should be clear that the one Jacob wrestled was not the pre-incarnate Son, Jesus.[3] Hosea 12:5 identifies Jacob's rival as an angel, but surely this is a reference to the angel of the Lord who in Genesis is often identified or associated with God himself, not specifically Jesus (see The Angel Who Saves, Gen 16).

But for the Christian, God makes his presence known preeminently in Christ. "The Word became flesh and made his dwelling among us" (John 1:14). Those who have seen the Son have seen the Father (John 14:9). Thus, it is not inappropriate for us to think that we strive with Jesus in the difficulties of life.

Jesus wants us to struggle with him in our afflictions and troubles, not abandon him. He wants us to cling to him as Jacob/Israel clung to his divine opponent after his hip was touched and he developed a limp.

### Leading with a Limp

When people think of a leader, they often conjure an image of a strong individual that "has it all." The leader is smart, physically attractive, able to take

3. See Malone, *Knowing Jesus in the Old Testament?*, for the position that the Old Testament does not have any distinctive "christophanies."

risks, has the aura of being in control and invincible, as well as to make decisions that cost (usually others).

Have you ever noticed how tall leaders are and how shorter ones stand out as odd? I was just at a gathering of seminary and university presidents and I felt like a midget. Of course, this anecdotal observation is not to suggest that tall leaders are bad or ineffective leaders. But the idea that physical power suggests strong leadership goes back to Israel's choice of tall Saul (1 Sam 10:23) and before. One might almost say it is built into our DNA.

Leaders, so we think, are self-sufficient, decisive, and resourceful. They may take advice, but they are the decision makers and then the ones who execute their ideas. Such leaders fear exposing weaknesses. If one is weak, how can one lead?

Even in our Christian institutions, leaders employ power plays and exploit procedure to achieve their ends rather than acting transparently, admitting weakness, and trying to effect change through persuasion. One well-known Christian leader gives the following advice to another institution about how to (in my words) "game the system" in order to reach a desired goal. He refers to successful efforts at other institutions in the past as he bemoans what he considers the weak efforts of another institution:

> The changes in those places (those that had success at change) had a number of things in common: the reformers organized and prepared for every eventuality, putting into place safety nets and multiple 'Plan Bs', they identified the places where influence could be wielded, mastered procedure, fought like the blazes when they had to, stood strong and immovable in the face of violent opposition, and outmaneuvered their opponents by continual attention to meeting agendas, points of order, procedural matters, and long-term coordinated strategy. They did not waste time and energy on irrelevant sideshows like rhetorical petitions that merely provided the material for public relations disasters. And guess what? In each case it actually worked. In fact, this way of approach sounds very like the strategy which frankly outflanked and then crushed the ill-prepared evangelical assault at last week's ... GA (General Assembly). It would seem that angry but sincere petitioners generally lose, while sincere but canny parliamentarians generally win. The evangelicals of [Name of Denomination] need new leadership that understand ... polity, the importance of procedure and, crucially, how institutions work and can therefore be changed.[4]

4. A public statement on the Internet (posted at http://thegospelcoalition.org/blogs/kevindeyoung/2009/05/27/carl-trueman-church-of-scotland-and/.

The use of such Machiavellian strategies as means to even a good end cannot be justified. It is leading out of human strength using worldly tactics. Unfortunately, such means succeed too often, but the goal, as is such in this leader's case, is an institution that is ingrown, under attack, fearful, circling the wagons, and losing influence in the broader world.

Dan Allender draws insight on the topic of leadership from the story of Jacob's wrestling with God. Indeed, the title of his book, *Leading with a Limp*, comes from this story.[5]

Allender rightly describes Jacob's life up to the present moment as one in which he tried to live and lead his family in his own strength, utilizing worldly means (deception) to protect himself and gain an advantage. "As a deceiver, he must be quick; he must get ahead of everyone else in his opportunistic hold over life."[6]

Allender rightly points out that his encounter with God that marks him with a limp, an obvious sign of weakness, effects a change that does not hurt but rather enriches him as a person and as one who can lead his family and interact with his world:

> The process of becoming a person who can lead others with a limp is not what we would have predicted. Do we really have to be that desperate and that deeply exposed to be freed from our narcissism, our fear, our dogmatism, and our tendency to hide? The story of Jacob exalts not the struggle but the goodness of God as he blesses a conniving, undeserving man. No matter how far off the mark we might be, we see in this account the promise that if we open ourselves to meet God, we will not come out of the encounter the same. We will walk a new path—with an unpredictable gait.[7]

As we will see, this encounter with God does not make Jacob a perfect person. He still has his flaws to be sure. But he can now face life with a new level of humility and with a confidence that is born not out of his own human resources, but out of a sense of his relationship with God.

If we lead with a limp, we follow the example of Jesus himself. Did he come with displays of power? Did he make people cower before him? Did he walk over and destroy his opponents?

Of course, the answer is no. He did not make the disciples wash his feet, but he washed his disciples' feet, and then told them to do the same for others (John 13:1–17). His path as leader was to suffer and die for others:

---

5. D. A. Allender, *Leading with a Limp: Turning Your Struggles into Strengths* (Colorado Springs, CO: Waterbrook, 2006).
6. Ibid., 47.
7. Ibid., 48.

Who, being in very nature God,
did not consider equality with God something to be used to his own
 advantage;
rather, he made himself nothing
by taking the very nature of a servant,
being made in human likeness.
and being found in appearance as a man,
he humbled himself
by becoming obedient to death—
even death on a cross! (Phil 2:6–8)

And this is the model of leadership Jesus imparted to his disciples. In response to the request of James's and John's mother that her sons sit at Jesus right side, Jesus responded: "You know that the rulers of the Gentiles lord it over them, and their high officials exercise authority over them. Not so with you. Instead, whoever wants to become great among you must be your servant, and whoever wants to be first must be your slave—just as the Son of Man did not come to be served, but to serve, and to give his life as a ransom for many" (Matt 20:25–28).

If you are a leader, seek to emulate Jesus. Lead out of weakness not out of strength.[8]

8. Thanks to Dr. Peter Enns of Eastern University for helpful comments that helped the writing of this essay.

CHAPTER 33

# Genesis 33:1 – 20

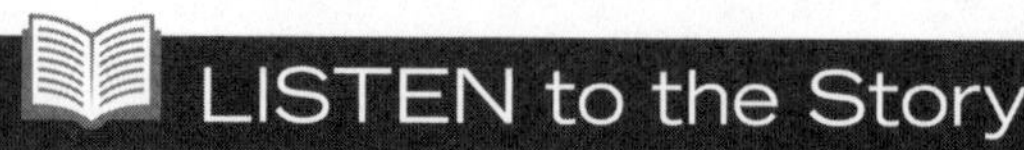

## LISTEN to the Story

[33:1]Jacob looked up and there was Esau, coming with his four hundred
men; so he divided the children among Leah, Rachel and the two female
servants. [2]He put the female servants and their children in front, Leah and
her children next, and Rachel and Joseph in the rear. [3]He himself went on
ahead and bowed down to the ground seven times as he approached his
brother.

[4]But Esau ran to meet Jacob and embraced him; he threw his arms
around his neck and kissed him. And they wept. [5]Then Esau looked up
and saw the women and children. "Who are these with you?" he asked.

Jacob answered, "They are the children God has graciously given your
servant."

[6]Then the female servants and their children approached and bowed
down. [7]Next, Leah and her children came and bowed down. Last of all
came Joseph and Rachel, and they too bowed down.

[8]Esau asked, "What's the meaning of all these flocks and herds I met?"

"To find favor in your eyes, my lord," he said.

[9]But Esau said, "I already have plenty, my brother. Keep what you
have for yourself."

[10]"No, please!" said Jacob. "If I have found favor in your eyes, accept
this gift from me. For to see your face is like seeing the face of God, now
that you have received me favorably. [11]Please accept the present that was
brought to you, for God has been gracious to me and I have all I need."
And because Jacob insisted, Esau accepted it.

[12]Then Esau said, "Let us be on our way; I'll accompany you."

[13]But Jacob said to him, "My lord knows that the children are tender
and that I must care for the ewes and cows that are nursing their young. If
they are driven hard just one day, all the animals will die. [14]So let my lord
go on ahead of his servant, while I move along slowly at the pace of the
flocks and herds before me and the pace of the children, until I come to
my lord in Seir."

[15]Esau said, "Then let me leave some of my men with you."

"But why do that?" Jacob asked. "Just let me find favor in the eyes of my lord."

[16]So that day Esau started on his way back to Seir. [17]Jacob, however, went to Sukkoth, where he built a place for himself and made shelters for his livestock. That is why the place is called Sukkoth.

[18]After Jacob came from Paddan Aram, he arrived safely at the city of Shechem in Canaan and camped within sight of the city. [19]For a hundred pieces of silver, he bought from the sons of Hamor, the father of Shechem, the plot of ground where he pitched his tent. [20]There he set up an altar and called it El Elohe Israel.

*Listening to the Text in the Story:* Biblical Text: Genesis 32

Jacob had informed Esau of his return to the promised land through messengers sent to his home in Seir. Esau then came to Jacob accompanied by four hundred men. Jacob did not know his brother's intentions, so he prepared for the worse. As he waited, he wrestled a "man," who turned out to be God and who changed his name from Jacob, connected to his reputation as a deceiver, to Israel, one who wrestles with God. As our present episode begins, Esau and his men have finally arrived.

## EXPLAIN the Story

### Jacob and Esau Meet (33:1 – 12)

In the previous episode, God had given Jacob a new name — Israel. Interestingly, unlike earlier when God changed Abram's name to Abraham or Sarai's to Sarah, the narrative continues to refer to Jacob as Jacob except in a few cases. As we will see, contrary to some interpretations, Jacob does not undergo a radical character transformation after his wrestling match with God. He remains a deceiver as well as one who struggles with God. Indeed, at the end of this very episode, he makes Esau think that he will follow him to Seir, though he apparently has no intention to do so.

Jacob's return to the land has been fraught with struggle. First, he had to deal with Laban who was irate with him for stealing away without announcement. Then he had to fight God himself. Now he must face his brother Esau, who, when he last left him (27:41), wanted to kill him for his past deceptions.

At the moment of decision, he divided his family into separate contingents and in an order that clearly indicates his own priorities based on his favoritism. First, he puts the two maidservants and their children (Dan, Naphtali, Gad, Asher) in front. This group would be the first one that Esau would meet. Next, he placed his unloved wife Leah and her children (Reuben, Simeon, Levi, Judah, Issachar, Zebulun), followed by Rachel with her one child Joseph in the rear. The narrative has made no secret of Jacob's favoritism toward Rachel, and in the Joseph narrative (chs. 37–50) we will see that he also favors Joseph over all his other children. By placing them in the rear, they stand the best chance of escape.

That said, Jacob himself went before all of them. He was the first person to meet his brother, unaware but probably suspecting that he had come to harm him. Thus, though he does show favoritism in the order in which he arranged his family, he puts himself on the line. If Esau had come to kill him, perhaps he would be satisfied with only his death.

Jacob approaches Esau and bows to him seven times. Such a gesture indicates total respect and even submission to a superior. We are reminded of a common expression in the Amarna Tablets where the city kings of Canaan begin their letters to their treaty overlord, the Egyptian Pharaoh, by saying "At the feet of my lord seven times and seven times I fall" (EA, No. 287; Abdu-Heba of Jerusalem to the Pharaoh).[1]

While some point back to the supposed ambiguity of the birth oracle of Genesis 25:23 (see discussion there) and argue that here we have the younger submitting to the older, Kaminsky rightly suggests that "one must note that the oracle in Gen 25:23 made clear that it would reach fulfillment only in the far future when the progeny of the younger child will rule over those descending from the elder one. Indeed, Israel did rule Edom for a considerable time during the Israelite monarchy (2 Sam 8:14; 2 Kgs 8:20)."[2]

Esau makes it clear immediately that he has not come to bring Jacob harm as he runs to him and embraces and kisses him. Our reticent narrator does not tell us what motivates Esau here. Perhaps he is satisfied that God has blessed him with wealth and no longer cares that Jacob himself is rich and the recipient of the covenantal blessings. Perhaps he was pacified by the gifts that Jacob had sent ahead. We are never told. It seems unlikely though that there is a more nefarious or dark reason for Esau's actions. That is, it is unlikely that he is reserving his punishment till he lures Jacob back to Seir. Why would he have to do that? Whatever the motivation or reason for the transformation, Esau's welcome was good news for Jacob and his family.

Esau asks the identity of those who accompany Jacob, and Jacob responds by introducing him to his family. He does so in the order that he had set them

1. ANET, 488.
2. Kaminsky, *Yet I Loved Jacob*, 52.

earlier, beginning with the families of the two servants, Bilhah and Zilpah, followed by the family of Leah, and concluding with his favorites, Rachel and Joseph. Like Jacob himself, they all bow to Esau out of respect and an acknowledgment that at present he is in a superior position.

Next Esau inquires concerning the flocks and herds that Jacob had set out in front of his entourage. Apparently Esau did not stop long enough for Jacob's servants to make a formal presentation to him or perhaps he wanted to hear that they were a gift from Jacob's own lips. Whatever the reason, Jacob informs his brother that their purpose was to please Esau and to put Jacob in a good light.

Esau at first declined the offer on the basis that he already had sufficient wealth and did not need it. Of course, his demurral could be simply the result of Near Eastern social custom, because Jacob insists and Esau ultimately accepts the gift from his brother. He too has all that he needs since God has been good to him. Considering that Jacob thought that Esau was coming to harm him, his statement that "to see your face is like seeing the face of God" rings sincere. Indeed, we should take note of the fact that Jacob had indeed just seen the face of God and lived the night before, even naming the place "Peniel," the face of God (32:22–32).

**Esau Desires Jacob to Accompany Him (33:13–19)**

At this point, Esau assumes that Jacob will now go home with him to Seir, and he offers to accompany him. Jacob, however, makes excuses to keep Esau from traveling with him. The excuse is a legitimate one in that he needs to travel slowly because of his young children and the flocks. He does, however, tell Esau that he will "come to my lord in Seir" (v. 14). Esau continues by offering to leave men, but does not insist on this when Jacob again declines the offer.

As it turns out, Jacob has no intention of going to Seir. Thus, he appears to be deceiving his brother again to make it appear as if he will go there. However, rather than traveling to Seir he goes to a place that is given the name Sukkoth or "shelters," named after his building of shelters for his livestock as well as for himself. Sukkoth (mentioned in later Scripture, Josh 13:27; Judg 8:5–9, 13–17) is near where the Jordan and the Jabbok meet, not far from where Jacob met Esau.

Of course, at least as modern readers, we wonder what motivates Jacob to act as he does toward Esau. Perhaps it would have been obvious to an ancient reader, but in any case we have another example of the reticence of Hebrew narrative style. Why does Jacob not want to go to Seir? Perhaps because he is still afraid of Esau, but, as earlier mentioned, if Esau wanted him harmed, he could do it right where they stood. Perhaps because God had called him back to the promised land and Seir was outside it. Perhaps, but why not tell Esau?

And what was Esau's reaction when he went back to Seir to wait for Jacob only to have him never show up? Again, we are not told, but apparently he did not retaliate. Is it possible that he was simply being hospitable toward his brother and when he did not accept the invitation, he was relieved because Jacob and his vast entourage would have cost him grazing land and other expenses? We cannot answer any of these questions definitively. However, we will see that the next and only time Jacob and Esau will be together again will be at Isaac's funeral, perhaps indicating that there is no deep-seated, abiding hatred between them (see 35:27–29).

In any case, the stay in Sukkoth appears to be a temporary location for Jacob's family because right after describing the building of Sukkoth, we now learn that he ended up in Shechem, a town in the northern central hill country of Canaan, the first town in which Abraham built an altar (12:6). Shechem was a bustling Canaanite city whose leaders were Hamor and a man named Shechem. As pastoralists, Jacob and his family dwelt in the outskirts of the city, but purchased a plot of ground from the leaders of the city, the second bit of real estate acquired by this family (see Gen 23). Like Abraham before him, Jacob too built an altar and named it El Elohe Israel, or "El is the God of Israel," or, less likely "mighty is the God of Israel." This land was acquired for one hundred *kesitahs*, which, since we do not know the exact amount of a *kesitah*, is taken by the NIV vaguely as one hundred pieces of silver. Shechem thus becomes the setting for the next important episode in Jacob's life (see Gen 34).

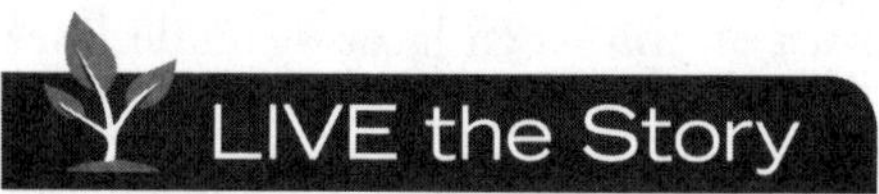


## Reconciliation among Brothers

Even if it is only momentary, our story presents a touching picture of two estranged brothers embracing in love and unity. Jacob fully expected hatred and violence from the brother he had angered in their youth when he stole his birthright and deceived their father to give him Esau's blessing. We have already commented on the text's silence about Esau's motivations for embracing rather than harming his brother, but we can still rejoice in this picture of reconciliation.

After all, this was the way it was meant to be. "Adam and his wife were both naked, and they felt no shame" (Gen 2:25). This comment is talking about more than sex; it is talking about the type of intimate, caring connection that characterized humanity before the introduction of sin. As we have seen in the commentary on Genesis 3, it was precisely humanity's rebellion against God that led to the estrangement in the relationship between his human creatures.

In a word, because of sin, self becomes preeminently important and other people are seen as posing threats to our own best interests, which leads to self-protection and the exploitation of others. But in reality, human beings, all of us, flourish not when we seek our own self-interest, but when we have peace with one another.

Gordon Wenham recognizes that many of the stories, including this one, present a picture of reconciliation in order to encourage such behavior in the readers of Genesis:

> Thus Genesis is not simply a justification for Israel's occupation of Canaan, it embodies a practical appeal as well. It urges brothers to make peace with each other and to forgive past wrongs. It insists that Israelites should live peaceably with their relatives, with fellow countrymen of different ethnic origins, and implies that as a nation it should not be afraid to make agreements with surrounding nations when they seek peace.[3]

The psalmist expresses joy at such unity. As we see Jacob and Esau embrace, we want to sing along:

> How good and pleasant it is
> when God's people live together in unity!
> It is like precious oil poured on the head,
> running down on the beard,
> running down on Aaron's beard,
> down on the collar of his robe.
> It is as if the dew of Hermon
> were falling on Mount Zion.
> For there the Lord bestows his blessing,
> even life forevermore. (Psalm 133)

Today, as during the Old Testament period, human relationships are fractured by sin and rebellion. This side of heaven there will not be perfect harmony among God's human creatures. But thanks to the reconciling work of Jesus, we can, like Jacob and Esau, experience glimpses of God's intention for human relationships.

Yes, it is Jesus' work on the cross that is the only hope for healthy human relationships. According to Paul it is Jesus himself who "is our peace, who has made the two groups one and has destroyed the barrier, the dividing wall of

---

3. Wenham, *Story as Torah*, 39.

hostility, by setting aside in his flesh the law with its commands and regulations. His purpose was to create in himself one new humanity out of the two, thus making peace, and in one body to reconcile both of them to God through the cross, by which he put to death their hostility. He came and preached peace to you who were far away and peace to those who were near. For through him we both have access to the Father by one Spirit" (Eph 2:14–18).

As the popular song goes, "they will know we are Christians by our love." Love and unity among Christians is hard but important work. Indeed, Jesus himself prayed that we might have that type of love for each other. Why? "Then the world will know that you sent me and have loved them even as you have loved me" (John 17:23).

## Jacob and Israel

In the aftermath of the wrestling match, God gave Jacob a new name, Israel. Duguid rightly points out that previously new names are significant but are slight variants of the original (Abram/Abraham and Sarah/Sarai), with Jacob's name change to Israel we have a total transformation.[4] Jacob, the deceiver, is now Israel, the one who wrestled with God.

And, indeed, on the other hand, as we read beginning with the story of his reconciliation with Esau, there are hints of change. This story, for instance, continues what we called Jacob's risk for reconciliation (see The Risk of Reconciliation after the Live the Story section in Gen 32:1–21). He humbles himself before Esau in order to seek forgiveness. More significantly, notice how he also attributes the size of his family and also the extent of his wealth not to his own efforts, but rather to the gracious acts of God (vv. 5, 11), in contrast to Esau who says nothing about God though his own well-being and wealth are the result of God's earlier blessing to him (21:13, 18).

On the other hand, we also can see that there are remnants in Israel of Jacob as he misleads Esau into thinking he is coming to Seir. In addition, rather than leaving and going directly to Bethel as he promised God (28:20–22), he will go to Shechem and settle there (see next chapter).

It is significant that from this point on the narrator will use both names in the narrative. This contrasts with the change of Abram's name to Abraham. After he is given the new name, the narrator never again uses the name Abram. It seems likely that the continued use of Jacob along with Israel is a way of saying that the transformation is there, but not complete.

As we follow the course of Jacob's life from now till the end we will see flashes of his grace-transformed life along with relapses to his old life of

4. Duguid, *Living in the Grip of Relentless Grace*, 114–15.

deception and favoritism (see The Ugly Consequences of Favoritism after Gen 37). Is this any different from any of us? Paul captured the struggle of our life when he talks about the war that goes on inside of our hearts:

"Although I want to do good, evil is right there with me. For in my inner being I delight in God's law; but I see another law at work in me, waging war against the law of my mind and making me a prisoner of the law of sin at work within me." Paul, however, is not paralyzed by this conundrum. He goes on: "What a wretched man I am! Who will rescue me from this body that is subject to death? Thanks be to God, who delivers me through Jesus Christ our Lord!" (Rom 7:21–25)

Yes, like Jacob, we will struggle with sin throughout our lives, but we can rejoice that we will not be judged on the basis of our own efforts. Jesus died on the cross to save us. Paul goes on to also assure his believing readers that "there is now no condemnation for those who are in Christ Jesus, because through Christ Jesus the law of the Spirit who gives life has set you free from the law of sin and death" (8:1–2, see the whole of Rom 8).

Still the Jacob story, and the reality of our continued struggle with sin, reminds us that we must call on God to give us the strength through the power of the Spirit who lives in us to obey him and presses upon us the need to turn to God in daily repentance.

CHAPTER 34

# Genesis 34

## LISTEN to the Story

34:1Now Dinah, the daughter Leah had borne to Jacob, went out to visit the women of the land. 2When Shechem son of Hamor the Hivite, the ruler of that area, saw her, he took her and raped her. 3His heart was drawn to Dinah daughter of Jacob; he loved the young woman and spoke tenderly to her. 4And Shechem said to his father Hamor, "Get me this girl as my wife."

5When Jacob heard that his daughter Dinah had been defiled, his sons were in the fields with his livestock; so he did nothing about it until they came home.

6Then Shechem's father Hamor went out to talk with Jacob. 7Meanwhile, Jacob's sons had come in from the fields as soon as they heard what had happened. They were shocked and furious, because Shechem had done an outrageous thing in Israel by sleeping with Jacob's daughter—a thing that should not be done.

8But Hamor said to them, "My son Shechem has his heart set on your daughter. Please give her to him as his wife. 9Intermarry with us; give us your daughters and take our daughters for yourselves. 10You can settle among us; the land is open to you. Live in it, trade in it, and acquire property in it."

11Then Shechem said to Dinah's father and brothers, "Let me find favor in your eyes, and I will give you whatever you ask. 12Make the price for the bride and the gift I am to bring as great as you like, and I'll pay whatever you ask me. Only give me the young woman as my wife."

13Because their sister Dinah had been defiled, Jacob's sons replied deceitfully as they spoke to Shechem and his father Hamor. 14They said to them, "We can't do such a thing; we can't give our sister to a man who is not circumcised. That would be a disgrace to us. 15We will enter into an agreement with you on one condition only: that you become like us by circumcising all your males. 16Then we will give you our daughters and take your daughters for ourselves. We'll settle among you and become one people with you. [17]But if you will not agree to be circumcised, we'll take our sister and go."

[18]Their proposal seemed good to Hamor and his son Shechem. [19]The young man, who was the most honored of all his father's family, lost no time in doing what they said, because he was delighted with Jacob's daughter. [20]So Hamor and his son Shechem went to the gate of their city to speak to the men of their city. [21]"These men are friendly toward us," they said. "Let them live in our land and trade in it; the land has plenty of room for them. We can marry their daughters and they can marry ours. [22]But the men will agree to live with us as one people only on the condition that our males be circumcised, as they themselves are. [23]Won't their livestock, their property and all their other animals become ours? So let us agree to their terms, and they will settle among us."

[24]All the men who went out of the city gate agreed with Hamor and his son Shechem, and every male in the city was circumcised.

[25]Three days later, while all of them were still in pain, two of Jacob's sons, Simeon and Levi, Dinah's brothers, took their swords and attacked the unsuspecting city, killing every male. [26]They put Hamor and his son Shechem to the sword and took Dinah from Shechem's house and left. [27]The sons of Jacob came upon the dead bodies and looted the city where their sister had been defiled. [28]They seized their flocks and herds and donkeys and everything else of theirs in the city and out in the fields. [29]They carried off all their wealth and all their women and children, taking as plunder everything in the houses.

[30]Then Jacob said to Simeon and Levi, "You have brought trouble on me by making me obnoxious to the Canaanites and Perizzites, the people living in this land. We are few in number, and if they join forces against me and attack me, I and my household will be destroyed."

[31]But they replied, "Should he have treated our sister like a prostitute?"

*Listening to the Text in the Story:* Biblical Texts: Genesis 12:1–3; 15:12–16; 28:20–22

Jacob was the recipient of the divine promises given to Abraham (12:1–3), promising that Abraham's descendants would become a "great nation," implying possession of land and many descendants. The promised land is the land that God showed Abraham and to which he journeyed. When God came to reassure Abraham of his intention to fulfill the promise as he began to doubt it, he specified the land as land that stretched from "the Wadi of Egypt to the great river, the Euphrates—the land of the Kenites, Kenizzites, Kadmonites, Hittites, Perizzites, Rephaites, Amorites, Canaanites, Girgashites and Jebusites" (15:18–20).

Jacob had returned to the promised land from Paddan Aram (northwest Mesopotamia) as God directed him to do, but rather than proceeding immediately directly to Bethel as he had promised (28:20–22), he ends up now settling near the Canaanite city of Shechem, where trouble now ensues.

### The Rape of Dinah (34:1–4)

At the end of the last story, Jacob settled in the city of Shechem. He had intentionally given the impression to Esau that he would follow him back to Seir at a slower pace. More disturbing, though, was the fact that Jacob had promised God that upon his safe return to the promised land he would go to Bethel (28:20–22). Perhaps his disobedience in this regard helps us understand the reason for the disaster that follows.

The narrator tells us one story about their stay in Shechem, and it is a story with present and future ramifications. The action begins with Dinah, who was already introduced as a daughter of Jacob and Leah (the only daughter ever mentioned, 30:21). Dinah went into town to visit some female Canaanite acquaintances and, while there, she was violated by Prince Shechem of the city of Shechem. The Hebrew which the NIV renders "took her and raped her" would be more literally rendered "took her, and lay with her and humbled her." The verb "humbled" (*ana*) clearly has a sexual meaning denoting rape in Deuteronomy 22:24 and 2 Samuel 13:14, so the NIV understanding seems justified, though it is possible to read the phrase as indicating consensual sex.

### Marriage Negotiations (34:5–17)

It seems, though, that Prince Shechem was truly attracted to her and so instructs his father to pursue marriage negotiations with her family in order to secure Dinah as his wife. Indeed, it says that he did love her and spoke tenderly to her. We are never, however, told what Dinah thinks about him. While from a modern perspective, this lack seems quite unfortunate, the ancient author did not think it important to the story, which, as we will see, is really concentrated on the issue of the relationship between the Canaanites (the Hivites are a subgroup of the inhabitants of the land, see 10:17; Exod 3:8; 23:23; Deut 7:1) and the covenant family.

Whether consensual or not, from the perspective of the narrator and apparently also Jacob, Dinah was defiled by this act of sex outside of the bounds of marriage. However, the narrator informs us that Jacob did nothing about it until his sons came back from working with the livestock in the fields. Perhaps we are to hear a subtle criticism of the patriarch at this point in the narrative.

In contrast to Jacob, when his sons who were out in the field heard about what had happened to Dinah, they returned. The narrator describes their reaction as being "shocked and furious." After all, Prince Shechem had done an "outrageous thing," by violating their sister. The term "outrageous thing" (*nebelah*) is often, but not exclusively used to refer to illegitimate sexual acts (see Judg 19:23; 20:6, 10; Deut 22:21). Typically, as here, the expression is "an outrageous act in Israel," though the NIV alternative given in the footnote ("against Israel") acknowledges that such a statement would be anachronistic during the period of the patriarchs.

At this point in the narrative, Jacob's sons are spoken of as a group, but soon we will see that it is in particular Simeon and Levi who are quick to act in response. The special role played by Simeon and Levi in the marriage negotiations is explained by the fact that they, along with Dinah, had Leah as their mother. In other words, they were the full brothers of Dinah, and in ancient Israel at this time brothers played a role in marriage negotiations for their sister.

Hamor begins the marriage negotiations by informing Jacob and her brothers that Shechem "has his heart set" on Dinah. He offers the family integration into Canaanite life. He envisions not just a marriage between Dinah and Shechem but more extensive intermarriage. His comment "give us your daughters" is an indication that Jacob has more daughters than Dinah, who is only specifically mentioned in Genesis because of her role in this story. He offers Jacob the opportunity to settle in the land, acquire property, and also the right to engage in trade (though note the NIV note that recognizes that the verb may indicate free movement rather than specifically trade, also at v. 21).

After his father speaks, Shechem then voices his desire for marriage with Dinah. He offers further inducements to the family, including a large bride price and a significant gift. The bride price was a customary payment from the groom's family to the bride's. According to Walton, "the transfer (of money from the groom's family to the bride's) is part of the socioeconomic system of provision and should not be thought of as purchase of chattel."[1]

1. Walton, "Genesis," 102.

Now that Hamor and Shechem have made their request and their offer, it is time for Jacob's side to respond. It is the "brothers," almost certainly referring specifically to Simeon and Levi, who respond. The narrator tells the reader right from the start that their answer is deceitful.

They appeal to their custom of circumcision. They do not go into a deep explanation; they only insist that intermarriage and integration between the two groups demands that the Hivite men undergo circumcision. If we go back to the time when God institutes circumcision at the time of Abraham, we do see that it is not only the blood relatives of the patriarch who must be circumcised but also even "those who are not your offspring" who are part of the household or community (17:12). And indeed, the consequence of this agreement would be that the family of God would "settle" among the Canaanites and "become one people" with them (v. 16). Even so, we will see that the sons of Jacob do not have ritual propriety in mind when they make this demand on the Hivites.

### Circumcision and Slaughter of the Shechemites (34:18–29)

The ruse worked, and Hamor and Shechem returned to the city of Shechem and laid out the agreement before the men of the city who were meeting at the gate where such decisions would be made. They appeal to the men that they allow Jacob's family to fully integrate with them based on self-interest that "their livestock, their property and all their other animals" will "become ours" (v. 23).

Hamor and Shechem's argument was persuasive to the men and they underwent a mass circumcision. It is at this point that we learn the specifics of the deception of the sons of Jacob. Two of the full brothers of Dinah, Simeon and Levi, now attack the men of Shechem when they are in a weakened condition right after the circumcision. The narrator mentions the killing of Hamor and Shechem in particular and the taking of Dinah from the house of Shechem. Not only do they kill all the men, but they also loot the city, aggrandizing themselves with "their flocks and herds and donkeys and everything else of theirs in the city and out in the fields" including "their women and children" (vv. 28–29).

### Jacob's Anger (34:30–31)

Not only were the inhabitants of the city of Shechem deceived by the sons of Jacob, but so was Jacob. He apparently had no clue what Simeon and Levi were up to. He is not at all pleased with their actions. He is angered that Simeon and Levi have made trouble between his family and the "people living in this land," named as "Canaanites and Perizzites" (v. 30). He considers their position vulnerable before the superior forces of their enemies.

Jacob, however does not get the last word. The chapter ends with Simeon and Levi simply saying, "Should he have treated our sister as a prostitute?" (v. 31).

What are we to make of the actions of Simeon and Levi in this chapter? Two positions are expressed at the end of the chapter. Jacob is upset that his sons' actions have made them obnoxious to the Canaanites, and Simeon and Levi argue that they should not let the Canaanites treat their sister like a prostitute. On whose side is the narrator?

Again, the narrator is reticent when it comes to making evaluation of action explicit. However, the narrator also controls how the story is presented and it is absolutely critical to our understanding of this story to see that he gives the last word to Simeon and Levi. This is a surefire indication that the narrator's sympathies lie with them.

And when we think about the story in the light of God's purpose for his people at this time, it makes sense that the narrator would be so disposed. After all, Jacob's response to Hamor and Shechem would have led to his family (the precursor of the people of Israel) becoming one with the Canaanites. This is not an outcome that God desires during this period of time. God wants his people to stay separate. Others may join themselves to God's people, but God's people must stay distinct and not be absorbed by another people group. After all, God had already informed Abraham that his people would inherit this land (see especially 15:12–16). Though it is a later text, Deuteronomy 7:3–6 expresses the principle for the nation that would have been relevant for the family of God at this earlier period of time. They were to stay separate from the Canaanites: "Do not intermarry with them. Do not give your daughters to their sons or take their daughters for your sons, for they will turn your children away from following me to serve other gods, and the Lord's anger will burn against you and will quickly destroy you."

That may be the narrator's/author's/God's view of the matter, but we know that Jacob maintains his animosity toward Simeon and Levi to the end of his life. To see this and also to see how this story has future ramifications for both the tribes of Simeon and Levi, see the commentary at Genesis 49:5–7.

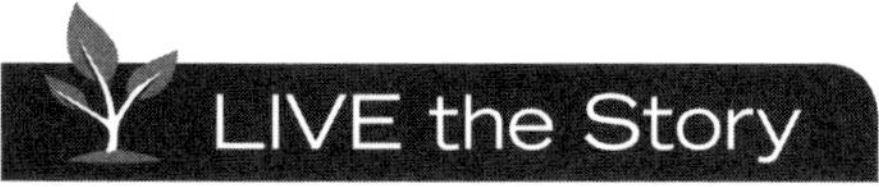


### Marrying Outside the Faith

Let's not mince words. The story of Jacob's family in Shechem is brutal. A woman gets raped and her brothers slaughter the men of the city. How can we derive any kind of lesson for today out of this account, especially in the modern West?

That is why it is so surprising to many to realize that the narrator, representing the perspective of the author of Genesis, takes sides with the brothers rather than with Jacob, and it is even more disturbing to those of us who affirm that the book of Genesis is the Word of God, that the author represents the perspective of God himself. What are we to make of this story for our lives today, if anything?

First, we must acknowledge that there is discontinuity between our place in redemptive history and Jacob's time. Indeed, it may be that even the narrator/author/God implies that Simeon and Levi's means of achieving a desirable end (prohibiting the marriage) was wrong, but there is no question that the marriage was wrong. At this point in redemptive history, Abraham's descendants should not marry Canaanites, and those who do (see, for instance, Esau and Judah) find trouble because of their marriages. If it is not certain whether the brothers' slaughter of the Canaanites was wrong at their time, there is no doubt about it today! Such acts of violence are sinful, pure and simple, in the period after Christ has come. After all, says Paul, "our struggle is not against flesh and blood, but against the rulers, against the authorities, against the powers of this dark world and against the spiritual forces of evil in the heavenly realms" (Eph 6:12).

But Paul also tells Christians, "do not be yoked together with unbelievers" (2 Cor 6:14). One might respond by saying, "but Paul is not talking about marriage in this context." True, but marriage is the most intimate form of human relationship available. Remember the words of Genesis 2:24 which establishes the institution of marriage: "That is why a man leaves his father and mother and is united to his wife, and they become one flesh." "One flesh!" That is very intimate.

And when one thinks about it, it makes sense. If a Christian marries a non-Christian, they do not share what is at their core; the most important part of their life, what makes them who they are. Paul goes on in 2 Corinthians to say, "For what do righteousness and wickedness have in common? Or what fellowship can light have with darkness? What harmony is there between Christ and Belial? Or what does a believer have in common with an unbeliever?" (2 Cor 6:14b–15). Yes, what does a believer have in common with an unbeliever? How can there be a marriage relationship of "one flesh" union when there is this divide between two people?

There are two dangers in such a marriage. The first is that because of this fundamental difference between a husband and a wife their marriage will not experience true spiritual intimacy. The other danger is that the Christian spouse will start losing their spiritual passion.

Now what we are saying here is directed to those who have not yet made a marriage choice. The purpose is to urge unmarried Christians not just to take the faith of a potential mate into consideration, but to make it an essential of entering into a marriage. But what about those who read or hear this advice who are already married to a non-believer? Perhaps they married someone thinking that they would change or that they could live well together in spite of their differences. Perhaps both husband and wife were unbelievers at the time of the marriage, but one became a Christian and the other did not. Perhaps both were believers at the time of the marriage and one later rejected the faith. What about circumstances like this?

Paul addresses this situation as well in his earlier letter to the Corinthians. He encourages those who are married to non-believers to take heart and not to leave the relationship. He tells the Christian that, even though their spouse is not a believer, that person is "sanctified through her believing" spouse (1 Cor 7:14). This statement, of course, does not mean they get a free pass to heaven, but rather that their children will be considered part of the covenant community. And second, Paul tells the believing spouse that their presence might very well lead to the conversion of their husband or wife (1 Cor 7:14). On the other hand, even though the Christian should not divorce their unbelieving spouse, if that person decides to leave the relationship, Paul says let them go (1 Cor 7:15).

So this disturbing, bloody narrative does inform Christians living in the twenty-first century. In the first place, it warns unmarried Christians to only marry a fellow believer. Second, it takes us to Paul's teaching that encourages those who find themselves in such a relationship.

### Levi and Christ

Levi plays a central role in this story, though one troubling, at least to modern readers. As the story of the people of God continues through Genesis and beyond, Levi and his descendants will occupy an important place in the furtherance of God's purposes of the world. As most readers of the Bible know, Levi's descendants will be chosen as the priestly tribe. Aaron, the Levite, will be the first high priest, and every Israelite priest will be one of his descendants.

Though it is hard to believe, the story of the choice of the Levites for such a holy and important role actually begins with this bloody story. Levi (along with Simeon) is here characterized as a calculating and violent man, willing to use deception in order to find vengeance against the one who violated his sister. We have argued that, though Jacob was outraged, the narrator, whose perspective represents that of the author, supports the brothers' desire to undermine intermarriage with the Canaanites. Even so, by cunningly slaughtering the men of the town in their weakness, Levi and Simeon may have exercised excessive force in an uncontrolled manner, leading to a dire situation for Jacob and his family. They likely could have chosen simply to refuse the marriage, but instead they act out of their anger. Certainly that is Jacob's perspective at the end of the chapter and it leads to Jacob's death bed curse on Levi and Simeon that they not receive a tribal allotment in the future (Gen 49:5–7).

And indeed, if we fast-forward to the second half of the book of Joshua, we see that neither the descendants of Levi or the descendants of Simeon receive a separate allotment, but rather territory within the land of the other tribes. Even so, though the Simeonites lose status among the tribes, as Jacob's curse intended, the Levites, on the other hand, become the most distinctive tribe of all. They are chosen to function as the priestly tribe serving God within the holy sanctuary.

What led to the choice of the Levites? Interestingly, and germane to the present story, it was their propensity to violence.

The turning point comes in Exodus 32, which recounts Israel's sin of worshipping the golden calf. While Moses and Joshua are on Mount Sinai receiving the law, the people convince Aaron to construct a golden calf so they can worship it. The passage is unclear whether the calf is a pedestal for the deity or represents the deity itself (note Aaron's call for a "festival to the LORD," in v. 5). In one sense, the ambiguity does not matter. Whichever is the case, Aaron leads the Israelites in a clear violation of the second commandment, which prohibits the construction of idols.

When Moses returns he is enraged and breaks the stone tablets of the law, signaling a rupture in the covenant relationship between God and Israel. He then calls for aid, "Whoever is for the LORD, come to me" (Exod 32:26) and it is the Levites who come to him.

Moses then instructs them to get their swords and "go back and forth through the camp from one end to the other, each killing his brother and friend and neighbor" (v. 27). They comply and then Moses announces to the Levites, "You have been set apart to the LORD today, for you were against your own sons and brothers, and he has blessed you today" (v. 29).

Here we have the origins of the Levites as the priestly tribe. They have demonstrated that they can now channel their violent tendencies to the service of the Lord, and, though again difficult from a modern Western perspective, such a quality is precisely what makes them good priests. After all, what is the purpose and function of the priesthood in ancient Israel? To state it most succinctly, the priests were the bodyguards of God's holiness. Or, as Moses puts it at the end of his life, the priestly Levites guarded the covenant

(Deut 32:9). They did this by guarding the sanctuary and determining when people were ritually unclean and could not enter the sanctuary and in some cases even the camp. They defended God's holiness preemptively by teaching the law and then offering sacrifices to restore relationship after the law was broken.

What then is the connection between Jesus and Levi? Of course, Jesus is presented in the New Testament as the ultimate priest. However, rather than using physical violence to keep a community holy, he wages war in a different way, by offering himself on the cross. After all, Jesus wages war, not against flesh and blood, but against the spiritual powers and authorities, and these enemies are defeated not by killing but by dying.

We, however, must further acknowledge that when the New Testament speaks of Jesus as the ultimate priest, it does so not by connecting him with Levi but rather by connecting him with Melchizedek (Heb 4:14–5:10; 7:1–8:13), the obscure priest-king from Salem who greets Abraham after his victory over the Near Eastern kings (see commentary at Gen 14). In this way, Jesus is said to a priest-king and far superior to the high priests in the line of Aaron (Heb 7:4–11).

See related essay: Jesus, a "High Priest Forever, in the Order of Melchizedek" (Heb. 6:20; after Gen 14).

CHAPTER 35

# Genesis 35:1 – 15

## LISTEN to the Story

[35:1]Then God said to Jacob, "Go up to Bethel and settle there, and
build an altar there to God, who appeared to you when you were fleeing
from your brother Esau."

[2]So Jacob said to his household and to all who were with him, "Get
rid of the foreign gods you have with you, and purify yourselves and
change your clothes. [3]Then come, let us go up to Bethel, where I will
build an altar to God, who answered me in the day of my distress and
who has been with me wherever I have gone." [4]So they gave Jacob all the
foreign gods they had and the rings in their ears, and Jacob buried them
under the oak at Shechem. [5]Then they set out, and the terror of God fell
on the towns all around them so that no one pursued them.

[6]Jacob and all the people with him came to Luz (that is, Bethel) in the
land of Canaan. [7]There he built an altar, and he called the place El Bethel,
because it was there that God revealed himself to him when he was fleeing
from his brother.

[8]Now Deborah, Rebekah's nurse, died and was buried under the oak
outside Bethel. So it was named Allon Bakuth.

[9]After Jacob returned from Paddan Aram, God appeared to him again
and blessed him. [10]God said to him, "Your name is Jacob, but you will no
longer be called Jacob; your name will be Israel." So he named him Israel.

[11]And God said to him, "I am God Almighty; be fruitful and increase
in number. A nation and a community of nations will come from you,
and kings will be among your descendants. [12]The land I gave to Abraham
and Isaac I also give to you, and I will give this land to your descendants
after you." [13]Then God went up from him at the place where he had
talked with him.

[14]Jacob set up a stone pillar at the place where God had talked with
him, and he poured out a drink offering on it; he also poured oil on it.
[15]Jacob called the place where God had talked with him Bethel.

*Listening to the Text in the Story:* Biblical Texts: Genesis 12:1 – 3; 28:10 – 22; 34

At the end of the previous chapter, Jacob feared reprisal for the actions of Simeon and Levi from regional Canaanites. Their violent outburst had left the local Shechemites decimated, but other Canaanites might come to attack them. Even so, it is God who tells Jacob to move on. God wants Jacob to return to Bethel, the place where God had first made himself known to Jacob as he began his flight to Paddan Aram (28:10–21). Here Jacob saw angels ascending and descending a ladder from heaven. Here he heard God affirm that the covenant promises given to Abraham (12:1–3) would flow through him. He thus names the place Bethel, "house of God," on this occasion. Here too Jacob made a vow, "If God will be with me and will watch over me on this journey I am taking and will give me food to eat and clothes to wear so that I return safely to my father's household, then the Lord will be my God and this stone that I have set up as a pillar will be God's house, and of all that you give me I will give you a tenth" (28:20–22).

### Jacob Finally Journeys to Bethel (35:1–8)

Jacob thus promised God that if he returned safely from his sojourn in Paddan Aram, then "the Lord will be my God." Interestingly, then Jacob immediately demands that all his household "get rid of the foreign gods you have with you, and purify yourselves and change your clothes" (v. 2). We are to see the change of clothes as part of the purification process. They are not to wear the clothes that they are presently wearing but to change them to symbolize the move from the realm of the common to the presence of God, which is the realm of the holy. Besides ridding themselves of the accoutrements of false religions, Jacob tells them that they are heading to Bethel to build an altar to the God who has taken care of him even when he traveled outside the promised land.

Jacob's household responded by giving him their foreign gods and their earrings, which must have had religious significance, and Jacob buried them under the oak at Shechem before they departed from Bethel. We are not told at this time who had false gods, but we know from an earlier story that Rachel had stolen the household idols of Laban (31:32); perhaps we are to think that they too were turned over to Jacob at this time for disposal.

Jacob's family is now cleansed from objects of false worship. They move out and do so safely because God put the fear of them into the hearts and minds of the surrounding Canaanites who might have been tempted to harm them. The passage wants us to connect the dumping of the idols to the fear that the Canaanites felt toward them. Thus, Jacob's family made it safely to the city that used to be called Luz, but whose name was changed because of Jacob's past experience to Bethel, which is given here in its longer form El Bethel, "The God of Bethel." Again, we are reminded that it was here that God had revealed himself to Jacob at the time he was fleeing Esau to head to Paddan Aram. At this time, Jacob constructed an altar to the Lord on which he could offer sacrifices and also call on God's name.

Interestingly, the narrator then reports the death of Deborah, Rebekah's nurse. We have not heard about Rebekah for quite some time, and one wonders why her nurse was living with Jacob at this time. Does it indicate that Rebekah and Isaac were now with their son? We cannot be sure. In any case, the nurse was buried under an oak tree in Bethel and the place where she was buried was then named Allon Bakuth, "Oak of Weeping."

**God Blesses Jacob at Bethel (35:9–15)**

Then the narrator again informs us of Jacob's name change. The change was actually instituted at the time he wrestled God (32:22–32). We are likely to understand this simply as a reiteration of that moment rather than a second time when God tells Jacob about his name change. Perhaps it is repeated here because now Jacob had fully moved into the promised land. He had divested his household of foreign gods and was now focused on the worship of the God who had brought him safely back from Paddan Aram. Thus, we are reminded that God changed his name from Jacob ("he grasps by the heel," an idiom for "he deceives," see NIV footnote) to Israel ("he struggles with God," see NIV footnote).

As at his first visit to Bethel, so here, God again reiterates the covenant promises, first delivered to Abraham (12:1–3), then passed down to Isaac and now to Jacob. God identifies himself as El Shaddai, rendered God Almighty by the NIV, though etymologically probably from "God of the Mountains." God had told Abraham that his descendants would be a "great nation," and here God promises that from Jacob would come "a nation and a community of nations" (v. 11), so he tells Jacob to "be fruitful and increase in number," which also reminds the reader not only of the Abrahamic promises, but also the original command to Adam and Eve (Gen 1:28).

God also tells Jacob that "kings will be among your descendants," something he also earlier told Abraham (17:7). However, with Abraham, we cannot be absolutely certain that God meant that Israel would have a future king. After all, Abraham's descendants include those through Ishmael and through Esau, the latter of whom fathers nations that have kings (Gen 36:31–39). Jacob's/Israel's sons are the fathers not of other nations but of the tribes of Israel. Here God is speaking about the rise of kingship in Israel, a promise that is also communicated through Jacob's blessing on Judah (Gen 49:8 – 12). Kingship is also anticipated in Balaam's fourth oracle (Num 24:17 – 19) and the Deuteronomic law of kingship (Deut 17:14 – 20). When kingship does come to Israel (1 Sam 8 – 12), it is not a second thought, as one might think since it comes in response to a sinful request of the people, but kingship was God's intention all along. After all, it is also a response to the political fragmentation, moral depravity, and spiritual confusion of the period of Judges ("In those days Israel had no king; everyone did as they saw fit," Judg 17:6; 18:1; 19:1; 21:25). It also anticipates the messiahship of Jesus (see Jesus, the Messiah in the Live the Story section after 49:1 – 28).

God's promise that he would make Abraham's descendants a great nation includes more than the promise of numerous descendants. It also includes the promise of land. God had assured Abraham and Isaac that their descendants would receive the land and now he assures Jacob.

Jacob had set up a stone pillar at Bethel to commemorate his meeting with God as he journeyed toward Paddan Aram; now he sets up a second stone pillar. He also offered a drink offering and poured oil on the stone. Standing stones apparently were a common feature of the religion of the day since archeologists have found many examples in Israelites sites during the Old Testament and Canaanite periods. Sometimes they represented deities and thus could be considered images forbidden by the later second commandment. On other occasions, they could be memorial stones, as here, marking an important meeting between God and his servant. Once again we hear that Jacob named this site Bethel or "house of God."

## Dumping the Idols of Our Life

At God's command, Jacob returned to the land. God had kept him safe through dangerous times in Paddan Aram in keeping with his promise to the patriarch given in Bethel (28:20 – 22). After crossing into the promised land, Jacob had fought both God and Esau and survived. It is now that Jacob orders his entire household to dump their idols (35:2 – 5). Among those idols were likely the household gods that Rachel stole from her father, probably in an attempt to get their blessing on their journey and to strike at her father who had used her and others.

Most of the readers of this commentary have likely never been tempted to worship objects that represented gods in the same way that Jacob's household had. There is no need for us to clear off our mantelpiece of idols and throw them in the fire. But, truth be told, everyone struggles with idols, though our idols are not made of wood or precious metals.

After all, an idol is anything or anyone that displaces the true God in our hearts and minds. Whatever we hold most important and most dear and whatever occupies our minds and energies more than anything else is our God, and if that God is not the Triune God of the Bible, then it is an idol.

John Calvin called the human mind a factory of idols because we are constantly tempted to make other things more important than the true God. Our idol might be money, work, sex, status, power, alcohol, or some other thing. Our idol might be our marriage, our children, or our friends. Our idol might be church. In other words, even very good things can become an idol if they are more important to us than God.

The book of Ecclesiastes makes it very clear that even good things will let us down if we make them the most important thing in our lives. Qohelet (commonly translated the Teacher or the Preacher) tried to find the ultimate meaning in life in work, status, money, and other things, and they constantly let him down as he indicates to us by constantly concluding "meaningless, meaningless ... everything is meaningless," starting in 1:2 and ending in 12:8. The second wise man tells his son (12:12) what is truly important in the final verses of the book: "Now all has been heard; here is the conclusion of the matter: Fear God and keep his commandments, for this is the duty of all mankind. For God will bring every deed into judgment, including every hidden thing, whether it is good or evil" (Eccl 12:13–14).

Our minds are a factory of idols. Therefore, we must daily dump the idols and reaffirm our primary allegiance to God: As Jesus said the most important commandment, since it summarizes all the commandments is, "Love the Lord your God with all your heart and with all your soul and with all your mind and with all your strength" (Mark 12:30). Loving God in this whole-personed manner is the way we dump our other idols and bury them deeply.

### "And Kings Will Be among Your Descendants" (Gen 35:11)

God reiterates his covenant promises to Jacob. He had earlier told Abraham that kings would descend from him (Gen 17:6). In the Live the Story section after our commentary on Genesis 17, we described how this promise played itself out first in the rise of the Davidic dynasty in the history of Israel. We also saw how that promise was fulfilled in Jesus Christ, the ultimate king of God's kingdom (see " ... I Will Make Nations of You, and Kings Will Come from You" [Gen 17:6] in the Live the Story section after Gen 17).

### "The Land I Gave to Abraham and Isaac I Also Give to You" (Gen 35:12)

In addition to the promise that kings would descend from Jacob, so God reiterates to Jacob the promise concerning land that he gave to Abraham. In the Live the Story section after our commentary to Genesis 13, we also saw that this promise, while finding its initial fulfillment when the Israelites took possession of the promised land finds its ultimate fulfillment in Jesus (see Jesus and the Land after the commentary at Gen 13).

CHAPTER 36

# Genesis 35:16–29

## LISTEN to the Story

35:16Then they moved on from Bethel. While they were still some
distance from Ephrath, Rachel began to give birth and had great
difficulty. 17And as she was having great difficulty in childbirth, the
midwife said to her, "Don't despair, for you have another son." 18As she
breathed her last — for she was dying — she named her son Ben-Oni.
But his father named him Benjamin.

19So Rachel died and was buried on the way to Ephrath (that is,
Bethlehem). 20Over her tomb Jacob set up a pillar, and to this day that
pillar marks Rachel's tomb.

21Israel moved on again and pitched his tent beyond Migdal Eder.
22While Israel was living in that region, Reuben went in and slept with his
father's concubine Bilhah, and Israel heard of it.

Jacob had twelve sons:

23The sons of Leah:

Reuben the firstborn of Jacob,

Simeon, Levi, Judah, Issachar and Zebulun.

24The sons of Rachel:

Joseph and Benjamin.

25The sons of Rachel's servant Bilhah:

Dan and Naphtali.

26The sons of Leah's servant Zilpah:

Gad and Asher.

These were the sons of Jacob, who were born to him in Paddan Aram.

27Jacob came home to his father Isaac in Mamre, near Kiriath Arba
(that is, Hebron), where Abraham and Isaac had stayed. 28Isaac lived a
hundred and eighty years. 29Then he breathed his last and died and was
gathered to his people, old and full of years. And his sons Esau and Jacob
buried him.

*Listening to the Text in the Story:* Biblical Texts: Genesis 29:31–30:24

Much earlier in the Jacob narrative we learned about the baby wars that ensued between his two wives Leah and Rachel (29:31–30:24). God had pity on the unloved Leah and allowed her to have children first. In response, Rachel had given Jacob her servant who bore children that counted as Rachel's but were not from her womb. Leah then countered by giving Jacob her servant and more children came. Leah even had more children of her own after this. At last, Rachel bore Joseph, but even that is not the end of the story as the present narrative will tell. With the birth of Jacob's final son, we also hear about the end of Isaac's life.

## EXPLAIN the Story

### The Birth of Benjamin and Death of Rachel (35:16–20)

We are not told why Jacob/Israel moved on from Bethel, but we do know that he will end up at the end of the chapter back at Mamre near Hebron (called Kiriath Arba at the time) where his father Isaac lived. On their way, while they were still some distance from Ephrath, Rachel died. Ephrath is associated with Bethlehem, some four miles south of Jerusalem. While Ephrath and Bethlehem may have started as separate towns, they eventually were associated and by the time of the prophet Micah the place was referred to as Bethlehem Ephrathah (Mic 5:2).

Rachel died in childbirth, giving birth to her second son, Benjamin. Rachel has bemoaned the fact that she remained childless for so long while her sister Leah produced many sons for Jacob. She eventually had given birth to Joseph, but she dies in the process of giving birth to her second son. In other words, "the childbearing contest eventually kills Rachel."[1] While her midwife tried to encourage her in the midst of her suffering, Rachel expressed her anguish by naming the son Ben-Oni, or "son of my affliction." Jacob, however, presumably not wanting his son to bear the onus of such an ill-omened name, renames him Benjamin, or "son of my right hand," the right hand being a position of power and prestige.

The narrator then reports that Jacob buried her at the spot on the way up to Bethlehem/Ephrath. He also marked the grave site with a pillar. Interestingly the narrator reminds his later audience that the pillar is still there to this day.

### Reuben Betrays His Father (35:21–22)

We are not told how long Jacob and his family sojourned in the vicinity of Bethlehem/Ephrath, but we are next told that he stops and encamps "beyond

1. I. Provan, *Seriously Dangerous Religion*, 211.

Migdal Eder" (v. 21). We are not sure exactly where this site is located. However, the Hebrew translates into English as "watchtower of the flock." It has been noted that this phrase occurs in poetic parallelism with "stronghold of Daughter Zion" in Micah 4:8, which would be a reference to the city of Jerusalem, so perhaps Migdal Eder is somewhere near Jerusalem.

While at Migdal Eder, his oldest son Reuben slept with his father's concubine Bilhah. At this point, we just are simply told that "Israel heard of it." Later we will see that this act will disqualify Reuben from the benefits of being the first born (see 49:3–4).

### The Twelve Sons of Jacob (35:21–26)

We are now near the end of the "account (*toledot*) of the family line of Isaac" that had begun in 25:19, and which had concentrated on Jacob as the son through whom the covenant promises would continue to flow to future generations. Thus, it is appropriate that the narrator give a final tally of the next generation. His twelve sons are named in order based on their birth mother. Leah, the oldest wife, is listed first. She had given birth to Reuben, who had just sullied himself in the eyes of his father but still is called the "firstborn of Jacob." Simeon, Levi, Judah, Issachar, and Zebulon are her other children. Next comes Rachel, the younger but favored wife. Her children number just two, Joseph and Benjamin, but because their mother was favored by Jacob, so were they as we will see in the "account of Jacob's family line" (37:2) that will conclude the book of Genesis. Third, we learn that Dan and Naphtali were born to Rachel's concubine Bilhah and Gad and Asher to Leah's servant Zilpah.

### The Death of Isaac (35:27–29)

At last, Jacob returned to Mamre, near Hebron (Kiriath Arba), a location about eighteen miles south of Jerusalem in the Judean hills. The narrator notes that both Abraham and Isaac had lived there, thus it is appropriate that the one to whom the promises have come, the third patriarch, Jacob, renamed Israel, would settle there. The transition to Jacob is complete when it is reported that Isaac died after his arrival home. Isaac had lived a long life of one hundred and eighty years and received a proper burial by his two sons Jacob and Esau. The presence of Esau with Jacob at the burial of Isaac indicates that whatever hostility had existed between them was no longer an issue.

## The Consequences of Sin

Reuben's sin is given the briefest mention possible, a single verse: "While Israel was living in that region, Reuben went in and slept with his father's concubine Bilhah, and Israel heard of it" (v. 22). Indeed, the act is narrated, but there is no discussion of punishment or any negative consequence. Reuben betrayed his father and committed adultery and incest as judged by the later Mosaic law (Lev 18:6, 8; 20:11). But again, this act seems mentioned only in passing. Will Reuben suffer no consequences?

Of course, those who have read through the whole book of Genesis know that he will pay dearly for this act. He was, after all, the first born and by all rights according to ancient law he should have been the dominant son and in the long run his descendants should be the chief among the tribes.

However, later, when Jacob announces curses and blessings on his various sons, he will pronounce a curse on Reuben (see commentary at 49:3–4). Because of his sin, Reuben will forfeit his status as the most important son and the tribe that descends from him will be superseded by others, and in particular the tribe of Judah (see Jesus, the Messiah, after Gen 49:1–28).

See related essays: Reconciliation among Brothers in the Live the Story section (after Gen 33:1–20).

## LISTEN to the Story

36:1 This is the account of the family line of Esau (that is, Edom).
2 Esau took his wives from the women of Canaan: Adah daughter of
Elon the Hittite, and Oholibamah daughter of Anah and granddaughter
of Zibeon the Hivite— 3 also Basemath daughter of Ishmael and sister of
Nebaioth.

4 Adah bore Eliphaz to Esau, Basemath bore Reuel, 5 and Oholibamah
bore Jeush, Jalam and Korah. These were the sons of Esau, who were born
to him in Canaan.

6 Esau took his wives and sons and daughters and all the members of
his household, as well as his livestock and all his other animals and all the
goods he had acquired in Canaan, and moved to a land some distance
from his brother Jacob. 7 Their possessions were too great for them to
remain together; the land where they were staying could not support
them both because of their livestock. 8 So Esau (that is, Edom) settled in
the hill country of Seir.

9 This is the account of the family line of Esau the father of the
Edomites in the hill country of Seir.

10 These are the names of Esau's sons:

Eliphaz, the son of Esau's wife Adah, and Reuel, the son of Esau's wife Basemath.

11 The sons of Eliphaz:

Teman, Omar, Zepho, Gatam and Kenaz.

12 Esau's son Eliphaz also had a concubine named Timna, who bore
him Amalek. These were grandsons of Esau's wife Adah.

13 The sons of Reuel:

Nahath, Zerah, Shammah and Mizzah. These were grandsons of Esau's wife Basemath.

14 The sons of Esau's wife Oholibamah daughter of Anah and
granddaughter of Zibeon, whom she bore to Esau:

Jeush, Jalam and Korah.

15 These were the chiefs among Esau's descendants:

The sons of Eliphaz the firstborn of Esau:
Chiefs Teman, Omar, Zepho, Kenaz, 16Korah, Gatam and Amalek.
These were the chiefs descended from Eliphaz in Edom; they were
grandsons of Adah.
17The sons of Esau's son Reuel:
Chiefs Nahath, Zerah, Shammah and Mizzah. These were the chiefs
descended from Reuel in Edom; they were grandsons of Esau's wife
Basemath.
18The sons of Esau's wife Oholibamah:
Chiefs Jeush, Jalam and Korah. These were the chiefs descended from
Esau's wife Oholibamah daughter of Anah.
19These were the sons of Esau (that is, Edom), and these were their
chiefs.
20These were the sons of Seir the Horite, who were living in the region:
Lotan, Shobal, Zibeon, Anah, 21Dishon, Ezer and Dishan. These sons
of Seir in Edom were Horite chiefs.
22The sons of Lotan:
Hori and Homam. Timna was Lotan's sister.
23The sons of Shobal:
Alvan, Manahath, Ebal, Shepho and Onam.
24The sons of Zibeon:
Aiah and Anah. This is the Anah who discovered the hot springs in
the desert while he was grazing the donkeys of his father Zibeon.
25The children of Anah:
Dishon and Oholibamah daughter of Anah.
26The sons of Dishon:
Hemdan, Eshban, Ithran and Keran.
27The sons of Ezer:
Bilhan, Zaavan and Akan.
28The sons of Dishan:
Uz and Aran.
29These were the Horite chiefs:
Lotan, Shobal, Zibeon, Anah, 30Dishon, Ezer and Dishan. These were
the Horite chiefs, according to their divisions, in the land of Seir.
31These were the kings who reigned in Edom before any Israelite king
reigned:
32Bela son of Beor became king of Edom. His city was named
Dinhabah.
33When Bela died, Jobab son of Zerah from Bozrah succeeded him as
king.

[34]When Jobab died, Husham from the land of the Temanites
succeeded him as king.
[35]When Husham died, Hadad son of Bedad, who defeated Midian in
the country of Moab, succeeded him as king. His city was named Avith.
[36]When Hadad died, Samlah from Masrekah succeeded him as king.
[37]When Samlah died, Shaul from Rehoboth on the river succeeded
him as king.
[38]When Shaul died, Baal-Hanan son of Akbor succeeded him as king.
[39]When Baal-Hanan son of Akbor died, Hadad succeeded him
as king. His city was named Pau, and his wife's name was Mehetabel
daughter of Matred, the daughter of Me-Zahab.
[40]These were the chiefs descended from Esau, by name, according to
their clans and regions:
Timna, Alvah, Jetheth, [41]Oholibamah, Elah, Pinon, [42]Kenaz, Teman,
Mibzar, [43]Magdiel and Iram. These were the chiefs of Edom, according to
their settlements in the land they occupied.
This is the family line of Esau, the father of the Edomites.
[37:1]Jacob lived in the land where his father had stayed, the land of
Canaan.

*Listening to the Text in the Story:* Biblical Texts: Genesis 12:1–3; 25:12–18; 25:19–34; 26:34–28:9

Earlier we saw that the "account" (*toledot*) of the non-chosen son Ishmael (25:12–18) preceded that of the much longer "account" (*toledot*) of the chosen son Isaac (25:19–35:29). As we move to the next generation, we see the same dynamic. The narrator begins with the "account" (*toledot*) of Esau (see also 1 Chr 1:35–37); indeed there are two "account" (*toledot*) introductions in chapter 36 (vv. 1 and 9). The most important observation to be made about the inclusion of the "accounts" of Ishmael and Esau is that, even though they are not "chosen," neither are they neglected. In the description of their offspring we see God's continuing care for them. After all, the promise to Abraham was that God would use his descendants to be a "blessing" to the nations (12:3). Indeed, the reminder that Esau's other name was Edom is a way of connecting this family genealogy to a national story.

Often we wrongly think there are just two categories in the book of Genesis: the chosen and the unchosen, and we often believe that the unchosen are completely on the outside, while the chosen are on the inside. Kaminsky rightly suggests that there are actually three categories: elect, nonelect, and antielect. He further cautions that we should not confuse the latter two categories. The elect are those through whom God administers the covenant promises, but the nonelect (Lot, Ishmael, Esau, etc.) are the beneficiaries of many of the blessings of God. On the other hand, there are those who are antielect.[1]

## EXPLAIN the Story

### Esau's Wives and Sons (36:1 – 8)

In the introduction to the first account (v. 1), we are reminded that Esau's other name was Edom. Edom will be the name of the nation that descends from Esau. We are first introduced to Esau's Canaanite wives. They were earlier introduced at 26:34 – 35 and we there noted that there was some tension between their names there and here. What was clear, though, was that they were a source of annoyance to Isaac and Rebekah and were the pretense used by Rebekah to send Jacob to Paddan Aram to find a "proper wife." The mention of Basemath daughter of Ishmael here (different than the Basemath mentioned in 26:34 – 35) reminds us that at a later point in his life Esau did marry closer relatives, non-Canaanites, in an effort to appease his parents (28:6 – 9). The "account" goes on to name the offspring of Esau through Adah (Eliphaz, interesting the name of the Edomite "friend" of Job), Basemath (Reuel), and Oholibamah (Jeush, Jalam, and Korah).

After naming the wives and children of Esau, the narrator goes on to describe his move to the hill country of Seir. By moving to Seir (which is a term used later in near synonymity with Edom), Esau departs the promised land, leaving it to his brother Jacob, which reflects his giving up his birthright as well as his father Isaac's blessing. The move is described in terms similar to the description of Lot's departure from Abraham in chapter 13. The narrator seems to be intentional in invoking the connection back to the Abraham and Lot story since by so doing he makes it sound like Esau packs up and departs while in the vicinity of Jacob, which is not what actually happened. After all, Esau was living with Isaac and Rebekah when Jacob departed for Paddan Aram and he was already living in Seir when Jacob returned (32:2).

Why would the narrator evoke the memory of Lot's departure from Abraham then? In the first place, the comparison highlights the wealth of both brothers. Just as with Abraham and Lot, so Esau had to depart from Jacob because they were both so wealthy that "the land where they were staying could not support them both" (13:6; 36:7). More subtly the comparison may

1. Kaminsky, *Yet I Loved Jacob*.

also indicate that Jacob and Esau's departure was an amicable one as was Abraham and Lot's. We have already seen that Jacob and Esau's presence at their father Isaac's funeral also supports the idea that there was a type of reconciliation between the brothers. There may also be a third implication of the comparison between the two stories. After Lot departed, he ran into serious problems by locating himself near the nefarious cities of Sodom and Gomorrah, leading to all kinds of negative consequences (Gen 14; 18–19). We have to look further ahead in Israel's history, but even if we are correct to say that Jacob and Esau achieved some kind of reconciliation, the relationships between Jacob's descendants, the Israelites, and Esau's descendants (the Edomites) was one characterized by tension and outright conflict.

In the first place, Edom, like Moab and Ammon, refused Israel passage during the wilderness wanderings (Num 20:14–21); however, it appears that Israel had some options at that time, so they found another way, avoiding violent confrontation. But there were later battles between Edom and Israel. For instance, David is described as having taken Edom as a vassal (2 Sam 8:14). Jehoshaphat had control over it (1 Kgs 22:47). An Edomite monarchy came about the time of Jehoram (2 Kgs 8:20), and Elath, an important seaport, was taken by the Edomites during the reign of Ahaz.

At the time of the Babylonian destruction of Jerusalem, Edom had taken advantage of the situation in some way. While not precisely described, this point can be established by reference to texts like Psalm 137:7; Lamentations 4:22; Ezekiel 35:15; Obadiah 10–14.

### A Second Account of Esau's Wives and Sons (36:9–20)

Verse 9 presents the second "account" (*toledot*) of Esau. Here again we learn about Esau's wives and children (see the first "account" of Esau), but here we also learn about the grandchildren of Esau, at least through two of his wives (Adah and Basemath). We also learn that his son Eliphaz had a concubine (Timna) through whom he had a son named Amalek, likely the father of the Amalekites, who had a very turbulent relationship with Israel. The Amalekites were the first to attack the Israelites as they left Egypt, picking off the stragglers (Exod 17:8–16). While Israel was able to defeat them there, God issued a decree that they should be completely destroyed (see Exod 17:14 and Deut 25:17–19). While Saul had his opportunity to do it, he failed (1 Sam 15). The Amalakites (Haman the Agagite [an Amalekite clan] and his people) are completely destroyed at the time of Esther, thanks to the hidden providence of God. These children and grandchildren of Esau are the "chiefs" of the Edomites (36:15–19).

### The Sons of Seir the Horite (36:20–30)

The second section under the second "account of Esau" actually lists the sons of Seir, the Horite (see also 1 Chr 1:38–42), who are the people with whom the Edomites intermarried and ultimately displaced from the southern Transjordan region (36:20–30). They are living in the region at the time of Abraham (Gen 14:6). Deuteronomy 2:12 states that the "Horites used to live in Seir, but the descendants of Esau drove them out. They destroyed the Horites from before them and settled them in their place, just as Israel did in the land the Lord gave them as their possession." Interestingly Deuteronomy 2:22 informs the reader that it was the Lord who drove the Horites out of the region: "The Lord had done the same for the descendants of Esau, who lived in Seir, when he destroyed the Horites from before them. They drove them out and have lived in their place to this day." That God drove the Horites out before the Edomites is yet another indication of God's blessing on this non-chosen son of Isaac.

It is also possible that besides displacing the Horites, the Edomites also intermarried with them. For instance, the Timna mentioned as a sister of Lotan (v. 22) may be the same as the Timna who is the concubine of Eliphaz who gave birth to Amalek (v. 12). It is also possible that we should identify the Zibeon of the Esau genealogy with the Seir genealogy (vv. 2 and 20). Esau married Oholibamah, the daughter of Anah (v. 2). Anah is mentioned among the Horites as one who discovered hot springs in the desert, a crucial find for the survival in this region (vv. 24 and 25).

As is well known, the territory occupied by the descendants of Esau is not only known as Edom, but also as Seir (32:3; 33:14, 16; Judg 5:4). Indeed, Mount Seir is a prominent geographical feature of the region (Deut 1:2). One would think that this name comes from the Seir who heads the genealogy of 36:20–30, but then we should remember as well that another name for Esau is not only Edom ("Red"), but also Seir ("Hairy").

Seir is a Horite. The name may be related to the Hebrew word for "hole" or "cave." There are plenty of caves in the region where they lived, so perhaps the name comes from the fact that at some point they lived in caves. It is unlikely that the name is related to Seir's grandson through Lotan, Hori, though some believe it to be a possibility. Finally, some argue that the Horites are Hurrians, but then Hurrians are Indo-European and many of the names in this genealogy are clearly Semitic, and there is no reason to think that Hurrian expansion came this far south.

The structure of the genealogy of Seir the Horite begins by naming his seven sons who are identified as "Horite chiefs" (vv. 20–21) and ends by naming the same seven sons (vv. 29–30). The section between lists nineteen sons and one daughter (Oholibamah mentioned above) of the sons of Seir.

**Edomite Kings (36:31–39)**

The third list of the chapter provides the names of the first Edomite kings along with their place of origin (compare 1 Chr 1:43–53). That Esau's descendants developed into a nation state with kings is another indication of the blessing that God had given them. Indeed, their society had kings long before the Israelites (as is noted by 36:31). The promise that Abraham would have kings among his descendants (Gen 17:7) is first realized here with the Edomites before the Israelites. Indeed, we should note that the comment that these kings "reigned ... before any Israelite king reigned" likely is an addition added after the introduction of the monarchy to Israel.

The kings are listed in succession by name typically, but not always, with patronymic and place of origin. We learn some additional information about the two Hadads.

Bela son of Beor from Dinhabah
Jobab son of Zerah from Bozrah (the ancient capital of Edom)
Husham from the land of the Temanites
Hadad son of Bedad from Avith

Here we are told that he had victory over the Midianites who were living in neighboring Moab to the north.

Samlah from Masrekah
Shaul from Rehoboth on the river
Baal-Hanan son of Akbor
Hadad (or Hadar) from Pau
He was married to Mehetabel daughter of Matred, the daughter of Me-Zahab

The final list connected of the chapter is one dedicated to the "chiefs descended from Esau" (vv. 40–43).

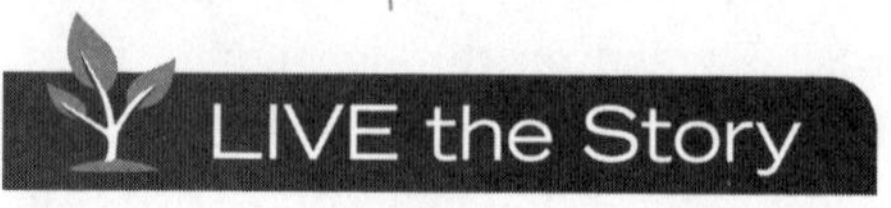


See related essay: A Promise for All Nations (after Gen 25:12–18).

CHAPTER 38

# Genesis 37:2 – 11

## LISTEN to the Story

[37:2]This is the account of Jacob's family line.

Joseph, a young man of seventeen, was tending the flocks with his brothers, the sons of Bilhah and the sons of Zilpah, his father's wives, and he brought their father a bad report about them.

[3]Now Israel loved Joseph more than any of his other sons, because he had been born to him in his old age; and he made an ornate robe for him. [4]When his brothers saw that their father loved him more than any of them, they hated him and could not speak a kind word to him.

[5]Joseph had a dream, and when he told it to his brothers, they hated him all the more. [6]He said to them, "Listen to this dream I had: [7]We were binding sheaves of grain out in the field when suddenly my sheaf rose and stood upright, while your sheaves gathered around mine and bowed down to it."

[8]His brothers said to him, "Do you intend to reign over us? Will you actually rule us?" And they hated him all the more because of his dream and what he had said.

[9]Then he had another dream, and he told it to his brothers. "Listen," he said, "I had another dream, and this time the sun and moon and eleven stars were bowing down to me."

[10]When he told his father as well as his brothers, his father rebuked him and said, "What is this dream you had? Will your mother and I and your brothers actually come and bow down to the ground before you?" [11]His brothers were jealous of him, but his father kept the matter in mind.

*Listening to the Text in the Story:* Biblical Text: Genesis 29:1 – 30:24

As we have observed before, the *toledot* of x is about the children of x, and thus we are not surprised that the *toledot* of Jacob (37:2) is about the twelve sons of Jacob. As we learned in 29:1–30:24, these twelve sons were born to four women, two of which, the primary wives Leah and Rachel, were enmeshed in a jealous rivalry. Jacob, their husband, was deceived into marrying Leah and thus he not only favored Rachel, his beloved wife, but he also favored her son, Joseph.

### Jacob's Favoritism (37:2–4)

The final section of the book of Genesis, one of the longest, begins with the announcement of the "account" (*toledot*) of Jacob, which, since *toledot* actually follow the child(ren) of the named person, is called the "account of Jacob's family" in the NIV. And indeed, while Jacob does continue as a major figure in the final chapters of Genesis, the focus now shifts to Jacob's children. The major emphasis is on Joseph, his first child with Rachel, but there is also a great interest in Judah. Indeed, one of the chapters focuses exclusively on Judah (ch. 38). While some scholars believe that this provides an interruption to the Joseph narrative, we will see that it is actually pivotal to the development of Judah's character, an important theme throughout the entire "account" of Jacob.

We are introduced first to Joseph, who is only seventeen at the time, and we should remember that with the exception of his full brother Benjamin, he was the youngest among the brothers. Right at the start the narrator tells us a story that will explain the brothers' antipathy toward Joseph.

Jacob had sent him out with his brothers, at least the children of the concubines Bilhah and Zilpah, and afterward he gave a bad report about them. We are not told exactly what they did to earn (assuming they did) the bad report, but we can imagine how the brothers felt about it. It is notable that the children of Leah are not mentioned here (Reuben, Simeon, Levi, Judah, Issachar, and Zebulun), but we will soon see that they share in the negative assessment of their younger brother.

Besides being a tattletale, Joseph brought on his brothers' anger as the favorite of their father Jacob. We already know that Jacob shows favorites as we consider his relationship with Rachel and Leah. Indeed, Joseph's status is because he is the son of his beloved and departed wife Rachel. The text does not mention this fact, but rather points to his birth when the patriarch was old. This notice reminds one of Isaac's birth to Abraham which also took place in his old age. Granted by the time Joseph was born in his old age, he already had ten sons, but it was Rachel's first and she, like Sarah, had been barren for a long time. The implicit analogy between Isaac and Joseph again explains Jacob's favoritism which causes the family dysfunction.

Jacob's special love for Joseph was made public by the gift of an ornate robe. Traditionally this robe has been understood to be a many-colored robe, but this understanding is unlikely, even impossible for the phrase *ketonet passim*. What is clear was that it was a distinctive robe, perhaps long-sleeved or ornate. Whatever the exact meaning of the phrase (maybe it was simply that it was not a "working coat"[1]), the gift of the robe served to set Joseph apart from his brothers thus feeding their envy. It was not so much the robe itself, but that it stood for the special love that their father had for their younger brother.

## Jacob's Dreams (37:5 – 11)

Jacob's brothers also hated him for his dreams. We will see that Joseph's ability as a dream interpreter plays a major role in the story. Here he interprets his own dreams; later he will interpret the dreams of two high level Egyptian officials, the chief cupbearer and the chief baker (40:1 – 41:40), and then, crucially, he will interpret the dreams of Pharaoh himself. We should notice that on all three occasions the dreams come in duplicate, the second dream confirming the message of the first in some way, though also occasionally carrying the message further.

Joseph's first two dreams both point to his future high status among his brothers, and the second one not only reaffirms this message but also adds his mother and his father. He reported his first dream to his brothers. They were all binding sheaves of grain in the field, when all of a sudden his sheave stood upright and their sheaves bowed down to it. The clear message is that Joseph will assume predominance of some kind among his brothers, and of course they hate him for this. They understand the dream to mean that Joseph will rule over them. After all, he is their younger brother, favored by their father. Perhaps they are further anxious because they know that their father was the younger, chosen son of Isaac, and Isaac himself was the younger son of Abraham. The sheaves may point to the future when Jacob will be in a position to provide food for his family during the great coming famine.

The second dream makes an even bolder claim. This dream has a cosmological setting as he sees the sun, the moon, and eleven stars bowing to him. The number eleven clearly points to the brothers, and the sun and the moon naturally point to Jacob and Rachel. Jacob himself expresses alarm at the

1. Provan, *Seriously Dangerous Religion*, 257.

claim of this dream, but the narrator informs us that he also kept the matter in his mind. In other words, he does not reject the idea out of hand. On the contrary, his brothers just grew in their jealousy and hated him even more.

The future will prove the dreams correct. Joseph will achieve high status among his brothers and even in relationship with his father. However, what the brothers do not understand is that this high status will serve their interests. But, of course, perhaps even more significantly, we certainly get no sense that Joseph understands that his future power is for service. Indeed, the narrator tells us the story of Joseph's dreams in a way that makes us understand, but not approve of, the brothers' reaction. Joseph is here acting very foolishly, and without condoning the brother's evil actions, he illustrates Proverbs 16:18: "Pride comes before a disaster, and before stumbling comes an arrogant attitude."[2]

To the brothers, it just seems that this upstart brat is asserting his superiority, and indeed, since portentous dreams like these would have been thought to come from God, giving his claims divine authority. Knowing the relationship between Joseph and his brothers helps us understand, but again not condone, their actions in the next episode.

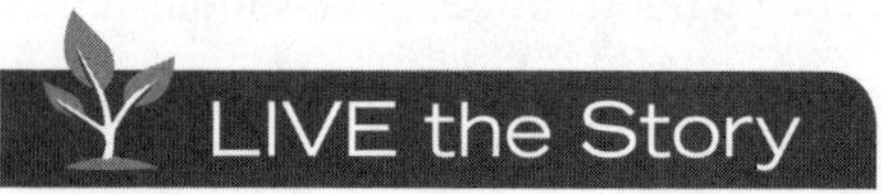


### The Ugly Consequences of Favoritism

Jacob is best known as a deceiver; indeed his very name evokes a Hebrew idiom which means "he deceives" (Gen 25:26). However, deception is not Jacob's only habitual sin. Jacob also demonstrates the ugly consequences of an illegitimate favoritism.

Jacob's favoritism starts with his love and his treatment of Rachel over Leah. Granted, Leah was imposed on Jacob by the scheming Laban (29:14b–31); however, from what we know Leah is not at fault for the situation. As far as we know, Jacob's treatment of Leah never stepped over the line to physical abuse, but it meant that Leah led a lonely, sad life (29:31).

We are even more disturbed by Jacob's treatment of his children. Here, his favoritism for Rachel over Leah extends to their children. Jacob not only shows that he favors Joseph over his brothers by giving the gift of an ornate robe, but also by his speech and actions throughout the whole Joseph narrative. As far as we can see, Jacob never stepped back from demonstrating favoritism toward Rachel's children, first Joseph and then later Benjamin.

2. Translation and commentary from Longman, *Proverbs*, 334.

Favoritism involves preferential treatment of some over others particularly in relationships that should be equal. Polygamy is not God's ideal (see The Nature of Marriage and the Gift of Sex after Gen 2:4b–25), but even here the later Mosaic law calls for equal treatment of a man's multiple wives (Exod 21:10–11). When it comes to children, they should all be treated with equal love in word and deed.

The story of Jacob's family is told in such a way that it becomes a warning to parents today about the dangers of favoritism. That favoritism is wrong is manifest through the common aversion to Jacob's behavior, but if parents are honest with themselves, and they should be, they will find that it is quite easy to fall into the trap of choosing favorites among children. Truth be told, some children are easier and more pleasant than others. The temptation is to try to correct the behavior of the difficult child by heaping praise on the "good" one and using his or her behavior as a standard for the unfavored child to emulate.

The Jacob narrative captures the typical results of such favoritism. It does not make things better, but much worse. It gives the favored child a puffed up sense of themselves (see Joseph and his presentation of the dreams), while it fuels anger on the unfavored child toward the family as a whole.

One might respond to this by charging God with favoritism. After all, he favored Abraham over others, and then favored Isaac over Ishmael, and Jacob over Esau. Doesn't he favor Christians over everyone else?

Such a view confuses chosenness with favoritism. As we have already seen throughout the book of Genesis, the chosen are not given preferential treatment. Indeed, their status as chosen if anything means that they will suffer more. No ornate coats for God's chosen, but rather famine, conflict, barrenness, and struggles of all sorts. As we have seen in the treatment of Ishmael and Hagar, the non-chosen are not cast off or neglected or unloved by God. Indeed, God uses the chosen as his instruments for the spiritual benefit of all people (Gen 12:3). As we turn to the New Testament, we often read of God's love for all. He loves everyone so much that he sent his son to die on the cross one of the best-known and most beloved passages of the Gospel of John tells us: "For God so loved the world that he gave his one and only Son, that whoever believes in him shall not perish but have eternal life. For God did not send his son into the world to condemn the world, but to save the world through him" (3:16–17).

See related essay: Does God Communicate to Us through Our Dreams? (after Gen 41).

CHAPTER 39

# Genesis 37:12–36

## LISTEN to the Story

[37:12]Now his brothers had gone to graze their father's flocks near
Shechem, [13]and Israel said to Joseph, "As you know, your brothers are
grazing the flocks near Shechem. Come, I am going to send you to them."

"Very well," he replied.

[14]So he said to him, "Go and see if all is well with your brothers and
with the flocks, and bring word back to me." Then he sent him off from
the Valley of Hebron.

When Joseph arrived at Shechem, [15]a man found him wandering
around in the fields and asked him, "What are you looking for?"

[16]He replied, "I'm looking for my brothers. Can you tell me where
they are grazing their flocks?"

[17]"They have moved on from here," the man answered. "I heard them
say, 'Let's go to Dothan.' "

So Joseph went after his brothers and found them near Dothan. [18]But
they saw him in the distance, and before he reached them, they plotted to
kill him.

[19]"Here comes that dreamer!" they said to each other. [20]"Come now,
let's kill him and throw him into one of these cisterns and say that a
ferocious animal devoured him. Then we'll see what comes of his dreams."

[21]When Reuben heard this, he tried to rescue him from their hands.
"Let's not take his life," he said. [22]"Don't shed any blood. Throw him into
this cistern here in the wilderness, but don't lay a hand on him." Reuben
said this to rescue him from them and take him back to his father.

[23]So when Joseph came to his brothers, they stripped him of his
robe—the ornate robe he was wearing—[24]and they took him and threw
him into the cistern. The cistern was empty; there was no water in it.

[25]As they sat down to eat their meal, they looked up and saw a caravan
of Ishmaelites coming from Gilead. Their camels were loaded with spices,
balm and myrrh, and they were on their way to take them down to Egypt.

[26]Judah said to his brothers, "What will we gain if we kill our brother
and cover up his blood? [27]Come, let's sell him to the Ishmaelites and

not lay our hands on him; after all, he is our brother, our own flesh and
blood." His brothers agreed.
[28]So when the Midianite merchants came by, his brothers pulled
Joseph up out of the cistern and sold him for twenty shekels of silver to
the Ishmaelites, who took him to Egypt.
[29]When Reuben returned to the cistern and saw that Joseph was not
there, he tore his clothes. [30]He went back to his brothers and said, "The
boy isn't there! Where can I turn now?"
[31]Then they got Joseph's robe, slaughtered a goat and dipped the robe
in the blood. [32]They took the ornate robe back to their father and said,
"We found this. Examine it to see whether it is your son's robe."
[33]He recognized it and said, "It is my son's robe! Some ferocious
animal has devoured him. Joseph has surely been torn to pieces."
[34]Then Jacob tore his clothes, put on sackcloth and mourned for his
son many days. [35]All his sons and daughters came to comfort him, but he
refused to be comforted. "No," he said, "I will continue to mourn until I
join my son in the grave." So his father wept for him.
[36]Meanwhile, the Midianites sold Joseph in Egypt to Potiphar, one of
Pharaoh's officials, the captain of the guard.

*Listening to the Text in the Story:* Biblical Text: Genesis 37:1–11

The previous section provides the background for the present story. There we learned about Jacob's favoritism and the brothers' deep envy of their younger brother Joseph.

## EXPLAIN the Story

### Joseph Goes to Dothan (37:12–17)

The brothers, without Joseph, had gone near the city of Shechem to pasture the flocks. The home base of Jacob's family at this time was Hebron. The trip was around eighty miles up the central ridge route that passed by Jerusalem, so their journey to Shechem would take some time. They are pastoral nomads, though, and they were following the available grazing land. Shechem was the first Canaanite city Abraham visited, and he had built an altar there (Gen 12:6). Of course, more recently the family had fled Shechem after Simeon and Levi had massacred the men of the city (Gen 34). We are not told the details, but they appear to feel comfortable enough to take the flocks to the vicinity of the city.

Jacob, here referred to by his other name Israel, decides to send Joseph to his brothers. We don't know what is going through Jacob's mind here, but he seems oblivious to the potential danger to his youngest son or oblivious to his other sons' jealousy. He would have to be utterly insensitive to the latter, so perhaps we are to think that he cannot imagine that they would harm their brother in any way.

He wants him to visit his brothers and then report on them and the flocks. We can imagine how the brothers would feel about this, considering the bad report Joseph had given his father at an earlier time (37:2).

Joseph goes dutifully to Shechem only to discover that his brothers had moved on. An unnamed man informs him that they had moved to Dothan, which is another day's walk (about thirteen miles), taking him even further from home and the protection of his family. Dothan was due west of Shechem, at the southern end of the Carmel mountain range) and, significantly for the rest of the story, on the international trade route that ran from the north down to Egypt.

### The Brothers Sell Joseph (37:18–28)

The narrator now (v. 18) shifts from following Joseph to reporting the action from the brothers' point of view, beginning when they spot him coming toward them from a distance. This gives them time to plot to do away with him. They don't refer to him by his name, but dehumanize him by calling him "that dreamer" (v. 19), calling to mind Joseph's galling dreams that asserted his future superiority to them.

Their immediate reaction was to kill him, and they devise a plot in order to cover up their crime. They will first kill him, then throw his body into a cistern (a pit used to store water) and then report that he was killed by a ferocious animal. By doing this they hope to subvert the message of his dreams. If he is dead, he certainly can't rule over them! It is unlikely that they actually believed that the dreams were from God, so we are to take their words as sarcasm.

Reuben intervenes at this point. He is the eldest of the brothers, and the supposed leader. He is also the one who would be held most responsible for anything that happened while they were gone. He advises his brothers not to kill him first, but simply to throw him into a cistern and leave him there. The result would be the same, but they would not have to actively shed Joseph's blood. Reuben, however, had an ulterior motive that he keeps hidden from his brothers. The narrator informs the reader that Reuben intended to come back and take his brother out of the cistern and return him to his father.

Thus, Reuben is the most admirable of the brothers. But even he is not acting as he should. As the eldest, he should have protected his young brother right from the start. Rather than devising a plot to subtly rescue him (which will backfire on him), he should have immediately quelled his brothers' plot. Since the Joseph narrative is also interested in answering the question why Judah and not Reuben is the father of the most important later tribe, we should also point out that at this stage Judah is one of the brothers who is plotting the death of Joseph. So relatively speaking, here at the beginning of the Joseph narrative Reuben outshines Judah. As time goes on, though, we will see dramatic development in Judah's character as Reuben will melt into the background.

They wasted no time when Joseph arrived, but ripped off the offending ornate robe that symbolized Jacob's preferential treatment of his youngest son. After this humiliation, they threw him into the cistern. The narrator mentions that there was no water in this cistern to explain why he did not drown. In this way, the brothers doomed him to a slow death from exposure, hunger, and thirst.

Fortunately for Joseph in the light of the brothers' intentions (though unfortunately as we will see for Reuben's plan to save him), they see a caravan working its way down the international highway from the north. The caravan was made up of Ishmaelite traders on their way to sell spices, balm, and myrrh in Egypt. Of course, as the name implies, they were the descendants of Ishmael according to Genesis 25:12–16 (see also 39:1; Judg 8:24; Ps 83:6), and their native homeland was the Arabian peninsula, but here they are also called Midianites, another people descended from Abraham, but through Keturah, the concubine of his old age (Gen 25:1–2) rather than through Hagar as was the case with Ishmael. While some believe the alternation between Ishmaelite and Midianite for the traders is the result of a merging of previously existing sources, it is also possible that Ishmaelite is a general term for inhabitants of northern Arabia and that the Midianites are the specific people meant.[1] That Ishmaelite and Midianite are used interchangeably for the same people may also be seen in Judges 8:22–24.

Now Judah steps to the fore for the first time. He is the fourth born son of Leah and Jacob, but we have already seen that Reuben (see 35:19–20) as well as Simeon and Levi (Gen 34) have sullied their reputations with Jacob. Thus, he is a potential leader among the brothers, and he offers a plan by which they can get rid of their annoying younger brother without killing him and in the process they can make a profit.

He comes across as a pragmatist, not someone who is morally outraged with the idea of killing Joseph, though he does appeal to the fact that he is

1. According to Provan (*Seriously Dangerous Religion*, 258), the brothers named them Ishmaelites from afar and then when they got closer, they recognized that they were more specifically Midianites.

their brother. He suggests selling Joseph to the Ishmaelite caravan. Thus, they can avoid taking bloodguilt on themselves and needing to cover up that crime (though they will have to cover his disappearance).

The brothers agree and they sell Joseph to the traders for twenty shekels of silver, which, as the NIV note indicates, is about eight ounces or two hundred and thirty grams. Interestingly, and in support of the authenticity of Joseph narrative as history, Kitchen has pointed out that this price for a male adult slave fits best for the first half of second millennium, not for a later period of time when some scholars think the narrative was created and placed in an earlier period of time.[2]

### Cover Up (37:29–36)

Judah's plan foiled Reuben's intention to rescue Joseph from his brothers. For reasons we are not told explicitly, Reuben was not there when Joseph was sold to the Ishmaelites. Perhaps it was his turn to tend the flocks. When he heard the news, he immediately panicked, tearing his clothes in grief and worry, not about Joseph necessarily but about the consequences for himself as the oldest brother who was ultimately responsible for what happened to Joseph.

Thus, they executed a cover up. They dipped Joseph's distinctive ornate robe into some goat's blood and took it back to Jacob. They asked him to examine it in order to determine whether it was Joseph's. Their request probably indicates that they were claiming that Joseph never actually met them. If he had, they would know it was the brother's garment and not need Jacob's affirmation. In this way, they also allow Jacob to reach his own conclusion on what happened. To him, it was obvious he had been eaten by a ferocious animal.

Jacob immediately plunges into grief, ripping his clothes, donning sackcloth. Attempts on the part of his sons and daughters (here we learn that Dinah is not the only one) to comfort him are refused. He is not able to be consoled and announces that he will never stop until he is united with Joseph in death.

The narrator ends the episode by informing the reader that the traders made it to Egypt where they then sold Joseph to Potiphar, who was a high ranking Egyptian official. Specifically, he was in the military. The Hebrew phrase translated "captain of the guard" by the NIV is more literally rendered "chief butcher," indicating that the Egyptians named their high offices after domestic servants (see later concerning the cupbearer and the baker).

---

2. K. Kitchen, "Genesis 12–50 in the Near Eastern World," in *He Swore an Oath: Biblical Themes from Genesis 12–50*, ed. R. S. Hess et al. (Cambridge, England: Tyndale House, 1993), 79–80.

## LIVE the Story

### "You Meant It for Evil ...," Part 1: God Uses the Evil Actions of Joseph's Brothers

As we read through the Joseph narrative for the first time, we are struck by the horrible treatment that Joseph receives from many parties, beginning in this chapter with his brothers. He may indeed be an arrogant, brash, insensitive younger brother, but he certainly does not deserve the treatment that he receives here, sold into slavery and reported dead to his father.

Where is God in all of this? While we suspect that he was indeed the one who sent the two dreams to Joseph, he is not explicitly mentioned in the text. There is no mention of God with Joseph in the cistern. At this moment it is not unlikely that Joseph would have thought that God had abandoned him.

However, reading the account of Joseph being sold into slavery in the light of the end of the story (a second reading of the narrative) sheds a totally different light on the matter. Looking back over the course of his whole life, Joseph could tell his brothers, "You intended to harm me, but God intended it for good to accomplish what is now being done, the saving of many lives" (Gen 50:20). We will develop this theme more extensively later (see "You Meant It for Evil ...," Part 4 in the Live the Story section after Gen 50:15–21).

For now we can already see that God was not at all absent when Joseph was thrown into the cistern and sold to the Ishmaelite traders, he was using the sinful motives and actions of the brothers to begin a process that would lead to the rescue of the family of God from the effects of a devastating famine.

Readers today should take encouragement from this story. Is life a mess? Does God seem absent? Remember that God can use the difficulties and pain of life to accomplish his purposes through you and for you.

Again, touching on a point to be developed at much further length later, Joseph here anticipates an even greater rescue. Jesus, like Joseph, suffered at the hands of others who just wanted to harm him. Indeed, as Peter told the crowd on Pentecost, "you, with the help of wicked men, put him to death by nailing him to the cross" but this was all according to "God's deliberate plan and foreknowledge" (Acts 2:23). The evil perpetrated against Jesus resulted in a far greater salvation, one from sin and death, than the salvation that resulted from Joseph's actions.

Greidanus goes even further and proposes that Jesus' suffering is also anticipated in Joseph's silent suffering at the hands of his brothers. While aware that later the brothers will feel guilty when they remember how Joseph pled for his life with them (42:21), he rightly points out that the narrative that recounts the sale pictures Joseph as silent. He goes on to suggest that Joseph in this chapter illustrates the silence of the suffering servant as will later be described by the prophet Isaiah:

> He was oppressed and afflicted,
> yet he did not open his mouth;
> he was led like a lamb to the slaughter,
> and as a sheep before its shearers is silent,
> so he did not open his mouth. (Isa 53:7)

In this too, he models the future suffering servant Jesus who, as Philip will later tell the Ethiopian eunuch was the one the prophet was ultimately speaking of (Acts 8:35) and who faced his suffering and death in silence (Mark 14:61; 15:5; Luke 23:9).[3]

## The Ugly Consequences of Envy

Right from the beginning of the Joseph narrative we have witnessed the tremendous envy that the brothers feel toward Joseph. Joseph has something that they desire: their father's special love. We have already described the wrongness of Jacob's favoritism toward Joseph (see The Ugly Consequences of Favoritism in the Live the Story section after 37:2–11). In a word, it elicits the envy of the brothers toward Joseph.

What is envy but "the desire for what another has that we don't have. It is resentful desire."[4] The brothers certainly resent Joseph, and they do so obsessively. They can't get him and his privileged family life out of his mind.

In an analysis of the Cain and Abel story, Miroslav Volf notes the pattern that we see in the story of Joseph and his brothers: "First came envy ... then came anger, that 'passionate againstness,' directed both at God and Abel."[5]

The brothers' envy-driven rage toward Joseph is obvious, but what about toward God? While it is not as clearly articulated as it is in the story of Cain and Abel, we see it in the brothers' unwillingness to control their hatred toward their brother. They are not content with what God has given them and so they lack trust in God and use malicious means in order to remove the source of their envy.

Psalm 73 provides an anatomy of a person who struggles against God because of his envy of the wicked who have more than he does:

---

3. Greidanus, *Preaching Christ from Genesis*, 352.

4. D. B. Allender and T. Longman III, *Cry of the Soul: How Our Emotions Reveal Our Deepest Questions about God* (Colorado Springs, CO: NavPress, 1994), 109.

5. M. Volf, *Exclusion and Embrace: A Theological Exploration of Identity, Otherness, and Reconciliation* (Nashville: Abindon, 1996), 95.

> ... my feet almost slipped;
> I had nearly lost my foothold.
> For I envied the arrogant
> when I saw the prosperity of the wicked. (Ps 73:2–3)

The brothers envied Joseph, who had his father's love and gifts and whose arrogance was manifest in his explanation of his dreams in the first part of Genesis 37. Unlike the brothers, the psalmist was in no position to harm the ones he envied, but he would have if he could.

The brothers, though, did act on their hate-filled envy by selling Joseph into slavery, faking his death, and reporting the fact to his father. By doing this, did they get what they wanted? After Joseph was gone from the scene, did Jacob love the other brothers more? Did the family move from dysfunction to happiness? Of course, the answer to both questions is no. "This is the irony of these dark desires: they actually destroy what we want."[6]

How do we handle envy then? Again, we turn to the psalmist for an answer. The composer of Psalm 73 wrote the song after he had come to grips with his envy. After all, the psalm begins with "Surely God is good to Israel, to those who are pure in heart" (73:1). The latter part of the psalm explains that his obsessively envious heart was calmed by going into the presence of God. He goes to the sanctuary, where during the Old Testament period, God made his special presence known, and he realized that God was with him and that the prosperity of the wicked was only apparent and short lived, not real.

Those of us who live in the twenty-first century encounter many things that can evoke our envy. We are exposed to the lives of the rich and powerful on television shows; constant advertisements play on our desires for more and better luxury items. No matter how much money and how many possessions we have, there is always an appetite for more. Like the psalmist we need to go into the presence of God and have our priorities corrected. If we have a vibrant, intimate relationship with God what else do we need?

---

6. Allender and Longman, *Cry of the Soul*, 115.

CHAPTER 40

# Genesis 38

## LISTEN to the Story

[38:1]At that time, Judah left his brothers and went down to stay with
a man of Adullam named Hirah. [2]There Judah met the daughter of a
Canaanite man named Shua. He married her and made love to her;
[3]she became pregnant and gave birth to a son, who was named Er. [4]She
conceived again and gave birth to a son and named him Onan. [5]She gave
birth to still another son and named him Shelah. It was at Kezib that she
gave birth to him.

[6]Judah got a wife for Er, his firstborn, and her name was Tamar. [7]But
Er, Judah's firstborn, was wicked in the LORD's sight; so the LORD put him
to death.

[8]Then Judah said to Onan, "Sleep with your brother's wife and
fulfill your duty to her as a brother-in-law to raise up offspring for your
brother." [9]But Onan knew that the child would not be his; so whenever
he slept with his brother's wife, he spilled his semen on the ground to
keep from providing offspring for his brother. [10]What he did was wicked
in the LORD's sight; so the LORD put him to death also.

[11]Judah then said to his daughter-in-law Tamar, "Live as a widow in
your father's household until my son Shelah grows up." For he thought,
"He may die too, just like his brothers." So Tamar went to live in her
father's household.

[12]After a long time Judah's wife, the daughter of Shua, died. When
Judah had recovered from his grief, he went up to Timnah, to the men
who were shearing his sheep, and his friend Hirah the Adullamite went
with him.

[13]When Tamar was told, "Your father-in-law is on his way to Timnah
to shear his sheep," [14]she took off her widow's clothes, covered herself with
a veil to disguise herself, and then sat down at the entrance to Enaim,
which is on the road to Timnah. For she saw that, though Shelah had
now grown up, she had not been given to him as his wife.

[15]When Judah saw her, he thought she was a prostitute, for she had
covered her face. [16]Not realizing that she was his daughter-in-law, he went
over to her by the roadside and said, "Come now, let me sleep with you."
"And what will you give me to sleep with you?" she asked.
[17]"I'll send you a young goat from my flock," he said.
"Will you give me something as a pledge until you send it?" she asked.
[18]He said, "What pledge should I give you?"
"Your seal and its cord, and the staff in your hand," she answered. So
he gave them to her and slept with her, and she became pregnant by him.
[19]After she left, she took off her veil and put on her widow's clothes again.
[20]Meanwhile Judah sent the young goat by his friend the Adullamite
in order to get his pledge back from the woman, but he did not find her.
[21]He asked the men who lived there, "Where is the shrine prostitute who
was beside the road at Enaim?"
"There hasn't been any shrine prostitute here," they said.
[22]So he went back to Judah and said, "I didn't find her. Besides, the
men who lived there said, 'There hasn't been any shrine prostitute here.' "
[23]Then Judah said, "Let her keep what she has, or we will become a
laughingstock. After all, I did send her this young goat, but you didn't
find her."
[24]About three months later Judah was told, "Your daughter-in-law
Tamar is guilty of prostitution, and as a result she is now pregnant."
Judah said, "Bring her out and have her burned to death!"
[25]As she was being brought out, she sent a message to her father-
in-law. "I am pregnant by the man who owns these," she said. And she
added, "See if you recognize whose seal and cord and staff these are."
[26]Judah recognized them and said, "She is more righteous than I, since I
wouldn't give her to my son Shelah." And he did not sleep with her again.
[27]When the time came for her to give birth, there were twin boys in
her womb. [28]As she was giving birth, one of them put out his hand; so the
midwife took a scarlet thread and tied it on his wrist and said, "This one
came out first." [29]But when he drew back his hand, his brother came out,
and she said, "So this is how you have broken out!" And he was named
Perez. [30]Then his brother, who had the scarlet thread on his wrist, came
out. And he was named Zerah.

*Listening to the Text in the Story:* Biblical Texts: Genesis 34; 35:21–22; 37:2; 37:21–36; Ancient Near Eastern Texts: Middle Assyrian Laws; Hittite Laws

Genesis 37–50 is frequently referred to as the Joseph narrative. Joseph is certainly the main character in this final section of the book of Genesis, and so Genesis 38 presents something of an anomaly. Joseph is never mentioned. Instead the narrator follows Judah who for unspecified reasons departs from his brothers and settles down with some Canaanites. Many scholars feel that Genesis 38 is an intrusion into the plot of the Joseph narrative. Such a view is shortsighted.

In actuality, these chapters are described as the "account" (*toledot*) of Jacob (Gen 37:2). And, as we have seen throughout the book, an "account" of x concerns the family, particularly the offspring, of x, so the final section of Genesis is not only about Joseph, but about all the sons of Jacob.

Indeed, we might also see Genesis 38 as an intentional insertion into the story about Joseph since it bears the mark of a " 'repetitive resumption' which 'mark the insertion of a self-contained unit into a given context' and which are 'characteritized by the partial repetition after the insert of the verse which closed the preceding part of the comprehensive unit, generally with some textual variation.' "[1] We can see this partial repetition by comparing 37:36 and 39:1.

Furthermore, Judah plays a special role in this final story. As mentioned earlier, this narrative seeks to answer the question of the tribe of Judah's later importance, even though Judah is the fourth born son of Jacob. After all, the first born son, Reuben (35:21–22), and the second and third born, Simeon and Levi (34), have disqualified themselves by alienating their father Jacob. Thus, attention now moves to Judah.

Genesis 38 imparts a story which helps us understand the nature of Judah's character at the beginning of the "Joseph narrative." We have already seen that he, unaware to be sure, spoiled Reuben's plan to rescue Joseph (37:21–30). The present story only deepens Judah's negative characterization at this point in his life. As time goes on, we will witness a significant transformation.

In the Explain the Story section, we will see that Judah's actions in marrying his widowed daughter-in-law to another son can be explained by reference to later (Mosaic) biblical law (Deut 25:5–6 quoted below). This procedure, though, is held in common with other ancient Near Eastern societies. The relevant Assyrian law states, "If a man with her pours oil on her head or brings (dishes for) the banquet, (after which), the son to whom he assigned the wife either dies or flees, he shall give her in marriage to whichever of his

1. M. Boda, "Flashforward: Future Glimpses in the Past of Ezra 1–6," in *Let's Go Up to Zion: Essays in Honour of H. G. M. Williamson on the Occasion of His Sixty-Fifth Birthday* (Leiden: Brill, 2012), 250, citing S. Talmon in "Ezra and Nehemiah (Books and Men)," in *Interpreter's Dictionary of the Bible Supplementary Volume*, ed. K. Crim (Nashville: Abingdon, 1976), 322.

remaining sons he wishes, from the oldest to the youngest of at least ten years of age."[2] According to the Hittite law, "If a man has a wife, and the man dies, his brother shall take his widow as wife. (If the brother dies,) his father shall take her. When afterwards his father dies, his (i.e., the father's) brother shall take the woman whom he had."[3] Though the Hittite and Middle Assyrian laws also postdate the action of this chapter, all of these sources testify to a widespread custom that predated all of these law codes.

### Judah Marries a Canaanite (38:1–5)

The story opens (vv. 1–5) by setting the scene and the background for the plot of the chapter. As just mentioned, Judah left his brothers and settled among Canaanites for a period of time, specifically at a place called Adullam where he associated himself with a man named Hirah. Indeed, his leaving is shocking in an ancient Near Eastern setting where extended families tended to stay together, leaving one to wonder whether there is an unexplained falling out with the family.

Adullam is about ten miles northwest of Hebron, where Jacob's family was settled and about fifteen miles southwest of Jerusalem. At this time, it is controlled by Canaanites, but many years later it is defeated by Joshua (Josh 12:15). It played an important role as a refuge for David at different points during his life (1 Sam 22:1–2; 2 Sam 13:13–17). It is also one of the cities warned by the prophet Micah (1:10–15). We do not know anything more about Hirah than is related in this chapter, but he appears to be Judah's friend who drew him to Adullam in the first place.

That Judah is associating closely with a Canaanite is a red flag about his relationship with God at this point. That it turns out that he marries a Canaanite, an unnamed woman identified as the daughter of Shua, is a sure danger sign. God wants his people to stay separate from the Canaanites. We noted Isaac and Rebekah's chagrin at Esau's marriages to Canaanites (26:34–35; 27:46), marriages that he too came to regret (28:6–9). This situation led Rebekah to convince Isaac to send Jacob off to Paddan Aram to marry someone within the family (27:46). We also argued that the story of Jacob at Shechem was told in a way that criticized Jacob's intention to allow his offspring to intermarry with the local Canaanite population (34).

2. Walton, "Genesis," 125, citing translation by M. Roth, *Law Collections from Mesopotamia and Asia Minor* (2nd edition; Atlanta: Society of Biblical Literature, 1997).

3. Walton, "Genesis," 126, citing Roth, *Law Collections.*

## The Death of Tamar's Husbands (38:6–11)

This marriage led to three sons: Er, the firstborn, then Onan, and finally Shelah. We learn that Shelah was born in another town named Kezib. The name Kezib only occurs here in all the Old Testament, but some scholars suggest that it is the same city as Akzib, which is listed as a town in Judah (of course the tribal region that Judah's descendants will be given by God; Josh 15:44) and, like Adullam, it is mentioned in the list of towns threatened with destruction at the time of the prophet Micah (see Mic 1:14).

The narrative sprints ahead from the birth of the three boys to the marriage of Er, the oldest. He marries a woman named Tamar. Though it is not explicitly mentioned, it is almost certain that Tamar was a Canaanite herself, an implication supported by the fact that her father's house seems to be in the area.

The marriage did not last long enough to produce a child. We are tersely told that God found Er to be wicked (though not told explicitly why), and so God put him to death. Biblical teaching makes it clear that such punishment does not always follow evil behavior (see the book of Job for a major example). There are other reasons for suffering, and wicked people do not always die young. But sometimes, as here, they do.

When Er dies, Judah does the right thing by instructing his next oldest son, Onan, to do his "duty" as a brother-in-law and impregnate her so she can have a child. Later Mosaic law describes the procedure in Deuteronomy 25:5–6:

> If brothers are living together and one of them dies without a son, his widow must not marry outside the family. Her husband's brother shall take her and marry her and fulfill the duty of a brother-in-law to her. The first son she bears shall carry on the name of the dead brother so that his name will not be blotted out from Israel.

Of course, the Mosaic law is not yet instituted at the time of Er's death, but the Mosaic law is probably making normative a social custom that was known from a much earlier time.

Onan, however, does not want to do his duty as a brother-in-law and spills his seed on the ground rather than impregnating Tamar so she has a child that would not be his. Interestingly, the law in Deuteronomy goes on to describe what happens if a brother-in-law does not want to fulfill his duty:

> However, if a man does not want to marry his brother's wife, she shall go to the elders at the town gate and say, "My husband's brother refuses to carry on his brother's name in Israel. He will not fulfill the duty of a brother-in-law to me." Then the elders of his town shall summon him

> and talk to him. If he persists in saying, "I do not want to marry her," his brother's widow shall go up to him in the presence of the elders, take off one of his sandals, spit in his face and say, "This is what is done to the man who will not build up his brother's family line." That man's line shall be known in Israel as the Family of the Unsandaled. (Deut 25:7–10)

The closest we see this scenario work out is in Ruth 4, when Boaz approaches a relative who is closer to Naomi than he is about marrying Ruth. Onan makes no public protest, but privately refuses to follow through on his duty. Since he does not protest publicly, Tamar would not have the option, if it was even available to her in this environment which is earlier and non-Israelite, to challenge his refusal. God, however, knows what Onan does in private, and for his evil actions, God put him to death.

After the deaths of Er and Onan, Judah advises his daughter-in-law to return to her father's household (ironic since Judah himself had left his father's household[4]) until his third son Shelah grows up. However, the narrator informs us that Judah is now worried about the possible fate of his third son considering that the two older sons had died young after marriage to Tamar. Being an obedient daughter-in-law, Tamar returned to her home to wait for the time when Shelah came of age.

### Judah Sleeps with a Prostitute (38:12–23)

A "long time" passes (v. 12), and the narrator tells the reader that Judah's wife died. We soon become aware that even though a long time has passed Judah has not given Shelah to Tamar as a husband. Tamar has come to the realization that Judah has no intention of giving her Shelah as a husband (v. 14). Thus, she takes matters into her own hands when she hears that Judah traveled to the city of Timnah with his friend Hirah in order to get his sheep sheared. This Timnah, not to be confused with the city of the same name seen in the Samson story (Judg 14), is located to the southeast of Hebron.

Tamar presents herself as a prostitute on the road to Timnah at the entrance to the town (or perhaps fork in the road) of Enaim. She had removed her widow's garb and presumably dressed like a prostitute, including a veil,[5] which also served to hide her identity from her father-in-law.

Judah, whose wife was dead, propositioned Tamar disguised as a prostitute. She asks for payment, and he promises a young goat from the flock. Since he

4. Mark Boda, personal communication.

5. While Walton ("Genesis," 126) says that the veil does not indicate that she was a prostitute but is mentioned only to explain why he did not recognize his daughter-in-law, v. 15 seems to be most straightforwardly understood as connecting the veil with prostitution ("he thought she was a prostitute, for she had covered her face").

does not have the goat at present, she asks for some kind of surety for the payment and specifically requests Judah's seal with its cord as well as his staff or walking stick. These are identity markers. A seal was used on soft clay to leave an impression that was unique to Judah. The walking stick would also have features that would connect it to Judah. Leaving these items with this prostitute would be equivalent to leaving a driver's license or a credit card today.

Thus, Judah slept and impregnated Tamar his daughter-in-law. She then left and put her widow's clothes back on and acted as if nothing had happened. Judah, on the other hand, asked Hirah to take the payment to the prostitute, but when he went to the location where they had met, she was nowhere to be found.

Hirah asks some of the locals where he might find the woman, and they respond that they know of no such person. Interestingly, Hirah refers to the woman as a "shrine prostitute" (*qdeshah*). The word is related to the verbal root *qdsh* which means to "be holy" or "set apart." The assumption is that she was not a regular prostitute but one associated with a local holy place. Shrine prostitution is prohibited in the later law of Deuteronomy (23:18), and even later Kings Asa and Jehoshaphat removed shrine prostitutes from the land (1 Kgs 15:12; 22:47). What made Hirah refer to the disguised Tamar as a shrine prostitute as opposed to a regular prostitute is not stated in the text, but perhaps she located herself near a shrine. Perhaps too it was a way of rationalizing the payment as a gift to the shrine rather than an out-and-out payment for sexual favors. Interestingly, when Judah actually approached her, the text says that he thought that she was a "prostitute" (*zonah*, the term used for a regular prostitute). The biblical text actually never talks about the function of a shrine prostitute, but prostitutes associated with holy places are known from other ancient Near Eastern sources.[6] Some ancient Near Eastern religious ideas are associated with fertility of womb and field and perhaps having intercourse with a woman associated with the gods was a way of assuring fertility, though this understanding has recently been questioned.

It is hard to determine whether the fact that Judah thought he was sleeping with a shrine prostitute further darkens his character. However, the association with false religion as well as having intercourse outside of marriage would seem to further vilify him in the eyes of the reader.

In any case, Hirah returns to Judah and reports to him his failure to locate her. Rather than keeping up the search, he tells Hirah that he did his best to pay her and is willing to give up the seal with its cord as well as the staff rather than becoming a laughing stock. Rather than being a laughing stock

6. Ibid., 126–27.

for sleeping with the shrine prostitute, it is more likely that the abuse would come because he kept up the search.

**Tamar Gives Birth to Twins (38:24–30)**

Three months pass; about the length of time it takes for a pregnancy to become noticeable. At this point, someone informs Judah that his daughter-in-law Tamar is guilty of prostitution and is pregnant. We do not know who informs him, and as events unfold it is not even beyond the realm of possibility that an agent of Tamar told him. After all, for her plan to work, Judah needed to know her condition, and she could anticipate his reaction. Without hesitation, he issues a harsh, but perhaps not unexpected judgment, "Bring her out and have her burned to death" (v. 24).

Due to the time period, we do not know whether burning at the stake was the normal punishment for a widow acting like a prostitute. Later Mosaic law only prescribes death by fire to the case of a man who marries a woman and her mother (Lev 20:14) and a priest's daughter who becomes a prostitute (Lev 21:9). Burning by fire is a particularly horrific way to die and also means that the person will not get a honorable burial.

However, before the sentence can be carried out, Tamar had his seal with its cord and his staff sent to him. Judah immediately understood that she was the "prostitute" and that she was pregnant by him. His assessment immediately changed, declaring that "she is more righteous than I" (v. 26). He recognized his guilt in withholding his third son Shelah from her. He thus does not have her executed, and he also refrains from sleeping with her again.

The chapter thus presents a predominantly negative portrait of Judah. He lives among and befriends Canaanites. He does not do the right thing by his widowed daughter-in-law. He sleeps with a prostitute, and callously orders the death of his daughter-in-law with no further inquiry. However, Judah is not totally reprobate. When confronted, he is able to recognize his guilt. Perhaps here we see the beginning of Judah's turnaround. Indeed, as the Joseph narrative continues, Judah is back with his brothers and the assumption is that he is no longer living among the Canaanites.

The chapter ends with an account of the birth of the twin boys born to Judah and to Tamar. The unusual nature of the birth indicates a struggle for primacy and explains the names given to the children. While one of the children stuck his hand out of the womb and was declared the "first," having a scarlet thread tied to his wrist, he soon drew the hand back into the womb. Thus, unexpectedly, the other child actually emerged first, receiving the name Perez or "breaking out." Then the child with the scarlet thread was born, receiving the name Zerah, which means "brilliance" or perhaps "scarlet."

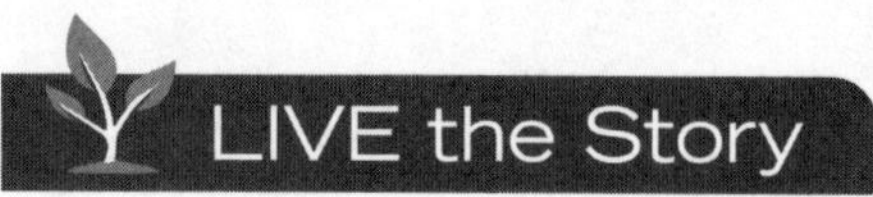

## "Judah the Father of Perez and Zerah, Whose Mother Was Tamar" (Matt 1:3)

The story of Judah and Tamar at first sight appears like an interruption of the Joseph narrative. In the Explain the Story section, we have pointed out that, though it does disturb the narrative flow from Genesis 37 to 39, it has an important function in the "*toledot* of Jacob" and also reminds us that Judah is a central character in the broader Joseph story and that his tribal descendants will play an incredibly important leadership role in the future history of Israel.

Wenham rightly goes further: "So this story, which at first sight seems to be so marginal to biblical history, records a vital link in saving history. Tamar, through her determination to have children, secured for Judah the honor of fathering both David and the Savior of the world."[7]

Perez and Zerah are the fruit of the liaison between Judah and Tamar. We next hear about them in the book of Ruth. The story of Ruth is a story of love and loyalty set in the dark period of Judges, but one of its purposes seems to be to explain the Moabite background of David.[8] The book, after all, ends with a genealogy that actually begins with Perez the son of Tamar and Judah:

> This, then, is the family line of Perez:
> Perez was the father of Hezron,
> Hezron the father of Ram,
> Ram the father of Amminadab,
> Amminadab the father of Nahshon,
> Nahshon the father of Salmon,
> Salmon the father of Boaz,
> Boaz the father of Obed,
> Obed the father of Jesse,
> and Jesse the father of David. (Ruth 4:18–22)

With the mention of David, of course, we see the connection to Jesus. Thus, Perez is named in both Matthew 1:3 and in Luke 3:33 as an ancestor to Jesus. Famously, the Matthew genealogy also mentions Tamar as one of four women who are mothers of ancestors of Jesus. Besides Tamar, they include Rahab, Ruth, and Bathsheba. All four are almost certainly foreign, with Tamar

7. G. Wenham, *Genesis 16–50*, WBC (Dallas: Thomas Nelson, 1994), 370, quoted in Greidanus, *Preaching Christ from Genesis*, 366.

8. For a fascinating account of how the story of Ruth (a Moabite and thus descended from the illicit union of a father and daughter [Lot and his daughter]) and Boaz (a descendant of the illicit union of a father and his daughter-in-law [Judah and Tamar]), see H. Fisch, "Ruth and the Structure of Covenant History," *VT* 32 (1982): 425–37.

and Rahab being Canaanites, Ruth a Moabite, and Bathsheba a Hittite. Their mention shows that the line that leads to Jesus is not an ethnically pure one, but includes people from other nations. All four women also have sexual pasts that are troubled in one sense or another, even if only by perception in the case of Ruth. Tamar gave birth to Perez (and Zerah) as a result of her deception of Judah. Ruth offered herself sexually to Boaz on the threshing floor before they were formally married. Rahab was a prostitute, and Bathsheba slept with David while she was married to another man. Jesus did not come from a long line of ethically pure ancestors, but from women (and men) who were ethically compromised in one way or another. Further, even it is only by perception, Mary, an unmarried pregnant woman, would have had questions surrounding her sexual purity.[9]

## Onan's Sin

Sometimes it is important to point out misapplications of biblical texts to modern life. In the introduction (see Reading from the Perspective of the Twenty-First Century), we discussed the issues surrounding taking this ancient historical narrative and applying it to our lives together. It is not easy navigating the question what is normative and what is unique to the time or considering how the coming of Christ might have created a new situation that renders the passage irrelevant for application to our lives today. One's case for relevance is often bolstered by appeal to didactic teaching elsewhere in Scripture.

Historically, Onan's act in Genesis 38 and God's response to it have been seen as relevant to the question of masturbation. Indeed, this episode inspired the technical name for masturbation (onanism). And if Onan's sin is maturbation, God's condemnation of it is clear, "he spilled his semen on the ground ... What he did was wicked in the LORD's sight; so the LORD put him to death ..." (38:9–10).

A careful, close reading of the narrative reveals that this text has nothing to do with masturbation and certainly should not be used as a prooftext indicating that masturbation is a sinful act. In the first place, Onan is not masturbating, he is pulling out his penis before ejaculating (*coitus interruptus*). And then he is doing that in order to avoid impregnating Tamar. Thus, his sin is not spilling his seed as such but rather he "spilled his semen on the ground to keep from providing offspring for his brother" (38:9).

Indeed, there is no biblical condemnation of masturbation in the Bible. There is a purity law that says, "If one of your men is unclean because of a

9. Thanks to Mark Boda, who drew my attention to J. Schaberg, *The Illegitimacy of Jesus* (New York: Crossroad, 1990).

nocturnal emission, he is to go outside the camp and stay there. But as evening approaches he is to wash himself, and at sunset he may return to the camp" (Deut 23:10–11). However, this law is not a moral law but rather a purity law. Indeed, if a man ejaculates during marital intercourse, he is ritually unclean for a short period of time (Lev 15:16–18). There is certainly nothing morally wrong with having intercourse with one's wife. This law is understandable in that Israel's law recognizes that one way a person can become ritually unclean is by coming into contact with something holy, and fluids (semen and blood connected to a woman's reproductive system) are considered holy because of their connection with life.

Thus, there is no biblical teaching that calls masturbation a sin, an important point to make because generations of people have been made to feel guilty about their God-given sexual desires. This issue has certainly become more pressing since in the modern period people tend to get married much, much later than during the biblical period. Masturbation, which actually begins in the womb, is a way to relieve sexual pressure that might otherwise lead to the sin of sleeping with a person who is not one's spouse.

CHAPTER 41

# Genesis 39

## LISTEN to the Story

39:1Now Joseph had been taken down to Egypt. Potiphar, an Egyptian who was one of Pharaoh's officials, the captain of the guard, bought him from the Ishmaelites who had taken him there.

2The LORD was with Joseph so that he prospered, and he lived in the house of his Egyptian master. 3When his master saw that the LORD was with him and that the LORD gave him success in everything he did, 4Joseph found favor in his eyes and became his attendant. Potiphar put him in charge of his household, and he entrusted to his care everything he owned. 5From the time he put him in charge of his household and of all that he owned, the LORD blessed the household of the Egyptian because of Joseph. The blessing of the LORD was on everything Potiphar had, both in the house and in the field. 6So Potiphar left everything he had in Joseph's care; with Joseph in charge, he did not concern himself with anything except the food he ate.

Now Joseph was well-built and handsome, 7and after a while his master's wife took notice of Joseph and said, "Come to bed with me!"

8But he refused. "With me in charge," he told her, "my master does not concern himself with anything in the house; everything he owns he has entrusted to my care. 9No one is greater in this house than I am. My master has withheld nothing from me except you, because you are his wife. How then could I do such a wicked thing and sin against God?" 10And though she spoke to Joseph day after day, he refused to go to bed with her or even be with her.

11One day he went into the house to attend to his duties, and none of the household servants was inside. 12She caught him by his cloak and said, "Come to bed with me!" But he left his cloak in her hand and ran out of the house.

13When she saw that he had left his cloak in her hand and had run out of the house, 14she called her household servants. "Look," she said to them, "this Hebrew has been brought to us to make sport of us! He came in here to sleep with me, but I screamed. [15]When he heard me scream for help, he left his cloak beside me and ran out of the house."

[16]She kept his cloak beside her until his master came home. [17]Then she told him this story: "That Hebrew slave you brought us came to me to make sport of me. [18]But as soon as I screamed for help, he left his cloak beside me and ran out of the house."

[19]When his master heard the story his wife told him, saying, "This is how your slave treated me," he burned with anger. [20]Joseph's master took him and put him in prison, the place where the king's prisoners were confined.

But while Joseph was there in the prison, [21]the LORD was with him; he showed him kindness and granted him favor in the eyes of the prison warden. [22]So the warden put Joseph in charge of all those held in the prison, and he was made responsible for all that was done there. [23]The warden paid no attention to anything under Joseph's care, because the LORD was with Joseph and gave him success in whatever he did.

*Listening to the Text in the Story:* Biblical Texts: Genesis 12:1–3; 37; Ancient Near Eastern Text: The Tale of Two Brothers (Egyptian)

After the interlude that focusses on Judah, the narrative returns to the story of Joseph. Joseph's brothers sold him into slavery to the Ishmaelite/Midianite traders at the end of Genesis 37, and at the beginning of our present chapter they finally arrive in Egypt where he is sold to a leading Egyptian official, Potiphar. Since God is with Joseph, Potiphar's house prospers bringing to mind God's promise to Abraham in Genesis 12:3 that "all peoples on earth will be blessed through you."

It is not uncommon for scholars to compare Genesis 39 with an Egyptian composition known as The Tale of Two Brothers. The two brothers are named Anubis and Bata, and the similarity comes when Anubis's wife tries to convince Bata to sleep with her, but when he refuses, she accuses him of rape. After that, the two story lines diverge sharply. In the final analysis, there is not substantial connection between these two stories. The similarities are of a general type and do not depend on any knowledge of the other.[1]

1. J. Hoffmeier, *Israel in Egypt: The Evidence for the Authenticity of the Exodus Tradition* (Oxford: Oxford University Press, 1999), 81.

## God Is with Joseph (39:1–6a)

Genesis 39 returns to the story of Joseph. In 37:36 we had heard that the Midianite caravan had sold Joseph as a slave to Potiphar a captain of the guard and one of Pharaoh's officials. Genesis 39:1 reminds the reader of this fact (though here Ishmaelite rather than Midianite is used to refer to the traders [see earlier discussion of 37:25–28]).

After this introduction, the narrator gets right to the point by informing the reader that "the LORD was with him" (v. 2), a phrase that signals that Joseph enjoys a covenantal relationship with God.[2] The heart of the covenant is expressed by the phrase, "I will be your God, and you will be my people." We should note that Israel's God is not just the God of Israel; he is the God of all the nations. He is active on Joseph's behalf even in Egypt.

In the same verse, we see that blessing follows the presence of God. Because of Joseph, God brought prosperity to Potiphar "in the house and in the field" (v. 5). Potiphar noted that the success of his household was the result of the presence of Joseph, so he gave him great responsibility to manage his household. According to verse 5, Joseph's rise in the household was accompanied by even more prosperity. He turned over the management of his house to the point that Potiphar did not have to worry about anything "except the food he ate" (v. 6).

At this point we should be reminded again of the promises given to Abraham in 12:1–3. God will not only bless Abraham and his descendants, but through them "all peoples on earth will be blessed through you." Joseph's presence blesses the household of the Egyptian Potiphar. We also hear that God will "bless those who bless you." As Potiphar promotes Joseph and entrusts him with more and more responsibility, so the prosperity of the house only grows.

## False Accusation (39:6b–18)

All is well for Joseph in Potiphar's household until Potiphar's wife takes notice of him. The narrator informs us that "Joseph was well-built and handsome" (v. 6). Hebrew narrative does not describe physical appearances gratuitously, but only if it is relevant to the plot, so we are not surprised that the next verse describes Potiphar's wife's proposition. She gets right to the point, "Come to bed with me!" (v. 7).

---

2. According to Robertson (*Christ of the Covenants*, 2), "The result of a covenant commitment is the establishment of a relationship 'in connection with,' 'with' or 'between' people."

Joseph refused her advances. He considered it an affront to his master who had entrusted him with the matters of his household. He reminds her that she is his wife and therefore should not be sleeping with another man. But this is not his only reason for his refusal. Adultery would also be sin against God. Adultery did not become sinful with the publication of the Ten Commandments (Exod 20:14; Deut 5:18). The Ten Commandments simply formalize God's will for his people at the point when the people of God become a nation state. She did not take no for an answer, but daily she kept trying to seduce him.

Joseph clearly did the right thing. He did not want to offend either God or his master. He fulfilled the law by loving his neighbor and God. The book of Proverbs was written much later than the time period of Joseph, but he clearly embodied the wisdom of the father who warned his son against sleeping with the "strange, foreign woman." One excerpt of the extensive teaching on this subject will have to do:

> Protect, my son, the command of your father;
> don't abandon the instruction of your mother.
> . . . .
> For the commandment is a lamp, and the instruction a light,
> and the path of life is disciplined correction
> to guard you from the evil woman,
> for the flattering tongue of the foreign woman.
> Don't desire her beauty in your heart;
> and don't let her absorb you with her eyelashes.
> For a prostitute costs a loaf of bread,
> but a married woman hunts for a man's life.
> Can a man scoop fire into his lap
> and his clothes not get burned?
> Or can a man walk on hot coals
> and his feet not get singed?
> Thus, the person who goes to the wife of his neighbor;
> all who touch her will not go unpunished.
> One does not despise a thief when he steals
> to fill his stomach if he is starving.
> If he is caught, he must pay sevenfold;
> he must give all the riches of his house.
> He who commits adultery with a married woman lacks heart;
> the one who does it destroys himself.
> He will find affliction and shame,
> and his reproach will never be blotted out.

> For passionate is the anger of a man,
> and he will not forgive on the day of vengeance.
> He will not regard the repentant face,
> and he will be unwilling, though the fine is large.
> (Prov 5:20, 23–35)[3]

In this passage and many others in Proverbs, the father warns his son about the advances of a woman. He backs up his teaching by reminding the son of the horrible consequences that follow such behavior.

Joseph is showing the type of wise behavior advocated by the father. We expect him to be rewarded. The exact opposite happens.

The moment of crisis comes when Joseph finds himself in the house alone with Potiphar's wife. The household servants are gone; we are not told why. Perhaps they were sent away from the house by Potiphar's wife. We also do not know whether Joseph was aware of the situation, but we do know that he was in the house in order to take care of his duties. Potiphar's wife seized the opportunity to once again proposition him, "Come to bed with me!" (v. 12). This time she also grabbed him by the cloak in order to force him, but he ran out of the house leaving the cloak behind.

Once again a garment of clothing plays a role in Joseph's fate. Earlier the ornate robe was used as evidence that he had been mauled by a wild beast. Potiphar's wife uses his cloak as evidence that he had tried to rape her. As Provan puts it, "Joseph is not a lucky man where clothing is concerned."[4]

Thus, she frames Joseph, first by calling the household servants, who must have been nearby though not in the house. She tells them that she had screamed when Joseph tried to force himself on her. Notice that she does not refer to him by name but as "the Hebrew," probably evoking the well-known disdain that Egyptians had for Asiatics (see also 43:32–34 and the Instructions of Merikare, which castigates "the wretched Asiatic").[5]

Potiphar's wife complained to the household servants and to her husband when he finally returned home that Joseph had made sport of her. The verb "make sport" (*tshq*) has sexual connotations as we saw in Genesis 26:8 when Abimelek saw Isaac "caressing" (from the verb *tshq*) Rebekeh. This sexual meaning is likely also at play in the description of the revelry of the Israelites in the presence of the golden calf (Exod 32:6). Interestingly, Potiphar's wife recruits the support of the household servants by saying that he was making sport of "us," thus including the servants. By trying to rape her, she claims,

3. Translation from Longman, *Proverbs*, 168–69.
4. Provan, *Seriously Dangerous Religion*, 258.
5. *ANET*, 416.

Joseph was raping all of them. We do not know what Joseph's relationship to the other household servants was like, but his favored status and his ethnicity may have already engendered a level of jealousy that she is here attempting to intensify.

**Joseph Thrown in Prison (39:19–23)**

Potiphar reacted like any offended husband would—with anger. What is rather surprising, however, is that rather than seeking his execution, he had him thrown into prison. We do not have Egyptian legal texts from this period that would indicate whether or not this is the normal penalty for attempted rape or not. Even if it were, we have to remember that Potiphar is a high Egyptian official, the chief of the guard (literally, "the chief butcher"). Such a person would likely not stand on formalities in terms of revenge. All of this raises the possibility that he may have suspected his wife's account of the story, and that he may still maintain regard for Joseph and what he had done for him.

Whatever the reason, and we are speculating here about the narrative gaps of the story, Joseph ends up in prison. Specifically, he ends up in the prison where the king's prisoners were held.

Joseph was sold into slavery because of the evil actions of his brothers. He is now thrown into prison by the evil actions of Potiphar's wife. Even so, just as we saw during his time in the service of Potiphar, we now learn that God was "with him" in prison. Above, we observed that this is shorthand for reminding us that God remains faithful to his covenant partner. And further, just like in Potiphar's house, God's presence with Joseph meant that the prison prospered. Accordingly, the warden gave him more and more responsibility, even putting him in charge of the prisoners. In this way, he came to meet two very important Egyptian officials, and this relationship will propel him to the next stage of his remarkable life.

**"You Meant It for Evil . . . ," Part 2: God Uses the Evil Actions of Potiphar's Wife and His Fellow Prisoners for His Greater Purposes**

As we noted at the beginning of the Joseph story, the reader processes the narrative differently whether reading for the first or second (or more) time. In Genesis 37, on the first reading all we know is that Joseph is being badly treated by his brothers and God seemed absent (see "You Meant It For Evil . . . ," Part 1 in the Live the Story Section of Gen 37:12–36). On the second reading, in the light of Genesis 50:20, we know that God is actually using the very evil acts of the brothers to move Joseph to Egypt in order to eventually bring him to a place where he can save his family from a severe famine.

Genesis 39 recounts further evil actions against Joseph. Potiphar's wife frames him for adultery, and he is thrown in jail. As the next chapter will inform us, even after successfully interpreting the cupbearer's dream that signals his release from prison, Joseph is quickly forgotten. His good deed goes unrewarded.

But again, as throughout his life, God is using these evil acts for good. Joseph is getting closer and closer to meeting the Pharaoh and getting the position that will allow him to provide food for the people of God. For the relationship between Joseph and Jesus on this theme, see "You Meant It for Evil . . . ," Part 4 in the Live the Story Section after Genesis 50:15–21.

The difference between Genesis 37 and 39 is that while God seemed (but actually wasn't) absent during Joseph's travails, now the narrator makes it very clear that God is "with him." We turn now to that important topic.

**Immanuel: The Lord is with Us**

God blessed Potiphar's household because God was "with Joseph" (v. 2, 3; cf. v. 5). In the exposition of the passage, we noted that this phrase is indicative of a covenant relationship. God enters into a relationship with his people in order to bring a blessing to them and to others who associate with them (Gen 12:3). The phrase indicates God's benificent presence.

The Christian reader's mind goes to the opening chapter of the Gospel of Matthew where the author cites (in Matt 1:22–23) the virgin birth of Jesus as the ultimate fulfillment of Isaiah 7:14: "The virgin will conceive and give birth to a son, and will call him Immanuel" (which means "God with us").

We will not be distracted for the purpose of this reflection with the interesting and knotty question of the connection between Matthew's use of Isaiah 7:14 and its Old Testament context. As all careful readers know, Isaiah speaks of the birth of Immanuel as something that will happen in the relatively near future as a sign that the kings of Syria and Israel will not threaten the Judah of King Ahaz. Thus, in its original fulfillment the woman who was a virgin (or perhaps a young, unmarried woman) at the time of the oracle was not a virgin (or unmarried) when the birth took place. However, the name Immanuel takes on what appears to be wider ramifications in its use in Isaiah 8:8 where Immanuel is addressed as one who possesses all the land of Israel. In addition, the Septuagint translates the Hebrew term *almah* as *parthenos*, a Greek term that specifically means virgin, not just a young, unmarried woman. These factors lend credence to Matthew's use of the passage to point to its ultimate fulfillment in Jesus' virgin birth.

What is important for us in this reflection is the identification of Jesus as Immanuel. He is, in other words, the ultimate expression of God's intent to be "with" his people. He is, after all, God himself. When he is with us, God is present with us. In his earthly ministry he made God's presence known to his disciples. After all, according to John: "In the beginning was the Word, and the Word was with God and the Word was God ... The Word became flesh and made his dwelling among us" (John 1:1, 14). But even after he ascended to heaven, he still remains with his people. According to Matthew, his final words included this promise: "And surely I am with you always, to the very end of the age" (Matt 28:20).

### A Sin against Potiphar and against God

Potiphar's wife wants to sleep with Joseph. She is attracted to him because he was "well-built and handsome" (Gen 39:6). We have no idea whether she was beautiful or not, but she was a person of power and to refuse her took courage. Joseph, after all, was a slave; she was the mistress of the house.

Why did he refuse her? For Potiphar and even more importantly for God. As Provan puts it, sleeping with Potiphar's wife "would represent a failure to love God and to love his neighbor."[6]

Surprisingly, even some wonderful scholars and preachers balk at looking at this passage as a moral lesson to avoid the temptations of adulterous sex. Greidanus, for instance, says that preachers should avoid using the text in a moralistic way, as a warning to young men to avoid the temptations of sex outside of marriage.[7] He makes a distinction between preaching the text moralistically and preaching it according to its place in redemptive history. In my opinion, this is not an either/or issue (as Paul himself points out in 2 Tim 3:14–17). We will see that Genesis 39 has a place in redemptive history, but the passage also has a clear moral lesson. The godly, wise person will avoid sexual intercourse outside of marriage.

John Calvin taught that the Bible, besides being a history of redemption, is also a mirror of the soul, though it functions as such in different ways in various books (see Introduction: Reading from the Perspective of the Twenty-First Century). When it comes to narrative texts, the reader should identify with the characters and learn to emulate their righteous behavior as well as to avoid their wicked actions.

But how do we know what is right and wrong in the actions of the characters? It is true that the stories themselves often don't help us decide. It is also true that sometimes righteous behavior in the Old Testament or at a

6. Provan, *Seriously Dangerous Religion*, 258.
7. Greidanus, *Preaching Christ from Genesis*, 378.

certain time during the Old Testament period is not righteous behavior today. Abraham married his half sister Sarah, but the later Mosaic law prohibits such a marriage. Joshua fought bloody wars at God's command, but Jesus heightens and intensifies the battle for Christians so that it is no longer directed toward flesh and blood but toward the spiritual powers and authorities (Eph 6:10–20).

However, both the Old Testament and the New Testament agree that sleeping with another man's wife is a violation of God's will for how we live. Thus, Joseph's behavior here models for later Christian readers the right response to an inappropriate sexual advance. And it is precisely Joseph's robust relationship with God that gives him the strength to resist Potiphar's wife.

Not only does the Law teach us, most notably in the seventh commandment ("You shall not commit adultery," Exod 20:14), that sleeping with another person's spouse is wrong, but so does the book of Proverbs. However, here an interesting problem presents itself.

Proverbs 5–7 provides lengthy teaching of a father to a son about the dangers of sleeping with another man's wife. Rather than appealing to ethical principles, the father warns his son of dire consequences of such evil action. If the son sleeps with a married woman, her husband will seek his harm and even death (Prov 6:30–35). Thus, the son should control himself for his own good.

Joseph does precisely what the sages of Proverbs recommend. But by doing so, he does not avoid punishment. He resists temptation, but still gets thrown in jail.

Reading the Joseph story in the light of Proverbs' teaching reminds us that the sages are not giving us guarantees.[8] They are rather saying that wise behavior, which includes not committing adultery, is the best way to achieve certain desired goals all other things being equal. In the Joseph narrative, not all things are equal. God is using the evil actions of many, including Potiphar's wife, to accomplish his purpose of bringing Joseph to a place of political power where he can help the future suffering of the people of God.

In the final analysis, Joseph illustrates what Paul urges: "Flee from sexual immorality" (1 Cor 6:18). Joseph does this immediately and literally as he runs away from Potiphar's wife's grasping hands. As Hoon Kim points out, Joseph's example also encourages us to stay away from temptation in the first place. Don't go to places or do things or be with people that may lead to sexual sin.[9]

8. Longman, *Proverbs*, 33 and B. Waltke, "Does Proverbs Promise Too Much?" *Andrews University Seminary Studies* 34 (1996): 319–36.

9. H. Kim, *Creative Bible Lessons in Genesis* (Grand Rapids: Zondervan, 2007), 152.

CHAPTER 42

# Genesis 40 – 41

## LISTEN to the Story

[40:1]Some time later, the cupbearer and the baker of the king of Egypt
offended their master, the king of Egypt. [2]Pharaoh was angry with his
two officials, the chief cupbearer and the chief baker, [3]and put them in
custody in the house of the captain of the guard, in the same prison where
Joseph was confined. [4]The captain of the guard assigned them to Joseph,
and he attended them.

After they had been in custody for some time, [5]each of the two
men — the cupbearer and the baker of the king of Egypt, who were being
held in prison — had a dream the same night, and each dream had a
meaning of its own.

[6]When Joseph came to them the next morning, he saw that they were
dejected. [7]So he asked Pharaoh's officials who were in custody with him in
his master's house, "Why do you look so sad today?"

[8]"We both had dreams," they answered, "but there is no one to
interpret them."

Then Joseph said to them, "Do not interpretations belong to God?
Tell me your dreams."

[9]So the chief cupbearer told Joseph his dream. He said to him, "In my
dream I saw a vine in front of me, [10]and on the vine were three branches.
As soon as it budded, it blossomed, and its clusters ripened into grapes.
[11]Pharaoh's cup was in my hand, and I took the grapes, squeezed them
into Pharaoh's cup and put the cup in his hand."

[12]"This is what it means," Joseph said to him. "The three branches are
three days. [13]Within three days Pharaoh will lift up your head and restore
you to your position, and you will put Pharaoh's cup in his hand, just as
you used to do when you were his cupbearer. [14]But when all goes well
with you, remember me and show me kindness; mention me to Pharaoh
and get me out of this prison. [15]I was forcibly carried off from the land of
the Hebrews, and even here I have done nothing to deserve being put in a
dungeon."

[16]When the chief baker saw that Joseph had given a favorable
interpretation, he said to Joseph, "I too had a dream: On my head were

three baskets of bread. [17]In the top basket were all kinds of baked goods for
Pharaoh, but the birds were eating them out of the basket on my head."

[18]"This is what it means," Joseph said. "The three baskets are three
days. [19]Within three days Pharaoh will lift off your head and impale your
body on a pole. And the birds will eat away your flesh."

[20]Now the third day was Pharaoh's birthday, and he gave a feast for all
his officials. He lifted up the heads of the chief cupbearer and the chief
baker in the presence of his officials: [21]He restored the chief cupbearer
to his position, so that he once again put the cup into Pharaoh's hand—
[22]but he impaled the chief baker, just as Joseph had said to them in his
interpretation.

[23]The chief cupbearer, however, did not remember Joseph; he
forgot him.

[41:1]When two full years had passed, Pharaoh had a dream: He was
standing by the Nile, [2]when out of the river there came up seven cows,
sleek and fat, and they grazed among the reeds. [3]After them, seven other
cows, ugly and gaunt, came up out of the Nile and stood beside those on
the riverbank. [4]And the cows that were ugly and gaunt ate up the seven
sleek, fat cows. Then Pharaoh woke up.

[5]He fell asleep again and had a second dream: Seven heads of grain,
healthy and good, were growing on a single stalk. [6]After them, seven other
heads of grain sprouted—thin and scorched by the east wind. [7]The thin
heads of grain swallowed up the seven healthy, full heads. Then Pharaoh
woke up; it had been a dream.

[8]In the morning his mind was troubled, so he sent for all the
magicians and wise men of Egypt. Pharaoh told them his dreams, but no
one could interpret them for him.

[9]Then the chief cupbearer said to Pharaoh, "Today I am reminded
of my shortcomings. [10]Pharaoh was once angry with his servants, and
he imprisoned me and the chief baker in the house of the captain of the
guard. [11]Each of us had a dream the same night, and each dream had a
meaning of its own. [12]Now a young Hebrew was there with us, a servant
of the captain of the guard. We told him our dreams, and he interpreted
them for us, giving each man the interpretation of his dream. [13]And
things turned out exactly as he interpreted them to us: I was restored to
my position, and the other man was impaled."

[14]So Pharaoh sent for Joseph, and he was quickly brought from the
dungeon. When he had shaved and changed his clothes, he came before
Pharaoh.

[15]Pharaoh said to Joseph, "I had a dream, and no one can interpret
it. But I have heard it said of you that when you hear a dream you can
interpret it."

16“I cannot do it,” Joseph replied to Pharaoh, “but God will give Pharaoh the answer he desires.”

17Then Pharaoh said to Joseph, “In my dream I was standing on the bank of the Nile, 18when out of the river there came up seven cows, fat and sleek, and they grazed among the reeds. 19After them, seven other cows came up — scrawny and very ugly and lean. I had never seen such ugly cows in all the land of Egypt. 20The lean, ugly cows ate up the seven fat cows that came up first. 21But even after they ate them, no one could tell that they had done so; they looked just as ugly as before. Then I woke up.

22“In my dream I saw seven heads of grain, full and good, growing on a single stalk. 23After them, seven other heads sprouted — withered and thin and scorched by the east wind. 24The thin heads of grain swallowed up the seven good heads. I told this to the magicians, but none of them could explain it to me.”

25Then Joseph said to Pharaoh, “The dreams of Pharaoh are one and the same. God has revealed to Pharaoh what he is about to do. 26The seven good cows are seven years, and the seven good heads of grain are seven years; it is one and the same dream. 27The seven lean, ugly cows that came up afterward are seven years, and so are the seven worthless heads of grain scorched by the east wind: They are seven years of famine.

28“It is just as I said to Pharaoh: God has shown Pharaoh what he is about to do. 29Seven years of great abundance are coming throughout the land of Egypt, 30but seven years of famine will follow them. Then all the abundance in Egypt will be forgotten, and the famine will ravage the land. 31The abundance in the land will not be remembered, because the famine that follows it will be so severe. 32The reason the dream was given to Pharaoh in two forms is that the matter has been firmly decided by God, and God will do it soon.

33“And now let Pharaoh look for a discerning and wise man and put him in charge of the land of Egypt. 34Let Pharaoh appoint commissioners over the land to take a fifth of the harvest of Egypt during the seven years of abundance. 35They should collect all the food of these good years that are coming and store up the grain under the authority of Pharaoh, to be kept in the cities for food. 36This food should be held in reserve for the country, to be used during the seven years of famine that will come upon Egypt, so that the country may not be ruined by the famine.”

37The plan seemed good to Pharaoh and to all his officials. 38So Pharaoh asked them, “Can we find anyone like this man, one in whom is the spirit of God?”

39Then Pharaoh said to Joseph, “Since God has made all this known to you, there is no one so discerning and wise as you. 40You shall be in

charge of my palace, and all my people are to submit to your orders. Only
with respect to the throne will I be greater than you."

41So Pharaoh said to Joseph, "I hereby put you in charge of the whole
land of Egypt." 42Then Pharaoh took his signet ring from his finger and
put it on Joseph's finger. He dressed him in robes of fine linen and put a
gold chain around his neck. 43He had him ride in a chariot as his second-
in-command, and people shouted before him, "Make way!" Thus he put
him in charge of the whole land of Egypt.

44Then Pharaoh said to Joseph, "I am Pharaoh, but without your word
no one will lift hand or foot in all Egypt." 45Pharaoh gave Joseph the name
Zaphenath-Paneah and gave him Asenath daughter of Potiphera, priest of
On, to be his wife. And Joseph went throughout the land of Egypt.

46Joseph was thirty years old when he entered the service of Pharaoh
king of Egypt. And Joseph went out from Pharaoh's presence and traveled
throughout Egypt. 47During the seven years of abundance the land
produced plentifully. 48Joseph collected all the food produced in those
seven years of abundance in Egypt and stored it in the cities. In each city
he put the food grown in the fields surrounding it. 49Joseph stored up
huge quantities of grain, like the sand of the sea; it was so much that he
stopped keeping records because it was beyond measure.

50Before the years of famine came, two sons were born to Joseph by
Asenath daughter of Potiphera, priest of On. 51Joseph named his firstborn
Manasseh and said, "It is because God has made me forget all my trouble
and all my father's household." 52The second son he named Ephraim and
said, "It is because God has made me fruitful in the land of my suffering."

53The seven years of abundance in Egypt came to an end, 54and the
seven years of famine began, just as Joseph had said. There was famine
in all the other lands, but in the whole land of Egypt there was food.
55When all Egypt began to feel the famine, the people cried to Pharaoh
for food. Then Pharaoh told all the Egyptians, "Go to Joseph and do
what he tells you."

56When the famine had spread over the whole country, Joseph opened
all the storehouses and sold grain to the Egyptians, for the famine was
severe throughout Egypt. 57And all the world came to Egypt to buy grain
from Joseph, because the famine was severe everywhere.

*Listening to the Text in the Story:* Biblical Text: Genesis 39; Ancient Near Eastern Text: Famine Stele of Sehel Island (see description in Explain the Story)

Genesis 39 provides the immediate background to the present episode that concerns Joseph in prison and his encounter with the chief cupbearer and the chief cupbearer, which will eventually lead him to the royal court. There we learn that his master Potiphar's wife framed him for attempted rape and he was thrown in jail.

**Joseph and the Cupbearer and the Baker (40)**

Joseph had been thrown into prison on the false charge of attempted rape. While there, the prison prospered because God was "with him." Accordingly, the warden turned over more and more of the management to Joseph.

We now learn that "some time later" (v. 1) two new people were added to the prison population. They are identified not by name but by position, Pharaoh's chief cupbearer and his chief baker. In spite of the names, we are not to think of them simply as kitchen staff. It appears that Pharaoh's closest advisors were called by such names. In this vein, we should remember that Potiphar's title was literally "chief butcher" (39:1).

We do not know the exact function of the chief baker, but we get a picture of a cupbearer in the person of Nehemiah who served in the Persian court of Artaxerxes 1 (reigned 464–424 BC). It is true that he did serve the king his wine (Neh 1:2), but from their interchange we see that he also was a trusted advisor, not simply a lackey. A cupbearer would need to be trusted because of the danger of political assassination by poisoning. The fact that Nehemiah was more than a household servant is demonstrated by the fact that Artaxerxes is comfortable naming him governor of the Persian province of Yehud. We will soon see that the Egyptian chief cupbearer in this story also has the same advisory role as Nehemiah enjoyed much later in Persia.[1]

The chief baker and the chief cupbearer were thrown into prison for an unspecified offense against Pharaoh. The prison here is called the "house of the captain of the guard" (40:3) the same title that was used for Potiphar (39:1). Potiphar apparently was in control, and the fact that he did not have Joseph killed may be yet another line of evidence that Potiphar was not totally convinced of his wife's charges. In any case, Joseph soon found himself in charge of these two prisoners.

After an unspecified amount of time passed, the two Egyptian officials each had a dream. The dream was on the same night which likely, along with the content of the dreams, suggested to them that the dreams had significance.

1. E. M. Yamauchi, *Persia and the Bible* (Grand Rapids: Baker, 1990), 258–60.

Again, as we saw with Joseph's initial dreams (37:5–11) and soon will see with Pharaoh's dreams (41:1–7), the dreams come in pairs (duplication showing reliability); however, this time each person has their separate dream and here "each dream had a meaning of its own" (v. 5).

Joseph, noticing that they were disturbed, asked them why they looked dejected. They responded by telling him about the dreams, but lamenting the absence of an interpreter. In Egyptian dream interpretation, as in Mesopotamia, a professional interpreter was needed who had access to dream commentaries.[2] The dreamer would inform the interpreter of the content of the dream and then would do research in the commentaries to determine the meaning of the dream. Indeed, this dynamic was also at play in Daniel 2 when Nebuchadnezzar had a dream which disturbed him. He summoned his wise men and told them to tell him the dream and then also the interpretation. They responded with disbelief that he would ask such a thing: "There is no one on earth who can do what the king asks! No king, however great and mighty, has ever asked such a thing of any magician or enchanter or astrologer. What the king asks is too difficult. No one can reveal it to the king except the gods, and they do not live among humans" (Dan 2:10–11).

Nebuchadnezzar is so upset that he orders the death of all the sages in his realm. When Arioch comes to the place where Daniel and the three friends are living, Daniel asks for some time to pray. God responds by telling Daniel the content of the dream as well as its interpretation.

While the chief baker and the chief cupbearer do not withhold knowledge of the content of their dreams, Joseph demonstrates, as he tells them, that "interpretations belong to God" (v. 8). He does not need dream books in order to interpret their dreams.

The cupbearer's dreams centered on a grapevine, appropriate for his position at court. This vine had three branches that produced grapes. In the dream, the cupbearer squeezed the grapes into Pharaoh's cup and served him wine. Joseph informs him that this dream foretold his restoration to Pharaoh's good graces after three days. Joseph also uses this moment as an opportunity to tell the soon-to-be restored Egyptian official to speak to Pharaoh about his incarceration. He tells the cupbearer that he was kidnapped to Egypt and then sent to prison on trumped-up charges.

While the cupbearer's dream portended good, the baker's dream announced a different, dire consequence. He had three baskets of bread on his head, presumably one stacked on another. This bread was meant for Pharaoh, but

2. For an example from around the time of Joseph, see R. K. Ritner, "Dream Oracles," in *COS* 1:52–4.

birds ate it instead. Joseph told the baker that that meant that in three days, he would be executed by being beheaded and impaled. Birds will eat his flesh.

Three days later it was Pharaoh's "birthday" (v. 20). There is no Egyptian evidence for a birthday celebration for Pharaoh until the Persian period, but Hoffmeier intriguingly suggests that this day was "not a celebration of his physical birth, but of his divine birth, at the 'festival of accession,' "[3] for which there is evidence much earlier than the time of Joseph. He also points out that times of coronation and also presumably then on the anniversary of the coronation were known as times when the king would release prisoners.

Whatever the exact occasion, God's interpretation of the dreams as related by Joseph proved true. The narrator says the heads of both the cupbearer and the baker were "lifted up" (v. 20) on that day. For the cupbearer that meant restoration to his position at court; for the baker, it meant beheading and impaling.

Thus, Joseph again demonstrates that he is a divinely authorized dream interpreter. And once again, Joseph is treated poorly as the cupbearer forgets about him and does not tell the Pharaoh about him as Joseph had requested.

### Pharaoh's Dreams and Joseph's Advice (41:1–40)

In the previous episode, Joseph had interpreted the chief cupbearer's dream that foresaw his restoration to court. However, far from demonstrating his gratitude by informing Pharaoh about him and trying to get him out of prison, the cupbearer forgot completely about him. That changed when Pharaoh himself had two disturbing dreams.

The action of the first dream took place by the Nile River, the source of all fertility in in Egypt. At first there were seven well-nourished cows grazing among the reeds by the water. However, seven other cows appeared that were ugly and thin. Amazingly, the thin cows ate the fat cows.

Pharaoh then had a second dream. On two previous occasions (37:5–11; 40:9–19), we have observed that dreams come in duplicate, two witnesses to the same truth. The duplication strengthens the reliability of the message of the dreams.

The second dream centers on grain. At first he sees a stalk with seven healthy heads of grain. Then he observes seven other heads of grain that were thin and scorched by the hot east wind. The latter then swallowed up the former.

Pharaoh does the expected and calls for his magicians and wise men, those trained in dream interpretation (see comments on 40:8). However, they are

3. Hoffmeier, *Israel in Egypt*, 89–91.

stumped. Apparently the dream books did not refer to anything like the dreams that the Pharaoh had that evening.

Due to the difficulty of interpreting Pharaoh's dreams, the cupbearer finally remembered Joseph. He then told the king the story of Joseph interpreting his dream as well as the dream of the now deceased baker.

Thus, the king summoned the prisoner Joseph. After Joseph is shaved and given a change of clothes, he appears before the Pharaoh. He asks Joseph to interpret the dreams, but he immediately confesses that he cannot do it. Rather he gives God the credit, "God will give Pharaoh the answer he desires" (v. 16).

Pharaoh then recounted his dreams to Joseph (vv. 17–24). To the first, he adds that even after the thin, ugly cows ate the fat ones, they remained ugly. He does not add any new substantial information to the content of the second dream.

Joseph is able to interpret the dreams immediately. He recognizes that the message comes from God to Pharaoh in order to inform Pharaoh so that he can do what is necessary. The two dreams have a single message. There will be seven years of plenty followed by seven years of famine. Throughout the Old Testament, seven is a symbolic number of completion or totality. Whether literal or symbolic here, a period of seven years is a long time and would have disastrous consequences if there were not preparation. The dream warning allows for the necessary preparation.

Interestingly, Joseph tells Pharaoh that the dreams came in a pair in order to communicate that the message was both certain and urgent. Thus, Joseph gives Pharaoh advice about how to handle the upcoming crisis.

As a side note, at this point in the story, commentators will often mention The Famine Stele of Sehel Island,[4] which mentions a seven year famine. The text sets the famine in the time of Djoser of the Third Dynasty (ca. twenty-seventh century BC), though the inscription itself comes from the much later Ptolomaic period (third to first centuries BC). In any case, there is no connection between this seven year famine and the famine at the time of Joseph. At best, the comparison is of interest to note that a seven-year famine was not unique to the time of Joseph.[5]

Joseph advises Pharaoh to appoint a "discerning and wise man" to head up the effort to collect surplus food during the seven years of abundant crops. Such a person would have the practical skill necessary to navigate the complexity of the situation. Joseph would not be using the terms discerning (*nabon*) and wise (*hakam*) in the full theological sense found, say, in the book of Proverbs. However, we will see that he will choose Joseph, who indeed

4. *COS* 1:130–34.

5. Walton, "Genesis," 130.

surpasses the practical definition of wisdom to include the ethical ("doing what is right and just and fair," Prov 1:3b) as well as the theological ("the fear of the LORD is the beginning of knowledge," Prov 1:7a).

Indeed, Joseph displays his discernment and wisdom to Pharaoh by providing the blueprint of a plan to deal with the challenge. Pharaoh should appoint his agents ("commissioners") to take a fifth of the harvest during the first seven years and then gather the grain in storehouses that were under the king's authority. This surplus would be used during the years of famine.

Pharaoh then turned to his officials and asked if they could find anyone like Joseph ("this man") who through his interpretation of the dreams and through the proposal of his plan has demonstrated that the "spirit of God" is in him. As the NIV note indicates, there is a question whether Pharaoh says the "spirit of God" or the "spirit of the gods." Either is possible in regard to the term *'elohim*. The latter may be preferred, since there is no question here of Pharaoh believing that there was only one God. The counterargument is that Joseph has made it plain to Pharaoh that the dream interpretation comes from his God.

What is clear is that the question to his officials was rhetorical; Pharaoh had already made up his mind. Joseph was the right person for the job; so he promotes Joseph to a position that is second only to his own.

## Joseph Prepares for the Famine (41:41–57)

Pharaoh makes his decision concerning Joseph public by means of an investiture ceremony where after announcing his high position, he gives Joseph his signet ring, a gold chain for his neck, and linen robes. In terms of the robe, we have earlier noted that garments have gotten Joseph into trouble before this time (the ornate robe his father gave him and the garment taken by Potiphar's wife). As Provan puts it, "at last, Joseph once again possesses the clothing of nobility."[6] In addition, Pharaoh also let him ride through the city in his own royal chariot, while heralds shouted "Make way!"

Hoffmeier notes the Egyptian evidence that speaks to the authenticity of this account of Joseph's public advancement. He points out that the Pharaohs of Egypt had a propensity to include such scenes in the paintings found in their tombs. There are both investiture ceremonies as well as reward ceremonies. Hoffmeier suggests that Joseph's ceremony might include both, reward for the dream interpretation and investiture for his new position as second in command. Of particular interest is the tomb painting which relates to a ceremony for Huy, Viceroy of Cush, during the reign of Tutankamun

6. Provan, *Seriously Dangerous Religion*, 259.

(ca. 1361–1352 BC). According to Hoffmeier, citing a study by Kitchen, "the painting shows Huy receiving a rolled up linen object along with a gold signet ring. Here we recall Joseph's gift of linen (Gen 41:42)."[7] He also notes that the word used here for linen (*shesh*) is of Egyptian derivation and was probably reserved for Egyptian linen.

Hoffmeier also comments on the reliability of the idea that a Semite would assume such a high office in Egypt.[8] We have no Egyptian record of Joseph's role, though that is not surprising since we don't have anything like a full record of even important officials at this time. Even so, some hesitate to take this story as historically reliable because, as we already commented, Asiatics were deeply resented in Egypt. That said, Hoffmeier points out that we do have record of Semites assuming high office in Egypt. Specifically he notes a high official who was Syrian-born named Bay who became important after the death of Seti II in 1194 BC as well as a man who was called vizier (the second highest office in Egypt) who had the Semitic name Aper-el dated to the Amarna period (fourteenth century BC).

Pharaoh goes even further and grants Joseph incredible authority. Though surely hyperbolic, the idea that Egyptians could not do anything (even something so minimal as to move hand or foot) shows the level of trust and power that Joseph could now wield throughout the land of Egypt. He has come a long way, from hated brother, to Egyptian slave, to prisoner, now to second in command in Egypt.

Pharaoh also gave Joseph an Egyptian name Zaphaenath-Paneah as well as a wife, Asenath, daughter of the priest of On, another name for the important city of Heliopolis (seven miles northeast of Cairo), named Potiphera. The precise meaning of these names is not certain and has been much discussed, but, according to Hoffmeier, they are undeniably Egyptian and appropriate for this period of Egyptian history.[9]

While the name and the marriage were certainly honors from an Egyptian perspective, they do raise a question of the appropriateness of Joseph's assimilation into the culture.[10] Later in the narrative, we will see that Joseph likely adopts Egyptian dress and even possesses a diviner's cup (44:5). Of course, marriage to an Egyptian princess leads Solomon astray and in other places the Old Testament treats marriage with foreign women as suspect, and this woman is a daughter of an Egyptian priest (see "In the World, But Not of It" in the Live the Story section after Gen 42).

---

7. Hoffmeier, *Israel in Egypt*, 92.
8. Ibid., 93–95.
9. Ibid., 84–88.
10. As noted by Provan, *Seriously Dangerous Religion*, 268.

While the question is naturally raised, the biblical portrait of Joseph never raises any questions about his fidelity to the true God who is the source of all his success. We might compare Joseph's acceptance of these gifts to Daniel and his three friends whose names are also changed and who not only allow themselves to be educated according to the toxic curriculum of Babylon which would include divination, but they graduate at the top of their class.[11]

Joseph was only thirty years old when he assumed this high office in Egypt. After his investiture, he takes steps to make certain that Egypt would have the necessary resources during the forthcoming seven years of famine. During the seven years of plenty, he traveled throughout Egypt making sure that the surplus grain was stored in the local areas where it was grown (v. 48). The years of plenty were plenteous indeed. The narrator describes the grain as numerous as the "sand of the sea" (v. 49). Indeed, there was so much grain that it was impossible to keep an official record of it.

Before moving on to the years of famine, the narrator comments on the two sons who were born to Joseph and his Egyptian wife. These sons will be very important for the future history of Israel (see Gen 48), being the father figure of two important tribes of Israel that will bear their name. As with the names of the sons of Jacob, these two also have names which bear significance. The first is Manasseh, a name connected by sound or etymology with the Hebrew verb "to forget" (see NIV footnote). Joseph explains that name: "It is because God has made me forget all my trouble and all my father's household" (v. 51). Joseph has indeed suffered first at the hands of his brothers, then at the hand of Potiphar's wife, and even due to the forgetfulness of the chief cupbearer. But now Joseph recognizes God's hand in bringing him to a better place. The name of the second son, Ephraim, gets at the same idea though from a more positive perspective. The name means "twice fruitful" (see NIV note), and Joseph explains the significance of this name when he says, "It is because God has made me fruitful in the land of my suffering" (v. 52). Joseph thus bears witness that joy can be had in the midst of suffering, a theme that will continue into the future.

As God had foretold and Joseph had announced, the seven years of plenty gave way to seven years of famine. The famine was severe and widespread, affecting not only Egypt but the surrounding lands. Thanks to Joseph, though, there was grain available in Egypt (showing that a descendant of Abraham would bring blessing on the nations [12:3]). This grain was under the ultimate control of Pharaoh who put Joseph in charge of distributing it. However, the grain was not distributed for free, but was sold to the Egyptians

11. T. Longman III, *Daniel*, NIVAC (Grand Rapids: Zondervan, 1999), 41–69.

as well as to foreigners who came to Egypt to get the only food that was available. This situation will now bring Joseph's family back into the action of the story.

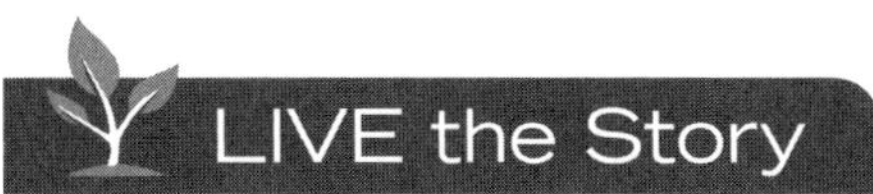


### "You Meant It for Evil . . . ," Part 3: The Cupbearer Forgets Joseph

As we will explain more fully in an essay that follows the commentary on Genesis 50 (see "You Meant It for Evil . . . ," Part 4 in the Live the Story section after Gen 50:15–21), the major theme of the Joseph narrative, articulated by Joseph himself in 50:19–20, is that God can bring salvation even using evil acts of those who want to harm God's people. Genesis 40–41 clearly illustrate this theme as the chief cupbearer forgets Joseph's appeal to remember him when he is restored to Pharaoh's favor. However, God's timing is perfect as he finally remembers his promise to Joseph when Pharaoh himself has a dream.

### Joseph and Jesus: From Humiliation to Exaltation

In this scene from the Joseph narrative, Joseph is brought out of prison and made the second most powerful person in Egypt. In this many see an anticipation of the humiliation and exaltation of Jesus. Greidanus puts it well when he says, "in New Testament times, God liberated Jesus from his imprisonment in the tomb and exalted him through his resurrection and ascension to be the King of kings in order to save the world."[12]

He goes on to cite John 3:16: "God so loved the world that he gave his one and only Son, that whoever believes in him shall not perish but have eternal life." Also relevant is Philippians 2:6–11:

> Who, being in very nature God,
> did not consider equality with God something to be used to his own advantage;
> rather, he made himself nothing
> by taking the very nature of a servant,
> being made in human likeness.
> And being found in appearance as a man,
> he humbled himself
> by becoming obedient to death—
> even death on a cross!
> Therefore God exalted him to the highest place
> and gave him the name that is above every name,

12. Greidanus, *Preaching Christ from Genesis*, 399.

> that at the name of Jesus every knee should bow,
> in heaven and on earth and under the earth,
> and every tongue acknowledge that Jesus Christ is Lord,
> to the glory of God the Father.

Greidanus continues his meditation on the redemptive-historical relationship between Joseph and Jesus:

> As Joseph was exalted to the right hand of Pharaoh to rule as king of Egypt, so Jesus was exalted to the right hand of God the Father to rule the nations as the "King of kings and Lord of lords" (1 Tim 6:15; Rev 17:14; 19:16). As all were commanded to bow before Joseph (v 43), so "at the name of Jesus every knee should bow in heaven and on earth and under the earth" (Phil 2:10). And as Joseph, with bread, saved many people from death, so Jesus, the bread of life, saves many people from eternal death. Jesus proclaims, "Whoever eats of this bread will live forever" (John 6:51).[13]

## Does God Communicate to Us through Our Dreams?

The book of Genesis makes it clear that God spoke to people in their dreams. What is particularly interesting is that he communicated through dreams not only with his people but also with others.

For instance, God warned Abimelek, the Philistine king, not to sleep with Sarah because she was married to Abraham (20:6–7). He also warned Laban not to harm Jacob as the latter fled back to the Promised Land (31:24). In the Joseph narrative, we hear of God sending the Egyptian cupbearer and baker (ch. 40) as well as Pharaoh (41:1–40) dreams that portended the future. But significant dreams were not restricted to the nonelect in Genesis; God communicated with both Jacob and Joseph through dreams.

Jacob had a dream where he saw angels ascending and descending from a stairway to heaven (28:10–15). He named the place Bethel, the "house of God." Later he claims that God gave him the strategy for enlarging his flocks at Laban's expense through a dream (31:10–13). While Joseph more typically plays the role of dream interpreter, his story begins with his report and interpretation of two dreams that God sent to him (37:5–11).

Of course, dream reports are not only found in the book of Genesis. Gideon overheard the report of a dream by someone from the enemy camp and took it as a sign from God that he would have victory (Judg 7:13–14). It was in a dream that God said to Solomon, "Ask for whatever you want me to give you" (1 Kgs 3:5). In response, Solomon asked for wisdom, and God gave him wisdom as well as wealth and honor.

---

13. Ibid., 409.

However, it is the book of Daniel in which dreams play a major role. Indeed, as has often been pointed out, the role of dreams in both the Joseph as well as the Daniel narratives is one of a number of parallels between these two wise men who play a significant role in the court of a foreign ruler.

The first half of the book of Daniel (chs. 1–6) contains stories of Daniel in the court of the Babylonian kings Nebuchadnezzar and Belshazzar as well as the Persian Darius. Two of the stories describe dreams of Nebuchadnezzar that Daniel interprets for him (chs. 2 and 4).

The first is the most telling for the nature of biblical versus ancient Near Eastern dream interpretation. Nebuchadnezzar has a troubling dream and he instructs "the magicians, enchanters, sorcerers and astrologers to tell him what he had dreamed" (Dan 2:2). However, based on what we know about Mesopotamian (and Egyptian) dream interpretation, Nebuchadnezzar's demand is quite outrageous.

In the ancient Near East, a dreamer would report a dream to a professional dream interpreter and then the dream interpreter would consult dream commentaries to figure out the meaning of a dream. As the Babylonian wise men insisted, "There is no one on earth who can do what the king asks! No king, however great and mighty, has ever asked such a thing of any magician or enchanter or astrologer. What the king asks is too difficult. No one can reveal it to the king except the gods, and they do not live among humans" (Dan 2:10–11).

Of course, the Babylonian wisdom teachers fail, but Daniel is able to tell the king his dream as well as interpret it, but not because of his own insight or ability, but because of God. As he puts it, "No wise man, enchanter, magician or diviner can explain to the king the mystery he has asked about, but there is a God in heaven who reveals mysteries" (Dan 2:27–28a). Joseph makes the same point when he responds to the Pharaoh's request that he interpret his dream by saying, "I cannot do it, but God will give Pharaoh the answer he desires" (41:16).

Daniel also interprets Nebuchadnezzar's dream in Daniel 4. Interestingly, Daniel himself has a dream in chapter 7, but he is unable to interpret it. An angel comes and interprets it for him.

Thus, though there are not many examples, it is clear that God does communicate through dreams to both his people and foreigners during the Old Testament time period. In Numbers 12:6 God tells Aaron and Miriam that "When there is a prophet among you, I, the Lord, reveal myself to them in visions, I speak to them in dreams." Of course, this mode of revelation is in contrast to the superior method of speaking to Moses "face to face" (12:8).

God clearly used dreams as one way of speaking to his human creatures. However, there is a risk involved. After all, not all dreams are revelatory. They might be a delusion. The prophet Jeremiah blasts the false prophets, who say "I had a dream! I had a dream!" Then he goes on to say, "How long will this continue in the hearts of these lying prophets, who prophesy the delusions of their own minds?" (Jer 23:25–26; see also 27:9; 29:8; Zech 10:2).

Indeed, one of the two laws of the prophet (see Deut 13:1–5 and 18: 14–21) warns of false prophets who will speak of a dream but then lead people away from God. In other words, dreams can lead deceive and lead people astray. When we turn to the New Testament, we note that dreams play a very minor role, particularly after the death and resurrection of Christ.

They do play a significant role in Matthew's narrative of Jesus' birth. An angel appears to Joseph in a dream to tell him to marry Mary even though she is pregnant. He announces to Joseph that "she will give birth to a son, and you are to give him the name Jesus" (1:21). Joseph and Mary are warned by an angel not to return to their country by a familiar route and to seek refuge from Herod's murderous intent by going to Egypt (2:12; see also v. 22). The Gospel of Matthew also speaks about a disturbing dream of Pilate's wife concerning the arrest of Jesus, an innocent man (Matt 27:19).

In summary, one cannot read the Bible and deny the fact that God on occasion used dreams to communicate with his human creatures. Though not frequent, he spoke to Abimelek, Jacob, Laban, Joseph, an unnamed Midianite, Solomon, Daniel, Jesus' father Joseph, and Pilate's wife through dreams.

Does God continue to speak to us today through dreams? One might respond that God no longer speaks to people through dreams now that Jesus has died and been raised by the Father. We have the Scriptures which are God's clear revelation to us.

However, we should be extremely cautious and avoid saying that God never speaks to people today through dreams. After all, listen to what Peter says concerning the "last days," by which we can understand the period of time after the resurrection of Christ. He sees in the events surrounding Pentecost the fulfillment of the prophecy of Joel 2:

> In the last days, God says,
> I will pour out my Spirit on all people.
> Your sons and daughters will prophesy,
> your young men will see visions,
> your old men will dream dreams. (Acts 2:17, quoting Joel 2:28)

While we must not deny that God uses dreams to speak to people today, we must also be very careful in ascribing divine meaning to our dreams. After all, though dreams can communicate God's message to us, it can also be simply an expression of our subconscious or our own wish fulfillment. The Bible would call this delusion.

Here is a principle that is inviolable. Though God can speak to us through dreams, he speaks most clearly to us through Scripture, which is the Word of God. Any message we get through a dream or through any other mode of revelation will never contradict or work against the Word of God as presented in Scripture.

As I reached the Joseph narrative in writing my commentary, I knew that I had to think through the question of whether or not God speaks to people through dreams today. I had already concluded, as I stated above, that there was no good reason to deny that God could speak to people in dreams today, provided it led them toward God and did not contradict God's revelation in Scripture.

But this was a conclusion in principle only and not my own personal experience. I have never had a dream in which I was convinced that God was trying to speak to me. That, of course, did not mean that God did not speak to other people through dreams. It may also be, I confess, that I was not open to God speaking to me in such a way and thus was not attuned to hearing God in such a way. But I had recently heard an interview on Christian radio where a Muslim convert talked about the not infrequent phenomenon of God reaching Muslims through their dreams, and so I decided to pursue the matter by reading a book by Nabeel Qureshi.[14]

Qureshi recounts how God spoke to him through three dreams in order to bring him eventually to Christ. These dreams were vivid to him, and he certainly questioned the direction that they were leading him since they were highly symbolic. He questioned whether the dreams were some kind of wish fulfillment, but in his own mind, he was not certain whether he was interested in Christianity. From his Muslim perspective, he even played with the idea that Shaitan was sending the dreams to tempt him to leave Islam.

What was most fascinating was that a Christian friend specifically drew his attention to Joseph (both the Old Testament Joseph as well as the father of Jesus) as recipients of prayers with messages from God. Eventually, especially after receiving the third dream (serving as a confirmation just like the second of the two that Joseph received), he became convinced and thus began his journey out of the mosque, as he puts it, and to Christ.

Qureshi's experience is not isolated among Muslims. What are we to make of this? In the final analysis, these dreams are driving people to a relationship

14. N. Qureshi, *Seeking Allah, Finding Jesus: A Devout Muslim Encounters Christianity* (Grand Rapids: Zondervan, 2014).

with Jesus and thus do not violate the principle that we stated above. While we cannot be certain, we should not deny that God is indeed using this means to reach Muslims to turn them to Christ today. And if Muslims, why not others?

### The Wisdom of Planning for the Future

Earlier (see To Depend on God or to Take Action in the Live the Story section after Gen 32:1–21), we admired how Jacob both took action in terms of planning and also prayed for God's help as he encountered his brother Esau for the first time after returning to the promised land. We observed how the patriarch modeled the wisdom offered by the book of Proverbs to plan but then to commit those plans to the will of God (Prov 16:1–3). In this, he also reflects the teaching found in the book of James that planning without consideration for the will of God is fruitless:

> Now listen, you who say, "Today or tomorrow we will go to this or that city, spend a year there, carry on business and make money." Why, you do not even know what will happen tomorrow. What is your life? You are a mist that appears for a little while and then vanishes. Instead, you ought to say, "If it is the Lord's will, we will live and do this or that." As it is, you boast in your arrogant schemes. All such boasting is evil. If anyone, then, knows the good they ought to do and doesn't do it, it is sin for them. (4:13–17)

Jesus delivers the same message in his parable of the rich man who, like Joseph, stores grain for the future, but unlike Joseph does not take into account the fact that God may well change his plans. The parable ends with the statement: "This is how it will be with whoever stores up things for themselves but is not rich toward God" (Luke 12:21). On the contrary, Joseph is an example of a person who stores things up and is rich toward God.

In Genesis 40–41 we discover that Joseph is an assiduous planner. Knowing that severe famine will bring a horrendous humanitarian crisis, he begins planning for it immediately. In this he demonstrates his wisdom. He knows that his goal is to provide food for people when the famine hits and he devises an effective strategy to meet that goal. Later he will develop a secondary goal, buying all the land of Egypt for Pharaoh (47:13–26), and he again devises a plan to accomplish his purpose on behalf of the king. As Proverbs 21:5a states, "The plans of the determined end up in profit."[15]

But, as we observed above, not all planning is wise planning. Proverbs also talks about foolish planning. Foolish planning is fraudulent (Prov 12:5b, 20a)

---

15. Translations from Proverbs come from Longman, *Proverbs*.

and will not succeed (14:22). Foolish planning also is presumptuous if it does not, as the sage points out in Proverbs 16:1–3, referred to above, commit the plans to the Lord. Jacob acknowledged that by praying along with planning, but what about Joseph? We don't see Joseph planning and then committing his plans to the Lord. Why not? Is this an example of foolish planning?

A close reading of the story affirms that Joseph is yet another example of wise, godly planning. After all, his plans flow from his dreams that he rightly understands come from God himself. God has told him that seven years of famine will follow seven years of plenty. God has definitively shown him what the future is going to bring, and so he plans accordingly.

Once again modern readers are presented with a model of wise planning. Yes, plan and plan carefully, but realize that God is in control and your plans may need to change. We should not grow frustrated or feel we waste our time by planning, but rather feel comfort knowing that our lives and the lives are others are guided by the merciful and compassionate hand of God.

CHAPTER 43

# Genesis 42

## LISTEN to the Story

42:1When Jacob learned that there was grain in Egypt, he said to his
sons, "Why do you just keep looking at each other?" 2He continued, "I
have heard that there is grain in Egypt. Go down there and buy some for
us, so that we may live and not die."

3Then ten of Joseph's brothers went down to buy grain from Egypt.
4But Jacob did not send Benjamin, Joseph's brother, with the others,
because he was afraid that harm might come to him. 5So Israel's sons were
among those who went to buy grain, for there was famine in the land of
Canaan also.

6Now Joseph was the governor of the land, the person who sold grain
to all its people. So when Joseph's brothers arrived, they bowed down to
him with their faces to the ground. 7As soon as Joseph saw his brothers,
he recognized them, but he pretended to be a stranger and spoke harshly
to them. "Where do you come from?" he asked.

"From the land of Canaan," they replied, "to buy food."

8Although Joseph recognized his brothers, they did not recognize him.
9Then he remembered his dreams about them and said to them, "You are
spies! You have come to see where our land is unprotected."

10"No, my lord," they answered. "Your servants have come to buy
food. 11We are all the sons of one man. Your servants are honest men,
not spies."

12"No!" he said to them. "You have come to see where our land is
unprotected."

13But they replied, "Your servants were twelve brothers, the sons of
one man, who lives in the land of Canaan. The youngest is now with our
father, and one is no more."

14Joseph said to them, "It is just as I told you: You are spies! 15And this
is how you will be tested: As surely as Pharaoh lives, you will not leave
this place unless your youngest brother comes here. 16Send one of your
number to get your brother; the rest of you will be kept in prison, so that
your words may be tested to see if you are telling the truth. If you are not,

then as surely as Pharaoh lives, you are spies!" 17And he put them all in custody for three days.

18On the third day, Joseph said to them, "Do this and you will live, for I fear God: 19If you are honest men, let one of your brothers stay here in prison, while the rest of you go and take grain back for your starving households. 20But you must bring your youngest brother to me, so that your words may be verified and that you may not die." This they proceeded to do.

21They said to one another, "Surely we are being punished because of our brother. We saw how distressed he was when he pleaded with us for his life, but we would not listen; that's why this distress has come on us."

22Reuben replied, "Didn't I tell you not to sin against the boy? But you wouldn't listen! Now we must give an accounting for his blood." 23They did not realize that Joseph could understand them, since he was using an interpreter.

24He turned away from them and began to weep, but then came back and spoke to them again. He had Simeon taken from them and bound before their eyes.

25Joseph gave orders to fill their bags with grain, to put each man's silver back in his sack, and to give them provisions for their journey. After this was done for them, 26they loaded their grain on their donkeys and left.

27At the place where they stopped for the night one of them opened his sack to get feed for his donkey, and he saw his silver in the mouth of his sack. 28"My silver has been returned," he said to his brothers. "Here it is in my sack."

Their hearts sank and they turned to each other trembling and said, "What is this that God has done to us?"

29When they came to their father Jacob in the land of Canaan, they told him all that had happened to them. They said, 30"The man who is lord over the land spoke harshly to us and treated us as though we were spying on the land. 31But we said to him, 'We are honest men; we are not spies. 32We were twelve brothers, sons of one father. One is no more, and the youngest is now with our father in Canaan.'

33"Then the man who is lord over the land said to us, 'This is how I will know whether you are honest men: Leave one of your brothers here with me, and take food for your starving households and go. 34But bring your youngest brother to me so I will know that you are not spies but honest men. Then I will give your brother back to you, and you can trade in the land.' "

[35]As they were emptying their sacks, there in each man's sack was his pouch of silver! When they and their father saw the money pouches, they were frightened. [36]Their father Jacob said to them, "You have deprived me of my children. Joseph is no more and Simeon is no more, and now you want to take Benjamin. Everything is against me!"

[37]Then Reuben said to his father, "You may put both of my sons to death if I do not bring him back to you. Entrust him to my care, and I will bring him back."

[38]But Jacob said, "My son will not go down there with you; his brother is dead and he is the only one left. If harm comes to him on the journey you are taking, you will bring my gray head down to the grave in sorrow."

*Listening to the Text in the Story:* Biblical Texts: Genesis 37; 39–41

In Genesis 37 we learn about the dysfunction of Jacob's family and in particular the alienation between Joseph and his brothers. When they had the opportunity, the brothers sold Joseph into slavery, and he came to Egypt where he worked for a high level Egyptian official named Potiphar (ch. 39). After Potiphar's wife framed him for rape, Joseph was thrown into jail where he met two fellow inmates who were themselves in jail after falling out of favor with Pharaoh. He successfully interpreted their dreams and when the one surviving official came back to court, he eventually informed the Pharaoh who had just had two dreams that portended the future of Joseph's ability to interpret dreams. Joseph, giving glory to God, told the king that his dreams indicated seven years of plenty followed by seven years of famine. The king in turn placed Joseph in a position of authority to prepare for the coming disaster. As the scene turns back to Canaan and Jacob's family, we see that they are in desperate need of help due to the lack of grain in their own land.

## EXPLAIN the Story

### Joseph's Brothers' First Trip to Egypt (42:1–26)

The scene shifts from Egypt and Joseph to Canaan and Jacob's household. Jacob hears there is grain in Egypt so he orders his sons to make the trip to Egypt in order to buy grain. Jacob's words do not show much respect or affection for his children. He berates them for not taking initiative or action, "Why do you just keep looking at each other?" (v. 1).

Thus, ten of Joseph's brothers head to Egypt along with others from Canaan in order to buy grain. We learn that Jacob is still showing favorites since he does not send Benjamin, the second son born to his beloved wife Rachel. He is afraid to lose him as he lost Joseph. Apparently, he could care less about the other ten.

As we have seen in the previous chapter, Joseph was in charge of the distribution and sale of the grain. Thus, upon arrival in Egypt, the ten brothers go to Joseph in order to get grain. They did not recognize Joseph. After all, a period of time has passed and Joseph had likely adopted Egyptian dress. In addition, the brothers would not have thought that it was their brother whom they had sold into slavery who was now such a powerful figure in Egypt. On the other hand, Joseph recognized his brothers.

Of course, after the treatment he had received at their hands, Joseph was not about to reveal his identity to them. Indeed, he embarks on a strategy that will test their character. He wants to know if they are the same self-seeking, envious brothers who sold him into slavery or whether they are now capable of putting others, including their father, before themselves.

On one level, the reader, particularly the modern reader, can feel sympathy for the ten brothers. They are ill treated by their father, and they were envious of their brother whose dreams portended his superiority over them. That said, at this stage of the story of God's people, God has made it clear that it is Joseph who will have ascendancy over his brothers. Joseph has needed to learn that his position is for service, and the brothers need to know that Joseph is the one chosen for this moment, not them. This does not make them, in the terminology of Kaminsky, antielect, but rather nonelect.[1] God does love them and cares for them and has a purpose for their lives and for the lives of their descendants, but they need to learn how to submit themselves before God's chosen, Joseph.

Joseph's strategy begins by his harsh questioning of them. After they bow to him (reminding Joseph [v. 9] and the reader of Joseph's earlier dreams [37:5–11]), he asks them where they came from. They tell him the truth that they came from Canaan and also their purpose, which was to buy grain.

Joseph knows that this is true, but he accuses them of being spies, a serious accusation. In spite of their protests, Joseph keeps pressing the case that they had come to see where the land was unprotected and they could attack the land. We have already commented on the Egyptian disdain and fear of the Asiatics to their north and east. Such a charge would not be out of the question during a period of Egyptian weakness.

---

1. Kaminsky, *Yet I Loved Jacob.*

The accusation leads the brothers to tell more specifics about their family background. They inform Joseph that they are the sons of one man, of course Jacob, and ten of twelve brothers, one was left home (Benjamin) and one is "no more" (Joseph). Of course, they did not know whether Joseph was still alive or not, but the public story was that he was killed by a wild animal, so they present Joseph as dead.

Now that they have revealed that there was a brother still at home, Joseph had the means to test them. At first, he tells them that only one of them can return to Canaan. That one needed to bring back Benjamin in order to prove their story. The other nine he will keep in prison. He then incarcerates all ten to give them time to think about their situation.

However, when he retrieves them from prison after three days, he presents a more generous plan. Only one will stay in Egypt, while the other nine can return to Canaan, with grain, in order to get Benjamin and bring him to Joseph.

They agree to this condition, but before they leave his presence, they make a startling confession, not knowing that Joseph could understand them speaking in their native language. They see their present predicament as payment for their abusive treatment of Joseph. They remember how he cried for mercy when they threw him in the pit. Reuben, the oldest, protests that he tried to dissuade them from their course, but if we remember back to the story (39), we have no indication that he tried to talk them out of the plot. Rather his plan to come back and secretly pull him out of the pit backfired on him when Judah convinced the brothers to sell him to the traders who took him down to Egypt.

So the brothers believe that they are in trouble because of their earlier treatment of Joseph. And indeed, they are correct. Little do they know it, but the one that they had treated so badly is pulling the strings and purposefully creating the situation that they now bemoan. That is, they are indeed, "being punished because of our brother" (v. 21).

Though he does so intentionally, he does not do it with cold calculation. Unbeknownst to his brothers, Joseph understands what they are saying and he weeps. We are not told exactly what motivates the tears, but it is likely that he is remembering his treatment at their hands and perhaps also he sees the beginnings of their remorse. Certainly it shows his longing for his family. Even so, Joseph is not ready to trust them, so he carries through on his strategy by keeping Simeon in Egypt while the other brothers return to Canaan.

Joseph gives them grain to take back to Canaan and provisions for the journey. Even more surprisingly, he places their payment of silver back in their sacks.

**Return to Jacob (42:27–38)**

At the end of the previous section, we learned that Joseph had not only given grain and provisions to his brothers, but he had also returned their payment of silver without their knowledge, placing it in the sacks of grain. Thus, that evening when they stopped to rest, one of the brothers opened his sack of grain and discovered the silver. Rather than rejoicing, this discovery distressed them greatly. They did not know how the silver got in his sacks. Not knowing that the Egyptian governor was their brother Joseph, they feared how much trouble they could get into. What would keep the suspicious Egyptian from thinking they had stolen the silver?

They blame God. After all, who else could have put the silver in their sacks? The guilt that they felt and expressed before Joseph (vv. 21–23) made them think that God was out to punish them.

Upon their return, they reported the turn of events to their father. Little did they or their father realize that the one whom they refer to as "the man who is lord over the land" is none other than Joseph. They narrate the trip pretty much as it happened, pointing out their harsh treatment and the accusation that they were spies. They tell their father how they asserted their innocence, saying that they were honest and not spies. They were just representing their family, which had twelve brothers, but one was back home and one was no more.

They then tell their father that the "Egyptian" lord wanted to test their honesty by having them bring the son at home with them on their return to Egypt. He would hold one brother as hostage. It is at this point that they unload and inspect all their sacks of grain. Lo and behold, they discover that all of them have their silver. This realization panics brothers and father alike. Jacob blames them for the loss of Joseph and now Simeon and the potential loss of Benjamin.

Reuben, the eldest, offers his own two sons as hostages for Benjamin, saying that Jacob could have them killed if he does not bring Benjamin safely back from Egypt. We have earlier seen how Reuben failed to rescue Joseph (37:29–30), and here he fails to convince his father. In the first place, we might question just how Jacob might take Reuben's offer. In effect he is telling Jacob that if he does not return with Benjamin, then he can kill two of his own grandchildren. What kind of deal is that? Even allowing for the possibility he did not like his grandchildren, Jacob would not be interested in lessening his progeny.

Jacob quickly refuses. Not only is Reuben's plan deeply flawed, there are already good reasons why Jacob would not trust him. After all, his eldest son has slept with his concubines (35:22). In addition, as the eldest, he would have been the most responsible for Joseph when he was lost.

Furthermore, Benjamin occupies a special place among the remaining brothers. How it must have cut the other brothers to the heart to hear Jacob says, "My son will not go down there with you; his brother is dead and he is the only one left" (v. 38). He is so fearful of losing Benjamin, the remaining son of the beloved Rachel, that he is willing to sacrifice Simeon, a son who had also compromised himself in his father's eyes (Gen 34).

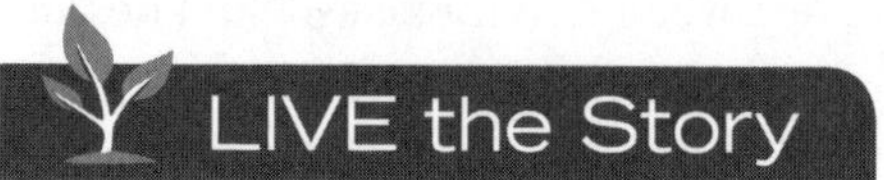


**"In the World, But Not Of It"**

Joseph's brothers don't recognize him when they arrive from Canaan, either on the first or the second journey to get grain. Why not? Well, it has been a number of years to be sure, but more to the point, Joseph has had a fairly significant cultural transformation.

Upon his promotion to high position, Pharaoh "dressed him in fine linen" (41:41) which surely denotes a distinctive Egyptian dress. The brothers did not even recognize him as a fellow Semite. To them he was an Egyptian official, which likely implies that he not only had Egyptian clothes, but also hairstyle. He was married to "Asenath daughter of Potiphera, priest of On" (41:45). He spoke to his brothers in Egyptian, though he understood the Semitic dialect of his childhood (42:23). In the next chapter, we will see he even has a cup for divination (44:2–5).

Joseph's behavior raises the question how far can a person of faith embrace a culture that is toxic to that faith? This question comes to the fore especially when combined with the very similar story of Daniel in the Babylonian court.[2]

Daniel and his three friends were brought to the Babylonian court where they were trained to serve in the court of Nebuchadnezzar (Dan 1). In the process their Hebrew names that praised the true God were changed to Babylonian names that praised false gods. They were also taught "the language and literature of the Babylonians" (1:4), which would have included the study of myths that extolled gods like Marduk as well as a heavy dose of divination literature, including dream commentaries to help them interpret dreams. They not only subject themselves to this training that was hostile to their faith, they graduated at the top of their class. Do these Old Testament stories teach us anything today about living in a culture that is toxic to our faith?

First, we need to recognize that indeed our culture is toxic to our faith and that statement is true no matter what your culture in the modern world.

2. I talk at length about the implications for the Daniel story for the question of cultural engagement in *Daniel*, 62–69.

While it is clearly true that at the beginning of the twenty-first century it is much more dangerous to be a Christian in parts of the Middle East than in the West, which allows for the freedom of religion, there are other types of issues that confront the believer. What should our attitude be toward the culture in which we find ourselves?

The Joseph and Daniel stories raise the question, but certainly do not provide a clear blueprint that allows us to answer all our pressing questions. What they do tell us is that a simple rejection of or withdrawal from the culture is not the answer. We might say that Daniel and his friends and Joseph had no choice in the matter. They could either conform or die. But that is to say that they had a choice, and indeed from the Daniel story we know that when they were confronted with that choice, they were willing to die for their faith rather than to fully embrace the idolatrous culture in which they found themselves (Dan 3 and 5). As far as we know from Genesis, Joseph never found himself in a position where he had to make a choice between his faith and his life, but since the narrator never implicitly or explicitly criticizes his integration into Egyptian culture as well as his actions and attitudes (see especially 50:19–20), we have to assume that he too maintained his faith.

We can also confidently say that the Joseph and Daniel narratives also indicate that the person of faith does not fully embrace the culture in which they find themselves. Granted this is clearer in Daniel narrative, where he and the three friends refuse to worship the gods of Babylon at the risk of their lives and may also be seen in their refusal to eat the food provided by the king.[3]

So there is no simple answer to the question of how we as people of faith live in a world that is hostile to that faith. The implicit lesson of Joseph and Daniel is illustrative of the teaching of Jesus that we are to be in the world, but not of it (see John 17:16) as well as to be as "shrewd as snakes and as innocent as doves" (Matt 10:16). By adopting Egyptian dress and customs and even an Egyptian wife (we do not know the status of her religious commitments after her marriage to Joseph), he is "in the world" by his maintaining his faith, but he is "not of it." He certainly shows himself to be as shrewd as a snake in his dealings with his brothers as well as with Egyptians like the chief cupbearer and baker. But he maintains his innocence as well.

The message to the modern Christian reader is that living in the world consistent with our faith commitments is no easy task. To live in, but not of the world is not as easy as applying a formula to a problem, but we are called to prayerfully ask whether our decisions and actions betray our commitment to Jesus.

3. Though this refusal may be more a matter of letting God have room to work than a refusal to participate in pagan religious rites (for which, see Longman, *Daniel*, 51–54.

### Testing Others

Earlier (in the Live the Story section after Gen 22:1–19), we addressed the questions Does God Test Us? and Can We Test God? The Joseph narrative raises the question, can we test other people? After all, when his brothers come to Egypt seeking grain, he works hard to create a situation to test whether his brothers have changed since the moment when they sold him into slavery.

But, really, is it ever permissible today to test other people? After all, we are talking about an ancient people, and Old Testament narrative does not always provide models for our behavior today (see Introduction: Reading from the Perspective of the Twenty-First Century). We cannot simply assume that Joseph's actions, even when affirmed as wise by the narrator, is permissible for today.

However, in response to that attitude, we can see that there are also New Testament passages that talk about testing others.[4] Particularly interesting passages include Paul's statement that by urging the Corinthians to give generously to support the Jerusalem church that he was not "commanding you, but I want to test the sincerity of your love by comparing it with the earnestness of others" (2 Cor 8:8), referring specifically to the generosity of the Macedonians. Special cases include the testing of those who might be made deacons. Here Paul advises Timothy that "they must first be tested; and then if there is nothing against them, let them serve as deacons" (1 Tim 3:10). In the book of Revelation the angel of the church in Ephesus commends it for knowing that they "cannot tolerate wicked people" and "have tested those who claim to be apostles but are not, and have found them false" (Rev 2:2). In this the church is following the admonition of John who called on his readers to "not believe every spirit, but test the spirits to see whether they are from God, because many false prophets have gone out into the world" (1 John 4:1). He goes on to say that "every spirit that acknowledges that Jesus Christ has come in the flesh is from God, but every spirit that does not acknowledge Jesus is not from God" (4:2–3).

Indeed, Joseph's testing his brothers is the height of wisdom. After all, they had abused him and even came close to killing him. Certainly, it would have been folly to "forgive and forget," as some people wrongly suggest is the Bible's teaching. Such an attitude is not only unbiblical but is downright dangerous when it comes to situations of abuse.[5]

---

4. In this essay we are exploring the testing of others, there are also passages that speak of the need to test ourselves (2 Cor 13:5; Gal 6:4).

5. As explained in D. Allender and T. Longman III, *Bold Love: The Courageous Practice of Life's Ultimate Influence* (Colorado Springs, CO: NavPress, 1992).

To affirm Joseph's actions here and recognize that testing others is a wise course of action in certain situations is certainly not open permission for suspicion and snooping around people's lives. The cases of testing other people in the Bible are only connected with situations where there are solid reasons for doubt about a persons character or if a person is seeking positions of influence over the community.

CHAPTER 44

# Genesis 43 – 44

## LISTEN to the Story

[43:1]Now the famine was still severe in the land. [2]So when they had eaten all the grain they had brought from Egypt, their father said to them, "Go back and buy us a little more food."

[3]But Judah said to him, "The man warned us solemnly, 'You will not see my face again unless your brother is with you.' [4]If you will send our brother along with us, we will go down and buy food for you. [5]But if you will not send him, we will not go down, because the man said to us, 'You will not see my face again unless your brother is with you.' "

[6]Israel asked, "Why did you bring this trouble on me by telling the man you had another brother?"

[7]They replied, "The man questioned us closely about ourselves and our family. 'Is your father still living?' he asked us. 'Do you have another brother?' We simply answered his questions. How were we to know he would say, 'Bring your brother down here'?"

[8]Then Judah said to Israel his father, "Send the boy along with me and we will go at once, so that we and you and our children may live and not die. [9]I myself will guarantee his safety; you can hold me personally responsible for him. If I do not bring him back to you and set him here before you, I will bear the blame before you all my life. [10]As it is, if we had not delayed, we could have gone and returned twice."

[11]Then their father Israel said to them, "If it must be, then do this: Put some of the best products of the land in your bags and take them down to the man as a gift—a little balm and a little honey, some spices and myrrh, some pistachio nuts and almonds. [12]Take double the amount of silver with you, for you must return the silver that was put back into the mouths of your sacks. Perhaps it was a mistake. [13]Take your brother also and go back to the man at once. [14]And may God Almighty grant you mercy before the man so that he will let your other brother and Benjamin come back with you. As for me, if I am bereaved, I am bereaved."

[15]So the men took the gifts and double the amount of silver, and Benjamin also. They hurried down to Egypt and presented themselves to

Joseph. [16]When Joseph saw Benjamin with them, he said to the steward of his house, "Take these men to my house, slaughter an animal and prepare a meal; they are to eat with me at noon."

[17]The man did as Joseph told him and took the men to Joseph's house. [18]Now the men were frightened when they were taken to his house. They thought, "We were brought here because of the silver that was put back into our sacks the first time. He wants to attack us and overpower us and seize us as slaves and take our donkeys."

[19]So they went up to Joseph's steward and spoke to him at the entrance to the house. [20]"We beg your pardon, our lord," they said, "we came down here the first time to buy food. [21]But at the place where we stopped for the night we opened our sacks and each of us found his silver—the exact weight—in the mouth of his sack. So we have brought it back with us. [22]We have also brought additional silver with us to buy food. We don't know who put our silver in our sacks."

[23]"It's all right," he said. "Don't be afraid. Your God, the God of your father, has given you treasure in your sacks; I received your silver." Then he brought Simeon out to them.

[24]The steward took the men into Joseph's house, gave them water to wash their feet and provided fodder for their donkeys. [25]They prepared their gifts for Joseph's arrival at noon, because they had heard that they were to eat there.

[26]When Joseph came home, they presented to him the gifts they had brought into the house, and they bowed down before him to the ground. [27]He asked them how they were, and then he said, "How is your aged father you told me about? Is he still living?"

[28]They replied, "Your servant our father is still alive and well." And they bowed down, prostrating themselves before him.

[29]As he looked about and saw his brother Benjamin, his own mother's son, he asked, "Is this your youngest brother, the one you told me about?" And he said, "God be gracious to you, my son." [30]Deeply moved at the sight of his brother, Joseph hurried out and looked for a place to weep. He went into his private room and wept there.

[31]After he had washed his face, he came out and, controlling himself, said, "Serve the food."

[32]They served him by himself, the brothers by themselves, and the Egyptians who ate with him by themselves, because Egyptians could not eat with Hebrews, for that is detestable to Egyptians. [33]The men had been seated before him in the order of their ages, from the firstborn to the youngest; and they looked at each other in astonishment. [34]When

portions were served to them from Joseph's table, Benjamin's portion
was five times as much as anyone else's. So they feasted and drank freely
with him.

44:1Now Joseph gave these instructions to the steward of his house:
"Fill the men's sacks with as much food as they can carry, and put each
man's silver in the mouth of his sack. 2Then put my cup, the silver one, in
the mouth of the youngest one's sack, along with the silver for his grain."
And he did as Joseph said.

3As morning dawned, the men were sent on their way with their
donkeys. 4They had not gone far from the city when Joseph said to his
steward, "Go after those men at once, and when you catch up with them,
say to them, 'Why have you repaid good with evil? 5Isn't this the cup my
master drinks from and also uses for divination? This is a wicked thing
you have done.' "

6When he caught up with them, he repeated these words to them.
7But they said to him, "Why does my lord say such things? Far be it from
your servants to do anything like that! 8We even brought back to you
from the land of Canaan the silver we found inside the mouths of our
sacks. So why would we steal silver or gold from your master's house? 9If
any of your servants is found to have it, he will die; and the rest of us will
become my lord's slaves."

10"Very well, then," he said, "let it be as you say. Whoever is found to
have it will become my slave; the rest of you will be free from blame."

11Each of them quickly lowered his sack to the ground and opened it.
12Then the steward proceeded to search, beginning with the oldest and
ending with the youngest. And the cup was found in Benjamin's sack.
13At this, they tore their clothes. Then they all loaded their donkeys and
returned to the city.

14Joseph was still in the house when Judah and his brothers came in,
and they threw themselves to the ground before him. 15Joseph said to
them, "What is this you have done? Don't you know that a man like me
can find things out by divination?"

16"What can we say to my lord?" Judah replied. "What can we say?
How can we prove our innocence? God has uncovered your servants'
guilt. We are now my lord's slaves—we ourselves and the one who was
found to have the cup."

17But Joseph said, "Far be it from me to do such a thing! Only the
man who was found to have the cup will become my slave. The rest of
you, go back to your father in peace."

[18]Then Judah went up to him and said: "Pardon your servant, my lord, let me speak a word to my lord. Do not be angry with your servant, though you are equal to Pharaoh himself. [19]My lord asked his servants, 'Do you have a father or a brother?' [20]And we answered, 'We have an aged father, and there is a young son born to him in his old age. His brother is dead, and he is the only one of his mother's sons left, and his father loves him.'

[21]"Then you said to your servants, 'Bring him down to me so I can see him for myself.' [22]And we said to my lord, 'The boy cannot leave his father; if he leaves him, his father will die.' [23]But you told your servants, 'Unless your youngest brother comes down with you, you will not see my face again.' [24]When we went back to your servant my father, we told him what my lord had said.

[25]"Then our father said, 'Go back and buy a little more food.' [26]But we said, 'We cannot go down. Only if our youngest brother is with us will we go. We cannot see the man's face unless our youngest brother is with us.'

[27]"Your servant my father said to us, 'You know that my wife bore me two sons. [28]One of them went away from me, and I said, "He has surely been torn to pieces." And I have not seen him since. [29]If you take this one from me too and harm comes to him, you will bring my gray head down to the grave in misery.'

[30]"So now, if the boy is not with us when I go back to your servant my father, and if my father, whose life is closely bound up with the boy's life, [31]sees that the boy isn't there, he will die. Your servants will bring the gray head of our father down to the grave in sorrow. [32]Your servant guaranteed the boy's safety to my father. I said, 'If I do not bring him back to you, I will bear the blame before you, my father, all my life!'

[33]"Now then, please let your servant remain here as my lord's slave in place of the boy, and let the boy return with his brothers. [34]How can I go back to my father if the boy is not with me? No! Do not let me see the misery that would come on my father."

*Listening to the Text in the Story:* Biblical Texts: Genesis 37, 39–42

In this episode of the narrative, the brothers will make their second journey to Egypt for grain. This scene has as its immediate background the first journey recounted in chapters 40–41, where Joseph had begun the test of his brothers' character. Now this test will come to its climax, determining whether or not there will be a successful reconciliation between Joseph and his family. The fracture in the family came in Genesis 37 where Joseph's arrogance about his special position in the family thanks to Jacob's favoritism and the brothers' inordinate envy resulted in their selling him into the slavery that brought him initially to Egypt.

## EXPLAIN the Story

### Jacob Agrees to Send Benjamin to Egypt (43:1–34)

In the previous chapter, Jacob utterly refused to allow the brothers to take Benjamin to Egypt in order to get more grain and retrieve Simeon. Benjamin was his new favorite son, and he did not want to risk him.

The famine, however, forced his hand, since it remained severe. Thus, as they were running out of the grain that they brought back from their first trip to Egypt, he told them to return and get more food.

It is Judah who then speaks up on behalf of the brothers, reminding him of the condition that Joseph had set regarding Benjamin. He knows that the man was serious, and so he tells his father that they will not go down to Egypt. Such a trip would not only be fruitless, but also dangerous.

Jacob petulantly blames the brothers for even telling the man that they had a brother back home. Jacob seems little concerned about the ten brothers, the nine who came back from Egypt and Simeon whom they left there. He feels personally assaulted ("Why did you bring this trouble on me...?" [v. 6]).

Judah responds by expressing surprise that the "Egyptian" man questioned them so much about the family. What could they do but answer this powerful person's inquiries?

Judah then makes himself responsible for Benjamin's safety. Unlike Reuben (42:37), he does not make an outrageous promise that Jacob could kill his offspring, but rather simply that he would bear the blame before his father. He urges his father to hurry, since they have already delayed their departure too long.

Jacob, here called by his other name Israel, gives reluctant permission for Judah to lead the brothers back to Egypt to get food. He gives Judah instructions about how to approach the "man," bearing gifts of native produce (balm, honey, spices, myrrh, pistachio nuts, and almonds; see Approaching Conflict

Wisely in the Live the Story section after Gen 32:1–21). They must return the silver that was returned to them from their first trip; indeed, they must double it. The only explanation that Jacob can come up with was that the return of the silver was a mistake.

Jacob's advice here sounds similar to the strategy that he used earlier with Esau (32:13–16). Perhaps these gifts will mollify the potential hostility of the man. That said, Jacob also realizes that the ultimate outcome of this venture will be the mercy of God Almighty. Even with these preparations, Jacob understands that there are no guarantees and resigns himself to the fact that he might be bereaved.

The narrator does not waste space getting them to Egypt and into Joseph's presence (v. 15). When he sees them, and in particular when he sees Benjamin, he issues orders that his steward is to prepare a meal and eat with him at noon.

The brothers did not know what kind of reception that they would receive, and indeed they feared the worse. After all, they feared that the Egyptian would think they stole the silver. They think he will take advantage of the crime and take their goods and enslave them. Thus, upon their arrival at Joseph's house, they tell the steward who greeted them that they did not know how the silver came to be placed back in their sacks. The steward assures them that he had received their payment and attributes the return to their God, something that had not even crossed the brothers' minds. Indeed, though Joseph was the human agent, what the Egyptian steward said was in the final analysis true. Even if the steward himself did not believe it, he spoke better than he knew.

The steward then ushered the brothers into Joseph's house where they were greeted as respected guests. They were given water to wash the grime of their travel off their feet and their donkeys were fed. Joseph was scheduled to arrive at noon for the midday meal that he invited them to share with him and the brothers prepared their gifts.

When Joseph arrived, he treated them with great respect, and the brothers treated him, whom they only knew as an Egyptian overlord, with honor. Joseph inquired after their father, and he blessed Benjamin, who was his one full brother. He was so moved by the sight of Benjamin that he had to remove himself from the room to compose himself.

When he returned, he ordered the food to be served. We have already noted several times that Egyptians found Asiatics distasteful and the seating arrangements reflected this with the Semitic brothers sitting apart from the Egyptians and Joseph eating alone as befitted his high office. We have no reason to think that the brothers were offended by this arrangement. Far from it! They thought they might be enslaved by this strange Egyptian leader, but here they were being feasted.

Even more surprising, they were seated according to birth order. How could the Egyptians know their respective ages! The Egyptian must be a wise man indeed. Though Benjamin as the youngest would have been seated last, he was served a portion five times that of his brothers. Who knows what might have gone through the minds of the brothers, but the reader certainly understands the significance of his special treatment.

### Judah's Plea for Benjamin (44:1 – 34)

In the previous chapter, we saw that Joseph treated the brothers with great respect, but he was not yet ready to reveal his identity to them. He is setting up a situation that will nearly replicate the moment when the brothers sold him into slavery. He wants to know whether they have changed or whether they are still the same envious, self-serving men that they were when they were younger.

Thus, he orders his steward to give them an abundance of food to take back with them and to again return their payment by placing the silver in the sack. The new wrinkle was the addition of Joseph's silver divining cup in the sack meant for Benjamin.

Not surprisingly, a lot of ink has been spilled over Joseph's divining cup. A divining cup was a cup in which one would pour oil into water. The shape that the oil would take would portend the future in some way. But what is Joseph doing with a divining cup in the first place? Later Israelite law condemns such practices (Deut 18:9 – 13), and the principle that leads to its prohibition would seem to be relevant even here at an earlier time. That is, divination of this sort automatically works and presumes that humans can basically wrest some knowledge of the future from the divine realm. In other words, it violates God's freedom to choose not to answer. Even the later priestly Urim and Thummim (Exod 28:30), though it sounds like a prohibited divinatory practice, was permitted because however it was manipulated, it was possible for God to choose to remain silent as he did when Saul tried to use it at the end of his life (1 Sam 28).

Though we are interested in the question of Joseph's possession of such a cup, in the final analysis we cannot say much. Some would defend Joseph by saying that though he had a cup he did not use it. Perhaps it was a part of his Egyptian disguise. We just cannot be sure. In any case, we don't need to know to follow the story. The cup's purpose is to create an occasion to bring a charge against Benjamin, which will test the other brothers' loyalty.

That charge is lodged soon after the brothers depart from Joseph's house. He instructs his steward to overtake them when they had not traveled far from the city. Once the steward overtakes them he is to charge them with the theft of the silver cup.

When confronted, the brothers are offended. After all, they had brought back the silver returned to them from the first trip. Their response has resonance with Jacob's words to Laban when the latter overtook Jacob and charged him with stealing his household idols (31:22–37). In that case, Jacob did not know that Rachel had indeed stolen them. In the present situation, they were unaware that the silver divining cup had been placed in Benjamin's sack of grain. Not knowing and indeed being confident of their innocence, the brothers say that if the divining cup is found on a person, that person will die while the rest will become Joseph's slave.

The steward agrees but lessens the penalty. The one on whom the cup is found will become a slave, while the others will be free to go.

Tension mounts for the characters as well as the reader as the inspection moves from oldest brother to Benjamin the youngest, the difference being that the reader knows what the brothers do not. The steward will find the cup in Benjamin's sack.

The brothers are stricken with grief when the discovery is made, demonstrated by tearing their garments. They have no recourse except to return to the city. Reaching Joseph's house, they throw themselves at his mercy. Joseph then berates them for trying to pull one over on him. He reminds them that he is a diviner and he can find such things out.

They are dumbfounded. This must be none other than God uncovering their guilt. Of course, they are not guilty of stealing the cup. They must be thinking of their guilt at selling Joseph. God is using this means to bring them to justice. They thus all agree to become Joseph's slaves. Joseph, however will not condemn the innocent with the guilty. He tells them that only Benjamin will be kept.

At this point Judah steps forward to speak. The sheer length of his speech (vv. 18–34) indicates its significance. We earlier commented on the characterization of Judah in the Joseph narrative. At the beginning he is a morally compromised person. He was the one who urged his brothers to sell Joseph to the Ishmaelites, spoiling Reuben's secret plan to save him (37:26–33). He refused to give his daughter-in-law his third son as a husband, leading her to force his hand by posing as a prostitute with whom he slept (ch. 38). Here we witness his transformation from self-seeker to one willing to sacrifice himself for the good of his family.

He approaches Joseph whom he only knows as second-in-command to Pharaoh himself with great respect and deference. He requests the privilege of speaking to him. He begins by reminding Joseph of their earlier interchange where, in answer to his questions, the brothers had informed him of the make-up of their family, particularly their father and their two other brothers, one who was no more and one who stayed home with his father. The latter, Benjamin, is called "the only one of his mother's sons left," significant because this mother was the father's beloved and favored wife. He is also described as the one whom his father loved. He goes on to remind Joseph that, though he had told them to bring Benjamin with him, that their father would refuse because he could not bear to part from him. Even so, Judah reminds him, Joseph had insisted that they not return without their brother.

Judah then says that the time finally came when the need for food was so grave that Jacob finally relented to allow the beloved son to travel with them to Egypt. Even so, Jacob reminded Judah of Benjamin's importance to him particularly with the loss of Joseph. Jacob told Judah that if Benjamin should come to harm his grief would "bring my gray head down to the grave in misery" (v. 29).

Judah now brings out the implications of Benjamin's loss to his family. In essence, Jacob would die of grief. Judah had earlier guaranteed the safety of his brother to his father (see 43:8–10). Thus, if Benjamin is not permitted to return to his father, then it would be Judah's fault and he would bear the blame for the rest of his life.

This speech leads to Judah's offer to Joseph that Joseph take him as a slave rather than Benjamin. Judah here takes full responsibility for the safety of his brother in the name of his love of his father. He puts his father's well-being ahead of his own, even though Jacob has shown no great love toward him.

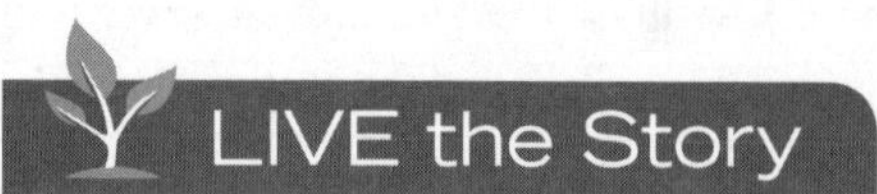


### Judah, a Model of Self-Sacrificial Love

At the beginning of the Joseph narrative, Judah is an out-and-out rogue. He leads the brothers in their sale of Joseph to the Ishmaelites. He marries a Canaanite woman and then mistreats his daughter-in-law Tamar, who tricks him into sleeping with her in order to produce an heir.

Judah's speech in 45:18–34 reveals a transformed man. No longer is he looking out just for himself to the harm of others. Rather as Waltke points out here "Judah ... is the first person in Scripture who willingly offers his own life for another. His self-sacrificing love for his brother for the sake of his father prefigures the vicarious atonement of Christ, who by his voluntary sufferings heals the breach between God and human beings."[1]

Greidanus thinks this is a weak parallel, but I tend to agree with Waltke that Judah anticipates an even greater act of self-sacrifice. In other words, the parallel comes out both in the similarities as well as the differences.

Judah offers himself as a prisoner. Jesus offers his very life. Judah's offer is ultimately not accepted by Joseph, while Jesus did die on the cross. Judah offers himself in place of Benjamin a family member; Jesus offered his life on behalf of those who were his enemies (Rom 5:9–11).

Jesus died in our place while we were still his enemies; now we are called to sacrifice ourselves for others in service of Jesus. We do not live for ourselves but for the glory of God and the betterment of others.

1. See Waltke, *Genesis*, 567, cited by Greidanus, *Preaching Christ from Ge*nesis, 419.

CHAPTER 45

# Genesis 45 – 47

##  LISTEN to the Story

45:1Then Joseph could no longer control himself before all his
attendants, and he cried out, "Have everyone leave my presence!" So there
was no one with Joseph when he made himself known to his brothers.
2And he wept so loudly that the Egyptians heard him, and Pharaoh's
household heard about it.

3Joseph said to his brothers, "I am Joseph! Is my father still living?"
But his brothers were not able to answer him, because they were terrified
at his presence.

4Then Joseph said to his brothers, "Come close to me." When they
had done so, he said, "I am your brother Joseph, the one you sold
into Egypt! 5And now, do not be distressed and do not be angry with
yourselves for selling me here, because it was to save lives that God sent
me ahead of you. 6For two years now there has been famine in the land,
and for the next five years there will be no plowing and reaping. 7But God
sent me ahead of you to preserve for you a remnant on earth and to save
your lives by a great deliverance.

8"So then, it was not you who sent me here, but God. He made me
father to Pharaoh, lord of his entire household and ruler of all Egypt.
9Now hurry back to my father and say to him, 'This is what your son
Joseph says: God has made me lord of all Egypt. Come down to me; don't
delay. 10You shall live in the region of Goshen and be near me—you,
your children and grandchildren, your flocks and herds, and all you have.
11I will provide for you there, because five years of famine are still to
come. Otherwise you and your household and all who belong to you will
become destitute.'

12"You can see for yourselves, and so can my brother Benjamin, that
it is really I who am speaking to you. 13Tell my father about all the honor
accorded me in Egypt and about everything you have seen. And bring my
father down here quickly."

14Then he threw his arms around his brother Benjamin and wept, and
Benjamin embraced him, weeping. 15And he kissed all his brothers and
wept over them. Afterward his brothers talked with him.

[16]When the news reached Pharaoh's palace that Joseph's brothers had
come, Pharaoh and all his officials were pleased. [17]Pharaoh said to Joseph,
"Tell your brothers, 'Do this: Load your animals and return to the land of
Canaan, [18]and bring your father and your families back to me. I will give
you the best of the land of Egypt and you can enjoy the fat of the land.'

[19]"You are also directed to tell them, 'Do this: Take some carts from
Egypt for your children and your wives, and get your father and come.
[20]Never mind about your belongings, because the best of all Egypt will
be yours.' "

[21]So the sons of Israel did this. Joseph gave them carts, as Pharaoh had
commanded, and he also gave them provisions for their journey. [22]To each
of them he gave new clothing, but to Benjamin he gave three hundred
shekels of silver and five sets of clothes. [23]And this is what he sent to his
father: ten donkeys loaded with the best things of Egypt, and ten female
donkeys loaded with grain and bread and other provisions for his journey.
[24]Then he sent his brothers away, and as they were leaving he said to
them, "Don't quarrel on the way!"

[25]So they went up out of Egypt and came to their father Jacob in the
land of Canaan. [26]They told him, "Joseph is still alive! In fact, he is ruler
of all Egypt." Jacob was stunned; he did not believe them. [27]But when
they told him everything Joseph had said to them, and when he saw the
carts Joseph had sent to carry him back, the spirit of their father Jacob
revived. [28]And Israel said, "I'm convinced! My son Joseph is still alive. I
will go and see him before I die."

[46:1]So Israel set out with all that was his, and when he reached
Beersheba, he offered sacrifices to the God of his father Isaac.

[2]And God spoke to Israel in a vision at night and said, "Jacob! Jacob!"

"Here I am," he replied.

[3]"I am God, the God of your father," he said. "Do not be afraid to
go down to Egypt, for I will make you into a great nation there. [4]I will
go down to Egypt with you, and I will surely bring you back again. And
Joseph's own hand will close your eyes."

[5]Then Jacob left Beersheba, and Israel's sons took their father Jacob
and their children and their wives in the carts that Pharaoh had sent to
transport him. [6]So Jacob and all his offspring went to Egypt, taking with
them their livestock and the possessions they had acquired in Canaan.
[7]Jacob brought with him to Egypt his sons and grandsons and his
daughters and granddaughters—all his offspring.

[8]These are the names of the sons of Israel (Jacob and his descendants)
who went to Egypt:

Reuben the firstborn of Jacob.

[9]The sons of Reuben:
Hanok, Pallu, Hezron and Karmi.
[10]The sons of Simeon:
Jemuel, Jamin, Ohad, Jakin, Zohar and Shaul the son of a Canaanite woman.
[11]The sons of Levi:
Gershon, Kohath and Merari.
[12]The sons of Judah:
Er, Onan, Shelah, Perez and Zerah (but Er and Onan had died in the land of Canaan).
The sons of Perez:
Hezron and Hamul.
[13]The sons of Issachar:
Tola, Puah, Jashub and Shimron.
[14]The sons of Zebulun:
Sered, Elon and Jahleel.
[15]These were the sons Leah bore to Jacob in Paddan Aram, besides his daughter Dinah. These sons and daughters of his were thirty-three in all.
[16]The sons of Gad:
Zephon, Haggi, Shuni, Ezbon, Eri, Arodi and Areli.
[17]The sons of Asher:
Imnah, Ishvah, Ishvi and Beriah.
Their sister was Serah.
The sons of Beriah:
Heber and Malkiel.
[18]These were the children born to Jacob by Zilpah, whom Laban had given to his daughter Leah — sixteen in all.
[19]The sons of Jacob's wife Rachel:
Joseph and Benjamin. [20]In Egypt, Manasseh and Ephraim were born
to Joseph by Asenath daughter of Potiphera, priest of On.
[21]The sons of Benjamin:
Bela, Beker, Ashbel, Gera, Naaman, Ehi, Rosh, Muppim, Huppim and Ard.
[22]These were the sons of Rachel who were born to Jacob — fourteen in all.
[23]The son of Dan:
Hushim.
[24]The sons of Naphtali:
Jahziel, Guni, Jezer and Shillem.
[25]These were the sons born to Jacob by Bilhah, whom Laban had given to his daughter Rachel — seven in all.

[26]All those who went to Egypt with Jacob—those who were his direct
descendants, not counting his sons' wives—numbered sixty-six persons.
[27]With the two sons who had been born to Joseph in Egypt, the members
of Jacob's family, which went to Egypt, were seventy in all.

[28]Now Jacob sent Judah ahead of him to Joseph to get directions to
Goshen. When they arrived in the region of Goshen, [29]Joseph had his
chariot made ready and went to Goshen to meet his father Israel. As soon
as Joseph appeared before him, he threw his arms around his father and
wept for a long time.

[30]Israel said to Joseph, "Now I am ready to die, since I have seen for
myself that you are still alive."

[31]Then Joseph said to his brothers and to his father's household, "I
will go up and speak to Pharaoh and will say to him, 'My brothers and
my father's household, who were living in the land of Canaan, have
come to me. [32]The men are shepherds; they tend livestock, and they have
brought along their flocks and herds and everything they own.' [33]When
Pharaoh calls you in and asks, 'What is your occupation?' [34]you should
answer, 'Your servants have tended livestock from our boyhood on, just
as our fathers did.' Then you will be allowed to settle in the region of
Goshen, for all shepherds are detestable to the Egyptians."

[47:1]Joseph went and told Pharaoh, "My father and brothers, with
their flocks and herds and everything they own, have come from the land
of Canaan and are now in Goshen." [2]He chose five of his brothers and
presented them before Pharaoh.

[3]Pharaoh asked the brothers, "What is your occupation?"

"Your servants are shepherds," they replied to Pharaoh, "just as our
fathers were." [4]They also said to him, "We have come to live here for a
while, because the famine is severe in Canaan and your servants' flocks
have no pasture. So now, please let your servants settle in Goshen."

[5]Pharaoh said to Joseph, "Your father and your brothers have come
to you, [6]and the land of Egypt is before you; settle your father and your
brothers in the best part of the land. Let them live in Goshen. And if you
know of any among them with special ability, put them in charge of my
own livestock."

[7]Then Joseph brought his father Jacob in and presented him before
Pharaoh. After Jacob blessed Pharaoh, [8]Pharaoh asked him, "How old
are you?"

[9]And Jacob said to Pharaoh, "The years of my pilgrimage are a
hundred and thirty. My years have been few and difficult, and they do
not equal the years of the pilgrimage of my fathers." [10]Then Jacob blessed
Pharaoh and went out from his presence.

11So Joseph settled his father and his brothers in Egypt and gave them property in the best part of the land, the district of Rameses, as Pharaoh directed. 12Joseph also provided his father and his brothers and all his father's household with food, according to the number of their children.

13There was no food, however, in the whole region because the famine was severe; both Egypt and Canaan wasted away because of the famine. 14Joseph collected all the money that was to be found in Egypt and Canaan in payment for the grain they were buying, and he brought it to Pharaoh's palace. 15When the money of the people of Egypt and Canaan was gone, all Egypt came to Joseph and said, "Give us food. Why should we die before your eyes? Our money is all gone."

16"Then bring your livestock," said Joseph. "I will sell you food in exchange for your livestock, since your money is gone." 17So they brought their livestock to Joseph, and he gave them food in exchange for their horses, their sheep and goats, their cattle and donkeys. And he brought them through that year with food in exchange for all their livestock.

18When that year was over, they came to him the following year and said, "We cannot hide from our lord the fact that since our money is gone and our livestock belongs to you, there is nothing left for our lord except our bodies and our land. 19Why should we perish before your eyes—we and our land as well? Buy us and our land in exchange for food, and we with our land will be in bondage to Pharaoh. Give us seed so that we may live and not die, and that the land may not become desolate."

20So Joseph bought all the land in Egypt for Pharaoh. The Egyptians, one and all, sold their fields, because the famine was too severe for them. The land became Pharaoh's, 21and Joseph reduced the people to servitude, from one end of Egypt to the other. 22However, he did not buy the land of the priests, because they received a regular allotment from Pharaoh and had food enough from the allotment Pharaoh gave them. That is why they did not sell their land.

23Joseph said to the people, "Now that I have bought you and your land today for Pharaoh, here is seed for you so you can plant the ground. 24But when the crop comes in, give a fifth of it to Pharaoh. The other four-fifths you may keep as seed for the fields and as food for yourselves and your households and your children."

25"You have saved our lives," they said. "May we find favor in the eyes of our lord; we will be in bondage to Pharaoh."

26So Joseph established it as a law concerning land in Egypt—still in force today—that a fifth of the produce belongs to Pharaoh. It was only the land of the priests that did not become Pharaoh's.

[27]Now the Israelites settled in Egypt in the region of Goshen. They
acquired property there and were fruitful and increased greatly in number.
[28]Jacob lived in Egypt seventeen years, and the years of his life were
a hundred and forty-seven. [29]When the time drew near for Israel to die,
he called for his son Joseph and said to him, "If I have found favor in
your eyes, put your hand under my thigh and promise that you will show
me kindness and faithfulness. Do not bury me in Egypt, [30]but when I
rest with my fathers, carry me out of Egypt and bury me where they are
buried."
"I will do as you say," he said.
[31]"Swear to me," he said. Then Joseph swore to him, and Israel
worshiped as he leaned on the top of his staff.

*Listening to the Text in the Story:* Biblical Texts: Genesis 12:3; 37 – 44

The Joseph story has been building up to this moment ever since it began at 37:2. Right from the start, we learned that Joseph has the divinely given gift of dream interpretation. However, Jacob's favoritism, Joseph's arrogance, and the brothers' envy led to his being sold into slavery in Egypt (ch. 37). He was sold to Potiphar, a high-ranking Egyptian official, and, because God was with him, Potiphar's household flourished. However, Potiphar's wife framed him for rape and Joseph's hardships continued as he was thrown into prison. God was still with him in prison, and there he had contact with the chief cupbearer and chief baker. He was able, through the enablement of God, to interpret their dreams. The relationship with the chief cupbearer ultimately brought him to the attention of the Pharaoh, who had dreams that Joseph was able to interpret as portending a forthcoming famine. Joseph's wisdom and God's presence enabled him to rise to a high position in Egypt.

At that point in the narrative, focus returned to the family in Canaan who were suffering the effects of the famine, and, accordingly, Joseph's brothers came to Egypt to get grain. Their journey led to Joseph, whom they did not recognize. Joseph did not reveal himself to them, but rather used the occasion to test their brothers' character. Were they still the angry, vengeful people they were when they sold him into slavery?

At the end of the previous section, Judah stepped forward to substitute his freedom for Benjamin, whom Joseph had framed for theft of his divination cup. Joseph had done this precisely to see how his brothers would react. Would they simply turn their back on Benjamin? Judah's actions revealed that the brothers had changed. The focus on Judah is particularly significant because at the beginning of the story Judah was a person of low moral character (see particularly 37:26 and ch. 39).

We should also be sensitive to the echoes of the divine promises to Abraham in the present episode. God there told Abraham that his descendants would become a great nation, which implies a numerous people. In the list of the members of Jacob's family in 46:8–27 we should see the beginnings of the fulfillment of this promise. We should also read Jacob's blessing of Pharaoh in the light of the promise that Abraham's descendants would bring a blessing to the nations.

## EXPLAIN the Story

### Reconciliation (45:1–28)

Joseph had arranged matters so they would replicate the moment when his brothers sold him into slavery. He manipulated events so that Jacob's other favored son, Benjamin, would be put at risk. Would the brothers take the opportunity to rid themselves of this beloved son in spite of the grief it would bring their father? In the light of Judah's speech in the previous chapter, the happy answer is no. Judah offers himself as a substitute for his younger brother for the happiness of their father.

Thus, the moment of revelation has arrived. Joseph had his answer; his brothers have changed. Thus, he tells them who he is. He is Joseph the brother they had sold into slavery.

First, he commands his Egyptian attendants to depart, leaving himself alone with his brothers. Joseph's weeping is so loud, though, that the Egyptians heard it and the news even spread to Pharaoh's very household.

Joseph announces his identity and asks if his father were still living. At first, the brothers could not respond. One might imagine their shock as well as their fear. After all, this powerful Egyptian turns out to be none other than their brother Joseph whom they had abused.

But Joseph moves quickly to assure him that he is not interested in revenge. Yes, Joseph says, I am the one you sold into slavery, but, for the first but not the last time (see particularly "You Meant It for Evil ..." Part 4 in the Live the Story section after Gen 50:15–21), he acknowledges that God's saving providence lies behind the events of his life. He now knows that it was God who used the brothers' sinful acts to bring him to Egypt where he would come to a place where he could help his family from the effects of the devastating famine. Indeed, they were only two years into the seven year famine, but because of his position he was confident that the family of God would survive.

Again, Joseph exclaims, behind the brothers' actions was the hand of God. It was God who made him "father to Pharaoh," in that he gave Pharaoh advice which he took in order to navigate the famine.

He then instructs them to return to Jacob and bring him down to Egypt where the whole family can live near him. They will live in Goshen (a location in the eastern Nile Delta). If they stay in Canaan, they "will become destitute" (v. 11), but if they return to Egypt, they will be well provided for.

Joseph goes first to his full brother Benjamin, and the two weep with joy as they embrace each other. He then with similar emotion greeted his other brothers.

Pharaoh's appreciation for Joseph extends to his family. He tells Joseph that his family can move to Egypt and avoid the ravages of the famine. Even though Joseph had invited them to move to Goshen earlier, the Pharaoh's invitation gives the necessary imprimatur for that move. He even tells them just to bring themselves and not worry about their property since they can live well with what will be provided for them in Egypt.

Joseph then sent his brothers off and well provides for their journey. While all of them benefit, Benjamin gets a larger portion of Joseph's gifts due to his special relationship with his brother. Three hundred shekels of silver (v. 22) is a large amount (seven and a half pounds according to the NIV note). He also sends twenty donkeys loaded with gifts to his father.

As they leave, Joseph admonishes them not to fight with each other. Of course, the natural tendency would be for them to bicker over who was responsible for sending Joseph into slavery in the first place. Joseph assumes the position of leadership among his brothers, trying to bring them into harmony.

Upon their return, they excitedly inform Jacob that his son Joseph is still alive. He initially greets the news with disbelief, but upon seeing the gifts that Joseph had sent with his brothers, he believes not only that he is alive, but also that "he is ruler of all Egypt" (v. 26).

### Jacob's Journey to Egypt (46:1–34)

Jacob, here named Israel, then set out for Egypt at the invitation of not only Joseph but also Pharaoh. When they camped at Beersheba, he offered sacrifices to God, here called the "God of Isaac." The title derives from the fact that Isaac lived in the area around Beersheba and built an altar there (26:25).

As we have seen before at Bethel (35:1–15) and elsewhere, God responds to Jacob's sacrifice with a personal appearance. Here God affirms Jacob's move to Egypt. God will go with him and his family to Egypt and will eventually bring him back. He will be with Joseph until the very end.

With the confidence of the blessing of God, Jacob then leaves Beersheba with his extended family and heads toward Egypt. At this point the narrative lists the individuals who accompanied Jacob/Israel to the land of Egypt. The list begins with the thirty-three sons and daughters of Jacob born to him through Leah (vv. 8 – 15), followed by the sixteen children and grandchildren born to Jacob through Leah's concubine Zilpah (vv. 16 – 18). Next comes the sons of Rachel, fourteen of them (vv. 18 – 21), and the seven sons and grandchildren born to Jacob by Rachel's concubine Bilhah.

Thus, there were sixty-six individuals heading down to Egypt. The narrator gives a final tally of seventy people which includes Joseph and his family (see also Exod 1:5). As the NIV footnote indicates, there is a variant number of seventy-five given in the Septuagint and this is the number picked up by Stephen in his speech in Acts 7:14.

After enumerating the names of those who went with Jacob to Egypt, the narrator returns to the journey to Egypt. It is significant that it is Judah whom Jacob sends ahead to Joseph to get directions to Goshen (v. 28) since it indicates that Jacob finds Judah a responsible son due to his earlier offer to save Benjamin. Jacob and his entourage eventually arrive in Egypt and are greeted by Joseph. The reunion with his father is emotional, and Jacob, here called by his other name Israel, proclaims himself satisfied and ready to die now that he knows that his beloved son Joseph still lives.

Joseph then informs his family that he will announce their arrival to Pharaoh. He will also tell them their occupation, shepherd. Since Egyptians detest shepherds Pharaoh will allow them to settle in Goshen and maintain a distinctive identity.

### Pharaoh Settles Jacob's Family in Goshen (47:1 – 12)

Now that Jacob and his family had arrived in Egypt, Joseph presents them to Pharaoh. He first brought five of his brothers to him, though the narrator does not inform the reader which five. At the meeting, Pharaoh asks them their occupation, and, following Joseph's earlier instructions (46:33 – 34), they inform him that they are shepherds. They explain that they have come to Egypt because of the famine. They request that they be allowed to occupy Goshen. Interestingly, they say that they will live in Egypt "for a while," seemingly giving the impression that they will leave after the famine abates. Of course, they do not do this, and this raises the question whether the family's continued presence in Egypt was an act of unbelief. Of course, while we might consider the question, the Bible itself never names their continued stay in Egypt a sin. Even so, it might explain why God allowed his people to be later enslaved by the Egyptians.

Pharaoh answers the brothers' inquiry in an address to Joseph. He says that they may indeed live in the land, even a luxurious part of the land like Goshen. He even permits Joseph to appoint a competent brother over Pharaoh's own livestock.

Joseph then introduced his father to Pharaoh. Of course, on a human level, the latter was superior to the former, but still the meeting began and concluded with the patriarch blessing Pharaoh. If this interpretation is correct (and as the footnote indicates, it is possible, though in my opinion not likely, that the narrator simply has Jacob greeting Pharaoh), then the narrator is presenting Jacob as the superior to Pharaoh, since the superior is the one who blesses an inferior. In addition, Jacob's blessing Pharaoh is reminiscent and illustrative of the divine promise that God would bless the nations through Abraham and his descendants (12:3).

Pharaoh inquires after Jacob's age. Jacob replies that he was one hundred and thirty years old (he would die at the age of one hundred and forty-seven [47:28]), a lengthy period by modern standards to be sure, but compared to his father Isaac who died at one hundred and eighty and Abraham who died at one hundred and seventy-five, he was young as he approached death. He attributes his frailty to his difficult life.

After these formal introductions, the family of God settled in the best part of the land, here described as "the district of Rameses" (v. 11). In addition to excellent pasture land, Joseph made sure that they had plenty of food.

## Joseph Acquires All the Land for Pharaoh (47:13–31)

Now that the narrator has completed the story of the reconciliation of the family (at least for the moment, see 50:15–21), the story returns to the famine. The region (including Egypt and Canaan) was still in the throes of the devastating seven-year famine. Joseph was in charge of the distribution of the stored grain on behalf of Pharaoh, and already the people of the land had exhausted their wealth in purchasing the grain.

The bottom line is that Joseph's plan enriched the central government at the expense of the people of the land. Thus, they had to come to Joseph and essentially beg him to give them grain.

Joseph comes up with a plan that continues to enrich Pharaoh at the expense of the people. For the next year they give their livestock in return for the food they need to survive. But at the end of that year, they still need food. All they have left is their land and their own selves. Thus, they sell themselves and their lands to Pharaoh. Thus, "the land became Pharaoh's" (v. 20) and the people became their slaves. The one exception was the priests, who did not have to sell themselves because Pharaoh had them already on a regular allotment of food.

Pharaoh owned the land and thus the people were essentially sharecroppers working the land for him. Thus, Joseph gives them seed and tells them that in the future they would have to give Pharaoh a tax of twenty percent on their crops. According to the narrator, the twenty-percent tax was still in force years later when the Genesis account was composed.

Of course, the alterative for the people was certain death. So rather than being bitter toward Joseph they thanked him for saving their lives.

At this point, we should remember that Genesis was written at a later time, certainly after the experience of the Israelites' own slavery in Egypt and the exodus. Imagine reading this story from that perspective. The Pharaoh who had abused Israel was an ingrate. After all, the power that he used to oppress the Israelites was achieved through the agency of Joseph. Though reluctant, we should see the gifts which the Egyptians give to the Hebrews as they leave (Exod 12:33–36) as due payment for labor and for Joseph's work on behalf of Pharaoh.

In verse 27 the narrator shifts attention from the Egyptians to Jacob's family. While the Egyptians had to sell their land to Pharaoh, Jacob's family "acquired property" in Goshen. Moreover, they flourished in Egypt. That they "were fruitful and increased greatly in number" (v. 27) is reminiscent of both God's command to Adam and Eve (Gen 1:28) as well as the promise to Abraham that his descendants would become a "great nation" (Gen 12:2). Furthermore, it looks forward to the opening of the book of Exodus (1:7), which will repeat this phrase.

Jacob had moved to Egypt at the age of one hundred and thirty and lived there for seventeen years before he died. While Genesis 48–49 will inform us about some of Jacob's last acts and words, at this point in the story he calls Joseph to him in order to elicit a promise from him concerning the disposition of his body. He does not want to be buried in Egypt but back in the promised land. He makes Joseph promise and indicate his commitment by swearing an oath while placing his hand under his thigh. Here "thigh" is clearly a euphemism for genitals, representing his progeny.

Joseph agrees. Jacob, here called Israel, then responds with worship. As the NIV note indicates, there is some debate over whether Jacob worships while he leaned on his walking staff or at the head of his bed.

### "God Sent Me Ahead of You to Preserve for You a Remnant on Earth" (45:7)

Joseph tells his brothers that God was behind their evil act of selling him into slavery. God has brought him out of slavery and prison (his humiliation) to a powerful position in Egypt (his exaltation) for a purpose: to see that the family of promise would survive a devastating famine (see also the essay Joseph and Jesus: From Humiliation to Exaltation in the Live the Story section after Gen 40–41).

The immediate consequence of the survival of the remnant would be the people of Israel, who themselves will be placed in slavery (their humiliation) but freed and brought into the promised land (their exaltation) by God. But there is of course a longer term and more powerful consequence for the survival of the family who received the promise of the seed. This family will become a nation that will produce the Messiah.

Paul sees the ultimate fulfillment of the promise of the seed to be Jesus. Indeed, he states this in a most shocking way when he says: "The promises were spoken to Abraham and to his seed. Scripture does not say 'and to seeds,' meaning many people, but 'and to your seed,' meaning one person, who is Christ" (Gal 3:16). Paul's citation of the promise in Genesis 12:2 is shocking because he knew, like all readers of the book of Genesis, that the promise did anticipate the many people of Israel, but what Paul is saying here is that that was just an anticipation of the ultimate fulfillment in Christ. Readers are directed to a fuller discussion of this intriguing passage in Jesus, the Seed of Abraham in the Live the Story section following Genesis 11:27–12:9. But here we note that the significance of Joseph's work is not exhausted in the continuation of the family line of Abraham, but more specifically in the future Messiah who will save the world ("If you belong to Christ, then you are Abraham's seed, and heirs according to the promise, " Gal 3:29)

### "I Will Go Down to Egypt with You" (Gen. 46:4a)

To understand the full theological import of this divine word to Jacob, we need to remember that the gods of the ancient Near East were local gods. Marduk was the god of Babylon, Baal the god of Canaan (and likely there were specific manifestations of the god Baal for specific regional locations); Amon-Re was a god of Egypt. They all had their territory.

The God of Jacob, however, was not restricted by real estate. Thus, God assures Jacob that he would go with him to Egypt. Of course, by this time in the narrative this is not surprising. After all, we have already seen how God was "with Joseph" in Potiphar's household (39:2, 3, etc.) and in prison (39:21). The consistent witness of Scripture is that Israel's God is the only God,[1] so of course God can move freely to Egypt.

Imagine the comfort that this statement would bring later generations of Israelites.[2] In particular, we can think of the Babylonian exiles, whose temple had been destroyed, and then they had been forcibly removed to the land of their captors. Even later, those who still lived away from the promised land after the return could know that their God was with them in faraway lands. The book of Esther teaches this important truth by way of the "hidden providence" of God that saves God's people from their foes.

With the coming of Christ and the inclusion of the Gentiles into the covenant, the universal claims of Israel's God are even more evident to those who read the New Testament. Indeed, for this reason, we may have lost the sense of the distinctiveness of this claim within its Old Testament context. Even so, the awareness that our God is a God not just of a local place, nation, or even the planet earth should stagger us. Yahweh is the God of the cosmos that he created.

Just as God assured Jacob he would be with him as he descended into Egypt, so God will assure Moses and Joshua as they lead Israel back to the promised land and face the Canaanites (Deut 31:6; Josh 1:5). In the New Testament, Jesus assures his disciples that he will be with them even after he ascends into heaven (Matt 28:20). The book of Revelation comforts God's suffering people with a picture of the New Jerusalem where God will be present with his people forever (Rev 21:3).[3]

### "And I Will Surely Bring You Back Again" (Gen. 46:4b)

In his speech to Jacob, God again anticipates the exodus. The exodus is in the future of God's statement, but in the past of its inclusion in the book of Genesis. Thus, the original readers, like readers today, read it in the light of the historical event. What differentiates Christian readers from the original audience is that we read it in the light of the greater exodus provided by Jesus Christ (see the essay God Delivers His People in the Live the Story section following the commentary on Gen 12:10–20).

See related essay: The Risk of Reconcilitation (after Gen 32:1–21).

1. Though sometimes this is expressed henotheistically (there is only one God who counts because he created the other gods), other spiritual beings (angels and demons) being on occasion called "gods" (cf. Exod 12:12; Ps 82).

2. As pointed out by Greidanus, *Preaching Christ from Genesis*, 438.

3. Ibid., 439.

CHAPTER 46

# Genesis 48:1 – 49:28

## LISTEN to the Story

48:1 Some time later Joseph was told, "Your father is ill." So he took his
two sons Manasseh and Ephraim along with him. 2 When Jacob was told,
"Your son Joseph has come to you," Israel rallied his strength and sat up
on the bed.

3 Jacob said to Joseph, "God Almighty appeared to me at Luz in
the land of Canaan, and there he blessed me 4 and said to me, 'I am
going to make you fruitful and increase your numbers. I will make
you a community of peoples, and I will give this land as an everlasting
possession to your descendants after you.'

5 "Now then, your two sons born to you in Egypt before I came to you
here will be reckoned as mine; Ephraim and Manasseh will be mine, just
as Reuben and Simeon are mine. 6 Any children born to you after them
will be yours; in the territory they inherit they will be reckoned under the
names of their brothers. 7 As I was returning from Paddan, to my sorrow
Rachel died in the land of Canaan while we were still on the way, a little
distance from Ephrath. So I buried her there beside the road to Ephrath"
(that is, Bethlehem).

8 When Israel saw the sons of Joseph, he asked, "Who are these?"

9 "They are the sons God has given me here," Joseph said to his father.

Then Israel said, "Bring them to me so I may bless them."

10 Now Israel's eyes were failing because of old age, and he could hardly
see. So Joseph brought his sons close to him, and his father kissed them
and embraced them.

11 Israel said to Joseph, "I never expected to see your face again, and
now God has allowed me to see your children too."

12 Then Joseph removed them from Israel's knees and bowed down
with his face to the ground. 13 And Joseph took both of them, Ephraim on
his right toward Israel's left hand and Manasseh on his left toward Israel's
right hand, and brought them close to him. 14 But Israel reached out his
right hand and put it on Ephraim's head, though he was the younger, and

crossing his arms, he put his left hand on Manasseh's head, even though Manasseh was the firstborn.

[15]Then he blessed Joseph and said,
"May the God before whom my fathers
Abraham and Isaac walked faithfully,
the God who has been my shepherd
all my life to this day,
[16]the Angel who has delivered me from all harm
—may he bless these boys.
May they be called by my name
and the names of my fathers Abraham and Isaac,
and may they increase greatly
on the earth."

[17]When Joseph saw his father placing his right hand on Ephraim's head he was displeased; so he took hold of his father's hand to move it
from Ephraim's head to Manasseh's head. [18]Joseph said to him, "No, my
father, this one is the firstborn; put your right hand on his head."

[19]But his father refused and said, "I know, my son, I know. He too will become a people, and he too will become great. Nevertheless, his younger brother will be greater than he, and his descendants will become
a group of nations." [20]He blessed them that day and said,
"In your name will Israel pronounce this blessing:
'May God make you like Ephraim and Manasseh.' "
So he put Ephraim ahead of Manasseh.

[21]Then Israel said to Joseph, "I am about to die, but God will be with
you and take you back to the land of your fathers. [22]And to you I give
one more ridge of land than to your brothers, the ridge I took from the Amorites with my sword and my bow."

[49:1]Then Jacob called for his sons and said: "Gather around so I can tell you what will happen to you in days to come.

[2]"Assemble and listen, sons of Jacob;
listen to your father Israel.
[3]"Reuben, you are my firstborn,
my might, the first sign of my strength,
excelling in honor, excelling in power.
[4]Turbulent as the waters, you will no longer excel,
for you went up onto your father's bed,
onto my couch and defiled it.
[5]"Simeon and Levi are brothers—
their swords are weapons of violence.

6Let me not enter their council,
let me not join their assembly,
for they have killed men in their anger
and hamstrung oxen as they pleased.
7Cursed be their anger, so fierce,
and their fury, so cruel!
I will scatter them in Jacob
and disperse them in Israel.
8"Judah, your brothers will praise you;
your hand will be on the neck of your enemies;
your father's sons will bow down to you.
9You are a lion's cub, Judah;
you return from the prey, my son.
Like a lion he crouches and lies down,
like a lioness—who dares to rouse him?
10The scepter will not depart from Judah,
nor the ruler's staff from between his feet,
until he to whom it belongs shall come
and the obedience of the nations shall be his.
11He will tether his donkey to a vine,
his colt to the choicest branch;
he will wash his garments in wine,
his robes in the blood of grapes.
12His eyes will be darker than wine,
his teeth whiter than milk.
13"Zebulun will live by the seashore
and become a haven for ships;
his border will extend toward Sidon.
14"Issachar is a rawboned donkey
lying down among the sheep pens.
15When he sees how good is his resting place
and how pleasant is his land,
he will bend his shoulder to the burden
and submit to forced labor.
16"Dan will provide justice for his people
as one of the tribes of Israel.
17Dan will be a snake by the roadside,
a viper along the path,
that bites the horse's heels
so that its rider tumbles backward.

[18]"I look for your deliverance, LORD.
[19]"Gad will be attacked by a band of raiders,
but he will attack them at their heels.
[20]"Asher's food will be rich;
he will provide delicacies fit for a king.
[21]"Naphtali is a doe set free
that bears beautiful fawns.
[22]"Joseph is a fruitful vine,
a fruitful vine near a spring,
whose branches climb over a wall.
[23]With bitterness archers attacked him;
they shot at him with hostility.
[24]But his bow remained steady,
his strong arms stayed limber,
because of the hand of the Mighty One of Jacob,
because of the Shepherd, the Rock of Israel,
[25]because of your father's God, who helps you,
because of the Almighty, who blesses you
with blessings of the skies above,
blessings of the deep springs below,
blessings of the breast and womb.
[26]Your father's blessings are greater
than the blessings of the ancient mountains,
than the bounty of the age-old hills.
Let all these rest on the head of Joseph,
on the brow of the prince among his brothers.
[27]"Benjamin is a ravenous wolf;
in the morning he devours the prey,
in the evening he divides the plunder."

[28]All these are the twelve tribes of Israel, and this is what their father said to them when he blessed them, giving each the blessing appropriate to him.

*Listening to the Text in the Story:* Biblical Texts: Genesis 35:21–22; 34; 38 and 44:18–34; 37; 39–47

As we learn from 47:28 – 31, Jacob knows that the end of his life is near. Thus, in our present passage, we see that he looks to the future and thus confers his blessings (and curses) on his progeny, beginning with his grandchildren by Joseph and then on to his twelve sons.

Specific stories lie behind the blessings of some of his sons. These stories will be evoked in the commentary that follows and only mentioned here. Of course, Joseph and his grandchildren are singled out because he was his father's favorite and also his meritorious acts as recorded in Genesis 37; 39 – 47. Reuben's future is affected by his sleeping with his father's concubines (35:21 – 22). Simeon and Levi are chastised because of their actions at Schechem (34), while Judah's positive assessment is understandable on the background of his transformation from the beginning of the Joseph story (see especially Gen 38) to the end (44:18 – 34).

## EXPLAIN the Story

### Jacob Adopts Joseph's Sons (48:1 – 7)

In the previous chapter, Jacob had secured Joseph's promise that he would be buried in the promised land and not in Egypt. He knew he was in his last days.

Thus, it is not surprising that chapter 48 announces that Jacob was ill. Upon the news, Joseph took his two sons Manasseh and Ephraim to his father. When Jacob hears that Joseph has come to see him, he manages to sit up in his bed.

Jacob recounts to Joseph his encounter with God at Luz (the city whose name he changed to Bethel based on his experience; see 28:10 – 22). He tells Joseph that God had reaffirmed the covenantal promises that God had made to his grandfather Abraham (12:1 – 3), passed on to his father Isaac (26:1 – 6), and then to Jacob himself on the evening he stayed in Luz/Bethel. God blessed him at Luz and told him that his descendants would "increase [in] numbers" so that his descendants would become a "community of peoples" (v. 4). He also told Jacob that he would receive the promised land.

Jacob now turns his attention from the past to the present. He tells Joseph that he will reckon Joseph's two sons, Ephraim and Manasseh, as his own. He will treat them just like his other children. He specifically mentions Reuben and Simeon because they are his two firstborn sons. In effect, this means that they will inherit along with Jacob's other sons. In the future we will see that Ephraim and Manasseh will both receive allotments of lands (Josh 13:29 – 31; 16 – 17) along with the other tribes descended from Jacob's sons. In effect, this decision means that Joseph will have a double allotment among his brothers.

Indeed, the book of Chronicles says as much when it says that when Reuben forfeited his rights as firstborn, these were passed on to the sons of Joseph (1 Chr 5:1–2). Other children born to Joseph will not receive the same treatment, but will be treated as Joseph's, not Jacob's, sons. As far as the biblical record is concerned, however, Joseph did not have any other children.

Verse 7 does not seem to connect clearly with the context as Jacob describes the death of Rachel as they were returning from Paddan. He tells Jacob that he buried her near Ephrath/Bethlehem (35:19–20). Perhaps this event is mentioned here to indirectly answer the question why Jacob treats Joseph and his children in a special way.

### Jacob Blesses Ephraim and Manasseh (48:8–22)

Jacob, whose sight was failing, asks Joseph the identity of the two children who are with him. A weak-sighted Jacob blessing the next generation reminds us of the time that Jacob tricked his blind father into blessing him rather than Esau (Gen 27), but there is no trickery here. Still, as Kaminsky recognizes "the passage strongly indicates that the narrator of Genesis and the character of Jacob himself affirm the correctness of what Jacob did those many years ago."[1]

Jacob expresses his wonder and thanks to have the opportunity at the end of his life not only to be restored to his lost son Joseph but also Joseph's children, so he asks to bless them. Joseph then prepared his sons for their blessing. After bowing to Jacob, Joseph placed his oldest son Manasseh so that Jacob could bless him with his right hand, indicating the primacy of the firstborn, and Ephraim, the younger son, where Jacob could bless him with his left. Surprisingly, though, Jacob crossed his hands and blessed the younger with his right hand and the older with his left.

He then blessed Joseph by blessing his two sons. He asks God to bless them. This is the God of Abraham and Isaac, the God who saved him from harm. In his last days, Jacob recognizes God as the shepherd who guided him through his tumultuous life. He also calls him an angel who protected him from harm. He adopts them as his own ("may they be called by my name," v. 16). And he asks that their descendants be numerous.

Joseph thought that his father made a mistake when he crossed his hands. He wanted Jacob to treat his firstborn son as his first and tried to move his father's hands to what he thought were the right positions. But Jacob told Joseph that he knew what he was doing. The younger brother (the tribe that descends from him) will be greater than (the tribe that will descend from) the

---

1. Kaminsky, *Yet I Loved Jacob*, 51. In our commentary at Genesis 27 we questioned Rebekah and Jacob's ethics ("the ends justify the means") even though the right results (the blessing of Jacob rather than Esau) was achieved.

older brother, though both tribes will be powerful. As history shows, both the tribe of Manasseh and the tribe of Ephraim were great tribes, but Ephraim was more dominant than Manasseh. Indeed, Ephraim was so dominant that during the period of the divided monarchy the northern kingdom was sometimes simply referred to as Ephraim.

The episode ends with Jacob/Israel anticipating his impending death. He reassures Joseph that God will be "with him," something that Joseph has experienced throughout his life as an indication of his covenant relationship with God (see Immanuel: The Lord is with Us in the Live the Story section after Gen 39). He also anticipates return to the promised land. Joseph's own return is intertwined with that of Israel since his bones will be taken for burial in the promised land by the Israelites when they return with Moses at the time of the exodus (Exod 13:19). Joseph will ultimately be buried at Shechem (Josh 24:31). This may explain the rather enigmatic statement that Jacob will "give one more ridge of land than to your brothers," since "ridge of land" is the Hebrew word Shechem. Jacob goes on to claim that he took this ridge from the Amorites through military action ("with my sword and my bow"). Could this be a reference to Levi and Simeon's violence which Jacob disowned in Genesis 34? Perhaps. Or it could be a reference to an otherwise untold story. In any case, Jacob's comment again shows Joseph's favored position and preeminence among his brothers as anticipated by his initial dreams in Genesis 37.

### Jacob Gathers His Sons (49:1–2)

Jacob is approaching death (47:28–31). Before he dies, he now blesses and curses his children in ways that will have ramifications for the tribes that will derive from them. Jacob may not always be operating from proper evaluation of his children (particularly Levi and Simeon), but still his words have consequences. He thus calls his children together and then speaks to them one by one beginning with the oldest and moving to the youngest.

### Reuben Forfeits His Birthright (49:3–4)

Reuben is treated first as the oldest (vv. 3–4). Jacob acknowledges Reuben as his firstborn. As firstborn, Reuben was a sign of Jacob's sexual vitality (my strength). As firstborn, he was exceptional. However, through his actions he forfeited his special status as firstborn. He slept with his father's concubines and thus will not enjoy primacy among his brothers (35:21–22). In the future, Reuben's descendents will receive a tribal allotment (Josh 13:15–23) but will not be distinguished from the other tribes.

## Simeon and Levi Will Be Scattered (49:5–7)

Next, Jacob turns his attention to Simeon and Levi. These brothers are treated as one because of their joint actions concerning their sister Dinah (see commentary at ch. 34). There they were involved in their sister's marriage negotiations with the prince of the Canaanite city of Shechem. They agreed that the man who had sexually violated their sister could marry him, but they were just setting up an elaborate plan to kill him and the other men of the city. Their agreement to the marriage was contingent on the men of Shechem undergoing the ritual of circumcision. They agreed, but when the men were circumcised and thus physically weakened, Simeon and Levi took the opportunity to slaughter them. While we noted earlier in the commentary that the narrator agreed with the brothers over Jacob (though perhaps indicating they were overzealous), Jacob had not forgiven them and thus curses their descendants.

They will be scattered through the land. The intent of this curse was that these two tribes would lose their distinctive identity as they got cities within the land controlled by other tribes (see Josh 19:1–9 [Simeon]; 21 [Levi]). Interestingly, Simeon's scattering resulted in loss of their identity, while Levi's did not (see below for the explanation for the difference).

## Judah's Royal Future (49:8–12)

Judah is next in line and the blessing that Jacob confers on his fourth son has long-lasting consequences and is certainly the best known verses of the chapter. Judah, whose name is based on the Hebrew verb "to praise" (see 29:35), will be the recipient of his brothers' praise. The tribe that derives from him will also dominate his enemies, the message of the image of having his hand on their neck (v. 8a). The other tribes ("your father's sons," v. 8b) will bow down to him. This picture reminds us of the dreams that Joseph has when all the brothers will bow to him (37:5–11). The Joseph tribes (Manasseh and Ephraim, see ch. 48) will dominate northern Israel while Judah will dominate the south.

In verse 9 Jacob uses a lion metaphor to refer to Judah's power and dominance. He will get his prey and no one will dare challenge Judah.

As the footnotes indicate, verse 10 is full of difficulties. However, one thing is clear. Kingship will emerge from the tribe of Judah and will stay there. The scepter was a symbol of kingship, being an ornamental mace showing the power of one who bore it. The same may be said about the ruler's staff. Indeed, as time unfolds, kingship will emerge from Judah in the person of David, and the descendants of David will rule Judah for the next four hundred plus years. But even after the last Davidic ruler in Jerusalem (Zedekiah who ended his reign in 586 BC), Jesus showed himself to be the true fulfillment of the Davidic covenant that David would have a descendant on the throne forever (see 2 Sam 7:11b – 16). This truth is proclaimed every time Jesus is called the Christ or "anointed one" (see below, Jesus, the Messiah).

The final description of Judah emphasizes his prosperity. The grape vine and the wine made from it will be so abundant that he will use it to tether his donkey and wash his clothes. He will have dark eyes like wine and teeth that are white like milk. In other words, he will be outstandingly handsome.

### Zebulun on the Seashore (49:13)

The fifth son is Zebulun. The description highlights the tribe's future location in the north and on the coast. Sidon is to the north of Israel and was an extremely important port. Zebulun too would prosper through trade by sea. Its allotment is described in Joshua 19:10 – 16.

### Issachar, a Rawboned Donkey (49:14 – 15)

According to the NIV, Issachar, the next born, is like a rawboned donkey. According to the NLT translation, Issachar is like a "sturdy donkey." The preferred reading is rawboned, which means gaunt, with bones showing through the skin. But this gaunt animal will find a pleasant resting place in the sheep pens. As verse 15 points out the metaphor seems to refer to Issachar's future pleasant location in the land of Israel. Because of its pleasant location, Issachar, though weak, will submit to forced labor. Its allotment is described in Joshua 19:17 – 23.

### Dan, a Snake (49:16 – 18)

Next comes the tribe of Dan, whose name comes from the Hebrew word for "justice." Thus, the first characteristic named by Jacob is that Dan will bring justice to the tribes. Though not strong, Dan will be dangerous like a snake that bites the heels of a horse and causes the rider to stumble and fall down. At this point Jacob interrupts his speech to his children to call the Lord to deliver him. Dan's allotment is described in Joshua 19:40 – 48.

### Gad, Repeller of Raiders (49:19)

After Dan comes Gad, whose name (as the NIV footnote indicates) is connected to the Hebrew word for "attack" or "band of raiders." But rather than being a band of raiders themselves, they will be beset by raiders. Still Gad will rally and attack those that raid it. Its allotment is described in Joshua 13:24 – 28.

### Asher's Rich Food (49:20)

Asher, whose name means "happy," will be rich and will even provide delicacies fit for a king. Its allotment is described in Joshua 19:24 – 31.

### Naphtali, a Doe (49:21)

Jacob's description of Naphtali is a beautiful one comparing that son and the future tribe that comes from him as a free doe that gives birth to beautiful fawns. As the NIV footnote indicates, the second colon could alternatively be read as "he utters beautiful words." This tribe's allotment is described in Joshua 19:32–39.

### Joseph, a Fruitful Vine (49:22–26)

The second youngest son of Jacob is Joseph, who was favored by his father in life and now we learn favored in terms of his blessing for the future of his descendants. Indeed, Joseph's blessing is only rivaled by Judah's and, like Judah's, indicates that the tribal descendants of Joseph will play a leadership role in Israel's future history. This is clearly the case with Ephraim, one of the two (the other being Manasseh) children of Joseph who will father two tribes that bear their names. For good reasons, these two tribes are often referred to as the Joseph tribes in contemporary scholarship.

Joseph is first described using the metaphor of a vine, a symbol of life and fruitfulness. The vine produces grapes that will produce wine that "gladdens human hearts" (Ps 104:15a). And this vine is no ordinary vine. It is planted near a water source ("a spring," v. 22b) and thus is lush, even growing over obstacles like a wall.

The NIV note indicates an alternative rendering to verse 22: "Joseph is a wild colt, a wild colt near a spring, a wild donkey on a terraced hill." This rendering is less likely, but if it is correct, it reminds us of the picture of the lover in the Song of Songs who is pictured as an animal gamboling on the hills (Song 2:8). This picture indicates vitality and energy. In either rendering, the Joseph tribes are pictured in a positive manner as having a vital role in the future of God's people.

Though vital, Joseph (the tribes that descend from him) will not go unchallenged. They will be attacked, though the attackers are not specifically named. Even so, with God's help the Joseph tribes will endure (the NIV note indicates that the verbs of vv. 23–24 could be translated with a future tense, but the change would make no notable difference to the message of the text). God will aid Joseph's descendants and will bless them from the skies (with rain) and with water from the deeps. They not only will be blessed with abundant water resources that will lead to bumper crops, but they will also be blessed with large families ("blessings of the breast and womb," v. 25).

These blessings will surpass even those of the mountains and their abundant bounty. They will come to Joseph, who significantly is called the "prince among his brothers" (v. 26e). This reference looks back on Joseph's two initial dreams (37:5 – 11), where he saw himself as dominant among his brothers. It also looks forward to the time that the Joseph tribes (particularly Ephraim) will dominate the northern kingdom from 931 – 722 BC. Its allotment is described in Joshua 10; 13:29 – 33; 16 – 17. That said, Judah's dominance (anticipated in vv. 8 – 12) will exceed that of the Joseph tribes since the Davidic dynasty will emerge from that tribe.

### Benjamin, a Ravenous Wolf (49:27)

Jacob began with the oldest (Reuben) and worked down the birth order to end with Benjamin, the youngest. Like Joseph, Benjamin was a favored son because he too was a son of the beloved Rachel. Even so, unlike Joseph (and Judah), Benjamin receives a brief statement from Jacob. In a culture that prizes power, we are likely to understand this statement positively as a blessing. Benjamin is likened to a wolf, a dangerous animal, an animal that hunts its prey. Indeed, the metaphor is unpacked to say that Benjamin the wolf hunts its prey during the day (morning and evening here are likely a merism meaning all day and all night). At night, after the hunt, the wolf Benjamin then divides the prey. Its allotment is described in Joshua 18:11 – 28.

### Looking to the Future (49:28)

The narrator concludes Jacob's words by making it clear that these blessings and curses have significance for the tribes that will descend from his children (which we have presumed throughout, but will develop now). He also indicates that Joseph's words are appropriate to each of his children. Looking forward, what can we say in terms of fulfillment of Jacob's words? Not surprisingly, we learn most about the tribes that receive the longest treatment in Jacob's last testament.

*Reuben*: We have already commented that Reuben forfeited the blessing of the firstborn by sleeping with his father's concubines. Thus, the tribe of Reuben does not have a distinguished or even notable history in the rest of the Old Testament. After the conquest, God through Moses assigned it territory in the Transjordan region to the south of Gad (Josh 13:15 – 23).

*Simeon*: Though the narrator sided with Simeon (and Levi) in terms of their actions in Shechem (Gen 34), Jacob cursed him to being dispersed in the land. They are indeed scattered within the tribal boundaries of Judah (Josh 19:1 – 9) and only occasionally are given a distinctive identity.

*Levi*: Levi shared Jacob's wrath along with Simeon. They too would be scattered through the land and not given a tribal allotment. Indeed, when Joshua and the high priest distributed the land among the tribes, they gave the Levites cities within the territory of other tribes (Josh 21). At this point, however, the similarity with Simeon breaks down. Rather than losing its tribal identity, the Levites become the most distinctive tribe of all through the history of Israel and beyond. What made the difference?

The account of the sin with the golden calf answers our question (Exod 32). When Moses and Joshua descended from Mount Sinai with the tablets containing the Ten Commandments, they saw that Aaron had constructed a golden calf at the insistence of the people. Moses was so angered that he smashed the tablets, symbolizing the breaking of the covenant between God and Israel.

After confronting Aaron, he called out: "Whoever is for the LORD, come to me" (Exod 32:26). The Levites responded to Moses, and he told them to arm themselves and "go back and forth through the camp from one end of the camp to the other, each killing his brother and friend and neighbor" (Exod 32:27). The Levites did so and killed three thousand calf worshipers.

Afterward, Moses announced, "You have been set apart for the LORD today, for you were against your own sons and brothers, and he has blessed you this day" (32:29). Thus, Jacob's curse is transformed into the blessing of being chosen as a tribe to be consecrated for special service in the holy place of God.

By their actions, they showed themselves to be ideal priests. What after all is a priest? A priest is a bodyguard of God's holiness. We may see this in Moses' later blessing on the tribe of Levi:

> Your Thummim and Urim belong
> to your faithful servant.
> You tested him at Massah;
> you contended with him at the waters of Meribah.
> He said of his father and mother,
> "I have no regard for them."
> He did not recognize his brothers
> or acknowledge his own children,
> but he watched over your word
> and guarded your covenant.
> He teaches your precepts to Jacob
> and your law to Israel.
> He offers incense before you
> and whole burnt offerings on your altar.
> Bless all his skills, LORD,
> and be pleased with the work of his hands.
> Strike down those who rise against him,
> his foes till they rise no more. (Deut 33:8–11)

The gist of the matter is stated in verse 9, where Moses says that the tribe of Levi guards God's covenant. This guarding includes preemptive actions such as teaching the law to Israel and discerning God's will through the use of the oracular device named the Urim and Thummim (see Exod 28:29–30). In this way, Israel knows God's will for how they should live and by so living they do not bring on his displeasure. But if Israel does sin, the priests administer the sacrifices that appease God's wrath, and if all else fails then, like with the calf worshipers, they administer God's punishment.

Indeed, another telling example of priests as guardians of God's holiness comes at Numbers 25. Here Israelite men have succumbed to the temptation of sleeping with Moabite women who lure them to the worship of their gods. Phinehas son of Eleazar, the son of Aaron, responds when an Israelite man has intercourse with a Moabite woman by driving his spear into the pair as they copulated. For this, God announced that he was making a covenant of peace with him wherein "he and his descendants will have a covenant of a lasting priesthood, because he was zealous for the honor of his God and made atonement for the Israelites" (Num 25:13).

*Judah*: Most significant for later Israelite history and beyond is Jacob's blessing of Judah in verse 10, "The scepter will not depart from Judah, nor the ruler's staff from between his feet, until he to whom it belongs shall come and the obedience of the nations shall be his" (49:10). We have already commented that this statement is an announcement that kingship will emerge from the tribe of David.

The story begins, as we have already described, with the transformation of the character of Judah within the Joseph narrative. At the beginning (see especially chs. 37 and 38) Judah is a deeply flawed character, but at the end he courageously represents his brothers before Joseph, whom they only know as a powerful Egyptian official (44:18–34). Even so, by the end of the narrative per se it is unclear whether it will be Joseph or Judah who will be the father of the dominant tribe in the future. While we have already seen that the Joseph tribes will be important, it is with this verse that we understand that kingship will emerge from Judah.

Of course, that will not happen for a number of centuries after the time of the patriarchs, though the Pentateuch does anticipate the rise of the institution in future Israel (Gen 17:7; Num 24:17–19; Deut 17:14–20). And when it does happen, it begins not with fanfare but with a kind of sad whimper.

First Samuel 8 narrates the time, when Samuel is old, that the people come and demand "appoint a king to lead us, such as all the other nations have" (v. 5). Samuel recognizes this request to be sinful and takes it as a personal affront. Even worse, God tells Samuel that it is an insult against him, not

Samuel. Nonetheless, God tells Samuel to give them their request. After all, as Deuteronomy 17 indicated, he had intended to institute kingship in Israel. However, though kingship is his will, the people's sinful request means that it will not come easily.

First Samuel 9 turns the reader's attention to Saul, a young man not from Judah but rather from Benjamin, in search of his father's lost donkeys. He cannot find them and so he goes to the town where Samuel lives in order to, through him, inquire about the location of the donkeys.

To Saul's great surprise Samuel warmly welcomes him, feasts him, and anoints him as the first king of Israel. After the anointing, Samuel gives Saul a detailed description of what would happen to Saul after he left Samuel's presence (1 Sam 10:1–8). First, Saul would encounter two men near Rachel's tomb who would tell him that the donkeys had been found and that his father was now worried about him. Afterward, he will meet three men going to worship God at Bethel. Saul tells them precisely what they would be carrying and that they would offer Saul two loaves of bread.

After this, Samuel tells him to go to "Gibeah of God, where there is a Philistine outpost" (v. 5). On the approach to Gibeah he will meet a group of prophets at which time the spirit of the Lord will come on him and he will also prophesy. It is at this point that Saul is to "do whatever your hand finds to do, for God is with you" (v. 7). After this, Saul is to go meet Samuel at Gilgal where he will offer sacrifices and where the prophet will give him further instructions.

Samuel's detailed description of what would happen to Saul after he left him is to confirm to Saul that Samuel's anointing is from the Lord. They are to encourage him to "do whatever your hand finds to do" after the spirit of God comes on him at Gilgal where there is a Philistine garrison.

To understand what Samuel means here we must remember what happened to the judges after the spirit came on them. They delivered God's people in extraordinary ways (e.g., Judg 14:19). In other words, Saul is here commissioned to attack and defeat the Philistine garrison at Gibeah.[2]

Samuel is a true prophet of Yahweh so everything he said would happen did happen (Deut 18:21), but what did Saul do? He went home neither acting against the Philistines nor meeting Samuel at Gilgal. He does not even tell his uncle what Samuel had told him; he simply went back to his life as normal.

Thus, Samuel has to "out" Saul. He does so by gathering all the people of Israel to Mizpeh, he cast the lots to chose the tribe of Benjamin out of all the tribes, then the clan of Matri out of all the clans of Benjamin, then finally

2. See V. P. Long, *The Reign and Rejection of King Saul: A Case for Literary and Theological Coherence*, SBLDS 118 (Atlanta: Scholars, 1989).

Saul the son of Kish. But where was Saul? He was hiding among the supplies. Even so, when he came out, the people saw that he was taller than anyone else, and to the people who wanted a "strong man" to lead them against their enemies, "there is no one like him among all the people" (10:24) and they publicly make him king.

At this point, Saul functioned, at least for the moment, like a real king by rescuing the people of Jabesh (1 Sam 11). After this, Samuel led the people in a renewal of the covenant since their sinful request threatened their fundamental relationship with God (1 Sam 12).[3] Indeed, Israel can have a human king as long as they and the king recognized God as their ultimate king and obeyed him as such.

However, right from the start Saul showed himself a disobedient king. Indeed, before too long, Saul demonstrates his inadequacy by not waiting for Samuel to offer the necessary pre-battle sacrifices. Samuel's tardiness and his resultant anxiety over the desertion of soldiers are no excuse for a king who should know that God battles for Israel (see Deut 20:3–9). When Samuel does arrive, he informs him that "your kingdom will not endure" and the Lord "has sought out a man after his own heart" (1 Sam 13:14).

That man, of course, is David from the tribe of Judah. With David, Jacob's pronouncements concerning Judah come to fruition. David, indeed, is the king after God's own heart, which means that he is a king of God's choosing.[4] Of course, God's choosing is pure grace, but there is a difference between Saul and David.

David, like Saul, does sin; we only need to refer to his adultery with Bathsheba (2 Sam 11–12) to understand that David, like Saul, is not perfect. The difference, however, is in David's heart to repent, and for this God grants David a covenant of kingship that ensures that "your house and your kingdom will endure forever before me; your throne will be established forever" (2 Sam 7:16), a promise that we will see below has messianic consequences (see Jesus, the Messiah below in the Live the Story section).

*Zebulun*: Jacob simply describes the tribal location of future Zebulun (Josh 19:10–16).

*Issachar*: Future Issachar will be located north of the massive tribe of Manasseh and south bordered on the north by Zebulun and Naphtali. Its tribal territory is just south of the Sea of Galilee, and the Jordan River defines its eastern boundary (Josh 19:17–23).

---

3. J. R. Vannoy, *Covenant Renewal at Gilgal: A Study of 1 Samuel 11:14–12:25* (London: Mack Publishing, 1978).

4. For the best biblical-theological treatment of the David story, see M. Boda, *After God's Own Heart: The Gospel according to David* (Phillipsburg, NJ: P & R, 2007).

*Dan*: Jacob's statement about Dan begins with a play on its name, which means "judge." Its original location made it one of the most southern of the northern tribes just to the northwest of the tribe of Judah and to the immediate west of Benjamin and Ephraim (Josh 19:40–48). Its western border was on the Mediterranean. The reference to the roadside may be a reference to the north-south international highway that was later referred to as the Via Maris or "Way of the Sea" that ran through its borders. Thus, they could harass those who traveled the road.

However, after settling in this region, they were dissatisfied and sought a new homeland. Perhaps they were squeezed by the larger tribes that bordered it, and certainly they were being troubled by the Philistines who were pressing in from the coast. However, their move to a new location to the north was an act of cowardice and lack of confidence in God that they could take care of their gift of land (Judg 17 and 18). Settling to the far north ironically meant that they were the first attacked by those who invaded from the north (Arameans and Assyrians).

*Gad*: Moses allocated territory in the Transjordan to Gad (Josh 13:24–28). It was immediately to the east of the Jordan River between the half-tribe of Manasseh to the north and Reuben to the south.

*Asher*: Asher was assigned territory on the Mediterranean coast and was one of the most northern tribes (especially before Dan relocated; Josh 19:24–31). This land was particularly fertile and was known in particular for its production of olive oil, thus the emphasis on the royal quality of the food that it provides.

*Naphtali*: Naphtali was given land to the north of Issachar and Zebulun, east of Asher, and the Jordan River provided its eastern boundary (Josh 19:32–39). It was, along with Asher, the northernmost tribe until Dan moved from its original location to north of it.

*Joseph*: Above we commented on Joseph's importance as signaled by the length of the blessing that his father bestowed on his favorite son. In Genesis 48, we saw how Joseph received a double portion, thus when we speak of the Joseph tribes, we are speaking of the large and influential tribes of Manasseh (with territory to the east [Josh 13:29–31] and west [Josh 17] of the Jordan River) and Ephraim (Josh 16:5–10; see Gen 48).

*Benjamin*: Benjamin was also a favorite of Jacob, but the blessing is short and its future tribal allotment was relatively small, being located between the massive tribes of Judah to its south and Ephraim to its north (Josh 18:11–28). Its location meant that it was in the center of the future conflict between the northern and southern kingdoms.

### The Second Born Becomes the Firstborn

Jacob blesses Ephraim the second born as if he were the firstborn. We have seen this before when Isaac is chosen but not Ishmael and Jacob receives the blessing of the firstborn rather than Esau, but there we emphasized the fact that God chooses the foolish over the wise (see the essay "God Chose the Foolish Things of the World," 1 Corinthians 1:27 in the Live the Story Section after Gen 25:19–34). Here we see again that God also gives preference to the second born over the first. Why?

It appears that God does not choose based on human entitlement or custom. Ancient Semitic ideas gave preference to the firstborn, but God does not work according to those expectations. On what basis does he choose?

Grace. There is nothing about Ephraim or Manasseh that determines this choice, only God.

What does this mean for us? As we think about our own "status" before God, we have to recognize that there is nothing in us that led to God's choice. We are not smarter, bigger, more spiritually sensitive, stronger than others. We can thank only God.

For this reason there is no boasting. As Paul reminds us, "For it is by grace you have been saved, though faith—and this is not from yourselves, it is the gift of God—not by works [or in the case of Jacob or Ephraim—by birth order], so that no one can boast. For we are God's handiwork, created in Christ Jesus to do good works, which God prepared in advance for us to do" (Eph 2:8–10).

### Jesus, the Ultimate High Priest

Jacob had cursed Levi to a scattering or dispersal in the future land, and above we followed the consequences of his words in the surprising consecration of the Levites to special service in the presence of God. Due to their actions during the golden calf incident, they became the divinely appointed "guardians" (Deut 33:9) of the covenant.

In their priestly role, the Levites and in particular Aaron, the high priest, model the function of the future Messiah, who is not only the ultimate Davidic king (see below Jesus, the Messiah), but also the ultimate priest. That Jesus is the ultimate high priest is taught particularly in the book of Hebrews, but in a very surprising way. Rather than seeing Jesus as a priest according to the model of Aaron, he is described as a high priest "according to the order of Melchizedek" (Heb 7–8), and since we encounter Melchizedek earlier in the book of Genesis, I refer the reader to Genesis 14 for a consideration of how Jesus is the ultimate fulfillment of the role represented by the Levites (see Jesus, a "High Priest Forever, in the Order of Melchizedek" [Heb 6:20] in the Live the Story section after Genesis 14).

### Curse Does Not Get the Last Word

Levi's characterization in the book of Genesis is admittedly not an easy one to describe, though there is no doubt that the characterization of Levi (as well as the other sons of Jacob) has consequences in the later history of the twelve tribes of Israel.

In Genesis 34, we see how he and Simeon took revenge against Prince Shechem and the Canaanite inhabitants of the city of Shechem for the sexual violation of their sister Dinah. In our interpretation of that chapter, we noted that the narrator (who best represents the author's perspective) sided with them over Jacob, who wanted to integrate with the Canaanite inhabitants of the land. That said, the narrator's preference for Levi and Simeon over against Jacob should not be taken as a total affirmation of their actions. Like Jehu at a later time (1 Kgs 19; 2 Kgs 9–10), they may have been overreaching in their slaughter (for a negative appraisal of Jehu, see Hos 1:4). In short, perhaps their violence was both unrestrained and done out of a personal sense of harm rather than to further the purposes of God. If so, then their actions in Exodus 32 demonstrate that the Levites have now channeled their violence in the service of God, thus, as we have observed, leading to their priestly consecration.

What is perfectly clear, however, is what Jacob meant as a curse (scattering and thus losing their distinctive tribal identity) becomes a blessing (consecration and resultant tribal distinctiveness in spite of not receiving an allotment of land). Thus, with the Levites we have an example of curse not being the final word, providing the lesson that it is never too late to turn to God and receive blessing. No one should ever think that they are irreparably doomed.

This is good news to all who are in relationship with Jesus. Apart from Christ, Paul tells us that that "cursed is everyone who does not continue to do everything written in the Book of the Law," (Gal 3:10, quoting Deut 27:26). We all fall short of this standard (Rom 3:28). However, rather than wallowing in guilt, Paul reminds us that "Christ redeemed us from the curse of the law by becoming a curse for us" (Gal 3:13). Curse does not have the final word in the life of the Christian.

### Jesus, the Messiah

Above, we saw how Jacob's blessing on Judah led to the emergence of kingship in the tribe of Judah after a fitful start with Saul the Benjaminite. It was

David with whom God entered into a covenant of kingship, promising him a descendant on the throne forever (2 Sam 7).

Of course, anyone who knows the history of Israel knows that, all in all, David's descendants proved to be a great disappointment. God anticipates the inadequacies of the future kings and announces "when he [a royal descendant of David] does wrong, I will punish him with a rod wielded by men, with floggings inflicted by human hands" (2 Sam 7:14). This conditional element to the covenant, however, is couched within the unconditional promise, "but my love will never be taken away from him, as I took it away from Saul, whom I removed from before you" (2 Sam 7:15).

After David comes Solomon, who started with such great promise, but ended with disaster. The "rod wielded by men" came in the form of Jeroboam, who led the northern tribes in secession from Judah, which continued to be ruled by a son of David, Rehoboam. Indeed, God permitted David's descendants to stay on the throne in Jerusalem for slightly over four centuries (ca. 1000–586 BC), making it the longest known dynasty of kings in the ancient Near East. This longevity is amazing especially in the light of the continued apostasy and disobedience of the descendants of David. Only two of the twenty kings (Hezekiah and Josiah) are commended for honoring the law of centralization (Deut 12), which called for sacrifices to take place exclusively at the temple. They both eradicated the problematic high places and also kept the temple pure. Even though God's attitude toward the sinful dynasty illustrates his longsuffering patience, four centuries is still not "forever."

What were the faithful to make of the situation after Zedekiah, the last king, was carted off in chains to Babylon and Judah lost its independence as a nation state? Was God a liar?

The faithful knew better. In the light of the failures of the Davidic dynasty, they likely already expected that God's promise of a king was better than those sinful, often oppressive kings in Jerusalem. But it was likely during the postexilic period that the expectation of a future, ideal Davidic "anointed" (messianic) king grew and grew.[5]

Of course, according to the New Testament, this expectation is met in Jesus. That Jesus is the expected Messiah is announced to Mary when the angel Gabriel announces to her that God will give the son growing in her virginal womb "the throne of his father David, and he will reign over Jacob's descendants forever; his kingdom will never end" (Luke 1:32–33). This

5. See T. Longman III, "The Messiah: Explorations in the Law and Writings," and M. J. Boda "Figuring the Future: The Prophets and Messiah," chapters 1 and 2 in *The Messiah in the Old and New Testaments*, ed. S. E. Porter (Grand Rapids: Eerdmans, 2007).

announcement is only the beginning of the extensive New Testament teaching that Jesus is the fulfillment of the Davidic covenant. Indeed, this truth lies behind the epithet Christ (Greek for Messiah or "anointed one") that is pervasive throughout the New Testament.

See related Essay: The Angel Who Saves (after Gen 16).

CHAPTER 47

# Genesis 49:29 – 50:26

## LISTEN to the Story

[49:29]Then he gave them these instructions: "I am about to be gathered to my people. Bury me with my fathers in the cave in the field of Ephron the Hittite, [30]the cave in the field of Machpelah, near Mamre in Canaan, which Abraham bought along with the field as a burial place from Ephron the Hittite. [31]There Abraham and his wife Sarah were buried, there Isaac and his wife Rebekah were buried, and there I buried Leah. [32]The field and the cave in it were bought from the Hittites."

[33]When Jacob had finished giving instructions to his sons, he drew his feet up into the bed, breathed his last and was gathered to his people.

[50:1]Joseph threw himself on his father and wept over him and kissed him. [2]Then Joseph directed the physicians in his service to embalm his father Israel. So the physicians embalmed him, [3]taking a full forty days, for that was the time required for embalming. And the Egyptians mourned for him seventy days.

[4]When the days of mourning had passed, Joseph said to Pharaoh's court, "If I have found favor in your eyes, speak to Pharaoh for me. Tell him, [5]'My father made me swear an oath and said, "I am about to die; bury me in the tomb I dug for myself in the land of Canaan." Now let me go up and bury my father; then I will return.' "

[6]Pharaoh said, "Go up and bury your father, as he made you swear to do."

[7]So Joseph went up to bury his father. All Pharaoh's officials accompanied him—the dignitaries of his court and all the dignitaries of Egypt—[8]besides all the members of Joseph's household and his brothers and those belonging to his father's household. Only their children and their flocks and herds were left in Goshen. [9]Chariots and horsemen also went up with him. It was a very large company.

[10]When they reached the threshing floor of Atad, near the Jordan, they lamented loudly and bitterly; and there Joseph observed a seven-day period of mourning for his father. [11]When the Canaanites who lived there saw the mourning at the threshing floor of Atad, they said, "The

Egyptians are holding a solemn ceremony of mourning." That is why that place near the Jordan is called Abel Mizraim.

12So Jacob's sons did as he had commanded them: 13They carried him to the land of Canaan and buried him in the cave in the field of Machpelah, near Mamre, which Abraham had bought along with the field as a burial place from Ephron the Hittite. 14After burying his father, Joseph returned to Egypt, together with his brothers and all the others who had gone with him to bury his father.

15When Joseph's brothers saw that their father was dead, they said, "What if Joseph holds a grudge against us and pays us back for all the wrongs we did to him?" 16So they sent word to Joseph, saying, "Your father left these instructions before he died: 17'This is what you are to say to Joseph: I ask you to forgive your brothers the sins and the wrongs they committed in treating you so badly.' Now please forgive the sins of the servants of the God of your father." When their message came to him, Joseph wept.

18His brothers then came and threw themselves down before him. "We are your slaves," they said.

19But Joseph said to them, "Don't be afraid. Am I in the place of God? 20You intended to harm me, but God intended it for good to accomplish what is now being done, the saving of many lives. 21So then, don't be afraid. I will provide for you and your children." And he reassured them and spoke kindly to them.

22Joseph stayed in Egypt, along with all his father's family. He lived a hundred and ten years 23and saw the third generation of Ephraim's children. Also the children of Makir son of Manasseh were placed at birth on Joseph's knees.

24Then Joseph said to his brothers, "I am about to die. But God will surely come to your aid and take you up out of this land to the land he promised on oath to Abraham, Isaac and Jacob." 25And Joseph made the Israelites swear an oath and said, "God will surely come to your aid, and then you must carry my bones up from this place."

26So Joseph died at the age of a hundred and ten. And after they embalmed him, he was placed in a coffin in Egypt.

*Listening to the Text in the Story:* Biblical Texts: Genesis 23; 47:28–31 (49:29–14); 37; 45:4–11 (50:15–21); 37:1–50:21 (50:22–26)

Jacob was aware that he was approaching his end (47:28–31). Now he has conferred his blessings and curses on his children (49:1–28) and was buried in the plot that Abraham purchased on the occasion of Sarah's death (v. 23). As we will see, the brothers now fear for their lives, thinking that Joseph will now seek vengeance for their past wrongs (v. 37). When they submit themselves to Joseph, we are not only reminded of Joseph's earlier dreams (37:5–11) but also of Joseph's earlier recognition (45:4–11) that his difficult life has been used by God for redemptive purposes.

## EXPLAIN the Story

### Jacob's Death (49:29–50:14)

The story of Jacob's life spans almost half of the book of Genesis. The narrative focus is on Jacob in the "account of the family line of Abraham's son Isaac" (25:19–35:9) that begins with an account of his (and Esau's) birth in 25:21–26. After a relatively brief consideration of Esau's family line (Gen 36), the book concludes with a lengthy final "account of Jacob's family line" (37:2–50:26). While the focus here shifts to Jacob's children (particularly Joseph and Judah), Jacob still remains a major character.

But now his life comes to an end. He has blessed Ephraim and Manasseh, his grandchildren through Joseph (Gen 48), and has announced blessings and curses on his twelve sons (Gen 49).

He has already made Joseph swear to bury him not in Egypt but in the promised land at the place where his fathers are buried. It is to that subject that the patriarch returns at the end of chapter 49.

Jacob again tells Joseph to bury him with his fathers, but here he is more specific. He describes the place as "the cave in the field of Ephron the Hittite" (49:29), thus recalling the earlier story of Abraham's purchase of the cave at the time of the death and burial of Sarah (Gen 23). In the commentary on that chapter, we noted the significance of this purchase as the first bit of real estate possessed by God's people in the land that will ultimately be theirs according to divine promise (Gen 12:1–3). Thus, it is a kind of earnest or down payment of the promise. Thus, it had (and has) great significance for the descendants of Abraham.

At this place, which is again described as "the field of Machpelah, near Mamre in Canaan" (v. 30; thus approximately forty miles south of Jerusalem near the city of Hebron), Abraham and Sarah, Isaac and Rebekah, and Leah were already interred. Only Rachel among the patriarchs and matriarchs is missing, having pre-deceased Leah on the journey back from Paddan Aram. She was thus buried on the way to Ephrath (Bethlehem; 35:19–20).

Jacob thus gave his final instructions to his sons. Now that everything was done, he simply crawled into bed and quietly died and was "gathered to his people" (v. 33).

Not surprisingly, Joseph mourned the death of his father. He was a man of faults to be sure, but those faults were not directed toward Joseph. Indeed, Joseph was his favorite. He may have made others suffer, but he too suffered in life.

Not only did Joseph mourn Jacob, so, we will see, did the rest of the family, but first we hear of the public mourning of the Egyptians, who appear to have a formal mourning period for a public figure of seventy days. Of course, their mourning for Jacob would be due to Joseph's status in Egypt, but this will contrast with the attitude toward the Israelites at the beginning of the book of Exodus when a new king arises "to whom Joseph meant nothing" (Exod 1:8). Not only did the Egyptians mourn him; they also embalmed him.

Joseph may be the second most powerful person in Egypt, but even he cannot do anything without the approval of the Pharaoh. He had earlier sought Pharaoh's permission to bring Jacob and his family to Egypt; now he seeks permission for his family to return to Canaan in order to bury his father. As before, Pharaoh quickly grants permission and they make the journey to Mamre to bury the patriarch. Amazingly not only did all the adults of the family and "those belonging to his father's household" make the trip, but also Egyptian officials as well as an Egyptian military guard go along. After all, Joseph was an important official. Only the children and livestock were left behind, indicating that they did not intend to stay in the promised land.

Interestingly, the mourning began well before they got to Mamre. It appears that it began formally once they crossed the Jordan River into the promised pand at a place called the threshing floor of Atad. They spent seven days there, the typical period of mourning for Hebrews as opposed to the period of seventy days earlier associated with the Egyptians, mourning Jacob.

The local Canaanite population was likely startled by such a company of mourners in their midst. It certainly left an impression since they named that place Abel Mizraim, or "the mourning of the Egyptians."

Thus, the account of Jacob's death ends with the assurance that his burial had been done exactly according to his wishes. Notice here that it is not just Joseph who is said to have received and carried out these instructions, but all the sons (v. 12). After the burial, they then returned to Egypt.

## God Meant It for Good (50:15–21)

While the account of Jacob's life closes with the story of his burial, the book of Genesis continues at least for a brief span. The narrator returns his attention to the relationship between the brothers. While it appeared that the dysfunctional family had been made whole again, there were still fissures. The brothers seem to have worried that Joseph was still angry with them and only repressed his anger out of respect for their father. But now their father was dead.

The brothers, presumably the ones who sold him to the Ishmaelites, confer and worry that Joseph had just been waiting for this moment to bring his vengeance to bear on them. They realize that they would be helpless before him, so they decide to beg mercy from him even before he acts.

First they inform Joseph, apparently through an intermediary ("they sent word to Joseph," v. 17), that Jacob had told them to tell him to show them mercy for their earlier actions. We have absolutely no reason to think that Jacob had said any such thing to his sons. After all, if he did want to send this message to Joseph, why wouldn't he have spoken directly to Joseph? The brothers' appeal to Joseph was an act of desperation and, as we will see, an unnecessary one at that. If we learn anything positive about the brothers here, it is that they now clearly recognize "the sins and wrongs they committed in treating you so badly" (v. 17). Interesting too is their characterization of themselves as "the servants of the God of your father" (v. 17) to Joseph, putting themselves in relationship to both their father and to God.

When Joseph received this message from his brothers from the intermediary, he wept. We are not told the reason for his tears, but it seems likely that they were for his brother's misunderstanding of his intentions toward them.

After their message was delivered, the brothers then presented themselves before Joseph. They then prostrated themselves before him and announced: "we are your slaves" (v. 18). At this point, the reader and perhaps also the characters remember Joseph's early dreams showing his dominant position among his brothers (37:5–12).

At this point, Joseph makes something clear that he did not understand those many years ago when he had his dreams. His position of dominance was not to exert power over his brothers. He was to use his God-given status to serve the interests of his family. After all, this family was no ordinary one; it was the family that God would use to continue the promises originally given to Abraham (12:1–3).

Thus, at the end of the story, Joseph articulates the awareness that his difficult life was not the result of whims of fate but was guided by God. While this was not the first time he expresses this thought (45:4–11), its reiteration at this climactic moment in the narrative shows its central importance to the story.

Joseph assures them that they should not fear reprisal from him because he knows that God's good purposes lie behind his life. It is not that they don't deserve punishment. God's use of their actions does not exonerate them from responsibility. After all, they "intended to harm me" (v. 20), but he will leave it to God to determine their fate ("Am I in the place of God?," v. 19). Surely while he lived his life Joseph wondered about the meaning of his suffering, but from the vantage point of the end of the story, Joseph could determine its meaning.

The reader can also look back over the account of Joseph's life and recognize God's providential hand that brought Joseph to the place where he could save the people of God from destruction due to the famine that ravished the region.

The brothers, after all, meant it for evil when they sold Joseph into slavery to the Ishmaelites. They were motivated by jealous hatred of their favored younger brother, but God meant it for good to bring Joseph to Egypt. Potiphar's wife meant it for evil when she framed Joseph for rape. She was angry that Joseph had spurned her advances, though he was just a slave. God, however, meant it for good when he met two high Egyptian officials who were also in prison, providing the opportunity to demonstrate his skills at dream interpretation. Joseph experienced yet more harm when the chief cupbearer forgot all about Joseph in prison. Even so, when Pharaoh experienced disturbing dreams, the cupbearer knew who could be counted on to interpret the dream. Thus, the harm wrought on Joseph by people who wished to hurt him ultimately brought him to a high position in Egypt, a position from which he could provide grain not only for the Egyptians but also for his own family. And his family was no ordinary family, but the one chosen by God to bring a blessing on all the nations of the world (12:3).

Joseph was not exonerating his brothers' wrongdoing, but he was also aware of God's overruling their evil actions and using them for good. Thus, Joseph not only refrains from vengeance, but he also provides for his brothers and their children. Indeed, Joseph goes out of his way to comfort his brothers.

### Joseph's Death (50:22–26)

The book of Genesis concludes with an account of the death of Joseph. While providing a sense of closure to the book, it also clearly suggests that the story will eventually continue. In other words, the way Joseph's death is narrated indicates that the story will eventually continue.

Joseph lived the rest of his life in Egypt as did his extended family. Joseph was blessed with a long life (one hundred and ten years), though not as long as his father Jacob (one hundred and thirty), his grandfather Isaac (one hundred and eighty), or his great-grandfather Abraham (one hundred and seventy five). He was blessed to see the third generation of Ephraim's children and the children of Makir son of Manasseh, whose children "were placed on his knees," a ritual that made his great-grandchildren like his own children.

Joseph, like his father Jacob, made his brothers promise to bury him in the promised land. Unlike Jacob, Joseph's bones were not immediately taken to Canaan but rather embalmed and stayed in Egypt until the Israelites returned after the exodus. Perhaps that is why the narrator says that he "made the Israelites" (rather than the brothers) swear this (see Keeping the Promise below).

The book of Genesis thus comes to a close, but we must remember that Genesis is simply the first part of a coherent story that encompasses the whole Pentateuch. Genesis is best understood as the prequel to the story of the exodus. Thus, the ending of Genesis (chs. 37–50) explains how the Israelites came to live in Egypt, where they are at the beginning of the book of Exodus, which begins after a gap of several centuries after the death of Joseph.

### "You Meant It for Evil ...," Part 4: God Uses Evil for Good throughout Joseph's Life

At the end of his life, Joseph could plainly see the providence of God guiding him even using the wicked intentions of other people (50:19–20). Not even the evil actions of his brothers, Potiphar's wife, or even the neglect of the chief cupbearer could prevent God using these very events to bring Joseph to a position where he could save the people of God.

This story of God's providence should serve as an encouragement to all God's people. The account of Joseph's life gives flesh to one of the most often quoted verses of the New Testament: "And we know that in all things God works for the good of those who love him, who have been called according to his purpose" (Rom 8:28). In the light of the story of Joseph, we can assert that not even those who harm us can thwart God's purpose to work good in our lives. This realization leads Paul to the astounding pronouncement that "we [those who love him] are more than conquerors through him who loved us. For I am convinced that neither death nor life, neither angels nor demons, neither the present nor the future, nor any powers, neither height nor depth, nor anything else in all creation, will be able to separate us from the love of God that is in Christ Jesus our Lord" (Rom 8:37–39).

We must remember, however, that the good God works in our life will not necessarily feel like it. God worked the "good" of being a slave in Egypt for the purpose of saving the family of God. Still there is great comfort in knowing the our ultimate good, being in a loving relationship with God, cannot be hindered by the evil actions of others.

The ultimate expression of God using the evil actions of wicked men to accomplish redemption is not the Joseph story, but Jesus' death on the cross. Peter expresses this truth in his Pentecost sermon:

> Fellow Israelites, listen to this: Jesus of Nazareth was a man accredited by God to you by miracles, wonders and signs, which God did among you through him, as you yourselves know. This man was handed over to you by God's deliberate plan and foreknowledge; and you, with the help of wicked men, put him to death by nailing him to the cross. But God raised him from the dead, freeing him from the agony of death, because it was impossible for death to keep its hold on him. (Acts 2:22–24)

Peter's point is that the greatest salvation event of all was accomplished through the agency of wicked men who nailed Jesus to the cross. They meant it for evil, but God meant it for good, "freeing him" and us from the agony of death.

Those who nailed him to the cross are not exonerated for their act. They are guilty, as were Joseph's brothers and any who harm us. However, knowing that even those evil actions do not hinder God working his purposes through us both comforts us in our pain and keeps us from working out our revenge on those who hurt us.

### Working in the Ordinary

Throughout the Joseph narrative, we have observed how God's hand of providence has guided Joseph to a place where he could provide the needed resources for the family of God to survive the severe famine that hit the region. Here we see God working through the ordinary events of life. Rather than working through miraculous events (as he can), he works through the everyday actions and decisions (even bad ones) that people make. Mark Lanier connects this with our lives, when he asks: "How often do we feel removed from Bible stories because we fail to see the miraculous in our lives? Yet, the hand of God could not have been more involved or more evident than we have in this story of God's providential care. We need to see God at work in the details of our daily lives, and give him credit for doing so."[1]

---

1. M. Lanier, "Survey of the Old Testament," (unpublished manuscript), 220.

### Vengeance is Mine Says the Lord

Joseph's recognition that God directed his life even when bad things happened to him allowed him to refrain from judgment and even provide for those who had hurt him. By so doing Joseph is not exonerating the evil actions of his brothers, but turning it over to God ("Am I in the place of God?" [50:19]).

Paul advises Christians to do the same. He urges his readers to "bless those who persecute you; bless and do not curse" (Rom 12:14). He continues:

> Do not repay evil for evil. Be careful to do what is right in the eyes of everyone. If it is possible, as far as it depends you, live at peace with everyone. Do not take revenge, my dear friends, but leave room for God's wrath, for it is written: "It is mine to avenge; I will repay," says the Lord. On the contrary:
>
> "If your enemy is hungry, feed him;
> if he is thirsty, give him something to drink.
> In doing this, you will heap burning coals on his head."
>
> (Rom 12:17–20)

Knowing that God can overrule even the evil actions of others for our good, we can refrain from working our own vengeance. We can turn it over to God. God will do as he sees fit. Perhaps our enemy will be convicted of his sins and be forgiven.

### Dying in the Knowledge of God's Faithfulness

The book of Genesis achieves closure with an account of Joseph's death. Joseph's request that his brothers take his bones to the promised land anticipates a sequel to be sure, a sequel that begins with the book of Exodus.

Joseph's final words express a sure confidence that God will remain faithful to the people of promise. They will eventually return to the land that God said he would give the descendants of Abraham.

Joseph dies with the confidence that God will fulfill his promises. Readers of the New Testament have also received promises. As Christians face death, we should remember Jesus' words:

> Do not let your hearts be troubled. You believe in God; believe also in me. My Father's house has many rooms; if that were not so, would I have told you that I am going there to prepare a place for you? And if I go and prepare a place for you, I will come back and take you to be with me that you also may be where I am. You know the way to the place where I am going. (John 14:1–4)

Joseph died peaceably knowing that his descendants and his bones would eventually end up in the land God promised Abraham. How much more should we face death with confidence in the knowledge that we will dwell in God's heavenly mansion?

**Keeping the Promise**

The book of Genesis ended with Joseph's request that his brothers take his bones back to the promised land. Joseph is speaking directly to his brothers when he makes them swear to do so when God "come[s] to your aid" (50:24). The brothers are not the ones to take his bones to Canaan for burial as we might think Joseph intended. We might question why the brothers of Joseph, or any of their descendants decided not to return to Canaan. Surely the famine ended. Were they too comfortable in Egypt? Were they compelled to stay? We are never told, but when the book of Exodus opens, the descendants of Jacob are enslaved in Israel. Nowhere in Scripture is this explicitly stated to be a consequence of a wrong decision to stay in Egypt, but it is suggestive.

We remarked above that, while Joseph made the request of his brothers, the narrator informs us that "Joseph made the Israelites swear" to take his bones to Canaan (50:25). The brothers here transition to the "Israelites," and, of course, it is the later Israelites who take his bones years later after the exodus. After Israel called for God's aid in the midst of their slavery, God responded and used Moses to lead them out of Egypt and toward the promised land. Thus, we learn, "Moses took the bones of Joseph with him because Joseph had made the Israelites swear an oath. He had said, 'God will surely come to your aid, and then you must carry my bones up with you from this place'" (Exod 13:19).

# Conclusion

## From Creation to Egypt

The book of Genesis is indeed a book of beginnings. In its first part (1:1–11:27), we learn about the start of the cosmos and the creation of the first humans who received the blessing of life from God. We also read about the introduction of sin and death, which led to the forfeit of that original blessing as Adam and Eve were ejected from Eden. At the same time, we hear about the beginning of the history of redemption as God seeks to restore his blessing on his beloved, yet rebellious, creatures. The early account of humanity after the rebellion is a story of sin, judgment, yet also divine grace.

In the patriarchal narratives (11:27–37:1), we hear of the beginning of a chosen people starting with Abraham and Sarah, who acted on the divine command to go to Canaan ("the land I will show you," 12:1) and thus received the divine blessings that God would make their descendants a "great nation" and bless them as well as the rest of the nations of the world through them (12:2–3). The patriarchal narratives describe the tumultuous generations that come after, following the account of Abraham's struggle of faith with that of his son Isaac and his grandson Jacob.

Finally, the book closes with a narrative that focuses on Joseph but concerns all the sons of Jacob (37:2–50:26). Here we see that God is with his chosen family, even using evil actions of others to bring them safely through crisis.

The book of Genesis is about beginnings, but we are far from the end of the story. The death of Joseph does bring some closure to the book, but the chosen family remains in Egypt. More is surely yet to come. That more, of course, continues in part 2 of the Torah, the book of Exodus and then the rest of the Torah, but for the Christian the story will continue far beyond the Torah, indeed far beyond the Law, the Prophets, and the Writings, to their fulfillment in Jesus Christ, the Logos, in whom "all things were created" and through whom God will "reconcile to himself all things, whether things on earth or things in heaven, by making peace through his blood, shed on the cross" (Col 1:16, 20).

# Scripture and Apocrypha Index

## Genesis

**Exodus**

**Joshua**



**Judges**



**Ruth**



**1 Samuel**

**2 Samuel**



**1 Kings**



**2 Kings**



**1 Chronicles**



**2 Chronicles**



**Ezra**



**Nehemiah**



**Esther**



**Job**

**Psalms**



**Proverbs**

# Subject Index

# Author Index